York Medieval Texts, second series

General Editors: Elizabeth Salter and Derek Pearsall
University of York

Piers Plowman

by William Langland

An Edition of the C-text
by Derek Pearsall

University of California Press
Berkeley and Los Angeles
1979

© Derek Pearsall 1978

University of California Press
Berkeley and Los Angeles

ISBN 0-520-03793-6

Library of Congress Catalog Card Number 78-64463

PR
2010
P4
1979

Printed in Great Britain

Contents

Preface

This is the first annotated edition of either of the longer texts of *Piers Plowman* to appear since the great editions of Skeat. No-one could be more conscious than I have become of the foolhardiness of the undertaking, and both text and notes are presented here in the full recognition that they may be merely interim statements in a continuing process of discovery. It seemed important, however, that readers and students of the poem should have, without further delay, an up-to-date text which would at least answer their preliminary needs and questions; the reasons for choosing the C-text are given in the Introduction. The Notes aim to provide, within their practical limits, what is essential to the understanding of the poem, and to incorporate whatever is immediately relevant to that understanding from the criticism and scholarship of recent decades. A particular function of the Notes is to provide cross-reference within the poem, which is long enough and complex enough to act as a commentary, and often the only relevant one, on its own developing structure. The Glossary serves purely pragmatic needs. The Introduction gives necessary information on the poem and the text, but it makes no claim to be a critical essay on the poem or a considered 'interpretation' of it; it will be found to work most usefully as a guide to the contents of the Notes.

I should like to thank the Trustees of the Huntington Library of San Marino, California, for permission to publish the text of *Piers Plowman* from their MS HM 143, and for supplying me with microfilm both of this MS and of MS HM 137. The kindness of the Librarian of University College London in allowing me to borrow the Library's copy of the rare facsimile of MS HM 143 (Chambers Papers 21) made the task of transcribing the MS much easier. My thanks are due also to the British Library Board and to the Master and Fellows of Trinity College Cambridge for supplying me with microfilm of MSS in their possession, and particularly to the staff of the Palaeography Room of the University of London Library for their care in supplying excellent photostat copies of the much mutilated MS [S.L.] V.88. In the later stages of the preparation of the edition I was very grateful for the help of Brenda Cornell, who typed up the whole of the text of the poem; Simon Pearsall helped me with the Glossary. Professor George Russell answered my questions about his forthcoming critical edition of the C-text with unfailing courtesy.

Many friends and colleagues have given me help in the preparation of the Notes to this edition, and would have given me more if I had known where I needed it. I should like to thank them all, with a special mention of John Alford, Denise Baker, Anna Baldwin, James Binns, Norman Blake, David Fowler, Albert Friedman, Helen Houghton, Andy Kelly, Carl Marx, Peter Newton, Oliver Pickering, Elizabeth Salter, Geoffrey Shepherd, Ron Waldron, Siegfried Wenzel and Rosemary Woolf. I owe a particular debt to Tom Hill, of Cornell, who has been generous with information on specific passages. I continue to be grateful to Talbot Donaldson for having written the best book on *Piers Plowman*, and having written it on the C-text; this has been a source of constant comfort to me. The notes of J. A. W. Bennett to his edition of the B-text, Prologue and Passus I–VII, have been invaluable, and I have plundered them mercilessly; the passage into the storm-tossed seas of the *Vita* was infinitely more forbidding in the absence of his guidance, and infinitely more precarious, as will become readily apparent to the informed reader. Finally, I should like to acknowledge the debt I owe, like all students of the poem, to W. W. Skeat. His knowledge of the poem remains unrivalled, and the magnitude of his contribution to the understanding of the poem, in the midst of all his many other labours, remains a cause for wonderment. To his memory this edition, I hope without presumption, is dedicated.

List of Abbreviations

Abbreviations for the names of books of the bible are included only where the Vulgate form of the name of a book is used in the notes, conventionally abbreviated, as being different in substance from the AV form.

AN	Anglo-Norman
Apoc.	Apocalypsis B. Ioannis Apostoli (The Revelation to St John in AV)
AV	The Authorized Version of the Bible (the King James Bible of 1611)
BJRL	Bulletin of the John Rylands Library
BL	British Library
Cant.	Canticum Canticorum (Song of Songs in AV)
CT	Chaucer's *Canterbury Tales*
E & S	*Essays and Studies*
EC	*Essays in Criticism*
Ecclus.	Ecclesiasticus (apocryphal in AV)
EETS	Early English Text Society, Original Series (ES, Extra Series; Supp., Supplementary Series)
EGS	*English and Germanic Studies*
EHR	*English Historical Review*
ELH	*English Literary History*
EStn.	*Englische Studien*
HF	Chaucer's *House of Fame*
JEGP	*Journal of English and Germanic Philology*
JWCI	*Journal of the Warburg and Courtauld Institutes*
MÆ	*Medium Ævum*
ME	Middle English
MED	Middle English Dictionary
MnE	Modern English
MLN	*Modern Language Notes*
MLR	*Modern Language Review*
MP	*Modern Philology*
MS	*Mediaeval Studies*
NM	*Neuphilologische Mitteilungen*
NQ	*Notes and Queries*
n.s.	new series
NT	New Testament
OE	Old English
OED	Oxford English Dictionary
OF	Old French
ON	Old Norse
OT	Old Testament

Para.	Paralipomenon (1 and 2 Chronicles in AV)
PBA	*Proceedings of the British Academy*
PF	Chaucer's *Parlement of Foules*
PG	*Patrologia Graeco-Latina*
PL	*Patrologia Latina*
PMLA	*Publications of the Modern Language Association of America*
PQ	*Philological Quarterly*
Reg.	Liber Regum, Book of Kings (1 and 2 Reg. correspond to 1 and 2 Samuel in AV, and 3 and 4 Reg. to 1 and 2 Kings in AV)
RES	*Review of English Studies*
Sap.	Sapientia (The Wisdom of Solomon, apocryphal in AV)
SP	*Studies in Philology*
Spec.	*Speculum*
TC	Chaucer's *Troilus and Criseyde*
TRHS	*Transactions of the Royal Historical Society*
Vg.	Vulgate (Latin) version of the Bible (see Reference List)
YES	*Yearbook of English Studies*

Select Bibliography

1 Editions, Selections and Translations

The Vision of William concerning Piers the Plowman, in Three Parallel Texts, ed. W. W. Skeat, 2 vols. (Oxford, 1886; reprinted 1954, with additional bibliography by J. A. W. Bennett).

Piers Plowman: The A Version. Will's Vision of Piers Plowman and Do-Well, ed. G. Kane (University of London, Athlone Press, 1960). Part I of *Piers Plowman: The Three Versions*, general editor, G. Kane.

Piers Plowman: The B Version. Will's Visions of Piers Plowman, Do-Well, Do-Better and Do-Best, ed. G. Kane and E. Talbot Donaldson (University of London, Athlone Press, 1975). Part II of *Piers Plowman: The Three Versions*, general editor, G. Kane.

Piers Plowman (selections from the C-text), ed. E. Salter and D. Pearsall (York Medieval Texts, London, 1969).

Langland, *Piers Plowman*. The Prologue and Passus I–VII of the B text, ed. J. A. W. Bennett (Oxford, 1972).

William Langland, *The Book concerning Piers the Plowman*, translated into modern English verse by D. and R. Attwater (London, Everyman, 1957).

Piers the Ploughman, translated into modern English prose by J. F. Goodridge (Harmondsworth, Penguin, 1959).

2 Collections of Critical Essays

E. Vasta, ed., *Interpretations of Piers Plowman* (Notre Dame, 1968).

R. J. Blanch, ed., *Style and Symbolism in Piers Plowman* (Knoxville, 1969).

S. S. Hussey, ed., *Piers Plowman: Critical Approaches* (London, 1969).

3 General Studies

G. Hort, *Piers Plowman and Contemporary Religious Thought* (London, n.d.).

T. P. Dunning, *Piers Plowman: An Interpretation of the A-Text* (Dublin, 1937).

R. W. Chambers, *Man's Unconquerable Mind* (London, 1939), pp. 88–171.

E. T. Donaldson, *Piers Plowman: The C-Text and its Poet* (New Haven, 1949).

D. W. Robertson and B. F. Huppé, *Piers Plowman and Scriptural Tradition* (Princeton, 1951).

R. W. Frank, *Piers Plowman and the Scheme of Salvation* (New Haven, 1957).

J. Lawlor, *Piers Plowman. An Essay in Criticism* (London, 1962).

E. Salter, *Piers Plowman: An Introduction* (Oxford, 1962).

M. W. Bloomfield, *Piers Plowman as a Fourteenth Century Apocalypse* (New Brunswick, N.J., 1963).

E. Vasta, *The Spiritual Basis of Piers Plowman* (The Hague, 1965).

B. H. Smith, *Traditional Imagery of Charity in Piers Plowman* (The Hague and Paris, 1966).

R. M. Ames, *The Fulfilment of the Scriptures: Abraham, Moses, and Piers* (Evanston, 1970).

E. D. Kirk, *The Dream Thought of Piers Plowman* (New Haven, 1972).

D. Aers, *Piers Plowman and Christian Allegory* (London, 1975).

4 Articles and Special Studies

H. W. Wells, 'The Construction of *Piers Plowman*', *PMLA* 44 (1929), 123–40.

—— 'The Philosophy of *Piers Plowman*', *PMLA* 53 (1938), 339–49.

N. Coghill, 'The Character of Piers Plowman considered from the B-Text', *MÆ* 2 (1933), 108–35.

—— 'The Pardon of Piers Plowman', *PBA* 30 (1944), 303–57.

—— 'God's Wenches and the Light that Spoke (Some notes on Langland's kind of poetry)', in *English and Medieval Studies presented to J. R. R. Tolkien*, ed. N. Davis and C. L. Wrenn (London 1962), pp. 200–218.

R. W. Frank, 'The Pardon Scene in *Piers Plowman*', *Speculum* 26 (1951), 317–31.

—— 'The Art of Reading Mediaeval Personification Allegory', *ELH* 20 (1953), 237–50.

T. P. Dunning, 'The Structure of the B-text of *Piers Plowman*', *RES*, n.s. 7 (1956), 225–37.

S. S. Hussey, 'Langland, Hilton and the Three Lives', *RES*, n.s. 7 (1956), 132–50.

—— 'Langland's Reading of Alliterative Poetry', *MLR* 60 (1965), 163–70.

A. G. Mitchell, 'Lady Meed and the Art of *Piers Plowman*', Chambers Memorial Lecture (London, 1956).

J. A. Burrow, 'The Audience of *Piers Plowman*', *Anglia* 75 (1957), 373–84.

—— 'The Action of Langland's Second Vision', *EC* 15 (1965), 247–68.

J. Lawlor, 'The Imaginative Unity of *Piers Plowman*', *RES*, n.s. 8 (1957), 113–26.

E. Zeeman (Salter), 'Piers Plowman and the Pilgrimage to Truth', *E & S* 11 (1958), 1–16.

R. E. Kaske, 'Patristic Exegesis in the Criticism of Medieval Literature: The Defense', in *Critical Approaches to Medieval Literature*, ed. D. Bethurum (New York, 1960), pp. 27–60.

R. Woolf, 'Some Non-Mediaeval Qualities of *Piers Plowman*', *EC* 12 (1962), 111–25.

J. A. Yunck, *The Lineage of Lady Meed: The Development of Medieval Venality Satire* (Notre Dame, 1963).

P. M. Kean, 'Love, Law and *Lewte* in *Piers Plowman*', *RES*, n.s. 15 (1964), 241–61.

—— 'Langland on the Incarnation', *RES*, n.s. 16 (1965), 349–63.

J. A. Longo, *Piers Plowman* and the Tropological Matrix: Passus XI and XII', *Anglia* 82 (1964), 291–308.

A. C. Spearing, 'The Art of Preaching and *Piers Plowman*', in *Criticism and Mediaeval Poetry* (London, 1964; 2nd ed., 1972), pp. 107–34.

G. Kane, *Piers Plowman: The Evidence for Authorship* (London, 1965).

—— 'The Autobiographical Fallacy in Chaucer and Langland Studies', Chambers Memorial Lecture (London, 1965).

G. H. Russell, 'The Salvation of the Heathen: The Exploration of a Theme in *Piers Plowman*', *JWCI* 29 (1966), 101–16.

A. V. C. Schmidt, 'Langland and Scholastic Philosophy', *MÆ* 38 (1969), 134–56.

B. J. Harwood, '"Clergye" and the Action of the Third Vision in "Piers Plowman",' *MP* 70 (1972–3), 279–90.

—— '*Liberum-Arbitrium* in the C-Text of *Piers Plowman*', *PQ* 52 (1973), 680–95.

—— 'Imaginative in *Piers Plowman*', *MÆ* 44 (1975), 249–63.

M. C. Davlin, 'Kynde Knowyng as a Major Theme in *Piers Plowman* B', *RES*, n.s. 22 (1971), 1–19.

B. Palmer, 'The Guide Convention in *Piers Plowman*', *Leeds Studies in English*, n.s. 5 (1971), 13–27.

J. S. Wittig, '*Piers Plowman* B IX–XII: Elements in the Design of the Inward Journey', *Traditio* 28 (1972), 211–80.

—— 'The Dramatic and Rhetorical Development of Long Will's Pilgrimage', *NM* 76 (1975), 52–76.

S. A. Barney, 'The Plowshare of the Tongue: The Progress of a Symbol from the Bible to *Piers Plowman*', *MS* 35 (1973), 261–93.

K. B. Trower, 'Temporal Tensions in the *Visio* of *Piers Plowman*', *MS* 35 (1973), 389–412.

R. Adams, 'Langland and the Liturgy Revisited', *SP* 73 (1976), 266–84.

J. A. Alford, 'The Role of the Quotations in *Piers Plowman*', *Speculum* 52 (1977), 80–99.

Introduction

Piers Plowman[1] exists in three recensions, known as the A, B and C texts. It is now generally accepted, as a necessary rather than a merely convenient hypothesis (see Kane, 1965), that all are the work of a single author, William Langland, of whom we know nothing but what we can deduce to be relevant to the poet from the characterization of the dreamer in the poem[2] and what we can accept as authoritative in some brief manuscript notes of the fifteenth century (see V 36n). The poem is, to all intents and purposes, Langland's whole known existence and his whole life's work. The A-text is the product of the 1360s, and was probably still being revised and rewritten in 1369–70 (see V 116n); the B-text, mainly to be assigned to the 1370s, contains much allusion to events of 1376–9 (see notes to Prologue 134, 139, 165, XV 171, XXI 428); while the C-text was probably complete by 1387, when Thomas Usk, who was executed in 1388, borrowed some phrases (which are in C only) in his *Testament of Love*.[3] Evidently, it is not possible to date with any exactness the different versions of a poem which, despite the testimony of the extant manuscripts to the integrity of the three versions, had such a continuous life in the mind of its creator over a period of some 25 years.

The poem is in two parts, as indicated by the Latinized rubrics or titles that appear in most manuscripts: the *Visio Willelmi de Petrus Plowman* and the *Vita de Dowel, Dobet et Dobest*. In the simplest form of the poem, the A-text, which is 2558 lines long, the *Visio* is an allegorical portrayal of the corruption of the social estate and of the attempts to remedy this corruption through the agency of Piers Plowman, representing the life of humble and honest obedience to God's law; the *Vita* is a vision of the dreamer's search for the good Christian life, conducted in allegorical terms through a series of interviews with personified faculties and ways of life (Thought, Wit, Study, etc.). The *Vita* is thus more introspective, seeking a rational basis for individual faith through intellectual enquiry after the failure of the attempts to reform the community in the *Visio*. The A-text has an ending, but the search is inconclusive. The B-text is an extensive rewriting of A, with much new material added incidentally, and with the further addition, after the omission of A's interim ending, of nine

1. For the sake of its traditional familiarity, *Piers Plowman* is kept as the title of the poem and the name of its hero in the title to the present edition and in this Introduction, though the form of the name in the text here presented is invariably *Peres (the plouhman)*.
2. See notes to Prologue 6, I 5, V 1, 2, 24, 36, VI 2, X 68, XI 168, XII 2, XVI 2, XVI 286, XX 472, XXII 183.
3. For this and other evidence supporting a date for C in the 1380s, see Sister Mary Aquinas Devlin, 'The Date of the C Version of *Piers the Plowman*', Abstracts of Theses, University of Chicago, Humanistic Series IV, 1925–6 (Chicago, 1928), 317–20. See also Donaldson, 1949, 18–19. Skeat's date in the 1390s (see III 207n) has little to support it.

long passus,[4] altogether trebling the length of the poem to 7302 lines. The quest for Dowel is continued at length, merging into Dobet, the life of Christ, and Dobest, the life of the Church, both allegorically represented in the person of Piers Plowman, brilliantly resurrected from the *Visio*. The C-text (7338 lines in the present edition) is an extensive but incomplete rewriting of B, with several major additions and omissions,[5] much radical reworking and transposition,[6] and much detailed line-by-line revision of less significance. This latest revision seems to have been prompted by an urgent desire to clarify the meaning of the poem and to reshape certain sequences, perhaps partly as a result of the trend of contemporary events and the new context in which they placed the poem (see below, p. 16). The C-reviser seems to have worked piecemeal, outward from certain cores of dissatisfaction, rather than systematically through B from beginning to end (see Russell, 1969, 39–40). The later passus are relatively little altered, and the last two not at all, but this may be because Langland was satisfied with them, understandably, rather than because he never reached them in the process of revision. The incompleteness of the C-revision is more clearly evidenced in the partially digested state of some of its additional lines (especially Prologue 106–17) and in the exposed seams where new material has been patched to B with little care for detailed congruence.[7]

It is proper that we should attend to all three versions of Langland's poem, separately and in relation to one another. The argument for presenting an edition of the C-text, therefore, needs no special enforcement, but it may seem to, in view of the virtual unanimity of scholars up to now in basing their discussions, with more or less consciousness of the issues involved, on the B-text. In the first place, then, the C-text has been ill-represented by the only text hitherto available, that of Skeat (see below, p. 20), which is based on a manuscript which has been fussily 'improved' by an intelligent and pedantic scribe or editor (the classic example is the substitution of *unwyse* for *wyse* in Prologue 49, where the scribe seemingly thought that the simple irony might escape the inattentive reader). Secondly, the C-revision, being the author's latest revision, presumably represents his latest thinking and therefore, *a priori*, what he is entitled to ask to be remembered by, unless it is marred by evident senility. Discrimination of relative merit is in such a case a highly subjective matter, as has been demonstrated in the discussion of the different versions of Wordsworth's *The Prelude*, but the *prima facie* authority of an authorial revision is not similarly arguable. Thirdly, though it would not be possible to argue

---

4. *Passus*, pl. *passūs*, is a Latin word meaning 'step' or 'stage'. It is used elsewhere to distinguish the parts of a poem in *Richard the Redeles* and *The Wars of Alexander*, both presumably under the influence of *Piers Plowman*. There may be some original or even partly surviving reference to the practice of dividing a poem for the purposes of oral delivery: in the text of the *Wars*, as distinct from the scribal rubrics, the reference is to *fittis*, e.g. line 3473 (ed. EETS, ES 47).

5. See notes to Prologue 95, III 77, 235, 290, V 1, VII 292, IX 70, 187, 291, X 254, XI 137, 163, 196, XII 153, XV 194, XVII 125, 187, XVIII 76, XX 283, 350. A list is provided in Skeat xv–xxi. On the C-revisions in general, see Donaldson, 1949, 20–32.

6. See notes to V 146, VI 3, 63, 170, 196, 309, VII 1, 70, X 51, 157, 184, XI 76, 163, XIV 11, XV 138, XVI 157, XVII 1, XVIII 8, 199; and Donaldson, 1949, 23–4.

7. See notes to Prologue 125, II 73, III 77, V 122, VI 37, VII 70, IX 294, X 170, XII 30, XIV, 16, 100, XV 11, 48, XVIII 179, XX 18.

that C is artistically superior at every point to B – indeed it is quite possible to show that in vividness, picturesque concretion and 'poetic' quality it is often inferior [8] – it is nevertheless clear that the excisions from B, ruthless as they are in their single-minded concentration on essentials, are the work of a man who knows what he is doing, while the great additions (viz. V 1–108, IX 70–161, 187–281, XII 153–XIII 99) reveal no waning of poetic power, passion or purpose. Fourthly, the C-text is substantially successful in achieving its overall purpose of reshaping and clarifying the general outline of the poem. There are still many blurs, and some new ones created in the process of revision, but there are not so many fundamental problems of interpretation as there are in the B-text, and fewer of those abrupt transitions and juxtapositions and dark meanderings that have earned B the epithet 'surrealistic' (Muscatine, 1972, 88, 106). C may be less exciting, but it makes better sense. Finally, however, the necessity of all such arguments is merely relative, and their importance diminished in the light of the great good fortune we have in possessing all three versions of Langland's poem, and a unique and compelling record, therefore, of the growth of a poet's mind over the whole of his mature life.

Before examining the nature and form of the poem, it will be necessary to give a brief analysis of its contents.

The poem begins with a Prologue,[9] the dreamer's vision of the world in its corrupted state as a 'field full of folk', dominated by self-seeking. A 'Westminster interlude' shows the higher levels of church and state subjected to the same turbulent misrule. In Passus I, Holy Church explains the dreamer's vision to him, shows him how a right use of worldly goods would be in accord with God's Law, and answers his urgent entreaty, How may I save my soul? (I 80), which in a sense initiates the whole movement of the poem, with a preliminary outline of the doctrine of Charity. But the dreamer wishes to understand more of the ways of the world, and is presented in Passus II–IV with the vision of Lady Meed, a brilliant allegorical portrayal of the corruption of every estate and activity of society through the influence of money. The king (an ideal king) wins a measure of control over Meed with the help of Conscience and Reason, whom he takes as his chief advisors, and a golden age, it seems, is about to begin. But administrative reform alone cannot bring this about: men's hearts must be purged of sin so that they may be reformed inwardly. After offering his own 'confession', therefore, the dreamer shows us Reason calling on the folk to repent and to seek Truth (V). The confessions of the Seven Deadly Sins follow (VI–VII), wound up by the prayer of Repentance for general forgiveness. The people rush forth in high enthusiasm to seek for Truth, but find no way until they meet Piers Plowman, who tells them where Truth may be found (in obedience to God's Law) and promises to lead them there when he has finished his ploughing (i.e. the well-organized Christian community must be based on a well-organized economy). All the folk, of all estates, are to help him. But not everyone works with a will: wasters

8. See notes to Prologue 10, 14, I 14, 176, VI 63, VII 136, 250, XI 297, XII 99, XVI 25, 157, XVIII 179. But cf. VI 136, VII 141, X 22.

9. The passus are numbered in the present edition as Prologue and Passus I–XXII, in accordance with the proposed numbering of passus in the forthcoming Athlone Press edition of the C-text by George Russell (see below, p. 20), as explained in Kane-Donaldson 78. Skeat numbers Passus I–XXIII.

and layabouts refuse to do their share and Piers has to call in Hunger to force them to work, an admission of defeat, since outward coercion is no substitute for inward and voluntary reformation. The passus (VIII) ends with Piers's programme of reform in some disarray, but he receives in the next (IX) a pardon from Truth granted to all those who help him: its terms as they apply to all estates of society are related in detail, but it is not in the end a satisfactory answer to the quest for Truth. It promises salvation for those who do well but does not explain what doing well consists of. Piers Plowman disappears at this point, and the dreamer, pondering on his dream and on dreams in general, takes up the search for Dowel.

At this point the poem makes a new beginning, as if to signal the movement from the outer to the inner, from the outward reform of society to the inward reform of the individual. The dreamer's search for Dowel is first within himself (X), for the answers provided by his own intellectual faculties (Thought, Wit). These answers are not fallacious, but they are partial, and as he goes on to meet a series of personifications of learning (Study, Clergy, Scripture) the dreamer, initially stubborn and complacent, becomes increasingly bewildered (XI). The answers he receives concerning Dowel and salvation are conflicting and confusing, and he falls into a stupor of worldliness, a fast subservience to Fortune, in which his life is dreamed away. The dreamer temporarily loses his identity, his place being taken by Rechelesnesse, who solaces the gnawing of doubt with his easy answers, crude simplifications and bold disparagement of what he does not understand. Witnesses of Truth, like Trajan and Leaute, are glimpsed briefly before being submerged in the prevailing murk, and hints of understanding on the part of Rechelesnesse, as of the virtue of poverty, are swallowed in presumption and vociferous anti-clericalism. This is without doubt the most difficult and in many ways the most profound part of the poem (XII). The dreamer resumes his identity only to make a grotesque misinterpretation of the vision of Middle-Earth (XIII) that he is granted, giving continued evidence of his unredeemed pride and presumption. At last he meets Imaginatyf, the sum of all the intellect can do. Imaginatyf provides interim answers to his questions about salvation and learning as they relate to the life of Dowel, but also, more importantly, embodies the first full and explicit recognition that Dowel consists precisely in not asking the kinds of question he has been asking, but in preparing the self, through humility and patience and voluntary submission of the will to God, for the admission of Charity (XIV). In the next passus, the dreamer is given an opportunity to exercise this active virtue of patience when he is invited to the feast with the learned and gluttonous friar (XV); for the first time speculation gives way to action, and talking about doing well gives way to doing well. After a momentary glimpse of Piers Plowman, an epiphany of Truth and promise of grace for the dreamer, Patience takes on the role of guide and instructs the dreamer and Activa Vita (another *alter ego* for the dreamer, through whom something of the life of common humanity is brought into the search for truth) in the true nature of patient poverty and the voluntary acceptance of God's will (XV–XVI). The achievement of this understanding of God's will is for man true freedom, and the next guide is appropriately Liberum Arbitrium (Free Will), the highest faculty of man as he lives in concord with God. Liberum Arbitrium offers the fullest understanding of true Charity that is accessible to man in his human state, unaided by grace or revelation, and shows the relation of the clergy and the Church to this true Charity (XVI–XVII). He also shows, in the vision of the Tree of Charity (XVIII), how man's growth towards charity is thwarted by the devil's work. Man stands in need of an act of divine grace, and the dreamer glimpses what form this will take in a brief account of the life of Christ. But before this vision of grace can be fully granted, Langland must show how the ascent of the soul to the full life of Charity in the reception of Christ reenacts and embodies the majestic processes of Christian history. So we return to Abraham (Faith) and Moses (Hope) and see how their partial understanding, under the Old Law, of divine truth and specifically of the Trinity is to be crowned in the New Law of mercy and love as it is expounded (XIX) by the Good Samaritan (Charity), a figure who subsequently merges into Piers Plowman and into Christ. The world and the dreamer's soul are now prepared for the great act of divine intervention, the fulfilment of the promise of redemption, and Passus XX is devoted to an account of the Crucifixion and Harrowing of Hell. From this high climax the poem returns to a vision of the establishment of Christ's Church on earth through the gift of grace; the dreamer, suffused with the glory of revelation, must still doggedly pursue the truth and be shown how the machinery of redemption is to operate, and how it has operated in the centuries of Christian history since the Redemption (XXI). The descent to the world of fourteenth-century England is swift, and the poem ends (XXII) with the Church of Unity besieged by the forces of Antichrist, the deadly sins, and infiltrated by the subtler temptations of the friars. The end of the poem is a resumption of the search for the true Christian life, as it is embodied in Piers Plowman.

Piers Plowman: the nature and form of the poem

Piers Plowman is a poem of crisis. It records in the minutest detail the conflict which racked late medieval society, as the feudal order and the Church of the west moved into their last stages of institutionalized decay, and as the antagonistic forces over which they had presided moved into the open arena. The strains and pressures between the shifting strata of society – between government and people, lords and commoners, clergy and laity, possessioners and mendicants – had built up during a long period of apparent stability, but the later fourteenth century saw the first release of tension, the first open fracture in the fabric of the traditional order, in two events to which Langland's poem provides both prelude and commentary – the Peasants' Revolt of 1381 and the condemnation of Wyclif's teaching in 1382. Langland's response to these conflicts is that of a devout medieval Christian, who sees all change as a form of decay, and who struggles to comprehend the nature of change within the categories of a hierarchic and traditional mode of thought. It is also the response of a poet, and a highly individual one, in whom the apprehension of conflict and change, the mood of apocalypse, the urgent personal sense of impending disaster, is transformed under the activity of a peculiarly powerful imagination. But above all it is the response of a prophet and a visionary, who attempts in his poem to initiate nothing less than an immense revolution in the moral and spiritual life of the individual, including his own, and of society. *Piers Plowman* is not a poem in the usual sense of the word, any more than Blake's *Prophetic Books*. It has no formal construction, no exclusively poetic ambition, no poetic self-consciousness, except perhaps of the inadequacy of poetry. It shifts and transforms through its three texts and within each text without ever coming nearer to achieved poetic form. Rather than a poem, it has for its writer, and often for the reader, the nature of a mortal combat.

In secular society, what Langland sees is the harmony of the estates, of a world structured in contractual obligation and mutual service (see e.g. Prologue 139–46, III 373–92, VIII 7–118), perverted through the influence of money. He shows with minute particularity in the Lady Meed passus (II–IV) how money dissolves all bonds of nature between man and man, and twists every relationship to its own remorseless ethic. The vigour of these passus, the pullulating ingenuity of innovation in malpractice that they portray, is ironic in its unspoken recognition that the vigour to transform society is there, and perhaps there alone, in money. Langland's answer is for the king to rule by Conscience and Reason, to sweep away Lady Meed: in practical terms, to abolish urban society and return to an idealized agrarian feudalism, though to be honest there are not many practical considerations involved, for Langland's vision of the true king and the true society drifts constantly into the language of apocalypse, where the king will be a new David and the Christ of the Last Days (e.g. III 441). At the same time, Langland observes the plight of the oppressed and the dispossessed with scrupulous fidelity and compassion, perhaps recognizing in them some of the victims of the new economic order, like the urban poor who have no alternative but to buy their food and must therefore suffer the petty exploitations of the hated *regraters* (e.g. III 86, VI 232), or the growing class of itinerant wage-labourers and unemployed vagrants created by economic change (see VIII 210n). The latter, particularly as they make part of the class of beggars, are a recurrent and acute problem for Langland (see Prologue 41n) and he finds the conflict they pose, between the demands of economic necessity and Christian compassion, almost irresolvable. A characteristic pattern develops, however, in which an irresistible compassion, moving against an impregnable political and social orthodoxy, produces in the end an appeal to posthumous rewards (e.g. IX 185, XV 290–99, XVI 17–21), in which poverty patiently borne is seen as the nurse of virtue and a privileged form of earthly purgatory. Langland's attitude here reflects the general movement from *Visio* to *Vita*, and the realization embodied there that there are no political and social problems which are not in the end moral and spiritual problems for the individual.[10]

Langland's more profound and unremitting engagement is with the corruption within the Church, which he traces again to the influence of money. The Church, by the fourteenth century, was a gigantic multi-national corporation, devoted, like all such institutions, to the perpetuation of its own power, privilege and wealth. Langland sees the Church perverted from its every

10. For some examples of the ways in which themes treated in the *Visio* are picked up again in the *Vita* and approached from a more purely spiritual point of view, see notes to VIII 2, X 1, XVI 4, 105, XXI 228, 230, 258, 401, XXII 80, 129.

spiritual office, from the Pope to the lowliest parish priest, by greed for money, and he circles with particular, almost obsessive insistence upon the friars as the spearhead of corruption. They are the focus of Langland's last despairing vision, the prime agents of Antichrist, and the theme of his last lines. Something of Langland's hostility to the friars, which is general in the fourteenth century, is explained by the hopes which the friars, as the true claimants to the inheritance of apostolic poverty and the true imitators of Christ, were felt to have betrayed. But Langland saw too how they struck at the very heart of the Christian community by their prostitution of the office of confession and the sacrament of penance.[11] Penitence, in its three stages (see VI 6n, XVI 25n), was the essential preliminary to inward reformation: the friars therefore obstructed the whole office of the Church and sowed damnation. The friar had no continuing relation with the person he confessed, no power, even if he wanted, of securing performance of the promises and vows he imposed. Confession became a service provided for money, a practice all the more insidious because it was satisfactory to both parties.

Langland is also part of a broader spiritual movement that was sweeping the fourteenth century, and of which the mystics and the Lollards are equally part. The growing isolation and rigidity of the Church as an institution, the growing élitism which identified the Church with the clergy and not with the whole Christian community, led to a movement away from the established Church among devout layfolk and the lower orders of the clergy, a demand for a more personal, non-sacerdotal kind of devotion and for a ministry which was closer to the original ideal of the gospels. Many men were touched by the movement, Chaucer among them, and Langland is at its very centre. It might be said that the heart of his endeavour is to reintegrate the Christian community, to see the potential of the perfected imitation of Christ in every Christian life, and furthermore to see 'the supernatural order of grace as founded and rooted in the natural order and the common life of humanity'.[12] This is why it seems to me that those interpretations of the poem which divide its progress through Dowel, Dobet and Dobest into stages appropriate to different kinds of life, or which identify the highest life with the withdrawn life of the contemplative,[13] are at odds with the poem's true meaning. The precept, to mean anything to Langland, must be universal (X 78n), and every soul must be recognized to be capable of Dobest.

In a way, therefore, Langland can be seen in close relation to the Lollards. He shares with them a general hostility to church endowment, an inveterate hostility to the friars, and a clear recognition that secular governors are responsible for the reform of the regular orders. But he makes little or no mention of the Pope as Antichrist nor of the Wycliffite doctrine of the eucharist, two themes reiterated with monotonous insistence in Wycliffite and Lollard writing. He is to be seen, therefore, as a representative of a broad radical movement which looked for change within the existing fabric of the Church, a movement from which Lollardy sprang but with which it is not to be identified. In fact, it can be strongly argued that one of the considerations

11. See notes to Prologue 62, III 38, VI 119, VIII 101, XII 6, XXII 283, 383.
12. C. Dawson, *Religion and the Rise of Western Culture* (London, 1950), 271.
13. See notes to I 86, X 78, XXI 228.

Langland has in mind in the C-text, maybe even one of the motives that prompted him to make the revision, is to clarify his thinking and his position in relation to those matters of ideology that the Lollards had made peculiarly their own. Many interventions in the C-text, and particularly the new role given to Rechelesnesse,[14] may reflect Langland's growing awareness in the 1380s that the Lollards had moved in directions in which he was not prepared to follow them, and his urgent desire to dissociate his poem from the kind of popular misuse it had suffered at the hands of the ideological leaders of the Peasants' Revolt (see Dobson, 1970, 381), men who themselves were subsequently branded by the establishment as Lollard heretics. In this and in every other way Langland's poem should be seen in close relation to the political and religious upheavals of his day, even to events month by month, like Blake's *Prophetic Books*, and not as a merely personal document.

It is nevertheless a highly individual response to the world of the late fourteenth century that Langland offers us, and cast in a highly idiosyncratic form. Its variety of procedures is bewildering, its conceptual vocabulary complex, and it seems at times designed to cast off the slothful reader. Its ostensible form is that of the dream-allegory, but Langland's use of the form constantly defies and transcends expectation. Much has been written, for instance, on Langland's use of allegory, and attempts have been made to offer a systematic interpretation of the poem in terms of the techniques of personification allegory or of biblical exegesis (e.g. Frank, 1957; Robertson-Huppé, 1951; Smith, 1966). Such techniques are certainly present: large parts of the poem consist of interviews between the dreamer and personified figures representing aspects of his own nature or of external authority; and the surface of the poem is always ready to open up and reveal its substructure in biblical commentary. But other varieties of allegory are equally present, ranging from full-scale allegorical episodes (Lady Meed, the Ploughing of the Half-acre, the feast of Patience, the founding of the Church, the coming of Antichrist) and great allegorical tableaux (the Seven Deadly Sins, the Tree of Charity) – which always have a tendency to develop into progressive narrative – through shorter inset narratives of an exemplary nature (the fable of the belling of the cat, the journey to Truth) down to those momentary flowerings of allegorical visualization which spring from every fissure in the surface of the text (e.g. IV 140, XV 22, XVI 330). Langland moves with breathtaking abruptness between these different allegorical modes, and intrudes the literal into all of them (e.g. the learned Doctor at the feast of Patience, the Annunciation into the allegory of the Tree of Charity); parts of the poem, furthermore, are not allegorical at all (the field full of folk, the Crucifixion and the Harrowing of Hell). Langland's commitment to allegory is both instinctive and casual: he moves towards and away from it with equal ease, and seems most characteristically active in exploring the borderland of the literal and the allegorical, where the allegorical is endorsed by the realities of the literal and the literal vivified by the possibilities of the allegorical. In its form, therefore, the poem reflects the nature of Langland's mind, and particularly his understanding of

---

14. See notes to XI 196, 208, XII 99, XIII 79, 99; and, for further references to relationships with Wycliffite doctrine, notes to Prologue 2, X 1, XIV 65, 115, XV 274, XVI 111, XVII 117, 121, 220, 227.

the bible, where, perhaps as an unexpected dividend of his not having received a full university training, he reveals an incurable literalism and a marked resistance to (or ignorance of) the neat and self-sufficient formulations of traditional biblical exegesis.[15] It reflects too the nature of his poetic imagination, which moves so readily between the concrete and the spiritual that the boundaries between the two are often blurred, or, to put it more positively, so as to effect a perfect fusion between image and reality.

All these varieties of allegorical procedure are contained within the encompassing framework of the dreams which constitute the governing principle of form in the poem. Some attempt has been made to see the eight visions of the poem[16] as intrinsically significant in themselves (e.g. by Frank, 1957; Burrow, 1965; Kirk, 1972), but the results are not convincing. Langland's handling of the mechanisms of dream-structure is too arbitrary (e.g. XI 168, XVIII 179), except in one or two striking passages (e.g. XIII 215, XX 471), to make one think that it is very important. On the other hand, his use of the dreamer, essentially as a first-person narrator, protagonist and observer, is of fundamental importance to the structure of the poem. Through the dreamer, who is both himself and not himself (see note 2, above), he engages the reader in the experience of the poem, so that its urgencies are shared, its discoveries seen and felt to be won. The characterization of the dreamer, stubborn, wary, irritable, but pressed upon always by the necessity of searching for the truth, is undeniably compelling, and there is no need to assume that it is all conscious artifice, since the poem certainly records at least in some measure its author's tortured progress towards understanding. This progress, at any rate, whether author's or dreamer's, is the dominant structure of the poem, insistent, urgent, irresistible, punctuated by reversals, blank fallings away into incomprehension, hard-won insights and hardly to be hoped for revelations of grace. It is the poem's great source of power, since it enforces participation rather than mere acquiescence; at the same time, it is the source of a recurrent paradox of interpretation, for the various 'authorities' who are shown leading the dreamer to higher understanding must be both right and partially wrong since what they say is governed by the dreamer's capacity to understand.[17] The general shape of the poem, however, is not in any doubt, and it is perhaps, of all things, most characteristic of Langland that it should end, after its twin patterns (i.e. in the *Visio* and *Vita*) of searching and finding and losing have been completed, with the return to the world of the Prologue and the beginning again of the search.

To ask what other writings of its time Langland's poem is most like is a profitable question, though in the end an amalgam of Blake's *Prophetic Books*, Wordsworth's *The Prelude* and Eliot's *The Waste Land* may seem to many

15. See notes to VIII 235, IX 261, X 89; and, for further evidence of Langland's imperfect theological training, notes to XIV 208, XVIII 81, XX 420. Whatever his intellectual background, Langland's attempt to wrestle free the authentic meaning of the gospels from the formalism and institutionalized interpretations of the centuries is a high kind of intellectual heroism.

16. Beginning at Prologue 8, V 109, X 67, XV 26, XVIII 183 (see 179n), XX 5, XXI 5, XXII 51. But see notes to XI 168, XIII 213.

17. See notes to X 89, 242, XI 196, 209, XIII 79, XIV 1, 90, 166, 207, XV 113, 126, XVIII 199, 215, XXI 409, XXII 37.

readers the most evocative analogy. Some of its contemporary affiliations are clear enough: the allegorical dream-poem provides its basic form, as has been said, and the traditions of venality satire supply full analogues for certain sequences (see Yunck, 1963; also Hussey, 1965; Salter, 1966). It should be emphasized, however, that Langland's poem, whatever imaginative harvest it may reap from other literature and, further, from its exploration of the poet's own struggles and dilemmas, is first and foremost, in intention, a poem of instruction. Its teaching is the whole Christian faith and, with a fine sense of dramatic suspense, the concentration of that faith in Christ. In a basic sense, therefore, its closest relatives are the manuals of religious instruction, particularly manuals of penitence and confession, which were appearing in increasing numbers in the vernacular, in both verse and prose, in the fourteenth century.[18] Here we find the endlessly reiterated analyses of the fourteen articles of faith, the ten commandments, the seven sacraments, the seven works of mercy, the seven virtues and, above all, and often with much vigorous detail, the seven deadly sins, which contribute much to the substance of Langland's poem. Their concerns are his concerns. Yet the differences are enormous: he breaks up the classifications, and conceals and redistributes the matter in terms of a seemingly organic process of discovery. The pretence (or the reality) is that he finds out to be true what other writers, with the whole weight of the Church's authority speaking through them, declare to be true.

Something similar is revealed if we compare *Piers Plowman* with sermon-literature. It has been said that *Piers Plowman* is no more than 'the quintessence of English medieval preaching gathered up into a single metrical piece of unusual charm and vivacity' (Owst, 1926, 295–6), and certainly there is much in the tone of address of many of the figures of 'authority', in the handling of local detail, in the processes of *inventio* by which materials are brought together (see XV 250n), even sometimes in the rhythmical and phrasal structures (see Prologue 72n) which would justify such a statement (see Owst, 1933; Salter, 1967, 48–50; Spearing, 1972). But Owst's comparisons, being partial, are often deceptive, and anyone who reads through a volume of contemporary English sermons, such as those of Wyclif or those edited by Ross, will become aware of the gulf that separates them from Langland's poem. The immersion of the professional homilists in the techniques of allegorical exegesis, the unvarying tone of voice and posture in relation to the audience, the absence of inner conflict or awareness of conflict, are all sufficient indications of this difference.

A special case might be made for the Wycliffite tracts which constitute the bulk of Matthew's collection and of Arnold's third volume (see Wyclif in Reference List). Whether by Wyclif or his followers (modern opinion would probably favour the latter), these tracts were being produced during the crucial period of Langland's literary career, and there are no writings which echo so insistently Langland's preoccupations, or at least certain of them (see

---

18. E.g. Robert Mannyng's *Handlyng Synne*, Dan Michael of Northgate's *Ayenbite of Inwit*, *The Vices and Virtues* (derived from the same source as the *Ayenbite*), *The Prick of Conscience*, Chaucer's Parson's Tale, the *Speculum Christiani*, the *Speculum Vitae*, *Dives et Pauper*, and *Jacob's Well*. These works are frequently referred to in the notes to the present edition.

note 14, above). However, the ideological differences between Langland and the Lollards, touched on above, are considerable, and there are whole areas of social and theological concern in *Piers Plowman* which Wycliffite writers hardly glance at. It should be remembered too that the Wycliffite tracts, though they allow much freedom of treatment, are basically homiletic in their form of address, and are rooted ultimately in university theology. Langland's poem is not so rooted, and the many attempts to prove him a scholar have perforce to seek their chief evidence outside the text. His knowledge of the bible, particularly the psalms, gospels and epistles, is deep and genuine (but see XVII 235n), though he knows the standard glosses only partially; he knows the Missal well, the Breviary much less well (see Adams, 1976). In fact, he knows just as much as we might expect of a partly-trained cleric in minor orders who performed spiritual offices for the community like a jobbing gardener (Donaldson, 1949, 218–19). As for theology and the writings of the Fathers, Langland knows enough to whet his appetite but not enough to satisfy it (see note 15, above). Most of his knowledge, including his non-biblical and non-liturgical Latin tags, was probably picked up from the collections of excerpts from patristic writings which were widespread, in a variety of forms, in the Middle Ages (see Dunning, 1937, 12); a surprising number of his Latin quotations are of general proverbial currency. His knowledge of law is likewise that of a magpie; he probably earned part of his living as a legal scribe[19] and may even have had some elementary legal training. The intensity of his interest in intellectual and theological matters is often that of a man who has not been to university (or not completed his course, at any rate – see V 36n, XIV 192n) but wishes he had. It should not be thought that this is a defect in Langland as a poet: it might be argued, without straining the paradox, that one of the hidden strengths of the poem is that its author is only partly-educated (in terms of a university education, that is), and that he is able to communicate the restless urgency of his search for truth because he is not liable to bury every question as it arises under a mountain of patristic authorities. Again, this may be the poem's artifice: if so, it is a brilliantly successful one.

Langland's use of other kinds of religious writing is similarly eclectic and arbitrary. His knowledge of devotional and contemplative writing is revealed at several points, but he makes his own use of what he knows; he rejects unworldly and élitist spirituality, at the same time absorbing much of the language and idiom of devotional writing into his own search for a full Christian life which will be every Christian's life (see notes to I 86, VII 256, X 78). It would not do to neglect the influence of this or any of the other kinds of writing mentioned above on Langland's poem, but in the final analysis it is differentiated from all of them by its dominant structure, that of the dreamer's search for truth, particularly as that truth is embodied in Piers Plowman. This is how the poem begins and how it ends, and this is what throughout provides the pressure which drives it forward through every morass and thicket of perplexity.

The poem is written in alliterative verse, and preserves, with not too much

---

19. See notes to IX 22, XIII 118, XVI 320, XIX 15; and see Skeat xxxvi.

fuss, a normal alliterative pattern of *aa/ax*. But Langland is never self-consciously 'poetic', except for possibly allusive or satirical purposes (see notes to Prologue 1, VI 43, X 61), and he shows as little regard for stylistic as for structural formalities. He certainly has few affiliations with the authors of the great poems of the 'alliterative revival',[20] and he draws close at times to the looser structures of semi-alliterative verse or even of alliterative prose. His choice of medium was probably determined by the simplicity of its formal demands as much as anything. His range and level of imaginative activity within it, however, is great, from the simplest, most unassuming, most prosaic exposition to the sublimity of Passus XX, and from the most colloquial conversational idiom (e.g. VI 93, VIII 164, XXII 187) to a lofty style replete with liturgical echoes (e.g. VII 123–51).[21] The characteristic power of Langland's poetry, however, is the operation of his imagination in fusing these different styles together, whirling the homely and the sublime into an extraordinary unity. He never learnt the decorum of the schools.

The Present Text

The three versions of *Piers Plowman* are extant in 51 manuscripts (excluding fragments). Of these, 16 are of the A-text (including 6 with C-text conclusions), 13 of B, and 18 of C, and the rest are scribal composites of other kinds. Texts of all three versions have been available since 1866–73 in the great editions of W. W. Skeat, and most conveniently in the Parallel-Text edition in one volume, with a separate volume of introduction, notes and glossary (Oxford, 1886). The number of manuscripts available to Skeat was limited, and his editions have long been in need of replacement. All three versions are now being presented in critical editions, with full apparatus of variant readings from all known MSS, in *Piers Plowman: The Three Versions*, under the general editorship of George Kane. The A-text, edited by George Kane (London, 1960), and the B-text, edited by George Kane and E. Talbot Donaldson (London, 1975), have already appeared. The publication of the C-text, to be edited by George Russell, will complete this formidable undertaking.

Meanwhile, the only complete text of C is that of Skeat. Skeat chose as his copy-text, and followed faithfully for the most part, a MS now in the Huntington Library in California (MS HM 137, *olim* Phillipps 8231 [P]). It is a carefully written and presented MS, organized to some extent according to the new principles of *compilatio*,[22] but the text that it contains is one that has been subjected to much scribal interference, 'improvement' and sophistication.

20. See J. A. Burrow, 'The Audience of *Piers Plowman*', *Anglia* 75 (1957), 373–84.
21. For discussion of the quality of Langland's poetry, see Donaldson, 1949; Lawlor, 1962; Salter, 1962, 1967; Muscatine, 1972; and also N. Coghill, 'God's Wenches and the light that spoke; some notes on Langland's kind of poetry', in *English and Medieval Studies presented to J. R. R. Tolkien*, ed. N. Davis and C. L. Wrenn (London, 1962), 200–218.
22. See M. B. Parkes, 'The Influence of the Concepts of *Ordinatio* and *Compilatio* on the Development of the Book', in *Medieval Learning and Literature: Essays presented to R. W. Hunt*, ed. J. J. G. Alexander and M. T. Gibson (Oxford, 1976), pp. 115–41.

Difficult passages have been smoothed out, readings that the scribe took to be errors have been 'corrected',[23] and many lines that the scribe thought to be over-long have been padded out into two.[24] Skeat's text can be held in some small measure responsible for the charges of prosiness, pedantry and fussiness which have often been laid against the C-reviser. The discovery of a new MS of C in the British Museum (MS Add. 35157 [U]) prompted a new classification of the C-text MSS (by Miss B. F. Allen in a London MA thesis of 1923) and a trial edition of C II–IV (Skeat III–V) by F. A. R. Carnegy (London MA thesis, 1923; published, London, 1934) based on the newly discovered MS. The subsequent appearance of another MS of C in a Sotheby's sale of 1924 (now Huntington Library MS HM 143 [X]), closely related to U, but superior in several readings, led R. W. Chambers to conclude: 'I think, therefore, that when a critical edition of the C-text is made, the manuscript which should be used as the base should not be, as it has hitherto been, *P* (*HM 137*), but rather *X* (*HM 143*). Although *U* (*Additional 35157*) comes very near in value to *HM 143*, its erratic spellings would make it a bad manuscript upon which to base a text.'[25]

It was this judgment that led us to choose X (corrected from U) as the basis of an earlier volume of selections from the C-text. There seems no reason to change this choice in the present edition of the complete C-text, especially since it is clear from the readings from Russell's projected C-text incorporated in the apparatus to the Kane-Donaldson B-text (on the basis explained there, p. 78) that Russell, like his predecessor, A. G. Mitchell, has also chosen X as his base MS. The superiority of X to U as a representative of the author's original is in fact marginal, and its spelling is barely if at all preferable (both X and U agree on *oe* spellings for long *ō*; U has some eccentric forms for pa.t.pl.; but X is manifestly inferior in its spellings *ho, hoes* for *who, whos*, and its use of *he* as well as *she* for the nom. of the 3sg.fem.pronoun, a form so gratuitously confusing that it is emended in the present edition)[26] but the two MSS together provide a good representation of the textual tradition to which they both belong, which in its turn is a good one. Therefore, X is used here as the base MS, and U is used for the correction of X where X is evidently faulty or inferior. No attempt is made to provide a complete apparatus of variant

---

23. Examples of the type of variation characteristic of P may be seen by comparing the following lines in the present edition with the corresponding lines in Skeat's text: Prologue 49, 72, II 19, III 73, 225, V 10, 44, VI 39, VII 134–5, VIII 295, etc. The activity of the scribe of P's exemplar, it should be stressed, is thoroughly reasonable and at times highly intelligent: it is this that makes him a dangerous guide for the editor. Nevertheless, P is sometimes used in the present edition for the emendation of the copy when it is defective.

24. Viz. I 99, III 140–41, 255, 304, V 115, VII 205, VIII 257–8, X 214, 236, XIII 9, 160, 191, XIV 121, XV 81, 142, 225, XVI 31, 93, XVIII 155, XIX 126, XX 332.

25. *Piers Plowman: The Huntington Library Manuscript* (*HM 143*), reproduced in Photostat, with an Introduction by R. W. Chambers and Technical Examination by R. B. Haselden and H. C. Schulz (San Marino, California, 1936: copy in University College Library, London, Chambers Papers 21), pp. 22–3. There was an earlier discussion by Chambers of the value of MS HM 143 in his essay, 'The Manuscripts of *Piers Plowman* in the Huntington Library and their value for fixing the text of the poem', *Huntington Library Bulletin* 8 (1935), 1–25. For a list and brief discussion of C-text MSS, see Donaldson, 1949, 227–31.

26. Other eccentricities of spelling are kept, since they are part of an actual language (e.g. *a* for 3 pers. pron.) and not of a tidied-up version of one.

readings in U which are not adopted into the text, though a few of the more interesting are recorded.

It is not to be supposed that the textual tradition represented by XU preserves in all cases what the C-reviser actually wrote. The XU text will inevitably contain inferior readings which have been introduced in the process of scribal transmission. It will be the business of Russell's critical edition to reconstruct, as far as possible, from the available evidence, what the author originally wrote. A particular complication is introduced by the fact that the text of B which the C-reviser used as the basis of his revision was already a copy corrupted by scribal transmission (Russell, 1969, 38; Kane-Donaldson 98), though not in such an advanced state of corruption as the archetype of all extant B MSS. Since the C-revision was neither systematic nor complete (see above, p. 10), it is difficult to determine what degree of authorial endorsement has been given to inferior readings carried over from the reviser's B MS (see Russell, 1969, n 21). An examination of this problem, as of the textual status of those parts of C which are additions to B or where the revision is not close enough to make textual comparison possible, must await Russell's full critical edition.

In the present edition, no attempt has been made to reconstruct the author's original from which XU are derived, though some effort has been made to correct readings that are evidently defective in sense or in form. For this purpose, two further MSS have been consulted, in addition to XU and P, in the hope that they may supply satisfactory readings where the joint testimony of XU is suspect. The first of these, Trinity College Cambridge MS R.3.14 [T], contains a text of C derived from a textual tradition regarded as superior even to that of XU by Chambers and Donaldson (though in my opinion subjected to some scribal improvement). The difficulty is that T is a composite AC text and is a C-text only from C XI 299 (Skeat XII 297). It cannot therefore be used as a base MS, though it can be used to correct manifest error in XU. The second is the MS formerly in the possession of the earl of Ilchester (now University of London MS [S.L.] V.88). Skeat knew this MS, and recognized its peculiar quality, but dismissed it from serious consideration because of the mutilated state in which it survives, due to the combined effects of damp and rats. He nevertheless incorporated occasional readings from it. The Ilchester MS [I] is in fact for the most part a worthy representative of the same textual tradition as XU and is used in this edition, where possible, to recover that tradition where XU are defective. A degree of confusion, however, surrounds the Prologue in I, which is an A-text with additions from C IX and C Prologue. The additions from C IX vary considerably from the usual XU text (which appears in I in its normal place in passus IX), more radically indeed than would normally be thought to be the result of scribal transmission. They could be an early draft by the author, a revision by the author, or a particularly prolonged piece of editorial rewriting. The addition from C Prologue, which consists of one long passage, contains a version of the Ophni and Finees episode (Prologue 106–17) which varies even more radically from the usual XU text. Russell considers that it represents a superior text of the passage (Russell, 1969, 29), from which other MSS differ because of the normal processes of scribal corruption. There are difficulties with this view, in the un-Langlandian syntax and vocabulary of the I version, but principally in the omission from I of an essential element in the biblical story (that corresponding to Prologue 111–13 here). I prefer to see the I-text of Ophni and Finees as an editorial revision (with particular attention to alliterative embellishment) of a passage which Langland had left half worked over. The scribe responsible for this rewriting was presumably also responsible for the transfer and rewriting of material from C IX which he recognized as being of particular power and which he wanted to present in a more prominent position in the Prologue. On the basis of this interpretation, I make no use of the readings of I Prologue. The argument that it is the start of a 'D-text' of *Piers Plowman* is not a strong one.

These four MSS, with the addition of Skeat's MS [P], which I have checked for all readings that I adopt or record from Skeat,[27] are the only MSS I have consulted for this edition, which has no claim, as I repeat, to be a critical edition of the C-text. Where the readings of all five MSS consulted are defective, some limited use is made of the B-text, as reconstructed by Kane-Donaldson, for emendation, especially in the later passus, where B and C are consistently closer, and where C revises sporadically or not at all.

X is presented with silent expansion of contractions according to normal editorial usage, but otherwise with every deviation from the MS, including the correction of mechanical errors, recorded in the footnotes. Scribal and other correction of the copy is not recorded unless it is relevant to the interpretation of the text. Contractions are expanded in accordance with the predominant spelling in uncontracted forms, where available; otherwise in accordance with normal London usage *c.* 1400. The main contractions are for vowel + *r*, for *r* + vowel, for nasals and for final *-es*; in addition, certain short words (e.g. *and, with, þou, quod*) and certain proper nouns (e.g. *Iesu, Dauid*) are abbreviated. Flourished final *r* is expanded *-re*; otherwise final flourishes are ignored. Punctuation and capitalization are modern. Word-division is modern, except that certain common compounds are hyphenated (e.g. *ho-so, pere-ynne*) in order to avoid gratuitous confusion.

The passus are renumbered Prologue and I–XXII, for the reasons outlined above (note 9). I have not, however, attempted to anticipate the line-numbering of Russell's edition, since no two editors will agree on the treatment of the Latin. The practice here is to number Latin lines which contain any word of English or which are integral to the syntax of the surrounding English lines. The remainder, mostly biblical quotations, are unnumbered and indented.

The textual notes record all deviations from X, the base MS. Emendation is backed by the citation of supporting MSS in the sequence UITP. The first MS in this sequence to contain the reading accepted is normally the last to be cited. Where I is omitted from the sequence, it may be presumed to be unusable (as in the Prologue) or defective (principally XI 276–XII 18, XV 294–XVII 58, XVIII 101–161, XXI 79–XXII end, and at many page edges and corners). Variants adopted from UITP are adapted to the spelling of X where the reading of X is closely comparable, and minor spelling variations in the sup-

---

27. A labour made easier by the availability of a complete collation of Skeat's text with MS HM 137 by J. A. W. Bennett, in *MÆ* 17 (1948), 21–31.

porting MSS (e.g. variation of *i/y*, variation of *i/e* in inflexions, omission or addition of final *-e*) not recorded. The name of *Peres . . . plouhman* is erased throughout MS X, with occasional omissions, and with additional obliteration of common noun *peres* and other names *Peres*. The erased readings have been recovered by ultra-violet light and are recorded in the technical introduction by Haselden and Schulz to the Chambers facsimile (note 25, above). No further remark on this feature is made in the textual notes.

Piers Plowman

The textual notes record readings from the following MSS:
  X (the copy-text) Huntington Library MS HM 143
  U   British Library MS Add.35157
  I   University of London MS [S.L.] V.88
  T   Trinity College, Cambridge, MS R.3.14
  P   Huntington Library MS HM 137
For a full account of the practice adopted in the treatment of the copy and variants, see Introduction, pp. 20–24.

Prologue

The Fair Field Full of Folk

In a somur sesoun whan softe was þe sonne
Y shope me into shroudes as y a shep were;
In abite as an heremite, vnholy of werkes,
Wente forth in þe world wondres to here,

1. Going out on a May-morning is frequently the prelude to a dream-vision in medieval poetry, as in Chaucer's *Legend of Good Women*, or it may be the first episode of the dream itself, as in the *Roman de la Rose* and Chaucer's *Book of the Duchess*. The use of the seasonal setting here is one of Langland's few allusions to fashionable poetic convention (cf. X 61–7): the description is characteristically curtailed in C by the omission of B Prol. 8–10. A similar setting is provided for the poet's dream in another alliterative poem, *Winner and Waster*, an allegorical debate on the social and economic state of England in the 1350s which may have influenced the original conception of Langland's poem (cf. 24, below, and see Coghill, 1944, 304–9; Hussey, 1965). Two other seasonal openings in alliterative poems, both of a didactic cast, look to be directly influenced by L, viz. *The Parlement of the Thre Ages* (ed. EETS 246) and *Somer Soneday* (ed. as a lament for Edward II in Robbins, 1959, no. 38, but now ascribed to *c*. 1400: see T. Turville-Petre in *RES*, n.s.25, 1974, 1–14). There seems to be allusion to L's opening lines also in a seasonal interlude in the romance of *The Sowdone of Babylone*, *c*.1400 (ed. EETS, ES 38), 963–78.

2. 'I dressed myself in (rough) outer garments as if I were a sheep (*or* a shepherd).' The coarse woollen outer garment of a shepherd (a possible sense of *shep*) might be presumed to resemble that of a hermit, mentioned in the next line, and L may be thinking of a shepherd as the simple, detached observer familiar in pastoral tradition. On the other hand, he associated himself elsewhere with 'ermytes' of dubious vocation (V 4) and a persistent hint of self-criticism is present in his frequent examinations of the justification of the hermit's life and of the distinctions of holy and unholy hermits (Prol. 30, 51, VIII 146, IX 188, XVII 8). A hermit's 'habit' seems, furthermore, to have been distinctive (see Chaucer's *Romaunt of the Rose* 6480–81, and X 1, below). On this reading, being dressed 'as a sheep' is an ironical reference to the woollen coat that disguises the hypocritical and predatory parasite on the Christian community – the wolf in sheep's clothing (symbol of the false prophet in Matt. 7:15). The true apostles, on the other hand, go out 'as lambs in the midst of wolves' (Luke 10:3). See IX 255n. In the light of X 1n, it is interesting that archbishop Courtenay called the Lollard poor priests 'wolves in sheep's clothing' (Workman, ii.204).

3. *vnholy of werkes*: 'without holy works to his credit' (but not, because of that, necessarily a man of sinful works: see Mills, 1969, 186).

4. Here, unobtrusively announced, is the dominant theme of the poem, the theme of journeying and seeking, later embodied in the pilgrimage to Truth and the quest for Dowel (see Salter, 1967, 41–7, and Sermons, ed. Ross, p. 74).

And say many sellies and selkouthe thynges.   5
Ac on a May mornyng on Maluerne hulles
Me biful for to slepe, for werynesse of-walked;
And in a launde as y lay, lened y and slepte,
And merueylousliche me mette, as y may telle.
Al þe welthe of the world and þe wo bothe   10
Wynkyng, as hit were, witterliche y sigh hit;
Of treuthe and tricherye, tresoun and gyle,
Al y say slepynge, as y shal telle.
     Estward y beheld aftir þe sonne
And say a tour – as y trowed, Treuthe was there-ynne.   15
Westward y waytede in a while aftir
And seigh a depe dale – Deth, as y leue,
Woned in tho wones, and wikkede spiritus.
A fair feld ful of folk fond y þer bytwene
Of alle manere men, þe mene and þe pore,   20
Worchyng and wandryng as þis world ascuth.

5. sellies U] X selles
7. of-walked XU] P of wandryng
15. y U] X *om*
21. wandryng U] X wondryng

6. On the basis of L's references to the Malvern Hills, in Worcestershire, as the setting of his dreams (cf. V 110, IX 293), it has often been presumed that he was educated at the priory of Great Malvern (e.g. Skeat xxxi). This is not unlikely (see Kaske, 1968, 160, and VI 157, 398), though the scenic detail of his vision should not be pressed in the interests of landscape realism (as in Bright, 1928). Nor should the 'I' of the poem be identified with L: his experiences and attitudes may at many points be the poet's but, as the dreamer, he is first of all, always, a literary fiction (see I 5n, V 1n, and Mills, 1969).

7. *of-walked*: 'exhausted with walking'. *of-* is an intensive adverbial prefix (cf. IX 85) comparable with *for-*, and suggestive of exhaustion caused by the action of the verb. The form *of walked* appears in MS W of B at XIII 204, though it is rejected in favour of *forwalked* by Kane-Donaldson.

10–13. These lines in C replace further scenic description and dream-setting in B, and are an example of the characteristic exclusion in C of non-functional 'poetic' ornament (Donaldson, 1949, 48–50, 71–4).

14–18. The prompt explanation of the significance of the tower and the dale (cf. I 1, 12, 55) is an innovation in C, though *Estward*, present already in B, would naturally suggest 'towards God', as the source of light and truth (for a long exposition, see *Dives et Pauper* 113–16), and the *tour* alludes to Ps. 60:4, Prov. 18:10. The rejection of the suggestive and mysterious in favour of the didactically explicit is typical of C. Suggestions have been made that the symbolic locale of the vision relates to the staging of medieval morality plays (e.g. Skeat 4, Bennett 82).

19. *A fair feld.* 'The field is the world,' says Christ, interpreting the parable of the tares (Matt. 13:38).

Somme potte hem to þe plogh, playde ful selde,
In settynge and in sowynge swonken ful harde
And wonne þat þis wastors with glotony destrueth.
And summe putte hem to pruyde and parayled hem þer-aftir   25
In continance of clothyng in many kyne gyse.
In preiers and penaunces potten hem mony,
Al for loue of oure lord lyueden swythe harde
In hope to haue a good ende and heuenriche blisse;
As ankeres and eremites þat holdeth hem in here selles,   30
Coueyten noȝt in contreys to cayren aboute
For no likerous liflode here lycame to plese.
    And summe chesen chaffare – þei cheueth þe bettre,
As it semeþ to oure sighte that suche men ythryueth;
And summe murthes to make as mynstrels conneth,   35
Wolleth neyther swynke ne swete, bote sweren grete othes,
Fyndeth out foule fantasyes and foles hem maketh   f.1^b
And hath wytt at wille to worche yf þei wolde.
That Poule prechede of hem preue hit y myhte;

26. of U] X and
39. That U] X Thay

22. Ploughmen appear first, as is appropriate to the first literal sense of the 'fair field' as the open level tract of arable land where the villagers have their acres or half-acres (cf. VIII 2), and appropriate too to the role of the ploughman in the poem as the type of the honest workman and faithful Christian. The field is almost immediately allegorized as the world of human activity.

24. *þat*: 'what'. The contrast of 'winning' and 'wasting' recalls the debate of *Winner and Waster*, mentioned above (1n). Cf. V 126, VIII 149.

25–6. 'And some devoted themselves to the satisfaction of their vanity, and dressed themselves accordingly, in outward show of clothing of many kinds.'

30. Stability of life was part of the vow of an anchorite or anchoress (see *Ancrene Wisse*, ed. Shepherd, xxxiv), and it is important for Langland as a way of distinguishing between true and false hermits (see above, 2n).

31–2. 'Are not over-anxious to go wandering about the countryside, nor to indulge their flesh in luxurious living.'

35. Minstrels, true and false, are, like hermits and beggars, one of Langland's persistent preoccupations (e.g. VII 82–119, VIII 48–52, IX 128–33, XI 31–5, XV 194–216, and see Donaldson, 1949, 136–55), presumably because their moral status in society, like that of hermits and beggars, is so blurred and open to challenge. He also perhaps sees his own life as a mirror of all three roles. Here he speaks with no mitigation (cf. B Prol. 34) of the coarsest kind of popular entertainer: the hostility to 'minstrels' is throughout C more clear-cut than in AB, perhaps because C has clarified the problem by recognizing a new class of 'God's minstrels' (VII 100, IX 138).

37–8. 'Invent filthy stories and make themselves fools and (yet) have the intelligence at their command to do something useful if they wanted to.'

39. Presumably a reference to 2 Thess. 3:10: 'If any man will not work, neither let him eat.'

Qui turpiloquium loquitur is Luciferes knaue.   40
 Bidders and beggers fast aboute ȝede
Til here bagge and here bely was bretful ycrammed,
Fayteden for here fode and foughten at þe ale.
In glotonye þo gomus goth þei to bedde
And ryseþ with rybaudrye þo Robardus knaues;   45
Slep and also slewthe sueth suche euer.
 Pilgrymes and palmers plighten hem togyderes
To seke seynt Iame and seyntes of Rome,
Wenten forth on here way with many wyse tales
And hadde leue to lye aftir, al here lyf-tyme.   50
Eremites on an hep with hokede staues
Wenten to Walsyngham, and here wenches aftir;
Grete lobies and longe þat loth were to swynke
Clothed hem in copis to be knowe fram othere
And made hemself heremites, here ese to haue.   55
 I fonde þer of freris alle þe foure ordres,
Prechyng þe peple for profyt of þe wombe,

44. þo U] X þe

40. The Latin ('He who speaks filth') is a reminiscence of Eph. 5:4, adapted to fit the syntax of the line. Cf. VII 117.

41. Beggars are a third group to whom L gives particular attention (e.g. VII 100, VIII 128, 209–90, IX 61–187, XII 102–19, XVI 10–89), for the reasons suggested above (2n, 35n; and see Donaldson, 1949, 130–36). He is influenced too by the debate about mendicancy as it concerned the friars (see below, 62n).

45. *Robardus knaues*. The form *roberdesmen*, 'Robert's men', was a cant term of the day for robbers (cf. VI 316), probably deriving from the similarity of sound. See Mustanoja, 1970, 62–3, and *Speculum Vitae* 3777–806, where *Robertmen* are also called *sneckedrawers* ('sneak-thieves') and a vivid description given of their activities.

47. A *palmer* was a pilgrim who had visited the Holy Land, in token of which he carried a palm leaf or badge; but the name often meant simply a professional pilgrim. There were, indeed, pilgrims who were literally 'professionals', who were hired to perform pilgrimages which others had accepted as a vow or a penance, and who often worked in confraternities, as here (see Workman, ii.407–8, and a note by L. Polak in *NQ* 215, 1970, 282–5). A barefoot pilgrimage to Canterbury cost 20s. in 1361.

48. *seynt Iame*: the shrine of Santiago at Compostella in Galicia, NW Spain, a famous place of pilgrimage. See VII 166n.

52. The shrine of Our Lady of Walsingham, in Norfolk, was second only to Canterbury as a place of pilgrimage in England.

55. For the punishment in the pillory of a false hermit, who feigned sanctity to win alms, see Riley's *Memorials*, 584.

56. *þe foure ordres*. Dominicans, Franciscans, Austin friars and Carmelites.

And glosede þe gospel as hem good likede;
For coueytise of copis contraryed somme doctours.
Mony of þise maistres of mendenant freres   60
Here moneye and marchandise marchen togyderes.
Ac sith charite hath be chapman and chief to shryue lordes

---

61. marchen P] XU maken

---

58. Friars were the professional preachers of the day, and it was a familiar complaint against them that they twisted the interpretation of scripture for their own purposes, and particularly for the purpose of claiming support from the gospels for their own practice of 'wilful begging' (*Defensio Curatorum*, 70). See Chaucer, Summoner's Tale, *CT* III. 1793; Wyclif, ed. Arnold, iii.180, 376–7. The 'glosing' of the friars is associated particularly with forced allegorical interpretation in Wyclif, ed. Arnold, ii.343.

60. *maistres*: masters of arts or divinity, learned men. Friars had a reputation for learning, but the contemptuous *þise* indicates the echo of Matt. 23:10. *of* introduces a loose apposition.

61. 'Their love of money and their trade (in souls) go hand in hand.' *marchen* may also mean 'have a common boundary', i.e. 'are linked'.

62. 'But ever since charity (i.e. the friars whose profession is charity) became a merchant and chief confessor to lords . . .' Friars were accused of making confession easy so as to win money (cf. III 38–67, XII 5–10, and *CT* I. 221–32) and of cultivating the favour of high-ranking nobles in the same way (most of the royal confessors of the 14th c. were friars). See Wyclif, ed. Arnold, iii.382, 393–6. It is their undermining of the necessary act of penance that makes the friars the main object of Langland's attack throughout the poem; it is the friars who bring the church to the brink of destruction in the poem's final vision (XXII 230–379). The specific criticisms of the friars, here and throughout the poem, echo the well-established traditions of estates satire (for which see J. Mann, *Chaucer and Medieval Estates Satire*, Cambridge, 1973, 37–54) and anti-mendicant propaganda. The friars had been under attack since the time of William of St Amour, whose *De periculis novissimorum temporum* (1256) associated the apocalyptic prophecies of 2 Tim. 3:1–10 (cf. XXII 340) with the coming of the friars (cf. 64–5, below). In England, two main waves of attack were those led by Richard FitzRalph, archbishop of Armagh, in his preaching in the vernacular in London in 1356 and in his *Defensio Curatorum*, translated by Langland's contemporary, Trevisa; and by Wyclif and his followers in the 1380s. The former attacked mainly the friars' usurpation of the rights of the parish clergy (*Defensio*, 41–55): burying, preaching and hearing confession (i.e. the most lucrative practices – FitzRalph also, like L, calls friars 'chapmen', 72). The latter concentrated more on the friars' perversion of the gospels. See Williams, 1953, 500–06.

62–5. The phrasing of this sentence recalls the many 14th c. poems of complaint against the abuses of the time (e.g. Robbins, 1959, no. 55, or *The Simonie* – see Salter, 1966) which, as here, are often accompanied by dire apocalyptic warnings as in the popular genre of admonitory political prophecy (e.g. Robbins, 1959, nos. 43–7, and cf. III 477, IV 108, V 168, VIII 343, XXII 53). Such works are important as the raw material of Langland's inspiration.

Mony ferlyes han falle in a fewe ʒeres,
And but holi chirche and charite choppe adoun suche shryuars
The moste meschief on molde mounteth vp faste. 65
    Ther prechede a pardoner as he a prest were
And brouth forth a bulle with bischopis selys,
Sayde þat hymself myhte assoylen hem alle
Of falsnesses of fastynges, of vowes ybrokene.
Lewed men leued hym wel and lykede his wordes 70
And comen and knelede to kyssen his bulles;
A bounchede hem with his bulles and blered here yes
And raughte with his rageman rynges and broches. f.2ᵃ
Thus ʒe gyue ʒoure gold glotons to helpe
And leneth hit lorelles þat lecherye haunten. 75
Were þe bischop yblessed and worth bothe his eres

69. of² P] XU and

66. A pardoner carried a papal bull, which was the formal statement of 'indulgence', and to it were affixed the seals of the bishops (67) in whose dioceses he was licensed to preach. Indulgences granted remission of punishment for sin imposed by the Church in this life (e.g. fasting, saying extra prayers) but not forgiveness from the guilt of sin (i.e. it was a pardon *a poena* but not *a culpa*). They were not 'sold', though recipients could make voluntary contributions to the church; pardoners were, in canon law, messengers who communicated indulgences from the pope and humbly requested alms (Kellogg, 1951, 253). The system was open to abuse, and unscrupulous pardoners could claim that they were offering absolution from sin (68–9), as if they were priests (66) with power of confession. The concept of personal sinfulness and the necessity of personal repentance were alike undermined by the practice of 'buying pardons', and pardoners were under constant attack in the later Middle Ages and were a major target for the reformers' criticism in the early 16th c. (for some examples of the kind of claims made for indulgences in 1517, see Krochalis and Peters, 1975, 62–70).

72–3. 'He tapped them on the head (in token of forgiveness, cf. *CT* VI. 909) with his papal letters of authority and deluded them thoroughly and raked in their rings and brooches with his roll of papal parchment.' The *bulles* and *rageman* are the same document; for the derivation of *rageman* (cf. rigmarole) see Bennett 90. *bounchede* and *blered* almost suggest a game of blind-man's buff (i.e. buffet). The following passage from a sermon (quoted by Owst, 1933, 373), describing the fate of those who trust pardoners, might support such an interpretation, and incidentally characterizes clearly the kind of semi-alliterative homiletic prose which L drew from and inspired: 'Alle such ben maad blynde or blyndefeld for a tyme, as men pleyen a-bobbid [i.e. Blindman's Buff]; for thei beth bobbid in hire bileve and in hire catel bothe, bi suche lepers over londe, that libbeth bi hire lesyngis'.

76. 'If the bishop were truly a bishop (as he was blessed at his consecration) and really worth his salt (i.e. worthy of his office) . . .' For a more specific interpretation of *worth bothe his eres* as 'worthy to have his ears because he made use of them' (i.e. was alert and vigilant), see a note by G. K. Johnstone in *NQ* 204 (1959), 244.

His seel sholde nouȝt be ysent in deseyte of þe people.
Ac it is nouȝt by þe bischop, y leue, þat þe boy precheþ,
For þe parsche prest and þe pardoner parten þe seluer
That þe peple in parsches sholde haue, yf þei ne were.   80
   Persones and parsche prestis pleyned to þe bischop
That here parsches were pore sithe þis pestelence tyme,
To haue a licence and a leue in Londoun to dwelle
And synge þer for symonye while seluer is so swete.
   Bischopes and bachelers, bothe maystres and doctours,   85
That han cure vnder Crist and crownyng in tokene
And ben charged with holy chirche charite to tylie,
That is lele loue and lyfe among lered and lewed,
Leyen in Londoun in lenton and elles.
Summe seruen þe kynge and his siluer tellen,   90
In þe cheker and in þe chancerye chalengen his dettes

87. And *supplied*] XUP *om*

78. *by þe bischop*: 'with reference to the bishop', i.e. with the bishop's permission. In other words, the pardoner had obtained the bishop's seal by bribing an episcopal official, or else had by-passed the bishop and gone directly to an official of the local archdeacon to obtain (by a bribe) permission to preach in his area (Kellogg, 1951, 267).

79. He then bribed the local priest with a share of the takings (as contrasted with Chaucer's Pardoner, *CT* I. 701–6).

80. *yf þei ne were*: 'if it were not for them'.

81. The *persone* was the incumbent priest, the one who received the living (he was often an absentee), while the *parsche prest* was his ill-paid deputy.

82. *pestelence tyme*. The Black Death made its first visitation in England in 1348–9 and broke out again in 1361–2, 1369 and 1375–6 (cf. V 115). The depopulation of the parishes meant a loss of tithes and income and many priests went to London, where there was a living to be made saying masses for the souls of the rich dead (i.e. as chantry priests). The practice was common enough for Chaucer to use his Parson's repudiation of it (*CT* I. 507–11) as a technique of moral idealization.

85–218 added in BC. There is a shift of focus from the opening scene.

85–94. Having mentioned the priests who resort to London, L is led on to speak of the higher ecclesiastics who hold official positions in law and government in London, and so neglect their priestly office – a frequent cause of complaint in Wycliffite writings, e.g. Wyclif, ed. Arnold, iii.215, 277; ed. Matthew, 13, 78, 149, 168, 242; but cf. V 69.

89. *lenton*. Lent was the busiest time of the year for a conscientious priest.

90–91. A notable contemporary example was William of Wykeham, bishop of Winchester, whose bishopric was a reward for secular office in the service of the king and who later became chancellor (1367–71). See further, Pantin, 1955, 14.

Of wardus and of wardemotis, wayues and strayues;
And summe aren as seneschalles and seruen oþer lordes
And ben in stede of stewardus and sitten and demen.
Consience cam and cused hem – and þe comune herde hit –   95
And seide, 'Ydolatrie ȝe soffren in sondrye places manye
And boxes ben yset forth ybounde with yren
To vndertake þe tol of vntrewe sacrefice.
In menynge of myracles muche wex hangeth there:
Al þe world wot wel hit myghte nouȝt be trewe,   100
And for it profiteþ ȝow into pursward ȝe prelates soffren
That lewed men in mysbileue lyuen and dyen.
I leue by oure lord for loue of ȝoure coueytise
That al þe world be the wors, as holy writ telleth
What cheste and meschaunce to þe children of Israel   105
Ful on hem þat fre were thorwe two fals prestis.
For Offnies synne and Fines his brother

95. cused] X cussed; U kuste; P acusede
105–6. Israel/Ful on P] XU Irael ful/On
107. Offnies synne] X offnies sone; U offny hely sone (hely [i.e. Heli's] *is a later insertion*); P the synne of Ophni

92. This line refers to various kinds of revenue that the king's officials would be engaged in collecting: money from the estates of minors in the king's guardianship (*wardus*); the dues payable by city wards, rendered at ward-meetings or *wardemotis*; and various kinds of lost property (*wayues*) and strayed animals (*strayues*) which, being unclaimed, passed to the king's possession.

95–124 added in C, a biblical exemplum of false priests. The introduction of the new material is characteristically abrupt, and anticipates the scene in parliament (139, below).

96–9. Iron-bound boxes were used for the reception of alms (Riley's *Memorials* 586); L suggests that the miraculous relics and images for which offerings were enjoined, and candles lit by the devout (99), were often false. The author of *Dives et Pauper* (quoted in Owst, 1933, 148) similarly attacks 'fals prechourys' for 'feynyng myracles of ymagis . . . to maynteyn ydolatrie for lucre of offerynge'. Attacks on relic-mongering were a feature of Wycliffite writing (e.g. Wyclif, ed. Arnold, iii.293, 462).

106–17. The story of Ophni and Phinees is told in 1 Reg. 1–4 as a contrast to the growth in grace of the young Samuel. Sons of the high priest Heli, they are the type of the false priest because they perverted to themselves the offerings of the people (1 Reg. 2:12–17). They were killed in battle, and Israel was punished for their sin by defeat in battle and the loss of the ark of the covenant to the Philistines. Heli, who had not effectively restrained them from their sinful course (2:22–5, 3:13), died by a fall when he heard the news of their death. The passage in L, developed from a brief allusion later in B (X 285–8), is remarkable for the failure of alliteration in many of its lines. It may be an unfinished piece of work: see Introduction, p. 23.

107. *Fines*: gen.sg., i.e. 'that of Phinees'.

Thei were discomfited in batayle and losten *Archa domini.*
And for here syre sey hem synne and suffred hem do ille f.2^b
And chastisid hem noght þerof and nolde noght rebuken hem, 110
Anon as it was tolde hym that þe children of Israel
Were disconfit in batayle and *Archa domini* lorn
And his sones slawe ther, anon he ful for sorwe
Fro his chayere þer he sat and brake his nekke atwene;
And al was for vengeance he bet noght his children. 115
And for þei were prestis and men of holy chirche
God was wel þe wrother and took þe raþer vengeance.
    Forthy y sey ȝe prestes and men of holy churche
That soffreth men do sacrefyce and worschipe maumettes,
And ȝe shulde be here fadres and techen hem betre, 120
God shal take vengeaunce on alle suche prestis
Wel hardere and grettere on suche shrewed faderes
Than euere he dede on Offnies and Fines his fader,
For ȝoure shrewed soffraunce and ȝoure oune synne.
Ȝoure masse and ȝour matynes and many of ȝoure oures 125
Ar don vndeuouteliche; drede is at þe laste
Lest Crist in his constorie acorse of hem manye.
    I parsceyued of þe power that Peter hadde to kepe,

111. Israel P] XU Irael
123. his fader X] U and hely þair fadre (*last three words a later insertion*)
125. ȝour, ȝoure²] X here, here *but marked thus for correction*

115. The need for fathers to correct and chastise their children is a theme to which L and other homilists frequently recur (e.g. IV 112, V 136–9, VIII 81). It is the use to which the present story is usually put, e.g. *Handlyng Synne* 4919–5044, *Dives et Pauper* 324, Wyclif, ed. Matthew, 55, 314.

123. *his* provides the equivalent of a gen.sg. inflexion for *Fines* (cf. IX 315). *Offnies* is already gen.sg.

125. The second and third ȝoure are written over *here* in MS X, indicating a transitional stage from the 3rd person construction of B (as C returns here to the matter of B). The mistake remains uncorrected in 127 (where IP read ȝow for *hem*). See Donaldson, 1949, 246.

127. The thought of the consistory courts (ecclesiastical courts, for the trial of any offence involving a cleric), at which the secular bishops of ll. 85–94 were accustomed to preside, makes L think of Christ's great consistory court at the Last Judgment, when they themselves will be judged. This in turn leads to a consideration of the papal consistory court (of cardinals) which inherits the power assigned by Christ to Peter.

128. *I parsceyued*. Conscience, who is apparently still speaking, inherits the visionary language of the dreamer from B, not altogether appropriately.

To bynde and to vnbynde, as þe boke telleth,
Hou he it lefte with loue as oure lord wolde   130
Amonge foure vertues most vertuous of vertues
That cardinales ben cald and closyng-ʒates
Thare Crist is in kynedom to close with heuene.
Ac of þe cardinales at court þat caught han such a name
And power presumen in hemself a pope to make,   135
To haue þe power þat Peter hadde inpugne hem y nelle,
For in loue and lettrure lith þe grete eleccoun;
Contreplede hit noght,' quod Consience, 'for holi chirche sake.'
   Thenne cam ther a kyng, knyghthede hym ladde,

133. Thare Crist U (*part of authentic late insertion*)] X thare/Crist
138. for holi U] X for men of holi (*with* men of *erased*)
139. ladde U] X lawe

129. Matt. 16:19, Christ's words to Peter: 'And I will give to thee the keys of the kingdom of heaven. And whatsoever thou shalt bind on earth shall be bound in heaven: and whatsoever thou shalt loose on earth shall be loosed in heaven.' This promise is the foundation of the Church's power of absolution from sin (cf. 66n, above). L sees this power as being exercised through love, and more specifically through the four cardinal virtues. See XXI 272–308, where the delivery of this power to Peter-Piers is dealt with in detail.

132. *cardinales*, adj., with pl. ending inherited from Latin or French. The cardinal virtues are the hinges (*cardinal*, in its various senses, is derived from Lat. *cardo*, 'hinge') upon which the gate of heaven opens and closes (and upon which a man's spiritual life 'hangs'). There is similar exploitation of the etymology of the word in Wyclif, ed. Matthew, 472. *closyng-ʒates*. Perhaps best understood as a type of participle + accus. compound, i.e. 'gate-closers', with a pun on the etymological meaning. But L may be using *cardinales* to refer to the virtues as both hinges and gates.

133. *to close with heuene*: 'to close heaven with'.

134. *caught* suggests that cardinals are not fully entitled to their name, with all its attached meanings, though L does not impugn their office nor their right to elect the pope. After the election by the French cardinals of an antipope in 1378, which began the Great Schism, there was much debate about the validity of the election of the 'true' pope, Urban VI, earlier in the same year (see Workman, ii.76–9).

139. Langland, who may, in this long BC interpolation, be thought of as analysing the organs of authority which rule in the corrupt state of the world, moves here from the papal court to the royal court and parliament. He attempts to establish first the nature of royal authority (a point much debated in the Middle Ages) by rehearsing allegorically the terms of the monarchic contract between the king and his estates (knighthood, clergy and commons). An examination of the nature of kingship would have had special point during the period when the infant Richard was heir-apparent (1376–7) or during the first years of his minority (see 206, below). See Bennett *MÆ*, 1943, 57–9.

Myght of tho men made hym to regne. 140
And thenne cam Kynde Wytt and clerkus he made
And Conscience and Kynde Wit and knyghthed togedres
Caste þat þe comunes sholde here comunes fynde.
Kynde Wytt and þe comune contreued alle craftes
And for most profitable a plogh gonne þei make, 145
With lele labour to lyue while lif on londe lasteth. f.3ᵃ
  Thenne Kynde Witt to þe kynge and to þe comune saide,
'Crist kepe þe, kynge, and thy kyneriche
And leue the lede so þy londe þat Lewte þe louye
And for thy rightful ruylynge be rewardid in heuene.' 150
  Consience to clergie and to þe kynge sayde,

---

140. tho XU] I þe mene; P the
141–2. and clerkus . . . Kynde Wit P] XU *om*
146. With P] XU And with

---

140. *Myght of tho men.* B has 'Might of þe communes' (Prol. 113). The change in C (cf. MS I) is interesting, even if *communes* in B is taken to mean 'the commonalty' and not 'the commons' (i.e. the lower house of parliament), though it does not suggest that L moved away in C from a 'more democratic' interpretation of the constitutional process in B. The fable that follows (165–216, below) and much else (e.g. I 90, VIII 84, IX 9, XXI 465–79) make it clear that L never entertained any such interpretation, though he stresses the obligations (e.g. XXI 476–9, and cf. III 377, IV 176, V 181) as well as the rights of kingship (see Donaldson, 1949, 88–120). But he may have wished, in C, to remove even the possibility of misinterpretation; the use of Piers Plowman as a rallying call at the time of the Peasants' Revolt (Dobson, 1970, 379–82) may have given him further encouragement to make the change.

141. *Kynde Wytt* is the inborn gift of intelligence, unillumined by divine revelation (cf. Reason, IV 5). Animals have a share in it (XIV 163), and it is the basis of all human knowledge and wisdom (see XIII 236, XIV 17, 30, 72, XXI 361, and Quirk, 1953, 182–5). *clerkus he made.* B makes it clear that these are the clerics who sat in parliament, but their role here is not explained. It may be that the archetype of XU has lost a line corresponding to B Prol. 115 ('For to counseillen þe kyng and þe commune saue') in addition to the line supplied here from P.

143. The lower estate (*communes*) is responsible for providing food (*communes*) for the whole community. Cf. I 20, VIII 24.

145. *for most profitable:* 'as a thing most profitable to all'.

149. *Lewte:* an important recurrent personification in the poem (see II 20, III 378, 443, 446, IV 36, 156, 174, XII 23, 78), variously interpreted as 'loyalty to truth, fair dealing', or 'legality, strict adherence to the letter of the law' (Donaldson, 1949, 66), or 'the justice which is a part of virtue' (Kean, 1964, 256). Essentially, it seems to have the colour, in political and legal contexts, of the feudal term *fealty*, and to signify a loving recognition of the mutuality of obligation between man and man, or between a king and his subjects, i.e. the mediation between law and love described in I 157 and represented later in the poem in the person of Piers Plowman (and of Christ).

'Sum Rex, sum princeps: neutrum fortasse deinceps.
O qui iura regis christi specialia regis,
Hoc vt agas melius, iustus es, esto pius.
Nudum ius a te vestiri vult pietate.   155
Qualia vis metere talia grana sere.
Si seritur pietas de pietate metas.'
    Consience and þe kynge in to court wente
Where houed an hundrid in houes of selke,
Seriantz it semede that serueth at þe barre,   160
Plededen for penyes and poundes þe lawe
And nat for loue of oure lord vnlose here lyppes ones.
Thow myghtest betre meten myst on Maluerne hulles
Than gete a mum of here mouth ar moneye were hem shewed.
    Than ran þer a route of ratones as hit were   165
And smale muys with hem, mo then a thousend
Comen til a conseyl for here comune profyt.
For a cat of a court cam whan hym likede
And ouerlep hem lightliche and laghte hem alle at wille

---

155. *vestiri* U] X *vestire*

152-7. The Latin verses (not original: see Bennett 99) are a warning of the responsibilities of kingship: '(You say) "I am king, I am prince": but neither perhaps one day. You who administer the supreme laws of Christ the king, that you may do it better, be merciful, as you are just. Naked justice should be clothed by you in mercy. Sow as you would reap. If mercy is sown, may you reap mercy.' Latin is used (leonine verse, with medial rhyme) to give added authority to the admonition.

158-64. The passage on lawyers is brought in from later in B (Prol. 210-16). It shows the king something of the problem he faces as the chief administrator of justice, and also provides for the evacuation of parliament in readiness for the next allegorical scene (which some, however, regard as taking place before the king in his court of law).

165-215. The fable of the belling of the cat was a favourite exemplum. Here it is used to demonstrate the futility of any attempt to curb royal authority (see Bennett *MÆ*, 1943). The cat is best understood as John of Gaunt, the rats and mice as the upper and lower houses of parliament. Gaunt was the most powerful man in the realm after the death of the Black Prince (1376) and during the early years of Richard's minority. He was much hated, particularly in London, and the Good Parliament of 1376 made some attempt, only temporarily successful, to curb his power. Bishop Thomas Brinton (Brunton) of Rochester used the same exemplum in a sermon (no. 69, ii.317) preached before a convocation of clergy on 18 May 1376 (see Kellogg, 1935; Owst, 1933, 576-88) while the Good Parliament was in session. The moral he draws, however, is quite different.

167. *comune profyt*: 'the good of the commonwealth', a term often significantly used in political writing of the period (and in *PF* 47, 75: see J. A. W. Bennett, *The Parlement of Foules*, Oxford, 1957, 33).

And playde with somme perilously and potte hem þer hym lykede.   170
'And yf we groche of his game a wol greue vs sore,
To his clees clawe vs and in his cloches vs halde
That vs lotheth þe lyf ar he lette vs passe.
Myghte we with eny wyt his wille withsytte
We myhte be lordes a-lofte and lyue as vs luste.'   175
   A ratoun of renown moste resonable of tonge
Sayde, 'Y haue seyen grete syres in cytees and in townes
Bere beyus of bryghte gold al aboute here nekkes
And colers of crafty werk, bothe knyghtes and squieres.
Wer ther a belle on here beygh, by Iesu, as me thynketh,   180
Men myghte ywete where þei wente and here way roume.
Ryȝt so,' quath the raton, 'reison me shewith
A belle to byggen of bras other of bryghte syluer
And knytten hit on a coler for oure comune profyt   f.3ᵇ
And hongen hit aboute þe cattes halse, thanne here we mowe   185
Wher he riht othere reste or rometh to pleye;
And yf hym lust for to layke than loke we mowe
And apere in his presence þe while hym pleye lyketh
And yf hym wratheth ben we war and his way roume.
   Alle thise route of ratones to þis resoun þei assentide,   190
Ac tho þe belle was ybroughte and on þe beygh hangid
Ther ne was non of al þe route for al þe reame of Fraunce
That derste haue ybounde þe belle aboute þe kattes nekke
Ne haue hanged it aboute his hals al Yngelond to wynne;
And leten here labour ylost and al here longe study.   195
   A mous þat moche good couthe, as me tho thoughte,
Strok forth sturnely and stod byfore hem alle

---

179. knyghtes U] X knyghte
181–3. way . . . other of P] X beyȝ (*inserted*) war (*over* way *erased*); U way shonye/Bot wolde
   we make vs a belle al of
187. hym P] XU vs

---

176. *A ratoun of renown.* Often identified as Peter de la Mare, the Speaker of the
Commons in the Good Parliament. But topical allusion is probably not of much
importance in C.
178–9. Some resentment was felt at these forms of ostentation (cf. 209, below),
especially when they were worn as part of the livery of great lords (see VI 248n).
196–216. L seems to approve the mouse's sentiments, which are those of resignation to
the status quo, reflecting perhaps a general reaction to the events of 1377, when
Gaunt re-exerted his authority over parliament after the short-lived excitements
of 1376 (Huppé, 1941, 36). A different view is that of E. M. Orsten (in *MS* 23,
1961, 216–39), who sees L using the fable still, like Brinton, as a stimulus to action,
and interprets the mouse, therefore, as an ironical presentation of a Gaunt-
inspired 'mediator'.

And to þe route of ratones rehersede thise wordes:
'Thow we hadde ykuld þe cat ȝut shulde ther come another
To crache vs and alle oure kynde thogh we crope vnder benches.   200
Forthy y conseile for oure comune profit lat þe cat yworthe
And be neuere so bold the belle hym to shewe.
For y herde my syre sayn, seuene ȝer ypassed,
Ther þe cat is but a kytoun þe court is ful elynge.
Wyttenesse at holy wryt, who-so kan rede: 205
Ve terre vbi puer est Rex.
Y seye it for me,' quod þe mous, 'y se so muche aftur,
Shal neuer þe cat ne kytoun be my conseil be greued
Ne carpen of here colers þat costede me neuere.
And thow hit costed my catel, byknowen y ne wolde   210
But soffre and sey nouȝt and that is þe beste
Til þat meschief amende hem þat many man chasteth.
For many mannys malt we muys wolde distruye
And þe route of ratones of reste men awake
Ne were þe cat of þe court and ȝonge kitones toward;   215
For hadde ȝe ratones ȝoure reik, ȝe couthe nat reule ȝow-suluen.'
    What þis meteles bymeneth, ȝe men þat ben merye,
Deuyne ȝe, for y ne dar, by dere god almyhten.
    Ȝut mette me more of mene and of riche,
As barones and burgeys and bondemen of thorpes,   220 f.4ᵃ
Al y say slepynge as ȝe shal here heraftur:
Bothe bakeres and breweres, bochers and other,
Webbesteres and walkeres and wynners with handes,
As taylers and tanners and tulyers of þe erthe,
As dykers and deluers þat doth here dedis ylle   225

---

202. to U] X *om*
216. reik B] X ryot (*over* reed *erased*); U rued; P reed
224. of þe] XU þe; P of

---

204. Richard II was 9 years old when he succeeded to the throne in 1377 on the death
of his grandfather, Edward III.
206. 'Woe to the land where a child is king' (cf. Eccl. 10:16). A favourite medieval
quotation (Walther 32852c).
209. *Ne carpen*: 'nor (shall I) speak'.
212. 'Until misfortune, that chastens many men, teaches them better'.
216. *reik*: the emendation recommended by C. T. Onions in *MLR* 3 (1908), 170–71,
and by A. G. Mitchell in *MÆ* 8 (1939), 118–20 (cf. Kane-Donaldson, 92, and B
Prol. 201), 'to have one's reik' being a set phrase meaning 'to have one's way.' *ryot*
in X is an interesting reading, perhaps meaning 'freedom (to follow whatever
scent one pleases)', a hunting term, suggested by the hunting references in B Prol.
207 (cf. MnE 'run riot').
222–31. The picture crowds and blurs, and dissolves in a chorus of street-cries.

And dryueth forth here days with '*Dew vous saue, dame Emme.*'
Cokes and here knaues cryede, 'hote pyes, hote!
Goode gees and grys! ga we dyne, ga we!'
Tauerners til hem tolde þe same:
'Whit wyn of Oseye and wyn of Gascoyne,
Of þe Reule and of þe Rochele the roost to defye!'   230
Al þis y say sleping and seuyn sythes more.

232. *line supplied from* U; X *om*

226. 'God save you, dame Emma', a line from a popular song, perhaps about the dame
Emma of Shoreditch who is mentioned in B XIII 339 and who was probably an
old 'wycche' (cf. VI 81), a dispenser of secret medicines, especially love-remedies,
i.e. a bawd, like Dame Sirith in the ME poem of that name (in *Early ME Verse and
Prose*, ed. J. A. W. Bennett and G. V. Smithers, Oxford, 1966, 77).
229. 'Innkeepers cried their wares to them in the same way'.
231. La Reole and La Rochelle are in the Bordeaux area.

Passus I

Holy Church

Passus primus de visione Pers le Ploghman
What the montaigne bymeneth and þe merke dale
And þe feld ful of folk y shal ȝou fair shewe.
A louely lady of lere in lynnene yclothed
Cam doun fro þe castel and calde me by name
And sayde, 'Wille, slepestou? seestow þis peple,   5
Hou bisy þei ben aboute þe mase?
The moste party of this peple þat passeth on þis erthe,
Haue thei worschip in this world, thei wilneth no bettere;
Of othere heuene then here thei halde no tale.'
    Y was afeerd of here face, thow she fayre were,   10
And sayde, 'Mercy, madame, what may this be to mene?'
    'The tour vppon þe tofte,' quod she, 'Treuthe is þer-ynne,
And wolde þat ȝe wroghton as his word techeth.

---

3. lere I] X glorie *over erasure*; U lore. yclothed] X in clothed; U clothid
8. Haue I] XU Hadde
10. of U] X of of

---

3. Similarly, in the *Roman de la Rose*, a beautiful lady, Raison, comes down from a
tower to instruct the dreamer and explain his dream (Chaucer's translation, 3191–
5); cf. also the lady Raison in Deguileville's *Pèlerinage de la Vie Humaine* (Lydgate's
translation, ed. EETS, ES 77, 1494) and the lady Philosophy in the *Consolation of
Philosophy* (I, pr. 1) of Boethius. Holy Church is commonly represented in
medieval art and literature as a beautiful woman because of the allegorical inter-
pretation of the bride of the Song of Songs as the Church and the similar inter-
pretation of the Bride of the Lamb in the Apocalypse (who is clothed in 'fine
linen', Apoc. 19:8) and of other passages in scripture (e.g. Matt. 15:22). Note also
'Mother Church' (this is how she treats the dreamer in 138, below) and the gender
of *Ecclesia*.
5. *Wille* (*sone* in AB: see Kane, 1965, 63) is a convenient as well as an actual name for
the dreamer (see Bennett 155, Kane, 1965, 52–70, and cf. V 24n, VI 2, X 71, XII
2) since it associates him with *Will* (self-will, wilfulness), conventionally set against
Wit (wisdom, good sense). There is an interesting alliterative poem of *The Conflict
of Wit and Will*, ed. B. Dickins (Leeds Texts and Monographs, no. IV, 1937).
6. *mase*. The literal meaning, 'maze', is very apt to the preceding vision of 'the
restlessness of people caught in the labyrinth of the search for worldly gain'
(Bennett 105).

For he is fader of fayth and formor of alle;
To be fayful to hym ȝaf ȝow fyue wittes   15
For to worschipe hym þer-with þe whiles ȝe lyuen here.
Wherfore he hette þe elementis to helpe ȝow alle tymes
And brynge forth ȝoure bilyue, bothe lynnen and wollene,
And in mesure, thow muche were, to make ȝow attese;
And comaundede of his cortesye in comune thre thynges;   20
Aren non nidefole but tho thre, and nemne hem y thenke
And rekene hem by rewe – reherse hem wher þe liketh.
    The firste is fode, and vesture þe seconde,
And drynke þat doth the good – and drynke nat out of tyme.   f.4^b
Loot in his lyue thorw likerous drynke   25
Wykkede wroghte and wrathed god almyhty.
In his dronkenesse a day his doughteres he dighte
And lay by hem bothe, as þe boke telleth,
In his glotonye bygat gurles that were cherles,
And al he witte þe wyn his wikkede dede.   30
    Inebriemus eum vino et dormiamus cum eo, vt seruare
        possimus de patre nostro semen. Genesis.
Thorw wyn and thorw woman there was Loot acombred;
Forthy drede delitable drynke bothe day and nyghtes.
    Mesure is medecyne, thogh þow muche ȝerne;
Al is nat good to þe gost þat þe gott ascuth,
Ne liflode to þe lycame þat lef is þe soule.   35
Leef nat thy lycame, for a lyare hym techeth,

17. See Gen. 1:11.

19. *thow muche were*: 'though abundance were available'.

20. *in comune*. All men are entitled, through God's grace, to the common necessities of life (cf. Prol. 143). For the *thre thynges*, see Ecclus. 29:28, 39:31, and XXII 11 here.

25–32. The story of Lot and his daughters (Gen. 19:30–38) was a standard homiletic exemplum of the consequences of drunkenness (e.g. Pardoner's Tale, *CT* VI. 485–7). The debt to the *Historia Scholastica* of Peter Comestor (the standard compendium of biblical history) is traced in Taitt, 1971. Cf. X 177.

29. The issue (*gurles* is common gender) of the incestuous union were Moab and Ammon, fathers of two tribes that were enemies of the Israelites.

30a. 'Let us make him drunk with wine and let us lie with him, that we may preserve seed of our father' (Gen. 19:32). In its OT setting, of course, the daughters' plan showed a misguided though otherwise admirable desire to preserve the race, since they thought themselves the sole female survivors of the destruction of Sodom and Gomorrah, their mother having been recently turned into salt.

33. 'Only let there be measure, that these things may not bind you by your loving of them: lest ye love that for enjoyment, which ye ought to have for use' (St Augustine, quoted by Dunning, 1937, 34).

34–5. 'What the stomach craves is not always good for the spirit, nor is what is dear to the soul always food for the body'.

Which is þe wrecchede world, wolde þe bigyle;
For the fend and thy flesch folewen togederes,
And þat seeth þe soule and sayth hit the in herte
And wysseth þe to ben ywar what wolde þe desseyue.'   40
  'A madame, mercy, me lyketh wel ȝoure wordes.
Ac þe moneye of þis molde, þat men so faste kepen,
Telleth me to wham þat tresour bylongeth?'
  'Go to þe gospel,' quod she, 'and se what god sayde,
Whenne þe peple aposed hym of a peny in þe temple,   45
And god askede at hem hoes was þe koyne.
"Cesares," thei sayde, "sothliche we knoweth."
"*Reddite Cesari*," sayde god, "þat Cesar byfalleth,
Et que sunt dei deo, or ȝe don ylle."
For riȝtfulliche resoun sholde reule ȝow alle   50
And kynde witte be wardeyn, ȝoure welthe to kepe,
And tutor of ȝoure tresor, and take it ȝow at nede;
For hosbondrye and he holdeth togederes.'
  Y fraynede her fayr tho, for hym þat here made,
'The dep dale and þe derke, so vnsemely to se to,   55
What may hit bymene, madame, y byseche?'
  'That is þe castel of care – whoso cometh þer-ynne
May banne þat he born was in body and in soule.   f.5ᵃ
Ther-ynne wonyeth a wyghte þat Wrong is his name,

---

39. seeth] X schenth *over erasure* (*for* schendeth? *cf. B.I.41*); U sueth; P seyþ (*cf.* seeþ *in Skeat's MSS EB*)

37–8. The world, the flesh and the devil are the enemies of the soul in numerous medieval allegories (e.g. Chaucer's *Melibeus, CT* VII. 970, 1421). The triad was developed in patristic commentary (see XVIII 29n) on the basis of scriptural texts such as Eph. 6:11–12. Cf. X 48, XVIII 31–52, and see esp. XI 175n. *wolde þe bigyle*: '(which) would like to deceive thee'.

39–40. 'And the soul sees that and tells you of it in your heart and advises you to be wary of what would deceive you'.

42–3. The dreamer's question – Is money one of the 'common' necessities of life? (cf. 20, above) – introduces the theme of the right use of worldly goods (Dunning, 1937, 16), which dominates succeeding passus and indeed the whole of the *Visio*.

48–9. 'Render unto Caesar (the things which are Caesar's), and unto God the things that are God's' (Matt. 22:21). The question in the gospel, of course, concerns the rendering of tribute to Rome: Christ's answer is in a delimitation of secular and spiritual spheres. It is supplemented here by insistence on reason and moderation in the use of money (50–53).

54. *for hym þat here made*: 'for the sake of Him that made her'.

59. *þat . . . his*: 'whose'.

59–67. The description of Wrong is inspired by John 8:44, where Jesus speaks to the unbelieving Jews of their father, the devil: 'He was a murderer from the beginning, and stood not in the truth, because there is no truth in him . . . he is a liar, and the father thereof'.

Fader of falshede, fond hit firste of alle. 60
Adam and Eue he eggede to ylle
And conseylede Caym to cullen his brother.
Iudas he byiapede thorw Iewene suluer
And afturward anhengede hym hey vppon an hellerne.
He is lettere of loue and lyeth alle tymes; 65
That tristeth in tresor of erthe he bytrayeth sonest;
To combre men with coueytise, þat is his kynde and his lore.'
    Thenne hadde y wonder in my wit what woman she were
That suche wyse wordes of holy writ shewede,
And y halsede here on the hey name or she thennes wente 70
What she were wytterly þat wissede me so and tauhte.
    'Holy churche y am,' quod she, 'þou oughtest me to knowe;
Y undirfenge þe formeste and fre man the made.
Thow broughtest me borewes my biddyng to fulfille,
Leue on me and loue me al thy lyf-tyme.' 75
    Thenne y knelede on my knees and criede here of grace
And preyede here pitously to preye for me to amende
And also kenne me kyndly on Crist to bileue:
'Teche me to no tresor, but telle me this ilke,
How y may saue my soule, þat saynt art yholde.' 80

68. she U] X he
70. halsede U] X hanslede
79. no U (*later insertion*)] X *om*

64. *hellerne*: elder-tree, a familiar medieval addition to the gospel story of Judas's suicide (Matt. 27:5).
66. *That*: 'He that'.
70. *on the hey name*: 'in the high name', i.e. in the name of Jesus (see Phil. 2:9–10).
72. The failure of the dreamer or poet-visionary to recognize his instructress is a characteristic feature of these allegorical scenarios: so in the *Consolation* of Boethius (3n, above) and in Alan of Lille's *De Planctu Naturae*, pr. 3, 449.
73–4. 'I received you at the beginning and made you free of sin (at baptism). You brought me sureties that you would fulfil my commands.' The *borewes* are given by the godparents, who stand surety for the child at baptism and make the necessary promises of faith in his name. Cf. XII 50–51.
79–80. The question, and its answer, are best illuminated by Matt. 19:16–22, where the rich young man asks 'What good thing shall I do, that I may have eternal life?' and Christ replies 'If thou wilt enter into life, keep the commandments,' and further 'If thou wilt be perfect, go sell what thou hast, and give to the poor, and thou shalt have treasure in heaven: and come follow me.' The question is the fundamental question of the poem, and the *Visio* and the *Vita* correspond in some ways to Christ's twofold answer. Holy Church's discourse, it should be understood, though it comes early in the *Visio*, comprehends the whole foundation of the Christian life in truth and love.
80. *þat saynt art yholde*: '(tell me, you) who are counted blessed'.

'When alle tresores ben tried, Treuthe is þe beste –
I do hit vppon *Deus caritas*, to deme þe sothe.
Hit is as derworthe a druerie as dere god hymseluen.
For who is trewe of his tonge and of his two handes
And doth þe werkes þerwith and wilneth no man ylle,   85
He is a god by þe gospel and graunte may hele
And also lyk oure lord, by saynt Lukes wordes.
Clerkes þat knowen hit is thus sholde kenne it aboute,
For cristene and vncristene claymeth it echone.

83. as¹ U] X a

81. *Treuthe* is both objective and subjective: it is at once God and God's law and also obedience to God's law.

82. 'I appeal for confirmation to the text *God is love*' (1 John 4:8, 16, said in daily grace: see III 339n). To love God, and to show a loving response to his love, is to obey his law and keep his commandments, as is repeatedly stressed in the same epistle: 'Whoso keepeth his word, in him verily is the love of God perfected' (2:5); 'This is the love of God, that we keep his commandments' (5:3). Cf. 'The lawe of God is the love of God' (Parson's Tale, *CT* X. 125).

86. 'He partakes of the divine nature, according to what the gospel says, and may grant (spiritual) health'. The man who brings his will into total conformity with God's will is the true follower of Truth, and to that extent he *is* God. This is close to the doctrine of 'deification', as developed in the writings of St Bernard (Vasta, 1965, 66). To the extent that this doctrine relates to the *image* of God in man and the blurring and restoration of that image through the Fall and Incarnation (God became man in order to make man God according to his nature), it can be seen as an important theme in *Piers Plowman* (see VII 255, XVII 72, XVIII 7, XX 22, and Raw, 1969). But there must be serious objections to the view that the allusion here is to the mystical interpretation of deification as the union of the contemplative soul with God, and to the attempt to interpret the whole poem, on the basis of this allusion, as the mystic's quest for perfection of life in communion with God (Vasta, 1965, 52, 92, 99). The most that can be said is that L is aware of such doctrines and that, as often, he is trying to adapt the language of contemplative devotion to a more general concept of the Christian life. *by þe gospel*. In Luke 6:35 it is said that selfless love of one's enemies (cf. 'wilneth no man ylle') makes man a son of God, and in Luke 8:21 Christ declares that his kin are 'those who hear the word of God and do it' (cf. 'doth þe werkes þerwith'). Cf. also Luke 16:10. But, though the influence of 1 John 4:16 ('He who abides in love abides in God, and God abides in him') is still strong (see 82n), the basic gospel text here is John 10:34, Christ's interpretation of the psalmist's 'You are Gods' (Ps. 81:6). *graunte may hele*. L is referring here to the granting of health (as in Acts 3:1–10), of spiritual health (as in Mark 16:17–18; see XV 219–22) and of the means to salvation (VII 89).

87. In Luke 6:40 Christ declares that the disciple, when he is fully perfect in the teaching of his master, will be like his master.

89. 'Both Christians and non-Christians claim to have it' (viz. the revelation of divine Truth). The reference is to Mohammedans and Jews rather than 'heathens'.

Kynges and knyghtes sholde kepen hit by resoun,   90
Rydon and rappe adoun in reumes aboute
And take *transgressores* and teyen hem faste
Til Treuthe hadde termyned here trespas to þe ende,
And halden with hem and here þat han trewe accion   f.5^b
And for no lordene loue leue þe trewe partie.   95
Treweliche to take and treweliche to fyghte
Is þe professioun and puyr ordre that apendeth to knyghtes,
And ho-so passeth þat poynt is appostata of knyghthed;
For thei sholde nother faste ne forbere the serk but fyghte and fende
    treuthe
And neuer leue for loue in hope to lacche syluer.   100
   Dauid in his daies dobbed knyghtes,
Dede hem swere on here swerd to serue treuthe euere.
And god, whan he bigan heuene in þat grete blisse,
Made knyghtes in his couert creatures tene,
Cherubyn and seraphyn, suche seuene and anoþer –   105
Lucifer, louelokest tho, ac litel while it duyred.

97–101. *lineation disordered* XUIP
105. *lineation as* U; X *mislineates* seuene/And

90. Having said that clerks are to teach Truth, Holy Church goes on directly to deal with the ruling orders of society (cf. Prol. 139n) and how they are to serve and keep Truth by defending the land and administering justice. It is well to recognize here the medieval commonplace that the function of the political organization of society (i.e. the State) is moral, that is, the maintenance of Christian truth and righteousness (Dunning, 1937, 46). See also II 203n.

91. *rappe adoun*: 'strike down (malefactors)' (OED) or 'hasten about' (Skeat). The suggestion is of a royal or judicial 'progress' or circuit.

92. *transgressores*, Jas. 2:9, where the word is used of those who transgress divine Law by showing partiality towards the rich (cf. 95). The whole chapter in James is of great importance to Langland (cf. 181 below), especially here, in connection with rulers as keepers of Truth, for its reference to divine Law as 'the royal law' (2:8), i.e. the law of Christ as king.

94–5. 'And support all those (*lit.* every him and her) who act in accordance with truth, and not abandon the cause of truth for any love of lords.' There seems no reason to regard *lordene* as anything other than gen.pl. (cf. Mitchell, 1939, 483–4).

96. *take*, i.e. receive what is due to them.

98. 'Whoever keeps the whole law but fails in one point has become guilty of all of it' (Jas. 2:10). An *apostata* was originally one who left a religious order after completing his novitiate; its use here emphasizes the religious character of the order of knighthood.

101. David, conceived of as a medieval feudal king (cf. 1 Para. 12:18) and a 'type' of Christ (cf. III 440, XXI 14) provides the transition to a consideration of the revolt in heaven, the primal un-Truth, as transgression against a celestial 'knighthood'.

104. The ten orders of angels were reduced to the familiar nine (seraphim, cherubim and thrones; dominions, virtues and powers; principalities, archangels and angels) by the defection of the company of Lucifer.

He was an archangel of heuene, on of goddes knyghtes;
He and oþer with hym helden nat with treuthe,
Lepen out in lothly forme for his fals wille
That hadde lust to be lyke his lord þat was almyghty.   110
    Ponam pedem meum in aquilone, et similus ero altissimo.'
  'Lord! why wolde he tho, þat wykkede Lucifer,
Luppen alofte in þe north syde
Thenne sitten in þe sonne syde þere þe day roweth?'
  'Nere hit for northerne men, anon y wolde ʒow telle –
Ac y wol lacky no lyf,' quod þat lady sothly.   115
'Hit is sikerore bi southe þer þe sonne regneth
Then in þe north by many notes, no man leue other;
For theder as þe fende fly his fote for to sette,
Ther he faylede and ful and his felawes alle,
And helle is þer he is, and he þere ybounde.   120
Euene þe contrarie sitteth Crist, clerkes wyteth þe sothe.
    Dixit dominus domino meo, sede a dextris meis.
Ac of þis matere no more nemnen y nelle;
Hewes in þe haliday after hete wayten,
Ac thei caren nat thow hit be cold, knaues, when þei worche.

---

120. he² U] X *om*
124. þei² U] X þe

110a. 'I will set my foot in the north, and I will be like the most high'. This (repeated XVI 212) is not an inaccurate memory of Isa. 13:13–14, but a quotation, probably through an intermediary such as the commentary on the *Fables* of Avianus (see Risse, 1966), from St Augustine's commentary on Psalm 47:2 in his *Enarrationes in Psalmos* (*PL* 36:534). To give a greater sense of physical vigour to Satan's action, Langland, apparently independently, changes the *sedem*, 'seat', of the original to *pedem* (cf. 118), probably on the basis of references elsewhere in St Augustine's *Enarrationes* to 'the foot of pride', *pes superbiae* (see Kellogg, 1949; 1958). The biblical association of Lucifer and the north, already well developed in St Augustine, was strengthened by the patristic association of heat with charity and of cold with unrepentant sin (see Hill, 1968), by Germanic mythology, which also placed Hell in the north (mount Hecla, in Iceland, according to some ecclesiastical historians), as well as by a more or less natural geographical prejudice (for which Holy Church half-playfully apologizes, 114) which can be found expressed in *The Owl and the Nightingale* (ed. E. G. Stanley, London and Edinburgh, 1960), 905–22, 995–1030. Cf. also the Friar's Tale, *CT* III. 1413.

115. 'But I will not speak ill of anyone'.

117. *no man leue other*: 'let no man believe otherwise'.

121a. 'The Lord said to my lord, Sit at my right hand' (Ps. 109:1, quoted frequently in NT, e.g. Matt. 22:44, etc.). Right and left (see II 5, VII 225, and Matt. 25:33) correspond symbolically to south and north; facing east, north is on the left hand.

123–4. 'Labourers look for holy days (holidays) to be sunny, but do not care if it is cold on work-days.' The sense is that people are content to suffer here and to hope for better weather in after-life, when they will live in the sunny south (with continuation of the association of heat with God's love, and of the pun on sun/Son).

Wonder wyse holy wryt telleth how þei fullen,   125
Summe in erthe, summe in ayr, summe in helle depe.
Ac Lucifer lowest lith of hem alle;   f.6ᵃ
For pruyde that hym pokede his payne hath non ende.
And alle þat worchen þat wikked is, wenden thei sholle
Aftur here deth-day and dwelle ther Wrong is,   130
And alle þat han wel ywrouhte, wende þey sholle
Estward til heuene, euere to abyde
There Treuthe is, þe tour that trinite ynne sitteth.
Lere hit thus lewed men, for lettred hit knoweth,
Than treuthe and trewe loue is no tresor bettre.'   135
   'I haue no kynde knowyng,' quod y, 'ȝut mot ȝe kenne me bettre
By what wey it wexeth and wheder out of my menynges.'
   'Thow dotede daffe,' quod she, 'dulle aren thy wittes.
To lyte lernedest þow, y leue, Latyn in thy ȝowthe:
Heu michi, quod sterilem duxi vitam iuuenilem!   140

128. that P] XUI ther
135. Than U] X That
139. þow U] X *om*

126. Not all the fallen angels fell into hell. Others inhabited the elements, as (more or less) evil spirits. See Chaucer, *HF* 930; Bartholomaeus, II. xix.

129–35. The example of Lucifer is now related to the main theme of Wrong and Truth, with anticipation of important lines in IX 288–93.

132. *Estward*. See Prol. 14n.

136. *kynde knowyng*: 'natural understanding'. This concept holds a position between Kynde Wytt (Prol. 141n) and Reason (IV 5n) which is not easy to define, but it is an important form of expression for Langland (cf. 141, 159, 161, below, and VII 183, X 56, XVI 213; and see Davlin, 1971), since he wishes to suggest by it that love of God (which is Truth) is 'natural', i.e. implanted in man by God's grace, without admitting the Pelagian heresy that man can love God and win salvation by his own efforts. The dreamer cannot grasp how Truth and Love (81–2, 135) are the same. The growth of the dreamer from 'knowing in the head' to 'knowing in the heart', realization, is one of the important controlling themes of the poem (persuasively explored in Lawlor, 1962, 88, 228–33, *et passim*).

137. 'How it grows and whether (in some way) out of my own intellectual capacities *or* intentions (powers of volition)'.

139. The reproach is not that he did not learn the Latin that follows but that he did not learn the elementary (Latin) lessons in theology.

140. 'Ah me, what a useless life I led as a youth!' This line (repeated in VII 55) of leonine verse (cf. Prol. 152) seems to have been a proverbial piece of sententiousness (Bennett 112, Alford 392, Walther 10736b). It occurs in a MS collection of Latin proverbs and other sayings in the John Rylands Library (MS 394: see W. A. Pantin, in *BJRL* 14, 1930, 81–114) which contains other quotations that L uses and which is perhaps typical of the kind of MS from which he may have culled his Latin *sententiae*.

Hit is a kynde knowynge that kenet in thyn herte
For to louye thy lord leuest of alle,
Dey rather þen do eny dedly synne.
  Melius est mori quam male viuere.
And this y trowe be treuth: ho-so kan tecche þe bettre,
Lok þow soffre hym to seye and so thow myht lerne.   145
  For Treuthe telleth þat loue ys triacle to abate synne
And most souerayne salue for soule and for body.
Loue is plonte of pees, most precious of vertues,
For heuene holde hit ne myghte, so heuy hit first semede,
Til hit hadde of erthe yȝoten hitsilue.   150
Was neuer lef vppon lynde lyhtere ther-aftur,
As when hit hadde of þe folde flesch and blode taken.
Tho was hit portatif and persaunt as is þe poynt of a nelde;

141–2. It was traditional theological teaching that man has a natural capacity to love God above all things (Vasta, 1965, 86). To that extent, *kynde knowyng* is not far different from that indwelling attachment to the sovereign good known to scholastics as *synderesis* (see Hort 72–81, and X 143).

143a. 'It is better to die than to live in sin': derived from the sense or a variant of Tob. 3:6: 'expedit enim mihi mori magis quam vivere', perhaps influenced by the proverb 'Better to die with honour than live in shame' (Whiting D 239, cf. Walther 14594). It is repeated by L in VI 290a and XVII 40a, and translated by Thomas Usk in his *Testament of Love* (in *Chaucerian and Other Pieces*, ed. W. W. Skeat, Oxford, 1897, 32). See also VII 209–10.

146. *triacle*: 'herbal medicine' (originally an antidote to a snake-bite; the modern meaning derives from the sweetness of the medicinal syrup). The imagery of sin as disease (or as a wound, XIX 83) and God's love as the cure was well-established in patristic writings; the symbolism of *triacle* (as the antidote provided by the Passion of Christ to the serpent-bite of Satan) was particularly influenced by the interpretation of Num. 21:8–9 (see Smith, 1966, 22–3; cf. XX 155). The idea of a herbal remedy leads directly to the image of the 'plonte of pees' (148 below, cf. Isa. 9:6, 53:2).

148–54. L draws here, briefly but evocatively, on a rich complex of biblical and patristic sources for the imagery of divine love as it is embodied in Christ. For detailed commentary, see Kean, 1965; Bennett 113–14; Smith, 1966, 21–34.

148. *most precious of vertues*: 'most precious in its healing-powers', as well as the obvious meaning.

149–50. Love is like a force of innate weight which draws God down to earth to beget himself on an earthly body. Cf. 'My weight is my love; by it I am carried wherever I am carried' (St Augustine, *Confessions*, xiii.9, cited in Kellogg, 1958, 388).

151. The lightness of love, weightless once it has fulfilled itself in the acts of Incarnation and Redemption, draws it back irresistibly to its source in God (referring to the Ascension and to the ascent of the redeemed soul).

153. The mobile activity and penetrativeness of love relates to the description of Wisdom in Sap. 7:22–4, to patristic commentary on the 'needle' of Luke 18:25, and to the image of the word of God as 'living and active, more piercing (*penetrabilior*) than any two-edged sword' in Heb. 4:12.

May non armure hit lette ne none heye walles.

Forthi is loue ledare of oure lordes folke of heuene, 155
And a mene, as þe mayre is, bitwene þe kyng and þe comune;
Ryht so is loue ledare and þe lawe shapeth;
Vp man for his mysdedes the mercement he taxeth.

And for to knowe hit kyndly, hit comeseth by myhte,
And in þe herte þer is þe hed and þe heye welle. 160
For of kynde knowynge of herte ther comseth a myhte
And þat falleth to þe fader þat formede vs alle, f.6ᵇ
Lokede on vs with loue, let his sone deye
Mekeliche for oure mysdedes to amende vs alle,
And ʒut wolde hem no wo þat wrouhte hym al þat tene 165
Bote mekeliche with mouth mercy he bysoughte
To haue pitee on þat peple þat paynede hym to dethe.

Here myhtow se ensaumples in hymself one
That he was myhtfull and meke, and mercy gan graunte
To hem þat hengen hym hye and his herte thorlede. 170
Forthy y rede ʒow riche, haueth reuthe vppon þe pore;
Thow ʒe be myhty to mote, beth meke in ʒoure werkes,
For þe same mesure þat ʒe meteth, amis other elles,
ʒe shal be weye þer-with whenne ʒe wende hennes.
   Eadem mensura qua mensi fueritis, remecietur vobis.

158. he U] X and he

154. The *armure* of the Roman soldiers set to guard the tomb and the *walles* of the tomb itself.

156–7. Christ, the incarnation of God's love, is compared, as 'mediator between God and men' (1 Tim. 2:5), to a mayor (the growing power of the mayor of London in the 14th c. makes this not inapposite); this in turn reintroduces the theme of love as law and obedience to law (90, above). Love, in the form of law, is the mediator between king and commons (see Prol. 149n, and Kean, 1964, 249), just as the law of God is the mediation of his love.

158. 'He imposes the fine on man for his misdeeds'. The amercement was the fine paid by a man who lay 'in the mercy' of the king, for some (often unspecified) misdemeanour (Yunck, 1963, 234). It was little different from extortion in practice, but L gives the word a new and paradoxical meaning by referring to a different kind of 'mercy'.

159–60. 'And so that you can grasp it (i.e. Love) by natural understanding, (let me explain how) it springs up through the divine power and in the heart, where its fountainhead and divine source is to be found.'

163–4. God's sending his Son into the world is the supreme example of love; cf. 1 John 4:9 (cf. 82n, 87n, above), John 3:16.

166–7. Luke 23:34.

170. *his herte thorlede.* John 19:34.

174a. 'The measure you give will be the measure you get back' (Luke 6:38).

For thow ӡe ben trewe of ӡoure tonges and treweliche wynne   175
And ben as chast as a child þat chyht noþer ne fyhteth,
But yf ӡe louye leeliche and lene þe pore,
Of such good as god ӡow sent goodliche parte,
Ӡe na haueth na more meryte in masse ne in oures
Then Malkyn of here maydenheed when no man here couayteth.   180
   For Iames þe gentele iugeth in his bokes
That fayth withouten þe feet is feblore then nauutht
And as ded as dore-nayl but yf þe dedes folowe:
    Fides sine operibus mortua est.
Chastite withouten charite worth cheyned in helle;
Hit is as lewed thyng as a laumpe þat no liht is ynne.   185
Mony chapeleynes aren chaste, ac charite hem fayleth;
Aren none hardore ne hungriore then men of holy chirche,
Auerous and euel-willed when þei ben avaunsed,
Vnkynde to here kyn and to alle cristene,
Chewen here charite and chiden aftur more,   190
And ben acombred with coueytise – thei can nouӡt crepe out,
So harde haþ auaryce yhapsed hem togederes.
And þat is no treuthe of þe trinite, but triccherye, synne,
And a luther ensaumple, leef me, as for þe lewed peple.
   For this aren wordes ywryten in þe ewangelie: 195
"*Date et dabitur vobis* – for y dele ӡow alle."   f.7ᵃ
And þat is þe lok of loue and vnloseth grace,
That conforteth alle carefole acombred with synne.

175–80. The syntax, as well as the theme (the nothingness of 'virtue' without love), echo 1 Cor. 13:1–3.

176. *þat chyht noþer ne fyhteth*, i.e. a very young child. Cf. B I 180: 'þat in chirche wepeþ'.

180. *Malkyn*: a familiar name (dim. of Matilda or Mary: see Mustanoja, 1970, 54–5, 71) for a woman of the lower classes (cf. Nun's Priest's Tale, *CT* VII. 3384), though to suggest, as Skeat does, that it implies wantonness (cf. *CT* II. 30) contradicts the sense here. Malkyn, a homely and unattractive drudge, is chaste by default, because no one wants her (see a note by F. G. Cassidy in *MLN* 63, 1948, 52–3). Trevisa uses the expression in a similar way (Whiting M 511).

184a. 'Faith without works is dead' (Jas. 2:26).

185. Alluding to the parable of the wise and foolish virgins (Matt. 25:1–13), traditionally interpreted (e.g. *Vices and Virtues* 257–8) as an example of the uselessness of virginity (the lamps) without love of God (the oil).

190–92. 'Their charity is swallowed up in greed and still they shout for more, and they are burdened with avarice, so firmly padlocked by greed (within their own money-boxes) that they cannot creep out'.

192. *yhapsed*. This transposition of letters (cf. yhasped U), known as metathesis, is common in ME.

196. 'Give, and it will be given to you' (Luke 6:38; cf. 174a, above).

197. *þat* refers to charitable almsgiving.

So loue is lecche of lyf and lysse of alle payne
And þe graffe of grace and graþest way to heuene.   200
Forthi y may seye, as y saide eer, by siht of this textes,
"Whenne alle tresores ben tried, treuthe is þe beste."
Loue hit,' quod þat lady, 'lette may y no lengore
To lere the what loue is' – and leue at me she lauhte.

199–200. 'So love is the healer of life and relief of all pain, and the stem from which grace grows and the most direct way to heaven'. Holy Church, summarizing her argument, echoes both *triacle* (146) and *plonte* (148). Cf. Matt. 7:13–14.

201–2. Cf. 81, above. The *textes* are those of ll. 48 and 82.

Passus II

The Marriage of Lady Meed

Passus secundus de visione vbi prius

And thenne y kneled vppon my knees and cried to here of grace
And sayde, 'Mercy, madame, for Mary loue of heuene
That bar þat blessid barn þat bouhte vs on þe rode,
Kenne me by sum craft to knowe þe false.'
    'Loke vppon thy left half and loo where he standeth.   5
Fals and Fauel and fikel-tonge Lyare
And mony mo of here maners of men and of wymmen.'
    Y lokede vppon my luft half as þe lady me tauhte
And say a womman as hit were wonderly yclothed.
She was purfiled in pelure, non puyrere on erthe,   10
And crouned with a croune, þe kyng haþ non bettre;
On alle here fyue fyngeres ful richeliche yrynged
And thereon rede rubies and othere riche stones.
Here robynge was rychere þen y rede couthe,
For to telle of here atyer no tyme haue y nouthe;   15

---

9. say U] X *om*

1. Cf. I 76.

2. *for Mary loue of heuene*: 'for the love of Mary of heaven'. The word-order is usual in ME, and genitives of proper names are often uninflected (cf. Prol. 107).

4. The dreamer's request, a natural one after Holy Church's instruction in the nature of Truth, initiates the action of Passus II–IV.

5. *thy left half*. Cf. I 111a and note. St Bernard assigns the goods of the body to the left side, the goods of the soul to the right, in his exegesis of Ps. 90:7 (Vasta, 1965, 77). So too *Speculum Vitae* 1469–82.

6. *Fauel*: 'deceit, fraud', also used as a personification in the OF *Roman de Fauvel* (dated 1310–14), where the thwarted allegorical marriage of Fauvel and Fortune is especially interesting in relation to L: see Yunck, 1963, 221–6; also R. D. Cornelius in *PMLA* 47 (1932), 363–7.

8. There is a deliberate echo here of the first appearance of Holy Church in I 3.

14–15. Some descriptive detail in B II 13–16 is thus peremptorily dismissed (see Prol. 10n), somewhat muffling the echo of the description of the *meretrix* of Apoc. 17:1–5, and also the probable allusion to Alice Perrers (Huppé, 1939, 44–52), mistress of Edward III in his last years and renowned for her extravagance of dress, her love of rings (l. 12 here) and her corrupt manipulation of royal favour.

Here aray with here rychesse raueschede my herte.
Whos wyf a were and what was here name,
'Leue lady,' quod y tho, 'layn nought yf ȝe knowen.'
     'That is Mede þe mayde, hath niyed me ful ofte
And ylow on my lemman þat Leute is hoten   20
And lakketh hym to lordes þat lawes han to kepe,
In kynges court, in comune court contrarieth my techynge,
In þe popes palays she is pryue as mysulue,
Ac sothnesse wolde nat so for she is a bastard.
Oon Fauel was her fader þat hath a fykel tonge   25
And selde soth sayth bote yf he souche gyle,
And Mede is manered aftur hym, as men of kynde carpeth: f.7ᵇ
     Talis pater, talis filia.
For shal neuer breere bere berye as a vine
Ne on a croked kene thorn kynde fyge wexe:

17. Whos U] X Heos
23. she U] X he

16. It is her *aray* that ravishes the dreamer, not her beauty; cf. the beauty and simple clothing of Holy Church (I 3).

17–18. The merging of indirect into direct speech is common in ME poetry. Taking line 17 as dependent on *raueschede* (so Mitchell, 1939, 485) only creates further difficulties.

17. *Whos wyf a were*: 'Whose wife she was'. A woman's nature, her moral and spiritual status as well as her social status, is known by her husband; hence the significance of Meed's forthcoming marriage (41, below).

19. Lady Meed ('reward') is the personification of the force that perverts men from the way of Truth – bribery, love of money, desire for gain, the acquisitive instinct, or, in theological terms, *cupiditas*, the love of worldly goods as an end in themselves (cf. I 42n). The development of capital in the 14th c., and the substitution of financial transaction and overt self-interest for the network of mutual obligation on which feudal society, at least in theory, depended, gave Meed a more and more powerful role in society, and one that was more and more bewildering to traditional moralists (see Yunck, 1963, 130, 232–7); hence the note of urgency in Langland's vision. For a comprehensive study of the medieval tradition of venality-satire, see Yunck, 1963. For the conflict between traditional morality and the emergent economic forces, see Tawney, 1926, 14–55.

20. *Leute*. See Prol. 149n.

24. *a bastard*. L frequently uses patterns of family relationship as allegorical signals of moral status (cf. 17n, above).

27. *of kynde*: 'concerning kinship'.

27a. 'Such as the father, so is the daughter'. The usual form of the Latin proverb (Alford 392; for the English, see Whiting F 80) is *Qualis pater talis filius* and derives from the Athanasian creed (see VII 236n). Cf. Ez. 16:44, 18:4.

Bona arbor bonum fructum facit.

Y ouhte ben herrore then she, y com of a bettere;   30
The fader þat me forth brouhte *filius dei* he hoteth,
That neuere lyede ne lauhede in al his lyf-tyme,
And y am his dere doughter, ducchesse of heuene,
That what man me louyeth and my wille foleweth
Shal haue grace to good ynow and a good ende,   35
And what man Mede loueth, my lyf y dar wedde,
He shal lese for here loue a lippe of trewe charite.
That helpeth man moste to heuene Mede most letteth –
Y do hit vppon Dauyd, the doumbe wil no3t lyen:
   Domine, quis habitabit in tabernaculo tuo.
And Dauyd vndoth hymself, as þe doumbe sheweth: 40
   Et super innocentem munera non accepit.
   Tomorwe worth Mede ymaried to a mansed wrecche,
To oon Fals Faythlesse of þe fendes kynne.
Fauel thorw his flaterynge speche hath Mede foule enchaunted
And al is Lyares ledynge this lady is thus ywedded.

---

30. she U] X he
37. a] X and *with* nd *erased*

29a. 'A sound tree bears good fruit' (Matt. 7:17), part of Christ's advice on how to recognize false prophets: 'You will know them by their fruits'. Cf. X 206, 242a. Lines 28–9 are based on Matt. 7:16.

32. *lauhede.* Jesus is not portrayed as laughing in the gospels, though he laughs scornfully in the apocryphal Infancy Gospels, e.g. *Evangelium Thomae*, XIII (Tischendorf, 178). In commenting on the weeping of Jesus at the death of Lazarus (John 11:35; see XVIII 146–7), patristic writers remarked on the absence of any mention of Jesus laughing (see the references in Ludolf of Saxony's *Vita Christi*, ed. Mabile and Guerrin, Paris and Rome, 1865, II. xvii, 459) and clearly regarded this as a significant act of asceticism. The contrast became a commonplace (e.g. *Cursor Mundi* 18855–56). Luke 6:25 was also glossed (e.g. by Bede in *PL* 92:404, and in the *Glossa Ordinaria*, *PL* 114:263) as a condemnation of laughing.

39. *Y do hit:* see I 28n. The reference is to the Psalms of David which, being a book, and therefore dumb, will not lie.

39a. 'O Lord, who shall sojourn in thy tent?' (Ps. 14:1). This is a cue-reference to the first line of the relevant psalm (cf. XV 135), which is then referred to more specifically (C only).

40a. 'And hath not taken a bribe against the innocent' (Ps. 14:5, in a list of those who, so doing, shall dwell with God).

41. The idea of an allegorical marriage for Meed may be drawn in part from the legend of the marriage of the devil's daughters, which was current in an AN poem attributed to Grosseteste (ed. P. Meyer in *Romania* 29, 1900, 54–72; cf. VII 232n) and widespread in sermon literature (Owst, 1933, 93–7).

Soffre and thow shalt see suche as ben apayed 45
That Mede is thus ymaried, tomorwe þou shalt aspye.
Knowe hem well yf þow kanst and kepe the fro hem alle
That loueth here lordschipe, lasse other more.
Lacke hem nat but lat hem worthe til Leutee be justice
And haue power to punyshe hem, thenne pot forth thy resoun. 50
For y bykenne the Crist,' quod she, 'and his clene moder,
And acombre thow neuere thy consience for coueityse of mede.'
   Thus lefte me that lady lyggynge as aslepe
And y say how Mede was maried, metyng as it were.
Al þe riche retenaunce þat rotheth hem o fals lyuynge 55
Were beden to þe bridale a bothe half þe contre,
Of many manere men þat of Mede kynne were,
Of knyghtes, of clerkes, of other comune peple,
As sysores, sompnores, shyryues and here clerkes, f.8ᵃ
Bydels and bailifs and brokeres of chaffares, 60
Vorgoers and vitalers and voketes of the Arches,
Y kan nouȝt rykene þe route þat ran aboute Mede.

47. þow U] X þat
50. punyshe U] X pynschen

43. Meed herself is morally neutral (17n, above; 120, below), and throughout she behaves according to her nature, believing that all she does is for the best (Mitchell, 1956, 191). But she is the cause of corruption in others, and is inclined to sin, being of illegitimate birth (24n, above), and now Favel, her father (25, above), is trying to wed her to the devil's kin.
49. The emphasis on the due order of law and rightful rule is important.
59. *sysores*: jury-men at the assizes, who might be bribed to give false verdicts (see XXII 161). *sompnores*: summoners, or 'apparitors', were the officers who summoned defendants to appear before ecclesiastical courts, where offences against morality (e.g. prostitution, drunkenness) were tried. The opportunities for bribery and corruption were extensive, as Chaucer shows (*CT* I. 623–68; and see Woodcock, 1952, 45–9, 111–12). Ll. 59–61 illustrate L's characteristic preoccupation with 'venality on the lower levels of officialdom' (Yunck, 1963, 302).
60. *Bydels*. Beadles were the officers who served the warrants of a court or demands for taxation.
61. *Vorgoers*. 'Foregoers' or purveyors were men who travelled in advance of a great lord to commandeer provisions and accommodation, or more generally commandeered supplies for a lord or king. The practice was much abused (see IV 45, 61) and frequent attempts were made to restrict purveying (e.g. Statutes of 1360–62, i.365, 371–3). *vitalers*: sellers of food and drink, especially those mentioned in III 80. *voketes of the Arches*: the advocates or proctors who pleaded in the archbishop of Canterbury's provincial court, which was held from about 1279 (see Woodcock, 1952, 11) in the London church of St Mary de Arcubus (St Mary le Bow, or Bow Church), so called from its being built on arches. Cf. 186, below, and XXII 136.

Ac Simonye and Syuile and sysores of contrees
Were most pryue with Mede of eny men, me thoghte.
Ac Fauel was þe furste þat fette here out of chambre   65
And as a brokor brouhte here forth to be ioyned wiþ False.
When Simonye and Syuile ysey þer bothe wille
Thei assentede hit were so at sylueres preyere.
   Thenne lup Lyare forth and saide, 'Loo! here a chartre
That Gyle hath gyue to Falsnesse and grauntid also Mede,'   70
And preyeth Syuile to se hit and Syimonye to rede hit.
Thenne Simonye and Syuyle standeth forth bothe
And vnfoldeth the feffament þat Fals hath ymaked.
Thenne saide Symonye þat Syuyle it herde:
'Al þat loueth and byleueth vp lykyng of Mede,   75
Leueth hit lelly this worth here laste mede
That foleweth Falsnesse, Fauel and Lyare,
Mede and suche men þat aftur mede wayten.
      Sciant presentes et futuri, etc.
   Wyten and witnessen þat wonyen on erthe
That Mede is maried more for here richesse   80

66. as P] XUI *om.* wiþ U] X to þe
67. ysey U] X yseyth
76. lelly U] X leuly

63. *Simonye*: strictly speaking, the sale or purchase of ecclesiastical office (see Acts 8:18), but here used to personify the practice of canon law in the ecclesiastical courts, as distinct from *Syuile*, civil law.
67. *þer bothe wille*: 'the will of both of them' (*bothe* is a relic of an old gen.pl. *botheres*).
69. Allegorical marriages are frequent in medieval literature (see 6n, 41n, above, and Bennett 125) and the marriage-charter is a natural extension of the allegory. Charters were used for the legal conveyancing or transfer of ownership of land and property, and the marriage-deed here takes the form of a granting of title (enfeoffment) to the territories of the seven deadly sins, as a kind of dowry from Meed's father. Compare also the 'Devil's Charter', a satirical form popular in the mendicant controversy, where a sect of religious is granted mock-legal authority by the devil to continue in wrong-doing (Bloomfield, 1961, 80).
73. *Fals* is used as a name for both Favel (as here) and Falsnesse (42, above), an ambiguity inherited from B which C attempted to remove by inventing a new name, Favel, for Meed's father (25, above), but without carrying out the substitution consistently (see 121, below, and Donaldson, 1949, 69).
78a. 'Let all men, present and future, know . . .' The legal formula for the opening of a charter; the construction is imitated in the next line. Medieval religious poetry often uses the legal forms and language of a charter for allegorical purposes: the most notable example is the Charter of Christ, in which the 'deed' of redemption is written on the parchment of Christ's skin, in the ink of his blood, etc. (Woolf, 1968, 210–14).

Then for holynesse oþer hendenesse oþer for hey kynde.
Falsnesse is fayn of here for he wot here ryche
And Fauel þat hat a fals speche feffeth hem by þis lettre
To ben princes in pruyde and pouert to dispice,
To bacbite and to boste and bere fals witnesse,   85
To skorne and to skolde and sklaundre to make,
Vnbuxum and bold to breke þe ten hestes.
The erldom of enuye and yre he hem graunteth
With the chastel of cheste and chaterynge out of resoun.
The counte of coueytise he consenteth to hem bothe,   90
With vsurye and auaryce and other fals sleythus
In bargaynes and brocages with the borw of thefte,
With al the lordschip of leccherye in lenghe and in brede,
As in werkes and in wordes and in waytynges of yes,   f.8ᵇ
In woldes and in weschynges and with ydel thouhtes   95
There þat wille wolde and werkmanschip faileth.
Glotonye a gyueth hem and grete othes togederes,
Al day to drynke at diuerse tauernes
And there to iangele and to iape and iuge here emcristene
And fastyng-dayes to frete before noone and drynke   100
With spiserye, speke ydelnesse, in vayne speke and spene,
And sue forth suche felawschipe til they ben falle in slewthe
And awake with wanhope and no wille to amende
For a leueth be lost when he his lyf leteth.
This lyf to folowe Falsnesse and folke þat on hym leueth,   105

---

84. princes U] X prunyse
90. counte U] X counteth. he P] XU and
96. werkmanschip I] X ne (*inserted*) wer manschip; U weremanshipe

---

95. *woldes*: a nonce-use of the verbal form as a substantive, as in Gower, *Confessio Amantis* (ed. EETS, ES 81–2), vi.923.
97. Gluttony (including drunkenness) and *grete othes* are commonly associated, as sins of the mouth, and of the tavern. See VI 361, 426; *CT* VI. 472, 629. The allegory of land-conveyancing dissolves here (97–104) into a tavern-scene, anticipating that of VI 350ff (for lechery, cf. VI 177, 193).
100. Only one meal was permitted on fast-days, and it was not to be taken before midday (cf. VI 434, VIII 146).
103. *wanhope*. The sin of sloth characteristically ends in despair of amendment (cf. VII 59).
104. *a* ('he') here is any sinful man; the charter is quite forgotten. *be lost*: '(himself to) be lost'.
105. *This lyf to folowe Falsnesse*: 'Those whose life is to (*or* Those who during life) follow Falseness'. The syntax is strained (with the inf. echoing the infs. of 98, 99, etc.), perhaps recalling the legal phrasing of a charter. It is unlikely that *This lyf to folowe* is to be construed independently (with *Falsnesse* and *folke* as antecedents of *þay*) as 'by following this life'.

After here deth þay dwellen day withouten ende
In lordschip with Lucifer, as this lettre sheweth,
With alle þe appurtinaunces of purgatorye and þe peyne of helle.'
   In wittenesse of þis thyng Wrong was the furste
And Peres þe pardoner of Paulines queste,   110
Butte þe bedel of Bannebury sokene,
Raynald þe reue and redyng-kynges manye,
Munde þe mullere and monye mo othere.
'In þe date of þe deuel þis dede is aseled,
By syhte of sire Simonye and Syuyles leue.'   115
   Thenne tened hym Teologie when he this tales herde
And sayde to Symonye, 'Now sorwe mot thow haue,
Suche a weddyng to worche þat wrathe myhte treuthe;
And ar this weddyng be wrouhte, wo to al ʒoure consayle!
For Mede is moilere, Amendes was here dame.   120
Althow Fals were here fader and Fikel-tonge her belsyre,
Amendes was here moder, by trewe menne lokynge,
And withouten here moder Amendes Mede may not be wedded.
For Treuthe plyhte here treuthe to wedde on of here douhteres
And god graunte hit were so, so no gyle were.   125
And thow haste gyue here as Gyle tauhte, now god ʒeue þe sorwe!

123. not U] X *om*

110. *Paulines queste.* Not clear: perhaps a 'quest', or collecting mission (pardoners were *quaestors, questors*), based on some church dedicated to St Paul. The minor order of friars known as the 'Crutched' Friars (see VIII 191n) were sometimes called Paulines, but an association of friars and pardoners is unlikely.

111. *Bannebury sokene.* Place-names like this were probably not chosen for any particular satirical reason, nor is the change from *Bokynghamshire* (AB) likely to be significant.

112–13. For the familiar charges of dishonesty against reeves and millers, see *CT* I. 545–622. The meaning of *redyng-kynges* (also VI 372) is obscure: *redyng* may refer to 'reeding' (i.e. thatching with reeds), 'redding' (red dye) or 'riding' (i.e. as a retainer), with *kynges* as an ironical term for a man who is master of his craft. The first seems most likely.

114. *In þe date of þe deuel.* A parody, again echoing the language of legal deeds, of 'in the year of the lord', as in B XIII 268: 'In þe date of oure driʒte'.

116. Theology inherits the role of Holy Church and, speaking for Truth, opposes the marriage. His point is that Meed, though sired by Fals (Favel), is *moilere* (adj., 'of legitimate birth') because her mother, Amends, was an honest woman. Allegorically, Meed is not essentially sinful (see 43n, above), since there is a proper reward, allowed by God, for honest work, just as there is proper 'amends' sanctioned by law for reparation in cases of injury and offence (and by God for sin).

122. *by trewe menne lokynge*: 'according to the witness of honest men'.

124. 'For Truth made a promise to her (Amends) that he would wed one of her daughters', i.e. Meed is already spoken for in marriage.

For Syuyle and thi-sylue selde fulfulleth
That god wolde were ydo withoute som deseyte.
   Y Theologie þe tixt knowe, yf trewe doom wittenesseth,
That Laurence the leuyte, that lay on þe gredyre,   130 f.9ᵃ
Lokede vp to oure lord and alowed sayde:
"God of thy grace heuene gates opene
For y, man, of thy mercy mede haue diserued."
And sethe man may, an eye, mede of god diserue
Hit semeth sothly riȝt so on erthe   135
That Mede may be wedded to no man bot Treuthe;
And thow hast feffed here with Fals, fy on suche lawe!
For by lesynges ȝe lacchen largeliche mede.
That ȝe nymeth, and the notaries, to nauhte gynneth brynge
Holy Churche, and charite ȝe cheweth and deuoureth.   140
Ȝe shall abyggen hit bothe but ȝe amende þe sonner.
For wel ȝe wyte, wernardus, as holy writ telleth,
That Fals is faythles, the fende is his syre,
And as a bastard ybore byȝete was he neuere.
And Mede is moylore and mayden of gode;   145
A myhte kusse the kyng as for his kynneswomman.
   Forthy worcheth by wisdom and by witt also
And ledeth here to Londone there lawe may declare
Where matrymonye may be of Mede and of Falshede.
And thow iustices enioynen hem thorw iuroures othes   150
Ȝut beth ywar of þe weddynge for witty is Treuthe
And Consience is of his consayl and knoweth ȝow alle;
And yf he fynde ȝow in defaute and with the fals holde
Hit shall sitte ȝoure soules ful sore at þe laste.'
   Here-to assenteth Syuyle, ac Symonye ne wolde   155

---

129. Theologie U] X Theogie
130. gredyre *with* y *over erasure* X
139. and U] X *om*
146. kynnes U] X kyne
150. iuroures U] X ieroures

---

130. St Lawrence was martyred by being roasted on a gridiron. The term *leuyte* is taken from the Latin (*Legenda Aurea*, CXVII, 488), where *levita* means a deacon or lesser priest (corresponding to the Levite in the Jewish priesthood). See also XVII 66.
132–3. Cf. 'Gratias tibi ago, domine, quia januas tuas ingredi merui' (*Leg. Aurea*, CXVII, 492).
139. 'What you and the lawyers take . . .' Theology is still addressing Simony, who was chiefly responsible for the legal sanctioning of the false marriage (74, above).
144. 'And, being a bastard from birth, he was never (true-)begotten'.
145. *of gode:* 'of good family'.

Til he hadde seluer for the seel and signes of notaries.
Tho fette Fauel forth floreynes ynowe
And bade Gyle to gyue gold al aboute,
'And nameliche the notaries þat noon of hem fayle,
And feffe Fals Witnesse with floreynes ynowe   160
For he may Mede amaystrye with his merye speche.'
  Tho this gold was ygyue grete was the thonkynge
That Fauel and Fals hadde for her fayre ʒeftes,
And comen ful courteysly to conforte the false
And sayde softly, 'Sese shal we neuere,   165
Til Mede be thy wedded wyf wolle we nat stunte,   f.9ᵇ
For we haue Mede amaystred thorw oure mery tonge
That she graunteþ to go with a goode wille
To Londone and to loke yf lawe wille iugge;
To be maried for mone Med hath assented.'   170
  Thenne was Fauel fayn and Falsnesse blythe
And leten somne alle his segges in vche syde aboute
And bade hem alle be bowen, beggares and othere,
To wende with hym to Westminstre his weddyng to honoure.
  Ac hakeneys hadde thei none bote hakeneys to huyre;   175
Thenne gan Gyle to borwen hors at many gret maystres
And shop þat a shereue sholde bere Mede
Softliche in saunbure fram syse to syse,
And Fals and Fauel fecche forth sysores
And ryde on hem and on reues righte faste by Mede.   180
Symonye and Syuyle seyden and sworen
That prestis and prouisores sholden prelates serue,

---

159. nameliche I] XU manliche
168. she U] X he
178. saunbure U] X schaunbre

---

164. *And comen*: 'And (they) came', i.e. the lawyers.
169. *iugge*: 'give a judgment in the matter'.
174. Westminster was where the law-courts were.
175–93. The imagery of this vivid satirical passage, of sins riding on wicked men, of wicked men riding on wicked men, of Liar actually, it seems, turned into a cart, is traditional in allegorical and satirical poetry (e.g. in *Le Char d'Orgueil* of Nicolas Bozon, ed. J. Vising, 1919; and cf. *The Simonie*, 326), and ultimately indebted to patristic commentary on Ex. 15:1–4, where Pharaoh is allegorized as Satan and his riders and chariots as the sins of the devil, and to further commentary by Bernard on the allusion to the Exodus passage in Cant. 1:8 (see Kellogg, 1958).
182. *provisores*. Provisors were clerics holding a papal provision or grant (usually obtained by bribery) to be presented to a benefice when it fell vacant. The Statutes of Provisors (the first was enacted in 1351) were designed to restrict this practice. See Pantin, 1955, 47–75, 82–98.

'And y my-sulue, Syuyle, and Symonye my felawe
Wol ryde vppon *rectores* and ryche men deuoutours,
And notaries on persones þat permuten ofte
And on pore prouisores and on appeles in þe Arches.   185
Somnours and sodenes that *supersedeas* taketh,
On hem þat loueth leccherye lyppeth vp and rydeth,
On secatours and such men cometh softly aftur.
And lat cople þe commissarie, oure cart shal he drawe · ·   190
And fecchen oure vitailes at *fornicatores*.
And maketh of Lyare a lang cart to lede al this othere,
As fobbes and faytours þat on her feet rennen.'
    Thenne Fals and Fauel ryde forth togederes
And Mede in þe myddes and al this men aftur.   195
Y haue no tome to telle the tayl þat hem folewede
Of many maner men, for Mede sake sende aftur,
Ac Gyle was forgoere to gyen al this peple
For to wisse hem þe way and with Mede abyde.
    Sothnesse seyh hem alle and sayde but lytel   200
And prykede forth on pacience and passed hem alle
And kam to þe kynges court and Consience tolde   f.10ᵃ

---

187. sodenes U] X sodones. that P] XUI *om.*   *supersedeas* U] X supersedias
190. cople P] XUI cope
191. at] XUI and; P of

184. *rectores*: rectors, priests holding the living of a parish (cf. *persone*, Prol. 81n).
185. *permuten*. The exchange of livings is condemned as a form of simony in *Jacob's Well*, 127, because it is accompanied by a cash-adjustment. See also OED, s.v. *chop-church*.
186. *appeles in þe Arches*. See 61, above.
187. *sodenes*, or sub-deans, were clerics appointed by a bishop with special responsibility for moral (e.g. matrimonial) matters. A *supersedeas* was a writ to suspend proceedings in a case (with the implication that ecclesiastical officials accepted bribes from offenders to take out such writs: cf. Chaucer's Summoner, *CT* I. 649–58).
188–9. *lyppeth*, *rydeth* and *cometh* can be taken as imp.pl.
190. A *commissarie* was a clerical official who acted as a bishop's deputy; the commissary-general, who may be referred to here, presided over the diocesan court, including the court of the Arches: like the others, he was open to bribes from canon-law offenders such as fornicators. The harnessing of the commissary to a cart recalls a tradition, in literature and art, in which allegorical beasts draw the chariots of the sins (Katzenellenbogen, 1964, 61).
192. The *lang cart* is the four-wheeled military cart used for transporting military supplies and provisions, allegorically often the cart in which Luxuria rides in the tradition described by Kellogg (175n, above).
200. *Sothnesse*; allegorically, not synonymous with *Treuthe*.

And Consience to þe kyng carpede hit aftur.
'Now by Crist,' quod þe kyng, 'and y cacche myhte
Fals or Fauel or here felawe Lyare,   205
Y wolde be awreke on tho wreches and on here werkes alle
And do hem hange by þe halse and alle þat hem maynteyneth.
Shal neuere man on þis molde maynpryse þe leste,
But riht as þe lawe loketh lat falle on hem alle.'
And comaundede a constable that cam at þe furste,   210
'Go atache tho tyrauntes, for eny tresor, y hote.
Lat fetere Falsnesse faste for enys-kynes ʒeftes
And gurdeth of Gyles heed, lat hym goo no wyddore,
And bryngeth Mede to me, maugrey hem alle,
And yf ʒe lacchen Lyare lat hym nat askape   215
Ar he be put on þe pylorye, for eny preyere, ich hote.'
    Drede stod at þe dore and þe dene herde,
What was þe kynges wille, and wyghtliche wente
And bad Falsnesse to fle and his feres alle.
Falsnesse for fere tho fleyh to þe freres   220
And Gyle doth hym to gone, agaste for to deye.
Ac marchauntes mette with hym and made hym abyde
And byschytten hym in here shoppes to shewen here ware
And paraylede hym lyke here prentys the peple to serue.
    Lyhtliche Lyare lep awey thenne,   225
Lorkyng thorw lanes, to-logged of moneye.
He was nawher welcome for his many tales,
Oueral yhouted and yhote trusse,

206. on[1] U] X in
217. þe[2] U] X *om*
222. Ac U] X And
223. shoppes U] X shoppe

203. *Consience to þe kyng.* The king, as he is referred to here and in the following passus, is
    literally the king, surrounded by his advisors, exercising his function as head of
    state (see I 90n). But, 'since men in their social relations are bound by exactly the
    same law as that which governs their moral life as individuals', namely, the law of
    charity (Dunning, 1937, 108), the king is also, allegorically, the individual will
    presiding over his interior commonwealth.
208. To *maynpryse* was to offer security for the release of a prisoner pending trial, i.e. to
    go bail; the practice was open to abuse by rich men's friends.
211. *for*: 'in spite of (the offer of)', as also in 212, 216.
217. *Drede.* Fear (of the king's justice) acts as an effective deterrent in dispersing the evil
    associates of Meed. Like much of Langland's primarily political and social al-
    legory, this can readily be interpreted as an allegory of the operation of personal
    morality (see 203n, above).
228. *yhote trusse*: 'told to pack off'.

Tyl pardoners hadde pite on hym and polleden hym into house.
Thei woschen hym and wypeden hym and wonden hym in cloutes 230
And senten hym on Sonendayes with seeles to churche
And gaf pardon for pans, pound-mele aboute.
Thenne lourede leches and lettres thei sente
That Lyare sholde wonye with hem, watres to loke.
Spysours speken to hym to aspye her ware, 235
For a can on here craft and knoweth manye gommes.
Ac mynstrals and mesagers mette with Lyare ones
And of-helden hym half-ȝere and eleue dayes. f.10^b

   Ac freres thorw fayre speche fetten hym thennes
And for knowyng of comeres they copeden hym as a frere. 240
Ac he hath leue to lep out as ofte as hym liketh
And is welcome when he cometh and woneth with hem ofte.

   Symonye and Syuile senten to Rome
And putte hem thorw appeles in þe popes grace.
Ac Consience to þe kyng accused hem bothe
And sayde, 'Syre kyng, by Crist, but clerkes amende 245
Thy kynedom thorw here coueytise wol out of kynde wende
And holy churche thorw hem worth harmed for euere.'

   Alle fledde for fere and flowen into hernes;
Saue Mede þe mayde no ma durste abyde.
Ac treuliche to telle a tremblede for fere 250
And bothe wepte and wrang when she was attached.

---

229. pite U] X spyes
233. lettres U] X lettre
240. comeres U] X countreys

---

229. *pite.* The irony was perhaps too much for the scribe of X.
230. *cloutes* suggests patched or ragged clothes. Perhaps the implication is that the pardoners, having cleaned Liar up, do not want him to appear too spruce an alms-seeker. They seem to know more tricks than Liar himself.
231–2. Cf. Prol. 66ff.
232. *gaf:* '(he) gave'. *pound-mele aboute:* 'a pound's worth here, a pound's worth there'.
234. *watres to loke.* Inspecting a patient's urine was an important means of diagnosis; the implication is that the mysteries of urinoscopy could be falsely used to invent expensive ailments.
237–8. *ones* suggests a specific occasion, and six months and eleven days was precisely the length of Edward III's French campaign in the winter of 1359–60 (see III 236n, and Bennett *PMLA*, 1943, 570), perhaps a notable period for the spreading of false rumours by itinerant minstrels and messengers. By the time of the C-text, the reference may well have seemed arbitrary in its precision.
240. *for knowyng of comeres:* 'to prevent recognition by visitors'.
243–8. Added in C to dispose more tidily of two characters who have been important in Passus II.

Passus III

Lady Meed at Westminster

Passus tertius de visione vt prius
Now is Mede þe mayde and na mo of hem alle
Thorw bedeles and baylifs ybrouhte byfor þe kyng.
The kyng callede a clerke – y can nat his name –
To take Mede þe mayde and maken here at ese.
'Y shal asaye here mysulue and sothliche appose   5
What man of this world þat here leuest hadde,
And yf she worche wysely and by wys men consayl
Y wol forgyue here alle gultes, so me god helpe.'
    Cortesliche þe clerk thenne, as þe kyng hyhte,
Took Mede by þe myddel and myldeliche here brouhte   10
Into boure with blisse and by here gan sitte.
Ac there was myrthe and mynstracie Mede to plese;
That wendeth to Westmynstre worschipede here monye.
Genteliche with ioye the iustices somme
Boskede hem to þe bour ther this buyrde dwelte   15
And confortede here as they couthe, by the clerkes leue,
And sayden, 'Mourne nat, Mede, ne make thow no sorwe
For we wol wisse the kyng and thy way shape
For to wedde at thy wille where the leef licketh

1–8. The court presided over by the king here is a blend of a law-court and a meeting of the King's Council (i.e. the chief men of the realm – here, allegorically, Conscience and Reason – meeting as an advisory council to the king and in effect, with him, supreme governing body, a kind of inner 'cabinet'). 'Meed is treated by the king like a ward in chancery who has got into bad company but is still an honest woman' (Bennett 135). He does not summon her until l. 127, which gives her ample time to go about her characteristic business.

6. *here leuest hadde*: a fusion of the two constructions *here were leuest* and *she leuest hadde* (see OED, s.v. *have*, 22c).

13. 'The many who go to Westminster paid her their respects'. The law-courts were at Westminster.

14. *the iustices somme*: 'the justices, some of them'.

For al Consiences cast and craft, as y trowe.'   20
   Myldeliche Mede thenne mercyede hem alle   f.11ᵃ
Of here grete goodnesse and gaf hem vchone
Coupes of clene gold, coppes of syluer,
Rynges with rubees and othere riche ʒeftes,
The leste man of here mayne a motoun of gold.   25
   Whenne they hadde lauhte here leue at this lady Mede
Thenne come clerkes to conforte here the same
And beden here be blythe, 'for we beth thyn owene
For to worche thy wille the while þou myhte dure.'
And Mede hendeliche behyhte hem þe same,   30
To louye hem leeliche and lordes to make,
'And purchace ʒow prouendres while ʒoure panes lasteth
And bygge ʒow benefices, pluralite to haue,
And in þe constorie at court do calle ʒoure names.
Shal no lewedenesse lette þe clerk þat y louye   35
That he ne worth furste vaunsed, for y am byknowe
There connynge clerkes shal clokke byhynde.'
   Thenne come þer a confessour ycoped as a frere,
To Mede þe mayde myldeliche he sayde:
'Thow lewed men and lered men haued layn by the bothe,   40
And Falshede yfonde the al this fourty wyntur,
Y shal assoyle the mysulue for a seem whete
And ʒut be thy bedman and brynge adoun Consience
Amonge kynges and knyhtes and clerkes, and the lyke.'
   Thenne Mede for here mysdedes to this man knelede,   45
Shrofe here of here synne, shameles, y leue,
Tolde hym a tale and toke hym a noble
For to ben here bedman and to bere wel here ernde,
Among knyhtes and clerkes Consience to turne.
   And he assoilede here sone and sethen a sayde: 50
'We han a wyndowe a worchynge wol stande vs ful heye;

26. Whenne U] X Thenne
41. And U] X *om*

34. *do calle*: 'cause to be called over'. Meed implies that she will ensure that they get
lucrative positions at the consistory court (Prol. 127n).
38–67. A vivid demonstration of the friar-confessor (see Prol. 62n) in action.
51–4. Friars often begged money for the improvement of their churches (as in the
Summoner's Tale, *CT* III. 1718, 2099–106). Donors of glass could have their
names inscribed in a corner of the window; they could also have prayers and
masses said for them, and be enrolled in the 'letters of fraternity' (54, 67, below) of
the order, which entitled them to share in the spiritual benefits of the order's prayers
and good works. See VII 27. For Wycliffite attacks on these and similar practices,
see Workman, i.107–8; Wyclif, ed. Arnold, i.67, 380, iii.299, 377, 420–24.

Wolde ȝe glase þat gable and graue ther ȝoure name
In masse and in mataynes for Mede we shal synge
Solempneliche and softlyche as for a suster of oure ordre.'
    Loueliche þat lady laghynge sayde: 55
'Y shal be ȝoure frende, frere, and fayle ȝow neuere
The whiles ȝe louyen this lordes that lecherye haunteth   **f.11**[b]
And lacketh nat this ladyes þat louyeth þe same.
Hit is but frelete of fleysche, ȝe fyndeth wel by bokes,
And a cours of kynde wherof we comen alle.   60
Ho may askape þe sclaundre, þe skathe myhte sone be mended;
Hit is synne as of seuene noon sannour relesed.
Haueth mercy,' quod Mede, 'on men þat hit haunteth
And y shal cuuere ȝoure kyrke and ȝoure cloistre make,
Bothe wyndowes and wowes y wol amende and glase   65
And peynten and purtrayen ho payede for þe makyng
That euery seg shal se y am a sustre of ȝoure ordre.'
    Ac god to alle good folk suche grauynge defendeth,
To writen on wyndowes of eny wel dedes,
An auntur pruyde be paynted there and pomp of the world;   70
For god knoweth thi consience and thy kynde wille,
Thi cost and here couetyse and ho þe catel ouhte.
Forthy, leue lordes, leueth suche writynges;
God in þe gospel suche grauynge nouȝt alloueth,
    Nesciat dextra quid faciat sinistra.

60. a U] X *om*
62. sannour X] U sonnere
64. cloistre U] X cloustre
71–2. thy kynde . . . couetyse and P] XUI *om*

53. *for Mede.* Modern capitalization obscures a neat pun.
59–62. A good example of the friars' *glosing* (Prol. 58n). Lechery was often assigned a lesser place among the deadly sins, as a sin of the flesh, and the promptings of the flesh, it was recognized, were not in themselves deadly; but nevertheless a man must resist them with all in his power (*Vices and Virtues* 4; *Handlyng Synne* 587–96).
68–76. This digression, totally intrusive in the allegorical drama, is inspired not by any objection to beautifying churches but by the need to castigate those who have their names recorded for pride's sake and who think that money can buy God's favour.
72. *ho þe catel ouhte*: 'to whom the money that is spent properly belongs', viz. the poor. The absolute obligation upon the rich of giving to the poor and distributing alms is constantly stressed by L (I 172, IX 27n, 61n).
74a. Properly, *Nesciat sinistra tua quid faciat dextera tua* (as in L's translation): 'Do not let your left hand know what your right hand is doing (so that your alms may be in secret)' (Matt. 6:3–4). As often, the biblical passage quoted is a cue to the context and not a summary of its theme, which is here the warning by Jesus against ostentation in almsgiving.

Lat nat thy lyft hand, oure lord techeth,   75
Ywyte what thow delest with thi ryhte syde.
ჳut Mede the mayr myldeliche she bysouhte,
Bothe schyreues and seriauntes and suche as kepeth lawes
To punischen vppon pilories and vppon pynyng stoles,
As bakeres and breweres, bocheres and cokes;   80
For thyse men don most harm to þe mene peple,
Rychen thorw regraterye and rentes hem beggeth
With that þe pore peple sholde potte in here wombe.
For tok thei on trewely they tymbred nat so heye,
Ne bouhte none burgages, be ჳe ful sertayn.   85
Ne thei han no pite on the peple þat parselmele mot begge,
And thow thei take hem vntidy thyng no tresoun þei ne halden hit;
And thow thei fillen nat ful þat for lawe is seled,
A grypeth þerfore as gret as for þe grayeth treuthe.

77. she] XI he; U *om*; P hure (*Skeat emends to* hue)
80. and[1] U] X at
88. thow] X how (*an erasure before* h); U þough
89. as[1] P] XUI a

77–114. This passage, on the malpractices of urban traders, retailers and money-
lenders, and the responsibility of the mayor and his officers to maintain true justice
and fair trading practice, was perhaps first suggested to L by the association of
ostentatious building (84). It was never clearly related to the context in AB, and
the attempt to clarify the relation in C (which extends the passage from 10 lines to
over 40) by introducing an anticipation of l. 115 at l. 77, only emphasizes its
digressive nature (though cf. Mitchell, 1939, 488–92). *bysouhte* is best treated as
intransitive for the time being.

79. Pillories were very commonly used as a punishment for those found guilty of
fraudulent trading practice, such as giving short measure (88–9) or selling adul-
terated or rotten food (87). Pining-stools, or cucking-stools (chairs in which
offenders were carried about to exhibit their disgrace; to be distinguished from
ducking-stools, for scolds), were similarly used, mainly for women (e.g. ale-wives,
cf. VI 225–33).

82. *regraterye*: the retail trade; more specifically, buying up goods in the market at
advantage, and selling them at a profit (Lipson, 1959, 300). Cf. 'forestalling' (IV
59). The ordinances of the craft-guilds constantly condemn the practice (*English
Gilds*, e.g. 343, 353, 381).

84. 'If they carried on (their trade) honestly, they would not (have the money to)
build so high'.

86. Poor people, who buy in small quantities (*parselmele*), are the ones most vulnerable
to the unscrupulous retailer who gives false measure.

88–9. 'And though they do not fill to the top the measure that is sealed and certified
according to the law, they take as much for it as for the exact true measure'. For
the sealing of measures, see *Liber Albus*, 233, 290; *English Gilds*, 366–7; Lipson,
1959, 298–9.

Many sondry sorwes in citees falleth ofte,   90
Bothe thorw fuyr and thorw flood, al thorw fals peple
That bygyleth goode men and greueth hem wrongly,
The whiche þat crien on here knees þat Crist hem auenge   f.12ᵃ
Here on this erthe or elles in helle
That so bigileth hem of here goed, þat god on hem sende   95
Feuer or fouler euel other fuyr on here houses,
Morreyne or other meschaunces; and mony tymes hit falleth
That innocence is herde in heuene amonge seyntes
That louten for hem to oure lord and to oure lady bothe,
Graunte gylours on erthe grace to amende   100
And haue here penaunce on puyre erthe and nat þe peyne of helle.
And thenne falleth ther fuyr on fals men houses
And goode mennes for here gultes gloweth on fuyr aftur.
Al this haue we seyn, þat som tyme thorw a breware
Many burgages ybrent and bodies þer-ynne,   105
And thorw a candle clemynge in a cursed place
Ful adoun and forbrent forth alle þe rewe.
      Forthy mayres þat maketh fre men, me thynketh þat ʒe ouhten
For to spyre and to aspye, for eny speche of suluer,
What maner muster oþer marchandise he vsed   110
Ar he were vnderfonge fre and felawe in ʒoure rolles.
Hit is nat seemely for sothe in citee or in borw-toun
That vsurers oþer regraters, for enys-kynes ʒeftes,
Be yfranchised for a fre man and haue a fals name.
      Ac Mede þe mayde þe mayre a bisowte   115
Of alle suche sullers seluer to take
Or presentes without pans and oþer priue ʒeftes.
'Haue reuthe on this regraters þat han riche handes –
      In quorum manibus iniquitates sunt –

---

106. a² U] X *om*

90–107. The sense of this passage (added in C on the suggestion of 121–6) is that when
the victims of this profiteering cry for vengeance on their oppressors, God may well
send it, and when it comes, as in the form of fire, good men suffer as well as bad.
The argument is the indivisibility of the community, in suffering as in true dealing.
95. *That*: 'on those that'.
100. *Graunte*: 'to grant' (i.e. pray to God that he may grant).
109. *for eny speche of suluer*: 'despite the persuasive language of silver'. The privileges of a
freeman of the city, it is implied, could be bought, contrary to all the provisions of
the city charters (*Liber Albus*, 127, 425).
118a. In Ps. 25:10 David prays not to be condemned with men 'in whose hands are evil
devices (and whose right hands are full of bribes)'. The text is a comment on what
Meed says (cf. XX 438a). Ps. 25:6–12 constitute the *Lavabo* prayer of the Mass
(Missale Romanum, ed. R. Lippe, 1899–1907, i.201).

Loue hem for my loue,' quod this lady Mede,
'And soffre hem som tyme to selle aȝeyne þe lawe.'   120
Salamon þe sage a sarmon he made
In amendement of mayres and oþer stywardes
And wittenesseth what worth of hem þat wolleth take mede:
Ignis deuorabit tabernacula eorum qui libenter accipiunt munera.
Amonge thise lettred lordes this Latyn is to mene
That fuyr shal falle and forbrenne al to blew aysches   125
The houses and þe homes of hem þat taketh ȝeftes.
The kyng fram conseyl come, calde aftur Mede   f.12ᵇ
And sente to se here—y myhte nat se þat ladde here.
Fol corteisliche þe kynge, as his kynde wolde,
Lacked here a litel whith for þat she louede gyle   130
And wilned to be wedded withouten his leue
And til Treuthe hadde ytolde here a tokene fram hymsulue;
And saide, 'Vnwittiliche, woman, wroft hastow ofte
And monye a gulte y haue the forgyue and my grace graunted
Bothe to the and to thyne in hope thow shost amende,   135
And ay the lengur y late the go the lasse treuthe is with the,
For wors wrouhtestou neuere then now, tho thow Fals toke.
Ȝut y forgyue the þis gult, god forbede eny more
Thow tene me and Treuthe; and thow mowe be a-take,
In the castel of Corf y shal do close the as an ancre   140
Or in a wel wors woen, be seynte Mary my lady,
That alle wantowen women shal be war be þe one
And bitterliche banne the and alle þat bereth thy name

123a. *tabernacula* I] XU tabernacla
138. god forbede I] X godes forbede; U godes forbode

123a. 'Fire shall consume the tabernacles of those who love to take bribes' (Job 15:34). Cf. 90–107, above. Wise biblical sayings were often thus attributed to Solomon.
127. This begins the interview with Meed that the king had promised (5–8, above) after consulting his council.
128. *y myhte nat se þat ladde here.* This is the same official, presumably, that L was unable to name before (3, above). There may be reluctance to name the incumbent of a real office, that of clerk to the king's council.
132. *And til*: 'and before'. The reference is to Truth's promise to marry Meed (II 124); the king, acting now as if Meed were a ward of court, will offer her to Truth's proxy, Conscience (146, below).
140. *the castel of Corf.* The dungeons of Corfe Castle, in SE Dorset, were notorious from King John's day as places of imprisonment (Skeat 45; R. B. Pugh, *Imprisonment in Medieval England*, Cambridge, 1968, 128). *as an ancre.* Rejected from a previous text (Carnegy, 1934, 12–13) as a mistaken incorporation of a scribal gloss (cf. III 421, XVI 184); but the sense is good (Mitchell, 1939, 486–8) and the line not unwieldy.

And teche the to louye treuthe and take consail of resoun.
Y haue a knyght, Consience, cam late fro beȝende;   145
Yf he wilneth the to wyue, wolt thow hym haue?'
   'Ȝe, lord,' quod that lady, 'lord hit me forbede
But y be holly at thyn heste, lat hange me elles!'
   Thenne was Consience ykald to come and apere
Byfore þe kyng and his consayl, as clerkes and oþere.   150
Knelyng, Consience to þe kyng loutede,
What his wille were and what he do sholde.
   'Woltow wedde this Mede yf y wol assente?
For she is fayn of thy felawschipe and for to be thy make.'
   Quod Consience to the kyng, 'Crist hit me forbede!   155
Ar y wedde suche a wyf, wo me bytyde!
For she is frele of here fayth and fikel of here speche
And maketh men mysdo manye score tymes.
In trist of here tresor she teneth fol monye;
Wyues and wedewes wantonnesse she techeth   160
And lereth hem to lecherye þat louyeth here ȝeftes.
Ȝoure fader she afelde, Fals and she togederes;
She hath apoisend popes, she appeyreth holy churche.   f.13ᵃ
Is nat a bettere baud, by hym þat me made,
Bytwene heuene and helle, and erthe thogh men soughte.   165
For she is tikel of here tayl, talewys of tonge,
As comyn as þe cartway to knaues and to alle,
To monekes, to alle men, ȝe, musels in hegge;
Lyggeth by here when hem lust lered and lewed.
   Sysores and somnours, suche men hire preiseth;   170
Shyreues of shyres were shent yf she nere,
For she doth men lesen here lond and here lyf bothe.
She lat passe prisones, paieth for hem ofte,

---

159. she U] X he; *so below*, 160, 163 (*twice*), 171, 172, 173, 180, 181, 183, 185, 186 (*twice*), 193
170. hire U] X he

162. In A, if taken literally, this would have referred to the then king's father, Edward II; by the time of C it would refer to Richard II's father, the Black Prince. The accusation would be appropriate to both, in a general way; Meed answers it in 232, below.
163. *apoisend popes*. The reference is to the legend of Constantine's gift of land to the pope (see V 175, XVII 220), which was regarded as laying the foundation for the corruption of the Church through wealth and property.
166. *tikel of here tayl*: 'sexually promiscuous'.
167. The proverb (Whiting C 64) suggests Meed's 'indiscriminate pliability' (Yunck, 1963, 295).

And gyueth the gaylers gold and grotes togederes
To vnfetere the fals and fle wher hym liketh;
And taketh treuthe by the top and teieth hym faste   175
And hangeth hym for hatrede þat harmede nere.
To be cursed in þe constorie a counteth nat a rusche;
For a copeth þe commissarie and coteth his clerkes
She is assoiled thus sone as heresulue lyketh.
She may ny as muche do in a monthe ones   180
As ȝoure secrete seel in sixe score dayes.
She is priue with þe pope, prouysours it knoweth,
For Symonye and heresulue seleth here bulles.
She blesseth this bischopes thow thei ben ny lewede;
She prouendreth persones and prestes she maynteneth   185
To holde lemmanes and lotebyes al here lyf-dayes,
And bringeth forth barnes aȝenes forbodene lawes.
Sunt infelices, quia matres sunt meretrices.
Ther she is wel with eny kyng, wo is þat rewme
For she is fauerable to þe fals, the whiche defouleth treuthe.   190
  By Iesu! with here ieweles the iustices she shendeth;
She lyth aȝeyn þe lawe and lettith hym þe gate
That fayth may nat haue his forth, here floreynes goth so thykke;
And leet þe lawe as here luste and louedayes maketh.
Thorw which loueday is loste þat Leute myhte wynne –   195
The mase for a mene man thow he mote euere!

188. barnes U] X barmes
193. lettith U] X leith

178–9. Cf. II 190, III 34.
181–2. Money acted more quickly in securing appointment to ecclesiastical office than the king's own decree. Cf. Wyclif, ed. Arnold, iii.307.
185–8. Conscience's comprehensive survey of Meed's activities here covers the appointment and consecration of ignorant secular men as bishops, the obtaining of prebends (ecclesiastical livings, presumably extra ones) for parsons, and the sanctioning of concubinage among the priesthood. *maynteneth*, as usual, has the sense of 'abet and support in wrong-doing'.
189. 'They are accursed, for their mothers are whores'. Source not identified.
193. *lettith hym þe gate*: 'puts obstacles in his way'.
195. *louedayes*: special days set aside at court-sessions, or more informally, for the settling of disputes by arbitration. They had a bad name, and bribery and intimidation rather than Christian forgiveness were often the effective arbiter, as we may deduce from the interest of Chaucer's Friar in such occasions (*CT* I. 258). Cf. V 158, XI 17, Wyclif, ed. Arnold, ii.77, iii.322, and see J. W. Bennett, 'The Mediaeval Loveday', *Speculum* 33 (1958), 351–70.
196. *Leute*. Cf. II 20n.

Lawe is so lordliche and loth to make eny ende;
Withoute presentes oþer pans he pleseth ful fewe.   f.13^b
   Trewe burgeys and bonde she bryngeth to nauhte ofte   200
And al þe comune in care and in coueytise.
Religioun she al to-reueth and oute of reule to lybbe.
Ther ne is cite vnder sonne ne noon so ryche reume
Ther she is alowed and ylet by þat laste shal eny while
Withouten werre oþer wo oþer wickede lawes   205
And custumes of coueytise þe comune to destruye.
Vnsittyng soffraunce, here suster, and heresulue
Han almest mad, but Marye the helpe,
That no lond ne loueth the and ӡut leeste thyn owene.
For clerkes and coueitise Mede hath knet togederes   210
That al þe witt of the world is woxe into gyle.
Thus lereth this lady thi lond, now lord ӡeue here sorwe!
For pore men dar nat pleyne ne no pleynt shewe,
Such a maister is Mede among men of gode.'
   Thenne mournede Mede and menede here to þe kyng   215
To haue space to speke, spede yf a myhte.
The kyng grauntede here grace with a goode wille:
'Excuce the yf thow kanst, y can no more segge,
For Consience acuseth the to congeye the for euere.'
   'Nay, lord,' quod þat lady, 'leueth hym þe worse   220
When ӡe wyteþ witterly in whom þe wrong liggeth.
Ther þat meschief is greet Mede may helpe;
And þat knowestou, Consience, y cam nat to chyde
Ne to depraue thy persone with a proed herte.
Wel thow wost, weye, but yf thow wille gabbe,   225

---

200. she] XUI he; P hue; *so below,* 202, 204
205. lawes U] X lawe

---

197. 'Nothing but confusion for an ordinary man, though he go on pleading his case for
ever'.
199. *he* refers to Law, personified in the preceding line. This causes the scribe of U some
confusion, and he uses *he* for Meed's activities in lines 200–04 (the confusion is not
apparent in X, which habitually uses *he* for both 'he' and 'she').
207. *Vnsittyng soffraunce*: 'improper indulgence', allowing things that ought not to be
allowed, with the suggestion of the law perverted to false leniency through
bribery. The occurrence of this phrase only in two passages added in C (202–9
here, and IV 187–94) was used by Skeat to suggest that both passages relate to
conditions around 1393 (Skeat xxxiv) but this was never very likely (see Intro-
duction, p. 9).
221. Meed addresses the king politely in the plural, but Conscience with familiar
contempt in the sg. (e.g. 223). These distinctions (cf. modern French) are consis-
tently maintained in the 14th c.

Thow hast hanged on my half enleuene tymes
And also grypen my gold and gyue hit where þe liked.
Why thow wrathest þe now wonder me thynketh;
ʒut y may, as y myhte, menske þe with ʒeftes
And maynteyne thi manhede more then thow knowest. 230
  Ac thow hast famed me foule byfore þe kyng here
For kulde y neuere no kyng ne conseilede so to done,
Ac y haue saued myselue sixty thousand lyues
Bothe here and elles-where in alle kyne londes.
Ac thow thysulue sothly, ho hit segge durste, 235 f.14ᵃ
Hast arwed many hardy man þat hadde wille to fyhte,
To berne and to bruttene, to bete adoun strenghtes.
In contrees there the kyng cam Consience hym lette
That he ne felde nat his foes tho fortune hit wolde
And as his wyrdus were ordeyned at þe wille of oure lorde. 240
Caytifliche thow, Consience, conseiledest þe kyng to leten
In his enemyes handes his heritage of Fraunce.
Vnconnynge is þat Consience a kyndom to sulle,
For þat is conquered thorw a comune helpe, a kyndom or ducherie,
Hit may nat be sold sothliche, so many part asketh 245
Of folk þat fauht þerfore and folwede þe kynges wille.
The leste ladde þat longeth with hym, be þe londe ywonne,
Loketh aftur lordschipe or oþer large mede
Wherby he may as a man for eueremore lyue aftur.
And þat is þe kynde of a kyng þat conquereth on his enemys, 250
To helpe heyliche alle his oste or elles graunte
Al þat his men may wynne, do therwith here beste.
Forthy y consayl no kynge eny conseyl aske
At Concience, þat coueiteth to conquere a reume.
For sholde neuere Consience be my constable were y a kyng,' quod 255
    Mede,
'Ne be marschal ouer my men there y moste fyhte.

---

227. grypen U] X gryp
244. is conquered I] XU conquereth

226–30. Meed claims that Conscience uses money and is therefore of her party (but cf.
I 42–53) and also offers to bribe Conscience more generously.
226. *hanged on my half*: 'clung to my side (i.e. party)'.
232. See 162, above.
233–4. A reference to bought truces and ransoms.
235–57. This passage replaces the more topical allusion in AB to the French campaign
of 1359–60 (cf. II 237n; for the argument that the reference in AB is to the later
campaign of 1373, see Huppé, 1939). Meed's argument is now more generalized
in its reference to the French wars; she argues that a king has a responsibility to
fight imperialistic wars of conquest and distribute the plunder among his men.
Conscience she portrays as mere pusillanimity.

Ac hadde y, Mede, ben his marchel ouer his men in Fraunce
Y durste haue yleyd my lyf and no lasse wedde
He sholde haue be lord of þat lond a lenghe and a brede
And also kyng of þat kuth his kyn for to helpe,   260
The leeste brolle of his blod a barones pere.
Vnconnyngliche thow, Consience, conseiledest hym thenne
To lete so his lordschipe for a litel mone.
   Hit bycometh for a kyng þat shal kepe a reume
To ȝeue men mede þat meekliche hym serueth,   265
To aliens and to alle men, to honoure hem with ȝeftes;
Mede maketh hym be byloued and for a man yholde.
Emperours and erles and alle manere lordes
Thorw ȝeftes haen ȝemen to ȝerne and to ryde.
The pope and alle prelates presentes vnderfongen   270
And ȝeuen mede to men to meyntene here lawes.   f.14ᵇ
Seruantes for here seruyse mede they asken
And taken mede of here maistres as þei mowen acorde.
Bothe begeres and bedemen crauen mede for here preyeres;
Munstrals for here minstracie a mede thei asken;   275
Maistres þat kenneth clerkes craueth therfore mede;
Prestes þat prechen and þe peple techen
Asken mede and mas-pans and here mete bothe.
Alle kyn crafty men crauen mede for here prentises;
Marchaundise and mede mot nede togederes.   280
Is no lede þat leueth þat he ne loueth mede
And glad for to grype here, gret lord oþer pore.'
   Quod þe kyng io Consience, 'By Crist, as me thynketh,
Mede is worthy, me thynketh, þe maistrye to haue.'
   'Nay,' quod Consience to þe kyng, 'clerkes witeth þe sothe   285
That Mede is euermore a mayntenour of gyle,
As þe sauhter sayth by such þat ȝeueth mede:

---

262. thow P] XU1 *om*

263. The return to the matter of AB (at l. 257) involves a reference here, apparently, to the treaty of Bretigny (1360). This was a bought peace, immensely profitable to the English, of exactly the kind that Meed claims credit for elsewhere (233–4, above); perhaps her point, with hindsight, is that the 'litel mone' it brought in was not to be compared with the potential profits of further plunder; but the possibility cannot be excluded that the reference is to some later campaign and some more petty truce (see Huppé, 1939, 55–9, and cf. Bennett, *PMLA*, 1943, 568–70). Or perhaps Meed is to be shown contradicting herself in order to win a point.

279. *mede* here refers to the heavy fee demanded by a master craftsman from a prospective apprentice (Lipson, 1959, 322, 414–16).

287. See 118a, above.

That vnlaufulliche lyuen hauen large handes
To ȝeue men mede more oþer lasse.
   Ac ther is mede and mercede, and bothe men demen   290
A desert for som doynge, derne oþer elles.
Mede many tymes men ȝeueth bifore þe doynge
And þat is nother resoun ne ryhte ne in no rewme lawe
That eny man mede toke but he hit myhte deserue,
And for to vndertake to trauile for another   295
And wot neuere witterly where he lyue so longe
Ne haue hap to his hele mede to deserue.
Y halde hym ouer-hardy or elles nat trewe
That *pre manibus* is paied or his pay asketh.
Harlotes and hoores and also fals leches   300
They asken here huyre ar thei hit haue deserued,
And gylours gyuen byfore and goode men at þe ende
When þe dede is ydo and þe day endit;
And þat is no mede but a mercede, a manere dewe dette,
And but hit prestly be ypayed þe payere is to blame,   305
As by the book þat byt nobody with-holde
The huyre of his hewe ouer eue til amorwe: f.15ᵃ
   Non morabitur opus mersenarii.
And ther is resoun as a reue rewardynge treuthe
That bothe the lord and the laborer be leely yserued.
The mede þat many prest taken for masses þat thei syngen,   310
Amen Amen, Matheu seyth, *mercedem suam recipiunt.*

---

293. in U] X on
294. hit U] X hihte
295. to² U] X þe
307a. *morabitur* U] X morabit

---

288. *That*: 'those that'.

290–405. In place of the distinction made by AB between the immoderate desire for gain and 'mesurable hire' (B III 256), C introduces a distinction between *mede* and *mercede*, the former still dependent on circumstance for its propriety, the latter a straightforward paying of a debt for services rendered; and also a long passage, entirely new, of grammatical analogy (332–405).

295–7. And, as an extreme case, a man should be prepared to work even if he has no certainty that his employer will survive to pay him his proper reward.

299. *pre manibus* is Langland's variant of the phrase *prae manu*, 'in hand', i.e. in advance. Cf. IX 45.

307a. 'The wages of a hired servant shall not remain (with you all night until morning)' (Lev. 19:13).

311. 'Truly, they have their reward' (Matt. 6:2, 6:5). The sense is ironical, as in the gospel, where the reference is to the praise sought by ostentatious almsgivers (see 74a, above), or by ostentatious prayer-mongers. Priests who say mass 'for hope of worldly wynnynge' are attacked in Wyclif, ed. Arnold, iii.286; ed. Matthew, 167.

In marchandise is no mede, y may hit wel avowe,
Hit is as a permutacoun apertly, on peneworth for another.
   And thow the kyng of his cortesye, cayser or pope,
ʒeue lond or lordschipe oþer large ʒeftes   315
To here lele and to lege, loue ys the cause,
And yf the lele and lege be luyther men aftur
Bothe kyng and cayser and þe crouned pope
May desalowe that thei dede and dowe þerwith another
And bynyme hit hem anone, and neuere-more aftur   320
Noyther eny of here ayres hardy to claymen
That kyng oþer kayser hem gaf catel oþer rente.
For god gaf Salomon grace vpon erthe,
Richesse and resoun the while he ryhte lyuede,
And as sone as god seyh a sewed nat his wille   325
A refte hym of his richesse and of his ryhte mynde
And soffred him lyue in mysbileue – y leue he be in helle.
So god gyueth nothyng þat *si* ne is the glose
And ryhte so sothly may kyng and pope
Bothe gyue and graunte there his grace lyketh   330
And efte haue hit aʒeyne of hem þat don ylle.
   Thus is mede and mercede as two maner relacions,

---

316. lele U] X om. ys P] XUI *om*
319. desalowe X (*over* desauowe *erased*)] UIP desauowe. dowe P] XUI do
327. soffred him lyue U] X hym lyue[re?]d

314–22. L introduces here already the idea of a necessary *relation* in the giving of reward – the recipient must be loyal to the giver and so repay the debt incurred in the gift.

320. *and neuere-more aftur*: 'and (they be) nevermore after'.

327. *y leue he be in helle.* The story of Solomon's apostasy in old age is told in 3 Reg. 11, but not in the corresponding section in 2 Para. 9, which may account for the uncertainty about whether he was in hell (or delivered thence at the Harrowing). Cf. XI 221.

328. 'So God gives nothing without an *if* in the margin'. The reference is probably to God's promises to Solomon after the dedication of the temple, where *si* marks a series of stern conditions (2 Para. 7:13, 17, 19).

332–405. This long section is difficult, and Skeat gave it up; but it is not uncharacteristically difficult (for its adaptation of grammatical terminology, cf. B XIII 151 and Kaske, 1963, 40; for its echo of scholastic method, cf. XIV 192; for the use of grammatical metaphor in venality-satire, see Yunck, 1963, 95, 120, and for its persistent use in Alan of Lille to describe unnatural sexuality, see *De Planctu Naturae*, 429, 463, 475–7), and the general argument is clear, if not all the details (see the analysis in Amassian, 1971, which I cannot always agree with). *Mede* and *mercede* are said to be analogous to certain kinds of grammatical relationship, viz. direct relation (e.g. of antecedent and relative pronoun, agreeing in gender, case and number: 'The man who is speaking') and indirect relation (e.g. of antecedent

Rect and indirect, reninde bothe
On a sad and a siker semblable to hemsuluen,
As adiectif and sustantif vnite asken
And acordaunce in kynde, in case and in nombre,
And ayther is otheres helpe – of hem cometh retribucoun,
And that þe gyft þat god gyueth to alle lele lyuynge,
Grace of good ende and gret ioye aftur.
  Retribuere dignare, domine deus.'
 Quod the kyng to Consience, 'Knowen y wolde
What is relacion rect and indirect aftur,
Thenne adiectyf, and sustantyf, for Englisch was it neuere.'
 'Relacoun rect,' quod Consience, 'is a record of treuthe,
  Quia ante late rei recordatiuum est,
Folowynge and fyndynge out þe fundement of a strenghe,
And styfliche stande forth to strenghe þe fundement
In kynde and in case and in þe cours of nombre.
As a leel laborer byleueth þat his maister
In his pay and in his pite and in his puyr treuthe

335

340
f.15ᵇ

345

342. and U] X an

and relative pron. not in the same case: 'The man to whom I spoke'). Proper and improper reward (it does not seem possible always to identify *mede* with indirect, *mercede* with direct relation, or vice versa) are distinguished by the different nature of the relationship between the parties, payer and payee. In the former the relationship is 'direct' and proper, and reflects the concord between God and man whereby man trusts in God's promises of salvation; in the latter the relationship is 'indirect' and confused. It is worth noting that 'indirect relation' in grammar is not in itself a solecism, which allows a complexity in the application of the metaphor whereby some degree of propriety is preserved for *mede*.

333–4. 'Direct and indirect, both of them dependent on a firm and sure (concept of relation), in which both have a part' – and which is further compared to the concord of adjective and substantive.

335–9. The grammatical parallel is applied abruptly to the relation of God and man, where God gives true repayment or 'retribution' (no pejorative sense) in return for true life.

339a. 'Deign, O lord God, to reward (with eternal life all of us who do good)'. A petition from the daily grace; it provides the sense of 337–9. The text of this, and of other echoes of the daily grace in L (e.g. I 82, III 402a, IX 125, XI 67, XV 264a, XVII 65) may be found in a collection of Latin graces in Balliol MS 354 printed in *The Babees Boke* (EETS 32), 382–5.

343–5. Direct relation is a remembrance of and witness to truth, reflecting in its nature the firm foundation of concord, and acting to strengthen that foundation.

343a. 'Because it is a record of that which has gone before': an explanation of grammatical relation common in Latin grammars (Amassian, 1971, 466).

345. *stande* is inf.

348. *In his pay*: 'for the sake of his own satisfaction'.

To pay hym yf he parforme and haue pite yf he faileth
And take hym for his trauaile al þat treuthe wolde;   350
So of holy herte cometh hope, and hardy relacoun
Seketh and seweth his sustantif sauacioun,
That is god the ground of al, a graciouse antecedent.
And man is relatif rect yf he be rihte trewe:
He acordeth with Crist in kynde, *Verbum caro factum est*;   355
In case, *Credere in ecclesia*, in holy kyrke to bileue;
In nombre, rotye and aryse and remissioun to haue,
Of oure sory synnes to be assoiled and yclansed
And lyue as oure crede vs kenneth with Crist withouten ende.
This is relacion rect, ryht as adiectyf and sustantyf   360
Acordeth in alle kyndes with his antecedent.
    Indirect thyng is as ho-so coueytede
Alle kyn kynde to knowe and to folowe
And withoute cause to cache and come to bothe nombres;
In whiche ben gode and nat gode to graunte here neyþer will.   365
And þat is nat resonable ne rect to refuse my syre name,

360. as U] X *om*
365. to] XUIP and. neyþer U] X nauht

351–4. Man is here the adjective seeking direct relation, or concord, with the substan-
tive, out of which concord will come salvation, while God is defined as antecedent,
since all notion of true concord depends upon him; yet he stands self-sufficient and
is not conditioned by the relationship. Likewise man, as adjective, is incidental,
yet he coheres in the nature of the antecedent. L seems to speak indiscriminately of
antecedent + relative pronoun and of substantive + adjective, two of the
four types of 'relation' (the others being subject + verb and partitive or super-
lative + genitive), all of which can be either 'direct' or 'indirect': for a simple
exposition of the subject, see the 15th c. ME translation of a treatise on Latin
grammar edited by S. B. Meech in *Essays and Studies in Comp. Lit.* (Univ. of
Michigan Pubs., Lang. and Lit., Vol. XIII, 1935), 81–125.

355–9. Grammatical agreement in *kynde* (i.e. gender), case and number is here made to
correspond to concord with Christ through observance of the key articles of the
Creed: belief in the Incarnation ('The Word was made flesh', John 1:14), belief in
holy Church, and belief in the resurrection of the body and the forgiveness of sins.

362–9. Indirect relation makes a chaos of concord, since it seeks to grasp everything to
itself: in terms of grammar, it seeks relationship on the basis of all genders and
both numbers. This is confusion, the more so because it confounds the one aspect
of the relation that is proper (i.e. *mede* makes part of *mercede*, as was expressed
earlier in Meed's pedigree, II 116). To refuse the claims of *mede* is good, but in a
way not good (365) since there is always some degree of direct relation or entitle-
ment, just as there is in matters of inheritance (366–9).

366–9. The implication of these references to family relationship (Conscience speaks
impersonally, not of his own family relations) is that social contracts, like gram-
matical relations, are binding in all their parts: the parties to the contract cannot
pick and choose which parts they are prepared to observe (Mitchell, 1956, 185).

Sethe y am his sone and his seruant sewe for his ryhte.
For ho-so wolde to wyue haue my worliche douhter
I wolde feffe hym with alle here fayre and here foule taylende.
So indirect is inlyche to coueyte   370
To acorde in alle kynde and in alle kyn nombre,
Withouten coest and care and alle kyn trauayle.
   Ac relacoun rect is a ryhtful custume,
As a kyng to clayme the comune at his wille
To folowe and to fynde hym and fecche at hem his consayl   375 f.16ᵃ
That here loue to his lawe thorw al þe lond acorde.
So comune claymeth of a kyng thre kyne thynges,
Lawe, loue and lewete, and hym lord antecedent,
Bothe heued and here kyng, haldyng with no parteyӡe
Bote standynge as a stake þat stikede in a mere   380
Bytwene two lordes for a trewe marke.
   Ac þe moste partie of peple now puyr indirect semeth,
For they wilnen and wolden as beste were for hemsulue
Thow the kyng and þe comune al the coest hadde.
Such inparfit peple repreueth alle resoun   385
And halt hem vnstedefast for hem lakketh case.
As relacoynes indirect reccheth thei neuere
Of the cours of case so thei cache suluer.
Be the peccunie ypaied, thow parties chyde,
He þat mede may lacche maketh lytel tale.   390
Nyme he a noumbre of nobles or of shillynges,
How þat cliauntes acorde acounteth mede litel.
   Ac adiectyf and sustantyf is as y her tolde,
That is vnite acordaunde in case, in gendre and in noumbre,
And is to mene in oure mouth more no mynne
But þat alle maner men, wymmen and childrene   395

---

372. *Skeat here adds a line from MS F*
373. Ac U] X As
375. fecche P] XUI seche
395. mene P] XUI nempne

---

369. *taylende*: tallying, reckoning up (of property), with the implication that not all she carries with her is equally desirable and perhaps with a pun on 'tail-end' (cf. *CT* VII. 434).

373–92. Direct relation in politics is the concord or balancing of mutual claims, of the king on the people (374) and of the people on the king (377). Indirect relation is self-seeking and neglect of community.

378. *Lawe, loue and lewete*. See Prol. 149n, XI 161n, XVII 126–40, and Kean, 1964. *antecedent*, i.e. having the same unconditional status as God (351, above, and see Kean, 1969, 98).

386, 388. *case* here means, generally, 'proper relationship'.

Sholde confourme hem to o kynde on holy kyrke to bileue
And coueyte þe case when thei couthe vnderstande
To syke for here synnes and soffre harde penaunces
For þat lordes loue that for oure loue deyede   400
And coueytede oure kynde and be kald in oure name,
    Deus homo,
And nyme hym into oure noumbre now and eueremore.
    Qui in caritate manet in deo manet et deus in eo.
Thus is he man, and mankynde in maner of sustantyf
As *hic et hec homo* askyng an adiectyf
Of thre trewe termisones, *trinitas unus deus*;   405
    Nominatiuo, pater et filius et spiritus sanctus.
  Ac ho-so rat of *Regum*, rede me may of Mede
How she Absoloun to hangynge brouhte;
And sethe, for Sauel saued a kyng for mede
Agaynes godes comandement, god tok such a vengeaunce   f.16^b
That Saul for þat synne and his sone deyede,   410
And ȝaf the kyndom to his knaue þat kept shep and lambren;

403. he I] XUP *om*
407. she U] X he

398. *case*: 'particular direct relationship', also 'occasion' (the normal non-specialized sense of the word).
401a. 'God (and) man', echoing the Athanasian creed (Breviary, II. 48).
402a. 'He who abides in love abides in God, and God abides in him' (1 John 4:16, said in the daily grace: see note to 339a, above). Cf. I 82, 87.
403–5. The noun *homo*, 'such-and-such a man' (*hic et hec*, 'this', masc. and 'this', fem.), now made substantive by the Incarnation and the life of man in Christ (Amassian, 1971, 474), needs to be in concord with an adjective which will be inflected according to the endings of the Trinity, here given in the nominative case (*nominatiuo*), with a pun on *in nomine*, 'in the name of' (the usual introduction to an invocation of the Trinity, as spoken when the sign of the cross is made, e.g. in the mass, Missale 577, 578, 581, etc.). Man, through Christ, may live in direct relation with the Trinity.
406. *Regum*: the books of Kings (the first and second books are called 1 and 2 Samuel in AV). The story of Absalom's conspiracy to win the kingdom from his father David is told in 2 Reg. 14–18; for his death, see 18:9–15.
408–41. Saul was commanded, through Samuel, to slay Agag, king of the Amalekites, and utterly to destroy the Amalekite people. This was to fulfil God's promise of revenge when the Amalekites opposed Israel on the journey through Sinai (Ex. 17:8–16). Saul's disobedience was punished by the withdrawal of God's favour, the provision of David as king and the eventual death in battle of Saul and his son Jonathan (1 Reg. 31). Agag was slain personally by Samuel. The story, told in 1 Reg. 15–16, is not intrinsically a very good one for the illustration of meed, since Saul's purpose in keeping back the best of the spoil was to offer it in sacrifice to God; Samuel's point was that God prefers absolute obedience (1 Reg. 15:21–2).

As me ret in *Regum*, aftur Ruth, of kynges,
How god sente to Sauel be Samuel þe prophete
That Agag of Amalek and alle his leege peple
Sholde deye derfly for dedes of here eldres.   415
  "Sauel," quod Samuel, "god hymsulue hoteth
To be buxum at my byddyng his bone to fulfille.
Haste the with al thyn oste to þe lond of Amalek
And alle þat leueth on þat lond oure lord wol þat thow sle hit,
Man and woman and wyf, childe, wedewe and bestes,   420
Mebles and vnmebles, man and alle þinges,
Bern hit, bere hit nat awey be hit neuer so riche,
For eny mede of money; al that thow myhte,
Spille hit, spare hit nat and thow shalt spede the bettere."
  And for a coueytede here catel and the kyng sparede,   425
Forbar hym and his beste bestes, as þe byble wittenesseth,
Otherwyse then god wolde and warnede hym by þe prophete,
God sayde to Samuel þat Sauel sholde deye
And al his seed for þat synne shentfolyche ende.
Thus was kyng Sauel ouercome thorw coueytise of mede   430
That god hated hym for euere and alle his eyres aftur.
The *culorum* of this kaes kepe y nat to shewe,
An auntur hit nuyede me noen ende wol y make.
For so is the world went with hem þat han þe power
That he þat sayth men sothest is sonnest yblamed.   435
  I, Consience, knowe this, for Kynde Wit me tauhte
That resoun shal regne and reumes gouerne
And riht as Agag hadde happe shal somme;
Samuel shal sle hym and Sauel shal be yblamed
And Dauid shal be ydyademed and adaunte alle oure enemyes   440

---

417. bone P] XUI loue
421. Mebles P] XUI That dwelleth in Amalek mebles. þinges U] X *om*
429. his seed B] XUI is; P hus
431. hated hym P] XUI *om*. his] X *om*; UI here; P hus
436. I U] X In

---

412. The first book of Kings (1 Sam. in AV) follows the book of Ruth.
421. *That dwelleth in Amalek* (see textual notes) was mistakenly incorporated into the
  text of XUI from a scribal gloss in the ancestor of all MSS of the [i] group
  (Carnegy, 1934, 12).
432. *culorum*: 'conclusion (to be drawn from this case)', an abbreviated form of *seculorum*,
  the last word of the last phrase (*in secula seculorum*, 'for ever and ever') of the *Gloria
  Patri*, commonly said at the end of prayers and graces, and of psalms and anthems
  in the church service (Breviary, II. 4).
433. L alludes to the dangers of making a contemporary application (cf. Prol. 218).

And o cristene kyng kepe vs echone.
Shal no Mede be maister neueremore aftur,
Ac loue and lownesse and lewete togyderes,
Tho shal be maistres on molde, trewe men to helpe.
And ho-so taketh aӡeyn treuthe or transuerseth aӡeyns resoun   445 f.17ᵃ
Lewete shal do hym lawe and no lyf elles.
Shal no seriaunt for þat seruicie werie a selk houe
Ne no pelure in his paueloun for pledyng at þe barre.
Muche euel is thorw Mede mony tymes ysoffred
And letteth the lawe thorw here large ӡeftes.   450
    Ac kynde loue shal come ӡut and Consience togyderes
And maky of lawe a laborer, suche loue shal aryse
And such pees among þe peple and a parfit treuthe,
That Iewes shal wene in her wit and wexen so glade
That here kyng be ycome fro þe court of heuene,   455
That ilk Moises or Messie, þat men ben so trewe.
For alle þat bereth baslard, briht swerd oþer launce,
Ax oþer hachet or eny kyne wypne,
Shal be demed to þe deth but yf he do hit smythye
Into sykel or into sythe, to shar oþer to coltur.   460
    Conflabunt gladios suos in uomeres et lancias in falces.
Vche man to pley with a plogh, a pikois oþer a spade,

447. seriaunt] X seruaunt; U seriant (i *over* u *erased*). þat U] X *om*
449. Muche euel U] X Muchel
451. Ac U] X As
452. a U] X *om*
456. That ilk] XUI The which; P *om*

441. David is here the type of the ideal king, the type of Christ (as was usual: see XXI
    14n) and the type of Christ ruling in the millennium. Despite the cautious hint of
    433, above, it is unlikely that this passage ever, even when it might have been
    topical (i.e. in A or B), contained a reference to the hopes and prophecies of the
    Black Prince's reign (Huppé, 1939, 54).
445. *taketh*: 'takes money'.
450. *letteth*: '(she) hinders'.
451–81. This prophecy of the golden age is not in A. It arises from the millennial
    suggestion of 436–41, and draws heavily on Isaiah's vision of the future Jerusalem
    (Isa. 2–5).
456. *þat*: 'as a result of the fact that'. The line is strained, even with emendation (see
    textual notes) and 455–6 may be a patch on B III 302–4 ('. . . wexen glade,/That
    Moyses or Messie be come into [myddel]erþe,/And haue wonder in hire hertes þat
    men beþ so trewe') to restore alliteration.
460a. 'And they shall beat their swords into ploughshares, and (their) spears into
    pruning-hooks' (Isa. 2:4).

Spynne oþer speke of god and spille no tyme.

   Prestes and persones *placebo* and *dirige*,

Here sauter and here seuene psalmes for alle synful preyen;

Haukyng or huntyng yf eny of hem hit vse   465

Shal lese þerfore his lyflode and his lyf parauntur.

Shal nother kyng ne knyght, constable ne mayre

Ouerkarke þe comune ne to þe court sompne

Ne potte men in panele to do men plihte here treuthe,

But aftur þe dede þat is ydo the doom shal recorde   470

Mercy or no mercy as most trewe acorden.

Kynges court and comune court, constorie and chapitre

Al shal be but a court and o buyrne be iustice

And þat worth Trewe-tonge, a tydy man, þat tened me neuere.

Batailes sholle neuere eft be, ne man bere eg-toel,   475

And yf eny smyth smethen hit, be smyte þerwith to dethe.

   Non leuabit gens contra gentem gladium, nec exercebuntur vltra ad prelium

Ac ar this fortune falle fynde me shal the worste

---

464. psalmes I] X phalmes; U spalmes
469. to U] X ne
472. chapitre U] X shaprie
473. buyrne U] X barn *marked for insertion*, buyrne *erased*

463–4. Priests will say their offices as they should (and not go hunting). *placebo* and *dirige* are the first words of two antiphons, based on verses from Psalms (viz. 114:9, 5:9), sung at the beginning of the Office for the Dead at vespers and matins respectively (Breviary, II. 271, 273) and which thus became short names for the whole service (whence MnE 'dirge'). The *seuene psalmes* are the seven Penitential Psalms (viz. 6, 31, 37, 50, 101, 129, 142), appointed to be read on particular service-days (e.g. Ash Wednesday) and also said over as a private penance or repeated by priests on behalf of the penitent (cf. V 47).

469. *panele*: the list on which a law-officer entered the names of jurymen. The implication is that jurors were often 'pressed', and intimidated or bribed into giving false verdicts.

472. *chapitre*: 'chapter', the administrative meeting of the body of clergy of a cathedral or monastery, here considered as a disciplinary court.

476a. 'Nation shall not lift up sword against nation, neither shall they be exercised to war any more' (Isa. 2:4, continuing 460a, above).

477–81. The portents which are to precede the establishment of the new order are a further reminder of its millennial character (441n, 451n), since they are based on prophecies of the signs before the Last Days (Matt. 24:7, Acts 2:19–20, quoting Joel 2:30–31; also Apoc. 6:12, *et passim*). There was much burlesque of this style of prophecy (cf. also Prol. 62n), but Langland's allusions, though cryptic (and troublesome to the scribes) are seriously meant (cf. IV 108, VIII 350–51), and faithfully in accord with the apocalyptic view of history as it is presented in such famous works as the *Prick of Conscience* (4047–924) or the sermon of Thomas Wimbledon (see IX 274) preached at St Paul's Cross in 1388 (Bloomfield, 1961, 87), where the date offered for the end of the world is 1400 (ll. 895–8).

Be sixe sonnes and a ship and half a shef of arwes;
And the myddell of þe mone shal make þe Iewes turne   f.17^b
And Saresines for þat syhte shal syng *Credo in spiritum sanctum*,   480
For Machameth and Mede shullen mishap þat tyme,
    Quia melius est bonum nomen quam diuicie multe.'
  As wroth as wynd wax Mede þeraftur:
'Loo! what Salamon sayth,' quod she, 'in *Sapiense*, in þe bible:
"That ȝeueth ȝeftes, taketh ȝeme, the victorie a wynneth
And muche worschipe therwith," as holy writ telleth: 485
    Honorem adquiret qui dat munera.'
  'I leue the, lady,' quod Consience, 'for þat Latyn is trewe.
Thow art lyk a lady þat a lessoun radde,
Was *omnia probate*, þat plesede here herte;
That line was no lengur and at þe leues ende.
Ac hadde she loked in þe luft half and þe lef turned   490
A sholde haue yfonde folwynge felle wordes aftur,
Quod bonum est tenete, a tixst of Treuthes makynge.
So ho-so secheth *Sapience* fynde he shall foloweth
A ful teneful tyxst to hem þat taketh mede,

---

478. sonnes U] X gonnes. and¹ P] XUI in
479. myddell P] X lyȝt (*insertion*); U croek; I *om*
481. shullen P] XUI and
489. line B] XUIP lef
491. felle U] X fele
492. Treuthes U] X treuthe
493. secheth P] XUI techeth

479–80. The Crucifixion took place at the time of the full moon (*myddell of þe mone*) and introduced a new order; the new order of which Conscience speaks will begin at the same time of the Paschal moon. The Jews will be converted (see XX 267n and *Prick of Conscience* 4534), and the Saracens, at the sight of that moon (or at the sight of the Jews' conversion), will advance from their present monotheism to full belief in the true Christian Trinity, including the Holy Ghost (see XIV 208, XVII 297, 317–22).
481. The Saracens are merely misled, but Mahomet is an apostate and a servant of Satan (XVII 165).
481a. 'For a good name is better than great riches' (Prov. 22:1).
485a. 'He who gives acquires (victory and) honour' (Prov. 22:9, not in AV). The book of Proverbs was attributed to Solomon, and L himself elsewhere calls it Sapience (B VI 235), not because he confuses it with the book of that name (apocryphal in AV), but perhaps because he regards both as 'the Wisdom of Solomon'. It is not, anyway, a 'significant' mistake on Meed's part. What she offers is a classic demonstration of how not to interpret the bible: she takes her biblical allusion out of context and neglects its true meaning, as Conscience acidly points out.
488, 492. 'Test everything; hold fast what is good' (1 Thess. 5:21).

The which þat hatte, as y haue rad, and oþer þat can rede,   495
    Animam aufert accipiencium.
Worschipe a wynneth þat wol ȝeue mede,
Ac he þat resceyueth here or recheth here is rescettour of gyle.'

495. and P] XUI an

495a. '(But) he corrupts the soul of the ones who receive' (Prov. 22:9, continuing 485a).

Passus IV

The Fall of Lady Meed

Passus quartus de visione vt prius
'Cesseth,' saide þe kynge, 'Y soffre ʒow no lengore;
ʒe shal sauhtene for sothe and serue me bothe.
Kusse here,' quod the kyng, 'Consience, y hote.'
   'Nay, by Crist,' quod Consience, 'congeie me rathir!
But Resoun rede me þer-tyl rather wolde y dey.'   5
   'And y comaunde,' quod the kyng to Consience thenne,
'Rape the to ryde and Resoun þat thow fecche.
Comaunde hym þat he come my consayle to here
For he shal reulen my rewme and rede me the beste
Of Mede and of mo othere and what man shal here wedde   10
And acounte with the, Consience, so me Crist helpe,
How thow ledest my peple, lered and lewed.'
   'Y am fayn of that foroward, in fayth,' tho quod Consience,
And rood forth to Resoun and rouned in his ere   f.18ᵃ
And sayde hym as þe kyng sayde and sennes he took his leue.   15
   'Y shal aray me to ryde,' quod Resoun, 'reste the while;'
And kalde Catoun his knaue, corteys of speche,

---

1. Cesseth P] XUI sethe
4. rathir U] X are
7. fecche P] XUI seche

5. The roles of Conscience and Reason are distinguished thus by Aquinas: 'Conscience is nothing else than the application of knowledge to a given act. But knowledge is the Reason' (quoted by Dunning, 1937, 100). Reason is thus the whole moral faculty as it participates in God's truth (see further Prol. 141n, I 136n), i.e. what we should normally call 'Conscience'; while Conscience signifies not a faculty but an act (cf. XVI 186–92). Dramatically, the scene resembles that in Alan of Lille's *Anticlaudianus* (I. viii–ix) where Prudence defers likewise to the judgment of Reason.

17–23. Reason's servants are basic good sense (as taught in the *Disticha Catonis*, a collection of aphoristic advice ascribed to Cato and used as an elementary Latin school-book in the Middle Ages: it consists of four books of two-line aphorisms in hexameter, preceded by a sequence of 56 brief prose *sententiae* of two or three words each) and honest speech (for the compound name, cf. VIII 80–83). His horse (cf. the allegory of II 175ff, and Jas. 3:2–3; also *Vices and Virtues* 226) is patience, fastened with the girth of prudent foresight, to curb his will.

And also Tomme Trewe-tonge-telle-me-no-tales-
Ne-lesynges-to-lauhe-of-for-y-louede-hit-neuere;
'And sette my sadel vpon Soffre-tyl-y-se-my-tyme   20
And lat warrokye hym weel with Auyseth-þe-byfore,
For hit is þe wone of wil to wynse and to kyke;
Forthy lat peytrele wil and pole hym with peynted withes.'
   Thenne Consience on his capel comesed to pryke
And Resoun with hym ryȝt, rounynge togederes   25
Whiche a maister Mede was amonges pore and riche.
   Ooen Wareyn Wisman and Wily-man his felawe
Fayn were to folowe hem and faste ryden aftur,
To take reed of resoun þat recorde sholde
Byfore þe kyng and Consience yf þe comune playne   30
Oon Wily-man and Witty-man and Wareyne Wryng-lawe.
Ac Consience knewe hem wel and carped to Resoun:
'Here cometh,' quod Consience, 'þat coueytise seruen.
Ryde forth, syre Resoun, and rech nat of here tales
For there is wrath and wranglynge there wol they abyde,   35
Ac there is loue and leutee hit lyketh nat here hertes.
     Contricio et infelicitas in viis eorum et viam pacis non
       cognouerunt; non est timor dei ante oculos eorum.
They gyue nat of good fayth, woet god the sothe,
For þey wolde do for a dyner oþer a doseyne of capones
More then for oure lordes loue oþer oure lady, goddes moder.'

    18. Tomme U] X thenne
    21. weel U] X wil
    23. withes] XUIP wittes
    30. and U] X an
    37. woet U] X woed
    38. doseyne] X deseyne; U dozene

23. 'Therefore let will be protected with a breast-plate and restrained with painted
    withies'. *withes*: restraining bands made of willow or other tough flexible twigs,
    painted and forming a kind of martingale. The reading of the MSS, *wittes*, can be
    preserved if *with* is taken to mean 'against' and *peynted wittes* to mean 'temptations
    exerted by specious shows of reason'.

27–31. The representatives of worldly wisdom (especially legal know-how) seem to
    think that they have a special claim on Reason's help and advice (i.e. that they
    are part of the proper activity of rational man), even though Reason is responsible
    for recording their misdeeds. *Wareyn* appears under two names, as he sees himself
    (*Wisman*) and as others see him (*Wryng-lawe*). It is Consience who recognizes
    them for what they are.

36a. 'Sorrow and misery are in their paths and they have known not the way of peace;
    nor is the fear of God before their eyes' (Rom. 3:16–18, quoting Ps. 13:3).

Thenne Resoun rood forth and took reward of no man   40
Bute dede as Consience hym kennede til he þe kyng mette.
   Corteyslyche þe kyng thenne cam and grette Resoun
And bytwene hymsulue and his sone sette tho sire Resoun
And speke wyse wordes a longe while togederes.
   And thenne cam Pees into parlement and putte vp a bille   45
How Wrong wilfully hadde his wyf forleyn
And how he raueschede Rose the ryche wydewe by nyhte
And Margarete of here maydenhod as he mette here late.   f.18ᵇ
'Bothe my gees and my grys and my gras he taketh.
Y dar nat for his felawschipe, in fayth,' Pees sayde,   50
Bere sikerlyche eny seluer to seynt Gyles doune;
And a wayteth ful wel when y seluer take,
What wey y wende wel ȝerne he aspyeth
To robbe me or to ruyfle me yf y ryde softe.
Ȝut is he bold for to borw ac baddelyche he payeth   55
For he borwed of me bayard, a brouhte hym hom neuere
Ne no ferthyng therfore, for nouhte y couthe plede.
A meynteyneth his men to morthere myn hewes
And forstalleth my fayres and fyhteth in my chepynges
And breketh vp my bernys dores and bereth awey my whete   60
And taketh me but a tayle for ten quarteres otes,

40. and U] X ac
57. no U] X *om*

43. *his sone.* An allusion to the Black Prince (d. 1376) would be merely historical by
the time of C. L, by this time, probably prefers the generalized allegorical sense.
45. *putte vp a bille*: 'put forward a petition'. Here begins a test-case for Reason, heard
before the king and his council sitting as a court and listening particularly to
complaints against the administration of the law. *Pees* is a private citizen: *Wrong* is,
in part, a representative of the hated class of purveyors (II 61n), whose activities
included all kinds of extortion and blackmail in the name of the lord who main-
tained them (VI 248n).
51. St Giles's down, near Winchester, where there was a famous fair (Lipson, 1959,
229).
57. *plede*: 'make legal complaint'.
59. *forstalleth my fayres*. To 'forestall the market' was, among other monopolistic prac-
tices, to buy up goods before they went on the market, create a shortage and so
force up prices. Cf. III 82n.
61. *tayle*: 'tally', a stick with notches cut in, and then split, so that each party to a
transaction could have an identical half as a record. A common complaint against
purveyors was that they would 'pay' with these tallies for the goods they comman-
deered, the tallies giving the recipient the right to deduct the amount from the
taxes he might pay in the future. But they were often dishonoured (Wyclif, ed.
Matthew, 233; Workman, i.244).

And ȝut he manascheth me and myne and a lyth be my mayde.
Y am nat hardy for hym vnnethe to loke.'
Þe kyng knew that he saide soþ, for Conscience him tolde
How Wrong was a wykked man and muche wo wrouhte.   65
    Tho was Wrong afered and Wisdom a souhte;
On men of lawe Wrong lokede and largelyche hem profered
And for to haue here helpe handy-dandy payde.
'Hadde y loue of the lord lytel wolde y reche
Of Pees and his power thow he pleyne euere!'   70
Thorw Wrong and his werkes there was Mede yknowe,
For Wysdom and Wyt tho wenton togyderes
And token Mede with hem, mercy to wynne.
    Ȝut Pees put forth his heued and his panne blody:
'Withouten gult, god wot, was gyue me this schathe;   75
Consience knoweth hit wel and al þe comune trewe.'
Ac Wyles and Wyt were aboute faste
To ouercome þe kyng thorw catel yf they myhte.
    The kyng swor by Crist and by his croune bothe
That Wrong for his werkes sholde wo tholye,   80
And comaundede a constable to caste Wronge in yrones
Ther he sholde nat in seuene ȝer see his feet ne handes.
    'God woot,' quod a wys oen, 'þat were nat the beste;
Yf he amendes may do lat maynprise hym haue
And be borw for his bale and buggen hym bote   85 f.19ᵃ
And amende þat is mysdo and eueremore þe betere.'
Witt acordede therwith and witnessede þe same:
'Betere is þat bote bale adoun brynge

---

62. manascheth *over* manestheth *erased* X
64. *line supplied from* U; X *om*
78. yf U] X y

---

68. *handy-dandy*: a game where children guess which hand a present is in. It came to
mean a covert way of giving a present or bribe, as here.
70. *his power*: presumably, the legal rights and sanctions that Pees could invoke.
71. It is Wrong who brings meed/Meed to the notice of the legal officials (whose
names vary through this passage, partly because of the development of the text
through ABC: see Donaldson, 1949, 69–70).
72. *Wysdom and Wyt* are terms for intelligence (*Wyt*) and the knowledge acquired by
intelligence (*Wysdom*) which are used here and elsewhere (e.g. XI 14, XVI 189,
XXII 133) to describe morally neutral and therefore corruptible human faculties
(cf. Prol. 141n, and 5n, above).
82. *seuene ȝer*: a conventional formula for 'a long time'.
84. *lat maynprise hym haue*: 'let him be bailed', with momentary personification of
maynprise as noun (cf. II 208).
88–9. 'It is better that a financial settlement should mitigate the offence than that the
offence should be punished and no-one be better off'. A neat play on *bale* and *bote*,
a familiar alliterative collocation (cf. 85, above, and XII 55).

Then bale be ybete and bote neuer þe betere.'
    Then gan Mede to meken here and mercy she bisouhte   90
And profrede Pees a present al of puyre golde.
'Haue this, man, of me,' quod she, 'to amende thy scathe,
For y wol wage for Wrong he wol do so no mare.'
    Pitousliche Pees tho preyede the kyng
To haue mercy on þat man that many tymes hym greuede: 95
'For he haþ waged me wel as Wysdom hym tauhte
And Mede hath made my mendes, y may no more asken,
So alle my claymes ben quyt by so þe kyng assente.'
    'Nay, by Crist,' quod þe kyng, 'for Consiences sake
Wrong goth nat so away ar y wete more.   100
Lope he so lihtliche, lawen he wolde
And efte the baldore be to bete myn hewes.
Bute Resoun haue reuth on hym he shal reste in my stokkes
As longe as y lyue for his luther werkes.'
    Summe men radden Resoun tho to haue reuthe vppon þat shrewe   105
And for to consayle þe kynge on Consience thei lokede;
That Mede myhte be maynpernour Reson thei bysouhte.
    'Rede me nat,' quod Resoun, 'no reuthe to haue
Til lordes and ladies louen alle treuthe
And hatien alle harlotrie, to heren hit oþer to mouthen hit,   110
And tyl Purnele porfiel be putte in here whicche
And childron chersyng be chasted with ȝerdes
And harlotes holynesse be an heye ferie;

---

96. haþ U] X *om*
102. be I] XU to be
107. Reson P] XUI Mede
112. childron U] X *om*

108–30. In medieval satirical writing, prophecies were often to be fulfilled or promises kept when a series of ideal (and unlikely) circumstances came about (see *Thomas of Erceldoune*, ed. Murray, Introd.; Robbins, 1959, no. 8; and a burlesque of the motif in *King Lear*, III. ii.81). The detailing of the circumstances provided the opportunity for satirical criticism. Cf. III 477n.

111. *Purnele* (gen.sg.): a type-name (dim. of Petronilla) for a vain and showily dressed woman (Mustanoja, 1970, 74–5). Cf. V 128, VI 3, 135, 367.

112. *childron chersyng*: 'the spoiling of children'. Medieval opinion was stern on the upbringing of children, and the theme was a common one in sermons (Owst, 1933, 461–8). Cf. Prol. 115n.

113. 'And the holiness of worthless scoundrels be (an occasion for) a high feast-day'. The logic of *impossibilia* (108n) would seem to demand that this should be a common occurrence, as in archetypal B IV 118 ('be holden for an hyne'), unless *harlotes holynesse* is taken to mean the superficial piety of *harlotes* as they are now and not as they will be, reformed, in which case it should be a matter of derision (as in Kane-Donaldson's [*hepyng*] for *hyne*). Perhaps the change in C was made to avoid this obscurity; the ref. now is clearly to the reformed state of *harlotes*.

Til clerkene coueytise be cloth for þe pore
And here pelure and here palfrayes pore menne lyflode   115
And religious outryderes be reclused in here cloistres
And be as Benet hem bad, Dominik and Fraunceys;
Til þat lerede men lyue as thei lere and teche
And til þe kynges consayl be alle comune profit
And til byschopes ben bakeres, breweres and taylours,   120
For alle manere men þat me fynt neodefole;   f.19^b
And til saynt Iames be souhte there pore sykke lyggen,
In prisones and in pore cotes be pilgrimages to Rome
So þat noon go to Galys but yf he go for euere;
And alle Rome-rennares for ruyflares in France   125
To bere no seluer ouer see þat sygne of kyng sheweth,
Nother ygraue ne vngraue, of gold oþer of suluer,
Vp forfeture of þat fee, ho fyndeth hem ouerward,
But he be marchaunt or his man or messager with lettres,
Prouisour or preest oþer penaunt for his synnes.   130
And,' quod Resoun, 'by þe rode, y shal no reuthe haue
Whiles Mede hath the maistrie þer motyng is at barres.

129. with U] X of

116. *religious outryderes*: monks or other members of the regular clergy with permission to ride out on the monastery's business (e.g. supervision of the estates), like Chaucer's Monk, *CT* I. 166 (cf. *CT* VII. 65).
117. *Benet*: Benedict, founder of the Benedictine order of black monks. *Dominik and Fraunceys* founded the two main orders of friars, and are only generally relevant here, since friars were not 'cloistered' like monks.
119. *comune profit*. See Prol. 167n.
120. i.e. till bishops provide real (spiritual) sustenance and help. Cf. XVII 285n.
122. Reason suggests that visiting the sick is a truer religion (cf. Jas. 1:27) than going on pilgrimage to St James (Prol. 48n).
124. 'So that none go (spiritually) to Galicia [Prol. 48n] who do not intend to make it their whole future life'.
125. *Rome-rennares* are those who travel to the Papal court with bribes (for clerical appointment, etc.) or with the proceeds of the papal levies in England. *for ruyflares in Fraunce*: 'for the sake of robbers in France'. The papal court was at Avignon from 1309 to 1408 (though 'Rome' continued to be used as a synonym for 'the papal court', cf. II 243).
128. *ouerward*: 'about to cross (the Channel)', replacing a reference to Dover in B. The export of sterling was forbidden by law, except in the cases cited (e.g. Statutes of 1381–2, ii.17–18; Lipson, 1959, 531–3), but the abuse of the law was a frequent theme of Wycliffite writing, part of the attack on papal power (e.g. Wyclif, ed. Matthew, 22–3, 66, 92, 144, 223; Workman, i.302–4).
130. A *prouisour* might seem a dubious exception (see II 182n), but presumably the distinction is that these are clerics going to receive benefices already granted to them (whatever may have produced the grant).

Ac y may seyen ensaumples as y see othere;
Y sey it for mysulf,' quod Resoun, 'and it so were
That y were kyng with croune to kepe my reume,   135
Shulde neuere wrong in this worlde þat y wyte myhte
Be vnpunisched in my power for perel of my soule
Ne gete my grace thorw eny gyfte ne glosynge speche
Ne thorw mede haue mercy, by Marie of heuene.
For *nullum malum*, man, mette with *inpunitum*   140
And bad *nullum bonum* be *irremuneratum*.
Lat thy confessour, syre kyng, construe this in Englische
And yf ȝe worche it in werke y wedde bothe myn handes
That lawe shal ben a laborer and lede afelde donge
And loue shal lede thi land as the leef lyketh.'   145
    Clerkes that were confessours couplede hem togederes
To construe this clause kyndeliche what it meneth.
Mede in the mot-halle tho on men of lawe gan wynke
In signe þat thei sholde with som sotil speche
Reherce ther anon ryhte þat myhte Resoun stoppe.   150
Ac al ryhtful recordede þat Resoun treuthe sayde
And Kynde Wit and Consience corteysliche thonkede;
Resoun for his ryhtful speche ryche and pore hym louede
And sayden, 'We seyn wel, syre Resoun, be thi wordes,
That mekenesse worth mayster ouer Mede at þe laste.'   155
Loue lette of Mede tho lyhte and Leutee ȝut lasse
And cryede to Consience, the kyng myhte hit here: f.20ᵃ
'Ho-so wilneth here to wyue,' quod he, 'for welthe of here goodes,
But he be knowe for a cokewold, kut of my nose.'
    Mede mornede tho and made an heuy chere,   160
For þe comune calde here queynte comune hore.
A sysour and a somnour tho softliche forth ȝede
With Mede þe mayde tho out of þe moet-halle.

134. for P] XI nat for; U not by
137. my² U] X *om*
138. speche U] X speke
139. haue I] X *om*; U do
143. worche U] X worthe
146. that were confessours P] XUI *om (with mislineation)*. couplede U] X complede
152. Wit U] X *om*
158. wyue U] X wynne

140–41. An allusion to a frequently quoted passage (cf. XX 433) from the *De Contemptu Mundi* (iii.15, in *PL* 217:746) of Innocent III: '(It is a just judge who leaves) no evil unpunished, no good unrewarded'. Langland, as often (see Salter, 1967, 13), introduces the text in a little allegorical narrative.
150. *þat*: 'something that'.

A shyreues clerk cryede, 'A! *capias* Mede
Et saluo custodias set non cum carceratis.'   165
    The kyng to consayl tho toek Consience and Resoun
And modiliche vppon Mede many tymes lokede
And lourede vppon men of lawe and lyhtlych sayde:
'Thorw ȝoure lawe, as y leue, y lese many chetes;
Mede and men of ȝoure craft muche treuthe letteth.   170
Ac Resoun shal rykene with ȝow yf y regne eny while
And deme ȝow, by this day, as ȝe haen deserued.
Mede shal nat maynprise ȝow, by Marye of heuene!
Y wol haue leutee for my lawe and late be al ȝoure iangling
And by lele and lyf-holy my lawe shal be demed.'   175
    Quod Consience to þe kyng, 'Withoute þe comune helpe
Hit is ful hard, by myn heued, herto to bryngen hit
And alle ȝoure lege lordes to lede thus euene.'
    'By hym þat rauhte vp þe rode,' quod Resoun to the kyng,
'But ich reule thus alle reumes, reueth me my syhte,   180
And brynge alle men to bowe withouten bittere wounde,
Withouten mercement or manslauht amende alle reumes.'
    'Y wolde hit were,' quod the kynge, 'wel al aboute.
Forthy, Resoun, redyly thow shalt nat ryden hennes
But be my cheef chaunceller in cheker and in parlement   185
And Consience in alle my courtes be a kynges iustice.'
    'Y assente,' sayde Resoun, 'by so ȝowsulue yhere,
Audiatis alteram partem amonges aldremen and comeneres,

---

173. ȝow I] XU *om*
174. iangling U] X iangle
180. ich P] XUI ȝe

164–5. 'Seize Meed and guard her securely, but do not put her in prison'. Sheriff's clerks were responsible for serving writs. *Capiatis et salvo custodias* is the usual form for a subpoena.

169. The king does not receive what is due to him, in this case *chetes*, 'escheats' (property that reverts to the crown when the owner is convicted of a felony or when there is no legitimate heir), because lawyers are bribed by Meed to manipulate the law falsely.

176. The need to involve the *comune* initiates the next stage in the movement of the poem, the repentance of the people (VI 1ff) and cleansing of the body politic in preparation for the new order. It is Reason, not Conscience, who takes the initiative (cf. IV 5n, and the distinction of executive and judicial function in 185–6, below) and preaches the sermon (V 114ff) that drives the people to repentance.

188. *Audiatis alteram partem*: '(provided that) you hear the other party'. A Roman law maxim, frequently quoted (Alford 397). The usual form begins *Audi* (as in MS P), but L seems deliberately to have introduced a 2 pl.subj. to fit the syntax of the preceding line.

And þat vnsittynge suffraunce ne sele ȝoure priue lettres
Ne no *supersedeas* sende but y assente,' quod Resoun.   190
'And y dar lege my lyf þat loue wol lene þe seluer
To wage thyn and helpe wynne þat thow wilnest aftur
More then alle thy marchauntes or thy mytrede bysshopes   f.20ᵇ
Or Lumbardus of Lukes þat leuen by lone as Iewes.'

  The kyng comaundede Consience tho to congeye alle his offeceres   195
And receyue tho that Resoun louede, and riht with þat y wakede.

190. *supersedeas* U] X supersedias

189. *vnsittynge suffraunce.* See III 207n.
190. *supersedeas.* See II 187n.
194. *Lumbardus of Lukes.* The Lombards of N. Italy (*Lukes* is Lucca in N. Italy) were the
    chief bankers and moneylenders in London after the expulsion from England of
    the Jews in 1290. Cf. VI 241. They were universally hated, as 'aliens', and were a
    particular object of the rebels' attention in London during the Peasants' Revolt of
    1381 (Dobson, 1970, 162, 189).

Passus V

The Author's Apologia and the Sermon of Reason

Passus quintus de visione vbi prius
Thus y awakede, woet god, whan y wonede in Cornehull,
Kytte and y in a cote, yclothed as a lollare,

1–108. This important passage, new in C, is introduced so that the dreamer can offer his own 'confession' before the people come to repentance; it is, with X 1–60 and XXII 1–51, the only significant waking episode in the poem. It is more in the nature of an *apologia pro vita sua* than a confession, and combines contrition with pugnacious self-justification in a characteristic way. The conventional nature of medieval 'autobiography' would encourage caution in the interpretation of the passage's biographical details (as in much of Hoccleve's 'autobiographical' writing: see the essay by E. M. Thornley in *NM* 68, 1967, 295–321) but they are not all necessarily fictitious (see Donaldson, 1949, 199–226). As Kane points out, in an important essay (*The Autobiographical Fallacy in Chaucer and Langland Studies*: the Chambers Memorial Lecture, University College London, 1965), the fiction of the dreamer, with all its potentialities for enigma and ambiguity, answered exactly to L's need to express the interest he felt as a man without sacrificing the freedom he needed as a poet (e.g. p. 15: 'The poets invite us to identify the narrators with themselves, and then, by the character of what is narrated, caution us not to carry out the identification').

1. *Cornehull.* Cornhill, in the city, had something of a reputation as a resort of London vagabonds; its pillories and stocks were famous, and there was a market that specialized in stolen clothes – as described in *London Lickpenny* (85–8), a lively portrait of the predatory city, much influenced by Langland (ed. Robbins, 1959, no. 50).

2. *Kytte.* The suggestion is that L, like many clerics in minor orders, had a wife. This, though generally tolerated (see Donaldson, 1949, 202–8), would have hindered his advancement in the church, since fully ordained priests were forbidden to marry by canon law. But he may of course be choosing details in order to provide a typical role for his dreamer, in which case the use of 'Kitte' as a type-name for 'a wife' in VII 304 is perhaps significant (and see XX 472n). *lollare* means 'loller, idler, vagabond', but during the 14th c. the word is confused, perhaps deliberately, with a new borrowing, *lollard* (from Dutch *lollaert*, a pious layman who mutters his prayers, from *lollen*, 'to mumble'), which is used to refer pejoratively to the followers of Wyclif (see IX 136n; Workman, i.327; Leff, 1967, 319, 559). The question is whether L's use of the term *lollare* indicates an awareness of this association; it probably does (but cf. IX 213–18), and if so would argue that he had little sympathy with the Wycliffites (see further the C additions in IX 71–281). By representing himself in the clothes of the false religious L is repeating the motif of Prol. 3.

And lytel ylet by, leueth me for sothe,
Amonges lollares of Londone and lewede ermytes,
For y made of tho men as resoun me tauhte.　　　　　　　　　5
For as y cam by Consience with Resoun y mette
In an hot heruest whenne y hadde myn hele
And lymes to labory with and louede wel fare
And no dede to do but to drynke and to slepe.
In hele and in inwitt oen me apposede;　　　　　　　　　10
Romynge in remembraunce, thus Resoun me aratede.
　　'Can thow seruen,' he sayde, 'or syngen in a churche,
Or koke for my cokeres or to þe cart piche,
Mowen or mywen or make bond to sheues,
Repe or been a rypereue and aryse erly,　　　　　　　　　15
Or haue an horn and be hayward and lygge þeroute nyhtes
And kepe my corn in my croft fro pykares and theues?
Or shap shon or cloth, or shep and kyne kepe,
Heggen or harwen, or swyn or gees dryue,
Or eny other kynes craft þat to þe comune nedeth,　　　　20
That þou betere therby þat byleue the fynden?'
　　'Sertes,' y sayde, 'and so me god helpe,
Y am to wayke to worche with sykel or with sythe
And to long, lef me, lowe to stoupe,
To wurche as a werkeman eny while to duyren.'　　　　　25
　　'Thenne hastow londes to lyue by,' quod Resoun, 'or lynage ryche
That fynde the thy fode? For an ydel man þow semest,
A spendour þat spene mot or a spille-tyme,
Or beggest thy bylyue aboute at men hacches
Or faytest vppon Frydayes or feste-dayes in churches,　　30
The whiche is lollarne lyf, þat lytel is preysed
There ryhtfulnesse rewardeth ryht as men deserueth.　　f.21ᵃ
　　　Reddet unicuique iuxta opera sua.

---

21. That þou betere X (*over* They ybetered *erased*)] U þey ybettered.　therby] X the(r?)by;
　　UI þe by. P *has the line* Hem that bedreden be by-lyue to fynde
30. feste-dayes U] X feste day

---

5. *made of*: 'composed verses about' (see Kane, 1965, 64).
6. Reason is the personification of the waking dreamer's own rational self-analysis
　　(cf. II 217n) as well as the authoritative figure of Passus IV.
21. 'By which you may improve the lot of those that provide you with food?'
24. *to long*: 'too tall'. L says his nickname is 'Longe Wille' in B XV 152. Hoccleve
　　refers to his incapacity for physical work in very similar terms in the *Regement of
　　Princes*, 981–7 (ed. EETS, ES 72). The general debt is to Luke 16:3.
32a. 'He will repay every man according to what he has done' (Matt. 16:27, cf. Ps.
　　61:12).

Or thow art broke, so may be, in body or in membre
Or ymaymed thorw som myshap, whereby thow myhte be excused?'
  'When y ȝong was, many ȝer hennes,
My fader and my frendes foende me to scole,   35
Tyl y wyste witterly what holy writ menede
And what is beste for the body, as the boek telleth,
And sykerost for þe soule, by so y wol contenue.
And foend y nere, in fayth, seth my frendes deyede,
Lyf þat me lykede but in this longe clothes.   40
And yf y be labour sholde lyuen and lyflode deseruen,
That laboure þat y lerned beste þerwith lyuen y sholde.
    In eadem vocacione in qua vocati estis.
And so y leue yn London and opelond bothe;
The lomes þat y labore with and lyflode deserue
Is *pater-noster* and my prymer, *placebo* and *dirige*,   45
And my sauter som tyme and my seuene psalmes.

35. ȝong U] X ȝong ȝong
43a. *in qua* U] X quia
44. opelond XUI] P on londene
47. psalmes I] X phalmes; U spalmes

36. The tradition of Langland's life (largely derived from some 15th c. notes in Trinity
College Dublin MS D.4.1 of the C-text) is that he was the son, perhaps il-
legitimate, of Stacy de Rokayle, a country gentleman of Shipton-under-
Wychwood, in Oxfordshire. His father and his *frendes* (i.e. his relations: see a note
by E. S. Olszewska in *NQ* 218, 1973, 205-7) paid for him to go to school,
traditionally at the priory of Great Malvern (see Prol. 6n; but *scole* probably
means 'university', where he was supported in the same way as Chaucer's Clerk,
CT I. 299), until they died, and he was left, half-trained for a clerical vocation, to
make a living as best he could. See Skeat xxvii–xxxviii; Kane, 1965, 25–35.

39. *by so y wol contenue*: 'provided that I will persevere (in well-doing)'.

41. *this longe clothes*, i.e. the dress of a cleric in minor orders.

43a. '(Remain) in the state to which you are called' (1 Cor. 7:20, varied).

44. *opelond*: 'in the country', i.e. anywhere outside London (*Liber Albus*, 602). L's
knowledge of both urban and rural life is exact, detailed and comprehensive.

46-7. See III 463n. The *prymer* is the basic private prayer-book (ed. EETS 105, 109),
a collection of psalms, prayers and services (e.g. Hours of the BVM, Seven
Penitential Psalms, Office of the Dead), selected for their simplicity (as opposed to
the complexities of the Breviary) and for their suitability for private devotion and
individual ownership. These are the 'tools' of L's trade, which is that of interces-
sion by prayer, as requested, for the souls of the living (l. 48) and the dead (to
accelerate their progress through purgatory). It may seem the kind of parasitic
existence scorned by Chaucer's Poor Parson (*CT* I. 507-11) and by L himself
(Prol. 83). The difference is that L has no choice, being unbeneficed, and leaves
no sheep 'encombred in the myre', and that he wins only enough for his daily
sustenance (l. 52).

This y segge for here soules of suche as me helpeth,
And tho þat fynden me my fode fouchen-saf, y trowe,
To be welcome when y come, oþer-while in a monthe,　　　　50
Now with hym, now with here; on this wyse y begge
Withoute bagge or botel but my wombe one.
　　And also moreouer me thynketh, syre Resoun,
Me sholde constrayne no clerc to no knaues werkes,
For by þe lawe of *Levyticy* þat oure lord ordeynede,　　　　55
Clerkes ycrouned, of kynde vnderstondynge,
Sholde nother swynke ne swete ne swerien at enquestes
Ne fyhte in no vawarde ne his foe greue.
　　　Non reddas malum pro malo.
For hit ben eyres of heuene, alle þat ben ycrouned,
And in quoer and in kyrkes Cristes mynistres.　　　　60
　　　Dominus pars hereditatis mee. Et alibi: Clemencia non constringit.
Hit bycometh for clerkes Crist for to serue
And knaues vncrounede to carte and to worche.
For sholde no clerke be crouned but yf he come were
Of frankeleynes and fre men and of folke ywedded.　　　　f.21^b
Bondemen and bastardus and beggares children,　　　　65
Thyse bylongeth to labory, and lordes kyn to serue
God and good men, as here degre asketh,
Somme to synge masses or sitten and wryten,
Redon and resceyuen þat resoun ouhte to spene.

---

58. vawarde U] X fanmewarde
62. knaues U] X knaue

---

52. *but my wombe one*: 'but only my stomach'. This is an important distinction in L's attitude to begging. See Prol. 41n and IX 98.
55. *Levyticy*. Lev. 21 deals with the injunctions laid upon the priesthood.
56. *of kynde vnderstondynge*: 'according to natural understanding'.
57. *ne swerien at enquestes*: 'nor have to give evidence on oath in courts of law'. Clerics had their own ecclesiastical courts and were exempt from the normal processes of law (see XIV 128).
58. There is a fierce attack on the arming of priests to war in Wyclif, ed. Matthew, p. 99.
58a. 'Do not repay evil for evil' (1 Thess. 5:15, varied).
59. *hit ben*: 'they are'.
60a. 'The lord is the portion of my inheritance' (Ps. 15:5). And elsewhere: 'Mercy is not restricted' (source not identified, but cf. 'The quality of mercy is not strained', *Merchant of Venice*, IV. i.179). Both texts relate to the privileges of tonsured clerics as 'eyres of heuene'; the former was actually used in the ceremony of tonsuring new clerks (e.g. *Pontifical* of Magdalen College, ed. H. A. Wilson, London, 1910, 57).
66. For the punctuation here, see a note by J. Sledd in *MLN* 55 (1940), 379–80.

Ac sythe bondemen barnes haen be mad bisshopes 70
And barnes bastardus haen be erchedekenes
And soutares and here sones for suluer han be knyhtes
And lordes sones here laboreres and leyde here rentes to wedde,
For the ryhte of this reume ryden aзeyn oure enemyes
In confort of the comune and the kynges worschipe, 75
And monkes and moniales, þat mendenantes sholde fynde,
Imade here kyn knyhtes and knyhtes-fees ypurchased,
Popes and patrones pore gentel blood refused
And taken Symondes sones seyntwarie to kepe,
Lyf-holynesse and loue hath be longe hennes, 80
And wol, til hit be wered out, or oþerwyse ychaunged.
    Forthy rebuke me ryhte nauhte, Resoun, y зow praye,
For in my consience y knowe what Crist wolde y wrouhte.
Preyeres of a parfit man and penaunce discret
Is the leuest labour þat oure lord pleseth. 85
Non de solo,' y sayde, 'for sothe *viuit homo,*
Nec in pane et in pabulo, the *pater-noster* wittenesseth;
Fiat voluntas dei – þat fynt vs alle thynges.'
    Quod Consience, 'By Crist, y can nat se this lyeth;
Ac it semeth no sad parfitnesse in citees to begge, 90
But he be obediencer to prior or to mynistre.'

---

76. mendenantes U] X mendenant
81. or U] X *om*
84. discret U] X desirede
90. begge I] X bygge; U bigge

70–81. This sentence is dependent on *Ac sythe* up to l. 80. It describes the perversion of the divinely established social order by money.

73–5. The implication is that the sons of lords have mortgaged their estates with wealthy city men (and to that extent become their *laboreres*) in order to raise money to fight for the realm.

79. *Symondes sones* are simoniacs, those who buy office in the church (cf. II 63n) and so take after Simon Magus, who tried to purchase with money the apostles' gift of laying on hands (Acts 8:18).

84. *a parfit man*: an allusion to the contemplative's life of perfection has been seen here (Vasta, 1965, 47; but cf. I 86n).

86–7. 'Man does not live by bread and food alone' (Matt. 4:4, quoting Deut. 8:3; L adds *et in pabulo*).

88. *Fiat voluntas dei*: 'God's will be done' (from the *pater-noster*, Matt. 6:10, with *dei* for *tua*). *fynt us*: 'provides us with' (cf. XV 250). The biblical text is used as a grammatical unit (cf. I 82, XXI 187) as if in itself it were substantive.

89. *lyeth*: 'applies, is to the point'. Conscience, catching up *parfit* (84), points out that L's theory of the perfect life is not what he practises. His sharpness on the matter of practice conforms well to his role in relation to Reason (see IV 5n, and Whitworth, 1972, 6).

'That is soth,' y saide, 'and so y beknowe
That y haue ytynt tyme and tyme myspened;
Ac ȝut, I hope, as he þat ofte hath ychaffared
And ay loste and loste, and at þe laste hym happed   95
A bouhte suche a bargayn he was þe bet euere,
And sette al his los at a leef at the laste ende,
Suche a wynnyng hym warth thorw wordes of grace.
    Simile est regnum celorum thesauro abscondito in agro.
      Mulier que inuenit dragmam, etc.   f.22ᵃ
So hope y to haue of hym þat is almyghty
A gobet of his grace, and bigynne a tyme   100
That alle tymes of my tyme to profit shal turne.'
   'Y rede the,' quod Resoun tho, 'rape the to bigynne
The lyif þat is louable and leele to thy soule' –
'Ȝe, and contynue,' quod Consience; and to þe kyrke y wente.

And to þe kyrke y gan go, god to honoure,   105
Byfore þe cross on my knees knokked y my brest,
Syȝing for my synnes, seggyng my *pater-noster*,
Wepyng and waylyng til y was aslepe.
   And thenne mette me muche more then y byfore tolde
Of þe matere þat me mette furste on Maluerne hulles.   110
Y saw þe felde ful of folk fram ende til oþer
And Resoun yreuestede ryht as a pope
And Consience his crocer byfore þe kyng stande.

---

95. and² U] X an
96. bouhte P] XUI boute
107. syȝing] X shyȝing; U sihing

---

98. *hym warth*: 'came his way' (lit. 'became to him'). *wordes*: 'destinies'.
98a. 'The kingdom of heaven is like treasure hidden in a field' (Matt. 13:44). 'The woman that found a silver coin': a cue-reference to the parable (Luke 15:10) which precedes that of the prodigal son and illustrates the joy in heaven over the sinner that repents. Both gospel texts have a poignant relevance to L's profession of faith (94–101).
101. *alle tymes of my tyme*: 'all the moments of my life'.
109–13. The second dream begins with an allusion to the opening of the first (Prol. 6, 19). The difference now is that the 'feld ful of folk' has been brought under the rule of law and truth, as is shown by the presence of the king's chief counsellors, Conscience and Reason, and the king himself.
113. *crocer*: 'cross-bearer'. Conscience carries the cross of Reason before him, as a bishop does for an archbishop (the scene is most strikingly reminiscent of a great episcopal visitation preaching: see Owst, 1926, 149). Reason's being dressed 'as a pope' is an added touch of grandeur, perhaps with the suggestion of a cardinal acting as papal legate (Reason addresses the pope in l. 191, below).

Resoun reuerentliche tofore al þe reume prechede,
And preuede þat this pestelences was for puyre synne 115
And the south-weste wynde on a Saturday at euene
Was pertliche for pruyde and for no poynt elles.
Pere-trees and plum-trees were poffed to þe erthe
In ensaunple, segges, þat we sholde do þe bettere.
Beches and brode okes were blowe to þe grounde 120
And turned vpward here tayl in tokenynge of drede
That dedly synne ar domesday shal fordon hem alle.
Of this mater y myhte mamele longe,
Ac y shal sey as y sayh, slepynge as hit were,
How Resoun radde al the reume to heuene. 125
    He bad wastoures to worche and wynne here sustinaunce
Thorw som trewe trauail and no tyme spille.
He preyde Purnele here purfyel to leue
And kepe hit in here cofre for catel at here nede.
Tomme Stoue he tauhte to take two staues 130

---

114. XUIP *mislineate* reume/Prechede
118. poffed U] X possed
122. hem XUI] P ous
130. two U] X to

---

114. Reason preaches in the open air, as was often the custom of the friars, particularly at some fixed site such as an open-air cross (e.g. St Paul's Cross in London, XI 56).
115. *this pestelences*. See Prol. 82n. The orthodox ecclesiastical view was that such disasters were God's punishment of man's wickedness.
116. A reference to the famous tempest of Saturday, 15 Jan., 1362, which is mentioned in several contemporary chronicles (Skeat 64, Bennett 152). The reference is important in establishing an earliest date for the A-text (see Bennett *PMLA*, 1943, 571–2), though the storm was long remembered, as by bishop Brinton in 1374 (Sermon 41, i.184).
122. *hem*: the *segges* of l. 119. There is some confusion of persons here (cf. *we* in 119), produced either by imperfect revision of B or by rapid shifting between direct and indirect speech (as below, 135–44).
126. *wastoures*. Cf. Prol. 24.
128. *Purnele*. Cf. IV 111.
130. *Stoue*, i.e. Stow, a surname common enough to be used as a general appellation.
130–39. A lesson in family discipline. Husbands were enjoined by the Church to chastise and discipline their wives, and fathers, of course, to beat their children. To do less was to neglect their Christian duty. A husband's responsibility for his wife's moral education derived from his superior moral status, as Chaucer explains in the Parson's Tale (*CT* X. 917–37).
131. *wyuene pyne*; 'women's punishment', presumably the punishment-chair of III 79. Tom is to bring her home from the public disgrace which his neglect of his duty brought upon her, and administer the long-overdue husbandly beating.

And fette Felyce hoem fram wyuene pyne.
He warnede Watte his wyf was to blame
For here hod was worth half-marc and his hoed nat a grote.
He bad Butte to kutte a bowhe or twene   f.22^b
And bete Betene þerwith but yf a wolde worche.   135
He chargede chapmen to chasten here children:
'Late no wynnynge forwanyen hem the while thei ben ȝonge,
For ho-so spareth the spryg spilleth here children
And so wrot the wyse to wyssen vs alle:
    Qui parcit virge odit filium.'
And sethe a preide prelates and prestes togyderes: 140
'That ȝe prechen to þe peple preue hit ȝowsylue;
Lyue ȝe as ȝe lereth vs – we shal leue ȝow þe bettere.'
And sethe he radde religioun here reule to holde,
'Laste þe kyng and his consayl ȝoure comunes apayre
And be stewardus of ȝoure stedes til ȝe be stewed bettere. 145
   Gregory þe grete clerk gart wryte in bokes
The reule of alle religious, rihtful and obedient:
"Ryht as fysches in þe floed whan hem fayleth water
Dyen for drouthe whenne they drye lygge,
Ryht so religioun roteth and sterueth   150

---

134. Butte XU] IP Bette
135. Betene X] UIP Betoun
140. a preide] X he apreide (he *inserted*); U he preyed

---

133. Expensive headdresses, like that of the Chaucer's Wife of Bath (*CT* I. 454), were a traditional object of satirical attack.

135. *Betene* is probably the daughter of *Butte*.

136. Rich merchants might be expected to spoil their children by lavishing expense upon them.

140. 'He who spares the rod hates his son' (Prov. 13:24). Cf. Prol. 115n.

144–5. The religious orders hold their temporalities (their land and property) of the king, who is entitled to appropriate their endowments if they do not live properly according to their rule. The question of temporalities was a vexed one, but L's position here is orthodox. At no point does he advocate the total disendowment of the Church, as Wyclif did (Leff, 1967, 542–5), or hint at the power to make and unmake priests appropriated to the king by Purvey (ibid. 581).

146–79. This passage is transferred from B X 298–332. It is immediately relevant to the theme of dispropriation, though the mode of address is not adapted to Reason's sermon.

148–51. The comparison is commonplace, and is alluded to also by Chaucer in his description of the Monk (*CT* I. 180: see Robinson's note). The attribution to pope Gregory is typical of the medieval habit of assigning well-known sayings to well-known authorities (cf. XII 172, XIV 189); however, Gregory has a place here as the original founder, through the mission of St Augustine in 597, of Benedictine monasticism in England.

That out of couent and of cloystre coueyteth to dwelle."
For yf heuene be on this erthe or eny ese to þe soule
Hit is in cloystre or in scole, by many skilles y fynde.
For in cloystre cometh no man to chyde ne to fyhte;
In scole is loue and louhnesse and lykyng to lerne.   155
Ac mony day, men telleth, bothe monkes and chanons
Haen ryde out of aray, here reule euele yholde,
Ledares of lawedays and londes ypurchaced
And pryked aboute on palfrayes fram places to maneres,
An hep of houndes at here ers as he a lord were,   160
And but if his knaue knele þat shal his coppe holde
He loketh al lourynge and lordeyne hym calleth.
Lytel hadde lordes a-do to ȝeue lond fro her heyres
To religious þat haen no reuthe thow it ryne on here auters.

158. lawedays XU] I ladies; P louedaies
159. to U] X and to
160. An U] X And
163. her I] XU *om*

152–3. This comment is important as a corrective to any misinterpretation of the tenor of L's criticism here and elsewhere of the regular clergy. The reference is explicitly to monks (cf. VI 155n, XVI 350) and regular canons (156n, below), the concept of the cloister as a 'heuene on erthe' being a medieval commonplace (Bloomfield, 1961, 72), though the friars are blended into the portrait.

153. *scole*: 'university' (see 36, above). University colleges were organized like monastic institutions.

156. *chanons*. Regular canons (principally those of the Augustinian and Premonstratensian orders) differed from secular canons and resembled monks in that they lived under a rule and in community.

158. *lawedays*: the days when a court of law was in session, e.g. the half-yearly sheriff's court. Clerics may be presumed to have played an improper part as *ledares* in managing suits. But *louedaies* (not very different in sense) is tempting (see III 195n).

159. Monks were often criticized for engaging in hunting; Chaucer's Monk was 'a prikasour aright' (*CT* I. 189). *fram places to maneres*: 'from one country residence to another'. Monastic estates were often scattered, and provided with residences for the benefit of the privileged 'outriders' (IV 116n).

163. *Lytel hadde lordes a-do*: 'Lords had little to do', i.e. surely they could have found something better to do. L disapproves of the secular endowment of the regular clergy, not only because wealth is a source of corruption in itself, but also because such a practice deprives heirs of their rightful inheritance (cf. XVII 55). Also, the endowment might include the living of the local parish church, which had been in the lord's patronage. The regulars, now the *persones* (165) or incumbents of the living, were expected to provide a *vicarius*, but they allowed the parish church to fall into ruin while they devoted the profits of the living to their own great churches.

164. *ryne on here auters*. This vivid image appears also in Wycliffite writings (e.g. Wyclif, ed. Arnold, iii.380; Workman, ii.105), where a fierce assault is maintained on secular endowment of the regular orders (e.g. Wyclif, ed. Arnold, i.308–9, 313–15, iii.213–18, 358–9, 433, 474–9; ed. Matthew, 117, 284–6, 386, 390, 392).

In many places ther thei persones ben, be hemsulue at ese,   165
Of þe pore haueth thei no pite and þat is here puyre chartre.
Ac ȝe leten ȝow alle as lordes, ȝoure lond lyth so brode.
　　Ac þer shal come a kyng and confesse ȝow alle
And bete ȝow, as þe bible telleth, for brekynge of ȝoure reule   f.23ᵃ
And amende ȝowe monkes, bothe moniales and chanons,   170
And potte ȝowe to ȝoure penaunce, *Ad pristinum statum ire,*
And barones and here barnes blame ȝow and repreue.
　　Hii in curribus et hii in equis; ipsi obligati sunt et ceciderunt.
Freres in here fraytour shal fynde þat tyme
Bred withouten beggynge to lyue by euere aftur
And Constantyn shal be here cook and couerour of here churches,   175

165. *be*: 'if they be'.
166. *þat is here puyre chartre*: 'that is the simple way in which they interpret their legal
responsibility' (i.e. as a charter of freedom).
167. *ȝe . . . ȝow.* The change from 3rd to 2nd person is made a line earlier than in the
corresponding passage in B (X 322).
168–71. There are suggestions of the millennium in the coming of this king (see 178–
9, and cf. III 441n), but a temporal king would not be going beyond his proper
authority in disciplining those regulars who were living out of rule. Henry V, for
instance, tried hard to introduce monastic reform (Knowles, ii.182–4). The idea
that the passage is a 'prediction', 'curiously fulfilled in the time of Henry VIII'
(Skeat 69), mistakes both Langland's purposes (see 152n) and Henry VIII's.
Wyclif and his followers, of course, arrogated an even greater authority to kings
and secular lords: see Wyclif, ed. Arnold, ii.88, iii.213–18, 240, 384, 435–6, 478,
514–17; ed. Matthew, 240, 287, 469. But a more cautious expression of the doc-
trine of secular lordship was perfectly orthodox, e.g. Sermons, ed. Ross, 282.
169. *as þe bible telleth.* It is hard to say where, unless perhaps a reference is intended to
Isa. 32:1 or Jer. 23:5, 11–12. There is a striking parallel to this apocalyptic
prophecy in a contemporary chronicle (Bloomfield, 1961, 215).
171. *Ad pristinum statum ire*: 'to go (back) to the first unsullied state'. A phrase used in
canon law (e.g. Friedberg, i.189, 1155) in discussion of the effectiveness of peni-
tence in reviving merit.
172a. 'Some (trust) in chariots and some in horses; (but we will call upon the name of
the lord our God). They are bound, and have fallen; (but we are risen, and set
upright).' (Ps. 19:8–9). Prompted perhaps by 159, above.
175. It was the emperor Constantine who originally endowed the church (III 163n,
XVII 220n). L's argument is that since monks have abused their wealth by living
luxurious worldly lives, and since it is the friars' poverty that drives them to beg
and flatter (XXII 383), therefore the friars should be endowed with enough to live
on and to roof their churches (cf. III 64), while monks and nuns (personified in
176) should feel the effects of partial ('a knok') disendowment.

For þe abbot of Engelonde and the abbesse his nese
Shal haue a knok vppon here crounes and incurable þe wounde.
>   *Contriuit dominus baculum impiorum, virgam dominancium, plaga*
>   *insanabili.*

Ac ar þat kyng come, as cronicles me tolde,
Clerkes and holy churche shal be clothed newe.'
   And sethe a consailede þe kyng his comune to louie:⁣   180
'For þe comune is the kynges tresor, Consience woet wel.
And also,' quod Resoun, 'y rede ȝow ryche
And comuners to acorde in alle kyn treuthe.
Lat no kyne consayl ne couetyse ȝow parte,
That o wit and o wil al ȝoure wardes kepe.   185
Lo, in heuene an heyh was an holy comune
Til Lucifer þe lyare leued þat hymsulue
Were wittiore and worthiore then he þat was his maister.
Holde ȝow in vnite, and he þat oþer wolde
Is cause of alle combraunces to confounde a reume.'   190
   And sethe a preyede þe pope haue pite on holy chirche
And no grace ne graunte til good loue were
Amonges alle kyne kynges ouer cristene peple.
'Comaunde þat alle confessours þat eny kyng shryueth
Enioyne hem pees for here penaunce and perpetuel forȝeuenesse   195
Of alle maner accions, and eche man loue other.
And ȝe þat seketh seynt Iames and seyntes of Rome,

177a. *virgam* P] XUI virga
183. to U] X *om*
195. forȝeuenesse] X forȝenesse; U forȝifnes

177a. 'The Lord has broken the staff of the wicked, the sceptre of rulers, (that smote the peoples in wrath) with an incurable wound' (Isa. 14:5–6). L has altered the syntax by omission, suggesting that the giving of the incurable wound is part of the lord's wrath and not the oppressor's fury; hence perhaps the difficult relation of the second half of 177 to the idea of monastic reform.

180. Reason's original sermon is here resumed, with a final series of exhortations to seek unity in the observance of truth, recapitulating many of the themes of political and religious governance of Passus I–IV.

181. The true source of the king's wealth is the love and loyalty of his people (cf. III 376).

186–8. Cf. I 108.

194. See Prol. 62n.

197. Cf. Prol. 48, IV 122–3.

Seketh seynt Treuthe in sauacoun of ʒoure soules;
Qui cum patre et filio, þat fayre hem byfalle
That sueth my sarmon.' Thus endede Resoun.   200

198. sauacoun U] X sauacouns

198. Reason's injunction to seek saint Truth is obeyed as soon as the confession of sins is
completed; see VII 155–81, where the contrast with conventional pilgrimages is
further developed. *Treuthe* is here identified with the Holy Spirit, antecedent of
Qui in the next line.

199. *Qui cum patre et filio*: 'Who with the Father and the Son' (from the Nicene Creed,
Breviary, II. 484). *þat*, introducing an adjuration: 'may prosperity attend on
those . . .'

Passus VI

The Confession of the Sins

Passus sextus de visione
Ryht with þat ran Repentaunce and rehersede his teme
And made Will to wepe water with his eyes.   f.23^b
  Purnele proude-herte platte here to þe erthe

3. Purnele U] X Prinele

1. *rehersede his teme*: 'announced the text of his discourse', which is, presumably (it is
not given), a direct and affecting (see l. 2) call to repentance. Repentance, as
priest-confessor, takes charge of the following scene, and offers up on behalf of all
the prayer for forgiveness at the end of it (VII 120–51).
2. *Will*. See I 5n, V 1n, 24n.
3. The confessions of the Seven Deadly Sins begin here, and are presented in the
following sequence: Pride, Envy, Anger, Lechery, Avarice, Gluttony, Sloth. They
are much expanded in C by the transfer of material from the description of
Haukyn's coat of Christendom, stained with the sins, in B XIII 273–456 (see here,
XV 194n). L uses a variety of dramatic, pictorial and iconographic techniques in
the representation of the sins, drawing on a rich repertoire of practice in sermons
(see 3n, 63n, 138n, below, and VII 30), treatises (see 93n, below) and allegorical
poems. He personifies the sins as individuals, and their accounts of their lives give
him the opportunity to include a mass of vivid and realistic circumstance of urban
and rural life (see V 44n). Much of this of course goes beyond the possible
experience of a single individual, and the sins should not be thought of as satirical
'characters'; often what L is doing is to offer individualized or personified versions
of different characteristic types of homiletic treatment of the vice in question
(Owst, 1933, 88). The contrast, in some of the confessions, between the vigour and
relish of the recital of sins and the brevity of the promise of amendment (e.g. VI
441) is in part the product of the literary method (personifications of sins can
hardly change their nature any more than their name) but it is allegorically
appropriate too as a warning of future backsliding. For an account of the tradition
of the Seven Deadly Sins, see M. W. Bloomfield, *The Seven Deadly Sins* (East
Lansing, 1952); Tuve, 1966, 57–143; S. Wenzel, in *Spec.* 43 (1968), 1–22. For some
further notable treatments of the Sins, see *Ancrene Wisse*, 99–112; *Vices and Virtues*
10–68; Chaucer's Parson's Tale; Spenser's *Faerie Queene*, I. iv.18–35. Simple ac-
counts of the practice of confession are given in Mirk's *Instructions* 787–1810, *Vices
and Virtues* 173–84, *Handlyng Synne* 11303ff, *Cursor Mundi* 25932–27523. *Purnele*.
Pride is the only sin represented as a woman, perhaps because vanity of dress (see
IV 111n) is such an obvious example of pride. Much of what follows is only
generally appropriate to a woman, and some is certainly more appropriate to a
man (see also 37n, below), not surprisingly, since much is from the account of
Haukyn in B XIII (viz. 30–60; 14–29 are new in C).

And long was ar she lokede vp and 'lord, mercy!' cryede
And bihyhte to hym þat vs alle made   5
A sholde vnsowen here serk and sette þeron an hayre
To affayten here flesshe þat fers was to synne.
'Shal neuere heyh herte me hente, but holde me lowe
And soffre to be mysseyde, and so dyde y neuere.
But now wol y meke me and mercy byseche   10
Of alle þat y haue hated in myn herte.'
     'Repente þe,' quod Repentaunce, 'as Resoun þe tauhte
And shryue the sharpeliche and shak of alle pruyde.'
     'Y, Pruyde, pacientlyche penaunce aske;
For y formost and furste to my fader and to my moder   15
Haue be vnbuxum, y byseche god of mercy,
And vnbuxum ybe, nat abaschet to agulte
God and goode men, so gret was myn herte;
Inobedient to holy churche and to hem þat þer serueth;
Demed for here vuel vices and exitede oþere   20
Thorw my word and my witt here euel werkes to shewe,
And scornede hem and oþere yf y a skil founde,
Lauhyng al aloude for lewede men sholde
Wene y were witty and wiser then another;
Scornare and vnskilful to hem þat skil shewede,   25
In alle manere maneres my name to be knowe;
Semyng a souerayn oen where-so me byfull
To telle eny tale, y trowed me wysor
To carpe and to consayle then eny clerk or lewed;
Proud of aparayle in port amonges þe peple   30
Otherwyse then y haue withynne or withouten,
Me wilnynge þat men wente y were, as in auer,

---

4. she] XU he; I ȝhe; P hue
14. Y Pruyde U] X In preueite (*over* pruyde *erased*)
26. manere U] X *om*

---

6. She will sew in hair-cloth as a new lining for her shift or undergarment. There are
   three stages of penitence (see XVI 32, Hort 130–55, and Chaucer's Parson's Tale,
   CT X. 107): contrition of heart, confession of mouth, and satisfaction of deed (i.e.
   some explicit penance or practical measure of amendment); Purnel has already
   reached the third, but she will soon resume the second (unless it be considered that
   a separate personification of Pride begins to speak at line 14). Any analysis of the
   confessions in C according to the stages of penitence is made difficult by the eclectic
   nature of the text.
8. *holde*: '(I shall) hold'.
20. *Demed*: 'judged (some men)'.
26. 'Desirous of making my name known in every kind of way'.
31. *Otherwyse then y haue*, i.e. 'far beyond my means'. Fine clothes are a sign of pride if
   they are not appropriate to one's station.
32. *Me wilnynge*: 'myself desirous'.

Ryche and resonable and ryhtful of lyuynge;
Bostyng and braggynge with many bolde othes,
Vantyng vp my vaynglorie for eny vnder-nymynge   35
And ȝut so synguler be mysulue, as to syhte of peple,
Was non such as mysulue ne non so pop-holy;
Summe tyme in o sekte, summe tyme in another;   f.24ᵃ
In alle kyne couent contreuede how y myhte
Be holden for holy and honoured by þat enchesoun;   40
Wilnynge þat men wente myne werkes weren þe beste,
And þe connyngest of my craft, clerkysh oþer other,
And strengest vppon stede and styuest vnder gyrdel
And louelokest to loke vppon and lykyngest abedde,
And likynge of such a lyf þat no lawe preiseth,   45
Prout of my fayre fetures and for y song shille.
And what y gaf for godes loue to gossipes y tolde,
They to wene þat y were wel holy and wel almesfull,
And non so bolde a beggare to bidde and to craue,
Tales to telle in tauernes and in stretes,   50
Thyng þat neuere ne was thouhte and ȝut y swor y seyh hit
And lyed o my lycame and on my lyf bothe;
Of werkes þat y wel dede witnesses take
And sygge to suche þat sytte me byside,
"Lo, yf ȝe leue me nat or þat y lye wenen,   55
Ascuth at hym or at here and he ȝow can telle
What y soffrede and seyh and some tymes hadde
And what y couthe and knewe and of what kyn y cam of." '
Of al a wolde þat men wiste when it to pruyde souneth,
As to be preised amonges þe peple thow he pore seme.   60

44. and² U] X a
51. y¹] X a; UI he; P ich. y² U] X a
59. a X] UI he; P ich

35. *for*: 'in spite of'.
37. *mysulue* (X *hymsulue*). L here allows the 3rd pers. pron. to slip through from the Haukyn passage he is adapting (B XIII 283). Cf. also 51 (B XIII 304) and 59 (B XIII 311). Emendation here does not pretend that the mistake was the scribe's, but assumes that L would himself have corrected such obvious errors in a perfected revision.
43. An echo of traditional alliterative formulae; *styuest vnder gyrdel* means little more than 'stoutest man alive'.
47–8. See III 74a.
59. 'He wanted men to know everything that contributed to his pride'.

> *Si hominibus placerem Christi seruus non essem. Nemo*
> *potest duobus dominis seruire.*

'Now god for his goodnesse gyue the grace to amende,'
Quod Repentaunce riht with þat, and thenne aroos Enuye.

Enuye with heuy herte asked aftur shrifte
And cryede *'mea culpa,'* corsynge alle his enemyes.
His clothes were of corsed men and of kene wordes.   65
A wroth his fust vppon Wrath; hadde he wesches at wille
Sholde no lyf lyue þat on his lond passede.
Chidynge and chalengynge, þat was his cheef lyflode,
And blame men byhynde here bak and bidde hem meschaunce.
And þat a wiste by Wille to Watekyn he tolde hit   70
And al þat he wiste by Watte tolde hit Wille aftur
And made of frendes foes thorw fikel and fals tonge;
'Or thorw myhte of mouthe or thorw mannes sleythes   f.24^b
Venged me vele tymes other vrete myself withynne
Lyke a schupestares sharre, and shrewed myn euen-cristene
Aʒeyn þe consayl of Crist, as clerkes fyndeth in bokes:

> *Cuius maledictione os plenum est et amaritudine; sub lingua*
> *eius labor et dolor.*
> *Filii hominum, dentes eorum arma et sagitte; et lingua*
> *eorum gladius acutus.*

---

65. corsed men U] XI corse men; P corsement
66. fust U] X furste
67. passede I] XU pissede

60a. 'If I were to please men, I should not be a servant of Christ' (Gal. 1:10). 'No one can serve two masters' (Matt. 6:24).
63. Envy's confession is considerably abbreviated from the corresponding passage in B V (69–85 is from B XIII 324–41), with omission of much vivid pictorial and narrative detail. There is still extensive debt to a favourite figure of the sermon-writers, the 'back-biter' (Owst, 1933, 450–58).
64. *mea culpa* (with *est* understood): 'I am to blame', part of the formula of confession (Missale 580), but ironically contradicted in the rest of the line (one of the most successful pieces of repair-work on a defective B text, according to Kane-Donaldson 107).
65. *corsed men* makes sense ('men that he had cursed') but is not very appropriate, since Envy's clothes ought allegorically to represent aspects of his envious nature; on the other hand, *corsement*, 'cursing', is not elsewhere recorded.
70. *by*: 'concerning'.
75. *a schupestares sharre*: 'a dress-maker's shears', which, with their serrated blades, provide an effective image for the inward gnawing of envy.
76a. 'Whose mouth is filled with cursing and bitterness; under his tongue are oppression and pain' (Ps. 9:7). 'The sons of men, their teeth are weapons and arrows; and their tongue a sharp sword' (Ps. 56:5).

And when y may nat haue þe maystrie suche malecolie y take
That y cache þe crompe, the cardiacle sume tyme
Or an ague in suche angre and som tyme a feuere
That taketh me al twel-monthe, til þat y despise   80
Lechecraft of oure lord and leue on a wycche
And segge þat no clerk ne can, ne Crist, as y leue,
To the soutere of Southewerk, suche is his grace,
For god ne goddes word ne gras helpe me neuere
But thorw a charme hadde y chaunce and my chef hele.   85
Y myhte nat ete many ȝer as a man ouhte
For enuye and euyl wil is euel to defye.
May no sugre ne swete thyng aswage my swellynge
Ne derworth drynke dryue hit fro myn herte
Ne noþer shame ne shryfte, but ho-so shrapede my mawe?'   90
    'Ȝus, redily,' quod Repentaunce, 'and thow be ryht sory
For thy synnes souereynly and biseke god of mercy.'
    'I am euere sory,' sayde Enuye, 'y am selde othur,
And þat maketh me so megre for y ne may me venge.
Ȝut am y brokour of bakbytynge and to blame menne ware   95
Amonges marchauntes many tymes and nameliche in Londone.
When he solde and y nat, thenne was y aredy
To lye and to loure and to lakke myn neyhebores,
Here werkes and here wordes, where þat y seete.
Now hit athynketh me in my thouhte þat euere y so wrouhte. 100
Lord, ar y lyf lete, for loue of thysulue,
Graunte me, gode lord, grace of amendement.'

---

81. *wycche.* 'Witches' could be of either sex: they sold herbal medicines and charms for fever, as here (85), and gave advice on matters of 'love' (see Prol. 226n). The 'cobbler of Southwark' (83) seems to have had a similar reputation.

86–7. Envy and ill-will upset the stomach (*euel to defye*: 'hard to digest') and stop a man eating properly; allegorically, they create a kind of moral constipation, which prevents him taking communion properly. For imagery of eating, cf. I 190.

88. *sugre.* Sugar was a rarity in the Middle Ages, and used in medicines.

91. *ȝus* is an emphatic form of 'yes', used instead of *ȝe* after negatives.

93. *sory.* Envy (deliberately ?) misunderstands Repentance's use of the word, just as Avarice misunderstands 'restitution' in l. 236 below. In the *Speculum Christiani*, each sin is introduced with a quatrain spoken by the sin personified: Envy has, 'I am ful sori in myn herte/for oþir mennis welfare & querte/I banne & bakbite wykkydli/and hindir al þat y may sekirli' (61).

99. *seete*: 'might be'.

Thenne awakede Wrathe, with two whyte eyes
And with a niuilynge nose, nippynge his lippes.
'I am Wrothe,' quod þat weye, 'wol gladliche smyte   105
Bothe with stoon and with staf, and stele vppon myn enemye;
To sle hym sleyliche sleythes y bythenke.   f.25ᵃ
Thow y sitte this seuene ȝer I sholde nat wel telle
The harm þat y haue do with hand and with tonge;
Inpacient in alle penaunces, and pleyned, as hit were,   110
On god, when me greued auht, and grochede of his sonde,
As som tyme in somur and also in heruest,
But y hadde weder at my wille, y witte god þe cause
In alle manere angres þat y hadde or felede.
Amonges alle manere men my dwellyng is som tyme,   115
With lewed and lered þat leef ben to here
Harm of eny man, byhynde or bifore.
Freres folewen my fore fele tyme and ofte
And preuen inparfit prelates of holy churche;
And prelates pleyneth on hem for they here parschiens shryuen 120
Withoute licence and leue, and herby lyueth wrathe.
Thus thei speke and dispute þat vchon dispiseth oþer.
Thus beggares and barones at debat aren ofte
Til y, Wrathe, wexe an hey and walke with hem bothe.
Or til they bothe be beggares and by spiritualte libbe   125

---

103. whyte U] X wyhte
104. niuilynge P] XUI niuilynges
118. fore U] X lore (*over erasure*)
125. spiritualte P] XUI spirituale

---

103. Wrath is omitted altogether in A (see Kane, 1965, 17–22), and in BC (which correspond, though not closely; there is no material from B XIII) is portrayed rather differently from the other sins. He is the only one who names himself, and he speaks of himself as the stirrer-up of anger in others, as a diabolical sower of discord, rather than as if he were the embodiment of anger. The reason may be that Anger as a personification might be expected to speak angrily, which would be too dramatically explicit for L's purposes. *whyte eyes*, i.e. with eyeballs rolling in anger and showing only the white.

117. *byhynde or bifore*: 'behind his back or in his presence'.

119. 'And prove prelates of holy Church to be imperfect', e.g. by pointing out that they do not observe apostolic poverty. The prelates meanwhile claim that the friars misuse their favoured position by selling shrift (see Wyclif, ed. Arnold, iii.374, 394, and Prol. 62n) and poaching on the financial preserves of the parish clergy. L refers here to the conflict of mendicants (friars) and possessioners (beneficed clergy and/or monks), which was one of the bitterest controversies of the 14th c. (cf. *CT* III. 1926). Wrath suggests (125–7) that it will not end until they are all either beggars or rich men.

123. *beggares and barones*, ironical terms for mendicants and possessioners.

Or alle riche and ryde, reste shal y nat, Wrathe,
That y ne mot folowe this folk – my fortune is non oþer.
  Y haue an aunte to nonne and an abbesse;
Here were leuer swowe or swelte then soffre eny payne.
Y haue be coek in here kychene and the couent serued,
Mony monthes with hem and with monkes bothe.
I was the prioresse potager and oþer pore ladies,
And made hem ioutes of iangelynge: "Dame Ione was a bastard,
And dame Clarice a knyhtes douhter, a cokewolde was here syre,
And dame Purnele a prestis fyle – prioresse worth she neuere;
For she hadde childe in the chapun-cote she worth chalenged at þe
    eleccioun."
Thus sytte they, þo sustres, sum tyme, and disputen
Til "thow lixt" and "thow lixt" be lady ouer hem alle;
And thenne awake y, Wrathe, and wolde be avenged.
And thenne y crye and crache with my kene nayles,
Byte and bete and brynge forth suche thewes
That alle ladyes me lotheth þat louyet eny worschipe.
  Amonges wyues and wydewes y am woned to sitte
Yparroked in pues; the persone hit knoweth
How lytel y louye Letyse at þe style;
For she had haly-bred ar y, my herte gan change.

130

135

140

f.25ᵇ

145

135. she U] X he; *so in 136 (twice)*
136. cote U] X coke
137. þo U] X *om*
142. lotheth I] X loteth; U louteth
143. y am woned U] X þan woned y
144. Yparroked U] X yparrokeded

128. *Y haue an aunte to nonne*: 'I have a nun for an aunt'.
133. *ioutes of iangelynge*: 'soups of squabbling', i.e. I provided them with food for argument. Cf. 86–7, above, and XV 43–61.
135. *Purnele* seems little more appropriate for a nun (see IV 111n), especially one who has ambitions to be prioress, than Chaucer's Eglentyne (*CT* I. 121).
136. *chapun-cote*: 'hen-house'. The change from B, which has *in chirietyme* (V 161), is maliciously apt, eliminating the overtones of romance and substituting ludicrous squalor.
138. 'Thus bygynneth stryf; and after that cometh chidynge, with "Thou lixte" and "Thou lixte" ' (from a sermon quoted in Owst, 1933, 459).
144. *pues*. On this evidence (the earliest recorded in OED) pews were not unknown in the Middle Ages; they were evidently introduced for the use of certain classes of people.
145. *at þe style*. The origin of the surname 'Stiles'.
146. It was other wives of the parish going to the offering before her that made Chaucer's Wife of Bath 'so wrooth' (*CT* I. 451). *haly-bred* is ordinary (leavened) bread, blessed, and distributed after mass as a mark of Christian fellowship (Mirk, *Instructions* 1458 and note).

Aftur mete aftirward she and she chydde
And y, Wrath, was war, and wrathe on hem bothe,
Tyl ayþer clepede oþer "hore" and on with the clawes
Til bothe here hedes were bar and blody here chekes.   150
    Amonges monkes y myhte be, ac mony tyme y spare,
For there aren many felle frekes myne aferes to aspye,
That is, priour and suppriour and oure *pater abbas.*
And yf y telle eny tales they taken hem togyderes
And doen me faste Fridayes to bred and to water.   155
Ȝut am y chalenged in oure chapitre-hous as y a childe were
And balayshed on þe bare ers and no brech bytwene.
Y haue no luste, lef me, to longe amonges monkes,
For y ete more fysch then flesche there, and feble ale drynke.
Ac other-while when wyn cometh and when y drynke late at euen   160
Y haue a flux of a foul mouth wel fyue daies aftur,
And al þat y wiste wykked by eny of oure couent
Y cough hit vp in oure cloystre, þat al þe couent woet hit.'
    'Now repente,' quod Repentaunce, 'and reherce neuere
Consayl þat thow knowest, by continaunce ne by speche.   165
And drynke nat ouer-delycatly no to depe neyther,
That thy wil ne thy wit to wrathe myhte turne.
Esto sobrius,' he saide, and assoiled hym aftur,
And bad hym bid to god, be his help to amende.

    Thenne seyde Lecherye 'Alas!' and to oure lady cryede,   170
'Lady, to thy leue sone loute for me nouthe,

---

148. wrathe] XUI warthe; P wroth
149. clawes I] XUP clothes
163. cough U] X couȝthe
167. wrathe U] X wreche

---

147. *she and she*: 'the one woman and the other'. Wrath changes abruptly here from
    angry participant in a quarrel (144–6) to personified agent of anger. Possibly
    144–6 could be regarded as a short speech by the unnamed wrathful woman.
154. *taken hem togyderes*: 'take counsel together (about my punishment)'.
155. Friday was the usual day for the performance of penances. The rigorous discipline
    of the monasteries is in striking contrast to the nunneries. L generally shows
    marked respect for the monastic orders (see V 152–3); it has been argued, in fact,
    that his point of view in the poem, particularly his apocalyptic view of history (see
    Prol. 62n, XXII 53n), is substantially that of 14th c. English monasticism
    (Bloomfield, 1961, 68–97).
157. *balayshed on þe bare ers.* Patience scourges Wrath thus in font-carvings in two west-
    country churches (Kaske, 1968, 161–2).
168. *Esto sobrius*: 'Be sober' (1 Pet. 5:8, with sg. for pl.).
170. Lechery comes earlier in AB, after the brief account of Pride, and is there very
    briefly treated; C expands, incorporating lines (176–85) from B XIII 343–51.

That he haue pite on me, putour, of his puyr mercy,
With þat y shal,' quod that shrewe, 'Saturdayes, for thy moder loue,
Drynke but with þe doke and dyne but ones.
    Y, gulty in gost, to god y me shryue   175
As in likynge of lecherye my lycames gultes,
In word and in wedes, in waytynge of eyes.
For eche mayde þat y mette y made here a signe
Semyng to synneward, and summe y gan taste   f.26ᵃ
Aboute þe mouthe, and bynethe bygan y to grope,   180
Til bothe oure wil was oen and to þe werk we ʒeden,
As wel fastyng-dayes as Frydayes and heye-festes euenes,
As leef in lente as out of lente, alle tymes ylyche –
Such werkes with vs were neuere out of sesoun –
Til we myhte no more; thenne hadde we mery tales   185
Of putrie and of paramours, and preueden thorw speche
And handlyng and halsyng and also thorw kyssyng,
Exited either oþer til oure olde synne;
Sotiled songes and sente out olde baudes
To wynne to my wille wymmen with gyle,   190
By sorserie sum tyme and sum tyme by maistrie.
Y lay by þe louelokest and louede here neuere aftur.
When y was olde and hoor and hadde ylore þat kynde,
Y hadde likyng to lythe of lecherye tales.
Now lord, for thy lewete, on lechours haue mercy!'   195

    Thenne cam Couetyse – y can hym nat descreue,
So hungrily and holow sire Heruy hym lokede.

172. putour U] X pitour
182. as² I] XU and
186. putrie U] X putour

173. Saturday was the mass-day of Our Lady, to whom, as the supreme example of chastity, Lechery has already declared special allegiance. One reason for the association of Saturday and Our Lady was that on the Saturday after Good Friday the mysteries of Christian faith were fastened in her alone (Bennett 157; see *Cursor Mundi* 16925–6).

182. Sexual abstinence was enjoined on such days, as well as the more usual kind of fasting. See *Vices and Virtues* 3, 248–9, *Handlyng Synne* 2009–24, and cf. X 291, XIII 153.

196. The confession of Avarice (for the medieval distinction of Avarice and Covetousness, see XVI 85) is the longest of all the confessions of the sins (260–85 incorporate lines from B XIII 361–98, and 309–30 anticipate B V 455–76), perhaps because of the opportunity it provides for detailed accounts of trading malpractice.

197. *sire Heruy. sire* is usually applied to a man in holy orders (e.g. 367, below, and see Mustanoja, 1970, 67), but the allusion contained in the name *Heruy* ('Harvey') has not been traced.

He was bitelbrowed and baburlippid, with two blered eyes,
And as a letherne pors lollede his chekes,
Wel syddore then his chyn ycheueled for elde;   200
And as a bondemannes bacoun his berd was yshaue,
With his hood on his heued and his hat bothe,
In a tore tabard of twelue wynter age –
But yf a lous couthe lepe, y leue and y trowe,
He ne sholde wandre vppon þat walch, so was hit thredbare.   205
    'Y haue be couetous,' quod this kaytif, 'y biknowe hit here.
For som tyme y serued Symme at þe style
And was his pretis yplyht, his profit to wayte.
Furste y lerned to lye a leef oþer tweye;
Wykkedliche to waye was my furste lessoun.   210
To Wy and to Wynchestre y wente to þe fayre
With many manere marchandise, as my maister hyhte;
Ne hadde þe grace of gyle go among my ware,
Hit hadde be vnsold this seuene ȝer, so me god helpe!
    Thenne drow y me amonge drapers, my donet to lere,   215 f.26ᵇ
To drawe the lyst along, the lenger hit semede.
Amonges the ryche rayes y rendrede a lessoun,
To brochen hem with a bat-nelde and bande hem togyderes,
Potte hem in pressoures and pynne hem þer-ynne,
Til ten ȝerde other twelue tolde out threttene.   220
    My wyf was a webbe and wollone cloth made;

---

201. *as a bondemannes bacoun*, i.e. roughly hacked, with tufts of hair showing here and there.
204–5. Proverbial (Whiting L 473).
206. The first part of Avarice's confession (to line 252) has to do largely with offences against lawful trading practice (cf. *Vices and Virtues* 40–41), especially the giving of fair weight and measure (cf. III 88–9). L's minute circumstantiality may seem trivial, but he sees wrongdoing, like the community it harms (III 90n), as indivisible.
207. *at þe style*. See 145n, above.
211. *Wy*: Weyhill, near Andover in Hampshire, site of a famous fair. *Wynchestre*. See IV 51n.
214. *seuene ȝer*. See IV 82n.
215. *my donet to lere*: 'to learn the rudiments of my subject'. *donet* is the elementary Latin grammar of Donatus (4th c.), widely used in medieval schools; the name was often used as a common noun in this kind of synecdoche.
216. 'To stretch the edge of the cloth, so that it would seem longer'.
217. *rendrede*: 'construed, showed that I had learnt off', punning on *donet*.
218–19. The pieces of cloth are sewn together with loose stitches with a coarse needle and then pinned in stretching-frames.

Sche spak to þe spynnesteres to spynnen it oute.
The pound þat she payede hem by peysed a quarter
More then myn auncel, when y wayed treuthe.
   Y bouhte here barly, she brew hit to sulle;   225
Peny-ale and poddyng-ale she poured togederes,
For laboreres and for louh folke – þat lay by hymsulue.
Ac þe beste ale lay in my bour and in my bedchaunbre
And ho-so bommode thereof a bouhte hit þeraftur
A galon for a grote – and ʒut no grayth mesure   230
When hit cam in coppe-mele; this crafte my wyf vsede.
Rose þe regrater was here ryhte name;
Sche hadde holde hokkerye this eleuene wynter.'
   'Repentedestow neuere?' quod Repentaunce, 'ne restitucioun madest?'
   'Ʒus, ones y was herberwed,' quod he, 'with an heep of chapmen; 235
Y roes and ryflede here males when they a-reste were.'
   'That was a rufol restitucioun,' quod Repentaunce, 'for sothe;
Thow wolt be hanged heye þerfore, here oþer in helle!
Vsedestow euere vsurye in al thy lyf-tyme?'

---

222. it I] XU *om*
223. þat she U] X tho he
225. she U] X and (nd *inserted*)
229. bommode] X bomnode; U bummeþ
234. Repentedestow I] XU Repentedest
236. they U] X the
239. Vsedestow I] XU Vsedest

222. *spynnen it oute*: spin out the yarn loosely, so that it would go further, in a process analogous to that of 218–19. For attempts to restrain such practices by statute, see Lipson, 1959, 461–5.
226. *Peny-ale*, thin or *feble ale* (159, above), at a penny a gallon (cf. VIII 328); *poddyng-ale*, thick or strong ale. For the practice of diluting the best ale, cf. XXI 400. For a dishonest alewife, see the Chester play of the Harrowing of Hell (and Axton, 1974, 183–4). The trade of brewing within the city of London was almost entirely confined to women (*Liber Albus* 307).
227. *þat lay by hymsulue*: that particular brew was kept apart in a separate place for those who could not afford anything better.
228–30. The best ale (usually three-halfpence a gallon) was kept in their living quarters and brought out as something special, to be sold at a groat (4d.) a gallon.
231. The people who suffer most from fraudulent retailers are those who buy in small quantities (cf. III 86).
234. *restitucioun* (of ill-gotten gains) is the practical demonstration of sincerity of repentance (i.e. *operis satisfactio*, see VI 6n) in confessions of avarice (it is used of other sins too, but not in the same literal sense). The sinner (deliberately ?) misunderstands, and thinks it has to do with robbing people when they are *at rest* (in B V 235 Avarice thinks *restitucion* is the French for *riflynge*). Cf. X 54.
239. Repentance's questions have the sharpness and precision recommended to the confessor by penitential manuals (e.g. Mirk, *Instructions* 1293).

'Nay, sothly,' he saide, 'saue in my ʒouthe   240
Y lernede among Lumbardus a lessoun and of Iewes
To weye pans with a peyse and parede þe heuegeste
And lente for loue of þe wed, the whych y lette bettere
And more worth then the moneye or men þat y lenede.
Y lene folk þat lese wold a lyppe of vch a noble   245
And with Lumbardus lettres lene gold to Rome,
So what buyrn of me borewede a bouhte the tyme.'
   'Lenedest euere eny lord for loue of his mayntenaunce?'
   'Y haue lent lordes and ladyes þat louede me neuere aftur
And haue ymad many a knyht bothe mercer and draper,   250
Payed neuere for his prentished nat a payre gloues;   f.27ᵃ
That chaffared with my cheuesaunces cheued selde aftur.'
   'Now redily,' quod Repentaunce, 'and by þe rode, y leue,
Shal neuere seketoure wel bysette the syluer þat thow hem leuest
Ne thyn heyres, as y hope, haue ioye of þat thow wonne,   255

---

240. With a full-stop after *ʒouthe*, the line could be a sniggering misunderstanding of 'usury' as 'lechery' (Bennett 167). The sense assumed here is that Avarice confesses to ostensibly innocuous practices in his youth which in effect constitute a disguised form of usury (Tawney, 1926, 42), as is made clear in *a bouhte the tyme* (247). The reason for this subterfuge is that usury was not only forbidden by canon law but was also regarded as a particularly odious sin, which no one would readily confess to outright.

241. *Lumbardus*. See IV 194.

243. Not only does Avarice lend clipped coins but he also lends, like Shylock, with an eye to the forfeit of the *wed* or pledge of security, which he considers more valuable than the sum borrowed (this in itself was usurious).

245. 'I lend to people who are willing to lose a bit of each coin'.

246. *Lumbardus lettres* are letters of exchange, drawn on the Lombard banks for the payment of papal dues (see a note by J. A. W. Bennett in *MLR* 40, 1945, 309–10). The bankers would charge for the service and the currency exchange, as is indicated in B V 249. C makes explicit the usurious nature of the transaction (*bouhte the tyme*).

248. *for loue of his mayntenaunce*: 'in order to get his support', i.e. in evading the law. There was mounting apprehension at the time at the way great lords would grant livery to large numbers of followers (i.e. give them the privilege of wearing their badge or suit and therefore the protection of their name), who then acted as private armies in influencing or openly defying the process of law or as gangs of protection racketeers (see the Commons petition of 1377 in *Rot.Parl.* iii.23). It was a particular criticism of Richard II that in the last years of his 'tyranny' (1397–9) he granted his badge of the white hart to all kinds of unscrupulous followers: see *Mum and Sothsegger* (ed. EETS 199), ii.1–112.

250–51. He forced his noble debtors into the position of forfeiting the rich cloths and garments which were the security on the loans they could not repay; thus they became like merchants or shopkeepers supplying him with goods, having served their apprenticeship in 'the trade' with him (and he had never even had to give the customary token present of a pair of gloves on indenture).

For þe pope with alle his pentauncers power hem fayleth
To assoyle the of this synne *sine restitucione.*
  Numquam dimittitur peccatum, nisi restituatur ablatum.'
  'With false wordes and weyhtes haue y ywonne my godes
And with gyle and glosynge ygadered þat y haue;
Meddeled my marchaundyse and made a good mostre,   260
The worste lay withynne, a greet wit y lat hit.
And yf my neyhebore hadde an hyne or eny beste elles
More profitable then myn, y made many wentes,
How y myhte haue hit al my wit y caste,
And but y hit hadde by other wey at the laste y stale hit   265
Or prieueliche his pors shoke and vnpiked his lokes.
And yf y ȝede to þe plough y pynched on his half aker,
That a foet lond or a forw fecchen y wolde
Of my neyhebore nexst, nymen of his erthe;
And yf y raap, ouer-reche, or ȝaf hem red þat repe   270
To sese to me with here sikel þat y ne sewe neuere.
  In haly dayes at holy churche when y herde masse
Ne hadde y neuere will witterly to byseche
Mercy for my mysdedes þat y ne mourned ofter
For loos of good, leef me, then for lycames gultes.   275
As, thow y deddly synne dede, y dradde nat so sore.
As whenne y lenede and leuede hit lost or longe or hit were payed.
And yf y sente ouer see my seruauntes to Bruges
Or in Pruys-lond my prenties my profit to awayte,
To marchaunde with my moneye and maken here eschaunges,   280
Myhte neuere me comforte in the mene tyme
Nother matynes ne masse ne no maner syhtes;

257a. *nisi restituatur ablatum* P] XUI *om*
258. weyhtes I] X whites; U wyghtes
270. yf U] X *om*
273–4. XUIP *mislineate* byseche mercy/For
274. ofter U] X aftur

257. *sine restitucione*: 'without restitution'. See 234n, above.
257a. 'A sin is never remitted unless what is stolen is given back'. A maxim of canon
  law, derived from St Augustine (Alford 398) and frequently quoted, as in the
  Speculum Christiani, p. 33. See also XIX 285, Frank, 1957, 106–7, and, for English
  versions, Whiting S 343.
260–85. These lines (see 196n) represent Avarice for the first time in a rural context,
  and as an overseas merchant.
267–71. These lines refer to farming on the open village field, where each villager had
  his half-acre strips, separated from those of his neighbour only by narrow
  unploughed strips of land (see VIII 2, 114).
273. The wreckage of this line is due to the loss of *woot god* after *wille* in the exemplar of
  B XIII 384.

Ne neuere penaunce parformede ne *pater-noster* sayde
That my muynde ne was more in my godes in a doute
Then in the grace of god and in his grete myhte.'   285
    Vbi tezaurus tuus ibi cor tuum.   f.27ᵇ
  'Now redily,' quod Repentaunce, 'y haue reuthe of thy lyuynge.
Were y a frere, in good fayth, for al þe gold on erthe
Y ne wolde cope me with thy catel ne oure kyrke mende
Ne take a meles mete of thyn, and myn herte hit wiste.
Ȝif thow were such as thow sayst y sholde rather sterue.   290
    Melius est mori quam male viuere.
Y rede no faythful frere at thy feste to sytte.
Ȝut were me leuer, by oure lord, lyue al by welle-cresses
Then haue my fode and my fyndynge of fals menne wynnynges.
Seruus es alterius cum fercula pinguia queris;
Pane tuo pocius vescere, liber eris.   295
  Thow art an vnkynde creature; y can the nat assoile
Til thow haue ymad by thy myhte to alle men restitucioun;
For alle that hauen of thy good, haue god my treuthe,
Ys haldyng at the heye dome to helpe the restitue.
Ȝe, þe prest þat thy tythe toek, trowe y non other,   300
Shal parte with the in purgatorye and helpe paye thy dette
Yf he wiste thow were such when he resseyued thyn offrynge.
And what lede leueth þat y lye, look in þe sauter glosed, on
    Ecce enim veritatem dilexisti,
And there shal he wite witterly what vsure is to mene,
And what penaunce the prest shal haue þat proud is of his tithes.   305

290. sterue U] X serue
294. *es* U] X *om. pinguia* U] X pingua
305. what P] XUI *om*

285a. 'Where your treasure (is), there (will) your heart (be also)' (Matt. 6:21).
290a. See I 143a.
294-5. 'Thou art the slave of another, when thou seekest after dainty dishes; feed rather upon bread of thine own, and thou wilt be a free man' (Skeat). Source not identified. Cf. Walther 28183.
297. *by thy myhte*: 'as far as lies in your power'. Some stolen things, of course, cannot be restored to their owners, as Augustine recognizes in the passage alluded to above (257a). See VIII 235, and Wyclif, ed. Arnold, iii.174.
303. *þe sauter glosed*. In medieval bibles, the text is usually accompanied by an elaborate apparatus of commentary derived from the writings of the fathers, the standard compilation being the *Glossa Ordinaria* (*PL* 113-14).
303a. 'For behold, you loved truth' (Ps. 50:8). The import of the gloss on this passage (e.g. Augustine, *Enarrationes in Psalmos, PL* 36:592), from the most widely known and frequently quoted of the 7 Penitential Psalms (the *Miserere*: see III 463n), is that sin, though to be forgiven, cannot go unpunished, and the inward truth that God desires must seek out and make restitution for every dubious act, including the receipt of tithes properly paid but ill-gotten.

For an hore of here ers-wynnynge may hardiloker tythe
Then an errant vsurer, haue god my treuthe,
And arste shal come to heuene, by Cryst that me made.'
    Thenne was there a Walschman was wonderly sory,
Hyhte Ʒeuan-ʒelde-aʒeyn-yf-y-so-moche-haue-
Al-þat-y-wikkedly-wan-sithen-y-witte-hadde: 310
'And thow me lyflode lakke, leten y nelle
That eche man ne shal haue his ar y hennes wende,
For me is leuere in this lyue as a lorel begge
Then in lysse to lyue and lese lyf and soule.'   315
    Robert the ruyflare on *reddite* lokede
And for þer was nat wherwith a wep swythe sore.
Ac ʒut þat synful shrewe saide to the heuene:
'Crist, þat on Caluarie on þe crosse deyedest   f.28ᵃ
Tho Dysmas my brother bisouhte ʒow of grace   320
And haddest mercy vppon þat man for *memento* his sake,

---

308. by . . . made P] XUI *om*
320. ʒow XU] P the

---

306. Whether *ers-wynnynge* could properly be tithed was a famous debate (see Wyclif, ed. Matthew, 433).

307–8. These two lines may be the product of archetypal error (inclusion of 307ᵇ from 298ᵇ) and subsequent amplification in MSS of the [p] group. The original line would have been 307ᵃ + 308ᵃ.

309–30. To enforce the theme of restitution, and to remove some apparent inconsistency in B, C here makes a penitent Welshman out of the last lines of Sloth's confession in B V 455–8, and transfers another penitent, *Roberd þe Robbere*, from the lines immediately following (B V 461–76), where his appearance seems difficult to explain (and was made an argument for the multiple authorship of *Piers Plowman*: see Kane, 1965, 19 and Dunning, 1937, 79–85), to what seems his proper place, in the present argument. The change is not without its flaws, however, for the ordering of B is not as arbitrary as it may seem: Robert is introduced as an *alter ego* of Dismas, the thief on the cross, whose penitence was the stock example against *wanhope* or despair (e.g. Chaucer, Parson's Tale, *CT* X. 702; *Handlyng Synne* 5203–34), the sin always associated with Sloth (II 103n, VII 59).

310. *Ʒeuan*: 'Evan', a Welsh name. For the compound name, cf. III 17n.

316. Robert's eyes fall upon the text *Reddite ergo omnibus debita*, 'therefore pay your debts to all' (Rom. 13:7, quoted by Augustine in the discussion of restitution noted above, 257a).

317. *nat wherwith*: 'nothing to pay back with'.

320. *Dysmas*. The two *latrones* (see 330, below) crucified with Christ (Luke 23:32–43) are named in the apocryphal *Gesta Pilati*, the first part of the so-called gospel of Nicodemus (regarded as an important supplement to the Passion narrative in the Middle Ages: see XX 259n) as Dismas and Gestas (*Gesta Pilati*, cap. X, in Tischendorf, 361). *my brother*, i.e. as a robber, and as a belated penitent.

321. *memento*: 'remember' ('Lord, remember me when you come into your kingdom', Luke 23:42).

So rewe on Robert þat *reddere* ne haue
Ne neuere wene to wynne with craft þat y knowe.
For thy mochel mercy mitigacioun y biseche;
Dampne me nat at domesday for þat y dede so ylle.'   325
   What byful of this feloun y can nat fayre shewe;
Wel y woet a wepte faste water with his yes
And knolechede to Crist his coupe ȝut eftsones,
That Repentaunce is pyk-staff a wolde polesche newe,
For he hadde layȝe by *Latro*, Luciferes aunte.   330
   'Be þe rode,' quod Repentaunce, 'thow romest toward heuene
By so hit be in thyn herte as y here thy tonge.
Trist in his mechel mercy and ȝut þou myhte be saued.
For al the wrecchednesse of this world and wikkede dedes
Fareth as fonk of fuyr þat ful amydde Temese   335
And deyede with a drop water; so doth alle synnes
Of alle manere men þat with goode wille confessen hem
And cryen hym mercy, shal neuere come in helle.
   Omnis iniquitas quoad misericordiam dei est quasi sintilla in medio maris.
   Repente þe anon,' quod Repentaunce ryhte to the vsurer,
'And haue his mercy in thy mynde and marchaundise, leue hit,   340
For thow hast no good, by good fayth, to gete the with a wastel.
For the good that thow hast gete bygan al with falshede
And as longe as thow lyuest therwith þou ȝeldest nat bote borwest.
And ȝif thow wyte neuere to whom ne where to restitue,
Bere hit to thy bischop and bide hym of his grace   345
To bysetten hit hymsulue as beste be for thy soule;
For he shal onswerie for the at the hey dome,

---

335. fonk P] X flowm (*over* flonke *erased*); UI flonk
337. P *lineates* wille/Confessen

---

322. *þat reddere ne haue*: 'that have not wherewith to pay back' (cf. Luke 7:42).
329. *is*: 'his'. To polish the pike-staff of repentance (cf. Eph. 6:14–17) is to cleanse the
   soul through the performance of penance in the form of a pilgrimage (a pike-staff
   was part of the characteristic equipment of a pilgrim, as in VIII 64).
330. *Latro*: 'robber', suggested by Luke 23:32 (see 320n, above).
337–8. Both alliteration and syntax are defective in these two lines.
338a. 'All the sin in the world in relation to God's mercy is like a spark of fire in the
   midst of the sea'. A very similar Latin text is quoted and attributed to St
   Augustine in the *Speculum Christiani* 73, 115, and in the *Prick of Conscience* 6316. The
   closest parallel in Augustine is in his commentary on Ps. 143:2: *Unda misericordiae
   peccati ignis exstinguitur* (*Enarr. in Psalmos, PL* 37:1861), 'The fire of sin is quenched
   in the wave of his mercy'. The reverse image (i.e. a drop of water in a furnace) is
   attributed to Augustine in Chaucer's Parson's Tale, *CT* X. 383.
341. 'For you have not enough truly-earned money to buy yourself a cake with'.
343. As long as you go on living on those ill-gotten gains, you are incapable of paying
   anything back in the way of restitution; indeed you are getting even more into
   debt to God's mercy.

For the and for many mo þat man shal ȝeue a rykenynge
What a lered ȝow to lyue with and to lette ȝow fram thefte.'

   Now bygynneth Glotoun for to go to shryfte   350
And kayres hym to kyrke-ward, his cowpe to shewe.
Fastyng on a Friday forth gan he wende
By Betene hous the brewestere, þat bad hym good morwen,
And whodeward he wolde the breuh-wyf hym askede.   f.28ᵇ
   'To holy churche,' quod he, 'for to here masse,   355
And sennes sitte and be shryue and synege no more.'
   'Y haue good ale, gossip Glotoun, woltow assaye?'
   'Hastow,' quod he, 'eny hote spyces?'
   'Y haue pepur and pyonie and a pound of garlek,
A ferthyng-worth fenkelsedes, for fastyng-dayes y bouhte hit.'   360
   Thenne goth Glotoun in and grete othes aftur.
Sesse þe souhteres saet on þe benche,
Watte þe wernare and his wyf dronke,
Tymme þe tynekare and tweyne of his knaues,
Hicke þe hackenayman and Hewe þe nedlare,   365
Claryce of Cockes-lane and the clerc of þe churche,

---

351. cowpe U] X conpte
353. Betene X] U Beton

---

349. *lyue with*: 'live upon' (implies spiritual sustenance).
350. The account of Gluttony follows B fairly closely, with only one line from B XIII (430 from B XIII 403). It is unique in being presented, up to line 421, in exclusively narrative (and powerfully dramatic) terms – a Glutton's long and lost week-end (see 352, 418).
351. *his cowpe to shewe*: 'to confess his guilt', by saying his *mea culpa* (64n, above).
353. *Betene hous*: 'the house of Betty'.
358. Hot spices are associated with heavy drinking in Chaucer's description of the Summoner (*CT* I. 634–5).
360. *fenkelsedes*, 'fennel-seeds', were taken to get rid of wind, and seem to have been an acceptable 'nibble' to stave off hunger on fast-days.
361. *grete othes*. Swearing is one of the 'sins of the tavern' traditionally associated with gluttony (11 97n), along with drunkenness and gambling (see 376–93 below), in homiletic literature (Owst, 1933, 427–41), as in the sermon of Chaucer's Pardoner (*CT* VI. 463–660). See 427, below.
366. *Cockes-lane* was a street of brothels, one of the few on the north side of the Thames (*Liber Albus* 395).

Syre Peres of Prydie and Purnele of Flaundres,
An hayward, an heremyte, the hangeman of Tybourne,
Dawe þe dikere, with a dosoyne harlotes
Of portours and of pikeporses and of pilede toth-draweres,   370
A rybibour and a ratoner, a rakeare and his knaue,
A ropere and a redyngkynge and Rose þe disshere,
Godefray þe garlek-monger and Gryffyth þe Walshe,
And of vphalderes an heep, herly by þe morwe
Geuen Glotoun with glad chere good ale to hansull.   375
    Clement þe coblere cast of his cloke
And to þe newe fayre nempnede hit forth to sull.
Hicke þe hackenayman hit his hod aftur
And bade Bitte þe bochere ben on his syde.
There were chapmen ychose this chaffare to preyse,   380
That ho-so hadde the hood sholde nat haue þe cloke,
And that the bettere thyng, be arbitreres, bote sholde þe worse.
Tho rysen vp rape and rounned togyderes

377. hit U] X *om*
379. Bitte X] U Bette
383. Tho X] U Two

367. *Syre Peres of Prydie*: a priest (197n, above). *pridie*, in Latin, means 'the day before'; it is used in the preparation for communion, just before the consecration of the bread and wine, when the priest speaks of the institution of the sacrament on the 'day before' Christ's crucifixion (Missale 616). A priest who made any subsequent mistake in the preparation of the bread and wine had to go back to this point and start again in order to make the consecration effective (Mirk, *Instructions*, 1902). The name is very appropriately associated with a priest who has his mind on other things (see a note by R. Oliphant in *NQ* 205, 1960, 167–8). *Purnele of Flaundres*. Cf. IV 111n. Flemish women had a reputation as prostitutes.

370. *Of*: 'in the form of' OED s.v.24b (cf. 'a fool of a man').

375. *to hansull*: 'as a gift or tip' (cf. *Liber Albus* 232), i.e. they bought his first drink, knowing they would profit in the end.

377. *þe newe fayre* seems to have been a game of exchanges. The two 'players' offer objects for exchange, which are appraised by selected *chapmen*, and the winner of what they deem the more valuable object offers compensation to the other player (382). If there is further argument, an umpire is appointed (388). Here the argument is settled, to everyone's satisfaction, by having Clement, who seems to have gained by winning Hick's hood, pay for a round of drinks. Anyone who wants his property back has to pay for a gallon of ale for the privilege (392–3). The point of the game is to 'beat one's neighbour', presumably by getting one's friends to acts as appraisers (379). The game had a bad name, and was probably used as a form of confidence trick. It was perhaps named after 'The Neue Feyre', the nickname of a disreputable street-market in Soper Lane, put down in 1297 because it was infested with thieves and beggars (Riley's *Memorials* 33). The use of 'marchaundye' in the alehouse to make deceitful gain is spoken of in *Handlyng Synne* 5977–80.

And preisede this peniworths apart by hemsulue,
And there were othes an heep, for on sholde haue þe worse.   385
They couthe nat by here consience acorden for treuthe
Til Robyn þe ropere aryse they bisouhte
And nempned hym for a noumper, þat no debat were.
    Hicke þe hostiler hadde þe cloke,
In couenaunt þat Clement sholde the coppe fulle,   390 f.29ᵃ
And haue Hickes hood þe hostiler and holde hym yserued;
And ho-so repentede hym rathest sholde aryse aftur
And grete syre Glotoun with a galon of ale.
    There was leyhing and louryng and 'lat go the coppe!'
Bargaynes and beuereges bygan tho to awake,   395
And seten so til euensong, and songen vmbywhile,
Til Glotoun hadde yglobbed a galoun and a gylle.
His gottes gan to gothly as two grydy sowes;
A pissede a potel in a *pater-noster* whyle,
A blew his rownd ruet at his rygebones ende,   400
That alle þat herde þe horne helde here nose aftur
And wesched hit hadde be wasche with a weps of breres.
He myhte noþer steppe ne stande til he a staf hadde,
And thenne gan he go lyke a glemans byche,
Sum tyme asyde and sum tyme arere,   405
As ho-so layth lynes for to lacche foules.
    And when he drow to the dore, thenne dymmede his yes,
And thromblede at the thresfold and threw to þe erthe,
And Clement þe coblere cauhte hym by þe myddel
And for to lyfte hym aloft leyde hym on his knees.   410
Ac Gloton was a greet cherl and greued in þe luftynge
And cowed vp a caudel in Clementis lappe;
Ys none so hungry hound in Hertfordshyre
Durste lape of þat lyuynge, so vnlouely hit smauhte.

---

384. peniworths U] X penworthis
396. euensong U] X euenson
398. two U] X to
400. rygebones] X ryngebones; U ruggebones
402. be U] X *om*

---

388. *þat no debat were*: 'so that there should be no argument'.
395. 'There was always some new bargaining and drinking starting up'.
398. *two grydy sowes*: used as an image of Gluttony in a carving on the elbow of a choir stall in the priory church at Little Malvern (Kaske, 1968, 161). Cf. *Sermons*, ed. Ross, 101.
404. *a glemans byche*: a blind minstrel's guide-dog, suggests Skeat, but popular entertainers often had a dog who took part in their act, as in *Dame Sirith* (see Prol. 226n, Axton, 1974, 21–2), or like Launce in *The Two Gentlemen of Verona*, II. iii.

With alle þe wo of this world his wyf and his wenche   415
Baren hym to his bed and brouhten hym þer-ynne,
And aftur al this exces he hadde an accidie aftur;
A sleep Saturday and Sonenday til þe sonne ȝede to reste.
Then gan he wake wel wanne and wolde haue ydronke;
The furste word that he spake was 'Who halt þe bolle?'   420
His wif and his inwit edwitede hym of his synne;
A wax ashamed, þat shrewe, and shrofe hym as swythe
To Repentaunce ryht thus: 'Haue reuthe on me,' he saide,
'Thow lord that aloft art and alle lyues shope!
  To the, god, y, Glotoun, gulty me ȝelde   425
Of þat y haue trespased with tonge, y can nat telle how ofte,   f.29ᵇ
Sworn "Godes soule and his sides!" and "So helpe me, god almyhty!"
There no nede ne was, many sythe falsly;
And ouer-sopped at my soper and som tyme at nones
More then my kynde myhte deffye,   430
And as an hound þat eet gras so gan y to brake
And spilde þat y aspele myhte – y kan nat speke for shame
The vilony of my foule mouthe and of my foule mawe –
And fastyng-dayes bifore noen fedde me with ale
Out of resoun, among rybaudes, here rybaudrye to here.   435
  Herof, gode god, graunte me forȝeuenesse
Of all my luyther lyf in al my lyf-tyme
For y vowe to verray god, for eny hungur or furste,
Shal neuere fysch in þe Fryday defyen in my wombe
Til Abstinence myn aunte haue ȝeue me leue –   440
And ȝut haue y hated here al my lyf-tyme.'

---

420. word P] XU *om*; I worlde.   Who U] X to
422. as U] X a
425. me I] XU y me
441. hated] X chasted; U ihatid

---

420. *Who halt þe bolle?* 'Who's got the bowl?' referring to the drinking-cup which was
passed round at the tavern (394, above).
427. For the association of gluttony and swearing, see 361n, above.
428. Idle, false and violent swearing were condemned, but not swearing 'in trouthe'.
For the orthodox view, and the relevant biblical texts, see Chaucer's Parson's Tale
(*CT* X. 587) and Pardoner's Tale (*CT* VI. 629).
434. See II 100n.
440. *myn aunte.* No particular allegorical significance need be attached to this suggestion
of family relationship (see also 128, 330, above, and cf. II 24n).
441. Gluttony's last words are a backward look at his old life. His penitence seems
peremptory and mechanical, and the allegorical suggestion is that formal confes-
sion will not prove adequate to cleanse society as a basis for reform.

Passus VII

The Shriving of the Folk; Piers Plowman's Guide to Truth

Passus septimus de visione
Thenne cam Sleuthe al byslobered with two slimed yes.
'Y moste sitte to be shryue or elles sholde y nappe;
Y may nat wel stande ne stoupe ne withouten a stoel knele.
Were y brouhte in my bed, but yf my tayl-ende hit made,
Sholde no ryngyng do me to ryse til y were rype to dyne.'   5
A bigan *benedicite* with a bolk and his breste knokkede,
Roxlede and romede and rotte at þe laste.
'What! awake, renke!' quod Repentaunce, 'and rape þe to shryfte!'
  'Yf y sholde deye be þis day y drede me sore;
Y can nat parfitly my *pater-noster* as þe prest hit syngeth.   10
Y can rymes of Robyn Hode and of Randolf erle of Chestre,
Ac of oure lord ne of oure lady þe leste þat euere was maked.
Y haue voued voues fourty and forȝeten hem a-morwen.
Y parfourmede neuere penaunces þat þe prest me hihte
Ne ryht sory for my synnes, y seyh neuere þe tyme.   15
And yf y bidde eny bedes, but yf hit be in wrath,
That y telle with my tonge is ten myle fro myn herte.
Y am occuepied vch a day, haliday and oþere,
With ydele tales at þe ale and oþer-while in chirches.
Goddes payne and his passioun is puyre selde in my thouhte.   20 f.30ᵃ

8. þe U] X *om*

---

1. Sloth, appropriately, brings up the rear. In the account of Sloth, C is close to B in the passages that correspond, but part of B is transferred to Avarice (VI 309n), and C incorporates lines from B XIII (70–119 from B XIII 409–56).
4. *but yf my tayl-ende hit made*: 'unless my rear-end forced me to'.
6. *benedicite*. The formula for confession begins, 'Bless me [*benedicite*], father, for I have sinned'.
11. *Robyn Hode*. There are documentary references to a Robin Hood as early as 1230, but this appears to be the earliest of a number of literary allusions where tales and songs of Robin Hood are cited as typical of idle and worthless entertainment (Bennett 177). *Randolf erle of Chestre*. The most famous Randolph earl of Chester was the first earl, who controlled all N. England during the reign of Stephen, but his grandson, the third earl, had more of a popular reputation (see J. W. Ashton, in *ELH* 5, 1938, 195–206).

Y visitede neuere feble man ne fetered man in prisone.
Y hadde leuere here an harlotrye or a lesyng to lauhen of
Or to lacke men or to likene hem in vnlikyng manere
Than al þat euere Mark made, Matheu, Iohn or Lucas.
Vigilies and fastyng-dayes y can forȝeten hem alle   25
And ligge abedde in lente and my lemman in myn armes
Til matynes and masse be ydo, thenne haue y a memorie at þe freres.
Y am nat shryue som tyme, but yf seknesse hit make,
Nat twies in ten ȝer and thenne telle y nat þe haluendele.
    I haue be prest and persoun passynge thritty wyntur   30
Ȝut kan y nother solfe ne synge ne a seyntes lyf rede.
Ac y can fynden in a feld and in a forlong an hare
And holden a knyhtes court and acounte with þe reue.
Ac y can nat construe Catoun ne clergialiche reden.
    Yf y begge and borwe ouht, but yf hit be ytayled,   35
I forȝete hit as ȝerne, and yf eny man hit aske
Sixe sithe oþer seuene y forsake hit with othes,

---

35. ouht P] XUI hit

21. Cf. 'I was hungry and you gave me no food, I was thirsty and you gave me no drink, I was a stranger and you did not welcome me, naked and you did not clothe me, sick and in prison and you did not visit me' (Matt. 25:42–3). Christ's rehearsal of the Last Judgment (Matt. 25:31–46) lists six works of mercy, as above, on the performance of which man will be judged. With burial of the dead added (from Tob. 2:7), they became the Seven Corporal Works of Mercy, frequently referred to in didactic literature (e.g. Gaytryge's *Sermon*, ed. EETS 26, 9).

27. *memorie*: 'commemorative mention'. He gets a mention in the prayers of the friars because he has bought letters of fraternity (III 51n) and become a 'brother' of their order, like Thomas in the Summoner's Tale (*CT* III. 1944–5).

28. *but yf seknesse hit make*: 'unless frightened into it by illness'. Cf. 65, below, and 4, above.

30. Sloth confesses largely in terms of his neglect of his duties and observances as a Christian (as was usual for *accidia*: see Mirk, *Instructions* 1177–1218, and S. Wenzel, *The Sin of Sloth*, Chapel Hill, 1967, 38, 88). For a moment (see VI 3n) he is here, explicitly, a priest, as L draws on the familiar homiletic type of the slothful parson (see Owst, 1933, 278–9; Sermons, ed. Ross, 53; and Wenzel, *op.cit.*, 139).

31. *a seyntes lyf*. Lives of saints were often read in church instead of or in addition to the more usual type of sermon. The South English Legendary is a collection of such lives, and there is a legendary attached to the Northern Homily Cycle.

32. The contrast is a preaching commonplace (Owst, 1926, 27). *forlong*: a strip of unploughed land on the open field, often overgrown (see VIII 114).

33. Priests were often involved in the business of local manorial estates (cf. the 'love-days' of III 195, V 158n) and of estate management (Prol. 93–4).

34. *Catoun*. See IV 17n.

35. *ytayled*: 'recorded on a tally' (IV 61n).

37. 'I repeatedly and vehemently deny all knowledge of the loan'. This is more like Avarice than Sloth, and indeed the two were often linked.

And thus haue y tened trewe men ten hundrit tymes.
And my seruauntes som-tyme here salerie is bihynde:
Reuthe is to here rekenynge when we shal rede acountes,   40
So with wikkede will my werkemen y paye.
Yf eny man do me a been-feet or helpeth me at nede
Y am vnkynde aȝen his cortesie, y can nat vnderstande hit,
For y haue and haue yhad sumdel haukes maners;
Y am nat luyred with loue but þer lygge ouht vnder þe tumbe.   45
The kyndenesse þat myn emcristen kud me ferne-ȝer,
Sixty sythes y, Sleuthe, haue forȝeten hit sethe
In speche and in sparyng of speche; yspilde many a tyme
Bothe flesch and fysch, and vitailes kepte so longe
Til eche lyf hit lothed to loke þeron or smylle hit;   50
Bothe bred and ale, botere, mylke and chese
Forsleuthed in my seruice, and yset hows a-fuyre,
And ȝede aboute in my ȝouthe and ȝaf me to no thedom,
And sethe a beggare haue ybe for my foule sleuthe.
Heu michi quod sterilem duxi vitam iuuenilem.   55
   'Repentest the nat?' quod Repentaunce, and ryht with þat he
      swowened,   f.30^b
Til *Vigilate* the veile fette water at his eyus
And flatte hit on his face and faste on hym cryede
And sayde, 'War the for wanhope þat wolde the bytraye!
"Y am sory for my synnes", sey to thysuluen   60
And bete thysulue vppon þe breste and bidde hym of grace,
For is no gult so greet þat his goodnesse is more.'
   Thenne sat Sleuthe vp and seynede hym ofte
And made vowe tofore god for his foule sleuthe:

---

60. to U] X to god (god *inserted*)

---

45. A hawk is persuaded to return to the hand by a tempting piece of meat or 'lure' (a technical term in falconry).

48. *In speche and in sparyng of speche*: (shown ingratitude) 'by the things I have said and the things I have not said'.

55. See I 140.

56. *Repentest the*: a fusion of impersonal (*repenteth* [*it*] *thee*) and personal (*repentest thow* or *repentest thow thee*, reflexive) constructions.

57. *Vigilate the veile*: '*Vigilate* the watchful one', from Matt. 26:41: 'Watch [*vigilate*] and pray that you may not enter into temptation; the spirit indeed is willing, but the flesh is weak'. *Vigilate* forces tears of contrition from Sloth and then dashes them in his face to revive him from his swoon.

59. *wanhope*, despair of amendment, is the characteristic final stage of Sloth (VI 309n). The symptoms were already present in l. 9, above.

61. To beat oneself upon the breast is a recognized gesture of contrition, recommended in a penitential treatise such as the *Prick of Conscience* (3408) and by Pandarus to Troilus (*TC* i.932).

'Shal no Sonday be this seuene ȝere, but yf seknesse hit make,   65
That y ne shal do me ar day to þe dere chirche
And here mateynes and masse as y a monke were.
Shal non ale aftur mete holde me thennes
Til y haue euensong yherd, y bihote to þe rode.'
    Ac wheche been þe braunches þat bryngeth men to sleuthe?   70
Is when men mourneth not for his mysdedes,
The penaunces þat þe prest enioyneth parformeth euele,
Doth non almesdede, drat hym nat of synne,
Lyueth aȝen þe bileue and no lawe kepeth
And hath no likynge to lerne ne of oure lord to here   75
But to harlotrie and to horedom or elles of som wynnynge.
When me carpeth of Crist or of clannesse of soule
A wexeth wroth and wol not here but wordes of murthe.
Penaunse and pore men and the passioun of seyntes
He hateth to here thereof and alle þat þerof carpeth.   80
This beth þe braunches, beth ywar, þat bryngeth a man to wanhope.
    Ȝe lordes and ladies and legates of holy churche
That feden foel sages, flateres and lyares,
And han lykyng to lythen hem in hope to do ȝow lawhe –
    Ve vobis qui ridetis –
And ȝeueth such mede and mete and pore men refuse,   85
In ȝoure deth-deynge y drede me sore
Laste tho manere men to muche sorwe ȝow brynge.
    Consencientes et agentes pari pena punientur.
Patriarkes and prophetes, precheours of goddes wordes,
Sauen thorw here sarmon mannes soule fram helle;
Ryht so flateres and fooles aren þe fendes procuratours   90 f.31ᵃ
To entise men thorw here tales to synne and to harlotrie.

70–119. These lines, incorporated from B XIII 409–56 virtually unchanged, are not adapted to the dramatic situation. *braunches* is a technical term for the subdivisions of a subject, but here seems to be used in reference to the branches of the bough of Sloth on the tree of the sins (cf. Chaucer, Parson's Tale, *CT* X. 388). Many allegorical pictures show the sins as a tree, with branches labelled accordingly (see XVIII 7n).

71. *Is*: '(It) is'. *whiche* in the preceding line could conceivably be a relative pronoun, 'that which, what', and not an interrogative.

82–119. This important passage on entertainers and minstrels (see Prol. 35n) is developed from the suggestion of 75–80. Jesters, flatterers, scandalmongers, tellers of frivolous and salacious stories, all cater for and encourage idleness, and are the instruments of the devil.

83. *foel sages*: 'foolish men who claim to be wise'.

84a. 'Woe to you that laugh now (for you shall mourn and weep)' (Luke 6:25, in a passage of prophecy following the Beatitudes).

87a. 'Those who consent to a deed and those who do it are to be equally punished'. A legal maxim (see Alford 395).

Clerkes þat knoweth this sholde kenne lordes
What Dauid sayth of such men, as þe sauter telleth:
   Non habitabit in medio domus mee qui facit superbiam, qui loquitur iniqua.
Sholde non harlote haue audiense in halle ne in chaumbre
There þat wyse men were, wittnesseth goddes wordes,   95
Ne no mysproud man amonges lordes be alouede.
   Clerkes and knyhtes welcometh kynges munstrals
And for loue of here lord liþeth hem at festes;
Muche more me thynketh riche men ouhte
Haue beggares byfore hem þe whiche ben goddes munstrals,   100
As he sayth hymsulf, seynt Ion bereth witnesse:
   Qui vos spernit me spernit.
Forthy y rede ȝow ryche, reueles when ȝe maketh,
For to solace ȝoure soules suche munstrals to haue:
The pore for a foul sage sittynge at thy table,
With a lered man to lere the what oure lord suffrede   105
For to saue thy soule from Satan thyn enemye
And fithele the withoute flaterynge of god Friday þe geste,
And a blynd man for a bordor or a bedredene womman
To crye a largesse tofore oure lord, ȝoure good loos to shewe.
Thise thre manere munstrals maketh a man to lauhe   110
And in his deth-deynge they don hym greet confort
That by his lyue lened hem and louede hem to here.

---

96. alouede U] X ylouede
98. liþeth U] X lyueth
100. munstrals U] X mnstrals
107. geste B] XUP feste

93a. 'No man who practises vanity or speaks wickedness shall dwell within my house' (Ps. 100:7).
97. *kynges munstrals*: high-class professional musicians, not to be confused with popular entertainers. The reference here is to a well-established practice whereby minstrels attached to the king's household, or to the households of noblemen, 'did the rounds', perhaps to save the expense of keeping them out of season (see E. K. Chambers, *The Mediaeval Stage*, 2 vols., Oxford, 1903, i.53, ii.247).
98. *here lord*, i.e. the king, their patron.
100. *goddes munstrals*. Cf. IX 128–38, where the same comparison is used, in a lengthy discussion of the ethics of begging.
101a. 'He who rejects you rejects me'. The quotation is actually from Luke 10:16 (Jesus sending out his disciples), but cf. John 12:48, 13:20.
107. *fithele* is used metaphorically: 'recite, with musical accompaniment'.
109. *crye a largesse*: 'ask for bounty'. 'Largesse!' was the familiar cry of minstrels (Owst, 1933, 11).

Thise solaseth þe soule til hymsulue be yfalle
In a wel hope, for a wrouhte so, amonges worthy seyntes,
There flaterers and foles with here foule wordes   115
Leden tho that lythed hem to Luciferes feste
With *turpiloquio*, a lay of sorwe and Luciferes fythele,
To perpetuel payne or purgatorie as wikke,
For a lythed and louede þat godes lawe despiseth.
   Dare histrionibus.

  Tho was Repentaunce aredy and redde hem alle to knele: 120
'Y shal byseke for alle synnefole oure sauiour of grace,
To amende vs of oure mysdedes, do mercy to vs alle.
  God, þat of thi goodnesse gonne þe world make   f.31^b
And madest of nauhte auhte and man liche thysulue,
And sethe soffredeste hym to synege, a sykenesse to vs alle –   125
And for oure beste, as y beleue, what-so þe boek telle:
   O felix culpa, et necessarium peccatum Ade!
For thorw þat synne thy sone ysent was til erthe
And bicam man of a mayde, mankynde to amende –
And madest thysulue, with thy sone, oure soule and oure body ilych:
   Ego in patre, et pater in me; et qui me videt, videt patrem meum;

118. as U] X a

117. *turpiloquio.* See Prol. 40n.
119. *þat:* 'them that'.
119a. 'To give to actors' (i.e. low entertainers), an allusion to a well-known saying quoted by Peter the Cantor (*Verbum Abbreviatum*, xlix.129, in *PL* 205:155) from St Jerome: *Paria sunt histrionibus dare et daemonibus immolare* ('Giving money to actors is just like sacrificing to devils').
121–2. Repentance, now acting as officiating priest, announces the prayer which he will say on behalf of all sinners. The prayer (123–51) takes the form of an invocation to God to have mercy on the penitent sinners, for Jesus's sake. The structure of the prayer, the syntax and the language are rich in quotation and echo from liturgy and scriptures (Bennett 182–6).
124. *madest of nauhte auhte:* 'made something out of nothing', a familiar form of expression which has reference to the doctrine of creation *ex nihilo* (see a note by A. L. Kellogg in *Traditio* 12, 1956, 406–7).
126. *for oure beste.* An allusion to the paradox of the Fortunate Fall, happily embroidered in one of the most famous of ME lyrics, 'Adam lay ybowndyn' (Gray, 1975, 1, 99; Woolf, 1968, 290). *what-so þe boek telle:* 'whatever the authorities (*or* the bible) say'. L may have been aware that there was a school of thought which regarded the paradox as doctrinally dangerous.
127. 'O happy fault, and necessary sin of Adam' (necessary, because it necessitated the Incarnation). From the canticle sung on Easter Eve (Holy Saturday) at the blessing of the Paschal candle (Missale 340).
129a. 'I (am) in the Father, and the Father (is) in me' (John 14:10). 'And whoever sees me, sees my Father' (John 14:9).

And sethe in oure secte, as hit semed, deyedest,   130
On a Friday, in fourme of man, feledest oure sorwe.
    Captiuam duxit captiuitatem.
The sonne for sorwe þerof lees liht for a tyme,
Aboute mydday, when most liht is, and mel-tyme of sayntes;
Feddest tho with thy flesch and blood oure forfadres in helle.
    Populus qui ambulabat in tenebris, vidit lucem magnam.
The lihte þat lup oute of the, Lucifer hit blente   135
And brouhte thyne yblessed fro thennes into þe blisse of heuene.
The thridde day þeraftur thow ȝedest into oure sekte;
A synful Marie þe sey ar seynte Marye þy dame,
And al so to solace synfole thow soffredest it so were.
    Non veni vocare iustos, set peccatores.

131a. *Captiuam duxit* U] X Captiuuam duxi

---

130. *in oure secte*: lit. 'in our suit of clothes', i.e. in our flesh (cf. XX 22). *as it semed* qualifies *deyedest*: Christ suffered (l. 131) and died only in his human nature, not in his divine nature (cf. XX 23).

131a. 'He led captivity captive' (Eph. 4:8, quoting Ps. 67:19; sung as a response on Ascension day, Breviary, I. dcccclxiv), i.e. he put an end to the thraldom of flesh to sin, and (following Eph. 4:9) led his people from hell to heaven.

132. The sun was eclipsed from the sixth to the ninth hour, the moment of Christ's death (Luke 23:44). See XX 61, 254. *nona hora*, 'the ninth hour', came later to mean midday ('noon').

133. *mel-tyme of sayntes* anticipates the sense of the next line; but there may also be an allusion to the legend found in *St Patrick's Purgatory*, where the blessed in the earthly paradise, who have passed through purgatory, are fed once a day by a light which shines for a short time out of heaven (see a note by M. Day in *MLR* 27, 1932, 317–18).

134. The crucifixion is an offer of spiritual food because it fulfils the promise of the Eucharist, which is conceived of here as being communicated instantly to the patriarchs and prophets in hell (properly, in limbo). Another associated image is that of Christ as the pelican (Ps. 101:7), which in the bestiaries revives its dead young by pecking at its own breast and feeding them on its flesh and blood.

134a. 'The people that walked in darkness have seen a great light' (Isa. 9:2, cf. Matt. 4:16). This passage was the source in prophecy of the apocryphal narrative of the Harrowing of Hell, the descent of Christ into hell to release the souls of the patriarchs. See XX 259n.

135. *lihte*. Christ's descent into hell was represented as the coming of a great light, in allusion to Isa. 9:2. *lup*. See XIV 84n. For the possibility of an allusion here to the generation of the Son, see T. D. Hill in *RES*, n.s.24 (1973), 444–9 (p. 446).

136. *brouhte*: B (V 495) *blewe*. An example of the tendency in C to tone down the vigour and physical concretion of B's verbs. The previous line, where MS P has *lemed* for *lup*, offers an example of an officious scribe trying to better his instruction.

138. *A synful Marie*: Mary Magdalene, alluding to her meeting with Jesus in the garden after the Resurrection (John 20:14). See XI 264n.

139a. 'I have not come to call the righteous, but sinners' (Matt. 9:13, cf. Luke 5:32).

And al þat Mark hath ymade, Matheu, Ion and Lucas,   140
Of thy douhtiest dedes, was don in oure sekte.
    Verbum caro factum est.
And by so muche hit semeth the sykerloker we mowe
Bidde and biseche the, yf hit be thy wille,
That art furste oure fadur and of flesch oure broþer,
And sethen oure sauyour, and seydest hit with thy tonge   145
That what tyme we synnefole men wolden be sory
For dedes that we han don ylle, dampned sholde we ben neuere,
Yf we knowlechede and cryde Crist þer-fore mercy.
    Quandocumque ingemuerit peccator, omnes iniquitates eius non recordabor amplius.
And for þi muchel mercy and Marie loue thi moder,
Haue reuthe of alle these rybaudes that repenten hem sore   150
That euere thei gulte aȝeyn þe, god, in gost or in dede.'
    Thenne hente Hope an horn of *Deus, tu conuersus viuificabis nos,*   f.32ᵃ
And blewe hit with *Beati quorum remisse sunt iniquitates et quorum*
      tecta sunt peccata,
That alle seyntes for synfol songen with Dauid:
    Homines et iumenta saluabis; quemadmodum multiplicasti
      misericordiam tuam, deus!

---

141. douhtiest U] X douhtiokest
146–7. *lineation as* P; XUI *mislineate* sory for dedes/That
149. þi U] X *om*
152. Hope U] X y˙
154a. *tuam* U] X meam

---

141. *in oure sekte.* The threefold repetition of this phrase (B uses three words, *secte, sute* and *armes*) is designed to focus the prayer on the central mystery and the central hope of the Incarnation, at once to acknowledge God's love in accepting Incarnation, and to make a claim on it.

141a. 'The Word was made flesh' (John 1:14). Also III 355.

142. *by so muche*: 'with so much (evidence of your intentions)'.

144. For Christ's 'brothers in the flesh', see XII 108, XX 418, and cf. VIII 217.

148a. 'Whenever a sinner shall repent, I will remember no more any of his sins' (partly from Jer. 31:34, with variation).

149. *Marie loue*: 'the love of Mary'.

152. 'Thou wilt relent, O God, and bring us to life' (spoken by the priest after the confession, early in the Ordinary of the Mass, e.g. *Missale Romanum*, ed. R. Lippe, 1899, 198; based on Ps. 70:20). The *horn* of Hope is the trumpet of salvation, *tuba salutaris*, referred to in the *Exsultet* sung at the mass on Holy Saturday, celebrating the Resurrection (see above, 127n).

153. 'Blessed are they whose transgressions are forgiven, whose sins are covered' (Ps. 31:1, one of the 7 Penitential Psalms).

154a. 'Men and beasts thou wilt preserve, (O lord); how hast thou multiplied thy mercy, O God!' (Ps. 35:7–8).

A thousend of men tho throngen togyderes, 155
Criede vpward to Crist and to his clene moder
To haue grace to go to Treuthe – god leue þat they mote!
  Ac þer ne was wye non so wys þat the way thider couthe,
But blostrede forth as bestes ouer baches and hulles,
Til late was and longe þat thei a lede mette, 160
Yparayled as a paynyem in pilgrimes wyse.
  He bar a bordoun ybounde with a brood liste,
In a wethewynde wyse ywrithe al aboute.
A bolle and a bagge a bar by his syde;
An hundret of aunpolles on his hat sette, 165
Signes of Syse and shelles of Galys,
And many a crouch on his cloke, kayes of Rome,
And þe vernicle bifore, for men sholde yknowe

155. One recalls here the mass confessions and mass pilgrimages that often followed on great public sermons in the Middle Ages, especially when they were associated with natural calamities like that of V 116 (see Burrow, 1965, 249).

157. The penitent folk, made clean by confession, now proceed to pilgrimage (a form of *satisfactio operis*: see VI 6n), following Reason's instruction (V 198).

161. *as a paynyem*: 'like a Saracen'. Pilgrims to the holy land would dress, for comfort, like the local inhabitants. Jerusalem had been in the hands of the Saracens since 1187, but Christian pilgrims had free access by Frederick II's treaty of 1229.

162–3. 'He carried a pilgrim's staff bound with a broad strip of cloth, twisted all round like bindweed'. This is probably a relic of the custom of carrying a slender rod bound to the pilgrim's staff, perhaps a penitentiary's rod in token of the indulgence gained at a particular shrine, or perhaps a formalized palm-branch, in general token of pilgrimage. See G. McN. Rushforth, *Medieval Christian Imagery* (Oxford, 1936), 93–6.

165. *aunpolles*: small phials containing holy water or oil from shrines he had visited (esp. Canterbury).

166. *Signes of Syse*: 'souvenirs from Assisi'. Each place of pilgrimage had its special 'sign' or souvenir, such as the *ampullae* of Canterbury, the scallop-shells of St James of Compostella in Galicia (St James the Greater, brother of John the Evangelist, who according to a late tradition preached the gospel in Spain; for the origin of the shells, see Rushforth, *op.cit.* in note to 162 above, p. 94), the *crouch* or cross, sewn on the cloak as a sign of a visit to the holy land, and the crossed keys of St Peter (guardian of heaven's gate) of Rome.

168. *vernicle*: Lat. *veronicula*, a copy of the kerchief (headcloth) of Veronica, which, according to legend, was miraculously impressed with a likeness of Christ when she gave it him to wipe his face with as he was led to crucifixion. The original was preserved at St Peter's, so that this was another sign of pilgrimage to Rome.

And se by þe signes wham a souht hadde.

 This folk frayned hym furste fro whennes he come.   170

'Fro Sinoye,' he sayde, 'and fro þe sepulcre of oure lord.

In Bedlem and in Babiloyne y haue be in bothe,

In Armonye, in Alisaundre, and in Damascle.

3e may se be þe signes þat sitten on my cappe

Y haue souht gode seyntes for my soule helthe   175

And ywalked ful wyde in wete and in drye.'

 'Knowest thow auht a cor-seynt,' quod they, 'þat men calleth
   Treuthe?

Kouthest wissen vs the way whoder out Treuth woneth?'

 'Nay, so me god helpe,' sayde þe gome thenne,

'I saw neuere palmere with pyk ne with scrippe   180

Axen aftur hym, but now in þis place.'

 'Peter!' quod a plouhman, and potte forth his heued,

'I knowe hym as kyndely as clerk doth his bokes.

Consience and Kynde Wyt kenned me to his place.

And maden me sykeren sethen to seruen hym for euere,   185

   173. and in Damascle P] XI y haue be in bothe; *line om* U
   177. cor-seynt] X cor sent; U cors seynt
   178. the way P] XUI today
   179. helpe U] X hehelpe
   180. scrippe U] X scripte
   185. sykeren] X sykerenesse; U sekeron

171–3. The palmer had visited the convent of St Katherine in the desert of Sinai, the Holy Sepulchre in Jerusalem, the Church of the Nativity in Bethlehem, Babylon the Less (near Cairo, with a shrine of St Barbara, and church of Our Lady, who dwelt there after the flight into Egypt), Armenia (where the Ark still rested on mount Ararat), Alexandria, home of the martyred St Katherine, and Damascus, where God created Adam before planting him 'eastward in Eden' (see Monk's Tale, *CT* VII. 2007). Mandeville's *Travels* (ed. EETS 153) record visits to all these places (e.g. *Babylone*, p. 21; *Damasce*, p. 44; *Ermonye*, p. 98).

180. *palmere*. See Prol. 47n. The ignorance of Truth displayed by the palmer is an example of the way institutionalized procedures (cf. pardons, IX 319–47) can lose sight of and in the end subvert the spiritual purposes they are designed to serve. The inadequacy of the professional pilgrim (cf. Prol. 47–50) is a sign that saint Truth (V 198) is likely to be found nearer home (see 255, below).

182. *Peter*: an oath, by St Peter, but also, appropriately enough, the baptismal form of the ploughman's own name, Piers (Peres). We imagine him poking his head through the hedge which separates the highway from his half-acre (VIII 2). *Peter* and *plouhman* are erased in MS X (see Introd., p. 24), as are *Peres* and *plouhman* throughout the MS, with occasional omissions.

183. *kyndely*. He has the kind of knowledge of Truth that the dreamer has long sought (I 136n).

Bothe to sowe and to sette þe while y swynke myhte,　　　　f.32^b
And to sowen his seed, suewen his bestes,
Withynne and withouten to wayten his profit,
Iich haue ybe his foloware al this fourty wynter
And yserued Treuthe sothly, somdel to paye.　　　　　　　　190
In alle kyne craftes þat he couthe deuise
Profitable as for the plouh, a potte me to lerne,
And, thow I sey hit mysulf, y serue hym to paye.
Y haue myn huyre of hym wel and oþer whiles more.
He is þe presteste payere þat eny pore man knoweth;　　　　195
He with-halt non hewe his huyre ouer euen.
He is as louh as a lombe and leel of his tonge,
And ho-so wilneth to wyte where þat Treuthe woneth,
Y wol wissen ʒow wel ryht to his place.'
　　'ʒe, leue Peres,' quod thise pilgrimes, and profrede Peres mede.　200
　'Nay, bi þe perel of my soule!' Peres gan to swerie,
'Y ne wol fonge a ferthynge, for seynt Thomas shryne!
Were it itolde Treuthe þat y toke mede
A wolde loue me þe lasse a long tyme aftur.
　　Ac ho-so wol wende þer Treuthe is, this is þe way theder.　205
　ʒe mote go thorw Mekenesse, alle men and wommen,
Til ʒe come into Consience, yknowe of god sulue,

188. 'To look after his interests both indoors and out'. There is no need to allegorize this as 'in both spiritual and material matters', since the whole passage describing the honest ploughman labouring in his vocation is at once real *and also* allegorical, in the most obvious way, of the spiritual life. It is a true 'figure' (see E. Auerbach, 'Figura', in *Scenes from the Drama of European Literature*, New York, 1959, 11–76, and Salter, 1967, 23–7). The Christian significance of the ploughman as archetype needs no explanation, which is why L chose it. Cf. Chaucer's Plowman, *CT* I. 529–41. 'If you want to hear Christ', said Peter Cantor (quot. Dunning, 1937, 117), 'you should go to ecclesiastics of good learning, but if you want to find Christ, you should go to peasants of good life'. Wyclif (ed. Arnold, ii.213) puts it more strongly: 'Good liif of a plowman is as myche worþ to þe soule as preier of þis frere'.

193. There is perhaps an allusion here, as in *wayten his profit* above (188), to the parable of the talents and the 'good and faithful servant' (Matt. 25:23).

196. *ouer euen*: 'beyond the evening', alluding to the text of III 307a.

200. *Peres*. That the pilgrims address him thus, without being told his name, suggests that *Peres* and *plouhman* were a traditional collocation.

203. *mede*. Peres knows the difference between payment offered before (III 292) and a fair wage for work done (194, above).

205. The directions that follow bear some general resemblance to Rutebeuf's *La Voie de Paradis* (ed. E. Faral and J. Bastin, Paris, 1959), where Pity directs the dreamer to the House of Confession, avoiding the Seven Deadly Sins: 'Si verrez a senestre main/Une meson moult orguilleuse' (150–51), etc. Cf. XV 47, XXII 70.

That ȝe louye hym as lord leely aboue alle;
That is to sey sothly, ȝe sholde rather deye
Thenne eny dedly synne do, for drede or for preyere.   210
And thenne ȝoure neyhebores nexst in none wyse apayre
Otherwyse then ȝe wolden they wrouhte ȝow alle tymes.

And so goth forth by þe brok, a brugge as it were,
Forto ȝe fynde a ford, Ʒoure-fader-honoureth;
Wadeth in at þat water and wascheth ȝow wel there   215
And ȝe shal lepe þe lihtloker al ȝoure lyf-tyme.
     Honora patrem et matrem.

And thenne shalt thow se Swere-nat-but-if-it-be-for-nede-
And-nameliche-an-ydel-þe-name-of-god-almyhty.

Thenne shalt thow come by a croft, ac com thow nat þer-ynne;
The croft hatte Coueyte-nat-menne-catel-ne-here-wyues-   220
Ne-none-of-here-seruauntes-þat-nuye-hem-myhte;   f.33ᵃ
Loke þou bere nat þere away, but yf hit be thyn owene.

Two stokkes þere stondeth, ac stynte thow nat þere;
Thei hatte Stele-nat and Sle-nat – stryk forth by bothe
And leueth hem on þe luft hand and loke nat þeraftur,   225
And hold wel þin haliday heye til euen.

---

208. as P] XUI *om*
219. nat P] XU *om*
223. Two U] X tho
225. nat P] XUI *om*
226. þin I] XU þe

209–10. See I 143.
210. *for drede or for preyere*: 'even though fear or the beseeching of others press you to it'.
212. *Otherwyse*: '(or act towards them) in any other way . . .'
213–31. The gospel summary of OT law having been referred to (206–12: 'Love God, and your neighbour as yourself', Luke 10:27), the journey to Truth passes through a countryside dotted with allegorical reminders of the Ten Commandments, seven of which are specifically mentioned. The form of the allegory here may well be designed to aid memory by associating the commandments (which every Christian was expected to know) with a sequence of things observed on a journey (see 232n, below). What is made clear is that knowledge of Truth is based on a hard-won rectitude of life in obedience to Law (I 82n), and that the journey to Christ is through the OT, which his teaching does not supersede but fulfils (Matt. 5:17).
216a. 'Honour (your) father and mother (and you shall live long upon the earth)' (Ex. 20:12).
217. *but-if-it-be-for-nede.* See VI 428n.
221. *þat-nuye-hem-myhte*: '(nor anything) that (i.e. the loss of which) might harm them'. Cf. Ex. 20:17, and for the elliptical construction, 212 above.
225. *on þe luft hand.* See I 121a and note.
226. The injunction to keep the sabbath (Ex. 20:8) was extended to cover all the church's holy days.

Thenne shaltow blenche at a berw, Bere-no-fals-witnesse,
Is frithed in with floreynes and othere fees monye;
Loke thow plokke no plonte þere, for perel of thy soule.

Thenne shaltow se Say-soth-so-hit-be-to-done-   230
In-none-manere-elles-nat-for-no-mannes-preyre.

And so shaltow come to a court as cleer as þe sonne.
The mote is of Mercy, the manere in þe myddes,
And al þe wallyng is of Wyt, for Wil ne sholde hit wynne.
The carneles ben of Cristendom, þat kynde to saue,   235
Ybotresed with Bileue-so-or-þow-best-not-ysaued;
And alle þe hous been yheled, halles and chaumbres,
With no leed but with loue, and with lele-speche.
The barres aren of buxumnesse, as bretherne of o wombe.
The brygge hatte Byde-wel-the-bet-may-þow-spede;   240
Vche a piler is of penaunces and preyeres to seyntes;

236. þow U] X two
240. þow U] X they

228. *frithed* usually means 'surrounded with a wattled fence', but the next line suggests that the 'fence' here is made up of attractive plants, the plucking of which (i.e. the taking of bribes: see Ex. 23:1, 8) gives free access to the hill of perjury (L's allegorical places tend to stand for the sin rather than the prohibition, cf. 223–5).

232. *a court*: the castle of Truth, of man dwelling in God, built of and inhabited by the Christian virtues of the soul redeemed by Christ. There is a rich allegorical tradition of the 'castle of the soul' or 'castle of the body' (cf. X 128, Owst, 1933, 77–85, and R. D. Cornelius, *The Figurative Castle*, Bryn Mawr, 1930), as in *Sawles Warde* (ed. R. M. Wilson, Leeds Texts and Monographs no. III, 1938), a free early 13th c. translation from the *De Anima* of Hugh of St Victor (d. 1146), and L may well have been influenced by Grosseteste's *Chateau d'Amour*, or a ME version of it, where the castle-of-the-body idea is adapted as an allegorical description of the Virgin (see Sajavaara, 1967, 90–98), as in *Cursor Mundi* 9879–10076. We are told (F. A. Yates, *The Art of Memory*, London, 1966) that imaginary buildings were often used in classical mnemotechnics (memory-training) as 'storehouses' of images and ideas (i.e. the things to be remembered would be associated with rooms or features of a building such as were already fixed in the memory). The allegorical castles of the Middle Ages, like the various schemes for representing the virtues and the vices (see above, 213n, and XVIII 7n), may owe a debt to this tradition.

234. *Wyt* and *Wil* are traditionally paired in medieval moral allegory, representing the divine gift of reason as opposed to the wilfulness of fallen nature – Milton's 'Reason' and 'Passion'. See I 5n.

236. 'This is the Catholic Faith: which except a man believe faithfully, he cannot be saved' (the closing words of the *Quicunque vult*, or Athanasian Creed, as recited on some special feast-days instead of the Apostles' Creed: Breviary, II. 46–8; see IX 288).

241. *Vche a piler*, i.e. each upright supporting the bridge.

The hokes aren almes-dedes þat þe ʒates hange on.
  Grace hatte þe gateward, a goed man for sothe;
His man hatte Amende-ʒow, many man hym knoweth.
Tel hym this ilke tokene: "Treuthe woet þe sothe,   245
Y am sory of my synnes and so y shal euere,
And parformed þe penaunce þat þe prest me hihte."
Biddeth Amende-ʒow to meke hym to his maister Grace,
To opene and vndo þe hye gate of heuene
That Adam and Eue aʒenes vs alle shette.   250
    Per Euam cunctis clausa est, et per Mariam virginem
        iterum patefacta est.
A ful leel lady vnlek hit of grace,
And she hath þe keye and þe clycat, thow þe kynge slepe,
And may lede in þat she loueth as here lef lyketh.
  And yf Grace graunte the to go in in this wyse
Thow shalt se Treuthe sitte in thy sulue herte,   255
And solace thy soule and saue the fram payne,   f.33ᵇ
And charge Charite a churche to make
In thyne hole herte, to herborwe alle trewe
And fynde alle manere folke fode to here soules,
Ʒef loue and leute and oure lawe be trewe: 260
    Quodcumque petieritis in nomine meo, dabitur enim vobis.

248. hym B] XUIP ʒow
250a. *cunctis* I] XU cuntis
252. she U] X he
253. she U] X he
254. in in P] XUI in
260. be P] XUI *om*

250a. 'Through Eve it was closed to all men, and through the Virgin Mary it was
  opened again': from an antiphon sung at Lauds between Easter and Ascension
  day (Breviary, I. dccclxx). The image of Mary as the gate of Paradise and as the
  key-bearer of Redemption (251–3) is derived from patristic commentary on OT
  texts such as Ez. 44:2, Ps. 117:20, and from the interpretation of the 'key of David'
  of Apoc. 3:7 (cf. Isa. 22:22) as the Virgin (Gray, 1975, 100), and is incorporated
  elsewhere in the liturgy in the antiphons of Advent (Bennett 194). See further,
  Woolf, 1968, 115–16.
252. *thow þe kynge slepe,* i.e. in her womb.
255. The journey to Truth ends in self-discovery, in the recognition of the spirit
  of Truth that dwells within (John 14:17), as Holy Church explained long ago
  (I 141, 160). L here touches on a theme frequently treated at length in mystical
  writing (see E. Zeeman, in *E & S* 11, 1958, 1–16; Vasta, 1965, 107–20; and see
  I 86n).
257–9. Through Love, the heart becomes a sanctuary for Truth and a source of spiri-
  tual nourishment for others.
260a. 'Whatever you shall ask in my name shall be given to you' (John 16:23, varied).

Ac be war thenne of Wrath, þat wikkede shrewe,
For he hath enuye to hym þat in thyn herte setteth
And poketh forth pruyde to preyse thysuluen.
The boldenesse of thy been-fetes maketh the blynd thenne;
So worth thow dryuen out as deux, and þe dore yclosed,   265
Ykeyed and yclyketed to close the withouten,
Hapliche an hundred wyntur ar thow eft entre.
Thus myhte thow lesen his loue, to lete wel by thysulue,
And geten hit agayne thorw grace, ac thorw no gifte elles.

Ac ther ben seuene susteres þat seruen Treuthe euere   270
And aren porteres ouer þe posternes þat to þat place bilongen.

261. þat I] XU nat þat

264. *boldenesse of thy been-fetes*: 'rash confidence in your good deeds'.
265. *as deux*: 'like dew'. Cf. Hos. 13:3.
267. *an hundred wynter*, i.e. in purgatory. The castle of Truth is thought of throughout as the life of Truth and spiritual grace on earth, and also as heaven.
268. *to lete wel by thysulue*: 'by thinking well of yourself'.
269. Grace is shown, in accordance with orthodox doctrine, to transcend, even to ignore, human desert. The doctrine of Grace, evolved by St Augustine (d. 430) in his treatises against Pelagius (who claimed that man could win salvation by good works) was designed to arrogate to God an absolute and arbitrary free will in judging man. Grace is not won, nor deserved, but given, out of God's overflowing love. The Augustinian doctrine of grace was vehemently reasserted in the 14th c. by Thomas Bradwardine, briefly archbishop of Canterbury (1348–9), in his *De Causa Dei*, against the emphasis on man's free will of those whom he called the 'modern Pelagians' (see Leff, 1957, 14–15). For him, merit or good works in man are in themselves valueless, since they are only the result of grace having already been given (ibid. 66, and see *Prick of Conscience* 2472). The debate in which Bradwardine participated is reflected in simpler, less scholarly but no less urgent form in *Piers Plowman* (see XI 205, 208, etc.).
270. *seuene susteres*. These are the seven Christian virtues (sometimes called 'chief' or remedial virtues), developed in penitential literature as *remedia* for the seven deadly sins (e.g. Chaucer's Parson's Tale). The seven virtues were less completely systematized than the sins, and there is some variation in the enumeration; the correspondence with the sins here is not perfect, for, if Charity be taken as *remedium* against Envy, Peace is left opposing Sloth (in the *Castle of Love*, one of the ME translations of Grosseteste mentioned in 232n, above, it is *gostliche gladynge*, line 841). The seven Christian virtues are to be distinguished from the three theological or spiritual virtues, Faith, Hope and Charity, and the four cardinal virtues (see XXI 274–310), which together formed another series of seven. The seven Christian virtues were often associated further in didactic treatises with the seven Gifts of the Holy Ghost (XXI 228a), the seven Beatitudes, the seven Works of Mercy (VI 21) and the seven Petitions of the Paternoster (see Tuve, 1966, 85–9, 442).
271. *porteres ouer þe posternes*. For a MS illustration of a castle of the Seven Virtues, with the virtues, represented as maidens, defending the castle against the assault of the vices, see Saxl, 1942, 104.

That on hatte Abstinence and Vmbletee annoþer,
Charite and Chastite ben his chief maydenes,
Pacience and Pees muche peple þei helpe,
Largenesse þat lady lat in ful monye –   275
Noen of hem alle helpe may in betere,
For she payeth for prisones in puttes and in peynes.
And ho is sib to þis seuene, so me god helpe,
Is wonderliche welcome and fayre vnderfonge.
Ho is nat syb to this seuene, sothly to telle,   280
Hit is ful hard, be myn heued, eny of ʒow alle
To geten ingang at eny ʒate, bote grace be þe more.'
    'By Crist,' quod a cotte-pors, 'y haue no kyn there.'
    'Ne y,' quod an hapeward, 'by auht þat y knowe!'
    'Wyte god,' quod a wafrestere, 'wiste y this for sothe,   285
Wolde y neuere forthere no foet for no frere prechynge!'
    'ʒus,' quod Perus þe plouhman, and pokede hem alle to gode,
'Mercy is a mayden there hath myhte ouer hem alle,
And she is sib to alle synfole, and here sone bothe.
And thorw þe helpes of hem two, hope þou non oþer,   290
Thow myhte gete grace there, so thow go bytymes.'   f.34ᵃ
    'ʒe, *villam emi*,' quod oen, 'and now y moste thedre
To loke how me liketh hit'; and toek his leue at Peres.
Anoþer anoen riht nede he sayde he hadde
To falewe with fiue ʒokes, 'Forthy me bihoueth   295
To goo with a good wil and graytheliche hem dryue.
Forthy y pray ʒow, Peres, parauntur ʒif ʒe meten

---

272. Abstinence U] X astinence
277. she U] X he.   puttes U] X places
295. ʒokes U] X ʒotes
297. meten U] X moten

---

277. *payeth for prisones*: 'ransoms prisoners'.
283. *y haue no kyn there*. The cutpurse and his fellows misunderstand the Ploughman's remarks (278, 280) by taking them literally. They are corrected in 289.
285. *Wyte god*: 'may God know', i.e. I am telling God. *wafrestere*: a female seller of cakes and confections. These cake-sellers were associated with taverns (as in the Pardoner's Tale, *CT* VI. 479) and had a bad reputation.
289. Mercy (cf. VI 333) is here identified with the Virgin.
292. *villam emi*: 'I have bought a field' (Luke 14:18). In lines 292–304 (added in C), dealing with those who excuse themselves from the pilgrimage, L paraphrases the answers of those who decline the invitation to the great supper (i.e. refuse to participate as Christ's disciples in the kingdom of heaven) in the parable of Luke 14:16–24. The poet of *Cleanness* does the same (ll. 63–72) in a similar context.

Treuth, telleth hym this, þat y be excused.'
    Thenne was oen hihte Actif, an hosbande he semede:
'Y haue wedded a wyf, wel wantowen of maneres;   300
Were y seuen nyhte fro here syhte, sighen she wolde
And loure on me and lihtly chyde and sygge y louede another.
Forthy, Peres the plouhman, y preye the telle hit Treuthe
I may nat come for a Kitte so a cleueth on me.
    Vxorem duxi et ideo non possum venire.'
    Quod Contemplacioun, 'By Crist, þogh y care soffre,   305
Famyne and defaute, folwen y wol Peres.
Ac þe way is ful wikked, but ho-so hadde a gyde
That myhte folowe vs vch a fote for drede of mysturnynge.'

---

301. sighen U] X shien[de]; I chiden; P seggen (*other MSS* synnen).   she U] X he
305. *line supplied from* U; X *om*

---

299. *Actif.* See X 78n, XV 194. According to the traditional interpretation of the Active and the Contemplative lives, the Active are not wicked men, but those who have chosen Martha's part (Luke 10:41–2; see XII 138), the way of the Commandments, the Active life of the world and not the way of perfection and renunciation (Matt. 19:21), i.e. the Contemplative life (305, below). C's addition here certainly hints at a more exclusively spiritual reading of the next passus (cf. VIII 2n), and to that extent is out of keeping, unless we assume that by *Actif* he means here (as in XV 194) the common body of sinning humanity.

304a. 'I have married a wife, and therefore I cannot come' (Luke 14:20). Taking a wife, in the context of the parable, was interpreted by the commentators as attaching oneself to delight in the pleasures of the flesh (e.g. Wyclif, ed. Arnold, i.5).

307. *but ho-so hadde*: 'unless one had'.

Passus VIII

The Ploughing of the Half-Acre

Passus octauus vt prius
Quod Perkyn þe plouhman, 'Be seynt Petur of Rome!
Ich haue an half-aker to erye by þe heye waye;
Haued ich y-ered þis half-aker and ysowed hit aftur,
Y wolde wende with ȝow and þe way teche.'
    'That were a long lettyng,' quod a lady in a sclayre,   5
'What sholde we wommen worche þe whiles?'

2. waye U] X *om*
4. wolde U] X wol
5. a² U] X þat. sclayre U] X slayre

1. *Perkyn*, i.e. Peterkin, dim. of Peter. See VII 182n.
2. *an half-aker*: the average area of one of the strips into which the open field was divided (see 114, below, and VI 267). Before the pilgrimage to Truth can begin (in fact, it never begins, though the theme of pilgrimage is taken up in the dreamer's search for Dowel, X 2), Piers must see to the ploughing of the half-acre, i.e. he must attend to the economic necessities and social obligations of life. (For this order of priorities, cf. Paul's explanation of the resurrection of the body: 'If there is a physical body, there is also a spiritual body . . . It is not the spiritual which is first but the physical', 1 Cor. 15:44, 46.) Piers gives instructions also to other classes as to how they are to participate, according to their station, in the work of the Christian community (a common theme of sermons: see Owst, 1933, 549–54), which is represented primarily through the ploughing (cf. Prol. 145). The reference of the allegory is political, social and economic; there is a spiritual dimension, of course, in so far as any allegory of the well-ordered community will adumbrate both the well-ordered soul and also the kingdom of heaven, but the secondary significance and inexplicit nature of that spiritual reference (see Aers, 1975, 109–31) is clearly brought out by comparison with the later ploughing scene of XXI 258, which is exclusively spiritual and totally non-literal. That later scene, in fact, provides a spiritual commentary on much of Passus VIII and IX. It is true, however, that some elements of the traditional imagery of the ploughman as preacher (XXI 258n) are absorbed into the portrait of Piers in this passus (see Barney, 1973, 287–9), perhaps progressively, as Piers's role develops (Trower, 1973).
6. It is in very similar terms that the people question John the Baptist ('What then shall we do?' Luke 3:10) after he has told them to prepare for the coming of the Lord. The situations are alike in other ways (see Trower, 1973, 399).

'Y preye ȝow, for ȝoure profit,' quod Peres to þe ladyes,
'That somme sowe þe sak for shedynge of the whete,
And ȝe worthily wymmen with ȝoure longe fyngres
That ȝe han selk and sendel to sowe whan tyme is   10
Chesibles for chapeleynes churches to honoure.
Wyues and wyddewes wolle an flex spynneth;
Consience conseyleth ȝow cloth for to make
For profit of the pore and plesaunce of ȝowsuluen.
For y shal lene hem lyflode, but þe lond faylle,   15
As longe as y leue, for the lordes loue of heuene.
And alle manere men þat by þe molde is susteyned
Helpeth hym worche wittiliche þat wynneth ȝoure fode.'   f.34ᵇ
    'By Crist,' quod a knyhte tho, 'a kenneth vs þe beste;
Ac on þe teme treuely ytauhte was y neuere.   20
Y wolde y couthe,' quod the knyhte, 'by Crist and his moder;
Y wolde assaie som tyme for solace as hit were.'
    'Sikerliche, sire knyhte,' sayde Peris thenne,
'Y shal swynke and swete and sowe for vs bothe
And labory for tho thow louest al my lyf-tyme,   25
In couenant þat thow kepe holy kerke and mysulue
Fro wastores and fro wikked men þat þis world struyen,
And go hunte hardelyche to hares and to foxes,
To bores and to bokkes þat breketh adoun myn hegges,
And afayte thy faucones to culle þe wylde foules   30
For þey cometh to my croft my corn to diffoule.'
    Courteisliche the knyhte thenne comesed thise wordes:
'By my power, Peres, y plyhte the my treuthe
To defende þe in fayth, fyhte thow y sholde.'
    'And ȝut a poynt,' quod Peres, 'y preye ȝow of more: 35
Loke ȝe tene no tenaunt but treuthe wol assente

---

10. han B] XUIP on.   sendel I] XU on sendel
20. on þe teme P] X in tyme; U on teme; I one tyme
22. assaie U] X *om*

8. *for*: 'to preȝent'.
16. *for the lordes loue of heuene*: 'for the sake of the love of the lord of heaven'.
20. *on þe teme*: 'on the subject' (with a pun on *teme*, 'plough-team').
24. The *comunes* provide for the whole community (Prol. 143n), but the other estates are expected to play their part in the social covenant. Knights are to defend the realm, and to hunt (to see the latter as an obligation is usual, and an example of strict orthodoxy in L's social thinking).
35. *ȝow*. 2pl. pronouns are introduced here and in the following lines, in the context of the usual 2sg. (Kane-Donaldson 170 suggest that it was scribes who preferred the more deferential form of address).
36. The line is not logical, given the usual sense of *tene*. The general argument recalls I 90–100. Cf. Wyclif, ed. Arnold, iii.206.

And when ȝe mersyen eny man late mercy be taxour
And mekenesse thy mayster, maugre Mede chekes.
And thogh pore men profre ȝow presentes and ȝyftes
Nym hit nat an auntur thow mowe hit nauht deserue,   40
For thow shalt ȝelden hit so may be or sumdel abuggen hit.
Misbede nat thy bondeman, the bette may the spede;
Thogh he be here thyn vnderlynge, in heuene parauntur
He worth rather reseyued and reuerentloker sitte.
        Amice, ascende superius.
At churche in the charnel cherles aren euele to knowe   45
Or a knyhte fro a knaue or a quene fram a queene.
Hit bicometh to the, knyhte, to be corteys and hende,
Treuwe of thy tonge and tales loth to here
Bute they be of bounte, of batayles or of treuthe.
Hoold nat with non harlotes ne here nat here tales,   50
Ac nameliche at þe mete suche men eschewe
For hit beeþ þe deueles dysors to drawe men to synne.
Ne countreplede nat Consience ne holy kyrke ryhtes.'   f.35ᵃ
  'Y assente, by seynt Gyle,' sayde the knyht thenne,
'For to worche by thy wit and my wyf bothe.'   55
    'And y shal parayle me,' quod Perkyn, 'in pilgrimes wyse
And wende with alle tho þat wolden lyue in treuthe.'
And caste on hym his clothes of alle kyn craftes,
His cokeres and his coffes, as Kynde Wit hym tauhte,
And heng his hopur on his hales in stede of a scryppe;   60
A buschel of breedcorn brouht was þer-ynne.
'For y wol sowen hit mysulf and sethe wol y wende

---

46. fro P] XUI or

38. *maugre Mede chekes*: 'in spite of Meed's power'.
44a. 'Friend, go up higher' (Luke 14:10), from the parable of the marriage feast, telling how humility will be rewarded in heaven.
45. *charnel*. The charnel-house is where bones dug up in the making of new graves are deposited indiscriminately. *euele to knowe*: 'hard to recognize'. The same argument is developed in Parson's Tale, *CT* X. 761–4.
50–52. See VII 82n.
52. *hit beeþ*: 'they are'.
58. Peres puts on the clothes and carries the equipment, not of the professional pilgrim (see VII 161ff), but of the hard-working Christian. The ploughing still seems to be a preliminary to the pilgrimage, but it is beginning to absorb it.

To pilgrimages, as palmeres doen, pardon to wynne.
My plouh pote shal be my pyk-staff and pyche a-to þe rotes
And helpe my coltur to kerue and clanse þe forwes.   65
And alle þat helpen me erye or elles to wedy
Shal haue leue by oure lord to go and glene aftur me
And maken hym merye þer-myde, maugrey ho bigruchen hit.
And alle kyne crafty men þat conne lyue in treuthe
Y shal fynde hem fode þat fayfulleche libbeth,   70
Saue Iacke þe iogelour and Ionet of þe stuyues
And Danyel þe dees-playere and Denote þe baude
And frere faytour and folk of þat ordre,
That lollares and loseles lele men holdeth,
And Robyn þe rybauder for his rousty wordes.   75
Treuthe telde me ones and bad me telle hit forthere:
Deleantur de libro viuencium, y sholde nat dele with hem,
For holy chirche is hote of hem no tythe to aske,
    Quia cum iustis non scribantur.
They ben ascaped good auntur, now god hem amende!'
    Dame Worch-when-tyme-is Peres wyf hehte;   80
His douhter hihte Do-rihte-so-or-thy-dame-shal-þe-bete;
His sone hihte Soffre-thy-souereynes-haue-her-wille-
Deme-hem-nat-yf-thow-doest-thow-shalt-hit-dere-abygge.
'Consayle nat so þe comune þe kyng to desplese,
Ne hem þat han lawes to loke lacke hem nat, y hote þe.   85
Lat god yworthe with al, as holy wryt techeth:

---

77. *Deleantur* U] X *Deliantur*

---

64. *plouh-pote*: 'plough-stick' (lit. 'pusher', from *pote*, 'to push, thrust'), a long-handled
   spade for clearing thick accumulations of earth and weeds from the coulter.
68. *maugrey ho bigruchen hit*: 'in spite of anyone who grumbles at it'.
71. *Iacke þe iogelour*, etc. L gives momentary vitality here to a pulpit commonplace, the
   familiar list of disreputable 'crafts of folly' (Owst, 1933, 371), as they appear for
   instance in *Jacob's Well*, 134.
77. 'Let them be blotted out of the book of the living' (Ps. 68:28).
78a. 'Because they may not be enrolled among the righteous' (Ps. 68:28, continuing
   77 above, with *quia* for Vg. *et* so as to adapt the clause to make it refer to those
   whose tithes are unacceptable to the church: cf. VI 300).
79. *They ben ascaped good auntur*: 'They have escaped (paying tithes) by good luck', or
   rather what seems to them good luck, for they are in peril of their souls.
80. The Ploughman's family exemplify by their names (cf. IV 18) the virtues of honest
   work, obedience to one's parents, and obedience to lawful authority. *Worch-when-
   tyme-is*, i.e. not on the sabbath: 'Six days you shall labour' (Ex. 20:9).
84. The son's name is distinguished neither in syntax nor theme from his father's
   advice. But this, though a product of textual accretion, is not entirely inappropriate,
   since his father gave him both.
86. *Lat god yworthe with al*: 'Leave it all to God'.

Super cathedram Moysi sedent.

Maystres, as þe mayres ben, and grete menne, senatours,   f.35^b
What þei comaunde as by þe kyng countreplede hit neuere;
Al þat they hoten, y hote, heiliche thow soffre hem
And aftur here warnynge and wordynge worche þou þeraftur.   90
    Omnia que dicunt facite et seruate.
Ac aftur here doynge ne do thow nat, my dere sone,' quod Peres.
  'For now y am olde and hoer and haue of myn owene,
To penaunces and pilgrimages y wol passe with this oþere.
Forthy y wol ar y wende do wryte my biqueste.
    In dei nomine amen: y make hit mysulue.   95
He shal haue my soule þat alle soules made
And defenden hit as fro þe fende, and so is my beleue,
Til y come til his acountes as my crede telleth
To haue a remissioun and a relees on þat rental y leue.
The kyrke shal haue my caroyne and kepe my bones   100
For of my corn and my catel he craued my tythe.
Y payede hit prestly for perel of my soule;
He is holdyng, y hope, to haue me on his masse
And menege me in his memorie amonges alle cristene.
My wyf shal haue of þat y wan with treuthe and no more   105

---

87. ben U] X is
90. and wordynge] XIP and worchynge; U *om*
93. pilgrimages U] X pilgrimes

86a, 90a. '(The scribes and the Pharisees) sit on Moses's seat; so practise and observe whatever they tell you, (but not what they do; for they preach, but do not practise)' (Matt. 23:2–3, Jesus advising the people on their behaviour to those set in authority over them).

94. *do wryte*: 'cause to be written down' (Peres is illiterate, cf. IX 282–3). It was a Christian's duty to make his will before setting out on any lengthy pilgrimage.

95. 'In the name of God, amen', the usual formula at the beginning of a will. The will itself, disposing in order of soul, body and property, follows the pattern of contemporary wills.

99. *rental*: a record of properties on which rent was due; here, metaphorically, a record of sins on which payment was due.

101. *he* identifies the parson of the church in the Ploughman's parish. The choice is important, for it was a frequent point of complaint against the friars that they offered easy confession and penance in return for burial rights (and the fees and bequests that went therewith). See Prol. 62n; Knowles, i.184–5; *Defensio Curatorum* 72.

103–4. Referring to the commemoration of the departed in the canon of the mass (Breviary II. 490). Cf. VII 27.

105. *of þat*: 'her portion [usually a third] of what'. *and no more*, i.e. there is no more than he 'wan with treuthe', for he has no ill-gotten gains to dispose of, and no debts to pay.

And delen hit amonges my douhteres and my dere childres.
For thouh y dey today my dette is yquited;
I bar hoem þat y borwed ar y to bedde ʒede.
And with þe resudue and þe remenant, by the rode of Lukes!
Y wol worschipe þerwith Treuthe al my lyue   110
And ben a pilgrym at þe plouh for profit to pore and ryche.'

   Now is Perkyn and þis pilgrimes to þe plouh faren;
To erien this half-aker holpen hym monye.
Dikares and deluares digged vp þe balkes;
Therwith was Perkyn apayed and payede wel hem here huyre.   115
Oþer werkemen þer were þat wrouhten fol ʒerne,
Vch man in his manere made hymsulue to done
And somme to plese Perkyn afeelde pykede wedes.

   At hey prime Peres leet þe plouh stande
And ouersey hem hymsulue; ho-so beste wrouhte   120
He sholde be huyred þeraftur when heruost tyme come.

   And thenne seet somme and songen at the ale   f.36ᵃ
And holpe erye this half-aker with 'hey trollilolly!'
Quod Peres þe plouhman al in puyre tene:
'But ʒe aryse þe rather and rape ʒow to worche   125
Shal no grayn þat here groweth gladyen ʒow at nede,
And thow ʒe deye for deul, þe deuel haue þat reche!'

   Tho were faytours aferd and fayned hem blynde
And leyde here legges alery as suche lorelles conneth
And maden here mone to Peres how þei may nat worche: 130

---

108. *ar y to bedde ʒede*: as laid down in Deut. 24:12. Cf. VII 196.

109. *Lukes*: Lucca, in N. Italy, where there was a famous crucifix. Irony (cf. IV 194) seems unlikely.

111. *pilgrym at þe plouh*. The pilgrimage has now, therefore, been completely absorbed into the ploughing (see 2n, 58n, above, and Burrow, 1965, 255), which is the allegory of the life of the Christian community on earth. There is no further mention (though cf. IX 5) of the pilgrimage of man's life.

112. The villagers go to work as a community on the common field, or, more appropriately allegorically, on the fields of the manorial lord. Peres acts as the (manorial) lord's reeve (cf. XXI 258) or farm-manager.

114. *balkes* were narrow unploughed strips of land separating the half-acre strips of individual villagers (VI 267n, VIII 2n), or they could be strips of land left unploughed because they were difficult to get at and therefore needed special attention, as here.

119. *At hey prime*: at 9 a.m., *prime* being the period from 6 to 9 a.m.

120–21. One of the many suggestions of spiritual allegory in this passus (see above, 2n); those to be hired at harvest-time are those judged worthy of the kingdom of heaven (harvest is a frequent figure for the Last Judgment, e.g. Matt. 13:39).

127. *haue þat reche*: 'take him who cares'.

129. *leyde here legges alery*: twisted their legs backwards so that they looked to be cut off at the knee (see a note by E. Colledge in *MÆ* 27, 1958, 111–13). These and other characteristic tricks of *faytours* are described in *Speculum Vitae* 3767–76.

'And we praye for ʒow, Peres, and for ʒoure plouh bothe
That god for his grace ʒoure grayn multiplye
And ʒelde ʒow of ʒoure almesse þat ʒe ʒeuen vs here.
We may nother swynke ne swete, suche sekenes vs ayleth,
Ne none lymes to labory with, lord god we thonketh.'   135
    'Ʒoure preyeres,' quod Peres, 'and ʒe parfyt weren,
Myhte helpe, as y hope, ac hey Treuthe wolde
That no faytrye were founde in folk þat goth a-beggeth.
Ʒe been wastours, y woet wel, and waste and deuouren
What lele land-tilynge men leely byswynken.   140
Ac Treuthe shal teche ʒow his teme to dryue
Or ʒe shal ete barly breed and of þe broke drynke,
But yf he be blynde or broke-legged or bolted with yren –
Suche poore,' quod Peres, 'shal parte with my godes,
Bothe of my corn and of my cloth to kepe hem fram defaute.   145
And ankerus and eremytes þat eten but at nones
And freres þat flateren nat and pore folke syke,
What! y and myn wolle fynde hem what hem nedeth.'
    Thenne gan Wastor to wrath hym and wolde haue yfouhte
And to Peres þe plouhman profrede to fyhte   150
And bad hym go pisse with his plogh, pyuische shrewe!
A Bretener cam braggyng, a bostede Peres also:
'Wolle thow, nulle thow,' quod he, 'we wol haue oure wille,
And thy flour and thy flesch feche whenne vs liketh
And maken vs murye þer-myde, maugreye ho begrucheth.'   155
    Peres the plouhman tho pleynede hym to þe knyhte
To kepe hym and his catel as couenant was bitwene hem:
'Awreke me of this wastors þat maketh this world dere;   f.36ᵇ

146. *ankerus and eremytes.* See Prol. 2n, 30n. *eten but at nones.* They treat every day as a feast-day, by not eating before noon (II 100n), and, furthermore, make the midday meal the only meal of the day.

149. *Wastor* (see Prol. 24) is a portrait of the itinerant labourers (see 331, below) who drifted into beggary and, according to the Commons petition of 1376, became 'mendinantz beggeres, pur mesner ocious vie . . . & lesquels sont fort de corps, & bien purroient eser la Commune pur vivre sour lour labour & service, si ils voudroient servir. Et plusours de eux devenent stafstrikers [see IX 159], & mesnent auxint ocious vie' (*Rot.Parl.* ii.340, trans. Dobson, 1970, 72–4). Another petition of the same year (*Rot.Parl.* ii.332) speaks of the 'fortz Ribauds mendinent' who pretend to be out-of-work soldiers (like the *Bretener* here, perhaps). Statutes were continually promulgated against these vagabonds: one of 1383 (Statutes, ii.32) renews a 1331 statute (i.268) against 'Roberdesmen [see Prol. 45], Wastours & Draghlacche'.

151. *pyuische shrewe.* Given the blending of direct and indirect speech common in ME, this could be Wasteɪ's opinion of Peres or the dreamer's opinion of Waster.

152. *Bretener.* Bretons had a reputation for bragging (Bennett 207), particularly in alliterative verse. He may be a hired Breton soldɪer, unemployed from the wars.

158. *maketh this world dere*: 'cause harm to the world' (*dere* being taken as noun and the phrase *maketh dere* as a variant of the common *do dere*).

They acounteth nat of corsynges ne holy kyrke nat dredeth.
For ther worth no plente,' quod Perus, 'and þe plouh lygge.'   160
  Courteisliche the knyhte thenne, as his kynde wolde,
Warnede Wastour and wissede hym betere:
'Or y shal bete the by the lawe and brynge þe in stokkes.'
  'I was nat woned to worche,' quod Wastour, 'and now wol y nat
    bygynne!'
And leet lyhte of þe lawe and lasse of the knyhte   165
And sette Peres at a pes to playne hym whare he wolde.
  'Now by Crist,' quod Peres the plouhman, 'y shal apayre ȝow
    alle,'
And houped aftur Hunger þat herde hym at the furste.
'Y preye the,' quod Perus tho, 'pur charite, sire Hunger,
Awreke me of this wastors, for þe knyhte wil nat.'   170
  Hunger in haste tho hente Wastour by þe mawe
And wronge hym so by þe wombe þat al watrede his yes.
A boffatede þe Bretoner aboute the chekes
Þat a lokede lyke a lenterne al his lyf aftur,
And beet hem so bothe he barste ner her gottes   175
Ne hadde Peres with a pese-loof preyede hym blyne.
'Haue mercy on hem, Hunger,' quod Peres, 'and lat me ȝeue hem
    benes,
And þat was bake for bayard hit may be here bote.'
  Tho were faytours afered and flowen into Peres bernes
And flapton on with flales fro morwen til euen,   180
That Hunger was nat hardy on hem for to loke.
For a potte ful of potage þat Peres wyf made
An heep of eremytes henten hem spades,

---

166. pes U] X mase
176. blyne X] U byleue
180. flales U] X fuales

---

166. *at a pes*: 'at the value of a pea'.
168. *at the furste.* Hunger needed no second telling: Famine was a real threat after a bad harvest. Peres's role here is a little blurred: his action is dramatically vivid but not entirely logical. Clearly Famine, though Peres might welcome him as a means of coercing recalcitrant workers, does not come because Peres calls, but because the harvest has been bad, owing to the slackness of the workers (160, above); unless, indeed, the suggestion is that Peres, as manager of the economy, is administering a 'sharp dose of deflation'. Hunger, as a form of coercion, is finally ineffective as an agent of reformation: see also XXII 8on.
174. *lyke a lenterne*: in allusion to the similarity of his hollow cheeks to the translucency or concavity of the walls (usually of horn) of a lantern.
176. *pese-loof*: a kind of 'bread' made, like pease-pudding, from dried peas and eaten by the poor.
178. Horses and hounds (see 225 below) were fed on a mash of beans and bran.

Sputeden and spradden donge in dispit of Hunger.
They coruen here copes and courtepies hem made   185
And wenten as werkemen to wedynge and to mowynge
Al for drede of here deth, such duntes ȝaf Hunger.
Blynde and broke-legged he botened a thousend
And lame men he lechede with longes of bestes.
Prestes and oþer peple towarde Peres they drowe   190
And freres of alle þe fyue ordres, alle for fere of Hunger.
For þat was bake for bayard was bote for many hungry,
Drosenes and dregges drynke for many beggares.
There was no ladde þat lyuede þat ne lowede hym to Peres   f.37ᵃ
To be his holde hewe thow he hadde no more   195
But lyflode for his labour and his lone at nones.
    Tho was Peres proude and potte hem alle a-werke
In daubynge and in deluynge, in donge afeld berynge,
In threschynge, in thekynge, in thwytinge of pynnes,
In alle kyne trewe craft þat man couthe deuyse.   200
Was no beggare so bold, but yf a blynd were,
Þat durste withsitte þat Peres sayde for fere of syre Hunger.
And Peres was proud þerof and potte hem alle to swynke
And ȝaf hem mete and money as þei myhte deserue.
    Tho hadde Peres pitee vppon alle pore peple   205
And bade Hunger in haste hye hym out of contraye
Hoem to his owene ȝerd and halde hym þere euere.
'Y am wel awroke of wastours thorw thy myhte.
Ac y preye the,' quod Peres, 'Hunger, ar thow wende,
Of beggares and biddares what beste be to done?   210

185. *here copes.* See Prol. 54, V 41.
189. *longes of bestes,* i.e. offal that would not usually be thought fit to be eaten.
191. *þe fyue ordres.* The usual reference is to four orders (Prol. 56n). The fifth is the order of Crutched or Cruciferous friars, so called from their habit, which bore a cross on the breast (Knowles, i.203). C alone has references to the five orders (IX 345, XV 81).
210. A recurrent question in Langland (Prol. 41n, IX 61ff, XI 29), particularly in the C-text (see a note by M. Day in *RES* 8, 1932, 445–6), and one in which he echoes an acute contemporary preoccupation with the problem of beggars, and of able-bodied beggars particularly. The petition presented before the Commons in 1376 (see 149, above) suggests imprisonment for vagrant beggars. Peres seems at one point, in anger, to advocate even more extreme measures (124–7, above); Hunger argues that Peres, as manager of the economy (i.e. the state), has a responsibility to ensure that no one should starve, though no responsibility to maintain life beyond the meanest level (224–8, below). Similar thinking concerning 'the dole' produced the Elizabethan Poor Law. The problem for a Christian community was in the conflict between economic realism (and the texts recommending discrimination in charity) and the clear exhortation of the gospels: 'Give to everyone who asks of you' (Luke 6:30, cf. also 2 Cor. 9:7 and 1 John 3:17), a conflict which was not entirely reconciled in canon law (Tierney, 1959, 55–61). Discrimination be-

For y woet wel, be Hunger went, worche þei wol ful ille.
Meschef hit maketh they ben so meke nouthe
And for defaute this folk folweth myn hestes.
Hit is nat for loue, leue hit, thei labore thus faste
But for fere of famyen, in fayth,' sayde Peres.   215
'Ther is no filial loue with this folk, for al here fayre speche;
And hit are my blody bretherne, for god bouhte vs alle.
Treuthe tauhte me ones to louye hem vchone
And to helpe hem of alle thynges ay as hem nedeth.
Now wolde y wyte ar thow wendest what were þe beste,   220
How y myhte amayster hem to louye and to labory
For here lyflode, lere me now, sire Hunger.'
  'Now herkene,' quod Hunger, 'and holde hit for a wysdom.
Bolde beggares and bygge þat mowe here breed byswynke,
With houndes bred and hors breed hele hem when þei hungren   225
And abaue hem with benes for bollyng of here wombe;
And yf þe gromes gruche bide hem go and swynke
And he shal soupe swettere when he hit hath deserued.
Ac yf thow fynde eny folke þat fals men han apayred
Conforte hem with thy catel for so comaundeth Treuthe,   230 f.37^b
Loue hem and lene hem, and so lawe of kynde wolde:
  Alter alterius onera portate.
And alle manere men þat thow myhte aspye
In mischief or in mal-ese, and thow mowe hem helpe,
Loke by thy lyue lat hem nat forfare.
Yf thow hast wonne auht wikkedliche, wiseliche despene hit.   235

226. abaue U] X bane
228. he² U] X *om*

tween the deserving and the undeserving poor became more acutely difficult in the late 14th c., since the fluidity of labour created by the Black Death (see 149, above, and 330, below) made it difficult to disentangle the problems of relieving poverty and of suppressing vagrancy. What was needed was 'a kind of scholastic critique of employability in able-bodied vagrants' (Tierney, 1959, 119), but it was not forthcoming from an ossified canon law system. L attempts to supply the deficiency in IX 61–186.

217. *hit are my blody bretherne*: 'they are my blood-brothers', i.e. through the blood of the redeeming Christ. Cf. XII 108, XX 418, 436.

226. *for bollyng of here wombe*: 'to prevent their stomachs from swelling' (ironical).

229. L here offers examples of the deserving poor, to whom help and alms should be given on a more generous scale. Cf. 289, below; IX 62, 175.

231a. 'Bear one another's burdens (and so fulfil the law of Christ)' (Gal. 6:2).

235. The import of this line (cf. XIX 245) may not seem to be in accord with the doctrine of restitution expounded earlier (VI 296–9). But canon law was practical on the matter, and declared that illicitly acquired wealth could be used for charitable purposes and for paying tithes provided that there was no injured party to claim restitution (Tierney, 1959, 50).

Facite vobis amicos de mammona iniquitatis.'
'Y wolde nat greue god,' quod Peres, 'for al þe good on erthe!
Myhte y synneles do as thow sayst?' sayde Peres þe plouhman.
'Ʒe, y bihote the,' quod Hunger, 'or elles þe bible lyeth.
Go to oure bygynnynge tho god the world made,
As wyse men haen wryten and as witnesseth Genesis,   240
Þat sayth with swynke and with swoet and swetynge face
Bytulye and bytrauayle trewely oure lyflode:
    In sudore and *labore vultus tui vesceris pane tuo.*
And Salomon þe sage with þe same acordeth:
The slowe caytif for colde a wolde no corn tylye;
In somer for his sleuthe he shal haue defaute   245
And go a-bribeth and a-beggeth and no man beten his hunger.
    Piger propter frigus noluit arare; mendicabit in yeme et
        non dabitur ei.
Mathew maketh mencioun of a man þat lente
His suluer to thre maner men and menyng they sholden
Chaffare and cheue þerwith in chele and in hete,
And þat best labored best was alloued   250
And ledares for here laboryng ouer al þe lordes godes.
Ac he þat was a wreche and wolde nat trauaile
The lord for his lachesse and his luther sleuthe
Bynom hym al þat he hadde and ʒaf hit to his felawe
Þat leely hadde ylabored, and thenne the lord sayde: 255

242. Bytulye U] X Bytuyle
242a. *sudore* U] X sudure
246a. *arare* U] X arrare. *mendicabit* I] XU mendicabitur

235a. 'Make friends for yourselves of the mammon of unrighteousness' (Luke 16:9), i.e.
     use ill-gotten wealth for good ends, and so benefit spiritually. The text concludes
     the parable of the unjust steward, which was commonly interpreted in this crude
     way (cf. Luke 16:10–13).
236. Peres's hesitation has to do with the harsh advice of Hunger in 224–8 above, as
     can be seen from the nature of Hunger's reply and especially 262–3, below.
242a. 'In labour and the sweat of your brow you shall eat your bread' (Gen. 3:19). L
     has added *labore* to the Vg. text from Gen. 3:17, or from the version of Gen. 3:16 in
     a lesson for Feria VI in Septuagesima (Breviary, I. div). Cf. B VI 233. All
     Hunger's texts have to do with the necessity of working for one's living.
246a. 'Because of the cold the sluggard would not plough; he shall beg in the winter
     and it shall not be given to him' (Prov. 20:4). The Vulgate reads *aestate*, 'summer',
     for *yeme* (i.e. *hieme*); this is the reading alluded to above (245) and of course the
     correct one in the context (no winter ploughing, no summer harvest). The reading
     hieme arises by sympathetic association of winter and deprivation. See XVI 13–14.
247. The parable of the talents, Matt. 25:14–30. The difficulty of the parable is that
     read literally it recommends usury (25:27). L refers only generally (*chaffare and
     cheue*) to the ways in which the servants are to labour on their lord's behalf.

"He þat hath shal haue and helpe þer hym liketh
And he þat nauht hath shal nauht haue and no man ʒut helpen hym
And þat he weneth wel to haue y wol hit hym bireue."
And lo, what þe sauter sayth to swynkares with handes:
"Yblessed be al tho that here bylyue biswynketh   260
Thorw eny lele labour as thorw lymes and handes."
   Labores manuum tuarum quia manducabis.   f.38ᵃ
This aren euidences,' quod Hunger, 'for hem þat wolle nat swynke
That here lyflode be lene and lyte worth here clothes.'
  'By Crist,' quod Peres þe þlouhman tho, 'this prouerbis
     y wol shewe
To beggares and to boys þat loth ben to worche.   265
Ac ʒut y praye ʒow,' quod Peres, 'pur charite, syre Hunger,
Yf ʒe can or knowe eny kyne thynges of fisyk,
For somme of my seruauntes and mysulf bothe
Of al a woke worche nat, so oure wombe greueth vs.'
  'Y wot wel,' quod Hunger, 'what sekenesse ʒow ayleth.   270
Ʒe han manged ouer-moche – þat maketh ʒow to be syke.
Ac ete nat, y hote, ar hunger the take
And sende the of his sauce to sauery with thy lyppes.
And kepe som til soper tyme and site nat to longe
At noon ne at no tyme, and nameliche at þe sopere   275
Lat nat sire Sorfeet sittien at thy borde,
And loke þou drynke no day ar thow dyne sumwhat.
And thenk þat Diues for his delicat lyf to þe deuel wente
And Lazar þe lene beggare þat longede after croumes –
And ʒut hadde he hem nat, for y, Hunger, culde hym,   280
And sethen y say hym sitte as he a syre were
In al manere ese and in Abrahames lappe.

---

278. Diues U] X. on.

256. *helpe*: '(have) help'.
261a. 'You shall eat the labour of your hands' (Ps. 127:2).
268. *and mysulf bothe.* For Peres to include himself as a victim of over-eating is at first puzzling. Allegorically, it confirms the suggestion that Peres, for all his competence as a spiritual guide, has the flaws of common humanity, at least at this point (see Troyer, 1932).
269. *Of al a woke*: 'for a whole week'.
278. The parable of the rich man (*dives*) and Lazarus is told in Luke 16:19–31. Cf. XIX 228–45.
282. *in Abrahames lappe*, i.e. in Limbo with prospects of heaven, under the protection of Abraham, to whom, with all who showed faith (Gen. 15:6, Gal. 3:6–18), God promised the inheritance of the kingdom of heaven. Cf. XVIII 272.

And ʒif thow haue pouer, Peres, y þe rede,
Alle þat grat in thy gate for godes loue aftur fode,
Part with hem of thy payne, of potage or of sowl,   285
Lene hem som of thy loef thouh thow þe lasse chewe.
And thouh lyares and lach-draweres and lollares knocke,
Lat hem abyde til the bord be drawe ac bere hem none croumes
Til alle thyne nedy neyhbores haue noen ymaked.
And yf thow dyete the thus y dar legge myn eres   290
That Fysik shal his forred hodes for his fode sulle
And his cloke of Callabre for his comune legge
And be fayn, be my fayth, his fysik to leete
And lerne to labory with lond lest lyflode hem fayle.
Ther ar many luther leches ac lele leches fewe;   295
They don men deye thorw here drynkes ar destyne hit wolde.'
'By seynte Poul,' quod Peres, 'thow poyntest neyh þe treuthe   f.38ᵇ
And leelyche sayst, as y leue, lord hit þe forʒeld!
Wende nouthe when thow wold and wel thow be euere
For thow hast wel awroke me and also wel ytauhte me.'   300
'Y behote the,' quod Hunger, 'þat hennes ne wol y wende
Ar y haue ydyned be þis day and ydronke bothe.'
'Y haue no peny,' quod Peres, 'polettes for to begge,
Ne noþer goos ne gries but two grene cheses
And a fewe croddes and craym and a cake of otes   305
And bred for my barnes of benes and of peses.
And ʒut y say, be my soule, y haue no salt bacoun
Ne no cokeney, be Crist, colloppes to make.
Ac y haue poret-ployntes, parsilie and skalones,
Chibolles and chiruulles and cheries sam-rede,   310
And a cow with a calf and a cart-mare

---

283. haue U] X *om*
287. lach U] X lech
307. say P] XUI sayde

---

288. *til the bord be drawe*: 'until the table be put away'. Meals in the hall were usually on trestle-tables, which were put away afterwards (unlike the Franklin's *table dormant*, *CT* I. 353).
289. *noen ymaked*: 'made their midday repast'.
292. *cloke of Callabre*: a cloak trimmed with Calabrian fur. Physicians often took rich clothes in lieu of fees.
299. *wel thow be*: 'good luck to you'.
302. *be þis day*: 'on this day' (i.e. had my food for the day), or possibly an oath. It is not forgotten that Hunger is the personification of real economic necessity as well as a temporary economic adviser. Here he must be fed on left-overs and the plainest seasonal foods during the difficult months before the harvest is in.
311. *a cart-mare*. Peres possesses the humblest kind of horse, like Chaucer's Plowman (who also leads afield the dung, *CT* I. 530, 541).

To drawe afeld my donge þe while þe drouthe lasteth.
And by this lyflode we mote lyue til Lamasse tyme
And by that y hope to haue heruost in my croftes;
Thenne may y dyhte my dyner as me dere lyketh.'
    Alle þe pore peple tho pese-coddes fette;
Benes and bake aples they brouhten in here lappe,
And profrede Pers this present to plese with Honger.
Hunger eet al in haste and askede aftur more.
Pore folk for fere tho fedde Honger ȝerne   320
With craym and with croddes, with cresses and oþere erbes.
By that hit nyhed neyh heruost and newe corn cam to chepyng
And thenne were folke fayn and fedde Hunger dentiesliche,
And thenne Gloton with gode ale garte Hunger slepe.
    And tho wolde Wastor nat worche bote wandren aboute,   325
Ne no beggare eten bred þat benes ynne were,
Bote of cler-matyn and coket and of clene whete,
Ne noon halpenny ale in none wyse drynke
Bote of the beste and of þe brouneste þat brewestares sullen.
Laborers þat han no lond to lyue on but here handes   330
Deynede noȝt to dyne a-day of nyhte-olde wortes;
May no peny-ale hem pay ne no pece of bacoun
But hit be fresh flesch or fisch, yfried or ybake,   f.39ᵃ
And þat *chaut* or *pluchaut* for chillyng of his mawe.

313. Lamasse I] XU lowe masse
315. my XI] UP þi
333. fresh U] X *om*

312. *þe drouthe.* Manure must be spread during the dry spells of March before the growing season properly begins.
313. *Lamasse*: Lammas (1 August), when a loaf (OE *hlaf*) made from the first harvest was offered at mass.
315. *my.* Other MSS have *þi*, but Hunger is Peres's hunger, of course, like everyone else's, if the allegory is momentarily depersonified.
327. *Bote of*: 'but (only bread made) of'.
328. *halpenny ale*. See VI 226, 228.
330. The Black Death of 1349 (see V 115) created a labour shortage, and many bondmen (tied labourers) left their villages to work as wage-labourers, often travelling about the country to get higher wages. The government introduced Statutes of Labourers (340, below) in 1361 and succeeding years, in an attempt to freeze wages and inhibit the movement of labour, but the attempt was by no means uniformly successful, and the tension created by this move was a general cause of the Peasants' Revolt of 1381. See Dobson, 1970, 59–74.
331–3. In an attempt to circumvent the provisions of the Statutes of Labourers concerning wages, employers often resorted to concealed payments in the form of meals.
334. *chaut or pluchaut*, i.e. *chaud* or *plus chaud*, 'warm or warmer': words from French cooking parlance used here contemptuously (like *manged* in 271).

And but yf he be heyliche yhuyred elles wol he chydde   335
And þat he was werkeman ywrouhte warien þe tyme.
Aȝenes Catones consayle comseth he to gruche:
Paupertatis onus pacienter ferre memento.
And thenne a corseth þe kyng and alle þe kynges iustices,
Suche lawes to lerne, laboreres to greue.   340
Ac whiles Hunger was here maister ther wolde non chyde,
Ne stryue aȝeynes his statuyt, a lokede so sturne.
    Ac y warne ȝow werkmen, wynneth whiles ȝe mowe,
For Hunger hiderwardes hasteth hym faste.
He shal awake thorw water, wastors to chaste,   345
And ar fewe ȝeres be fulfeld famyne shal aryse,
And so sayth Saturne and sente vs to warne.
Thorw flodes and thorw foule wederes fruyttes shollen fayle;
Pruyde and pestilences shal moche peple feche.
Thre shypes and a schaef with an viii folwynge   350
Shal brynge bane and batayle on bothe half þe mone.
And thenne shal deth withdrawe and derthe be iustice
And Dawe þe deluare dey for defaute
But yf god of his goodnesse graunte vs a trewe.

338. 'Remember to bear patiently the burden of poverty' (*Disticha Catonis*, i.21: see IV
  17n).

342. *his statuyt.* There is emphatic contrast between the law of Hunger and the ineffec-
  tive laws of 340, i.e. the Statutes of Labourers.

343–54. This prophecy, being a warning of the disasters that will happen unless God
  intervenes (354), is more straightforward than the similar prophecies of III 477
  and IV 108, where the circumstances that will precede the fulfilment of a certain
  prophecy are described. L's use of the popular genre of prophecy, represented
  elsewhere in such works as the Latin prophecies of John of Bridlington (see
  Reeves, 1969, 254–6), the alliterative prophecies (e.g. Robbins, 1959, no. 45) and
  Winner and Waster 11–17, 290–92 (see Prol. 1n), has an apocalyptic sense of
  urgency (cf. Prol. 62, III 477, XXII 53, and see Bloomfield, 1961, 91–4, 112–13).
  See further, *Thomas of Erceldoune*, ed. Murray, Introd.

345. *water*, i.e. flood (followed by other natural disasters: famine, tempest, plague and
  war).

347. *Saturne* is the most malignant and powerful of all planetary influences (Knight's
  Tale, *CT* I. 2453–69).

350. This line presumably contains a cryptic date-reference, like III 478 (which also
  includes *ship* and *shef*). A *schaef* might refer to the number of arrows in a sheaf (viz.
  24). See a note by H. Bradley in *MLR* 5 (1910), 342, and Bloomfield, 1961, 211–
  12.

351. *on bothe half þe mone*, i.e. in all parts of the world.

352. *deth*, i.e. the plague.

Passus IX

The Pardon sent from Truth

Passus nonus vt prius
Treuthe herde telle her-of and to Peres sente
To taken his teme and tilion þe erthe,
And purchasede hym a pardoun *a pena et a culpa*,
For hym and his ayres for euere to ben assoiled,
And bad hym holden hym at hoem and eryen his leyes   5
And alle þat holpe hym to erye, to sette or to sowe
Or eny manere mester þat myhte Peres auayle,
Pardoun with Peres þe plouhman perpetuelly he graunteth.
    Kynges and knyhtes þat holy kyrke defenden
And ryhtfulliche in reumes ruylen þe comune   10
Haen pardon thorw purgatorye to passe ful lyhtly,
With patriarkes and prophetes in paradis to sitton.
    Bishopis yblessed, yf they ben as they sholde,
Lele and fol of loue and no lord drede,   f.39ᵇ
Merciable to meke and mylde to þe gode   15
And bitynge in badde men but yf they wol amende,
Drede nat for no deth to distruye by here power
Lechery amonges lordes and here luyther custumes,
And suche liue as þei lereth men, oure lord Treuthe hem graunteth
To be peres to þe apostles, alle peple to reule   20

---

1. *Treuthe* is God and God's law (I 14, 81). *herde telle her-of* may refer to Saturn's warning and the last line of the previous passus, or, more probably, to God's knowledge of Peres's attempt to set up the true Christian community.

3. *a pardoun a pena et a culpa.* The pardon is superior to the usual kind of indulgence communicated to pardoners (Prol. 66n), which remitted the punishment (*pena* — what is called the 'debt of pain' in *Prick of Conscience* 3813) but not the guilt (*culpa*) of sin to the penitent. This pardon is, in this view, the power to absolve from the guilt of sin granted to the Church by Christ (Prol. 129), as is explained further in XXI 182–90, in a scene which acts, here and elsewhere, as a spiritual commentary on the events of VIII and IX (see VIII 2n). But the phrase *a pena et a culpa* was often loosely used (Dunning, 1937, 142), and the pardon may be no more than a conventional 'indulgence'.

5. *holden hym at hoem.* The pilgrimage has been abandoned (see VIII 110n): most folk must do the world's work and receive the conditional promise of salvation (only Contemplation, it will be remembered, welcomed the pilgrimage in the first place, VII 305). Hence, perhaps, Peres's impatience with the pardon (291, below), and the beginning of a new search, a new 'pilgrimage'.

And deme with hem at domesday bothe quyke and dede.

  Marchauntes in þe margine hadde many ȝeres,

Ac no *pena et a culpa* no Treuthe wolde hem graunte

For they holde nat here haliday as holi chirch hem hoteth,

And for they swere by here soule and god mote hem helpe   25

Aȝen clene consience for couetyse of wynnynge.

Ac vnder his secrete seal Treuthe sente hem a lettre

That bad hem bugge boldly what hem best likede

And sethe sullen hit aȝeyn and saue þe wynnynges,

Amende meson-dewes þerwith and myseyse men fynde   30

And wyckede wayes with here goed amende

And brugges tobrokene by the heye wayes

Amende in som manere wyse and maydones helpe,

Pore peple bedredene and prisones in stokkes

Fynde hem for godes loue, and fauntkynes to scole,   35

Releue religion and renten hem bettere:

'And y shal sende ȝow mysulue seynt Mihel myn angel

---

25. swere U] X swore
33. maydones U] X mayndones

---

21. For the participation of true-living Christians in judgment at Doomsday, see *Cursor Mundi* 23039–62, *Prick of Conscience* 6017–25.

22. *in þe margine*, i.e. in the form of a marginal addendum in a legal document, presumably because merchants are not a separate estate of society. *many ȝeres*, i.e. of remission of punishment in purgatory (as in 11, above), a normal interpretation of *a pena* and of the function of orthodox pardons, though strictly speaking *pena* referred only to the punishment imposed as penance in this life (Prol. 66n, and below, 327).

25. These are oaths, expressed in indirect speech.

27. *vnder his secrete seal*. The personal or privy seal of a pope or king (cf. 138, below, and III 182) was used on documents not intended for public proclamation. The distinction between this private letter and the open document (cf. XIX 7n) which constitutes the general pardon does not imply underhand dealing. It suggests that the Church (NB. *Treuthe* in line 23 replaces *the pope* in AB) recognizes the propriety of trade (cf. III 313) so long as the profits are devoted to good causes and works of charity, but cannot sanction trade as such. To engage in trade is not positively sinful, but it is a perilous business for the soul (Tawney, 1926, 33). As to its profits, according to canon law, a man who holds wealth is bound to give what is super-fluous to his needs to those who are needy; what he keeps more than he needs is theft (Tierney, 1959, 36–7; see I 171).

31. This and the following are well-recognized works of charity, frequently mentioned in bequests, and often financed by trade-guilds (see *English Gilds* 143, 194, 231, 249).

37. *seynt Mihel*. St Michael, the angel of death, was present at the moment of death to take the soul, if it were so decreed, from the grasp of devils, who gathered to terrify the dying man and tempt him to despair of salvation – a subject treated with characteristic relish in *Prick of Conscience* 2216–2373, 2902–19.

That no deuel shal ȝow dere ne despeyre in ȝoure deynge
And sethe sende ȝoure soules þer y mysulue dwelle
And abyde þer in my blisse, body and soule for euere.'
Tho were marchauntes mury; many wopen for ioye   40
And preyde for Peres the plouhman þat purchased hem þis bulles.

    Alle þe peple hadde pardon ynow þat parfitliche lyuede.
Men of lawe hadde lest þat loth were to plede
But they *pre manibus* were payed for pledynge at þe barre.   45
Ac he þat speneth his speche and speketh for þe pore
That innocent and nedy is and no man harm wolde,
That conforteth suche in eny caes and coueyteth nat here ȝiftes
And for þe loue of oure lord lawe for hem declareth
Shal haue grace of a good ende and greet ioye aftur.   50 f.40ᵃ
Beth ywar, ȝe wis men and witty of þe lawe,
For whenne ȝe drawe to þe deth and indulgences wolde haue
His pardoun is ful petyt at his partynge hennes
That mede of mene men for here motynge taken.
For hit is symonye to sulle þat sent is of grace,   55
And þat is wit and water and wynde and fuyre the ferthe;
Thise foure sholde be fre to alle folk þat hit nedeþ.

    Alle libbyng laborers þat lyuen with here handes
Lellyche and lauhfollyche, oure lord Treuthe hem graunteth
Pardoun perpetuel, riht as Peres the plouhman.   60

    Beggares and biddares beth nat in þat bulle
Bote the sugestioun be soth þat shapeth hym to begge.

---

38. deynge] X doynge; U dying
46. þat U] X *om*
48. here U] X he
57. nedeþ I] XU nedede

---

44. *lest*, i.e. fewest years' remission (see 22, above).
45. *pre manibus*: 'in advance'. See III 299.
51. *wis men and witty*. Cf. IV 27, 31, etc.
54. Lawyers were exhorted to give legal advice free to the poor.
56. The four elements were often adapted to suit a context, here by the substitution of *wit* for earth, signifying the five wits or senses (I 15) or perhaps *kynde witt* (Prol. 141), gifts of God which all men should enjoy in common.
61. Having dealt with the estates within society – knights, bishops, merchants, lawyers, labourers – L turns now to beggars (see Prol. 41n). Lines 70–161 are new in C, a prolonged meditation upon the opposed injunctions of Cato (69, below) and the gospels (VIII 210n) in relation to almsgiving (see I 171n). Having spoken earlier of a discriminating charity (VIII 210, 288), L now makes it clear that charity must positively seek out the truly needy (see 27, above) in order to fulfil the promise that God will provide (XV 250, XVII 8) whilst accepting the ban on beggary (162, below). Those who have must give so that those who have not need not ask (Wyclif, ed. Arnold, iii.411).

For he þat begeth or biddeth, but yf he haue nede,
He is fals and faytour and defraudeth the nedy
And also gileth hym þat gyueth and taketh agayne his wille.   65
For he þat gyueth for goddes loue wolde nat gyue, his thankes,
Bote ther he wiste were wel grete nede
And most merytorie to men þat he ȝeueth fore.
Catoun acordeth therwith: *Cui des, videto.*

   Woet no man, as y wene, who is worthy to haue;   70
Ac þat most neden aren oure neyhebores, and we nyme gode hede,
As prisones in puttes and pore folk in cotes,
Charged with childrene and chief lordes rente;
Þat they with spynnyng may spare, spenen hit on hous-huyre,
Bothe in mylke and in mele, to make with papelotes   75
To aglotye with here gurles that greden aftur fode.
And hemsulue also soffre muche hunger,
And wo in wynter-tymes, and wakynge on nyhtes
To rise to þe reule to rokke þe cradel,
Bothe to carde and to kembe, to cloute and to wasche,   80
And to rybbe and to rele, rusches to pylie,
That reuthe is to rede or in ryme shewe
The wo of this wommen þat wonyeth in cotes;
And of monye oþer men þat moche wo soffren,
Bothe afyngred and afurste, to turne þe fayre outward,   85
And ben abasched for to begge and wollen nat he aknowe   f.40ᵇ

---

63. he² I] XU they
68. to U] X and to
71–9. *mislineated in* X

---

69. 'Consider to whom you should give' (*Disticha Catonis*, Sententia 17: see IV 17n).
71. L stresses the immediate corporal works of mercy (VII 21n) due to one's neighbour (Luke 10:27), perhaps contrasting them with more ostentatious acts of charity.
74. *Þat they with spynnyng may spare*: 'What they can put aside from the money they earn spinning'. These lines (73–83) describe the poverty of widows left to bring up a family by themselves. It is important to recognize that all the 'deserving poor' of whom L speaks have fallen into poverty by mischance (see 175–82, below). There is no sense of the existence of a mass of rural poor like the urban poor of the industrial era (Tierney, 1959, 64).
75. *with*, as in the next line, would go after the direct object in MnE.
81. *rybbe*: scrape flax with a flat iron tool, to remove particles of core. *relye*: reel, wind yarn on to a reel. *rusches to pylie*: peel rushes, so as to make rushlights from the pith.
85. *afyngred and afurste*: from *of-hyngred, of-þurste*, with the intensive prefix *of–* (cf. Prol. 7n) obscured. *to turne þe fayre outward*: 'in order to keep up a respectable appearance (*or* a bold front)'.
86. *wollen nat be aknowe*: 'do not wish (it) to be known'.

What hem nedeth at here neyhebores at noon and at eue.
   This I woet witterly, as þe world techeth,
What other byhoueth þat hath many childrene
And hath no catel but his craft to clothe hem and to fede,   90
And fele to fonge þer-to, and fewe panes taketh.
There is payne and peny-ale as for a pytaunce ytake,
And colde flesche and fische as venisoun were bake.
Fridays and fastyng-days a ferthing-worth of moskeles
Were a feste with suche folk, or so fele cockes.   95
These are almusse, to helpe þat han suche charges
And to conforte such coterelles and crokede men and blynde.
   Ac beggares with bagges, þe whiche brewhous ben here churches,
But they be blynde or tobroke or elles be syke,
Thouh he falle for defaute þat fayteth for his lyflode,   100
Reche ʒe neuere, ʒe riche, thouh suche lollares sterue.
For alle þat haen here hele and here ye-syhte
And lymes to labory with, and lollares lyf vsen,
Lyuen aʒen goddes lawe and þe lore of holi churche.
   And ʒut ar ther oþere beggares, in hele, as hit semeth,   105

87. hem I] XU hym. nedeth I] XU nedede
88. I U] X he
90. hem I] XU hym

87. *at noon and at eue*, i.e. at every meal.
92. *pytaunce*: originally, in religious houses, an additional allowance of food (granted out of 'pity') on special occasions. Here, 'a special treat'.
93. *as venisoun were bake*: 'like roast venison'.
98. *beggares with bagges*, as opposed to true beggars, who beg only for their daily needs. See V 52n. *þe whiche . . . here*: 'whose'.
101. *lollares*. See V 2n.
105. L introduces here a consideration of beggars who are able-bodied but feeble-minded. Since they are God's creatures they must be serving God's purposes (115): they are, in fact, his secret apostles (118), capable of uttering hidden wisdom in their foolishness (114). L draws on a number of biblical texts here, particularly Christ's exhortation of his disciples to a divine 'carelessness' of worldly considerations (Luke 9:1–5, 10:1–12) such as is characteristic of the 'lunatyk lollares'; and Paul's epistles to the Corinthians, which stress that men of Christ must be fools to the world ('We are fools for Christ's sake', 1 Cor. 4:10; cf. 1:18–31, 3:18 as below, 127a, and see XXII 61). But L extends Paul's metaphor in a striking way, suggesting that 'real' fools and madmen have a special access to God and God's truth – a common belief in the Middle Ages (see P. B. R. Doob, *Nebuchadnezzar's Children: Conventions of Madness in ME Literature*, New Haven, 1974, 31) and an important theme in *King Lear* – and hints (125) that they are God's agents in engendering charity (cf. Wordsworth's *The Old Cumberland Beggar*). 'I have often applied to idiots, in my own mind,' says Wordsworth elsewhere, 'that sublime expression of Scripture, that *their life is hidden with God*' (*Early Letters*, ed. E. de Selincourt, Oxford, 1935, 296–7). For Wordsworth's biblical text, see Col. 3:3.

Ac hem wanteth wyt, men and women bothe,
The whiche aren lunatyk lollares and lepares aboute,
And madden as þe mone sit, more other lasse.
Careth they for no colde ne counteth of non hete
And aren meuynge aftur þe mone; moneyeles þey walke,   110
With a good will, witteles, mony wyde contreyes,
Riht as Peter dede and Poul, saue þat þey preche nat
Ne none muracles maken – ac many tymes hem happeth
To profecye of þe peple, pleyinge, as hit were.
And to oure syhte, as hit semeth, seth god hath þe myhte   115
To ȝeue vch a wyht wyt, welthe, and his hele,
And suffreth suche go so, it semeth, to myn inwyt,
Hit aren as his postles, suche peple, or as his priue disciples.
For a sent hem forth seluerles in a somur garnement
Withoute bagge and bred, as þe book telleth: 120
   Quando misi vos sine pane et pera.
Barfoot and bredles, beggeth they of no man.   f.41ᵃ
And thauh a mete with the mayre ameddes þe strete,
A reuerenseth hym ryht nauht, no rather then another.
   Neminem salutaueritis per viam.
Suche manere men, Matheu vs techeth,
We sholde haue hem to house and helpe hem when they come.   125
   Et egenos vagosque induc in domum tuam.
For hit aren merye-mouthed men, munstrals of heuene,
And godes boys, bourdyors, as the book telleth.

114. pleyinge U] X ple(n)inge
125a. *vagosque* I] XU vagos

107. *lepares aboute.* It may be that L is here echoing, for purposes of paradox (see below,
    127n, 136n), phrases such as *lepers over londe, ronners over contreys* (see Prol. 72n and
    Owst, 1933, 373) in which orthodox preachers condemned pardoners and itiner-
    ant priests.
108. *And madden as þe mone sit*: 'and (who) grow mad according to the phases of the
    moon' (the original derivation of *lunatyk*).
120a. 'When I sent you forth without bread or bag' (adapting Luke 22:35, alluding to
    Luke 9:3).
122–3. A characteristic piece of behaviour that L associates with himself in B XV 5.
    Like other classes of society with which L shows a particular preoccupation (Prol.
    35n), the *lunatyk lollares* contain features of self-portraiture (compare 105 with V 7,
    10; 111 with XV 1; 139 with V 52).
123a. 'Salute no one on the road' (Luke 10:4).
125a. 'And bring the homeless and the poor into your house' (Isa. 58:7, said in the
    grace for lent: see III 339n). The reference to Matthew is generally to 25:31–46.
127. *boys, bourdyors*: words of normally pejorative connotation, but Langland, prompted
    by *munstrals of heuene*, is already in process of recalling the audacious image of poor
    beggars as God's minstrels (VII 100), who should be welcome at lords' feasts.

Si quis videtur sapiens, fiet stultus vt sit sapiens.
And alle manere munstrals, me woet wel þe sothe,
To vnderfongen hem fayre byfalleth for þe ryche,
For þe lordes loue or þe ladyes þat they with longen.
Me suffreth al þat suche sayen and in solace taketh,   130
And ȝut more to suche men me doth ar they passe;
Men gyueth hem giftes and gold for grete lordes sake.
   Ryht so, ȝe ryche, ȝut rather ȝe sholde
Welcomen and worschipen and with ȝoure goed helpen   135
Godes munstrals and his mesagers and his mery bordiours,
The whiche arn lunatyk loreles and lepares aboute,
For vnder godes secret seal here synnes ben keuered.
   For they bereth none bagges ne boteles vnder clokes,
The whiche is lollarne lyf and lewede ermytes,   140
Þat loken louhliche to lache men almesse,
In hope to sitte at euen by þe hote coles,
Vnlouke his legges abrood or ligge at his ese,
Reste hym and roste him and his rug turne,
Drynke druie and depe and drawe hym thenne to bedde,   145
And whenne hym lyketh and luste, his leue is to ryse,
And when he is rysen, rometh out and riȝt wel aspyeth
Where he may rathest haue a repaest or a ronde of bacoun,
Suluer or sode mete and sum tyme bothe,
Loef oþer half-loef other a lompe of chese;   150
And caryeth hit hoem to his cote and cast hym to lyuene
In idelnesse and in ese and by otheres trauayle.

133. gyueth U] X syneth
137. arn U] X *om*
141. Þat U] X *om*
144. him U] X *om*
151. caryeth U] X cayreth

127a. 'If anyone thinks he is wise, let him become a fool that he may be wise' (1 Cor. 3:18).

136. *Godes munstrals.* Cf. *joculatores Domini*, a name taken by the early followers of St Francis, for their use of song, and their carelessness of the world. *mesagers*, like minstrels and *bordiours* (127, above, and VII 108), had a bad reputation (see II 237), but L is here engaged in establishing a vocabulary of spiritual paradox on the model of Paul's 'fools' (105n, above). See also XIII 32ff. This type of ironical usage is extended to 'lolleris and loselis' in a contemporary treatise by Sir John Clanvowe, *The Two Ways* (ed. V. J. Scattergood, Cambridge, 1975, 512), where it is said that such names are given by the world to meek folk of simple life. Clanvowe was a Lollard sympathizer.

138. They have a special dispensation from God for their sins.

140. *lollarne*, gen.pl. The term is used here in its normal, not its paradoxical (136, above) sense, as L returns to the castigation of 'sturdy beggars'.

And what freke on this folde fiscuth aboute
With a bagge at his bak a begyneld wyse,   f.41^b
And can eny craft in caes he wolde hit vse,   155
Thorw which craft a couthe come to bred and to ale
And ouer-more to an hater to hele with his bonis,
And lyueth lyke a lollare, goddes lawe hym dampneth.
'Forthy lollares þat lyuen in sleuthe and ouer-land strikares
Buth nat in this bulle,' quod Peres, 'til they ben amended,   160
Ne no beggare that beggeth, but yf they haue nede.'
The boek banneth beggarie and blameth hit in this manere:
   Iunior fui, etenim senui. Et alibi: Infirmata est virtus
      mea in paupertate.
Hit nedeth nat nouthe anoon for to preche
And lere this lewede men what þis Latyn meneth,
For hit blameth all beggarie, be ʒe ful certayn.   165
For they lyue in no loue, ne no lawe holden,
Ne weddeth none wymmen þat they with deleth;
Bringeth forth bastardus, beggares of kynde,
Or þe bak or som bon þey breke of here children
And goen and fayten with here fauntes for eueremore aftur.   170
Ther aren mo mysshape amonges suche beggares
Then of many oþere men þat on this molde walken.
And tho þat lyueth thus here lyf, leue ʒe non other,
Þai haue no part of pardoun, ne of preyeres ne of penaunces.
Ac olde and hore, þat helples ben and nedy,   175
And wymmen with childe þat worche ne mowe,
Blynde and bedredne and broken in here membres,
And alle pore pacient, apayed of goddes sonde,

---

157. an hater I] XU han after
162a. *in* P] XU *om*

---

154. *a begyneld wyse*: 'in the manner of a beggar'.
159. *ouer-land strikares*. Compare 107n, above, and also the phrase 'staff-strikers' used in the Commons petition against vagrants in 1376 (VIII 149n, 210n). This brief intervention of Peres as interpreter is appropriate enough to him, but not easily reconcilable with the authorial exposition of the whole of the rest of the pardon, and with the suggestion (283, below) that Peres cannot read the Latin document. Skeat attributes 159–281 to Peres.
162–85. C returns here briefly to the matter of B.
162a. 'I have been young, and now am old (and I have not seen the righteous forsaken nor his children begging bread)' (Ps. 36:25). And elsewhere: 'My strength is weakened through poverty' (Ps. 30:11). The latter text, added in C, refers to 'beggary' rather than begging, and seems equivocal in the context. It is explained later how the poor can live (on God's alms) without begging (XVII 8). Cf. XIII 101.
168. *beggares of kynde*: 'beggars by nature, born beggars'.
178. *apayed of goddes sonde*: 'content with what God has sent them'.

As mesels and mendenantes, men yfalle in meschief,
As prisones and pilgrimes and parauntur men yrobbed   180
Or bylowe thorw luther men and lost here catel after,
Or thorw fuyr or thorw floed yfalle into pouerte,
That taketh thise meschiefes mekeliche and myldeliche at herte,
For loue of here lowe hertes oure lord hath hem ygraunted
Here penaunce and here purgatorye vppon this puyre erthe   185
And pardon with the plouhman *a pena et a culpa.*
     And alle holy eremytes haue shal þe same.
Ac ermytes þat inhabiten by the heye weye
And in borwes among brewesteres, and beggen in churches –   f.42ᵃ
Al þat holy ermytes hatede and despisede,   190
As rychesses and reuerences and ryche menne almesse,
Thise lollares, lache-draweres, lewede ermytes
Coueyten þe contrarye, for as coterelles they libbeth.
For hit ben but boyes, bollares at þe ale,
Noyther of lynage ne of lettrure, ne lyf-holy as ermytes   195
That wonede whilom in wodes with beres and lyons.
Summe hadde lyflode of his lynage and of no lyf elles
And summe lyuede by here lettrure and labour of here handes
And somme hadde foreynes to frendes þat hem fode sente
And briddes brouhte somme bred þat they by lyuede.   200
Althey holy ermytes were of heye kynne,
Forsoken lond and lordschipe and alle lykynges of body.
     Ac thise ermytes þat edifien thus by the heye weye
Whilen were werkmen, webbes and taylours
And carteres knaues and clerkes withouten grace,   205
Holden ful hungry hous and hadde muche defaute,

---

201. Althey X] U al þe; I and þey; P alle these

179. *men yfalle in meschief.* See VIII 229–34, and above, 74n.
185. The idea that poverty and other mischiefs, patiently borne, are a form of earthly purgatory is alluded to further in XVI 17 (cf. XI 298). The Wife of Bath thinks that being married to her is likewise a form of earthly purgatory (*CT* III. 489).
186. *a pena et a culpa.* See above, 22n.
187. From here to line 281 is another long addition in C, a witty and vigorous study of hermits, true and false. Like minstrels and beggars, hermits are a persistent preoccupation for Langland (see Prol. 2n, 35n).
188–9. These hermits will (presumably) not receive the pardon: the sentence begun here is not completed.
190. *holy ermytes.* References throughout this passage are to the Desert Fathers, whose lives were favourite reading in the Middle Ages. See XVII 6ff.
202. *Forsoken:* '(they) forsook.
203. Hermits often set themselves up beside the high road or at bridges, ostensibly to carry out the charitable work of maintenance, but often, L suggests, for the purpose of living on the contributions to the upkeep of roads and bridges made by pious layfolk in their alms and bequests (31–2, above).

Long labour and litte wynnynge, and at the laste they aspyde
That faytede in frere clothinge hadde fatte chekes.
Forthy lefte they here labour, thise lewede knaues,
And clothed hem in copes, clerkes as hit were,   210
Or oen of som ordre or elles a profete,
Aȝen þe lawe of Leuey, yf Latyn be trewe:
>   *Non licet uobis legem voluntati, set voluntatem*
>   *coniungere legi.*
Kyndeliche, by Crist, ben suche ycald 'lollares',
As by þe Engelisch of oure eldres, of olde mennes techynge.
He þat lolleth is lame or his leg out of ioynte   215
Or ymaymed in som membre, for to meschief hit souneth.
Rihte so sothly such manere ermytes
Lollen aȝen þe byleue and þe lawe of holy churche.
     For holy churche hoteth alle manere peple
Vnder obedience to be and buxum to þe lawe;   220
Furste, religious of religioun a reule to holde
And vnder obedience be by dayes and by nyhtes;
Lewede men to labory, lordes to honte
In frithes and in forestes for fox and other bestes   f.42ᵇ
That in wilde wodes been or in waste places,   225
As wolues þat woryeth men, wymmen and childrene;
And vppon Sonendayes to cese, goddes seruice to here,
Bothe matynes and masse, and aftir mete in churches
To heren here euensong euery man ouhte.
Thus hit bylongeth for lordes, for lered and for lewed,   230
Vcche haly day to here holly þe seruise,
Vigilies and fastyng-days forthermore to knowe

---

212. of Leuey I] XUP he lyueth

208. *That*: 'that those who'.
211. *a profete*. Used satirically: see Matt. 7:15.
212. *of Leuey*: 'of Levi', i.e. according to the Judaic law appertaining to the priesthood, a good sense in the context, even though the Latin that follows is not to be found in Leviticus nor elsewhere in the bible.
212a. 'It is not lawful for you to make the law conform to your will, but (rather for you to conform) your will to the law'. There is something similar in the *De Contemptu Mundi*, ii.4 (*PL* 217:718), of Innocent III (Alford 398).
216. *to meschief hit souneth*: 'it (*sc.* lolling) implies some accident or injury'.
218. *Lollen* plays on the meanings 'lounge, slump awkwardly' and 'offend, being *lollares*'. The crucial question, developed in the following analysis of the three estates of society (religious, *lewede men* and *lordes*, is one of obedience to the law of Holy Church (i.e. Truth, I 81). False hermits and *lollares* acknowledge no rule of life (cf. V 90–91), and are therefore inobedient in their very life.
223. Cf. V 65–6, VIII 28.

And fulfille tho fastynges, but infirmite hit made,
Pouerte or oþer penaunces as pilgrimages and trauayles.
Vnder this obedience ar we vchone   235
And ho-so breketh this, be wel waer, but yf he repente,
Amenden hym and mercy aske and mekeliche hym shryue,
Y drede me, and he dey, hit worth for o dedly synne
Acounted byfore Crist, but Consience excuse hym.
   Loke now where this lollares and lewede ermites,   240
Yf they breke þis obedience þat beth so fer fram chirche.
Where se we hem on Sonendayes the seruise to here,
As matynes by þe morwe? Til masse bygynne,
Or Sonendayes at euensong, se we wel fewe,
Or labory for here lyflode as þe lawe wolde.   245
Ac aboute mydday at mele-tyme y mette with hem ofte,
Come in his cope as he a clerk were;
A bacheler or a bew-pere beste hym bysemede,
And for þe cloth þat keuereth hym ykald he is a frere,
Wascheth and wypeth and with þe furste sitteth.   250
Ac while a wrouhte in þe world and wan his mete with treuthe
He sat at þe syde benche and at þe seconde table.
Cam no wyn in his wombe thorw þe woke longe
Ne no blanked on his bed ne whyte bred byfore hym.
   The cause of al this caytiftee cometh of many bischopes   255
That soffreth suche sottes and oþere synnes regne.
Certes, ho-so durste sygge hit, Simon *quasi dormit*;
Vigilare were fayrere, for thow haste a greet charge.
For many wakere wolues ar wroken into thy foldes;

---

239. Crist U] X god
247. Come I] XU Somme
249. for U] X forth

---

233. *but infirmite hit made*: 'unless illness brought it about (otherwise)'.
240. *where*: 'whether' (possibly also in 242).
248. *bew-pere*, i.e. *beau pere*, 'good father', a term of address for a priest. Cf. XX 240.
255–81. Bishops are the direct mediators to the people of the spiritual authority and law of the church, and the representatives of Christ on earth through the apostolic succession. L treats them throughout with comparative restraint (e.g. Prol. 78), but here lays on them a heavy and direct responsibility for the spiritual guidance of their flocks, and in particular for controlling the wolves (e.g. false hermits, see Prol. 2n) who prey upon them.
257–8. 'Simon is as it were asleep; to watch were better'. L here adapts the words of Christ to Peter (whom he calls Simon) in the garden of Gethsemane: *Simon, dormis? non potuisti una hora vigilare?* 'Simon, are you asleep? Could you not watch one hour?' (Mark 14:37). Simon is the type-name for a bishop, since bishops are successors of Simon Peter, founder of the Church and first bishop of Rome. The injunction *vigilare* is applied specifically to bishops in Wyclif, ed. Arnold, i.261.

Thy berkeres aren as blynde that bringeth forth thy lombren,   260 f.43[a]
Dispergentur oues, þe dogge dar nat berke.
The tarre is vntydy þat to þe shep bylongeth;
Here salue is of *supersedeas* in sumnoures boxes.
Thy shep ben ner al shabbede, the wolf shyt þe wolle.
Sub molli pastore lupus lanam cacat, et grex   265
In-custoditus dilaceratur eo.
How, herde! where is thyn hound and thyn hardy herte
For to go worye þe wolf that the wolle fouleth?
Y leue for thy lacchesse thow lesest many wetheres

264. shyt þe wolle] XU shyt wolle; I bischit þe folde
265–6. *lupus . . . eo* P] XUI *om*
267. hound U] X hond
268. fouleth U] X foureth

260. *Thy berkeres aren as blynde* (as: 'as if'). L alludes here, and more clearly in the next line (*þe dogge dar nat berke*), to the 'dumb dogs that cannot bark' of Isa. 56:10 (see B X 293, and Kellogg, 1960), conflating them with those they serve, the blind and negligent watchmen whose responsibility it is to protect the flocks from devouring beasts (i.e. the spiritual leaders who should guide Israel in the keeping of the covenant). Important supporting texts for the present theme are the image of false prophets as wolves in sheep's clothing (Matt. 7:15, and Prol. 2n) and of Christ as the good shepherd (John 10:7–18). Cf. Parson's Tale, *CT* X. 721, 775, 792; Wyclif, ed. Arnold, i.139, 238, iii.37; ed. Matthew, 438.

261. *Dispergentur oues*: 'the sheep will be scattered', from a prophecy of the purification of Israel in fulfilment of God's will (Zech. 13:7, cf. 11:4–17), as used by Christ to foretell the scattering of the disciples after the arrest in the garden of Gethsemane (Matt. 26:31, Mk. 14:27). The use of the phrase here, quite out of context, is an example of L's readiness to catch up biblical texts in unglossed readings for his own immediate purposes.

262–3. Tar was used in the treatment of sores ('scab') in sheep; shepherds kept a box of it handy. But today's shepherds use a substitute made from *supersedeas* (i.e. letting people off for a consideration, II 187n), which is provided by summoners (II 59n). The allegorical meaning of sheep-scab and shepherds' tar is obvious from the familiar imagery of pastors and their flocks. The contrast of harsh antiseptic treatment (i.e. penance) and smooth unguents is developed in XXII 358–72.

265–6. 'Under a weak and negligent shepherd the wolf befouls the wool, and the unguarded flock is torn to pieces by him'. This saying, with *capit* (variant *rapit*), 'seizes', for *cacat*, is proverbial (Walther 30542, Alford 398), appears in the *Liber Parabolarum* of Alan of Lille (*PL* 210:581, cf. XX 453), and is alluded to by Chaucer in the Physician's Tale (*CT* VI. 101). The form *cacat* is appropriate enough for the allegorical reading, since 'false prophets' are the cause of uncleanness among the faithful (cf. Chaucer's *shiten shepherde* and *clene sheep* in the description of the Poor Parson, *CT* I. 504), but it has no literal sense.

And many a fayre flees falsliche is ywasche.   270
When thy lord loketh to haue allouaunce of his bestes
And of þe moneye thow haddest therwith his mebles to saue
And þe wolle worth weye, wo is the thenne!
Redde racionem villicacionis or in arrerage fall.
Thyn huyre, herde, as y hope, hath nat to quyte thy dette   275
Ther as mede ne mercy may nat a myte availle,
But 'haue this for þat tho þat thow toke
Mercy for mede, and my lawe breke.'
Loke now for thy lacchesse what lawe wol the graunte,
Purgatorye for thy paie ore perpetuel helle,   280
For shal no pardon preye for 30w there ne no princes lettres.

   'Peres,' quod a prest tho, 'thy pardon moste y rede,
For y can construe vch a word and kennen hit the an Englische.'
And Peres at his preyre the pardon vnfoldeth
And y byhynde hem bothe byheld alle þe bulle   285
In two lynes as hit lay and nat a lettre more,
And was ywryte ryhte thus in witnesse of Treuthe:

---

272 saue U] X haue

270. Presumably an allusion to the image of sheep-washing as the purification of the soul of the faithful in the love of Christ (Cant. 4:2).

271–2. 'When your master looks to have the profit on the fleeces (i.e. souls) and on the investment that he made in employing you to look after his property . . .' The reference is to the Last Judgment.

274. 'Render the account of (your) stewardship' (Luke 16:2, the beginning of the parable of the unjust steward, cf. VIII 235a). This was the text of a famous sermon preached by Thomas Wimbledon about 1388 (III 477n). See *Wimbledon's Sermon*, ed. I. K. Knight, Duquesne Studies, Philological Series 9 (Pittsburgh, 1967).

275. *hope*: 'think, expect'. *hath nat*: 'will not be enough'.

277. *for þat tho þat*: 'in return for that, that is, the occasion when (you offered mercy for money)'. The shepherd (bishop) will be brought to strict account, when neither *mede* (bribes, such as he received) nor *mercy* (forgiveness, such as he granted) will be of any use.

281. The mention of the inefficacy of pardons provides a transition back to the matter of B and an anticipation of the next stage of the action.

283. The suggestion is that Peres does not understand the Latin of the document. On the other hand, he clearly understands the spirit and purport of the document (see 159n, above), what Truth intends. Thus the conflict between the priest and Peres might well be seen to dramatize a contrast between the literal and the spiritual; Peres's impatience is with the 'letter that killeth' (2 Cor. 3:6).

285. An unexpected intervention in his own dream by the dreamer. *þe bulle*: the pardon is here conceived of as issuing from the pope (see 27n, above).

Qui bona egerunt ibunt in vitam eternam;
Qui vero mala in ignem eternum.
'Peter!' quod the prest tho, 'y kan no pardoun fynde,   290
Bote "Dowel and haue wel and god shal haue thy soule
And do yuele and haue euele and hope thow non oþere
Bote he þat euele lyueth euele shal ende." '
  The prest thus and Perkyn of þe pardon iangelede
And y thorw here wordes awoke and waytede aboute   295
And seyh the sonne in the southe sitte þat tyme.
Meteles and moneyles on Maluerne hulles   f.43ᵇ

289. *eternum* U] X eternam
291. god U] X *om*
294. and U] X and the
296. southe U] X souhe

288–9. 'They that have done good shall go into life everlasting; and they that have done evil into everlasting fire'. From near the end of the Athanasian creed (VII 236n). Cf. also Matt. 25:46, John 5:29.

291. *Bote*: 'but only'. The priest is right in recognizing that it is not a 'pardon' in the usual sense. On the other hand, he fails to realize that the promise of redemption, which makes the first clause (*Qui bona*) possible, is itself a form of pardon, that which was bought on Calvary, and one which would be familiar to a 14th c. audience, specifically in the form of a legal document conferring the benefits of the Redemption, in the 'Charter of Christ' (see II 378a, and Woolf, 1969, 56–60); Truth tells no lies, neither here, nor through Holy Church (I 129–35), nor in the later exposition of Peres's pardon (XXI 197–8, and see 3n, above). Peres, on the other hand, had expected rather more of the pardon than it contained. He seems to have interpreted the promise of redemption as if it were the gift of redemption, as if, like a papal or royal pardon, it constituted in itself the act of forgiveness. A famous episode in B (following the line corresponding to 293, below), where Peres tears the pardon in anger and frustration, is omitted in C, probably because the scenario, though highly dramatic, is not logical: Peres, the servant of Truth, can not tear Truth's pardon. (For discussion of the episode in B, see Coghill, 1944, 316–20; J. Lawlor, in *MLR* 45, 1950, 449–58; R. W. Frank, in *Spec.* 26, 1951, 317–31; Woolf, 1969; Kirk, 1972, 80–100. It must be said that those scholars who lay stress on the tearing of the pardon as itself a significant allegorical act must perforce ignore the evidence of C.) The conclusion, though, is the same in B and C: Peres retires from active contact with the community, and the dreamer is left to wonder on his dreams, and to make sense of the pardon by beginning his search for the whole truth of *dowel*. This he will find in the refounding and reforming of the inner life of the individual, rather than of society as in the *Visio*. But this process of reform is not detached from the social and ecclesiastical context in which the individual must live (see XXI 228). There is never that concentration on the inner life of contemplation which we find in the writing of the mystics.

294. Here C picks up B again, having omitted the argument of the priest and Peres (B VII 119–43), to which this line is evidently more apt.

297. *Maluerne hulles*. See Prol. 6n.

Musyng on this meteles a myle way y ȝede.
Mony tyme this meteles hath maked me to studie
Of that y seyh slepynge, if hit so be myhte,
And of Peres the plouhman fol pencyf in herte   300
And which a pardoun Peres hadde the peple to glade
And how þe prest impugnede hit thorw two propre wordes.

   Ac men setteth nat by sowngewarie for me seth hit often fayle;
Caton counteth hit at nauht and canonistres at lasse.   305
Ac for þe boek-bible bereth witnesse
How Danyel deuynede and vndede þe dremes of kynges,
Of Nabugodonasor þat no pere hadde,
And sethen aftur his sones, and sayde hem what they thouhte. –
And Ioseph mette merueilously how þe mone and þe sonne   310
And the eleuene sterres haylsede hym alle,
And thenne Iacob iuged Iosepes sweuene:
'Beau fitz,' quod the fadur, 'for defaute we shal,
Y mysulue and my sones, seche the for nede.'
Hit biful as his fadur saide in Farao his tyme   315
That Ioseph was iustice, Egipte to saue;
His eleuene bretherne hym for nede souhte
And his fadur Israel and also his dame. –

318. Israel] XUI Isaak; P Iacob

302. *which a*: 'what sort of'.
304. *sowngewarie*: the interpretation of dreams. Medieval writers often discuss dreams, especially when writing within the dream-form (e.g. *Roman de la Rose* 1–20), and it is a favourite subject with Chaucer, as in the *House of Fame* 1–110, *Parlement of Foules* 99–108, *Troilus* v.358–85, and the Nun's Priest's Tale (*CT* VII. 2896–3156). The usual conclusion, much influenced by the commentary of Macrobius on the *Dream of Scipio*, attributed to Cicero (trans. W. H. Stahl, New York, 1952), is that there are different kinds of dream, with different values for interpretation, ranging from divinely-inspired prophetic visions down to fantasies due to digestive disorder. Popular dream-lore was simpler, especially in so far as if derived from a widely-known manual called the 'Pseudo-Daniel) (a version in MS Harley 2253 is printed by M. Foerster in *Archiv* 127, 1911, 36). L's discussion is dominated by biblical examples of the veracity of dreams, which are also distinguished from ordinary dreams in *Handlyng Synne* 379–478.
305. *Somnia ne cures*, 'Take no heed of dreams' (*Disticha Catonis* ii.31: see IV 17n). See Nun's Priest's Tale, *CT* VII. 2940, 2971–7.
309. *his sones*: 'his son's'. Daniel interprets the dreams of Nebuchadnezzar in Dan. 2, 4, and the writing on the wall to Belshazzar (Nebuchadnezzar's son) in Dan. 5.
310. Gen. 37:9.
313–14. Cf. Gen. 37:10. L anticipates in Jacob's answer the fulfilment of the dream in Gen. 42–7. L makes no use, unexpectedly, of Pharaoh's dreams (Gen. 41).
318. *Israel*. The mistake of MSS XU (Isaac was Jacob's father) provides the clue to the correct reading. Israel was the name given to Jacob in Gen. 32:28, and it is used particularly in the account of the migration into Egypt (Gen. 45–7).

Al this maketh me on meteles to studie
And how þe prest preuede no pardon to Dowel   320
And demede þat Dowel indulgences passeth,
Bionales and trionales and bisshopes lettres.
For ho-so doth wel here at þe day of dome
Worth fayre vnderfonge byfore god þat tyme.
So Dowel passeth pardoun and pilgrimages to Rome.   325
Ʒut hath þe pope power pardoun to graunte
To peple withouten penaunce to passe into ioye,
As lettrede men vs lereth and lawe of holi churche:
    Quodcumque ligaueris super terram erit ligatum et in celis.
And so y leue lely, lord forbede elles,
That pardoun and penaunces and preyere don saue   330
Soules þat haue syneged seuene sythes dedly.
Ac to truste vp this trionales, treuly me thynketh   f.44ᵃ
Hit is nat so syker for þe soule, certes, as ys Dowel.
   Forthy y rede ȝow renkes þat riche ben on this erthe,
Vp truste of ȝoure tresor trionales to haue,   335
Be ȝe neuere þe baldere to breke þe ten hestes;
And nameliche ȝe maistres, mayres and iuges,
That haen the welthe of this world and wise men ben holde

---

333. ys U] X y
337. nameliche U] X manliche

321. *And demede*: 'and so I concluded'. *indulgences*. See Prol. 66n.
322. *Bionales and trionales* are arrangements to say masses for the soul of the beneficiary over a period of, respectively, two and three years, with the aim of speeding his passage through purgatory. *bisshopes lettres*, the letters of authorization for pardoners (Prol. 66n).
325. Cf. XVI 36–40.
326–33. L faces a familiar difficulty. It is not that pardons, etc., are false or even inefficacious; but they are less effective (since at best they only remit punishment in purgatory for those souls that are already saved) than truly striving to live the good Christian life according to God's law (342–3, 351, 353), and the rich, especially, would do well to remember this (334–9). 'Langland's fear, as so often, is that the external form or institution – even though it is acceptable in itself – may come to usurp the place of the inner spiritual reality' (Burrow, 1965, 260).
328a. 'Whatever you bind on earth shall be bound in heaven (and whatever you loose on earth shall be loosed in heaven)' (Matt. 16:19). This is the passage in the bible where Christ names Peter as the rock on which the Church will be built, and commits to him the keys of the kingdom of heaven. It is the fundamental authority for the Church's assumption of power to excommunicate and absolve; the efficacy of pardons, which all derive from the pope, is derived from the first delegation of power to Peter. See 3n, above, Prol. 129n, XXI 189. Wyclif denies all such power (ed. Arnold, iii.257, 362, 459).
331. *seuene sythes*. See X 21.
335. *Vp truste*: 'in trust', i.e. having trust.

To purchace 30w pardoun and the popes bulles.
At þe dredful dome when dede shullen ryse   340
And comen alle bifore Crist acountes to 3elde,
How we ladde oure lyf here and his lawes kepte
And how we dede day be day the doem wol reherce.
A pouhe-ful of pardon there, ne prouinciales lettres,
Thow we be founden in the fraternite of alle fyue ordres   345
And haue indulgences doublefold, but Dowel vs helpe
Y sette nat by pardon a pese ne nat a pye-hele!
    Forthy y consayle alle cristene to crye god mercy,
And Marie his moder be oure mene to hym
That god gyue vs grace here ar we go hennes   350
Suche werkes to worche the while we ben here
That aftur oure deth-day Dowel reherce
At þe day of dome we dede as he tauhte. Amen.

Explicit visio Willelmi .W. de Petro le plouhman
Et hic incipit visio eiusdem de Dowel

---

344. *prouinciales,* adj.pl. (see Prol. 132n). The letters of fraternity spoken of in the next line (cf. III 67, VII 27) would be granted under the authority of the 'provincial' of the order, responsible for the administration of a province containing a number of houses of the order.

345. *fyue ordres.* See VIII 191.

347. *pye-hele*: the pastry base of a pie (the part no-one values much).

352. *Dowel* has already begun the bewildering process of spiritual metamorphosis that occupies the following passūs. Dowel is here the record of well-doing (as in 346 above) but also the teacher of well-doing and the judge at Doomsday, i.e. Christ (alluding to Matt. 25:31–46).

Passus X

The Search for Dowel:
the Discourse of the Friars, Thought and Wit

Thus yrobed in russet y romede aboute
Alle a somur seson for to seke Dowel,
And fraynede ful ofte of folke þat y mette
Yf eny wiht wiste where Dowel was at ynne,
And what man a myhte be of mony men y askede.   5
 Was neuere wihte in þis worlde þat me wisse couthe
Where this leode longed, lasse ne more,
Til hit biful on a Fryday two freres y mette,

---

7. this leode B] XUI this; P that he
8. on a U] X in

1–2. Quite deliberately, here and in the dream-prologue (61–7, below), L echoes the opening of the poem, thus preparing us for a pattern of meaning in the *Vita de Dowel*, etc., in which the events and the sequence of events in the *Visio* are echoed, but on a more deeply spiritual level and within a different context (see X 100, XI 161, etc. and Wells, 1929, 126–8). Thus it is not an aimless wandering now (cf. Prol. 4) but a journey with a purpose, to find Dowel. He is, to start with, awake (see V 1n).

2. *russet*: a coarse woollen cloth, reddish-brown in colour, commonly associated with hermits (cf. Prol. 3), but by the late 14th c. having some particular association with the itinerant preachers of Wyclif's persuasion (see Walsingham's *Historia*, ed. H. T. Riley, Rolls series 28, 1863–4, i.324, and M. Aston, 'Lollardy and Sedition 1381–1431', *Past and Present* 17, 1960, 13). The word appears in the A-text, and may conceivably have contributed to the association (cf. Prol. 140n); in later texts, L may have been not unwilling to allow the Lollard implications to stand as a temporary characterization of the dreamer (cf. V 2n, XIII 80n). For the dreamer's attire as symbolic of his spiritual state, see XX 1n, and for the contrast with Holy Church's *lynnene* garment (I 3), see Deut. 22:11: 'Thou shalt not wear a garment of woollen and linen mixed'.

4. *at ynne*: 'in lodging'.

8. *two freres*. Friars usually went about in pairs; after 50 years' service they 'made their jubilee' and were permitted to go about alone (see Summoner's Tale, *CT* III. 1862).

Maystres of þe Menores, men of gret witte.
Y haylsede hem hendly, as y hadde ylered,   10
And preyde hem, pur charite, ar they passede forthere
Yf they knewe eny contre oþer costes aboute
Wher þat Dowel dwelleth, 'Dere frendes, telleth me,   f.44^b
For ȝe ar men of this molde þat moste wyde walken
And knowen contrees and courtes and many kynne plases,   15
Bothe princes paleis and pore menne cotes,
And Dowel and Do-euele, where þei dwellen both.'
    'Sothly,' saide þe frere, 'a soiourneth with vs freres
And euere hath, as y hope, and euere wol hereaftur.'
    '*Contra*,' quod y as a clerk, and comsed to despute,   20
And saide sothly, '*Septies in die cadit iustus*,
Fallyng fro ioye, Iesu woet þe sothe!
"Seuene sithe," sayth þe boek, "synegeth day by day
The rihtfulluste reng þat regneth in erthe."
And ho-so synegeth,' y sayde, 'certes, he doth nat wel;   25
For ho-so synegeth, sicurly doth euele,
And Dowel and Do-euele may nat dwelle togyderes.
Ergo, he is nat alwey at hom amonges ȝow freres;
He is other-while elleswher to wisse the peple.'
    'Y shal sey þe, my sone,' sayde þe frere thenne,   30
'How seuene sithes þe sad man synegeth on þe day.

9. *þe Menores*: 'the Minors', i.e. the Friars Minors (Franciscans), from Lat. *fratres minores*, 'lesser brothers', a name taken by early followers of St Francis as a mark of humility. Franciscans were the great scholars and theologians of the 13th and 14th c., especially in England.
20. *Contra*: 'against', i.e. 'I dispute that', a term used in scholastic debate (see XIV 192n). The dreamer's presumption, in arguing 'as a clerk', does not augur well for his readiness to receive spiritual illumination, though the friar's remark is admittedly provoking.
21. 'The righteous man falls seven times a day (and rises again)' (Prov. 24:16, with *in die* for Vg. *enim*, as in *Prick of Conscience* 3432, where it is clearly explained that the reference of the saying is to venial sins only). The dreamer would have done well to look at the immediate context of his biblical quotation (cf. III 488n).
22. This line, added in C, is a parenthetic exclamation playing on the double meaning of *cadit*, 'falls' and 'sins'.
28. *Ergo*: 'therefore'. The dreamer's argument has the trappings of scholarly disputation, but it is of course specious.

By a forbisene,' quod þe frere, 'y shal the fayre shewe.
  Lat bryng a man in a boet amydde a brood water;
The wynde and þe water and wagyng of the bote
Maketh þe man many tyme to stomble, yf he stande.   35
For stonde he neuere so stifliche, thorw steryng of þe bote
He bendeth and boweth, the body is so vnstable,
And ʒut is he saef and sound; and so hit fareth by þe rihtfole.
Thow he falle, he falleth nat but as ho-so ful in a boet
That ay is saef and sound, þat sitte withynne þe borde.   40
So hit fareth,' quod þe frere, 'by þe ryhtful mannes fallynge;
Thow he thorw fondynges falle, he falleth nat out of charite,
So dedly synne doth he nat, for Dowel hym helpeth.
The water is likned to þe world, þat wanyeth and waxeth;
The godes of this grounde ar like þe grete wawes,   45
That as wyndes and wederes waleweth aboute;
The boet is liknet to oure body, þat bretil is of kynde,
That thorw the fend and oure flesch and this freel worlde
Synegeth seue sithe þe saddest man on erthe   f.45ª
And þe lyf-holiest of lyf þat lyueth vnder sonne.   50

37. He U] X Ai.   so U] X *om*
39. as P] XUI *om*
44. world U] X word
49. sithe U] X *om*
50. þe lyf-holiest U] X lyfliost

32. *a forbisene.* The illustrative story, or exemplum, that follows is based on a figure which had wide currency in homiletic literature (Owst, 1933, 68–9), being ultimately derived from a passage in a sermon of St Augustine (Sermo LXXV, *PL* 38:475–6) in which the allegory of the ship of the Church is developed from the story of Jesus stilling the storm on the sea of Galilee (Matt. 14:24–33). Behind this allegory lies the image of baptism (i.e. entry into the Church of Christ) as the ark of the new covenant which will save the righteous as Noah was saved (1 Pet. 3:20–21). Though it may seem a fair example of comfortable 'glosing' of the gospel (Prol. 58n, III 59n) by the friars, the handling of the exemplum is perfectly orthodox; it is the application to which it is put that is disturbing (and which suggests the limitations of the intellectual approach), namely, to give support to a manifest falsehood (i.e. that Dowel dwells pre-eminently with the friars). Suspicion derived from this source attaches itself to the friar's discourse, which begins to seem like an argument that men are entitled to sin. C corrects this tendency (51–5). Wyclif, in a sermon on Matt. 14:24 (ed. Arnold, i.375), points out that it is not the association of the boat with the Church that is false, but the friars' identification of themselves with the true Church.

43. *So*: 'provided that'. Even the righteous man lives, by his very nature, in venial sin. But deadly sin can only be committed with the consent of free will.

44. A commonplace image, e.g. *Prick of Conscience* 1213–24.

45. *The godes of this grounde*: 'the goods of this world', i.e. the temptations of the world, which are likened to the storms that beset the boat.

48. See I 37n.

Ac fre wil and fre wit foleweth man euere
To repenten and to arise and rowe out of synne
To contricion, to confessioun, til he come til his ende.
For rather haue we no reste til we restitue
Oure lyf to oure lord god for oure lycames gultes.'   55
    'Y haue no kynde knowlechyng to conseyue al this speche,
Ac yf y may lyue and loke y shal go lerne bettere.'
    'Y bykenne the Crist,' quod he, 'þat on þe cross deyede.'
And y sayde, 'Þe same saue ʒow fro meschaunce,
And gyue me grace on þis grounde with good ende to deye.'   60

    I wente forth wyde-whare, walkynge myn one,
By a wilde wildernesse and by a wode-syde.
Blisse of þe briddes abyde me made,
And vnder lynde vpon a launde lened y a stounde
To lythen here layes and here louely notes.   65
Murthe of here mouthes made me ther to slepe,
And merueilousliche me mette amyddes al þat blisse.

---

53. To[1] XUP] I þorgh

51–5. C abandons further development of the *forbisene* in B (VIII 45–56) in order to stress that man is neither condemned nor entitled to sin, and that it is in the power of his free will (for *fre wit*, see a note by A. V. C. Schmidt in *NQ* 213, 1968, 168–9) always to 'rowe out of synne' by repentance (see VI 6n, and Parson's Tale, *CT* X. 1073). This added passage, which quite defies any suggestion that the friar speaks 'in character', illustrates a pervading concern on L's part in C with themes of penitence and restitution (cf. VI 309n, XVI 25–38), expressed here in terms of a contract with God by which the final act of restitution, and the final rest, is death (54–5). For the suggestion that the rewriting here is due the C-reviser's dissatisfaction with his corrupt text of B, see Kane-Donaldson 171.

54. *reste . . . . restitue.* See VI 234.

56. 'I have no natural understanding to enable me to grasp all that you say'. The dreamer recurs to an important theme of his conversation with Holy Church (I 136n), the difficulty of grasping expounded truth as inward and personal truth (unless it is simply a polite way of *congeying* the friar, cf. XV 176; his companion seems to have disappeared). It has been suggested (Davlin, 1971, 3) that the dreamer's allusions to *kynde knowyng* in the Dowel passūs are ironical: in his quest for theoretical formulations he has forgotten what *kynde knowyng* is (cf. XVI 213n).

60. Cf. B VIII 61: 'And ʒyue yow grace on þis grounde goode men to worþe'. The change eliminates any implication that the dreamer has a right to feel superior to the friars, especially if we accept the unexpected *me* for *yow*.

61–7. See 1–2, above. L here keeps the traditional dream-prologue more or less intact from AB (cf. Prol. 10n). The third vision begins here.

A muche man, as me thoghte ylike to mysulue,
Cam and calde me be my kynde name.
'What art thow?' quod y, 'þat thow my name knowest?'   70
'That wost þou, Wille,' quod he, 'and no wyht bettere.'
'Woet y,' quod y, 'who art thow?' 'Thouhte,' sayde he thenne;
'Y haue sued the this seuen ʒer, saw thow me no rather?'
'Art thow Thouht?' quod y tho; 'thow couthest me wisse
Where þat Dowel dwelleth, and do me to knowe.'   75
'Dowel and Dobet,' quod he, 'and Dobest the thridde
Aren thre fayre vertues and ben nat fer to fynde.
Ho is trewe of his tonge and of his two handes

---

71. wost P] XUI *om*

---

68. *A muche man*, a tall man, *ylike to mysulue*, as L describes himself in V 24. *Thouhte* (72) is the first of a series of personifications who represent aspects of the dreamer's own mind and developing understanding; the first two, *Thouhte* and *Wit*, being innate, are portrayed as the dreamer's doubles (cf. 115, below).

73. 'I have been with you for a long time; haven't you noticed me before?' The 'long time' (cf. IV 82n) might correspond to the years of L's maturity or the years since he began his poem.

76. Here, for the first time, the dreamer hears of Dobet and Dobest. A natural grammatical extension of Dowel, they push back the horizons of the dreamer's search, and suggest that the good life is not a state but a process of growth. Thought's analysis of the three lives is the first of many such attempts at definition (e.g. X 127, 301, XI 161, XV 125, XXI 109). The dreamer's understanding gradually evolves by a 'ruminative' process: 'Langland was a poet who liked to be seen feeling for his ideas; he tries out successive notions, and noses his way among opinions before the reader's eyes' (Coghill, 1933, 128). And elsewhere: 'The method of the poet is not so much to develop an argument as to make us undergo its development. He gives us thinking rather than thought; all the dreamer's perplexities are before us, the riddles he cannot solve as well as the truths he can triumphantly affirm' (Lawlor, 1962, 11).

78–98. According to Thought, Dowel is the life of obedience to the law and honest labour in one's vocation (cf. VII 184ff); Dobet adds to this a greater degree of humility and active charity towards one's neighbour; while Dobest puts all these qualities to the active service of the organized Church, which has power over sin. Generally speaking, Thought's definition provides a fair basis for understanding the nature of the three lives as they are developed in subsequent passūs, viz. Dowel in X–XVII, Dobet in XVIII–XX, and Dobest in XXI–II (see Kean, 1969, 95–6). But essentially they are inseparable, being no more than the degrees of progress towards understanding the law of love as the basis of the good life (Frank, 1957, 12, 34–44); and inseparable too in that Dowel and Dobet must always be inspired by the possibility of Dobest (cf. Wyclif, ed. Arnold, i.384–5), not only for those who seek perfection in the contemplative life, but for all men. 'The love of God and neighbour does not fall under the precept to a certain extent only ... The perfection of divine love falls under the precept universally' (Aquinas, quot. Goodridge, 1959, 365). The use of the bishop here (92) as the exemplar of Dobest

And thorw lele labour lyueth and loueth his emcristene
And therto trewe of his tayl and takeþ but his owene   80
And is nat dronklewe ne dedeynous, Dowel him foleweth.
    Dobet doth al this, ac ȝut he doth more;
He is logh as a lomb and loueliche of speche,
And helpeth alle men of þat he may spare.
The bagges and þe bigerdeles he hath tobroken hem alle,   85 f.45ᵇ
Þat þe erl Auerous held, and his ayres,
And of Mammonaes money maked hym many frendes,
And is ronne into religioun and hath rendred þe bible

---

80. takeþ but his owene B] XUI of his two handes; P halt wel his handes
81. him U] X hem

---

might suggest a reference to the traditional division of the Active, Contemplative and 'Mixed' lives (see XVIII 81), and indeed these have often been used as a basis for the interpretation of Dowel, Dobet and Dobest, as in the famous essays of Wells (1929) and Coghill (1933), of H. W. Wells again in *PMLA* 53 (1938), 339–49, and of R. W. Chambers in *Man's Unconquerable Mind* (London, 1939), 88–171. But the interpretation is only sporadically helpful (see Frank, 1957, 6–11, and important essays by S. S. Hussey in *RES*, n.s.7, 1956, 132–50, and by T. P. Dunning, ibid. 225–37) and L nowhere mentions the mixed life as such. The difficulty of establishing a definite correspondence with the Three Lives, or even of making much use of the terms Active and Contemplative (see VII 299n), is that such terms are mainly familiar in technical treatises for religious, where the 'Active Life' is the activity in good works of those dedicated to the cloister. L is clearly not much interested in this life: his Dowel, etc. relate primarily to the life of the secular Christian in the world. See further, Dunning in Hussey, 1969.

84. *of þat*: 'with what, out of what'.
86. *þe erl Auerous*, presumably the ruler of *the counte of coueytise* (II 90).
87. Luke 16:9. See VIII 235a.
88. *is ronne into religioun*: 'has taken up a religious vocation'. The expression would normally mean 'entered a religious order', but the only regular orders that preached on any scale were the friars, and L is unlikely to identify friars with Dobet. *rendred*: 'learnt and expounded', not 'translated'. There is no reason, therefore, to associate this with Wycliffite translation of the bible (the first version was completed *c.*1384: see M. Deanesly, *The Lollard Bible*, Cambridge, 1920, 224, 254), since there had always been much *ad hoc* exposition with translation of specific passages of the bible, as here, for purposes of preaching and instruction (orthodox fear of full vernacular translation of the bible was that it offered the text to the lay reader without the control of interpretation). The difficulty of this passage (88–91) is that it is not clear whether being 'a religious' is (a) essential to the life of Dobet, (b) one form that the life of Dobet can take, or (c) simply an opportunity to expound a particular text, that of 89a.

And precheth to þe peple seynt Paules wordes:
> *Libenter suffertis insipientes.*

"Ʒe wordliche wyse, vnwyse þat Ʒe soffre,   90
Lene hem and loue hem," this Latyn is to mene.

Dobest bere sholde þe bisshopes crose
And halie with þe hoked ende alle men to gode,
And with the pyk pulte adoun *preuaricatores legis.*
Lordes þat lyuen as hem lust and no lawe acounten,   95
For here mok and here mebles suche men thenketh
Sholde no bisshop be, here biddynges to withsite.
Ac Dobest sholde drede hem nat, but do as god hihte.
> *Nolite timere eos qui possunt occidere corpus.*

Thus Dowel and Dobet demede as Dobest
And crounede oen to be kyng, to kull withoute synne   100
That wolde nat do as Dobest deuinede and tauhte.
Thus Dowel and Dobet and Dobest the thridde
Crounede oen to be a kyng to kepen vs alle,
And to reule alle reumes by here thre wittes,
Bute oþere wise ne elles nat, but as they thre assentede.'   105

---

92. crose U] X corose
93. alle X] UIP ille
99. as U] X a

89a. 'For you gladly bear with fools (being wise yourselves)' (2 Cor. 11:19). Paul said this in rebuke of a weakness in the Christians of Corinth, of which he will, as a 'fool', take ironical advantage. The passage is rhetorically complex, and related to Paul's use of 'fool' as part of a vocabulary of spiritual paradox (IX 105n). L takes it quite simply as an exhortation (some A MSS have *sufferte*, imperative). It may be considered that he is deliberately misconstruing the passage 'in character' in order to indicate Thought's limitations (but cf. Robertson-Huppé, 1951, 104–5). Wyclif (ed. Arnold, ii.260) understands very well the scornful irony of the passage.

90. *þat*, introducing an adjuration (cf. V 199n).

92. The bishop was the usual exemplar of the 'mixed' life (see above, 78n), as one who brought the fruits of contemplation into the active life of the community. For the symbolic function of the crozier, see XVII 286–7.

94. *preuaricatores legis*: those who misuse or evade the law. A common phrase in the writings of St Augustine (Alford 398).

98a. 'Do not fear those who can kill the body (but cannot kill the soul)' (Matt. 10:28).

100. L moves here from the bishop as representative of ecclesiastical authority to consideration of the king as the secular arm of that authority. The sequence of ideas recalls early passūs (e.g. Prol. 139n), though we should not interpret 'king' literally; rather think of this as one of the occasions where L adapts the political concepts of the *Visio* to larger theological and spiritual meanings (cf. XI 161, and for a similar use see V 168). At this stage, the 'king' is the principle of order and stability, upon which the good life depends; later, the concept is to be made manifest in the kingship of Christ (XXI 83). See Kean, 1969, 96–108.

101. *That*: 'those that'.

Y thonkede Thoght tho, þat he me so tauhte:
'Ac ʒut sauereth nat me thy sawes, so me Crist spede;
A more kyndore knowynge coueyte y to here
Of Dowel and Dobet and ho doth best of alle.'
'Bote yf Wit wol the wisse,' quod Thouhte, 'where tho thre
     dwelleth,   110
Elles knowe y noen þat can, in none kyneryche.'

  Thouht and y thus thre dayes we ʒeden,
Disputyng vppon Dowel day aftur other,
And ar we ywar were, with Wit gan we mete.
He was long and lene, ylyk to noon other;   115
Was no pruyde on his parail, no pouerte noythere;
Sad of his semblant, and with a softe speche.
Y durste meue no matere to maken hym to iangle,
Bote as y bad Thouht tho to be mene betwene   f.46ᵃ
And potte forth som purpos to preuen his wittes,   120
What was Dowel fro Dobet and Dobest fro hem bothe.
  Thenne Thouht in þat tyme sayde this wordes:
'Whare Dowel and Dobet and Dobest ben in londe,
Here is oen wolde ywyte, yf Wit couthe teche;
And what lyues they lyue and what lawe þei vsen,   125
And what þey drede and doute, dere sire, telleth.'
  'Sire Dowel dwelleth,' quod Wit, 'nat a day hennes
In a castel þat Kynde made of foure kyne thynges.
Of erthe and ayer is hit maed, ymedled togyderes,
With wynd and with water wittyly enioyned.   130
Kynde hath closed ther-ynne, craftili withalle,
A lemman þat he louyeth ylyke to hymsulue.
Anima she hatte; to here hath enuye

---

108. *kyndore knowynge.* See 56, above, and I 136n.
114. *ar we ywar were.* 'Thought' (intellectual activity) leads imperceptibly to 'Wit' (rational understanding based on the senses). See above, 68n.
119. *Bote as*: 'except in so far as'.
128. *Kynde* is God as creator, i.e. that aspect of God which is manifested in his creation, and therefore knowable to rational understanding. The castle of Man is a familiar medieval allegory (see VII 232n, Prov. 4:23, *Ancrene Wisse* 29, 198 [ed. Shepherd, p. 21], *Prick of Conscience* 5820, and the tale of Melibeus, *CT* VII. 969, 1420): man's body, made of the four elements, encloses the soul (*Anima*), beloved of God, and is under the guardianship of Inwit and the five wits. Dowel, Dobet and Dobest are worked into the allegory without much difficulty.
129–30. If *wynd* means 'air', *ayer* must mean 'fire'. *aer* is used as an alternative for *ignis* in the explanation of fire in the body's composition in the *Liber de spiritu et anima*, claimed as a source for Langland here by Wittig, 1972, 217.
133. *hath enuye*: 'covets to possess'.

A proued prikeare of Fraunce, *princeps huius mundi*,
And wole wynne here awaye with wyles, and he myhte.   135
And Kynde knoweth this wel and kepeth here þe betere
And hath do here with sire Dowel, duk of his marches.
Dobet is here damysele, sire Doweles douhtur,
To serue þat lady leely boþe late and rathe.
Dobest is aboue bothe, a bishopis pere,   140
And by his leryng is lad þat ilke lady *Anima*.
Ac þe constable of þat castel þat kepeth hem alle
Is a wise knyhte withalle, sire Inwit he hatte,
And hath fyue fayre sones by his furste wyue:
Sire Se-wel and Sey-wel, sire Here-wel þe ende,   145
Sire Worch-wel-with-thyn-hand, a wyht man of strenghe,
And sire Goed-fayth Go-wel, grete lordes alle.
Thise sixe ben sette for to saue *Anima*
Til Kynde come or sende and kepe here hymsulue.'
    'What kynne thyng is Kynde?' quod y; 'canst thow me telle?'   150
    'Kynde is creatour,' quod Wit, 'of alle kyne thynges,
Fader and formour of al þat forth groweth,

148. sixe B] XUIP fyue
151. alle U] X two (*an insertion*)

134. *princeps huius mundi*: 'the prince of this world', a phrase used in John (12:31, 14:30,
16:11) to signify the devil. The portrayal of the devil as a French (armed) horse-
man contributes vividly to the military and chivalric suggestions of castle and
siege; it also indicates that an allusion to the pride and viciousness of the French,
whether serious or playful, was now recognizable as a motif.
140. *a bishopis pere*. See 92n, above.
143. *Inwit*. Not Conscience exactly, but the intellectual awareness of right and wrong
which when put into action is Conscience (Quirk, 1953, 185–8), with some addi-
tion too from the scholastic concept of synderesis, a 'cognitive attachment to the
sovereign good' (see 175, below) which survives in some measure the Fall. See B.
J. Harwood and R. F. Smith, 'Inwit and the Castle of *Caro*', *NM* (1970), 648–54;
also IV 5n.
144. *fyue fayre sones*: the five wits (cf. I 15, XV 256). Often in ME the five wits are the
five bodily senses, but sometimes the term 'wit' is extended, as here, to cover other
physical faculties, such as speech and locomotion (OED, s.v.3). In didactic and
penitential treatises (e.g. *Sawles Warde*, l. 18: see VII 232n) the five wits are
traditionally under the governorship of Conscience. *furste wyue*: perhaps the flesh in
its unfallen state, when the senses were uncorrupted (a more complex explanation
is provided by Wittig, 1972, 217–19, while Robertson-Huppé, 1951, 108 suggest
that 'the first wife represents the old law and the five sons the obedience to her
precepts which results in doing well').
148. *sixe*. The emendation (which counts Inwit with his five sons) is self-evident: so
Kane-Donaldson B IX 23.
152. Cf. I 14.

The which is god grettest, bygynnynge hadde he neuere,
Lord of lyf and of lyht, of lisse and of payne.
Angeles and alle thyng aren at his wille;
Man is hym most lyk of membres and of face
And semblable in soule to god but if synne hit make.
And as thow seest the sonne sumtyme for cloudes
May nat shyne ne shewe on schawes on erthe,
So let lecherye and other luther synnes
That god sheweth nat suche synnefole men and soffreth hem mysfare,
And somme hangeth hemsulue and oþer-while adrencheth.
God wol nat of hem wyte bute lat hem yworthe,
As þe sauter sayth by synnefole shrewes:
    Et dimisi eos secundum desideria eorum.
Such lyther-lyuyng men lome been ryche
Of gold and of oþer goed, ac goddes grace hem fayleth,
For they louyeth and bylyueth al here lyf-tyme
On catel more then on Kynde, that alle kyne thynges wrouhte,
The which is loue and lyf þat last withouten ende.
    Inwit and alle wittes closed been þerynne;
By loue and by leute, þerby lyueth *Anima*,
And lyf lyueth by inwit and leryng of Kynde;
Inwit is in the heued and *Anima* in herte.
And moche wo worth hym þat inwit myspeneth,
For þat is goddes oune goed, his grace and his tresour,
That many a lede leseth thorw lykerous drynke,
As Lote dede and Noe; and Herodes þe daffe
ʒaf his douhter for a daunsynge in a disch þe heued
Of þat blessed Baptist bifore alle his gestes.
Euery man þat hath inwit and his hele bothe

155 f.46^b

160

165

170

175

180

159. schawes U] X schalkes
165. lome I] X in lome (in *inserted*); U somme

157. *but if synne hit make*: 'unless sin causes it (to be otherwise)'. This passage (157–69), on how sin obscures the image of God in man, replaces a more adventurous disquisition in B IX 32–51 on the Word made flesh in the act of creation (Gen. 1:3, Ps. 148:5). Both take 156 as their starting-point.
160. *let*: 'causes a hindrance, creates an obstacle'.
161. *sheweth*: 'looks upon'.
164a. 'And I let them go their own way according to their desires [Vg. *desideria cordis eorum*]' (Ps. 80:13, God speaking of those who did not obey his law).
170. In the transition back to the matter of B, C omits mention of the antecedent of *þerynne*, viz. the castle of man (*caro* in B IX 50).
177. *Lote*. See I 25n. *Noe*. See Gen. 9:21. *Herodes*. See Mk. 6:21. Lot and Herod are examples of drunkenness in the Pardoner's Tale, *CT* VI. 485–91. The associations are traditional, based on Peter Comestor (Taitt, 1971).

Hath tresor ynow of Treuthe to fynden hymsulue.

   Ac fauntokynes and foles þe which þat fauten inwit,
Frendes shal fynde hem and fram folye kepe
And holy churche helpe to, so sholde no man begge
Ne spille speche ne tyme, ne myspende noyther   185
Meble ne vnmeble, mete noþer drynke.

   And thenne dede we alle wel, and wel bet ʒut to louye
Oure enemyes enterely and helpe hem at here nede.
And ʒut were best to ben aboute and brynge hit to hepe
That alle landes loueden and in on lawe bileuede.   190 f.47ᵃ
Bishopes sholde ben hereaboute and bryng this to hepe,
For to lese þerfore her lond and her lyf aftur.
The catel that Crist hadde thre clothes hit were;
Therof was he robbed and ruyfled or he on rode deyede
And seth he lees his lyf for lawe sholde loue wexe.   195
Prelates and prestes and princes of holy churche
Sholde nat doute no deth ne no dere ʒeres
To wende as wyde as þe worlde were
To tulie þe erthe with tonge and teche men to louye;
For ho-so loueth, leueth hit wel, god wol nat laton hym sterue   200
In meschief for defaute of mete ne for myssyng of clothes.
   Inquirentes autem dominum non minuentur omni bono.

187. And U] X Ac
191. Bishopes U] X Bishope
195. he lees U] X al
200. hit P] XUI hym

184–201. This passage of comparatively simple instruction, with its brief allusion to the
three lives (187–90) and its emphasis on the pastoral duties of bishops and
prelates, abandons some lively but loosely articulated material in B IX 71–108, on
godparents, Jews and time-wasting; B in turn is completely rewritten from a still
longer section in A.

184. *to*: 'too', or perhaps 'to' with the sense 'there-to' (OED, s.v.*to*, D6).

189. *brynge hit to hepe*: 'bring it together', i.e. bring it about as a single conclusion. So in
191 below.

192. *For to lese*: 'despite the fact that they might lose'.

193. *thre clothes*. This allusion may seem oddly oblivious of the allusion to the seamless
robe of John 19:23–4, but it is explained by a passage in the *Vita Christi* of Ludolf
of Saxony (II. lxii: see II 32n), as will be made clear by T. D. Hill, of Cornell
University, in a forthcoming published note: I am grateful to him for communi-
cating this information to me.

195. *for lawe sholde loue wexe*: so that the law of the old covenant might grow into the
love of the new. See e.g. Rom. 13:10, Gal. 5:14.

197. *dere ʒeres*: 'years of dearth', when food is scarce and expensive. In other words, fear
of want should not deter them from going about and preaching the gospel; the
point is taken up in 200, below.

201a. 'But those that seek the lord shall not be deprived of any good' (Ps. 33:11).

Ho-so lyueth in lawe and in loue doth wel,
As this wedded men þat this world susteyneth,
For of here kynde þey come, bothe confessours and martres,
Prophetus and patriarkes, popes and maydenes.   205
For god saith hymsulue, "Shal neuere goed appel
Thorw no sotil sciense on sour stok growe";
And is no more to mene but men þat ben bygeten
Out of matrimonye, nat moyloure, mowen nat haue þe grace
That lele legityme by þe lawe may claymen.   210
And þat my my sawe is soth þe sauter bereth witnesse:
   Concepit in dolore et peperit iniquitatem.
Caym þe corsede creature conseyued was in synne
Aftur þat Adam and Eue hadden ysyneged;
Withouten repentaunce of here rechelesnesse a rybaud þei
   engendrede.
As an hewe þat erieth nat auntreth hym to sowe   215
On a leye-land aȝeynes his lordes wille,
So was Caym conseyued and so ben corsed wreches
Þat lycame haen aȝen þe lawe þat oure lord ordeynede.
  Alle þat come of Caym caytyue were euere
And for þe synne of Caymes seed sayede god to Noe,   220

---

215. auntreth U] X ariketh (? *over* aunreth *erased*)

202–3. Marked as a question by Skeat. Here *As* in 203 is interpreted as 'such as', introducing an example of the general truth in 202. C returns here to the matter of AB, and follows to the end of the passus, with some variation and addition, the discussion of the foundation of the life of Dowel in sanctity of wedlock and legitimacy of birth. The abruptness with which the discussion is introduced is due to the omission in BC of a fine passage in A which describes how the sweet red rose of Dobest grows from the ragged root and rough briars of Dowel (i.e. of ordinary decent Christian lives).

206–7. 'A bad tree cannot bear good fruit' (Matt. 7:18). See II 29a, and 242 below.

209. *nat moyloure*: 'not of legitimate birth'. See II 120, 145. For L's concern with legitimacy, see II 17, 24, 43, V 65.

211a. 'He [the wicked man] conceived in misery and brought forth wickedness' (Ps. 7:15, etc.). L substitutes *in dolore* for Vg. *dolorem* under the influence of Gen. 3:16: *in dolore paries filios*, 'in pain you shall bring forth children'.

212. According to the story told in the apocryphal *Vita Adae et Evae* (ME trans. in Blake, 1972, 109–10), a period of penance was accepted by Adam and Eve for their sin in eating of the apple. Before the period of penance was completed, they came together and Cain was conceived.

219. The progeny of Cain are the sons of unrighteousness; they are, allegorically, all wicked men (cf. 1 John 3:12, Jude 11). The term was also applied to the race of giants (Gen. 6:4, with the gloss of Num. 13:33) destroyed in the Flood (224–5 below) and of monsters who survived the Flood, of whom Grendel was one descendant (*Beowulf* 107, 1261).

Penitet me fecisse hominem,
And bad go shapen a ship of shides and bordes.
"Thysulue and thy sones thre and sethen ȝoure wyues,
Boske ȝow to þat boet and abideth þerynne   f.47ᵇ
Til fourty daies be fulfild and floed haue ywasche
Clene awey þe corsed bloed þat of Caym spronge.   225
Bestes þat now beth shal banne þe tyme
That euere þat corsed Caym cam on þis erthe;
Alle sholle deye for his dedes by dales and by hulles
And þe foules þat flyeth forth with oþer bestes,
Excepte onliche of vch a kynde a payre   230
That on thi chingled ship shal be with þe ysaued."
      Here aboughte þe barn the belsires gultes
And al for here forfadres ferden þe worse.
The gospel is here-agayn, as gomes may rede:
      Filius non portabit iniquitatem patris.
Holy writ witnesseth þat for no wikkede dede   235
That þe sire by hymsulue doth þe sone sholde be þe worse.
Ac Westminstre lawe, y woet wel, worcheth þe contrarye
For thogh þe fader be a frankeleyn and for a felon be hanged
The eritage þat þe eyer sholde haue is at þe kynges wille.
Ac þe gospel is a glose ther and huydeth þe grayth treuthe,   240
For god seid ensaumple of suche manere issue,
That kynde folweth kynde and contrarieth neuere.

224. daies U] X *om*
229. flyeth I] X flueth; U fleeth
232. aboughte U] X aboute
237. Westminstre U] X Westninstre

220a. 'It grieves me to have made man' (Gen. 6:7).
229. *forth with*: 'along with'.
234a. 'The son shall not suffer for the iniquity of the father' (Ez. 18:20). L refers this to 'the gospel' presumably because it has a NT flavour (being a NT prophecy, cf. Jer. 31:29–30), which he constrasts with the indiscriminate vengeance of the Flood and the apparent meaning of texts like Ex. 20:5.
237–9. Since L is about to endorse the punishment of sons for the father's offence (on the grounds that sons are likely to be like their fathers), his reference here (added in C) to contemporary legal practice, that of escheating to the crown the goods of convicted felons and denying inheritance, cannot be intended as a criticism of that practice. On the other hand, *at þe kynges wille* hints at an important qualification, and a possibility of mercy which at the moment seems beyond Wit's understanding.
240. Wit's suggestion that the 'gospel' text is a misleading gloss is a piece of text-juggling reminiscent of III 488 or 21, above, and reveals the limitations of his understanding. Cf. the use of the same text in Ezechiel by the false sophists of B X 114.

Numquam colligunt de spinis vuas. Et alibi: Bona arbor
   bonum fructum facit.

Ac why þe world was adreynt holy writ telleth
Was for mariages makynge þat men made þat tyme.
Aftur þat Caym þat corsed hadde ykuld Abel,   245
Seth, Adames sone, seth was engendred
And god sente to Seth so sone he was of age
That for no kyne catel ne no kyne byheste
Soffre his seed seden with Caymes seed his brother.
And seth for he soffred hit god sayde, "Me forthynketh   250
Þat y man made or matrimonye soffrede,
For goode sholde wedde goode thouh they no goode ne hadde,
For y am *via et veritas* and may avauncen alle."
   Ac fewe folk now folweth this, for thei ȝeue her childrene
For coueytise of catel and connynge chapmen.   255
Of kyn ne of kynrede counteth men bote litel   f.48ᵃ
And thogh she be louelich to loken on and lossum abedde,
A mayde and wel ymanered and of gode men yspronge,
Bote she haue oþer goed haue wol here no ryche.
Ac lat here be vnlouely and vnlossum abedde,   260
A bastard, a bond oen, a begeneldes douhter,
That no cortesye ne can, bute late here be knowe
For riche or yrented wel, thouh she be reueled for elde

242b. *Bona* I] XU *bonus*
246. Seth U] X Syth (*over* Seth *erased*)
257. she] XU he; I ȝhe; P hue
258. ymanered I] XU ymaried
259. she] XU he; I sche; P hue
260. here] XUI hem; P hure
263. she U] X he

242a. 'Do they ever [Vg. *Numquid*] gather grapes from thorns' (Matt. 7:16). And elsewhere: 'A sound tree bears good fruit' (Matt. 7:17). See II 29a and above, 206.

247–9. The story of God's command to Seth is derived from patristic interpretation (e.g. Comestor's *Historia Scholastica*, PL 98:1081) of Gen. 6:4, where the intermarriage of the 'sons of God' (Seth's offspring) and the 'daughters of men' (Cain's offspring) is seen as the main cause of corruption in the world.

249. *Soffre*: 'to allow', i.e. he should allow.

253. *via et veritas*: 'the way and the truth' (John 14:4).

254–69. This passage of contemporary application is added in C. L condemns the practice of marrying for money because it subverts rank and perverts the divinely ordained hierarchy of class (cf. V 70–81). Preachers also commonly attacked the practice of marrying for money (Owst, 1933, 381–2; see also Wyclif, ed. Arnold, iii.188–201), though they place more emphasis on the sinful consequences (e.g. adultery) than on the subversion of social rank, and of course they recommend not marriage for love (see 280, below) but marriage in fulfilment of God's law.

Ther ne is squier ne knyhte in contreye aboute
That he ne wol bowe to þat bonde to beden here an hosebonde   265
And wedden here for here welthe and weschen on þe morwe
That his wyf were wexe or a walet ful of nobles.
In ielosye, ioyles, and iangelynge abedde,
Many a payre sethe this pestelences han plyhte treuthe to louye,
Ac they lyen lely, here neyther lyketh other.   270
The fruyt þat they brynge forth aren many foule wordes;
Haen þei no childerne bute cheste and choppes hem bitwene.
Thogh they do hem to Donemowe, bote þe deuel hem helpe,
To folwe for þe flicche, feccheth they hit neuere;
Bote they bothe be forswore þat bacon þei tyne.   275
     Forthy y conseyle alle cristene coueyte neuere be wedded
For no coueytise of catel in none kyne wyse;
Bote maydones and maydones marie ȝow togyderes
And wedewes and wedewares weddeth ȝow ayþer oþer,
And loke þat loue be more þe cause then lond oþer nobles.   280
And euery maner seculer man þat may nat contynue
Wisely go wedde and war þe fro þat synne
That lecherye is, a lykyng thynge, a lym-ȝerd of helle.
And whil þou art ȝong an ȝep and thy wepene kene

---

268. *Skeat here adds a line from MS F*
270. lely I] XU leix
272. choppes U] X shoppes
273. do U] X *om*
279. wedewes U] X wedewe

---

267. *wexe.* This could be a playful allusion, as Skeat suggests, to the practice of offering one's own weight in wax (an expensive commodity, much needed in churches) to the Church, often in the form of a 'man of wax' (OED, s.v.*wax*, sb¹, 2d). Alternatively, it is *wexe*, pp. 'become' (OED, s.v.*wax*, v¹, 9b), and *or* should be omitted.

273. *Donemowe.* Dunmow is in Essex; this is the first known reference to the custom in the village of offering a flitch of bacon to any married couple who are prepared to declare on oath (hence the allusion in *forswore*) that they have lived a year without quarrelling. Cf. *CT* III. 218.

281. *seculer man.* The usual reference of *seculer* in this sort of context would be to the secular clergy, i.e. those who lived 'in the world', as distinct from the regular orders. The recommendation that such clerics should marry would not be outrageous, and not an exclusively Lollard opinion; many did (Langland's Will amongst them), though canon law forbade it. On the other hand, the reference could be to 'layman'. *CT* IV. 1251 is equally ambiguous. *contynue* may mean 'continue (chaste)', or it may be a variant of *conteyne* (MED, s.v. *continue*, v, 6), translating Lat. *continent* in 1 Cor. 7:9: *Quod si non se continent, nubant* ('But if they cannot be continent, they should marry').

283. *lym-ȝerd*: 'lime-twig', a twig smeared with bird-lime (a sticky substance) to catch birds. Cf. Prov. 7:23.

Awreke the þerwith on wyfyng, for godes werk y holde hit. 285
Dum sis vir fortis, ne des tua robora scortis;
Scribitur in portis, meretrix est ianua mortis.

And ȝe þat han wyues, ben war and worcheth nat out of tyme,
As Adam dede and Eue, as y whil er ȝow tolde.
For sholde no bed-bourde be, bote yf they bothe were
Clene of lyf and in loue of soule and in lele wedlok. 290
For þat dede derne do no man sholde f.48ᵇ
Bote wyues and wedded men, as holy writ techeth:
> *Bonum est vt unusquisque uxorem suam habeat propter*
> *fornicacionem.*

That oþergatus ben gete for gadelynges ben holden
And fals folk and fondlynges, faytors and lyares, 295
Vngracious to gete goed or gete loue of peple,
Awayten and wasten alle þat they cacche mowe;
Aȝen Dowel they do yuele and þe deuel serue
And after her deth-day dwellen in helle
Bote god ȝeue hem grace here goynge here to amende. 300
And thus is Dowel, my frende, to do as lawe techeth,
To louye and to loue the and no lyf to greue.
Ac to louye and to lene, leef me, þat is Dobet.
Ac to ȝeue and to ȝeme bothe ȝonge and olde,
Helen and helpen, is Dobest of alle.
For þe more a man may do, by so þat a do hit, 305
The more he is worthy and worth, of wyse and of goed ypresed.'

293a. *vt* U] X *om*
300. goynge I] X doynge; U goande
303. lene P] XUI loue

286–7. 'While you are a virile man, do not spend your vigour on prostitutes; it is written on the gates, a prostitute is the gateway of death'. These lines of leonine verse (cf. Prol. 152) seem to have been widely known (Walther 4447, Alford 393); the second is quoted in the Prophecies of John of Bridlington (in Wright, *Pol. Poems*, ii.159). The original inspiration is in Prov. 29:3, 7:23.

288. *worcheth nat out of tyme*: 'do not have intercourse at improper times', e.g. during pregnancy (see XIII 143–55) or while performing penance (214 above). See VI 182n.

293a. 'It is good that every man should have his own wife for fear of fornication' (1 Cor. 7:2).

Passus XI

Learning and Salvation:
the Discourse of Study, Clergy and Rechelesnesse

Passus primus de visione de dowel
Thenne hadde Wit a wyf was hote dame Studie,
That ful lene lokede and lyf-holy semede.
She was wonderly wroth þat Wit me so tauhte.
Al staryng dame Studie sturneliche sayde:
'Wel artow wyse,' quod she to Wyt, 'suche wysdomes to shewe   5
To eny foel or to flaterere or to frentike peple!'
And sayde: '*Nolite mittere*, ʒe men, margerie-perles
Among hogges þat han hawes at wille;
They do bote dreuele theron – draf were hem leuere
Then al þe preciouse perye þat eny prince weldeth.   10
Y syg hit by suche,' quod she, 'þat sheweth by here werkes
Thei louyen lond and lordschipe and lykynge of body
More then holynesse or hendenesse or al þat seyntes techeth.
   Wysdom and wit now is nat worth a carse
Bote hit be cardet with coueytise, as clotheres kemben here wolle.   15
Ho can caste and contreue to disseyue þe rightfole
And lette with a loue-day treuthe, and bigile,
That coueite can and caste thus ar cleped into þe consayle.
Qui sapiunt nugas et crimina lege vocantur;   f.49ᵃ
Qui recte sapiunt, lex iubet ire foras.   20
He is reuerensed and yrobed þat can robbe þe peple

---

11. she B] XUI wit; P Studie
12. Thei P] XUI þat
16. rightfole] X rihgtfole

---

1. *dame Studie* is the first of these personified figures (see 94, 97, below) who repre-
sent external bodies of knowledge rather than innate faculties. See X 68n,
XIV 1n.
7. 'Do not throw (pearls before swine)' (Matt. 7:6).
15. *cardet*: 'combed out', as wool is 'carded' to improve its appearance; hence, 'made
to look better'.
17. *loue-day*. See III 195.
19–20. 'Those who know about trifles and slanders are called in by the law; those who
are truly wise the law commands to go away'. Source not identified.

Thorw fallas and fals questes and thorw fikel speche.
  Iob þe gentele in his gestes witnesseth
What shal worthen of suche when þei lyf leten:
    Ducunt in bonis dies suos, et in fine descendunt ad infernum.
The sauter saith the same of alle suche ryche:
    Ibunt in progenies patrum suorum, et usque in eternum non
      videbunt lumen.
    Et alibi: Ecce ipsi peccatores!
"Lo!" saith holy letrure, "whiche lordes beth this schrewes!"
Tho þat god most goed ȝeueth, greueth most riht and treuthe.
    Que perfecisti, destruxerunt.
Harlotes for here harlotrye aren holpe ar nedy pore;
And þat is no riht ne resoun, for rather me sholde
Helpe hym þat hath nauhte then tho that haen no nede.   30
  Ac he þat hath holy writ ay in his mouth
And can telle of Treuthe and of þe twelue aposteles
Or of þe passioun of Crist or of purgatorie þe peynes,
Litel is he loued or leet her-fore among lordes at festes.
  Nowe is þe manere at þe mete, when munstrals ben stille,   35
The lewed aȝen þe lered þe holy lore to dispute,
And tellen of þe trinite how two slowe þe thridde
And brynge forth ballede resones, taken Bernard to witnesse,
And putten forth presumpcioun to preue þe sothe.
Thus they dreuele at the deyes, the deite to knowe,   40

23. gestes U] X gistes
36. dispute U] X dispite
37. two U] X tho
40. at U] X as

24a. 'They spend their days in prosperity, and in the end go down into hell' (Job 21:13).
25a. 'They will go to the generation of their fathers, and they will never more see the light' (Ps. 48:20). And elsewhere: 'Behold, these are sinners', viz. the rich (Ps. 72:12). L. 26 translates this latter text.
27a. 'What thou hast made, they have destroyed' (Ps. 10:4, Vg. only, lamenting the depredations of the wicked).
31-4. Cf. VII 105-7. A brief reference to a favourite theme (see Prol. 35n).
37. An example of the kind of idle speculation indulged in by these ignorant intruders into the world of theological debate (Dame Study's province). Scribes of B, perhaps shocked by the violence of the line (which alludes to a heretical denial of the triune nature of the Trinity), substituted, for the second half, 'a tale ouþer tweye' (B X 54).
38. *Bernard.* St Bernard of Clairvaux (d. 1153), the driving force behind the monastic and spiritual revival of the 12th c. His works, it is suggested, are being 'glosed'.

And gnawen god with gorge when here gottes fullen.
Ac þe carfole may crye and quake at þe ȝate,
Bothe afyngred and afurst, and for defaute spille;
Is non so hende to haue hym yn, but hote hym go þer god is!
Thenne semeth hit to my sihte, to suche þat so biddeth,   45
God is nat in þat hoem, ne his helpe nother.
Lytel loueth he þat lord þat lente hym al þat blisse
That so parteth with þe pore a parsel, when hym nedeth.
Ne were mercy in mene men more then in riht riche,
Mony tymes mendenauntes myhte goen afyngred;   50
And so saith þe sauter, y say hit in *Memento*:   f.49ᵇ
    Ecce audivimus eam (i.e. caritatem) in Effrata.
    Clerkes and knyhtes carpen of god ofte
And haen muche in here mouth, ac mene in her herte.
Freres and faytours haen founde vp suche questions
To plese with proude men senes this pestelences,   55
And prechyng at seynt Poules for puyr enuye of clerkes,

---

41. fullen U] X fallen
44. yn P] XUI *om*
53. her U] X *om*
54. and U] X and and
56. for B] XUI and; *line om* P

---

41. *with.* Kane-Donaldson read *in þe* at the corresponding line in B X 58, translating 'bite God persistently in the throat', and suggest that *gnawen wiþ þe gorge* is 'actually non-sense' (p. 103). But if *gorge*, 'throat', is taken loosely to mean 'what is used in eating', the present reading fits better with the second half of the line, suggesting the idle picking at some savoury snack when stomachs are full. Cf. 53, below, and see the review of Kane-Donaldson by D. C. Fowler in *YES* 7 (1977), 23–42 (p. 32).

42. The suggestion for this stark image is in the story of Dives and Lazarus, Luke 16:20. Cf. VIII 278–84.

51. *Memento*: 'remember', the first word of the psalm referred to; psalms and texts were often briefly identified in this way.

51a. 'Behold, we have heard of it (that is, charity) in Ephratah, (we have found it in woodland glades)' (Ps. 131:6). The literal reference is to the ark of the covenant, symbol of God's truth revealed to Israel. The typological interpretation, stimulated by the identification of the humble village of Ephratah with Bethlehem (Mic. 5:2), suggests that the new covenant of charity is found amongst the poor and the lowly (Hort 100–101). It is possible that L intends an ironical contrast between what is *heard of* in Ephratah and what is *found* in the fields (Goodridge, 1959, 336), but unlikely.

53. *ac mene in herte*: 'but it is simple men who have God in their heart' (cf. VII 187n).

56. *seynt Poules.* St Paul's Cross in London was a famous open-air preaching place: see Owst, 1926, 13–14, 198–9, etc., and cf. XV 70 and V 114n, 115, where there is the same association of preaching with *pestelences* (a relic here of the specific reference to *pestilence*, the Black Death, in AB). Friars were skilful preachers, and the suggestion is that they used sermons not only to win favour for themselves (Prol. 58n, 62n) but also to attack their traditional enemies, the *clerkes* or possessioners. See VI 119, XII 33n.

That folk is nat ferme in þe faith ne fre of here godes
Ne sory for here synnes; so ys pruyde enhanced
In religion and in al þe reume amonges riche and pore
That preyeres haen no power this pestilences to lette.   60
For god is deef nowadayes and deyneth vs nat to here
And gode men for oure gultes he al togrynt to deth.
And ȝut this wreches of this world, is noen ywar by oþer,
Ne for drede of eny deth withdraweth hym fro pruyde
Ne parteth with þe pore, as puyr charite wolde,   65
Bote in gaynesse and in glotonye forglotten here godes
And breketh nat here bred to þe pore, as þe boke hoteth:
　　Frange esurienti panem tuum.
Ac þe more a wynneth and hath þe world at his wille
And lordeth in ledes, the lasse goed he deleth.
　Tobie techeth nat so; taketh hede, ȝe ryche,   70
How he tolde in a tyme and tauhte his sone dele:
　　Si tibi sit copia, habundanter tribue; si autem exiguum,
　　　illud impertiri libenter stude.
And is to mene no more bote "Who muche goed weldeth,
Be large þerof whil hit lasteth to ledes þat ben nedy;
And yf thow haue litel, leue sone, loke by þy lyue
Get þe loue þerwith, thogh thow worse fare."   75
Ac lust no lord now ne lettred man of suche lore to here,
Bote lythen how þey myhte lerne leest god spene.
And þat loueth lordes now and leten hit a Dowel,
For is no wit worth now but if hit of wynnynge soune,
And capped wiþ clergie to conspire wronge.   80

---

58. ys U] X *om*
71b. *impertiri* U] X impertire
80. *this line in* I *only*

67a. 'Share your bread with the hungry' (Isa. 58:7, said in the grace for Lent: see III 339a). Cf. IX 125a.
71a. 'If you have many riches, give generously; if only a little, be diligent to give willingly according to what you have' (Tob. 4:8, quoted in a similar context in *Speculum Christiani* 43).
78. 'And that is what lords enjoy now and consider "doing well"'.
79. Cf. 14–15, above.
80. *capped.* A contemptuous reference to the caps worn by masters of divinity. Wyclif often speaks scornfully of 'capped freris' (e.g. Wyclif, ed. Arnold, iii.376).

Forthy, Wit,' quod she, 'be waer holy writ to shewe
Amonges hem þat haen hawes at wille,
The which is a lykyng and a luste and loue of þe world.'
   And when Wit was ywar what Studie menede,   f.50ᵃ
I myhte gete no grayn of Wittes grete wittes,   85
But al lauhynge he louted and loked vppon Studie,
Semyng þat y sholde bysechen here of grace.
   And when y was war of his wille, to þat womman gan y louten,
And saide, 'Mercy, madame, ʒoure man shal y worthen
As longe as y lyue, bothe late and rathe,   90
And for to worche ʒoure wille þe while my lyf duyreth,
With þat ʒe kenne me kyndeliche to knowe what is Dowel.'
   'For thy mekenesse, man,' quod she, 'and for thy mylde speche
Y shal kenne þe to Clergie, my cosyn, þat knoweth
Alle kynne kunnynges and comsynges of Dowel,   95
Of Dobet, of Dobest, for doctour he is knowe,
And ouer Skripture þe skilfole and screueynes were trewe.
For she is sib to þe seuene ars and also my suster
And Clergices wedded wyf, as wyse as hymsulue
Of lore and of lettrure, of lawe and of resoun.   100

---

83. and² P] XU þe
93. man U] X *om*
98. she] XUI he; P hue

81–3. Dame Study returns to her argument that a little learning is a dangerous thing, that the Christian truths and mysteries are profaned and abused by the laity (a familiar argument against vernacular translation of the scriptures). True learning can only be sought within the strict clerical regime of the school and university (this is the difference between *Wit* and *Study*), and with particular reference to Theology (*Clergy*, see 97 below) and Biblical studies (*Scripture*). These arguments in A originally prepared for the conclusion of A (see 163, 306, below) that a university (i.e. theological) education is not necessary for salvation, and that the simple honest Christian life of Truth will suffice ('The A-text breaks off just where the education of the more enterprising layman would be expected to conclude', Wells, 1929, 125). In BC, Study's arguments begin a complex questioning of the value of learning which is only finally resolved by Imaginatyf.

97. 'And superior in authority to Scripture, with all her knowledge, provided that scribes have copied their texts accurately'. Scripture (Biblical studies) comes into her own where exegesis in relation to textual matters is in question (see B. Smalley, *The Study of the Bible in the Middle Ages*, Oxford, 1952, 214–42: 'The Literal Exposition'); at other times she is subordinate to Clergy, who understands biblical exegesis in relation to theology, which in its turn is the ultimate subject of all clerical learning.

98. *þe seuene ars.* The seven Liberal Arts were divided into the trivium (grammar, logic, rhetoric) and the quadrivium (music, arithmetic, geometry, astronomy), and in that order formed the elementary and advanced university course preliminary to the study of theology.

So with þat Clergie can and consail of Scripture
Thow shalt kunne and knowe kyndeliche Dowel.'
   Thenne was y as fayn as foul of faire morwen,
Gladdere then gleman þat gold hath to ȝefte,
And askede of here þe hey way whare þat Clergie dwelte: 105
'And telle me som tokene,' quod y, 'for tyme is þat y wende.'
   'Aske þe hey wey hennes to Soffre-
Bothe-wele-and-wo-yf-þou-wilt-lerne,
And ryde forth by Rychesse, reste nat þerynne,
For yf thow coueytest to be ryche to Clergie comest thow neuere.   110
Bothe wymmen and wyn, wrothe, ire and slewthe,
Yf thow hit vse oþer haunte, haue god my treuthe,
To Clergie shaltow neuere come ne knowe what is Dowel.
Ac if þow happe,' quod she, 'þat þou hitte on Clergie
And hast vnderstandyng what a wolde mene,   115
Sey hym thysulue ouerseye my bokes
And sey y grette wel his wyf, for y wrot here a bible
And sette here to *Sapience* and to þe sauter yglosed.
   Logyk y lerned here and al þe lawe aftur
And alle þe musons in musyk y made here for to knowe.   120
Plato þe poete y putte hym furste to boke;   f.50^b
Aristotel and oþere to arguen y tauhte.
Gramer for gurles y gart furste write
And beet hem with a baleyse bute yf þei wolde lerne.
Of alle kyne craftes y contreuede here toles,   125
Of carpentrie, of keruers, and contreuede þe compas,
And caste mette by squire, bothe lyne and leuele.
Thus thorw my lore ben men ylered thogh y loke demme.
   Ac Teologie hath tened me ten score tymes;
Þe more y muse þeron the mystiloker hit semeth   130
And þe deppore y deuine the derkore me thynketh hit.
Hit is no science sothly bote a sothfaste bileue,

107–9. *mislineated in* XUI
114. Ac] X As; U but. she] XUI he; P hue
116. ouerseye I] XU ouerse. my P] XUI many
124. beet U] X bed
127. mette I] XU ouet; P out

---

101. *with þat Clergie can*: 'with what Clergy knows'.
103. Proverbial (Whiting F 561).
108–10. Cf. Peres Ploughman's directions to Truth, VII 206ff.
116. 'Tell him that you have some acquaintance with the kind of learning I have to offer'.
118. *Sapience*: the book of Sapience, or Wisdom (but see III 485a). *þe sauter yglosed*: see VI 303n.
128. *thogh y loke demme*: 'though I myself can see but poorly'.

Ac for hit lereth men to louie y beleue þeron þe bettere,
For loue is a lykyng thyng and loth for to greue.
Lerne for to louie yf þe lik Dowel,   135
For of Dobet and Dobest here doctour is dere loue.'

    Tho wente y my way withouten more lettynge
And to Clergie y cam as clerkes me saide.
Y grette hym goodly and graythly y hym tolde
How þat Wit and his wyf wissede me to hym   140
To kenne and to knowe kyndeliche Dowel.
    'By Crist,' quod Clergie, 'yf thow coueyte Dowel
Kepe þe ten comaundementis and kepe þe fro synne
And byleef lely how goddes sone alyhte
On þe maide Marie for mankynde sake   145
And bycam a man of þat maide withoute mankynde.
And al þat holi churche herof can þe lere
Leue hit lelly and loke þou do þeraftur.
    Austyn þe olde herof made bokes:
Ho was his autor and hym of god tauhte?   150
Patriarkes and prophetes, apostles and angelis –
And þe trewe trinite to Austyn apperede
And he vs saide as he sey, and so y bileue,
That he seyh þe fader and þe sone and þe seynt spirit togederes
And alle thre bote o god, and herof he made bokes,   155
ʒe, busiliche bokes! ho beth his witnesses?
    Ego in patre et pater in me est; et qui me vidit, patrem
        meum vidit qui in celis est.   f.51ᵃ
Alle þe clerkes vnder Crist ne couthe this assoile,
Bote thus hit bilongeth to bileue alle þat liketh to Dowel.
For hadde neuere frek fyn wit the faith to dispute,
Ne man mouhte haue meryhte þerof, mouhte hit be ypreued: 160

    156. ʒe busiliche bokes P] XUI *om*
    159. wit U] X with
    160. þerof U] X *om*

137. C omits B X 194–221, in which Study offers further examples of the inferiority of
   'science' to Theology.
152. Probably this line does not embody any specific allusion to Augustine's life or
   writing, but the suggestion may have come from *Confessions*, xiii.5, or from the life
   of St Augustine in the *Legenda Aurea*, CXXIV, 564.
156a. 'I (am) in the Father, and the Father is in me' (John 14:10). 'And whoever has
   seen me has seen my Father who is in heaven' (John 14:9, with *qui in celis est*
   added, from the *pater-noster*). Cf. VII 129a.
158. 'But it is this that is necessary for all who desire to do well to believe'.

Fides non habet meritum vbi humana racio prebet experimentum.
Thus bileue and leute and loue is the thridde
That maketh men to Dowel and Dobet and Dobest.'
Thenne Scripture scorned me and mony skiles shewed
And continaunce made on Clergie to congeie me, hit semede,
And lakkede me in Latyn and lyhte by me sette   165
And saide '*Multi multa sciunt et seipsos nesciunt.*'
Tho wepte y for wo and wrathe of here wordes
And in a wynkynge y warth and wonderliche me mette,
For y was rauysched rihte there, for Fortune me fette

160a. *prebet experimentum* B] XU *om*; P possidet dominium
161. Thus P] XUI Thus in. leute] XUI lel; P leaute
165. me in P] XUI a

160a. 'There is no merit in faith where human reason supplies proof'. From Gregory's
Homily 26 on the Gospels (*PL* 76:1197), as used in the first lesson at matins on the
Sunday after Easter (Breviary, I. dccclx), and frequently quoted (e.g. *Speculum
Christiani* 12).
161. *bileue and leute and loue.* Cf. III 378: an example of L's adaptation of the political and
social concepts of the *Visio* to larger theological and spiritual meanings (see X 100).
163. C omits here B X 257–376 with the long discourse by Clergy on false clerics
(including the passage on monks and other regulars transferred to Reason's ser-
mon in C V 146–79), and the first announcement, in a dialogue with Scripture, of
the theme of the salvation of the righteous heathen. C meanwhile brings forward
Scripture's warning (166) and the dream of the land of longing from B XI 1–35.
The purpose of these changes seems to be to accelerate the coming-on of the crisis
of intellect which caused the suspension of the argument in A (see 81 above, and
306 below), and to clarify the process by which B, in a series of turbulent and
eddying developments, broke out of the dilemma.
166. 'Many men know many things, and know themselves not at all': the opening words
of the *Meditationes Piisimae de cognitione humanae conditionis* (*PL* 184:485), a popular
medieval compilation (falsely attributed to St Bernard) similar to the *Liber de spiritu
et anima* (see X 129n), dealing with the soul's ascent through self-knowledge (see
Wittig, 1972, 214, 231), Dame Scripture takes much the same attitude as Dame
Study to the dreamer's attempt to understand intellectually the nature of Dowel.
168. *in a wynkynge y warth*: 'I fell into a doze'. But the dreamer has been asleep since X
66. L may have forgotten; but perhaps the dream-within-a-dream of the land of
longing is an apt image, allegorically, for the dreamer's 'real' life, particularly his
life in all its futility as it follows on the crisis of intellect (see XIII 213). The dream
of the land of longing, in any case, represents the falling into a worldly stupor of
the dreamer in his fictitious life, an escape from despair of salvation. In some
senses, too, it corresponds to the interval in L's life between the symbolic 'death' of
Will in A XII 104 (assuming these lines to be genuine) and the resumption of the
struggle and search in B (see Chambers, 1924. Kirk, 1972, 114–26).
169. Fortune, as Boethius explains in his *Consolation of Philosophy*, book II, is the arbiter
of the destiny of those who dedicate themselves to the things of the world, that is,
to transient and mutable things, and blind themselves to the nature of God's
providence and the pursuit of the true good.

And in to þe lond of longyng alone she me brouhte 170
And in a myrrour þat hihte Myddelerd she made me to loke
And senes she saide to me, 'Here myhte thow se wondres
And knowe þat þou coueytest and come þerto parauntur.'
  Thenne hadde Fortune folwyng here two fayre maydenes:
Concupiscencia carnis men calde þe eldre maide 175
And Coueytise-of-yes ycalde was þat oþer.
And Pruyde-of-parfit-lyuynge pursuede me faste
And bade me for my continence counte clerkes techyng lihte.
Concupiscencia carnis confortede me of this manere
And saide, 'Þou art ȝong and ȝep and hast ȝeres ynowe 180
For to lyue longe and ladyes to louye,
And in þis myrrour thow myhte se murthes fol monye
That lede þe wol to lykynge al thy lyf-tyme.'
The seconde saide þe same: 'Y shal sewe thy wille;
Til thow be a lord and haue lond, leten y the nelle 185
That y ne shal folowe thy felowschipe yf Fortune lyke.'
'A shal fynde me his frende,' quod Fortune þeraftur;

---

172. she B] XUI he; P *om*
184. shal U] X *om*

---

170. *þe lond of longyng* may be the condition of longing for carnal things. But it is also the *regio dissimilitudinis*, the land of unlikeness (Augustine, *Confessions*, vii.10, cf. *Hali Meidenhad* in Blake, 1972, 41) into which the soul strays away from God; this in turn was often associated with the *terra longinqua*, the far-off land ('þis fer contre is þe liif of man in synne': Wyclif, ed. Arnold, ii.70) into which the prodigal son goes away from his father (Luke 15:13). *long of longyng*, in allusion to this, may mean 'land of being-distant (from God)'. See Wittig, 1972, 232–4.

171. *a myrrour þat hihte Myddelerd*. The world is a mirror because it is, as God's creation, an image of the mind of its creator, in its order and beauty (see also XIII 132). But in medieval usage, mirrors, since they reflect an exact image of falsehood as well as of truth, often have dual or ambiguous connotation (cf. *CT* IV. 1582, *Troilus*, i.365); here the mirror of the world merely reflects the dreamer's vanity and cupidity. See Wittig, 1972, 235–41; Kaske, 1968, 163–4, and for a general study of the use of the word *Speculum* in titles, Sister R. Bradley in *Spec.* 29 (1954), 100–115.

175–7. 'Do not love the world, or the things in the world . . . For all that is in the world, the lust of the flesh (*concupiscencia carnis*) and the lust of the eyes and the pride of life, is not of the Father but is of the world' (1 John 2:15–16). These three temptations to sin constitute the state of man in his life in the world; they were the three temptations to which Adam succumbed and which Christ resisted. They were often identified with Gluttony (or Lechery: see *Prick of Conscience* 1141), Avarice and Pride, and associated with another triad, the World, the Flesh and the Devil (see I 37n, and D. R. Howard, *The Three Temptations*, Princeton, 1966, 43–53).

178. *for my continence*: 'for the sake of my looks' or 'as far as self-restraint was concerned' (*continence* and *countenance* are cognate forms).

'The man þat me liketh to helpe myhte nat myshappe.'
   Thenne was þere oen þat hihte Elde, þat heuy was of chere.
'Man,' quod Elde, 'yf y mette with the, by Marie of heuene,   190
Thow shalt fynde Fortune þe fayle at thy moste nede   f.51ᵇ
And *Concupiscencia carnis* clene the forsake;
Bitterliche shaltow banne thenne bothe dayes and nyhtes
Couetyse-of-yes þat euere thow here knewe;
And Pruyde-of-parfit-lyuynge to moche perel the brynge.'   195
   'Ʒe? reche þe neuere,' quod Rechelesnesse, stod forth in
          ragged clothes;
'Folowe forth þat Fortune wole, þou hast ful fer to elde;
A man may stoupe tyme ynowe when he shal tyne þe croune!'
Sir Wanhope was sib to hym as som men me tolde,
For Rechelesnesse in his rybaudie riht thus he saide: 200
'Go y to helle or to heuene y shal nat go myn one!

---

189. þere U] X *om*
200. rybaudie U] X rybaude

---

189. The earlier introduction in C of the beginning of the dream of Fortune (see above, 163n) makes this reference to *Elde* a distant and not ineffective anticipation of XII 1–13.

196. *Rechelesnesse*. One of the major innovations in C is the extension of the role of Rechelesnesse (see Donaldson, 1949, 170–75), who was briefly introduced in B XI 34–41 in the lines corresponding to C XI 196–8, 306–11. Rechelesnesse is an aspect of the dreamer's consciousness (XII 3–4, XIII 128–33), and at first represents his careless reaction (cf. Parson's Tale, *CT* X. 710, where *reccheleesnesse* is a species of Sloth) to warnings of mortality and his desire to find easy answers to the problem of Dowel. The immediate purpose of extending his role in C is so as to allocate to him the intellectual questionings concerning learning and salvation attributed to the dreamer of AB, and in so doing to discredit them explicitly, or at least to withdraw from them any hint of authorial sanction. Later, taking over (XII 87) the speeches attributed in B to the dreamer (by Skeat to *Leaute*), Rechelesnesse seems to represent a quality of 'carelessness' not altogether unadmirable (e.g. freedom from worldly cares; see also XVI 348), as if L were trying to enforce the paradox (cf. IX 136n) involved in juxtaposing the usual pejorative sense of the word with the injunctions of Matt. 6:25–34. But much remains unclear, and there is no certainty that L completed his reworking of this difficult section of the poem. For the argument that changes in this section are due to changes in L's attitude towards the necessity of baptism for salvation, see Russell, 1966, 105–6. For the suggestion that L is dealing with issues raised by the Lollards, see XIII 79n. *ragged clothes* may have had a Lollard ring: a sermon against Lollards, quoted in Owst, 1933, 374, says: 'Thei the go to ragged and to rent and schewe out-ward, it is nothyng in her herte; for more prowder men, mor envyus men, than thei be with-inne, bethe none in this world'.

198. 'It will be time enough for a man to stoop when he finally loses his hair'. *stoupe* plays on the senses 'stoop (with age)' and 'stoop (in order to work)' (cf. V 24). *þe croune* was the circle of hair left after tonsure.

Were hit al soth þat ȝe seyn, thow Scripture and thow Clergie,
Y leue neuere þat lord ne lady þat lyueth her in erthe
Sholde sitte in goddis sihte ne se god in his blisse.
> *Ita possibile est diuiti intrare in regnum celorum*
> *sicut camelus, etc.*

For Clergie saith þat he seyh in þe seynt euaungelie   205
That y man ymaed was and my nam y-entred
In þe legende of lyf longe ar y were.
Predestinaet thei prechen, prechours þat this sheweth,
Or prescient inparfit, pult out of grace,
Vnwriten for som wikkednesse, as holy writ sheweth.   210
> *Nemo ascendit ad celum nisi qui de celo descendit.*

And y leue hit wel, by oure lord, and on no lettrure bettere.
   For Salomon þe sage þat *Sapience* made,
God gaf him grace of wit and of goed aftur,
Neuere to man so moche þat man can of telle,
To reule alle reumes and ryche to make,   215
And demede wel and wysly, wymmen bereth wittenesse:
> *Nec michi nec tibi, set diuidatur.*

204a. *regnum* U] X regno
209. prescient U] X precyet

204a. 'It is possible for a rich man to enter into the kingdom of heaven as (it is possible for) a camel (to go through the eye of a needle)' (Matt. 19:23–4, varied).

205. *Clergie saith.* Not an actual reference to anything that has passed in the poem, but a general reference to the Church's teaching on predestination (which was reinforced by the Augustinian revival of the 14th c.: see VII 269n).

207. *þe legende of lyf:* the book of life of Apoc. 20:12.

208. *Predestinaet thei prechen:* 'they preach [in the sense, proclaim] (men to be) predestinate (to be saved)'. L alludes here, with a direct transliteration of Lat. *predestinati,* 'those predestined to be saved', to the Wycliffite doctrine of the predestination of the elect (Leff, 1967, 516–19).

209. *Or prescient inparfit:* 'or known beforehand to be imperfect' (with use of another technical term from theology).

210. *Vnwreton.* 'And if anyone's name was not found written in the book of life, he was thrown into the lake of fire' (Apoc. 20:15; cf. John 3:13).

210a. 'No one has ascended into heaven but he who descended from heaven, (the Son of man)' (John 3:13). Rechelesnesse proceeds to interpret this text in a very simple-minded way.

212. *Sapience.* See above, 118n.

215. *ryche to make:* 'to give prosperity to his people'. Cf. *divites facit,* Prov. 10:22.

216a. '(It shall be) neither mine nor yours, but let it be divided' (3 Reg. 3:26). The allusion is to the famous judgment of Solomon in the dispute of the two mothers who claimed the same child as their own. He decreed that the living child should be divided into two, and half given to each. The true mother gave up her claim; the false agreed to the division, in the words above.

Aristotel and he, ho tauhte men bettere?
Maistres þat men techen of goddis mercy and prechen
Wittenesseth þat here wordes and here werkes bothe
Were wonder goed and wisest in here tymes,   220
And holi churche, as y here, haldeth bothe in helle!
And yf we sholde worche aftur here werkes to wynnen vs heuene
That for here werkes and wyt wonyeth now in payne
Thenne wrouhte y vnwysly for alle ȝoure wyse techynge.   f.52ᵃ
    Ac y countresegge the nat, Clergie, ne thy connyng, Scripture,   225
That ho-so doth by ȝoure doctrine doth wel, y leue.
Ac me were leuere, by oure lord, a lyppe of goddes grace
Thenne al þe kynde wyt þat ȝe can bothe and kunnyng of ȝoure bokes.
For of fele witty, in faith, litel ferly y haue
Thogh here gost be vngracious god for to plese.   230
For mony men in this molde more sette here herte
In goed then in god; forthy hem grace faileth.
At here moste meschef mercy were þe beste
And mercy of mercy nedes moet aryse,
As holy writ witnesseth, goddes word in þe gospel: 235
    Eadem mensura, etc.
Wel ywitted men and wel ylettred clerkes,
Seldom ar they seyen so lyue as they lere.

218. prechen B] XU techen; P *om*
227. Ac] X As; U but
233. here U] X he

221. L introduces here the question of the salvation of the righteous unbaptized, which
remains a preoccupation throughout the rest of the poem, as a test of the truth of
God's promise of love and redemption (see XIV 208n), and a challenge to the
more ruthless theology of predestination. Orthodoxy assigned all unbaptized,
before and after the act of Redemption, to hell (unbaptized babies to a special
region between hell and limbo); an exception was made for the patriarchs and
prophets of the OT, who were placed *in limbo inferni*, in a region on the outskirts of
hell (XVIII 116, 266), whence they were taken out by Christ at the harrowing of
hell (XX 269ff); and a particular exception was made for Enoch and Elias, who
went straight to heaven (Gen. 5:24, 4 Reg. 2:11, Nicodemus 25). Many, however,
accepted a modification of this opinion, which placed the righteous heathen (e.g.
Aristotle) in limbo, to dwell there until the day of judgment. The place of
Solomon was a matter of particular dispute, because of the contradictory accounts
of his later career in 3 Reg. 11 and 2 Para. 9; he was never mentioned among
those brought out of limbo by Christ, and was generally assumed to be in hell (cf.
III 327). It is worth nothing that Rechelesnesse introduces the question, not out of
any concern for Aristotle and Solomon, but in order to prove that learning is of no
use in winning salvation. He is answered by Imaginatyf in XIV 131ff.

235a. 'With the same measure (that you give, it shall be measured out to you in
return)' (Luke 6:38). Cf. I 174a.

Wittnesseth godes word þat was neuere vntrewe:
> *Super cathedram Moysi, etc.*

Ac y wene hit worth of monye as was in Noes tyme
Tho he shoop þe ship of shides and bordes: 240
Was neuere wrihte þat þeron wrouhte ne werkman ysaued
Bote briddes and bestis and þe blessed Noe
And his wyf with his sones and his sones wyues;
Of wryhtes þat hit wrouhte was noen of hem ysaued.
God leue hit fare nat so by folk þat þe faith techen   245
Of holy kirke, þat sholde kepe alle cristene soules.
For *Archa Noe*, nymeth hede, ys no more to mene
Bote holy churche, herborw to alle þat ben yblessed.
The *culorum* of this clause curatores is to mene,
That ben carpentares vnder Crist, holy kirke to make   250
For lewed folk, goddes foles and his fre bestes.
> *Homines et iumenta saluabis.*

At domesday a deluuye worth of deth and fuyr at ones;
Worcheth, ȝe wrihtes of holy churche, as holy writ techeth,
Laste ȝe be loste as þe laboreres were þat labered vnder Noe.

A Gode Friday, y fynde, a feloun was ysaued   255
That vnlawefulliche hadde ylyued al his lyf-tyme,
And for he biknewe on þe croes and to Crist shrof hym   f.52^b
He was sunnere ysaued then seynt Iohn þe Baptiste
And ar Adam oþer Ysaye oþer eny of the profetes
That hadde yley with Lucifer mony longe ȝeres.   260
A robbare was yraunsomed rather then thei alle;
Withoute penaunce oþer passioun oþer eny other peyne

238a. *cathedram* I] XU cathedra
250. ben U] X *om*

238a. See VIII 86a.
247–8. The interpretation of Noah's Ark as the Church is usual: see 1 Pet. 3:20–21, and
X 32n. The carpenters who built the ark are, according to this interpretation, the
priests of the Church.
249. 'The conclusion consequent upon this interpretation refers to priests'. For *culorum*,
see III 432n.
251a. 'Men and beasts thou wilt save' (Ps. 35:7, taken to allude to the Flood).
252. The Flood is a type of the Last Judgment in Matt. 24:37–9.
255. Having shown that learning is of no avail in winning salvation, Rechelesnesse now
turns to examples of salvation granted to the sinful and ignorant. For the penitent
thief on the cross, see Luke 23:42–3, and VI 320n.
258. According to the *Descensus Christi ad Inferos*, also known as the second part of the
gospel of Nicodemus (see VI 320, XX 259n), the penitent arrived at the gates of
paradise and was bid to enter and await the arrival of Adam and the others
released from hell. See Nicod. 26, i.e. *Descensus*, cap. X (Tischendorf 405).
261. *rather*: 'sooner'.

Passet forth paciently to perpetuel blisse.
   Then Marie Maudelene who myhte do worse
As in likyng of lecherye, no lyf denyede?   265
Or Dauid þe douhty þat deuyned how Vrye
Mouhte sleylokeste be slawe and sente hym to worre,
Lelly, as by his lokes, with a lettere of gyle?
Poul þe apostel, that no pite ne hadde
Cristene peple to culle to dethe?   270
And now beth this seyntes, by that men saith, and souereynes
     in heuene,
Tho that worste wrouhten þe while þat thei here were.
By that þat Salamon saith hit semeth þat no wyht
Woet ho is worthy for wele or for wykkede,
Wheþer he is worthy to wele or to wykkede pyne.   275
    Sunt iusti atque sapientes et opera eorum in manu dei sunt.
   Thus y, Rechelesnesse, haue yrad registres and bokes
And fonde y neuere in faith, for to telle treuthe,
That clergie of Cristes mouthe comaunded was euere.
For Crist saide to sayntes and to suche as he louede:
    Dum steteritis ante reges vel presides, etc.
"Thogh ȝe come bifore kynges and clerkes of þe lawe   280

---

266. deuyned P] XUI deuyed
268. lettere P] XUI leare
269. þat P] XUI *om*
269–70. *lineation as* U; X *mislineates as one line*
271. *lineation as* U; X *mislineates* souereynes/In heuene
273–4. *lineation as* P; XUI *mislineate* wyht woet/Ho
280. lawe U] X lawes

---

264. *Marie Maudelene.* Medieval tradition associated the Mary Magdalene of Luke 8:2 and of the passion and resurrection story (VII 138n) with the prostitute who washed Christ's feet with her tears in Luke 7:37–50. See also XII 134, XVII 21, and for general discussion of the legend, H. M. Garth, *St Mary Magdalene in Med. Lit.* (Baltimore, 1950); also, on the Mary Magdalene hymns, J. Szövérffy in *Traditio* 19 (1963), 79–146.

265. *no lyf denyede*: '(seeing that she) denied no man'.

266. David desired Bathsheba, wife of Uriah, and sent a letter, by Uriah, to Joab, the commander of his troops, ordering him to place Uriah in the forefront of the battle where he would be killed (2 Reg. 11:14–17).

268. 'In good faith, to all appearances, but with a letter full of deceit'.

269. Paul's persecution of Christians before his conversion is told in Acts 8.

274. *for wele or for wykkede*: 'for well or for wicked doing'.

275a. 'There are just men and wise men, and their works are in the hand of God: (and yet man knoweth not whether he be worthy of love, or hatred)' (Eccl. 9:1). The book of Ecclesiastes, like Proverbs and the book of Wisdom (Sapience), was attributed to Solomon.

279a. 'When you stand before kings or governors, etc.' (used as a response at matins on the Nativity of an Apostle, Breviary, II. 366, adapted from Mk. 13:9).

Beth nat aferd of þat folk for y shal ʒeue ʒow tonge
And connyng and clergie to conclude suche alle."
Dauid maketh mensioun he spake among kynges
And myhte no kyng ouercome hym as in connynge of speche.
Sothly,' saide Rechelesnesse, 'ʒe se by many euydences   285
That wit ne wihtnesse wan ʒeuere þe maistrie
Withoute þe gifte of god which is grace of fortune.
   For he þat most sey and saide of the sothfaste trinite
Was Austyn þe oelde þat euere man wiste,
Saide thus in his sarmon for ensaunple of grete clerkes: 290
   Ecce ipsi idiote rapiunt celum vbi nos sapientes in
       inferno mergimur.
And is to mene no more to men þat beth lewed,   f.53ᵃ
"Aren noen rather yraueschid fro þe rihte bileue
Comuneliche then clerkes most knowyng in konnyng,
Ne none sonnere ysaued ne none saddere in bileue
Then ploughmen an pastours and pore comune peple."   295
Lewed lele laboreres and land-tulyng peple
Persen with a *pater-noster* paradys oþer heuene
And passen thorgh purgatorie penaunceles for here parfit bileue.
   Breuis oratio penetrat celum.
   Selde falleth þe seruant so depe in arrerage
As doth the reue or contrerollor þat rykene moet and acounten   300
Of al þat they haen had of hym þat is here maister.

---

286. wihtnesse] XU witnesse; P wyghtnesse. maistrie U] X maistre
287. which is grace of] XU which grace of; P with hus grace and
288. sey U] X seith
294. sonnere ysaued U] X sauere ysanned
299. T *begins here as a C-text*

283. 'And I spoke of thy testimonies before kings, and I was not ashamed' (Ps. 118:46).
289. *þat euer man wiste* completes the sense of *most* in the previous line.
290. *Saide*: '(who) said'.
290a. 'Lo, these ignorant men seize heaven by force while we wise men are plunged into hell' (Augustine, *Confessions*, viii.8). *idiote* means 'simple people', with no connotation of idiocy. For the phrase *rapiunt celum*, see Matt. 11:12. Whether L appreciates the context of the Augustinian passage or not (see a note by C. D. Benson in *NQ* 221, 1976, 51–4), it is clear that some irony must attach to Rechelesnesse's use of the greatest doctor of the church in an attack on learning, and to the extravagantly generalized translation he provides.
298. Cf. IX 185n. The orthodox view was that purgatory might be by-passed by those who led devout ascetic lives of penance and self-denial and by baptized children who died young (*Prick of Conscience* 2637–42, 3286–3349). The views expressed throughout this passage are, of course, those of Rechelesnesse.
298a. 'A short prayer penetrates heaven'. Proverbial (Alford 390), ultimately from Eccl. 35:17. Cf. Jesus's condemnation of the long prayers of the scribes and Pharisees, Matt. 23:14.

So lewede laborers of litel vnderstondyng
Selde falleth so foule and so depe in synne
As clerkes of holy chirche þat kepe sholde and saue
Lewede men in good bileue and lene hem at here nede.'   305
'*Homo proponit*,' quod a poete tho, and Plato he hihte,
'*Et deus disponit*,' quod he, 'lat god do his wille.
All þat Treuth attacheth and testifieth for gode,
Thow thei folowe þat Fortune wole, no folye ich it holde.
Ne *Concupiscencia carnis* ne Coueytise-of-yes   310
Ne shal nat greue the grettly, ne bigyle the, but yf thow wolle.'
'Ʒe, farewel, Fyppe!' quod Fauntelete, and forth gan me drawe
Til *Concupiscencia carnis* acorded til al my werkes.
Of Dowel ne of Dobet no deynte me ne thouhte,
Ne Clergie ne his conseile – y counted hit ful litel!   315

302. So B] XUTP Ac (But)
304. kepe sholde U] X sholde socoure (socoure *inserted*)
307. lat U] X lad
309. no U] X in
310. ne Coueytise-of-yes B] XUTP *om with subsequent mislineation*
312. Fauntelete X] U a fauntelete

306. C returns at this point to the sequence of B, and the end of the dream of the land of longing (see above, 163n, 168n, 189n); A meanwhile is brought to an independent conclusion in its short passus XII. The allocation of speeches in 306–11 is not easy to determine: the inclusion of *tho* in 306 (C only) suggests that Plato is introduced as an independent witness, and not within the discourse of Rechelesnesse. The whole of 306–11 could be attributed to Plato (as here), though his direct address to the dreamer in 311 is not entirely appropriate; alternatively, R could resume speaking in 307 (as if to cap Plato's remark) or in 308. *Homo proponit*, etc.: 'Man proposes and God disposes', familiar as a proverb (Walther 11102), identical in sense with Prov. 16:9 and in form with a passage in Hugh of St Cher's commentary on that text (Alford 394). *Plato* is referred to in a general way, as an 'authority' for proverbial sayings; L commonly refers to him as 'a poet' (e.g. 121, above), perhaps for no other reason than the alliteration.

308. 'All those that Truth claims jurisdiction over and testifies to be good'. The argument, that to follow the way of the world is reconcilable with adherence to Truth, sounds suspect, but 309ª can be read as a simple acceptance of the condition of man in his worldly life.

312. *Fyppe*: Phip, a pet-name for a sparrow (either imitating its chirp, or dim. of Philip), used here of a trivial and tedious subject (suggesting that what Plato said was true and proper). *Fauntelete*: 'childishness', i.e. a trivial and frivolous part of the dreamer's character, speaking here in opposition to Elde.

Passus XII

The Debate about Salvation continued:
Discourse of Rechelesnesse on Humility and Patient Poverty

Passus secundus de Dowel

'Allas, eye!' quod Elde and Holynesse bothe,
'That wit shal turne to wrechednesse for Wil hath al his wille!'
  Couetyse-of-yes conforted me aftur
And saide, 'Rechelesnesse, reche the neuere; by so thow riche were,
Haue no consience how þou comst to good—confesse the to som frere;   5
He shal asoile the thus sone how so euere thow wynne hit.
For while Fortune is thy frende freres wol the louye
And festene the in ther fraternite and for the byseche
To here priour prouincial his pardoun to haue
And preye for the, pol by pol, yf thow be *peccuniosus*.'   10 f.53^b
  Pena peccuniaria non sufficit.
  By wissyng of this wenche y dede, here wordes were so swete,
Til y forȝet ȝouthe and ȝorn into elde.
And thenne was Fortune my foo for al her fayre biheste
And pouerte pursuede me and potte me to be lowe.
And flittyng fond y the frere þat me confessede   15

---

5. Haue . . . good T] XU *om with mislineation*
8. fraternite U] X flaternite

---

2. *Wil.* L takes advantage of the familiar contrast with *wit* and the play on the
dreamer's name (I 5n).

6–10. L refers here to familiar charges against the friars: that they looked to profit
from the granting of absolution (Prol. 62n, VI 120n) and of letters of fraternity
(III 51n, VII 27n), of pardon (cf. IX 344) and the gift of prayer.

6. *how so euere thow wynne hit*: thus defying the Church's ruling on restitution (VI 296–
9, cf. VIII 235). Friars are particularly warned against accepting alms of this kind
by Repentance (VI 287–93).

10. *pol by pol*: 'head by head', i.e. each benefactor will have a separate mass said for
him.

10a. 'A financial penalty is not enough' (a comment on the preceding argument that
money solves all problems). A maxim of canon law (Lyndwood, *Provinciale:
Constitutio D.Othoboni*, 99).

12. *forȝet*: 'passed right through' (i.e. *forȝede*).

And saide he myhte nat me assoile but y suluer hadde
To restitue resonably for al vnrihtfole wynnynge.
   'Ouh!' quod y tho to hym, and myn heued waggede,
'By my faith, frere,' quod y, 'ȝe fare lyke þe woware
That wilneth nat þe wedewe bote for to welde here godes.   20
Riht so, by þe rode,' quod y, 'rouhte ȝe neuere
Wher my body were yberied by so ȝe hadde my godes.'
   And thenne louhe Leaute for y loured on þe frere:
'Why lourest þou?' quod Leaute. 'Leue sire,' y saide,
'For this frere flaterede me þe while he fond me ryche   25
And now y am pore and penyles at litel pris he sette me.
Y wolde it were no synne,' y saide, 'to seien þat were treuthe;
The sauter sayth hit is no synne for suche men þat ben trewe
To segge as they seen and saue only prestis:
     Existimasti inique quod ero tibi similis; arguam te et
       statuam contra faciem tuam.
Thei wolle allegge also and by þe gospel preuen hit,   30
   Nolite iudicare quemquam.'
   'And wherof serueth lawe,' quod Leaute, 'and no lyf vndertoke

---

18. to hym T] XU *om*
22. yberied U] X ybered
24. þou I] XU *om*

16–17. The friar claims that he always accepted money as a form of restitution; if there is no money, therefore, he cannot grant absolution.

19–22. A similarly lively indictment of the friars' avarice appears in *The Simonie* 163–92 (see Prol. 62n).

27. L introduces here another important theme: the extent to which public criticism of falsehood, especially of false clerics, is a proper part of the love of Truth and the life of Dowel (cf. Ecclus. 4:23). It is closely related to the question of the role of learning, which dominates these passus, since learning is more or less exclusively the province of clerics. *Leaute* (31n) is introduced to provide a preliminary answer to the question – one which interests L acutely since he views his own role as a poet essentially as that of the 'sayer of truth'.

29. *saue only prestis*, i.e. priests should not publicly rebuke sinners if it involves revealing the secrets of the confessional.

29a. 'You have thought wrongly that I should be one like yourself; (but) I shall accuse you and lay the charge before you' (Ps. 49:21). The verse begins: 'These things you have done and I have been silent'. God is presented rebuking the wicked.

30. *Thei.* The adaptation from B XI 89 does not make it entirely clear that *Thei* are the opposition, namely the friars, who know how to 'glose the gospel' (Prol. 58).

30a. 'Do not judge anyone' (Matt. 7:1, varied).

31. *and no lyf vndertoke*: 'if no-one reproved'. For *Leaute*, see Prol. 149n, II 20, and below, 87, 91, 95.

Falsnesse ne faytrye? for sumwhat þe apostel saide:
   Non oderis fratrem tuum secrete in corde.
Thyng þat al þe world woet wherfore sholdest thow spare
To rehercen hit al by retoryk to arate dedly synne?
Ac be neuere more þe furste the defaute to blame;   35
Thouh thowe se, say nat sum tyme, þat is treuthe.
Thyng þat wolde be pryue publische thow hit neuere,
Nother for loue labbe it out ne lacke hit nat for enuye.
   Parum lauda, vitupera parcius.'
'A saith soth,' quod Scripture tho, and skypte an heyh and
     prechede.
Ac þe matere þat she meuede, if lewede men hit knewe,   40 f.54[a]
The lasse, as y leue, louyon þey wolde
The bileue of oure lord þat lettred men techeth.
Of here teme and here tales y took ful good hede;
She saide in here sarmon selcouthe wordes:
'*Multi* to a mangerye and to þe mete were sompned   45
And whan þe peple was plenere ycome þe porter vnpynnede þe gate
And plihte in *pauci* priueiliche and lette þe remenaunt go rome.'

32a. *tuum* U] X *om*
44. She] XUIT he; P hue

---

32. *for sumwhat*: 'for some good reason'. *þe apostel*: Paul, who echoes the following injunction on many occasions, e.g. 1 Tim. 5:20, Titus 1:13.

32a. 'You shall not hate your brother secretly in (your) heart (but lay your charge against him openly)' (Lev. 19:17). L takes advantage of the pun on biblical *fratrem*, 'neighbour', and *fratrem*, 'friar'.

33–8. The writer's responsibility, like the preacher's, is the denunciation of open and blatant sinfulness. But he must restrict himself to what is public knowledge (lest enthusiasm give way to self-righteousness) and show patience (cf. the poem, likewise inspired by gnomic tags of pseudo-classical provenance, 'See much, say little, and learn to suffer in time', in *Religious Lyrics of the XVth century*, ed. C. Brown, Oxford, 1939, no. 181; and cf. XIII 219); and he must avoid matters of private sin that are properly secret (see 29n) and personal attacks where he might be motivated by malice (like Chaucer's Pardoner, *CT* VI. 412–22). Wycliffite tracts are much concerned to assert the need to cry out openly against the sins of priests, especially friars (e.g. Wyclif, ed. Arnold, ii.75–6, 201–3, iii.349; ed. Matthew, 264–5, 271–4, 296–8, 312–15).

38a. 'Praise little, blame less'. Proverbial, wrongly attributed to Seneca (Alford 394, cf. Walther 13480, 13524).

39. *an heyh*, i.e. into a pulpit. Scripture's last appearance was in XI 166 (cf. XI 202, 225); her message now is similarly forbidding.

45–7. A summary of the parable of the marriage-feast, which in Matt. 22:14 concludes: 'Many (*multi*) are called, but few (*pauci*) are chosen. The version presented here eliminates altogether the suggestion of the early part of the parable (22:3–6) that the wicked, in refusing the invitation, choose to show themselves unworthy; it stresses therefore the idea of pre-election to God's grace, and raises again (cf. XI 208), more acutely, the problem of predestination.

Al for tene of here tyxst tremblede myn herte
And in a wer gan y wex and with mysulue to despute
Where y were chose or not chose; on Holy Churche y thouhte   50
That vnderfeng me at þe fonte for on of godes chosene.
For Crist clepede vs alle, come yf we wolde,
Sarrasynes and sismatikes, and so a ded þe Iewes,
And bad hem souke for synne sauete at his breste
And drynke bote for bale, brouke hit ho-so myhte: 55
    O vos omnes sicientes, venite ad aquas.
'Thenne may alle cristene come and clayme þerto entre
By þat bloed he bouhte vs with and bapteme as he tauhte:
    Qui crediderit et baptizatus fuerit, etc.
For thogh a cristene man coueitede his cristendom to renoye,
Rihtfolliche to renoye no resoun hit wolde.
For may no cherl chartre make ne his chatel sulle   60
Withouten leue of þe lord; no lawe wol hit graunte.
Ac he may renne in arrerage and rome fro home
As a recheles caytyf other reneyed, as hit semeth;
Ac reson shal rekene with hym and rebuken hym at þe laste
And consience acounte with hym and casten hym in arrerages   65
And potten hym aftur in prisoun in purgatorie to brenne
And for his rechelesnes rewarde hym þere riht to þe day of dome,
Bote yf contricioun and confessioun crye by his lyue

50. or not chose U] X *om*
54. sauete P] XUIT saue
64. Ac] X As; U But

51. Cf. I 73.
54. *for synne*: 'as a remedy against sin'. Christ, by shedding his blood, gave the hope of
salvation. Sinners were often represented, therefore, drinking the blood gushing
from the chief wound in his side. Associated here is the image of Christ the
mother, suckling his children, derived from texts like Isa. 49:15, 66:13 (see Woolf,
1968, 189–90), and the image of the pelican (VII 134n).
55a. 'O all you that thirst [Vg. *sitientes*], come to the waters' (Isa. 55:1), echoed in
Apoc. 21:6 and 22:17 as an allusion to the fountain of the water of life, i.e. of
Christ's redeeming blood.
56. A passage of direct speech must begin here (cf. B XI 123), possibly spoken by R
(but see 67 below), so that Scripture can reply in line 70.
57a. 'He who believes and is baptized (shall be saved)' (Mk. 16:16).
58–69. A man baptized into the faith can no more 'leave' that faith (cf. the friar's
argument, X 39) than a bond-man can deny his bondage by running away,
though both may suffer punishment for this 'rechelesnes'.
60. A bond-man had no legal property and no rights in law: what he possessed was
his lord's, as were his children and his own body. See R. Hilton, *Bond Men Made
Free* (London, 1973), 55–62.
68. *by his lyue*: 'during his life'.

Mercy for his mysdedes with mouthe and with herte.'
'That is soth,' saide Scripture; 'may no synne lette   70
Mercy þat she ne may al amende, and mekenesse her folowe.
They bothe, as oure bokes telleth, are aboue godes werkes:
   Misericordia eius super omnia opera eius.'
'ʒeʔ bawe for bokes!' quod oen, was broken out of helle.   f.54ᵇ
'I, Troianes, a trewe knyht, y take witnesse of a pope
How y was ded and dampned to dwellen in hell   75
For an vncristene creature, seynt Gregori woet þe sothe,
That al þe cristendoem vnder Crist ne myhte me crache fro thenne
Bote onlyche loue and leaute as in my lawes demynge.
Gregori wiste this wel and wilned to my soule
Sauacion for þe soethnesse a sey in my werkes.   80
And for a wilnede wepynge þat y were ysaued
God of his goodnesse ysey his grete will
And withouten mo bedes-biddyng his bone was vnderfonge
And y saued as ʒe may se withoute syngynge of mo masses.
Loue withoute lele bileue as my lawe rihtfoel   85
Saued me, Sarrasyn, soule and body bothe.'

71. she] XU he; T heo
72. aboue U] X boþe
72a. *eius²* U] X *om*

72a. 'His mercy is above all his works' (Ps. 144:9).
74. *Troianes.* Legends associated with Gregory the Great, pope 590–604, told (e.g.
   Legenda Aurea, XLVI, 196–7) how he prayed for the soul of the emperor Trajan (d.
   117), whose righteousness of life had impressed him. Trajan, who was in hell (not
   in limbo: cf. XI 221n, XIV 149), was promptly released, because in his life he
   lived according to truth as he knew it (XIV 208n). L does not accept, as do
   Aquinas and Dante (Dunning, 1943, 53), that Trajan was restored to life and
   christened. He apparently went straight to heaven (XIV 205: see Russell, 1966,
   108–9). For the legend and its interpretation in the Middle Ages, see Wittig, 1972,
   249–63. The legend was of crucial importance in discussions of grace, predestina-
   tion and salvation, as is made clear in the Introduction, pp. 19–30, to the edition
   of *St Erkenwald* by Ruth Morse (Cambridge and Totowa, 1975). Trajan's con-
   tempt for books will be readily taken up by R and made part of his attack on
   learning, but the lesson of Trajan's experience is two-edged: it offers comfort for
   the righteous unbaptized, but no comfort for the dreamer, who has sought (52–72)
   security in faith, baptism and knowledge of the law, and now finds that *loue and
   leaute* in good works are apparently more important. The question will be resolved
   by Imaginatyf (XIV 206) and Liberum Arbitrium (XVII 125).
78. 'But only love and loyalty to truth in the exercise of justice as I understood
   it'.
86. *Sarrasyn*: 'a pagan'. 'Saracen' was often applied to the followers of Mahomet
   (e.g. III 480, XVII 150–86), but often also generally, as here, to any pagan or
   infidel.

'Lo, lordes, what leute dede and leele dome y-used!
Wel ouhte ȝe lordes þat lawes kepeth this lesson to haue in mynde
And on Troianes treuthe to thenke alle tyme in ȝoure lyue
And louye for oure lordes loue and do leute euermore.   90
For lawe withouten leutee, ley þer a bene!
Or eny science vnder sonne, the seuene ars and alle,
Bote loue and leute hem lede ylost is al þe tyme
Of hym þat trauaileth heron bote treuthe be his lyuynge.
So loue and leute hit ben oure lordes bokes   95
And Cristis oune clergie, he cam fro heuene to teche hit,
And seynt Ion sethen saide hit of his techyng:
    Qui non diligit manet in morte.
And nameliche pore peple, here preyeres may vs helpe.
For god, as þe gospel saith, goth ay as þe pore,
And as þe euaungelie witnesseth, when we maken festes   100
We sholde nat clepie knyhtes þerto ne none kyne ryche:
    Cum facitis conuiuia, nolite vocare amicos.
"Ac calleth the carefole þerto, the crokede and the pore.
For vch a frende fedeth other, and fondeth hou beste to quite
Meles and manschipes, vch a riche man oþer;
Ac for þe pore may nat paye y wol pay mysulue;   105

87. *and leele dome y-used*: 'and true exercise of justice as practised by him'. The speaker is not immediately identifiable, but XIII 128 suggests that the long preceding discourse, starting here, is spoken by R, who first seizes on the story of Trajan as proof that love and truth can win salvation without learning, and then proceeds to develop this theme with characteristic energy (see XI 196n). As often, his interpretation is recklessly simple, and has later to be qualified (XIV 204).

92. *the seuene ars.* See XI 98n.

97a. 'He who does not love remains in death' (1 John 3:14).

98. The virtue of poverty dominates the rest of R's discourse. The essential theme is the equality of all men in the sight of God and in capacity to win grace, an orthodox belief which is being exploited by R as part of his strategy to discredit learning and prove it unnecessary to salvation. R's eulogy of poverty, though it may seem unobjectionable in itself, must be seen in relation to the great 13th and 14th c. debate about poverty, where St Francis's original insistence on the imitation of the poverty of Christ and his disciples was gradually developed, particularly by the extreme wing of the Franciscan movement, the Spirituals or Zealots, into an attack on all ecclesiastical possession. This view of poverty was condemned by the Church, but it was vigorously taken up by Wyclif, along with the demand for the disendowment of the Church. Even the poverty of Christ (see 99, 130, below, and XXII 37n) was decreed to be comparative, not absolute. See Leff, 1967, 51–166, 527–9; also XIII 99, XVI 111.

99. This line is a poor remnant of B XI 185–9. The gospel reference is to Christ's account of the Last Judgment, Matt. 25:37–40.

101a. 'When you give a dinner, do not invite your friends (or your brothers or your kinsmen or rich neighbours, lest they also invite you in return, and you be repaid)' (Luke 14:12). The following lines continue the paraphrase.

102. Cf. XI 42.

That louieth and leneth hem largeliche shal y quyte."
In Caluarie of Cristis bloed cristendoem gan sprynge   f.55ᵃ
And blody bretherne we bycome there of o body ywonne,
As *quasi modo geniti* gentel men vchone,
No beggare ne boy among vs but hit synne make.   110
      Qui facit peccatum seruus est peccati.
In þe olde lawe, as þe lettre telleth, mennes sones me calde vs
Of Adames issue and Eue ay til god man deyede,
And aftur his resureccoun *redemptor* was his name
And we his blody bretherne, as wel beggares as lordes.
Forthy loue we. as leue childerne, lene hem þat nedeth,   115
And euery man helpe other for hennes shal we alle
To haue as we haen serued as holy chirche witnesseth:
      Et qui bona egerunt, ibunt, etc.
   Forthy lerne we þe lawe of loue as oure lord tauhte
And pore peple fayle we nat while eny peny vs lasteth,
For in here likenesse oure lord lome hath be yknowe.   120
Witnesse in þe Paske-woke when he ȝede to Emaux:
Cleophas ne knewe hym nat þat he Crist were

---

112. god man U] X god and man (and *inserted*)
114. lordes U] X loddes
118. þe T] X to; U *om*

---

106. 'You will be paid at the resurrection of the just' (Luke 14:14). *That*: 'those that'.
108. *blody bretherne.* Cf. VIII 216; also 54 above.
109. *quasi modo geniti*: 'as if new born' (1 Pet. 2:2, varied according to the form used in the Introit for Low Sunday, the first after Easter, Missale 385). Christ's blood makes all men new born as gentle-men (i.e. free men), unless sin causes them to forego their new status and return to servility. There is some allusion too to Christ as the nobly born lover-knight (XX 11n) and to the association of sin and servility of the next line (cf. XX 107, XXI 34).
110a. 'Everyone who commits sin is a slave to sin' (John 8:34). But 'the truth will make you free' (8:32).
111. *mennes sones*: *filii hominum*, the term invariably used in the OT, where the NT uses *filii Dei*.
112. *god man*: 'god in the form of a man'.
115. *as leue childerne.* Perhaps suggested by Eph. 5:1: 'be followers of God, as beloved children'.
116. *euery man helpe other.* Cf. Gal. 6:2: 'Bear one another's burdens'.
117a. See IX 288.
121. The story of the appearance of the resurrected Christ on the journey to Emmaus is told in Luke 24:13–35. The failure of the witnesses to recognize Christ is a characteristic feature of the post-Resurrection stories (cf. John 20:14, 21:4). The speaker here takes advantage of a particular interpretation of this element in the story, which emphasizes the importance of *werkes* done in poverty and humility as against outward observance (*clothyng*) of the law (Robertson–Huppé, 1951, 141). Cf. XVI 99.

For his pore parail and pilgrimes clothes
Til þat he blessed here bred and brake hit hem bitwene.
So by his werkes thei wisten þat he was Iesu
Ac by clothyng they knewe hym nat, so caytifliche he ȝede.   125
And al was ensample sothly to vs synfole here
That we sholde be low and louelich, and lele, vch man til oþer,
And pacient as pilgrimes for pilgrimes are we alle.
In þe parail of a pilgrime and in pore likenesse   130
Holy seyntes hym sey, ac neuere in secte of riche.
    And seynt Marie his moder, as Mathew bereth witnesse,
Was a puyre pore mayde and to a pore man ywedded.
Marthe on Marie Maudelene an huge pleynte she made
And to oure sauyour sulue saide þis wordes: 135
    Domine, non est tibi cure quod soror, etc.
And here aytheres wille hastilich god assoiled
And aitheres werkes and will riht wel alowede,
Ac pouerte god potte byfore and preuede for þe betere:
    Maria optimam partem elegit, que non, etc.
    And alle þe wyse þat euere were, by auhte y can aspye,
Preisede pouerte for beste, if pacience hit folowe,   140 f.55ᵇ
And bothe bettere and blessedere by manyfold then richesse.
Althouh he be sour to soffre, þer cometh a swete aftur.
As on a walnote withoute is a bittere barke
And aftur þat bittere barke, be þe scale aweye,
Is a cornel of confort, kynde to restore;   145
So aftur, penaunce and pouerte, pacientliche ytake,
Maketh man to haue mynde in god and his mercy to craue,
The which is þe cornel of confort for alle cristene soules.

---

125. his T] XU this
135a. *cure* P] XUT cura
136-7. hastilich ... will U] X *om*

135a. 'Lord, do you not care that my sister (has left me to serve alone)?' (Luke 10:40). The identification of Mary, sister of Martha and Lazarus, with Mary Magdalene (see XI 264n, XVII 20n) was usual in the Middle Ages.
138a. 'Mary has chosen the best portion, which shall not (be taken away from her)' (Luke 10:42). The story of Martha and Mary was traditionally used to contrast the life of the world and the life of the spirit (or the active and contemplative lives). The *optima pars*, identified by the speaker here (unusually) as poverty, was traditionally interpreted as virginity, e.g. by Hugh of St Cher (*PL* 177:781); see XVIII 76n.
145. *kynde*: nature, natural strength. Walnuts were recognized to have excellent nutritive properties, though there is reference here also to patristic interpretation of biblical uses of 'nut', where the shell and kernel are likewise made to correspond to the winning, through tribulation, of the sweetness of divine consolation (see R. E. Kaske in *JEGP* 58, 1959, 650-54; also Kaske, 1960, 35-6).
146. *So aftur*: 'so likewise'.

And wel sikorere he slepeth, þe segg þat is pore,
And lasse drat by day or in derke to ben yrobbed,   150
Then he þat is rihte ryche, reson bereth witnesse:
Pauper ego ludo, dum tu diues meditaris.
    Holy Churche witnesseth, "Ho-so forsaketh
His fader or his frendes, fremde oþer sybbe,
Or eny welthe in this world, his wyf or his childrene,   155
For þe loue of oure lord loteth hym to be pore,
He shal haue an hundred fold of heuene-ryche blisse
And lyf lastyng for euere byfore oure lord in heuene."
    Quicunque relinquit patrem et matrem, etc.
Crist acordeth efte herwith; clerkes wyteth þe sothe,
What god saide hymsulue to a segg þat he louede: 160
"Yf thow likest to lyue," quod god, "þe lyf þat is parfit,
Al þat thow haste here, hastly go and sulle hit;
Ʒef pore peple þe panes, þerof pors þou none,
Ac Ʒef hem forth to pore folk þat for my loue hit aske;
Forsaek al and sue me and so is thi beste."   165
    Si vis perfectus esse, vade et vende, etc.
Ʒut conseileth Crist in commen vs all:
"Ho-so coueiteth to come to my kyneriche
He moet forsaken hymsulue his suster and his broþer
And al þat þe world wolde, and my will folowe."
    Nisi renunciaueritis omnia que possidetis, etc.

---

156. loteth] X lotheth; U loueth; I logeth; T lowiþ; P loweth
169a. *possidetis* U] X posidetis

---

152. 'I am poor and free from care, while you are rich and full of anxiety'. Proverbial (Walther 20907, Alford 394–5), apparently originating with Alexander of Ville-Dieu.

153. From here to XIII 100 is an addition in C, in praise of poverty.

158a. 'Everyone who leaves [Vg. *reliquerit*] father and mother, etc.' (Matt. 19:29). The preceding lines here are a paraphrase of the whole verse, which is part of Christ's explanation to the disciples of the difficulty for the rich of entering the kingdom of heaven (19:23).

165a. 'If you would be perfect, go and sell (all you have and give to the poor, and you will have treasure in heaven)' (Matt. 19:21). The preceding lines again paraphrase the surrounding text: it is characteristic of L to work closely with biblical texts in this way, particularly in C (cf. VII 292n). The whole passage in Matthew, of Christ's advice to the young man (19:16–22), is important to an understanding of the shift in the poem from the *Visio* to the *Vita*, from the good life to the perfect life, from the right use of worldly goods to renunciation (see I 79n, VII 299; the gospel text is similarly used in the prefatory dialogue on poverty in *Dives et Pauper*). Much of the discussion here of poverty and riches parallels the Meed episodes, but on a different spiritual level (cf. VIII 2n).

169a. 'Unless you renounce all that you possess (you cannot be my disciple)' (Luke 14:33, varied). The preceding lines echo 14:26.

Mo prouerbes y myhte haue of mony holy seyntes 170
To testifie for treuthe þe tale þat y shewe,
And poetes to preuen hit, Porfirie and Plato;
Aristotel, Ennedy, enleuene hundred, f.56ᵃ
Tulius, Tolomeus, y can nat tell here names,
Preueth pacient pouerte prince of alle vertues. 175
    And by þe grayn þat groweth god vs all techeth
Meschiefes on molde mekeliche to soffren:
    Nisi granum frumenti cadens in terram mortuum fuerit, etc.
Bote if þe seed þat sowen is in the sloo sterue,
Shal neuere spir sprynge vp, ne spiek on straw kerne.
Sholde neuere whete wexe but whete furste deyede, 180
And oþer sedes also in þe same wyse,
That ben layd in louhe erthe, ylore as hit were,
And thorw þe grace of god and grayn dede on erthe
At the laste launceth vp whereby we lyuen all.
    Ac sedes þat ben sowen and mowen soffre wyntres 185
Aren tidiore and touore to mannes byhofte
Then sedes þat sowe ben and mowen nat with forstes,

173. Ennedy X] U Eueyde; T euredie (?); P Ouidius
177. Meschiefes] X mesciefes; U mescheues
181. And T] XU on
185. Ac I] X As; U and þe

172–4. An example of rhetorical amplification through random citation of learned 'authorities' (cf. XIV 189). Porphyry (a 4th c. Greek philosopher), Plato (see XI 306n), Aristotle, Ennodius (a Christian–Latin poet of the 5th c.: other texts refer to Ovid), Tullius (Cicero) and Ptolemy the astronomer (2nd c.) were probably little more than names to L, though he may be remembering scraps attributed to them in *florilegia*, collections of *sententiae* and apophthegms, which were the source of much medieval knowledge of classical writers. One such saying, relevant here, is quoted by Chaucer and attributed to 'Senec and othere clerkes' in *CT* III. 1183: 'Glad poverte is an honest thyng' (Whiting P 331). For another poetic eulogy of patient poverty, see *Patience* (ed. J. J. Anderson, Manchester, 1969), ll. 35–48 (based on the Beatitudes, Matt. 5:3–10).

177a. 'Unless a grain of wheat falls into the earth and dies (it remains alone; but if it dies, it bears much fruit)' (John 12:24). One might suspect that L was led to this text from Luke 14:26 (see 169a, above) via John 12:25–6, and that in this way the whole of the following sequence was generated. The application made by Christ of the seed image is of course that death to the world is eternal life, but 'he who loves his life loses it' (12:25). This sense is not incompatible with the use of the text made here by R.

178. *Bote if*: 'unless'.

182. The gospel interpretation presses strongly in these lines: the planting of the seed is the source of life, just as burial underground or 'death' is the source of life, i.e. through Christ's resurrection from such a burial, 'whereby we lyuen all'.

187. *mowen nat with*: 'may not endure' (so too 190–91 below).

Ne wynde ne wederes, as in wynter tymes;
As lyn-sed, lek-sed, and lente-sedes all
Aren not so worthy as whete, ne so wel mowe   190
In þe feld with þe forst, and hit frese longe.
Riht so, sothly, þat soffry may penaunces
Worth allowed of oure lord at here laste ende
And for here pacience ben ypresed as for puyr martir,
Or for a confessour ykud, þat counteth nat a ruche   195
Fere ne famyne ne fals mennes tonges.
But as an hosebonde hopeth aftur an hard wynter,
Yf god gyueth hym þe lyf, to haue a goed heruost,
So preueth this profetes þat pacientliche soffren,
Mescheues and myshappes and many tribulacounes   200
Bitokeneth treuly in tyme comyng aftur
Murthe for his mornyng and þat muche plentee.
For Crist saide tho seyntes þat for his sake tholeden
Pouerte and penaunce and persecucoun of body
Schullen haue more worschipe to wages [and worthier ben yholde]   205
Then angelis in here owen degre; on this wyse hem grette:
      Tristicia vestra vertetur in gaudium.
"Ʒoure sorwe into solace shal turne at þe laste
And out of wo into wele ʒoure wirdes shal chaunge."   f.56ᵇ
   Ac ho-so rat of the ryche, the reuers may fynde,
How god, as þe gospelle telleth, gyueth hym foel to name,   210
And þat his gost shal go and goed bileue,

---

203. tho] XI to; U so to; TP to hise
205. *this line in* I *only* (*where the MS is defective; the last four words are by Skeat*)
206. owen degre I] XUTP anger
209. the U] X th
210. hym T] XUI *om*

---

192. *þat*: 'those that'.
195. *for a confessour ykud*: 'acknowledged as (equal in holiness to) a confessor'.
197. The farmer is similarly used as a model of the patient Christian in James 5:7. The whole passage in James (5:1–11) is important here.
199. 'As an example of suffering and patience, brethren, take the prophets' (James 5:10).
206a. 'Your sorrow will turn into joy' (John 16:20). Christ is speaking to the disciples, who are sorrowful (whence the reading *in here anger* in MSS XUP) and uncomprehending at his impending departure. He has already described the persecution they will suffer (John 15:18–16:4). His reference here is to the joy that the disciples will have in the Resurrection.
210. *gyueth foel to name*: 'calls (them) by the name of fool' (i.e. *stulte*, 214a), lit, 'gives fool as name' (see OED, s.v.*to*, sense 22). Skeat suggests 'evil nickname' for his reading *foul towname* (OED, *to-name*), but *stulte* is not really a nickname, and L is here paraphrasing the scriptural text.
211. *and good bileue*: 'and his goods remain'.

And asketh hym hertely, "Ho shal hit haue,
The catel þat he kepeth so in coffres and in bernis,
And art so loth to leue that lete shal thow nedes?
    O stulte, ista nocte anima tua egredietur.
    Tezaurisat, et ignorat, etc.
An unredy reue thy residue shal spene,   215
That many mothe was maister ynne, in a mynte-whyle;
Vpholderes on þe hulle shal haue hit to sulle."
   Lo, lordes, lo! and ladyes, taketh hede,
Hit lasteth nat longe þat is lycour swete,
As pesecoddes, pere-ionettes, plomes and cheries.   220
That lihtlich launseth vp litel while dureth,
And þat rathest rypeth rotieth most sonnest.
On fat lond ful of donge foulest wedes groweth:
Riht so, sothly, suche þat ben bischopes,
Erles and erchedekenes and oþere riche clerkes,   225
That chaffaren as chapmen and chide bote they wynne
And haen þe world at her wille oþerwyse to leuene.
Riht as wedes waxeth in wose and in donge,
So of rychesse ope rychesse arisen alle vices.
Lo, lond ouerleyd with marl and with donge,   230
Whete þat þeron wexeth worth lygge ar hit rype;
Riht so, sothly, for to segge treuthe,
Ouer-plente pruvde norischeth, þer pouerte hit distrueth.
   For how hit euere be ywonne, but hit be wel dispendid,
Worldly wele ys wykked thyng to hem þat hit kepeth.   235

---

212. hym hertely T] XI *om*; U him; P hym after
214a. *egredietur* U] X egrediatur
227. her U] X he
229. arisen U] X ariste
234. be wel dispendid U] X wel despeneth

213–14. The 3rd person gives way to the 2nd as L moves closer to the scriptural text.
214a. 'Fool! this night your soul will depart; (and the things you have accumulated, whose will they be?)' (Luke 12:20, varied). 'Man heaps up riches [Vg. *thesaurizat*], and knows not (who will gather)' (Ps. 38:7, suggested here by Luke 12:21).
216. The suggestion of the *mothe* could have come from either of the preceding texts, viz. Luke 12:33 (but Matt. 6:19 is fuller), Ps. 38:12.
217. *Vpholderes on þe hulle*: 'second-hand dealers (or worse) on Cornhill'. See VI 374, V 1, and *Liber Albus* 624–5.
222. Proverbial: 'Soon ripe, soon rotten' (Whiting R 142).
223. 'Most subject is the fattest soil to weeds' (*2 Henry IV*, IV. iv.54).
227. 'And have it in their power, if they wished, to live otherwise'.
231. *worth lygge*: 'will be laid flat to the ground under its own weight'. For *lygge*, see OED, s.v. *ledger*, adj. 5b. The theme is still of poverty as a form of spiritual toughening and purgation, but the image is now of hard soils rather than hard weather. The succession of agricultural images in this passage is interesting.

For if he be fer þerfro, fol ofte hath he drede
That fals folk fecche awaye felonliche his godes;
And ȝut more hit maketh men mony tymes and ofte
To synege, and to souche sotiltees of gyle,
For coueytyse of þat catel to culle hym þat hit kepeth.   240
And so is many man ymorthred for his moneye and his godes
And tho that dede þe dede ydampned þerfore aftur,
And he for his hard holdyng in helle, parauntur.   f.57ᵃ
So coueytise of catel was combraunce to hem alle.
Lo, how pans purchaseth fayre places and grete,   245
That rote is of robbares the rychesses withynne.

245. grete U] X deede; ITP drede
246. *Skeat here adds a line from MS M*

243. *hard holdyng*: 'close-fistedness' (Skeat).
246. 'The riches within which (i.e. the fine houses) make robbers what they are'. The
reading with *drede* is strained, and Skeat's additional line unnecessary.

Passus XIII

Rechelesnesse concludes; the Mirror of Middle-Earth

Passus tercius de Dowel
Ac wel worth Pouerte! for he may walke vnrobbed
Among pilours in pees, yf pacience hym folowe.
Oure prince Iesu pouerte chees, and his apostles alle,
And ay þe lengere they lyuede the lasse goed they hadde.
    Tanquam nichil habentes.
   Зut ret me þat Abraham and Iob weren wonder ryche,   5
And out of nombre tho men many mebles hadden.
Abraham for his auзte hadde moche tene,
For in greet pouerte he was put; a prince, as hit were,
Bynoem his hosewyf and Abraham not hardy ones to letten hym
Ne for brihtnesse of here beaute here spousehod to byknowe.   10
And for he soffrede and saide nauht, oure lord sente tookene,
That the kynde comely kynge criede hym mercy
And delyuerede the weye his wyf, with moche welthe aftur.
   Iob þe gentele, what ioye hadde he on erthe!
And how bittere he hit abouhte, as þe book telleth.   15
And for a song in his sorwe, "*Si bona accepimus a domino,*
Derworthe and dere god! do we so *mala,*"
Alle his sorwe to solace thorw that song turnede,
And Iob bykam as a iolyf man, and al his ioye newe.

---

7. auзte T] XUI *om*
10. spousehod to T] XU spouse to be
12. comely kynge T] XUI *om*

---

1. *wel worth Pouerte*: 'well may it be for Poverty', i.e. Poverty will be better off. Behind these two lines lies a familiar tag from Juvenal, to the effect that the poor man sings when he comes among thieves (*Sat.* x.21–2). Chaucer has it in the Wife of Bath's Tale (*CT* III. 1192) and in a gloss in his translation of Boethius (II, pr. 5, 202). See XVI 141n.
4a. 'As having nothing (and possessing all things)' (2 Cor. 6:10).
8. *a prince*: Abimelech. The story is told in Gen. 20.
10. Abraham, on journeying into Gerar, declares Sarah to be his sister, not his wife, so that he will not be killed by those who covet her beauty (Gen. 20); he did the same when he went down into Egypt (Gen. 12:13).
16. If we accept good from God (shall we not also accept) evil?' (Job 2:10). Job is the example of suffering and patience in James 5:11 (see XII 199n).

Lo, how pacience in here pouerte thise patriarkes releuede   20
And broughte hem all aboue, þat in bale rotede.
As grayn þat lith in greut and thorw grace at the laste
Spryngeth and spredeth, so spedde þe fader Abraham
And þe gentel Iob; here ioye hath non ende.
Ac leueth nat, lewede men, þat y lacke rychesse   25
Thogh y preyse pouerte thus and preue hit by ensaunples
Worthiore as by holy writ and wyse fylosofres.
Bothe þei·ben gode, be ʒe ful certeyn,
And lyues þat oure lord loueth and large weyes to heuene.
Ac þe pore pacient purgatorye passeth   30
Rather then þe ryche thogh they renne at ones.   f.57ᵇ
      For yf a marchant and mesager metten togyderes
And sholden wende o wey where bothe mosten reste
And rikene byfore resoun a resonable acounte
What oen hath, what anoþer hath, and what they hadde bothe,   35
The marchaunt mote nede be ylet lenger then the messager,
For þe parcel of his paper and oþer pryue dettes
Wol lette hym, as y leue, the lenghe of a myle,
Ther þe messager doth no more but with his mouth telleth his erende
And his lettre sheweth and is anoon delyuered.   40
And thogh they wente by the wey tho two togederes,
Thogh the messager make his way amydde the fayre whete
Wol no wys man be wroth ne his wed take –
      Necessitas non habet legem –
Ne non haiward is hote his wed for to taken.

20. in here P] XUIT and
28. þei T] XI to; U two
30. Ac] X As; U But.   purgatorye U] X þe purgatorye
37. paper U] X pauper

22. An echo of the theme of XII 184.
30–31. Cf. XI 299, and the contrast there of servant and reeve, similar to that of messenger and merchant here.
43a. 'Necessity has no law'. Proverbial (Walther 16295c). Cf. XXII 10.
44. The *haiward* was a manor official appointed to prevent trespass on the cultivated land by animals or persons (cf. V 16, and the poem *The Man in the Moon* in *Harley Lyrics*, ed. G. L. Brook, Manchester, 1948, 69). From trespassers he will extract a *wed*, or pledge of payment of a fine. The suggestion here seems to be that the messenger, because he has no money to pay the fine, commits no offence in breaking the law. This is dubious, and encourages the suspicion that R's praise of poverty, orthodox in itself for the most part, is motivated by a search for 'cheap grace', refusing the effort to learn and understand and settling for 'sinlessness for want of opportunity' (see B. J. Harwood in *MP* 70, 1972–3, 279–90, esp. p. 289: but Patience's arguments in XVI 43ff are similar). But haywards could be extortioners, and were much hated (see Wyclif, ed. Matthew, 444, for an allegorical use of the 'wickid hayward'), so that our attitude to Rechelesnesse's *exemplum* cannot be unambiguous.

Ac if þe marchaunt make his way ouer menne corne
And þe hayward happe with hym for to mete, 45
Oþer his hatt or his hoed or elles his gloues
The marchaunt mote forgo or moneye of his porse,
And ȝut be ylette, as y leue, for the lawe asketh
Marchauntz for here marchaundyse in many place to tolle.
   And ȝut thow they wende o way as to Wynchestre fayre 50
The marchaunt with his marchauntdyse may nat go so swythe
As þe messager may ne with so moche ese.
For þat on bereth but a box, a breuet þerynne,
Ther þe marchaunt latte a male with many kyne thynges
And dredeth to be ded þer-fore and he in derke mette 55
With robbares and reuares þat ryche men despoilen,
Ther þe messager is ay merye and his mouth ful of songes
And leueth for his lettres þat no lede wole hym greue.
Ac ȝut myhte þe marchaunt thorw his moneye and other ȝeftes 60
Haue hors and hardy men – thogh he mette theues
Wolde noon suche assailen hym for such as hym foloweth,
And as safly as þe messager and as sone at his hostiele come.
   Ȝe wyte, ȝe wyse men, what this is to mene:
The marchaunt is no more to mene but men þat ben ryche 65
Aren alle acountable to Crist and to þe kyng of heuene, f.58ᵃ
That holde mote þe hey way, euene the ten hestes,
Bothe louye and lene lele and vnlele
And haue reuthe and releue with his rychesse by his power
All maner men yn meschief yfalle; 70
Fynde beggares bred, bakkes for þe colde,
Tythen here goed treuthliche, a tol, as hit semeth,
That oure lord loketh aftur of vch a lyf þat wynneth
Withoute wyles or wronges or wymmen at þe stuyues;

59. lede T] XUIP wyht
63. as sone U] X asone
68. lele U] X lene
70. yn U] X *om*

51. *Wynchestre fayre.* See IV 51n.
58. *ful of songes.* See above, 1n.
65. *but*: 'but that'.
67. For the 'high way' of the Ten Commandments, see VII 205ff.
69. *by his power*: 'as far as lies in his power'. The responsibilities of the rich are described in terms similar to the conditions of the pardon granted to merchants, IX 27–36.
71. *bakkes for þe colde*: 'clothes for their backs as a protection against the cold'.
73. *loketh aftur*: 'expects'.
74. For discussion of the validity of tithes or alms derived from ill-gotten gains, see VI 287ff, VIII 235n.

And ȝut more, to maken pees and quyten menne dettes   75
And spele and spare to spene vppon þe nedfole
As Crist hymsulf comaundeth alle cristene peple:
   Alter alterius onera portate.
The messager aren this mendenantz þat lyuen by menne almesse,
Beth nat ybounde as beth ȝe ryche to bowe to þe lawes,
To lene ne to lerne ne lentones to faste   80
And other pryue penaunces þe which þe prest woet wel
That þe lawe ȝeueth leue such low folk to be excused,
As none tythes to tythe ne to clothe the nakede
Ne in none enquestes to come ne contuimax thogh he worche
Haly day or holy euene his mete to discerue.   85
For if he loueth and byleueth as the lawe techeth –
   Qui crediderit et baptizatus fuerit, etc. –
Telleth þe lord a tale as a trewe messager
And sheweth be seel and seth by lettre with what lord he dwelleth
And knowelecheth hym cristene and of holy kirke byleue,
Ther is no lawe, as y leue, wol lette hym þe gate   90
Ther god is gateward hymsulf and vch a gome knoweth.
So þe pore of puyr reuthe may parforme þe lawe
In þat a wilneth and wolde vch a wyht as hymsulue.
For þe wil is as moche worthe of a wrecche beggare
As al þat þe ryche may rayme and rihtfuly dele,   95
And as moche mede for a myte þer he offreth
As þe ryche man for al his mone and more as by þe gospell:
   Amen dico vobis, quia hec vidua paupercula, etc.
  So pore and pacient parfitest lyf is of alle;
Vch a parfit prest to pouerte sholde drawe.   f.58[b]

---

79. bowe to þe] X þe (*space preceding*); UP boþe þe two; I boþe þe; To boþe to þe
99. parfit U] X parfist

77a. 'Bear one another's burdens' (Gal. 6:2). So XII 116.
79. The argument, that poor beggars are released from obedience to the law (like the messenger, 44n, above), is contradictory to authorial statement in IX 220, 235, and is evidently a reckless exaggeration on the part of Rechelesnesse. The views expressed, not entirely unpersuasively, by R (see XI 196n, 208n, XII 87n, 98n) are similar in some ways to those of the Lollards (cf. 99 below).
86a. See XII 57a.
92. The poor man acts according to the law in feeling compassion for others (even though he can do nothing to help them). Skeat's reading, *porter* for *pore*, is attractive, but involves a sudden change of subject in 93.
97a. 'Truly I say to you, that this poor widow (has put in more than all the others)' (Mk. 12:43 and Luke 21:3, the story of the widow's mite).
99. The insistence on priestly poverty is characteristic of Wyclif's doctrines (Leff, 1967, 527–9; cf. XVI 111 and see XII 98n).

For *spera in deo* speketh of prestis þat han no spendynge suluer 100
That yf thay trauaile treulyche and trist in god almyhty
Hem sholde neuere lacke lyflode noþer lynnen ne wollene.
The tytle ȝe take ȝoure ordres by telleth ȝe ben avaunsed
And nedeth nat to nyme siluer for masses þat ȝe synge.
For he that toek ȝow a title sholde take ȝow wages 105
Or þe bischop þat blessed ȝow and enbaumed ȝoure fyngeres.

For made neuere kyng no knyhte but he hadde catel to spene
As byful for a knyht, or fond hym for his strenthe;
For hit is a carfol knyhte and of a caytif kynges makynge
That hath noþer lond ne lynage ryche ne good los of his handes. 110
The same y segge for sothe by suche þat beth prestes
That han noþer connyng ne kyn bote a croune one
And a title, a tale of nauht, to his lyflode as hit were.
Euele beth thei ysoffred, suche þat shendeth þe masse
Thorw here luyther lyuynge and lewede vnderstondynge. 115

A chartre is chaleniable byfore a chief iustice;
Yf fals Latyn be in þat lettre þe lawe hit enpugneth,
Or peynted par-entrelynarie, parseles ouerskipped.
The gome þat gloseth so chartres for a goky is halden.
So hit is a goky, by god! þat in þe gospel fayleth 120
Or in masse or in matynes maketh eny defaute.
    Qui offendit in vno in omnibus est reus.

---

112. han U] X *om*
114. shendeth] X syngeth (*inserted*); U segge (*inserted*); I *om*; T shenden; P shynden

100. C returns here to the matter of B (see XII 153). *spera in deo*: 'trust in God' (Ps. 36:3). The psalm, applied here to priests (because it is spoken by the priest as he goes up to the altar in the mass: Hort 51), speaks at length of the prosperity of the wicked and the poverty of the righteous, and of the inheritance promised to the latter, and sustenance in this life ('I have not seen the righteous forsaken or his children begging bread', 36:25, see IX 162a).

103. *The tytle ȝe take ȝoure ordres by*: 'the title you receive at ordination', i.e. the title of *priest*. *avaunsed*: 'placed in a position of special privilege and authority', *priest* being derived from Lat. *presbyter* (e.g. Titus 1:5), 'elder'.

105. *he that toek ȝow a title*: 'he that gave you the name (of priest)', i.e. the pope who, as vicar of Christ, was the ultimate authority for all ordination.

108. *or fond hym for his strenthe*: 'or else was able to provide for himself by strength of arms'. Skeat suggests *fond* = 'chose', with *kyng* as subject, but the sense of *fond* would be unusual.

112–13. 'Who have neither learning nor (influential) relations, but have to live on, as it were, only a tonsure and a title (of priest), which (in their case) is a mere name'.

118. 'Or drawn up with interlineation, (or with) bits left out'. Passages such as this (cf. A VIII 43) suggest that L himself worked as a legal scribe.

121a. 'Whoever fails in one point is guilty in all' (James 2:10). An example is provided by the priest of VI 367.

For ouerskipperes also in þe sauter sayth Dauid:
> *Psallite deo nostro, psallite; quia Rex terre deus, psallite*
> *sapienter.*

The bishop shal be blamed before god, as y leue,
That crouneth suche for goddes knyhtes that conne *sapienter*
Nother syng ne rede ne seye a masse of þe day.   125
Ac neuer noþer is blameles, the bischop ne þe chapeleyn,
For *ignorancia non excusat*, as ych haue herd in bokes.'

   Thus Rechelesnesse in a rage aresenede Clergie
And Scripture scornede þat many skilles shewede,
Til þat Kynde cam Clergie to helpe   130
And in þe myrour of Mydelerthe made hym efte to loke,
To knowe by vch a creature Kynde to louye.
   And y bowed my body, bihelte al aboute,   f.59ᵃ
And seyhe þe sonne and þe see and þe sond aftur,
And where þat briddes and bestis by here make þei ʒeden,   135
Wilde wormes in wodes and wondurfol foules
With flekede fetheres and of fele colours.
Man and his make y myhte se bothe,
Pouerte and plente, bothe pees and werre,
Blisse and bale bothe y sey at ones,   140

122a. *terre* U] X *om*
125. ne seye a masse of þe day B] XUITP *om with mislineation*

122a. 'Sing praises to our god, sing praises; since god is king of the earth, sing praises wisely [i.e. with proper understanding]' (Ps. 46:7–8, varied).
124. *goddes knyhtes* alludes to the analogy of 107–8 above, with some sense too of the tonsure, the mark of ordination, as a kind of spiritual 'dubbing'.
127. 'Ignorance is no excuse'. A maxim of canon law (Lyndwood, *Provinciale*, 1; Friedberg, ii.928, 1122), later proverbial.
128. Here the discourse of R ends (see XI 196n), with a decisive repudiation of his opinions.
130. *Clergie to helpe*. Clergy has been silent for a long time (since XI 162), and meanwhile R has dominated the poem with his assault on learning. Kynde now attempts to bring R (the dreamer) to an understanding of the value of Clergy by allowing him to read in the book of Nature, but it is not until the discourse of Imaginatyf (XIV) that the dreamer is completely brought round. He meets Clergie again in XV 26. See Chambers, 1924, 55–63.
131. *Mydelerthe*, i.e. between heaven and hell. The world of Nature (*Kynde*), or natural order, is the *myrour* of the order in the mind of its Creator. This is the second opportunity the dreamer has been given to see and understand the world in this *myrour* (cf. XI 171). Still only imperfectly distinguished from R (see 131, 133) in the trust he places in his unaided vision, he again seizes on a false issue and commits himself to a gross misunderstanding.
138. *bothe*: 'also'.

And how þat men mede toke and mercy refusede.
   Resoun y sey sothly sewe alle bestes
In etynge and drynkyng, in engendrure of kynde.
Aftur cors of concepcion noon toek kepe of oþer,
As when þei hadde roteyed anon they reste aftur;   145
Males drow hem to males a morwenynge by hemsulue,
And femeles to femeles ferddede and drowe.
Ther ne was cow ne cow-kynde þat conseyued hadde
That wolde bere aftur bole, ne boer aftur sowe.
Ther ne was no kyne kynde that conseyued hadde   150
That ne lees the lykynge of lost of flesch, as hit were,
Saue man and his make; and þerof me wondrede,
For out of resoun they ryde and rechelesliche taken on,
As in derne dedes, bothe in drynkyng and elles.
   Briddes y beheld þat in bosches made nestes;   155
Hadde neuere weye wyt to worche þe leste.
Y hadde wonder at wham and where þe pye
Lernede to legge stikkes þat ley on here neste;
Ther is no wriht, as y wene, sholde worch here nest to paye.
Yf eny mason made a molde þerto, moche wonder me thynketh.   160
   And ȝut me merueylede more, mony of þe briddes
Hudden and helede here egges dernely
For no foul sholde hit fynde but his fere and hymsulue.

141. men U] X *om*
146. a U] X and
148. was U] X *om*
153. taken P] XUIT token
154. in² T] XUI *om*
155. þat U] X *om*
157. wham] X whan; U whom
158. legge U] X begge

141. *mercy refusede*, i.e. refused God's gift of mercy and promise of redemption (by failing to follow Truth).
146. *a morwenynge*: 'in the morning'. Kane-Donaldson emend the corresponding line in B XI 339 to *al mornyng*, referring to the notion *post coitum est omne animal triste* (p. 160). This is attractive, though the anthropomorphic view of animal sexuality here will perhaps allow the equally whimsical notion of the morning-after.
150-52. Sexual intercourse during pregnancy was condemned by the Church: see *Vices and Virtues* 249. The whole contrast between the 'natural' sexual behaviour of animals and the unnatural lustfulness of man was homiletic commonplace, but it was normally used, of course, to stimulate man to an awareness of his own sinfulness (e.g. Alan of Lille, *De Planctu Naturae*, pr. 4, 462), not as a way of questioning the reasonableness of the natural order of creation.
153-4. 'For they have intercourse at unnatural times, and continue in it without restraint, with secret practices stimulated by drink and the like'.
160. *made*: 'should make', i.e. were able to make. The domed nest of the magpie is notably elaborate, in fact.

And som treden, y toke kepe, and on trees bredde,
And brouhte forth here briddes al aboue þe grounde.   165
In mareys and in mores, in myres and in watres,
Dompynges dyuede; 'Dere god,' y sayde,
'Where hadde thise wilde suche wit, and at what scole?'
And how þe pocok caukede, þerof toke y kepe,   f.59^b
How vncorteysliche þat cok his kynde for-strenede,   170
And ferlyede of his fayrenesse and of his foul ledene.

   And sethe y lokede on þe see and so forth on sterres;
Mony selcouthes y seyh, aren nat to segge nouthe,
Ne what on floures on felde, and of here fayre coloures,
And how out of greeut and of gras growe so many hewes,   175
And some soure and some swete, selcouthe me thouhte.
Of here kynde and of here colour to carpe hit were to longe.

   Ac þat moste meuede me and my moed chaungede
Was þat y seyh Resoun sewen alle bestes
Saue man and mankynde; mony tymes me thouhte   180
Resoun reuled hem nat, noþer ryche ne pore.

   Thenne y resonede Resoun and ryht til hym y sayde:
'Y haue wonder in my wit, so wys as thow art holden,
Wherefore and why, as wyde as thow regneste,
That thow ne reuledest rather renkes then other bestes?   185
Y se non so ofte sorfeten, sothly, so mankynde;
In mete out of mesure and mony tymes in drynke,
In wommen, in wedes, and in wordes bothe,
They ouerdoen hit day and nyhte and so doth nat oþer bestes;
They reule hem al by resoun, ac renkes ful fewe.   190

---

170. vncorteysliche U] X vncorteyliche. for- X] U forth
171. ledene U] X lenede
181. reuled U] X releued

---

168. The answer to this question is in the discourse of God to Job on the wonder of his creation and the littleness and feebleness of man (Job 38–41). This magnificent tirade, which also inspired Blake's *The Tyger*, is specifically echoed here in the mention of birds, their nests and their eggs (cf. Job 39:14, 27), and of the peacock (*struthio*, 'ostrich', in Job 39:13 was often understood to mean a peacock). God's demand, 'Shall a faultfinder contend with the Almighty?' (40:2) is very relevant here, as is Job's final reply: 'I have uttered what I did not understand, things too wonderful for me, which I did not know' (42:3).

169. A different and more authoritative view of the peacock is offered by Imaginatyf in XIV 172.

174. *Ne what on floures*: 'nor what (marvels I saw) in the flowers'.

182. *resonede*: 'reasoned with, argued with'. To reason with Reason is evidently not a very reasonable thing to do, as the dreamer recognizes in 243, below.

190. *by resoun*. The dreamer is confusing the issue; animals are not ruled by reason, but by natural instinct. Man alone has the power of reason, and the power of choice to follow its law. So much the more 'þan aght man ... noght to be of wers condicion/Þan þe creatours withouten reson' (*Prick of Conscience* 59–62).

And þerfore merueileth me, for man is moste yliche the of wit
    and of werkes,
Why he ne loueth thy lore and leueth as þou techest?'
    And Resoun aresounede me and sayde: 'Reche þe neuere
Why y soffre or nat soffre – certes,' he sayde,
'Vch a segge for hymsulue, Salamon vs techeth: 195
    De re que te non molestat, noli te certare.
Ho soffreth more then god?' quod he; 'no gome, as y leue!
He myhte amende in a mynte-while al þat amys standeth,
Ac he soffreth, in ensaumple þat we sholde soffren alle.
    Is no vertue so fair, ne of valewe ne profit,
So is soffrance souereynliche, so hit be for godes loue.   200
And so witnesseth wyse and wisseth þe Frenche:
Bele vertue est suffrance, mal dire est petit vengeance;
Ben dire e ben suffrer fait lui suffrable a bien venir.
Forthy,' quod Resoun, 'y rede thow reule thy tonge euere,   f.61ª *i.e.* f.60ª
And ar thow lacke eny lyfe, loke ho is to preyse.   205
For is no creature vnder Crist þat can hymsulue make,
And if creatures cristene couth make hemsulue
Vch a lede wolde be lacles, leef thow non other!
Man was made of such matere he may nat wel asterte
That some tyme hym bitit to folewen his kynde;   210
Caton acordeth therwith – *Nemo sine crimine viuit.*'
    Tho cauhte y colour anoen and comesede to ben aschamed,
And awakede þerwith; wo was me thenne
That y ne hadde met more, so murye as y slepte,
And saide anoen to mysulue, 'Slepynge hadde y grace   215
To wyte what Dowel is, ac wakynge neuere!'
    And thenne was ther a wyhte, what he was y neste.
'What is Dowel?' quod that wyhte. 'Ywis, sire,' y saide,

195a. 'Do not argue about a matter which does not concern you' (Ecclus. 11:9).
Reason offers no rational 'arguments' to answer the dreamer – to do so would be
to admit the validity of such intellectual questioning – but instead shifts the
ground of the debate, as does God in answer to Job's protestations of his innocence
and the unjustness of his affliction (Job 31), so as to remind the dreamer of the
inscrutability of God's wisdom and purpose. For homiletic use of the same
argument, see Sermons, ed. Ross, 223.

196. For God's patience and long-suffering, see e.g. 1 Pet. 3:20, 1 Pet. 3:15.

201. *wyse*: 'the wise man', i.e. Solomon, e.g. in Eccl. 7:8: 'The patient in spirit is better
than the proud in spirit'.

202–3. 'Patience is a fair virtue, evil speaking is a petty vengeance; gentle speech and
forbearance bring the patient man to a good end'. Source not identified, but cf.
the passage beginning 'pacience is an heigh vertu' in the Franklin's Tale (*CT* V.
773), which also includes an allusion (779–80) to the tag quoted below, 211.

211. 'No man can live without offending' (*Disticha Catonis*, i.5: see IV 17n).

213. *And awakede þerwith.* This could be regarded as the awakening from the inner
dream of XI 168. In XV 1 the dreamer awakens again without having gone to
sleep, i.e. from the 'outer' dream of X 67.

'To se moche and soffre al, certes, is Dowel.'

'Haddestow soffred,' he sayde, 'slepyng tho thow were,   220
Thow sholdest haue yknowe þat Clergie can, and conseyued mor
      þoruȝ Resoun;
For Resoun wolde haue rehersed þe riht as Clergie seide.
Ac for thyn entermetynge her artow forsake:
    Philosophus esses, si tacuisses. Et alibi: Locutum me
      aliquando penituit, tacuisse nunquam.
Adam, þe whiles he spak nat, hadde paradys at wille,
Ac when he mamelede aboute mete and musede for to knowe   225
The wisdom and the wit of god, he was pot out of blisse.
Rihte so ferde Resoun by the for thy rude speche,
And for thow woldest wyte why of Resones preuete.
For pruyde or presompcioun of thy parfit lyuynge
Resoun refusede the and wolde nat reste with the,   230
Ne Clergie of his connynge kepeth he nat shewe.
For shal neuere, ar shame come, a shrewe wel be chaste.
For lat a dronkene daffe in a dykke falle,
Lat hym lygge, lok nat on hym til hym luste to ryse;
For thogh Resoun rebuke hym thenne, recheth he neuere,   235
Ne of Clergie ne of Kynde Wyt counteth he nat a rusche;
To blame hym or to bete hym thenne y halde hit but synne.
Ac when Nede nymeth hym vp, anoen he is aschamed,   f.61ᵇ *i.e.* f.60ᵇ
And thenne woet he wherfore and why he is to blame.'

'Ȝe seggeth soth, be my soule,' quod y, 'I haue sey hit ofte: 240
Ther smyt no thyng so smerte, ne smelleth so foule
As Shame; ther he sheweth hym, vch man shoneth his companye.

---

221. þoruȝ T] XUI þen
228. of P] XUIT *om.* preuete] X preuede; U priueyte
229. For P] XUIT *om*
232. be P] XUIT *om*

---

219. The dreamer's reply (cf. XII 33) is rueful, but reveals a degree of enlightenment. His colouring with shame at his intellectual presumption (above, 212) was a more positive sign of his convalescence (for the appropriateness of this term, see Boethius, *Cons. Phil.* I, pr. 5. 11–12): see below, 232, 242.

221. *þat Clergie can*: 'what Clergy knows'.

223a. 'You might have been a philosopher, if you had been able to hold your tongue' (adapted from Boethius, *Cons. Phil.* II, pr. 7.20: the moral of a story in which a feigned philosopher is exposed when he reacts with impatience to unjust provocation). And elsewhere: 'I have sometimes regretted having spoken, but never (regretted) having kept silent' (cf. *Disticha Catonis* i.12; also Walther 30954b).

228. The danger and presumption of enquiring too closely into the mysteries of the universe is a common theme in the Middle Ages: see XVI 211–16.

229. 'Because of your pride and presumption in assuming that you knew all about the "perfect life" '. Cf. V 83, 89.

Why ȝe worden to me thus was for y aresonede Resoun.'
  'Ȝe, certes,' quod he, 'þat is soth,' and shop hym to walke;
And y aroes vp riht with that and reuerensed hym fayre,
And yf his wille were, a wolde his name telle?   245

245. y T] XUI *om*

243. The dreamer now shows something of the self-knowledge of which Scripture spoke
    much earlier (XI 166).

Passus XIV

Imaginatif

Passus quartus de dowel vbi prius
'I am Ymagenatyf,' quod he; 'ydel was y neuere
Thogh y sete by mysulue, suche is my grace.
Y haue folewed the, in fayth, mo then fourty wynter
And wissed the fol ofte what Dowel was to mene
And conseyled the for Cristes sake no creature to bygile,   5
Noþer to lye ne to lacke ne lere þat is defended
Ne to spille no speche, as for to speke an ydel,
Ne no tyme to tyne ne trewe thyng tene,
Lowe the and leue forth in þe lawe of holy chirche,
And thenne dost thow wel, withoute drede, ho can do bet, no force!   10
Clerkes þat conne al, y hope they can do bettere,
Ac hit soffiseth to be saued and be such as y tauhte.

---

11. bettere U] X no bettere

1. *Ymagenatyf*. In medieval psychology, *vis imaginativa* (from which L derives his form of the name) was the power of making pictures, ideas and abstractions from the data of experience, and the power, therefore, by which intellectual truth was gained through sensible objects (Bloomfield, 1961, 170–74, and cf. R. Quirk in *JEGP* 53, 1954, 81–3). Like Thought and Wit, he is personified as an innate faculty (see l. 3 here, and X 68n, 73), but in him understanding is enriched through the teaching of Study, Clergy and Scripture. He operates by the making of similitudes (as a form of mediation between sense-data and intellectual truth) and his discourse here, appropriately enough, shows a particular fondness for similes and metaphors (see 104, 166). He has no cognitive authority commensurate with Reason's (see B. J. Harwood in *MÆ* 44, 1975, 249–63, esp. p. 254) and he frankly admits ignorance in some matters (e.g. 153–5, 166–7, 212), but he sums up what the intellect can do as a preparation for the next move in the poem (see Wittig, 1972, 264–77).

7. *an ydel*: 'in idle, idly'.

11–12. From lines 4–16, C departs from B, and omits an interesting passage (B XII 16–29) in which Imaginatyf attacks and L defends his poetry-writing, his 'meddling with makings' (certain lines, however, are picked up in C V 47–8). C is more concerned to tackle squarely the central problem at this point, which is to reconcile the proffer of salvation to the poor and the ignorant (which the dreamer and Rechelesnesse have developed into an argument that learning is useless) with the necessity of learning and the clergy; in larger terms, to reconcile faith and grace

Ac for louye and to lene and lyue wel and byleue
Is ycalde *Caritas*, Kynde Loue an Engelysche,
And þat is Dobet, yf eny suche be, a blessed man þat helpeth   15
That pees be and pacience and pore withoute defaute.
    Beacius est dare quam petere.
  Ac catel and kynde wit acombreth fol monye:
Wo is hym þat hem weldeth but he hem wel despene!
    Scientes et non facientes variis flagellis vapulabunt.
Ac comunlyche connynge and vnkynde rychesse –
As loreles to be lordes and lewede men techares   20
And holy chirche horen helpe, auerous and coueytous –
Druyeth vp Dowel and distruyeth Dobest.
Ac grace is a graes þer-fore to don hem efte growe;
Ac grace ne groweth nat til gode-wil gyue reyne
And woky thorw gode werkes wikkede hertes.   25 f.60ᵃ *i.e.* f.61ᵃ
Ac ar such a wil wexe worcheth god sulue
And sent forth the seynt espirit to do loue sprynge:
    Spiritus vbi vult spirat.
So grace withouten grace of god and also gode werkes
May nat be, be þow syker, thogh we bidde euere.

18a. *Scientes, facientes, vapulabunt* P] XUIT Scienti, facienti, vapulabitur
19. rychesse U] X riche
21. auerous U] X auerours
22. Druyeth U] X Druyueth
24. gyue XT] UIP (by)gynne
25. woky T] X waky; U woke
29. be þow U] X þan

with reason and good works. The present lines offer the first hints of a strategy which is to lead to the declarations of 35 and 43, below; it is interesting that the scribes disagree completely on their significance.

16a. 'It is more blessed [Vg. *beatius*] to give than to ask' (Acts 20:35, with *petere* for Vg. *accipere*).

17. C returns here to the matter of B. The line in B refers to the preceding examples (B XII 40–54) of men whose riches and wisdom did not avail for 'soule helþe'. The transition in C is abrupt, but not obscure: wealth (as in 15–16, above) and intelligence (as in 11, above) have been hinted at.

18a. 'Those who know (God's will) and do not do it shall be beaten with many scourges' (adapted from Luke 12:47; cf. John 13:17).

23. *graes*: a herb of healing virtue (OED, *grass*, sb¹, 2a). The pun is exploited in the lines following, the sense of which is that the abusers of wealth, like all sinners, can be redeemed through God's grace provided that the infusion of his love through the holy spirit has prepared their hearts for grace in the performing of good works. See VII 269n.

27a. 'The spirit breathes where it wills' (John 3:8).

Ac clergie cometh bote of syhte and kynde wit of sterres,   30
As to be bore or bygete in such a constillacioun,
That wit wexeth therof and oþer wordes bothe.
    Vultus huius seculi sunt subiecti vultibus celestibus.
So grace is a gifte of god and kynde wit a chaunce
And clergie a connynge of kynde wittes techyng.
And ȝut is clergie to comende for Cristes loue more   35
Then eny connyng of kynde wit but clergi hit reule.
For Moyses witnesseth þat god wroet and Crist with his fynger;
Lawe of loue oure lorde wroet long ar Crist were,
And Crist cam and confermede and holy kyrke made
And in soend a signe wroet and saide to þe Iewes: 40
"That seth hymsulue synnelees, sese nat, y hote,
To strike with stoen or with staf this strompet to dethe."
    Quis vestrum sine peccato est.
Forthy y conseile vch a creature clergie to honoure.
    For as a man may nat se þat misseth his yes
No more can no clerk but if hit come of bokes.   45
Al-þeiȝ men made bokis god was here mayster
And þe seynt spirit þe saumplare and said what men sholde wryte.
And riht as syht serueth a man to se þe hye strete,
Riht so lereth lettrure lewed men to resoun.
And as a blynde man in bataile bereth wepene to fyhte   50
And hath non hap with his ax his enemye to hutte,
No more can a kynde-witted man but clerkes hym teche
Come for al his kynde wit thorw cristendoem to be saued,

37–8. and Crist . . . lorde wroet UIT (loue T; UI *om*)] X *om*
46. Al-þeiȝ men made bokis T] XUI *om with subsequent mislineation*
48. þe hye strete U] X hye þe sterre (sterre *over erasure*)

---

30. Learning comes only from what we have seen or learnt empirically (referring to John 3:11: 'We speak of what we know and bear witness to what we have seen', in which Christ contrasts earthly and heavenly knowledge) and learning in its turn is based on natural intelligence, which is a gift of fortune. Imaginatyf is acknowledging that learning, though it is to be commended (35 below), is not a gift of God's grace nor a means of special access to God's grace.

32a. 'The phenomena of this world are subject to the configurations of the heavens'. Source not identified.

37. God wrote on the tablets of stone on mount Sinai (Ex. 31:18) and Christ on the ground (John 8:6). These are acknowledgements of the importance of learning.

39. *confermede.* Christ wrote on the ground to signify that he was a law-giver like Moses (see Augustine, *Tractatus in Joannis Evangelium,* xxxiii.5, in *PL* 35:1649); his teaching both confirms the Law of Moses, with which the scribes and Pharisees had challenged him, and also fulfils it in the law of Love.

42a. 'Whoever of you is without sin (let him be the first to throw a stone at her)' (John 8:7).

The whiche is coffre of Cristis tresor, and clerkes kepeth þe keyes
To vnlouken hit at here lykynge, the lewed and lered to helpe, 55
To ȝeue mercy for mysdedes ȝif men hit wol aske
Buxumliche and benyngnelyche and bidden hit of grace.
    Arca dei in þe olde lawe Leuytes hit kepte;
Hadde neuere lewede leue to legge hand on þat cheste   f.60ᵇ *i.e.* f.61ᵇ
Bote hit were prestis or prestis sone, patriarke or prophete. 60
Saul for he sacreficede sorwe hym bytydde
And his sones for his synnes sorwe hem bytydde
And all lewede þat leide hand þeron loren lyf aftir.
    Forthy y conseyle all creatures no clerk to despice
Ne sette shorte be here science, what-so þei doen hemsulue. 65
Take we here wordes at worthe, for here wittenesses ben trewe,
And medle we nat moche with hem to meuen eny wrathe
Laste cheste chaufen vs alle to chide and schoppe vch man oþer.
And do we as Dauid techeth for doute of godes veniance:
    Nolite tangere Christos meos.
For clergy is Cristes vycary to conforte and to cure; 70
Both lewede and lerede were lost yf clergie ne were.
    Kynde-wittede men han a clergie by hemsulue;
Of cloudes and of costumes they contreuede mony thynges
And markede hit in here manere and mused þeron to knowe.
And of the selcouthes þat þei sye, here sones þerof þei tauhten 75
For they helden hit for an hey science here sotiltees to knowe.

---

55. vnlouken] X vlouken; U vnloke
56. mysdedes U] X mysdes
68. chide I] XU *om*

58. 'No one but the Levites may carry the Ark of God' (1 Para. 15:2). *Arca dei* was the Ark of God or the Ark of the Covenant, the chest containing the tablets of stone and other relics of the Mosaic covenant, kept in the holiest place in the Jewish temple. The Levites were the members of the tribe of Levi to whom were assigned the duties of ministering in the temple-worship. For Imaginatyf they are examples of a privileged caste of clergy, i.e. learned men.

61. 1 Reg. 13:9. For another story of Saul's disobedience, see III 408.

65. *what-so þei doen hemsulue.* In asserting that men should respect the learning of the clergy even if the clergy themselves are not of blameless life, Imaginatyf alludes slightingly to an important Wycliffite doctrine: that priests of unholy life lose the power of their priestly office, and that sacraments administered by them are invalid. See Leff, 1967, 525–7.

69a. 'Touch not my anointed ones' (Ps. 104:15). David is speaking of the way God gave special protection to the early patriarchs and prophets of Israel.

72. *Kynde-wittede men* are men of natural intelligence and wisdom (Aristotle, Hippocrates and Virgil are mentioned in the passage in B referred to above, 17n) who yet lacked the revelation of the Christian faith. See Prol. 141n.

73. *cloudes* and *costumes* ('customs') could refer to the two domains of natural science and moral philosophy.

Ac thorw here science sothly was neuere soule ysaued
Ne brouhte by here bokes to blisse ne to ioye.
For al here kynde knowyng cam bote of diuerse syhtes
Of briddes and of bestes, of blisse and of sorwe.   80
Patriarkes and prophetus repreuede here science
And saide here wordes ne here wysdomes was but a folye;
As to þe clergie of Crist thei counted hit but a tryfle.
    Sapiencia huius mundi stulticia est apud deum.
  For the hey holi gost heuene shal to-cleue
And loue shal lepe out aftur into þis lowe erthe   85
And clennesse shal cach hit and clerkes shollen hit fynde:
    Pastores loquebantur ad inuicem.
Hit speketh þer of ryche men riht nouht, ne of ryche lordes,
Bote of clennesse of clerkes and kepares of bestes.
    Ibant magi ab oriente.
Yf eny frere wer founde þere y ʒeue the fyue shillynges!
Ne in no cote ne caytyfs hous Crist was ybore   90
But in a burgeis hous, the beste of þe toune.

88a. *Ibant* I] XU Ibunt
89. wer U] X we
90–91. Crist . . . burgeis hous T] XUI *om*

79. *syhtes*: 'observations', used in the same sense of 'empirical learning' as in 30, above.
83a. 'The wisdom of this world is folly with God' (1 Cor. 3:19).
84–6. An allusion to the Annunciation (84), the Incarnation (85) and the Immaculate Conception (86), and a remarkable reminiscence of I 149–52. The lines could also be taken to refer simply to the Annunciation to the Shepherds.
85. *loue shal lepe out.* For the patristic tradition of the 'leaps' of Christ, based on interpretation of Cant. 2:8, see Smith, 1966, 30. Cf. VII 135n.
86a. 'The shepherds said to one another ("Let us go over to Bethlehem")' (Luke 2:15). The Annunciation to the Shepherds was traditionally interpreted as a sign that Christ had a special care for the poor and lowly; but the shepherds were also interpreted allegorically as priests (*pastores*; cf. IX 257–75) and learned men (e.g. *Northern Homily Cycle* 2970), and that sense is present here. The theme is reinforced by the story of the Magi, the wise and learned men to whom Christ also announced his coming. Both are evidence of God's respect for learning and learned men.
88. *clerkes* may refer to either the shepherds or the Magi, as in 86 above.
88a. 'There came wise men from the east' (Matt. 2:1).
89. Friars had a reputation for learning but not for 'clennesse'.
90–91. We are perhaps more used to an emphasis on the lowly setting of Christ's birth (from Luke 2:7), but Imaginatyf is interested here in dissociating Christ from beggars (or mendicants: suggested by the mention of friars, and specified in B XII 146) and the rascally poor. The *burgeis hous* does not contradict Matt. 2:11, and it is probably distinct enough from the house of a rich man or lord (87 above). Nevertheless, the lines are an example of the burr-like quality of Imaginatyf's arguments by association.

To pastours and to poetes appered þe angel   f.62ª
And bad hem go to Bedlem goddes berthe to honoure
And song a song of solace, *Gloria in excelsis deo.*
Ryche men rotte tho and in here reste were   95
Tho hit shoen to þe shepherdes, a sheware of blisse.
Clerkes knewe þe comet and comen with here presentes
And deden here homage honerably to hym þat was almyhty.
    Why y haue tolde þe al þis, y toek ful gode hede
How þou contraridest Clergie with crabbed wordes,   100
That is, how lewede men and luyther lyhtloker were ysaued
Then connynge clerkes of kynde vnderstondynge.
And thow saidest sothe of somme, ac yse in what manere.
Take two stronge men and in Temese cast hem
And bothe naked as a nedle, here noen heuegore then othere;   105
That oen hath connyng and can swymmen and dyuen,
That oþer is lewed as of þat labour and lerned neuere to swymme;
Which trowest of tho two in Temese is in moste drede?'
    'He þat can nat swymmen, y sayde, 'hit semeth to alle wittes.'
    'Riht so,' quod þat renk, 'resoun hit sheweth   110
Þat he þat knoweth clergie conne sounore aryse
Out of synne, and be saef thogh he synege ofte,
Yf hym liketh and luste, then eny lewede sothly.
    For yf þe clerke be connynge he knoweth what is synne

---

97. knewe þe U] X knowe here
99. þe U] X *om*
102. Then U] X The
108. is U] X *om*
114. he B] XUIP and

---

92. *poetes.* L uses 'poet' in a general sense (cf. XI 306, XII 172, and see OED, s.v. sense 1b) to mean any wise and learned writer. The shepherds, if thought of as priests (note to 86a, above), are men of learning (though they seem here to be distinguished from the *clerkes*, or magi, of 97, below). Skeat suggests they are 'composers' because they go away 'glorifying and praising God' (Luke 2:20), and is reminded of the neatherd and poet Caedmon.

94. *And song*, i.e. the angel sang. *Gloria in excelsis deo*: 'Glory to God in the highest' (Luke 2:14).

96. 'And the glory of the Lord shone around them' (Luke 2:9). 'And the angel said . . . "I bring you good news of a great joy" ' (Luke 2:10).

100. See XI 276–305. It was actually Rechelesnesse speaking at that point, but Imaginatyf's comment, inherited as it is from B, is appropriate enough in view of the close identification of R and the dreamer.

104. Boethius uses a similar illustration, but based on walking not swimming (*Cons. Phil.* IV, pr. 2. 17–25).

105. *here*: 'of them'.

And how contricion withoute confessioun conforteth þe soule,   115
And we seen in þe sauter, in psalmes oen or tweyne,
How contricioun is comended for hit cacheth awey synne:
>   *Beati quorum remisse sunt iniquitates.*
And þat conforteth vch a clerk and keuereth fro wanhope,
In whiche floed þe fende fondeth man hardest,
There þe lewede lyth stille and loketh aftur lente   120
And hath no contricion ar he come to shrifte, and thenne can he lytel
>   telle,
But as his loresman hym lereth byleueth and troweth,
And þat is aftur his person other his parsche preest, and parauntur
>   bothe lewede
To lere lewede men, as Luk bereth witnesse:
>   *Dum cecus ducit cecum, etc.*
Fol muchel wo was hym marked þat wade shal with þe lewede! 125 f.62ᵇ
Well may þe barne blesse þat hym to boek sette,
That lyuynge aftur lettrure saued hym lyf and soule!

124a. *cecus* I] XU secus. *cecum* I] XU secum
127. hym U] X hy

115–23. The ignorant man may undervalue contrition (see VI 6n, XVI 25–31) and assume that only the formality of confession is of value in relieving the burden of sin. He may then postpone confession until the time when it is compulsory (cf. VII 28), and be at that time in despair (cf. VII 59) because his soul is unprepared, and also because he does not know how to confess properly. It was orthodox doctrine that contrition alone, by itself, could deliver a man from sin (e.g. Parson's Tale, *CT* X. 308, Brinton's Sermons, i.81), but the question was much debated (see Frank, 1957, 98–9; *Cursor Mundi* 26062–91). L omits other references in B to the doctrine at XII 23 (cf. B XI 81) and XV 274, perhaps because the argument that confession was unnecessary had, by the 1380s, become associated with Wyclif and heresy (Hort. 155).

117a. 'Blessed are they whose sins are forgiven' (Ps. 31:1). Later verses of this psalm, the second of the seven penitential psalms (see III 463n), describe how forgiveness is to be sought through penitence.

123. *aftur*: 'according to what he is told by'. *paraunter bothe lewede.* The ignorance of parsons and parish-priests was often commented on. The great programmes of instruction that followed on the Lateran Council decrees of 1216 (which declared that all Christians must go to confession at least once a year) were directed as much at the education of parish-priests, so that they might understand the elements of the faith and be able to receive confession, as at laymen. See Pantin, 1955, 189–218.

124a. 'If a blind man leads a blind man (both will fall into a pit)' (Matt. 15:14 rather than Luke 6:39).

126. *þat*: 'him that'. See V 36.

Dominus pars hereditatis is a merye verset,
Hit hath take fro Tybourne twenty stronge theues;
There lewede theues ben lolled vp, loke how þei ben saued!   130
     The thef þat hadde grace of god a Gode Fryday, as thow toldest,
Was for a ȝeld hym creaunt to Crist and his grace askede.
And god is ay gracious to alle þat gredeth to hym
And wol no wikkede man be lost, bote if he wol hymsulue.
     Nolo mortem peccatoris.
Ac thogh the theef hadde heuene he hadde noen hey blisse   135
As seynt Iohan and oþer seyntes þat haen serued bettere.
Riht as sum man ȝeueth me mete and sette me amydde þe flore,
Ich haue mete more then ynow ac nat with so muche worschipe
As tho þat sitten at þe syde table or with þe souereyns in halle,
Bote as a beggare bordles be mysulue on þe grounde.   140
So hit ferde by þe feloun þat a Goed Fryday was saued;
A sit noþer with seynte Iohn ne with Simond ne Iude
Ne with maydenes ne with martires ne with mylde weddewes,
Bote as a soleyn by hymsulue yserued vppon þe grounde.
For he þat is ones a thef is eueremore in daunger,   145

134. be U] X *om*
136. As U] X Ac
138. so P] XUIT *om*

128. 'The Lord is the portion of (my) inheritance' (Ps. 15:5). This and the next line refer to the custom of pleading 'benefit of clergy', whereby condemned criminals could claim to be beyond the jurisdiction of lay courts by proving their literacy (equivalent to clerical status), usually by reading a passage from Psalms in the Latin (the 'neck-verse'). Ps. 50 was the usual choice; Ps. 15 is quoted here for the reasons made clear in the note to V 60a. Imaginatyf clearly regards the practice not as a gross abuse of the law, but as an instrument of God's mercy to the sinner, and he goes on to associate the *stronge theues* with the thief on the cross.
130. *þei*, i.e. the literate thieves.
131. Imaginatyf has come round, by a rather typical associative process (see 90n, above), to answering the questions of the dreamer (as Rechelesnesse) in XI 255–63.
132. *ȝeld hym creaunt*: 'acknowledged himself vanquished'. This was the usual chivalric phrase attributed to knights in battle. L has a nice place on *creaunt* in its etymological sense, 'believing'.
134a. 'I desire not the death of the sinner [Vg.*impii*] (but that the wicked turn from his way and live)' (Ez. 33:11, cf. 18:23, 32).
135. As a way of reconciling God's law and God's mercy in this matter, Imaginatyf takes advantage of the well-established doctrine that there are degrees of bliss in heaven (cf. IX 20), as expounded, for instance, by Peter Comestor in his discussion of the fate of the thieves on the cross (*Historia Scholastica, PL* 198: 1631). The scriptural basis is John 14:2.
142. *Simond ne Iude*. Simon (not Simon Peter) and Jude or Judas (not Iscariot) were two of the disciples. They have the same day.

And as þe lawe lyketh to lyue oþer to dye.
De peccato propiciato noli esse sine metu.
And for to seruen a seynt and suche a thef togyderes,
Hit were no resoun ne riht to rewarde bothe ylyche.
And riht as Troianes þe trewe knyhte telde nat depe in helle
That oure lord ne hauede hym lihtliche out, so lyueþ þat thef
    in heuene.   150
For he is in þe loweste of heuene, yf oure byleue be trewe,
And wel losliche he lolleth þere as by þe lawe of holy churche.
Et reddet unicuique iuxta opera sua.
  Ac why þat on theef vppon þe cros cryant hym ȝelde
Rather then þat oþer, thogh thow woldest apose,
Alle þe clerkes vnder Crist ne couthe hit assoille.   155
    Quare placuit? quia voluit.
And so y sey by þe þat sekest aftur þe whyes
How creatures han kynde wit and how clerkes come to bokes
And how þe floures in þe fryth cometh to fayre hewes;   f.63ᵃ
Was neuere creature vnder Crist þat knewe wel þe bygynnyng
Bote Kynde þat contreuede hit furst of his corteyse wille.   160
He tauhte þe tortle to trede, the pocok to cauke,
And Adam and Eue and alle othere bestes
A cantel of kynde wyt here kynde to saue.
Of goed and of wykke Kynde was þe furste,
Sey hit and soffred hit and saide hit be sholde.   165
    Dixit et facta sunt.

---

149. telde U] X dwelde (*over erasure*)
150. lyueþ T] XUI leue y; P leyueth of
152a. *unicuique* U] X unicuieque
155a. *quia* U] X qui
161. trede U] X trete

146a. 'Do not be over-confident about the forgiveness of sins' (Ecclus. 5:5).
149. *depe*, i.e. 'so deep'. See XII 74.
152. *losliche*: 'uneasily', i.e. he knows his right to be there, by the law, is arguable.
152a. See V 32a.
155a. 'Why did it please him? because he willed it'. Adapted from texts like Ps. 113b:3, 134:6, but with perhaps some echo of discussions like that of Peter Comestor, in his *Historia Scholastica* (*PL* 198:1075), on the Fall: 'Si quaeritur quare permisit Deus hominem tentari . . . dicimus . . . quia sic voluit. Si quaeritur cur voluit, insipida est quaestio quaerere causam divinae voluntatis, cum ipsa sit summa causa omnium causarum'.
157. Imaginatyf now deals with the dreamer's objections (XIII 134ff) to the natural order of creation. The mysteries of Nature the Creator, he says, are unfathomable to the intellect.
165a. 'He commanded, and they were created' (Ps. 148:5).

Ac why a wolde þat wykke were, y wene and y leue
Was neuere man vppon molde þat myhte hit aspie.
   Ac longe-lybbynge men lykened men lyuynge
To briddes and to bestes, as here bokes telleth
Þat þe fayrest foul foulest engendreth   170
And feblest foul of flyht is þat fleeth oþer swymmeth;
That is, þe pocok and þe popeiay with here proude fetheres
Bytokenen riht ryche men þat reygne here on erthe.
For pursue a pocock or a pohen to cacche
And haue hem an haste at þyn owen wille,   175
For þey may nat fle fer ne ful hey neyther,
For here fetheres þat fayre beth to fle fer hem letteth.
His ledene is vnloueliche and lothliche his careyne,
Ac for his peynted pennes þe pecok is honoured
More þan for his fayre flesch or for his merye note.   180
Riht so men reuerenceth more þe ryche for here mebles
Then for eny kyn he come of or for his kynde wittes.
Thus þe poete praiseth þe pecok for his fetheres
And þe ryche man for his rentes or for his rychesse in his shoppes.
The larke þat is a lasse foul is louelokere of ledene   185
And swettore of sauour and swyftore of wenges.
To lowe-lyuynge men þe larke is resembled
And to lele and lyf-holy þat louyeth alle treuthe.
Thus Porfirie and Plato and poetes monye
Likneth in here logik þe leste foul outen.   190
   And wher he be saef or nat saef þe sothe woet no clergie,

171. swymmeth U] X swymneth
178. ledene U] X lethene
181. reuerenceth U] X reuerenced
185. louelokere T] XUI louelokest

166. Imaginatyf does not tackle the question of the existence of evil in the world; it is not his province, any more than the nature and operation of man's free will (above, 153–5). Instead, he answers questionings of the order of nature with moralized lessons from 'natural history'. The usual function of animals in medieval didactic writing, such as the bestiaries, is to provide allegorical examples and types for homiletic purposes.

172. *þe pocok*. See XIII 169.

183. *þe poete*: 'the learned writer' (see above, 92n). Probably Aristotle is in mind, but the credit for general observations like this was rather indiscriminately distributed (see XII 172n).

189. Porphyry and Plato (see XII 172) replace Aristotle in B XII 268, but all are cited at random.

191. *he* is left over from B, where only Aristotle is referred to. By a typical process of association (see above, 131n), Imaginatyf comes now to a consideration of the question of the salvation of the righteous heathen (see XI 221n).

Ne of Sortes ne of Salamon no scripture can telle
Wher þat þey ben in hell or in heuene, or Aristotel þe wyse.
Ac god is so gode, y hope þat seth he gaf hem wittes   f.63ᵇ
To wissen vs weyes þerwith þat wenen to be saued,   195
And þe bettere for here bokes, to bidden we ben yholde
That god for his grace gyue here soules reste,
For letrede men were as lewede men ȝut, ne were þe lore of tho
        clerkes.'
    'Alle thise clerkes,' quod y tho, 'þat in Crist leuen
Segen in here sarmons þat noþer Saresynes ne Iewes   200
Withoute bapteme, as by here bokes, beth nat ysaued.'
    'Contra,' quod Ymagynatif tho, and comesed to loure,
And saide, '*Vix saluabitur iustus in die iudicii;*
Ergo saluabitur,' quod he, and saide no more Latyn.
'Troianes was a trewe knyhte and toek neuere cristendoem   205
And he is saef, saith the boek, and his soule in heuene.
Ac þer is follyng of fonte and follyng in bloed-chedyng
And thorw fuyr is fullyng, and al is ferme bileue.

192. no U] X ne
200. in U] X withoute

192. *Sortes.* The standard form of the name of Socrates in medieval treatises on logic,
and one of several suggestions that L had some university training (see V 36n, and
Bloomfield, 1961, 164–7).
199. Will has learnt some of the lessons of intellectual humility and patience (see XIII
219n) but he is not willing to leave the fate of the righteous heathen undecided
(*Saresynes* includes all pagans: see XII 86n).
202. *Contra.* See X 20.
203. 'The righteous shall scarcely be saved on the day of judgment' (1 Pet. 4:18,
varied).
204. *Ergo saluabitur*: 'Therefore he shall be saved' (a logical deduction from *vix*,
'scarcely'). See XV 23. *The Prick of Conscience*, predictably enough, makes precisely
the opposite deduction from the same text: If the just can hardly be saved, what of
the sinful? which is indeed the sense of the rest of the verse from the epistle (cf. III
486ff).
205. *Troianes.* For Trajan, see above, 149n, and XII 74.
207. Baptism in *bloed-chedyng* is martyrdom, the baptism of suffering to which Christ
refers in Luke 12:50.
208. The baptism of fire, *baptismus flaminis,* is described by Aquinas (see Dunning, 1943,
52) as the visitation upon a man of the Holy Ghost (see 208a), so that the heart is
moved to believe in and love God and repent of his sins. Such visitation might be
made upon any non-Christian who lived in truth as he knew it (209–17 below).
This theory of 'an immediate divine revelation to an infidel of good will'
(Dunning, 1943, 49) was designed to reconcile two apparently contradictory doc-
trines: (a) faith and baptism are necessary for salvation; (b) God wills the salva-
tion of all men, as Christ died for all men, and no man is damned but by his own
fault. Imaginatyf does not clearly expound this view (see 211), and relies more on
the righteous heathen keeping to the best faith he knows (see Frank, 1957, 65), but
he follows it in spirit, and in his recognition that belief in one God and one

Aduenit ignis diuinus non comburens set illuminans.

Ac treuth þat trespassed neuere ne trauersede aзens his lawe
Bote lyuede as his lawe tauhte and leueth þer be no bettere,   210
And yf þer were, a wolde leue, and in suche a wille deyeth –
Ne wolde neuere trewe god bote trewe treuthe were alloued,
And wher hit worth or worth nat, the bileue is gret of treuthe
And hope hangeth ay þeron to haue þat treuthe deserueth.

Quia super pauca fuisti fidelis, etc.

And þat is loue and large huyre, yf þe lord be trewe,   215
And a cortesye more þen couenant was, what so clerkes carpe,
For al worth as god wol'; and þerwith he vanschede.

208a. *Aduenit* U] X Auenit
211. leue T] XUIP *om*

providence (see III 480, XVII 132, 150, 317), with potential belief in a Mediator
(i.e. provided no false mediator is accepted, XVII 158), is sufficient for salvation.
As always, L speaks of the matters that concerned theologians, but not as a well-
trained theologian would speak (Hort 116). He provides here, at any rate, an
interim answer which accommodates the story of Trajan and softens the ruthless
predestinarianism of Bradwardine (see VII 269n, XI 205, 221).

208a. 'There came a divine fire, not burning but giving light'. From an antiphon sung
in matins at Pentecost (Breviary I.mvi), referring to the baptism of fire and the
Holy Spirit promised by John the Baptist in Matt. 3:11 and fulfilled in Acts 1:5,
2:3.

209. *treuth þat trespassed neuere*: 'he that never trespassed against truth'. For trans. use of
trespass, see OED, s.v. 3a. Skeat, however, takes 'truth' here and throughout the
following passage as the personification of the righteous heathen.

211. *And yf þer were, a wolde leue*: 'And if there were (a better law, that he knew of), he
would believe it (and live by it)'.

212. 'And the true God would never wish but that true obedience to law were com-
mended'.

213. 'And whether it is (commended) or not, the faith embodied in such obedience to
law is great'. The line is awkward, and emended by Kane-Donaldson in B XII
291 (see their Introd., p.209): 'And wheiþer it worþ [of truþe] or noзt, [þe] worþ
[of] bileue is gret'. The argument is based on Rom. 2:13–15.

214a. 'Because you have been faithful over a little (I will set you over much)' (Matt.
25:23). From the parable of the talents: the servant who was given a lesser number
of talents, but made good use of them, is like the righteous heathen.

215. *large huyre*: 'generous terms of service' (continuing the allusion to the parable).

Passus XV

The Feast of Patience and the Meeting with Activa Vita

Passus quintus de visione vt supra
And y awakede þerwith, witteles ner-hande,
And as a freke þat fay were forth can y walken
In manere of a mendenaunt mony ȝer aftur.
And many tymes of this meteles moche thouhte y hadde;
Furste how Fortune me faylede at my moste nede   5
And how Elde manased me – so myhte happe
That y lyuede longe – leue me byhynde
And vansche alle my vertues and my fayre lokes.
And how þat freres folewede folk þat was ryche
And people þat was pore at litel pris setten,   10 f.64ᵃ
Ne no cors of pore comune in here kyrke-ȝerde most lygge
Bote quyke he byquath hem auht or wolde helpe quyte here dettes.
And how þis coueytyse ouercome al kyne sectes,
As wel lered as lewede, and lorde as þe boende.
And how þat lewede men ben lad, but oure lorde hem helpe,   15
Thorw vnkunynge curatours to incurable peynes.
And how þat Ymaginatyf in dremeles me tolde
Of Kynde and his connynge, and what connynge he ȝaf bestes,
And how louyng he is to vch a lyf, a londe and o watere,
For alle a wisseth and ȝeueth wit þat walketh oþer crepeth.   20

---

3. a U] X *om*
6. manased U] X manced
8. lokes] XUIT lotes (loces?); P lockes

---

1. *y awakede þerwith*. See XIII 213n.
3. *mendenaunt*: a beggar, rather than a friar. Cf. Prol. 2n, X 1n.
5–24. The dreamer offers here a summary of scattered episodes from the preceding 'dream' (not clearly identified, however, as either the 'outer' or 'inner' dream of XIII 213n). Lines 5–12 refer to XII 13, XI 189–95 and XII 15–26; lines 13–16 are of general relevance; lines 17–24 refer to XIV 159–65, 201–3.
7. *leue*: 'to leave', inf. dependent on *manased*, 'threatened'.
8. *vansche alle my vertues*: 'cause all my powers to waste away'.
11. One of the privileges acquired by the friars in the late 13th c. was the right to bury laymen (usually appropriated to the parish), with all the fees and bequests accruing. See VIII 101n, also XII 22 (though the passage specifically referred to here, B XI 64–8, has been removed in C).

And y merueyled in herte how Ymaginatyf saide
That *iustus* bifore Iesu *in die iudicii*
Non saluabitur bote if *vix* helpe;
And when he hadde ysaide so, how sodeynliche he vanschede.
And so y musede vppon þis matere, þat me lust to slepe.   25
   And thenne cam Concyence, and Clergie aftur,
And beden me ryse vp and rome, and with Reson sholde y dyne.
And y aroos and romede forth and with Resoun we mette.
We reuerensede Resoun and romede forth softly
And metten with a mayster, a man lyk a frere.   30
Concience knewe hym, welcomede hym fayre;
They woschen and wypeden and wenten to þe dyner.
   And there cam Pacience as a pore thyng and preyede mete pur
      charite,
Ilyk Peres the ploghman, as he a palmere were,
Crauede and cryede, for Cristes loue of heuene,   35
A meles mete for a pore man, or moneye, yf they hadde.
Concience knewe him wel and welcomede hem all,
Woschen and wipeden and wenten to sytten.
   The maister was maed sitte furste, as for þe moste worthy;
Resoun stoed and styhlede, as for styward of halle.   40
Pacience and y prestly was pot to be mettes,
And seten by ouresulue at a syde-table.
   Clergie cald aftur mete and thenne cam Scripture
And serued hem thus sone of sondry metes monye,
Of Austyn, of Ambrose, of alle þe foure euaungelies,   45

---

21. merueyled T] XUI merueyle
37. him U] X hem
41. prestly T] XUI *om*

22–3. See XIV 203. The play on words, in this little allegorical narrative of Doomsday (cf. IV 140n), depends on the interpretation of *vix* as the Five *V*) wounds of Jesus (*I*) Christ (*X*). See Wyclif, ed. Arnold, i.337.

26–7. All these characters have been met before, and have dealt more or less harshly with an obstinate Will. The invitation to dinner is probationary reward for Will, who has shown recent signs of improvement (see XIV 199n). The fourth vision begins here.

30. *mayster*: a Master (later a *doctour*, 65) of Divinity. See Prol. 60n, X 9n, and Wyclif, ed. Arnold, iii.396.

33. Patience is the significant guest – an active virtue, not an intellectual faculty. The dreamer will now be tested in the practice of what he has been taught (e.g. XIII 201–7). Patience's resemblance to Peres Plowman is a very positive sign: last mentioned in IX 301, Peres is about to be resurrected as the embodiment of the lives of Dowel, Dobet and Dobest.

45. Augustine and Ambrose, with Gregory and Jerome, are the most important of the Church Fathers. See XI 149, XXI 269–70.

Edentes et bibentes que apud eos sunt. f.64^b

Ac of this mete þat mayster myhte nat wel chewe;
Forthy eet he mete of more cost, mortrewes and potages.
Of þat men myswonne they made hem wel at ese;
Ac here sauce was ouer-sour and vnsauerly ygrounde
In a morter, *post-mortem*, of many bittere peynes   50
Bote yf they synge for tho soules and wepe salte teres.

  Vos qui peccata hominum comeditis, nisi pro eis lacrimas et orationes
     effuderitis, ea que in deliciis comeditis, in
     tormentis euometis.

Thenne was Resoun radde, anoon riht aftur,
That Consience comaunde sholde to do come Scripture
And bringe breed for Pacience, bytyng apartye,
And to me þat was his mette tho, and oþer mete bothe.   55
He sette a sour loef, and saide, '*Agite penitenciam*,'
And sethe he drow vs drynke, *diu perseverans*:

---

46. chewe U] X shewe
52. was I] XUT as; P *om*
57. *diu* U] X dia

45a. 'Eating and drinking such things as they have' (Luke 10:7, Christ's advice to the disciples to receive hospitality when they go out before him).

47. The friar cannot manage the wholesome diet of scripture and patristic commentary, and must eat more expensively prepared stews and soups (perhaps suggestive of 'potted' versions of the scriptures). For the idea of the scriptures as portions of food, L need have gone no farther than the Lord's Prayer (see also 250 below, and XVI 318) and the spiritual interpretation of 'our daily bread' (Matt. 6:11), or Christ's declaration that he is 'the bread of life' (John 6:35), or, most obviously, Christ's words when tempted by the devil: 'Man shall not live by bread alone, but by every word that proceeds from the mouth of God' (Matt. 4:4). He may also have used patristic commentary specifying the food (viz. books of the bible) eaten at the nuptial feast of Luke 14:7–11 (Robertson-Huppé, 1951, 160); and he may have a debt to Raoul de Houdenc's *La Voie de Paradis* (ed. P. Lebesgue, Paris, 1908: to be distinguished from the poem of the same name by Rutebeuf, VII 205n), where the dreamer feasts with Confession upon 'souspirs et plainz … angoisses de cuer' and drinks 'lermes plorées' (371–8). Cf. also 186, below.

48. *they* is actually a relic of B, where the friar has a companion (cf. X 56n), but it can be readily understood as a reference to friars in general. The point about expensive foods is here taken up quite literally: the friars live well, on the ill-gotten gains of those they profess to minister to.

49–51. The sauce which goes with their expensive eating will turn out to have a bitter after-taste, after death (*post-mortem*), unless they truly do their duty by the souls of those who provide for them (cf. XII 19–22).

51a. 'You who feast upon the sins of men, unless you pour out tears and prayers for them, you shall vomit up amid torments the food you now feast on amid pleasures'. Source not identified.

56. *Agite penitenciam*: 'Repent' (Matt. 3:2).

57. *diu perseverans*: 'long enduring' (cf. Matt. 10:22: 'He who endures to the end will be saved').

'As longe,' quod he, 'as lyf and lycame may duyre.'
'This is a semely seruyce!' saide Pacience.
Thenne cam Contricion, þat hadd coked for hem all,   60
And brouhte forth a pytaunce, was *Pro hac orabit omnis sanctus
        in tempore oportuno.*
Thenne Consience confortede vs, bothe Clergie and Scripture,
And saide, '*Cor contritum et humiliatum, deus, non despicies.*'
    Pacience was wel apayed of this propre seruice
And made mery with this mete; ac y mournede euere   65
For a doctour þat at þe hey deys dranke wyn faste –
    Ve vobis qui potentes estis ad bibendum vinum! –
And ete manye sondry metes, mortrewes and poddynges,
Brawen and bloed of gees, bacon and colhoppes.
    Thenne saide y to mysulue, so Pacience hit herde:
'Hit is nat thre daies doen, this doctour þat he prechede   70
At Poules byfore þe peple what penaunce they soffrede,
Alle þat coueyte to come to eny kyne ioye;
And how þat Poul þe apostel, what penaunce he tholede
For oure lordes loue, as holy lettre telleth:
    In fame and *in frygore, etc.*
Ac me wondreth in my wit why þat they ne preche   75
As Poul þe apostle prechede to þe peple ofte:
    Periculum est in falsis fratribus!   f.65ᵃ
Holy writ byt men be waer and wysly hem kepe
That no fals frere thorw flaterynge hem bygyle;
Ac me thynketh loth, thogh y Latyn knowe, to lacken eny secte,
For alle be we brethrene, thogh we be diuersely clothed.   80

---

61. *hac* T] XUI hoc
66a. *potentes* U] X patentes
79–82. *mislineated in* XUI

---

58. A toast, based on the preceding text.
61. 'For this shall everyone that is holy pray in a seasonable time' (Ps. 31:6).
63. 'A contrite and humbled heart, O God, thou wilt not despise' (Ps. 50:19). This text, like the last, is from one of the seven penitential psalms (III 463n), the 'food of repentance' for the dreamer.
66. *a doctour,* i.e. someone of whom such behaviour would not be expected.
66a. 'Woe to you who are mighty in drinking wine' (Isa. 5:22).
71. *At Poules*: at St Paul's Cross, in London. See XI 56n.
74a. 'In hunger and . . . in cold' (2 Cor. 11:27, from Paul's list of the tribulations he has endured).
76a. 'There is danger in false brethren' (2 Cor. 11:26), with the usual pun on *fratres,* 'friars' (cf. XII 32a).
79. The dreamer makes an effort to show the patience that has been required of him (XIII 204–5).

Ac y wiste neuere freek þat frere is ycald of þe fyue
    mendynantz
That toek this for his teme and tolde hit withoute glose.
They preche þat penaunce is profitable to þe soule,
And what meschief and male-ese Crist for man tholede,
Ac this doctour and dyvynour,' quod y, 'and decretistre of canoen   85
(And also a gnedy glotoun with two grete chekes)
Hath no pyte on vs pore; he parformeth euele
That a precheth and preueth nat compacience,' ich tolde,
And wischede witterly with will ful egre
Þat in þe mawe of þat mayster alle þo metes were,   90
Bothe disches and dobelares, with alle þe deyntees aftur!
  'Y schal iangle to þis iurdan, with his iuyste wombe,
And apose hym what penaunce is and purgatorie on erthe,
And why a lyueth nat as a lereth!' 'Lat be,' quod Pacience,
And saide, 'Thow shalt se thus sone, when he may no more,   95
He shal haue a penaunce in his foule paunche, and poffe at vch
    a worde,
And thenne shal gothelen his gottes, and gynnen to galpe.
Now he hath dronke so depe a wol deuyne sone
And preuen hit by here Pocalips and þe passioun of seynt Aueroy
That noþer bacon ne brawn ne blaunmanger ne mortrewes   100
Is noþer fische ne flesche, but fode for penantes;
And take wittenesse at a trinite and take his felowe to witnesse

85. Ac] X As; U But
90. þe U] X þat
94–5. Pacience/And saide Thow *so* T; XUI Pacience and saide/Thow
102. to U] X no

81. *þe fyue mendynantz.* See VIII 191n.
82. *withoute glose.* See Prol. 58n, III 59n, X 32n, XII 16n.
92. *iurdan:* 'chamber-pot', but perhaps with a punning reference to friar William Jordan, a well-known Dominican controversialist of the 1370s (Gwynn, 1943, 2–4) and opponent of Uthred of Boldon (see XVII 124n). *iuyste wombe:* 'pot-belly'.
95. *may:* 'may do', i.e. eat.
99. *here Pocalips:* 'their version of the Apocalypse', i.e. the *Apocalipsis Goliae* (*c.* 1190), a famous parody of St John, satirizing corrupt and gluttonous clergy (printed in *Poems attrib. to Walter Mapes*, ed. T. Wright, Camden Society, 1841, pp. 1–21: see esp. ll. 345–408). *seynt Aueroy* is perhaps St Avoya, who was fed in her torment with fine bread from heaven – a useful twist to the doctor's argument that good food and suffering go together. The mistake in the spelling of the saint's name is readily attributable to a scribal misreading of *u* as *u + er* contraction, and to the fact that her cult was not widespread. Another possible identification is St Aurea, a Spanish solitary, better known, who is said to have drunk only what she could distil from cinders. See Skeat 193.
102. *take wittenesse at a trinite:* 'swear by the Trinity'.

What a fond in a forel of a frere lyuynge,
And bote þe furste leef be lesynges, leue me neuere aftur!
And thenne is tyme to take and to appose this doctour   105
Of Dowel and of Dobet, and yf Dobest do eny penaunce.'
   Y sat stille, as Pacience wolde, and thus sone this doctour,
As rody as a rose rodded his chekes,
Cowhede and carpede, and Consience hym herde
And tolde hym of a trinite and toward me he lokede.   110
'What is Dowel, sire doctour?' quod y. 'Is Dobest eny penaunce?'   f.65ᵇ
   'Dowel?' quod this doctour, and he dronke aftur,
'Do thy neyhebore non harm ne thysulue nother,
And thenne dost thow wel and wysly, y dar hit wel avowe.'
   'Certes, sire,' thenne saide y, 'hit semeth nouhte here,   115
In þat 3e parteth nat with vs pore, þat 3e passeth Dowel,
Ne lyueþ nat as 3e lereth, as oure lord wolde.
      Et visitauit et fecit redempcionem plebis sue.
And 3e fare thus with 3oure syke freres, ferly me thynketh
But Dowel wol endite 3ow *in die iudicii.*'
   Thenne Consience ful corteyslyche a continaunce he made   120
And preynte vppon Pacience to preie me be stille,
And saide hymsulue, 'Sire doctour, be so hit be 3oure wille,
What is Dowel and Dobet? 3e deuynours knoweth.'
   'Y have yseide,' quod þat segg, 'y can sey no bettre,
Bote do as doctours techeth for Dowel y hit holde;   125
That trauayleth to teche oþere y halde hit for a Dobet;

106. Dobest B] XUITP Dobet
107. sat U] X saed
109. carpede U] X capede
117. lyueþ T] XUI louyeth
117a. *plebis sue* U] X *om*
119. But T] XUI That

103. 'What (poor) fare he [i.e. *his felowe*] found in a friar's box of provisions'.
110. *tolde hym of a trinite*: 'told the friar briefly of the triad of Dowel, Dobet and Dobest on which he is about to be questioned'.
113. The doctor's answer is unobjectionable, especially in the context of Gal. 5:14: 'The whole law is fulfilled in one word, "You shall love your neighbour as yourself"' (cf. also Rom. 13:9, Matt. 19:19). If it seems that the doctor's phrasing gives what he says a dubious slant, comparison should be made with the words of Peres in VII 211. The lesson only recently taught by Imaginatyf (XIV 65) was that a bad priest can be true witness. See also X 32n. For a contrary interpretation, see Goodridge, 1959, 299–300, Robertson-Huppé, 1951, 163.
117a. 'And he has visited and redeemed his people' (Luke 1:68, the words of Zacharias at the naming of his son, John the Baptist).
126–7. The doctor's phrasing may again seem dubious, but it does not necessarily follow from his definition of Dobest that Dobet is *not* practising what you preach. *doth* in 127 means 'acts to the full', but some degree of *doing* well is implied for Dobet. The doctor is again speaking with correctness.

And he þat doth as he techeth, y halde hit for þe beste.
    Qui facit et docuerit, magnus vocabitur.'
'Now þou, Clergie,' quod Consience, 'carpe what is Dowel.'
'Haue me excused,' quod Clergie, 'be Crist, but in scole,
Shal no such motyef be meued for me, bote þere,   130
For Peres loue þe palmare ʒent, þat inpugnede ones
Alle kyne connynges and alle kyne craftes,
Saue loue and leute and lowenesse of herte,
And no tixst ne taketh to preue this for trewe
Bote *dilige deum et proximum*, and *domine, quis habitabit*,   135
And preueth by puyre skile inparfyt alle thynges,
    Nemo bonus,
Bote lele loue and treuthe, that loth is to be founde.'

    Quod Peres the ploghman: '*Pacientes vincunt.*
Byfore perpetuel pees y shal preue þat y saide
And avowe byfore god, and forsaken hit neuere,   140
That *disce, doce, dilige deum*

---

130. bote þere P] XUI bote oþere; T þer but
135. *proximum* U] X proxemum
136–8. *mislineated in* XUI
138. *vincunt* U] X vinciunt
141–4. *mislineated in* XUI

127a. 'He who does them and teaches them [sc. the commandments] shall be called great (in the kingdom of heaven)' (Matt. 5:19).

129. Clergy, perhaps offended by the contrast between the doctor's gluttony and the scholarly correctness of his exposition, does not wish to enter into similar definitions. He suggests they are appropriate only to scholarly debate, and prefers the simple love, faith and humility of Peres Plowman (who is again referred to as a palmer in MSS XU, as in 34 above: both references are in C only).

135. *dilige deum et proximum*: 'love God and your neighbour' (abbreviated from e.g. Matt. 22:37, 39). *domine, quis habitabit*: 'Lord, who shall dwell (in they tabernacle)?' (Ps. 14:1). As often, the first words of the psalm provide the cue to the relevant text, which is in the answer in the following verses, e.g. 'He who does what is right . . . and does no evil to his friend' (vv 2–3).

136a. 'No one is good (but God alone)' (Mk. 10:18).

138. The mysterious and dramatic appearance of Peres Plowman (see above, 33n) is an important innovation in C. He speaks now as Christ in his life upon earth, verifying, in the presence of his Father, his own words in the gospels, concerning the charity which grows out of patience (see 33, above). *Pacientes vincunt*: 'the patient conquer'. Proverbial: see Walther 20833f and Matt. 10:22.

139. *Byfore perpetuel pees*: 'In the presence of the everlasting peace', i.e. *byfore god.*

141. 'Learn; teach; love God'. C here cuts through the riddles of the B-text, and some complex redefinitions of the three lives, sweeping all aside in a demonstration of the ruthlessness of perfect love: 'Love your enemies' (Matt. 5:44, Luke 6:27), the revolutionary core of the Sermon on the Mount.

And thyn enemy helpe emforth thy myhte.
Caste hote coles on his heued of alle kyn speche,
Fond thorw wit and word his loue to wynne,
ȝef hym eft and eft, euere at his nede,   145 f.66ᵃ
Conforte hym with thy catel and with thy kynde speche,
And ley on hym thus with loue til he lauhe on þe;
And bote he bowe for this betynge, blynde mote he worthen!'
    And whan he hadde yworded thus, wiste no man aftur
Where Peres the plogman bycam, so priueyliche he wente.   150
And Resoun ran aftur and riht with hym ȝede;
Saue Concience and Clergie y couthe no mo aspye.
    Saue Pacience properliche spak, tho Peres was thus ypassed:
'That loueth lely,' quod he, 'bote litel thyng coueyteth.
Y wolde, and y will hadde to, wynnen all Fraunce   155
Withoute bruttenynge of buyren or eny bloed-shedynge;
Y take wittenesse,' quod he, 'of holy writ a partye:
    Pacientes vincunt.
For, by hym þat me made, myhte neuere pouerte,
Meseyse ne meschief, ne man with his tonge
Tene þe eny tyme and þou take pacience   160
And bere hit in thy bosom aboute wher þou wendest
In þe corner of a cart-whel, with a crow croune.
Shal neuere buyren be abasched þat hath this abouten hym,
Ne neuere hete ne hayl ne helle-pouke hym greue,

---

157. he XUI] T þe wy
162. cart U] X car

---

143. *Caste hote coles on his heued*: Prov. 25:22, Rom. 12:20. The 'hot coals' may be thought as the pangs of shame or remorse or fear of God's judgment, but the usual medieval interpretation (e.g. *Ancrene Wisse*, ed. Shepherd, 28) sees the hot coals as the heat of love which melts the hard heart of an enemy.

148. 'And if his resistance cannot be beaten down by such love, may he become blind!'

151. Reason does not appear again in the poem, and Conscience has to work alone (see Whitworth, 1972).

155. *Y wolde and y will hadde to*: 'I could, if I wished to'. Patience's claim is a literal illustration of *Pacientes vincunt.*

157a. See 138n, above.

162. This cryptic line replaces some even more cryptic lines in B. The reference is presumably to a symbolic 'Wheel of the Virtues' (see Kaske, 1963, 55–7), similar to the 'Wheel of Life' and 'Wheel of the Senses', which are used as a kind of allegorical diagram (cf. the trees of XVIII 7n) in medieval painting (see G. McN. Rushforth, in *Proc. Soc. Antiquaries* 26, 1914, 47–60), in the form of circles with radiating spokes like a cart-wheel, a virtue, vice, etc. in a medallion at the end of each spoke. *Patientia* here occupies a humble corner, hooded self-effacingly in black (perhaps with some allusion to the *corvus* of Cant. 5:11, as suggested by Kaske, 1963, 57–60).

Noþer fuyr ne floed, ne be aferd of enemye.   165
      Caritas expellit omnem timorem.
Ne þer is wyht in this world þat wolde the lette
To haue alle londes at thy likyng, and the here lord make
And maister of alle here mebles and of here moneye aftur,
The kyng and alle þe comune and clergie to þe loute
As for here lord and here ledare, and liue as thow techest.'   170
   'This is a *Dido*,' quod this doctour, 'a dysores tale!
Al the wit of this worlde and wyhte menne strenghe
Can nat parfourme a pees of the pope and his enemyes
Profitable for bothe parties' – and potte þe boerd fro hym
And toek Clergie and Consience to conseyle, as hit were.   175
   Ac Concience, y toek kepe, conieyod sone this doctour
And sethe a saide to Clergie, so that y hit herde,
'By Crist,' quod Consience, 'Clergie, y wol nat lye,
Me were leuere, by oure lorde, and y leue sholde,   f.66^b
Haue pacience parfitlyche then half thy pak of bokes!   180
Lettrure and longe studie letteth fol monye,
That they knoweth nat,' quod Concience, 'what is kynde Pacience.
Forthy,' quod Concience, 'Crist y the byteche,
With Pacience wol y passe, parfitnesse to fynde.'
   And wenten forth in here way, with grete wille y folowede.   185
Thenne hadde Pacience, as pilgrimes haen in here poke vitayles,
Sobrete and symple speche and sothfaste bileue,
To conforte hym and Consience yf they come in place

---

168. moneye XUTP] I maynye
170. liue U] X loue
172. the U] X this
187. and¹ U] X or

165a. 'Love casts out all fear' (1 John 4:18). Patience is an aspect of Charity, in which all three Lives are identified.

171. *a Dido*: a tale of Dido, an old tale, known to every popular entertainer. The doctor is a 'man of the world' and takes the sourly practical view that what Patience has been saying is irrelevant to the real problems of the world, like the war between the pope and his enemies (this could refer to the papal schism of 1378, as suggested in Bennett *MÆ*, 1943, 60–61, though the pope had enemies before). His impatient dismissal of the whole conversation (174), and turning to 'business', is a vivid gesture.

180. Conscience speaks on the limitations of learning with an authority denied to the dreamer or Rechelesnesse in the poem's hierarchy of witness. See also XVI 205–37.

184. *parfitnesse to fynde.* 'You, therefore, must be perfect, as your heavenly Father is perfect' (Matt. 5:48, the end of the passage in the Sermon on the Mount introduced above, 141).

There vnkyndenesse and coueytise is, hungry contreys bothe.
   And as they wente by the way of Dowel can they carpe;   190
They mette with a mynstral, as me tho thouhte.
Pacience apposede hym and preyede a sholde telle
What craft þat he couthe, and corteysliche he saide:
'Ich am a mynstral,' quod this man, 'my name is *Actiua Vita*,
Peres prentys þe plouhman, alle peple to conforte.'   195
   'What manere munstracye, my dere frende,' quod Concience,
'Hastow vsed or haunted al thy lyf-tyme?'
   'Munstracye can y nat moche bote make men merye;
As a wafrrer with wafres ay welcome godes gestes.
Of my labour thei lauhe, þe lasse and þe more.
The pore and the ryche y plese and payn fynde   200

189. is U] X *om*
193. corteysliche U] X corteyliche
199. ay I] X ar; U and
200. my T] XUI thy. thei U] X thu (*over* thy *erased*)

189. *hungry contreys*, i.e. lacking in spiritual food, the bread of life.
194. *Actiua Vita*: the Active life, the life of the Christian in the world, getting and spending, as contrasted with the Contemplative life, essentially that of the cloistered religious; the Mixed life often made a third (see X 78n). The Active life is a good and proper Christian life: Peres was its representative in VII 184ff (but cf. VII 299n), and the minstrel claims to be his apprentice. But minstrels have long been an object of suspicion in this poem (Prol. 35n) and apprentices have usually been scoundrels (II 224, VI 208). Through the minstrel we see what it means to be active in the world's work (cf. IX 5), and the inadequacy of such a life in relation to the possibility, increasingly clear to understand, of a higher spiritual life. He shows himself to be thoroughly bound up with the world, and yet to grudge all that he does; he is unable to think of anything but worldly reward (202, 209) or of prayers as anything but a poor substitute for such a reward (211–12); his scorn of other kinds of minstrel (203) seems mixed with envy; his hatred of idleness (214) is mere busy-ness about the world. He serves Peres, but does not understand Peres's ideal of service. It is important to note that the portrait of Active is rewritten and much reduced from B XIII, where he is given a personal name, Haukyn, and developed as a compelling portrait of sinful and repentant humanity (see S. Maguire, in *RES* 25, 1949, 97–109). C shifts the account of his sins to the earlier confession of the sins (see VI 3n), and is primarily interested in preparing Active as an erring pupil for instruction by Patience. In this, like Rechelesnesse, he again takes over, temporarily, the role of the dreamer.
195. *to conforte*: literally, 'to provide for', referring to Peres's role as the ploughman; also, 'to provide spiritual sustenance for', in accordance with Peres's higher role; but the only contribution Active makes to the work of Christ on earth and the life of the Church is to sell eucharistic wafers (199).
199. *wafres* were eucharistic wafers, sold to *godes gestes*, i.e. communicants. They were also fancy cakes, as sold in public places. *Wafrers*, sellers of the latter kind of wafer, had a bad reputation (see VII 285n): they would combine their wafer-selling with low popular entertaining, whence Active's claim to be a minstrel.

And fewe robes y fonge or forrede gounes.
Wolde y lye and do men lawhe thenne lacchen y scholde
Or mantel or mone amonges lordes munstrals.
Y can nat tabre ne trompy ne telle fayre gestes,　　　　　　　　　205
Farten ne fythelen at festes, ne harpe,
Iape ne iogele ne genteliche pipe,
Ne noþer sayle ne sautrien ne syngen with þe geterne.
Y haue no gode giftes of thise grete lordes
For no breed þat y betrauaile furste to bryng byfore lordes,　　　210
Nere hit þat þe parsche preyeth for me on Sonendayes.
Y am sory þat y sowe or sette but for mysulue,
Ac þe prest and oþere peple preyeth for Peres þe plouheman
And for me, Actyf, his man, þat ydelnesse hate;
Lordes and lorelles, luther and gode,　　　　　　　　　215 f.67ᵃ
Fro Mihel-masse to Mihel-masse y fynde mete and drynke.
　　Y fynde payn for þe pope and preyen hym ych wolde
That pestilences to pees and parfyt loue turnen.
For founde y þat his blessynge and his bulle myhte
Lette this luythere eir and leche þe sike –　　　　　　　　220
As þe boek bereth witnesse þat he bere myhte
In his mouthe mercy and amende vs all,
　　Super egros manus ponebant et bene habebunt –
And thenne wolde y be bysy and buxum to helpe
Vch a kyne creature þat on Crist leueth.
For sethe he hath þe power þat Peter hadde he hath þe pott with
　　　þe salue.　　　　　　　　　　　　　　　　　　225
　　Argentum et aurum non est michi; quod habeo tibi do

---

207. iogele U] X iangele
210. bryng T] XUI *om*
214. hate T] XUI hatte
217. pope U] X pote.　preyen U] X preen
220. eir P] XUT *om*; I folc

---

206. *Farten.* Skill in this form of entertainment was much admired in the Middle Ages,
not only in popular circles, as appears from an attack on such and similar enter-
tainers by John of Salisbury (quoted in Tho. Warton's *History of English Poetry*, ed.
W. C. Hazlitt, 1871, iii.162): 'Quodque magis mirere, nec tunc ejiciuntur, quando
tumultuantes inferius crebro sonitu aerem foedant, et turpiter inclusum turpius
produnt'. The art remained popular (it was still admired in the late 19th c. in
French popular theatre) and was presumably exploited at key moments in medi-
eval plays, e.g. the fall of Lucifer in the *Ludus Coventriae* (ed. EETS, ES 120), p. 19.
222a. 'They laid [Vg.*imponent*] their hands on the sick, and they will recover' (Mk.
16:18). Christ assigns power to the disciples, from whom the pope inherits.
225. Cf. IX 263.
225a. 'I have no silver and gold; what I have I give you' (Acts 3:6). What Peter has is
the power to heal.

Ac yf myhte of myracle hym fayle hit is for men beth nat worthy
To haue þe grace of god, and no gulte of þe pope.
For may no blessynge doen vs bote but yf we wol amende,
Ne mannes prayere maky pees amonges cristene peple
Til pruyde be puyreliche fordo and þat thorw payn defaute.   230
    Habundancia panis et vini turpissimum peccatum aduenit.
Plente of payn the peple of Sodoume
And reste and ryche metes rebaudes hem made.'
   'Pees!' quod Pacience, 'Y preye ȝow, sire Actyf!
For þoȝ nere payn ne plouh ne potage were,
Pruyde wolde potte hymsulf forth thogh no plough erye.   235
Hit am y þat fynde alle folke and fram hunger saue
Thorw the helpe of hym þat me hyder sente.'
And saide, 'Lo, here lyflode ynow, yf oure beleue be trewe.
For lente neuere was here lyf but lyflode were shape
Wherof or wherfore and wherwith to lyuene: 240
Þe worm þat woneth vnder erthe and in water fisches,
The cryket by kynde of þe fuyr and corleu by þe wynde,
Bestes by gras and by grayn and by grene rotes,
In menynge þat alle men myhte þe same
Leue thorw lele bileue as oure lord wittenesseth: 245
    Quodcumque pecieritis in nomine meo dabitur enim vobis. Et
    alibi: Non in solo pane viuit homo.'   f.67ᵇ
   'Hastow,' quod Actyf, 'ay such mete with the?'
   'Ȝe,' quod Pacience, and oute of his poke hente
A pece of þe *pater-noster* and profred hit to vs all.
And y lystnede and lokede what lyflode hit were

---

241. þat woneth T] XU and wonte; I þat wonde
243. gras U] X grace

---

230. *payn defaute*: 'lack of bread'. For the idea of pestilence and famine as the antidote to pride, see V 117, VIII 349–53.
230a. 'From abundance of bread and wine comes the most wicked sin'. There is a similar sentence in Peter the Cantor, 'Et abundantia panis causa fuit peccati Sodomorum' (*Verbum abbreviatum*, cxxxv, 300, in *PL* 205:331), also prompted by the verse from Ezekiel which follows here. A variant form appears in B XIV 77.
231–2. See Ez. 16:49.
233. C here returns to the matter of B (see above, 194n). Patience reminds Active that pride and sin will not be silenced by mere hunger, and thus also rebukes Active's preoccupation with worldly matters.
242. 'The cricket (lives) by the natural element of fire and the curlew upon air'. The cricket is here identified with the salamander. The four elements are represented in 242–3.
245a. 'Whatever you ask in my name shall be given to you' (John 14:13). And elsewhere: 'Man shall not live by bread alone (but by every word that proceeds from the mouth of God)' (Matt. 4:4; see above, 47n).

And thenne was hit *fiat voluntas tua* þat sholde fynde vs alle.   250
'Haue, Actyf,' quod Pacience, 'and eet this when þe hungreth
Or when thow claumsest for colde or clingest for eny drouthe,
And shal neuere gyues the greue ne grete lordes wrathe,
Prisoun ne oþer payne, for *pacientes vincunt*.
By so þat þou be sobre of syhte and of tonge,   255
In ondynge and handlynge, in alle thy fyue wittes,
Dar þe nat care for no corn ne for cloth ne for drynke,
Ne deth drede ne deuel, deye as god liketh
Wheþer thorw hunger or hete, at his wille be hit;
For if thow lyuest aftur his lore the shortere lyf þe betere.   260
Si quis amat Christum mundum non diligit istum.
Thorw his breth bestes wexe and abroed ȝeden:
Dixit et facta fuerunt.
Ergo, thorw his breth bestes lyueth, bothe men and fisches,
As witnesseth holy writ when we seggeth oure graces:
Aperis tu manum tuam, et imples omne animal benedictione.
Hit is founde þat fourty wynter folke lyuede and tylde nat,   265
And oute of þe flynt spronge þe floed þat folk and bestes dronke.
And in Elies tyme heuene was yclosed
That no reyn ne roen; thus rat men on bokes,
That manye wynter men lyuede and no mete ne tylede.

---

254. *pacientes* U] X pacience
256. *ondynge* P] XUIT etynge
258. *deth* U] X dieth
264. *et imples omne animal benedictione* U] X *om*
268. *rat* U] X þat *with* r *inserted*

250. 'Thy will be done' (Matt. 6:10). See above, 47n. The sequence of quotations in
245a and 250, and elsewhere in this section of the poem, illustrates well how the
discourse of the poem is generated from scriptural concordance, i.e. the association
of verbally related (here 'give', 'bread') scriptural texts (see Alford, 1977, 93),
though the original process of generative composition is often obscured in the
revisions of C.

254. *pacientes vincunt*. See above, 138n, 157a.

261. 'If anyone loves Christ he loves not the world', continuing, in one MS of C, *Sed
quasi fetorem spernes illius amorem* ('But you reject the love of it [the world] as if it
stank'). Leonine verses (Prol. 152n), proverbial (Walther 28959), based on 1 John
2:15.

262a. 'He commanded and they were created' (Ps. 148:5, Vg. *sunt*), as in XIV 165a.

264a. 'Thou openest thy hand, and fillest with blessing every living thing' (Ps. 144:16).
This text was used daily in saying grace (see III 339a).

265–6. The references are to the forty years' wandering of the Israelites in the wil-
derness (Num. 14:33, 32:13), and the flow of water from the rock struck by Moses
(Num. 20:11). A similar use of the two examples is made in Deut. 8:15–16.

267. See 3 Reg. 17:1, and cf. James 5:17.

Seuene slepen, as saith þe boek, more then syxty wynter,　　　　　270
Lyuede withouten lyflode and at the laste awakede.
And yf men lyuede as mesure wolde sholde neuere be defaute
Amonges cristene creatures, yf Cristes wordes be trewe:
　　Dabo tibi secundum peticionem tuam.'
　'What is parfit pacience?' quod *Actiua Vita.*
'Meeknesse and mylde speche and men of o will,　　　　　　275
The whiche wil loue lat to oure lordes place,
And þat is charite, chaumpion, chief of all vertues;
And þat is pore pacient, alle perelles to soffre.'　　　　　f.68ᵃ
　'Where pouerte and pacience plese more god almyhty
Then rihtfullyche rychesse and resonablelyche to spene?'　　280
　'Ȝe, *quis est ille?*' quod Pacience, 'quik *laudamus eum!*
Thogh men rede of rychesse rihte to þe worldes ende
I wiste neuere renke þat riche was, þat whan he rekene sholde
Then when he drow to þe deth, that he ne dradd hym sarrore
Then eny pore pacient, and þat preue y be resoun.　　　　285
Hit are but fewe folk of this ryche that ne falleth in arrerage,
There þe pore dar plede and preue by puyr resoun
To haue allouaunce of his lord; by puyre lawe he claymeth
Ioye þat neuere ioye hadde; of rihtfull iuge he asketh
And saith, "Loo! briddes and bestes þat no blisse ne knoweth　290
And wilde wormes in wodes, thorw wyntres thow hem greuest
And makest hem wel-neyh meke and mylde for defaute.

281. *laudamus* X] U laudabimus
283. *line supplied from* B; XUITP *om*

270. The story of the Seven Sleepers of Ephesus is told in the *Legenda Aurea*, CI (also in the *Alphabetum Narrationum*, 195: see XVII 165). They were walled up in a cave by the emperor Decius and awoke alive under Theodosius II, 362 years later.

273a. 'I will give you according to your request' (Ps. 36:4, varied; cf. Mk. 6:22).

274. The abruptness of Active's question (though patience has been in part the theme of the preceding discourse: see 254) has something to do with the omission of 25 lines in B (XIV 73–97) at this point. But C is preparing, with its customary directness and economy, for the next question (279–80) and the ensuing discussion of poverty and riches. The lines omitted assert the orthodox belief (see XIV 115n) that contrition alone suffices to deliver a man from sin. Faced again with the familiar difficulty of an orthodox point of doctrine that may well mislead a non-theologian, L omits the passage, content with his previous discussion in XIV 115–23.

276. *The whiche wil loue lat*: 'which same unanimity of purpose love directs'.

279. *Where*: 'Whether', introducing a question, perhaps in imitation of the *Utrum* of scholastic disputation (see XIV 192n).

281. 'Who is he? Let us praise [Vg. *laudabimus*] him' (Ecclus. 31:9). Patience's answer suggests ironically that rich men such as Active mentions will be hard to find.

286. Cf. XI 299.

Theraftur thow sendest hem somer þat is here souereyne ioye
And blisse to all þat been, bothe to wilde and to tame."
Thenne may beggares, as bestes, aftur a blisse aske   295
That al here lyf haen lyued in langour and defaute.
Bote god sende hem somtyme sum manere ioye
Other here or elliswher, elles hit were reuthe.
For to wroþer-hele was he wrouht þat neuere was ioye yschape.
Angeles þat in helle now ben hadden somtyme ioye,   300
And Dyues in his deyntees lyuede and in *douce vie*
And now he buyth hit bittere, he is a beggare of helle.
Many man hath his ioye here for al here wel dedes
And lordes and ladyes ben cald for ledes þat they haue
And slepeth as hit semeth and somur euere hem folleweth.   305
Ac when deth awaketh hem of here wele þat were er so ryche
Then aren hit puyre pore thynges in purgatorie or in hell.
Dauid in þe sauter of suche maketh mynde,
And sayth, *Dormierunt et nichil inuenerunt. Et alibi: Velud
        sompnum surgencium, etc.*

296. The speech of *þe pore* could end here, or at 298, or later.

297. *Bote*: 'unless'.

299. *to wroþer-hele*: 'with evil fortune' (a fossilized phrase: see OED, *wrother-heal*). *þat*: 'for whom'.

301. *Dyues.* Luke 16:19. See VIII 278. *douce vie*: 'a life of luxury'.

303. *for al here wel dedes*: 'despite all their good deeds', i.e. their good deeds will not excuse them from the payment they will have to make for their joy on earth.

307. *Then aren hit*: 'Then are they'.

309. 'They have slept, and (all the rich men) have found nothing (in their hands)' (Ps. 75:6). And elsewhere: 'Like the dream of one awaking (O Lord, so in thy city thou shalt reduce their image to nothing)' (Ps. 72:20).

Passus XVI

Patience and Liberum Arbitrium

Passus sextus de Dowel
Allas! þat rychesse shal reue and robbe mannes soule
Fro þe loue of oure lord at his laste ende.
Hewen þat haen here huyre byfore aren eueremore pore
And selde deyeth oute of dette þat dyneþ ar he deserue hit.   f.68^b
When his dyuer is doen and his dayes iourne   5
Thenne may men wyte what he is worth and what he hath deserued,
Ac nat to fonge byfore for drede of dessallouwynge.
So y sey by ʒow ryche, hit semeth nat þat ʒe sholle
Haue two heuenes for ʒoure here-beynge.
Muche murthe is in May amonge wilde bestes   10
And so forth whiles somur laste here solace duyreth,
And moche murthe among ryche men is þat han meble ynow and hele.
Ac beggares aboute myssomur bredles they soupe,
And ʒut is wynter for hem worse, for weet-shoed þey gone,
Afurste and afyngered and foule rebuked   15
Of this world-ryche men, þat reuthe is to here.
Now lord, sende hem somur somtyme to solace and to ioye
That al here lyf leden in lownesse and in pouerte!
For al myhtest þou haue ymad men of grete welthe

3–5. *lineation as* U; X *mislineates*
4. þat dyneþ T] XUP to dyne
7. of U] X *om*

---

1. It may often seem that L is returning to themes he has already fully discussed. But the ruminative processes of the poem are extraordinarily rich and productive, and Patience (an aspect of Charity) brings to the present discussion of poverty and riches not only a greater compassion for the poor but also compassion for the rich, who were treated by Rechelesnesse with a certain self-satisfied relish (e.g. XII 218ff). It is interesting to see that poverty, which was the worst of the world's problems in the *Visio*, is now the solution to them.

4. *þat*: 'he that'. L recurs here to a theme treated literally in III 292–303, that men should be paid after not before working. Here he is using it allegorically: the rich are those who are paid before (i.e. here) and who cannot therefore expect to be paid again hereafter.

8. *hit semeth nat*: 'it beseemeth not, it is not fitting'.

13. Even in summer the poor are badly off, since they can expect nothing better until harvest-time (see VIII 322).

And yliche witty and wys and lyue withoute nede –   20
Ac for þe beste, as y hope, aren som pore and ryche.
  Riht so haue reuthe on þi renkis alle
And amende vs for thy mercy and make vs alle meke,
Lowe and lele and louynge and of herte pore.
And sende vs contricion to clanse with oure soules   25
And confessioun to kulle alle kyne synnes
And satisfaccioun þe whiche folfilleth þe fader will of heuene.
And these ben Dowel and Dobet and Dobest of alle.
Cordis contricio cometh of sorughe of herte
And *oris confessio*, þat cometh of shrifte of mouthe   30
And satisfaccion, þat for soules paieth and for alle synnes quyteth.
Cordis contricio, Oris confessio, Operis satisfaccio:
Thise thre withoute doute tholieth alle pouerte
And lereth lewed and lered, hey and lowe to knowe
Ho doth wel or bet or beste aboue alle;   35
And holy churche and charite herof a chartre made.
And bote these thre þat y spak of at domesday vs defende
Elles is al an ydel al oure lyuynge here,
Oure preyeres and oure penances and pilgrimages to Rome.
Bote oure spensis and oure spendyng sprynge of a trewe welle   40
Elles is alle oure labour loest – loo, how men writeth   f.69ᵃ
In fenestres at þe freres yf fals be þe fondement!
Forthy cristene sholde be in comune ryche, noon coueytous for
              hymsulue,
For seuene synnes þat þer ben þat assailen vs euere;
The fend followeth hem alle and fondeth hem to helpe,   45

---

22. þi renkis alle T] XU vs alle (*with subsequent mislineation*); P ous alle that on the rode
    deydest
29. sorughe] X soruthe; U sorowe
44. assailen U] X assoilen

20. *and lyue*: 'and (made) to live'.
21. A reminder that Patience is speaking.
25. Some fine lines in B (esp. XIV 174–80) are omitted here, having earlier provided
    inspiration for C IX 72–85 (Donaldson, 1949, 26–7). C concentrates instead on an
    explicit statement of the necessity of penance, in its three stages (cf. VI 6n), and of
    the supreme importance of penance as the legal and sacramental instrument in
    which love and law are united (the *chartre* of line 36). The relation to the general
    theme is that penance is the declaration of spiritual poverty, or *herte pore* (24).
    Wyclif makes the same distinction of bodily poverty and 'poverte in spirit' in a
    sermon on the Beatitudes (ed. Arnold, i.407).
32a. 'Contrition of heart, confession of mouth, satisfaction of deed'.
41–2. See III 64–74.
44. In the following lines (44–99), Patience analyses the Seven Deadly Sins (VI 3n) in
    relation to the rich and the poor, showing how the poor are of necessity less
    vulnerable to sin. Only Envy is not mentioned.

Ac with rychesse tho rybaudes rathest men bigileth.
   For þere þat rychesses regneth reuerences folleweth,
And þat is plesant to Pruyde, in pore and in ryche;
Ac þe ryche is reuerenced by resoun of his rychesse
There þe pore is potte behynde and parauntur can more   50
Of wit and of wisdoem, þat fer away is bettere
Then rychesse or ryalte, and rather yherde in heuene.
For þe ryche hath moche to rykene and riht softe walketh;
The hey way to heuene-ward he halt hit nat fol euene,
There þe pore preseth byfore with a pak at his rugge –   55
   Opera eorum sequuntur illos –
Batauntliche, as beggares doen, and baldeliche he craueth
For his pouerte and his pacience perpetuel ioye.
   And Pruyde in rychesse regneth rather then in pouerte;
Or in þe mayster or in þe man som mansion he haueth.
Ac in pouerte þer pacience is Pruyde hath no myhte   60
Ne none of þe seuene synnes sitte ne may þer longe
Ne haue power in pouerte yf pacience hym folewe.
For þe pore is ay prest to plese þe ryche
And buxum at his biddyng for his breed and his drynke,
And buxumnesse and boost aren eueremore at werre   65
And ayther hateth oþer and may nat wone togyderes.
   Yf Wrathe wrastle with þe pore he hath þe worse ende,
For yf they bothe pleyne the pore is bote feble
And yf he chyde or chattere hym cheueth þe worse.
For louelyche he loketh and lowe is his speche   70
That mete or moneye of straunge men moet begge.
   And yf Glotonye greue pouerte he gadereth þe lasse
For his rentes wol nat reche ryche metes to bugge.
And thogh his glotonye be of gode ale he goth to a colde beddynge
And his heued vnheled, vnesylyche ywrye   75
For when he streyneth hym to strecche the strawe is his shetes.   f.69^b

---

47. þere T] XU *om*
49. Ac B] XUT And; P *om*
51. away U] X way
72. he T] X ho (*lines 72–3 om U*)

---

46. *tho rybaudes*, i.e. the devil and his companions.
55. *with a pak at his rugge*, containing his good works.
55a. 'Their deeds follow them' (Apoc. 14:13), i.e. the deeds of the virtuous, those who 'die in the Lord', accompany them to blessedness, where they 'may rest from their labours'.
59. *or in þe man*. The detail 'calls to mind', as Skeat says, 'the arrogant manners of the retainers in a great household'.
76. The sheets only partly cover the straw bedding. Proverbial (Whiting W 234).

So for his glotonye and his grete synne he hath a greuous penaunce,
Þat is welowo when he awaketh and wepeth for colde;
So he is neuere merye, so meschief hym folleweth.

   And thogh Coueytyse wolde with þe pore wrastle they may nat
      come togyderes   80
And by þe nekke namelyche here noen may henten other;
For men knowen wel þat Coueytise is of a kene will
And hath hondes and armes of a longe lenthe
And pouerte is bote a pety thyng, appereth nat to his nauele,
And louely layk was hit neuere bytwene a longe and a short one.   85
And thogh Auaryce wolde angry pouerte he hath bote lytel myhte
For pouerte hath bote pokes to potten in his godes
There Auaryce hath almaries and yre-bounden coffres.
And where be bettere to breke? lasse boest hit maketh
To breke a beggares bagge then an yre-bounden coffre.   90

   And Lecherye loueth no pore for he hath bote litel siluer
Ne doth men dyne delicatlyche ne drynke wyne ofte.
A straw for the stuyues! hit stoed nat hadde they noen haunt
      bote of pore!

   And thow Sleuthe sewe pouerte, and serue nat god to paye,
Meschief is ay a mene and maketh hym to thenke   95
That god is his gretteste helpe and no gome elles,
And he his seruant alway, he saith, and of his secte bothe.
And where he be or be nat, a bereth þe signe of pouerte
And in þat secte oure saueour saued al mankynde.

   Forthy alle pore þat pacient is of puyr rihte may claymen   100
Aftur here endynge here heuene-ryche blisse.
Moche hardyore may he aske þat here myhte haue his wille
In lond and in lordschipe, in lykynge of body,
And for goddes loue leueth al and lyueth as a beggare.

77–8. *lineation as* I; XU *mislineate*
97. his[1] B] XUTP is

---

81. *here noen*: 'none of them'.

86. *Auaryce.* L makes here the traditional distinction between Covetousness, desire for gain, and Avarice, desire to retain (e.g. *Handlyng Synne* 5325–42).

89. *where* (a contracted form of *whether*): 'which of the two'. *lasse boest hit maketh*: 'it makes less of a noise' or 'it causes less of an outcry', i.e. a poor man is not likely to be anxious about his property or make a fuss if it is stolen, and therefore is less prone to avarice.

94–8. A poor man may have tendencies to slothfulness, but adversity gives him less opportunity to be slothful, and makes him recognize that God alone is his help; in any event, he has still the advantage of being a poor man.

99. Cf. XII 120.

As a mayde for a mannes loue here moder forsoke,   105
Here fader and alle here frendes and goth forth with here paramours:
Moche is suche a mayde to louye of a man þat such oen taketh,
More then þat mayde is þat is maried by brocage,
As by assente of sondry persones and suluer to bote,
More for coueytise of catel then kynde loue of þe mariage.   110
So hit fareth by vch a persone þat possession forsaketh   f.70ᵃ
And potte hym to be pacient and pouerte weddeth,
The whiche is syb to Crist sulue and semblable bothe.'
　　Quod Actyf tho al angryliche and arguinge as hit were:
'What is pouerte, Pacience?' quod he, 'y preye þat thow telle hit.'   115
'*Paupertas*,' quod Pacience, '*est odibile bonum, remocio curarum,*
　　　possessio sine calumpnia, donum dei, sanitatis mater, absque
　　　solicitudine semita, sapiencie temperatrix, negocium sine dampno,
　　　incerta fortuna, absque solicitudine felicitas.'
'Y can nat construe al this,' quod *Actiua Vita*.
'Parfay,' quod Pacience, 'propreliche to telle hit,
Al this in Engelysch, hit is ful hard, ac sumdel y shal telle the.
　　Pouerte is the furste poynte þat pruyde moest hateth;   120
Thenne is pouerte goed, by goed skill, thouh hit greue a litel,
Al þat may potte of pruyde in eny place þer he regneth.
　　　Remocio curarum.
Selde syt pouerte þe sothe to declare,
Or a iustice to iuge men, me enioyneth þerto no pore,

---

116. *possessio* U] X posessio. *solicitudine*¹ P] XUT solitudine. *temperatrix* P] XUT temporatrix

---

105–10. Again (as in 4, above), L makes allegorical and spiritual use (prompted by texts like Matt. 19:5, 29, Eph. 5:21–33) of a theme treated literally in an earlier passus (X 254ff).

111. *persone*, in the context, seems to mean 'parson of a living', i.e. beneficed priest, or 'possessioner'. If so, Patience comes close here to endorsing the Wycliffite ideal of the poor priest (XIII 99n).

113. *bothe*: 'also'.

114. Active speaks angrily and argumentatively because it is his nature to do so, not because of anything that has been said. He is impatient and busy (see XV 212, 224), and provides a dramatic and edifying contrast with his tutor.

116. 'Poverty is a hateful good, freedom from cares, possession without dishonesty, a gift of God, mother of health, a pathway free from anxiety, a mediator of wisdom, innocent labour, uncertain fortune, happiness free from anxiety'. There are ten points here, of which Patience glosses nine (i.e. excluding *incerta fortuna*) in ll. 120–54. This aphoristic commendation of Poverty is attributed to the legendary Secundus Philosophus (Alford 396), and is well-known, in various forms, in encyclopaedic works such as the *Speculum Historiale* (x.71) of Vincent of Beauvais (Douai, 1624; repr. Graz. 1965, 393) and in collections of aphorisms. Chaucer makes use of it in the Wife of Bath's Tale (*CT* III. 1195–1200).

121. This line embodies the sense of *odibile bonum* (*goed . . . greue*).

122. *Al*: in apposition to *hit*, previous line. *potte of*: 'drive away'.

Ne to be a mair ouer men ne mynistre vnder kynges. 125
Selde is eny pore ypot to punyshe eny peple,
Ergo pouerte and pore men parforme þe comandement
   Nolite iudicare quemquam.
   Possessio sine calumpnia.
Selde is þe pore rihte ryche but of his rihtfole eritage;
Wynneth he nat with wightes false ne with vnselede mesures
Ne boreweth of his neyhebore but þat he may wel paye, 130
And me leneth lyhtly fewe men and me wene hem pore.
   The furthe hit is a fortune þat florischeth þe soule
With sobrete fro alle synnes and also ȝut more:
Hit defendeth þe flesche fram folies ful monye,
A collateral confort, Cristes oune sonde: 135
   Donum die.
ȝut is hit moder of myhte and of mannes helthe
And frende in alle fondynges and of foule eueles leche:
   Sanitatis mater.
The sixte hit is a path of pees, ȝe! thorwe þe pase of Aultoun
Pouerte myhte passe withoute perel of robbynge.
For þer as pouerte passeth pes folleweth comunely 140
And euere þe lasse þat on lede þe lihtere his herte is there,
As he þat woet neuere with wham on nyhtes tyme to mete. f.70ᵇ
   Seneca: Paupertas est absque solicitudine semita.
The seuethe is a welle of wysdoem and fewe wordes sheweth
For lordes alloueth hym litel or leggeth ere to his resoun;
A tempreth þe tonge to treuthe-ward þat no tresor coueyteth. 145
   The eyȝte hit is a lel labour and loeth to take more
Then he may sothly deserue in somur or in wynter,
And thogh he chaffare, he chargeth no loes, may he charite wynne:
   Negocium sine dampno.

126. punyshe U] X penesche
129. wightes U] X whittes

127a. See XII 30a.
129. *wightes*: 'weights'. *vnselede mesures*. Cf. III 88.
138. *þe pase of Aultoun* was a wooded stretch of the valley of the Wey near Alton (Jane Austen's home was nearby), reputed a favourite resort of robbers, who would lie in wait there to attack merchants on their way to or from Winchester fair. See IV 50–54, VI 211, XIII 51, and Skeat's note.
141–2. The general inspiration of these lines is the tag from Juvenal (quoted in B) referred to in XIII 1n: *Cantabit pauper coram latrone viator.*
142a. The name of Seneca has possibly been added by scribes. He expresses generally similar sentiments on poverty in Epist. 17, to which Chaucer refers in *CT* III. 1184 (see above, 116n), but L has already quoted the Latin text from which he draws. Seneca, of course, was often named as a vague 'authority' (cf. XII 172n) for proverbial tags.

The nythe hit is swete to soules ne no sucre swettore,
For pacience is his paniter and pouerte payn here fyndeth   150
And sobrete ȝeueth here swete drynke and solaceth here in all
        angrys.
Thus lered me a lered man for oure lordes loue, seynt Austyn,
That puyre pouerte and pacience was a louh lyuynge on erthe,
A blessed lyf withoute bisinesse bote onelyche for þe soule:
    Absque solicitudine felicitas.
Now god þat al gyueth graunte his soule reste   155
That wroet thus to wisse men what pouerte was to mene!'

    Thenne hadde Actyf a ledare þat hihte *Liberum Arbitrium*;
A knewe Consience ful wel and Clergie bothe.
'He þat hath lond and lordschipe,' quod he, 'at þe laste ende
Shal be porest of power at his partynge hennes.'   160
Thenne hadde y wonder what he was, þat *Liberum Arbitrium*,
And preyde Pacience þat y apose hym moste.
And ,he soffrede me and saide, 'Assay his oþer name.'
'Leue *Liberum Arbitrium*,' quod y, 'of what lond ar ȝe?
And yf thow be Cristes creature, for Cristes loue telle me.'   165
    'Y am Cristes creature,' quod he, 'and of his kynne a party,
And in Cristes court yknowe wel and of cristene in mony a place.
Is noþer Peter the porter ne Poul with the fauchen

161. *Liberum* U] X Leberum
166. of . . . party] XUTP cristene in mony a place
167. cristene . . . place] XUTP his kynne a party

150. *pouerte payn here fyndeth*: 'provides poverty with bread'. *his*, earlier in the line, refers to this last 'point' or personified virtue of poverty. *here* may mean 'here', adv., or, more probably, 'her', pron.obj. in apposition to 'poverty'.

152. *seynt Austyn*. Relevant remarks can be found in St Augustine, but his name appears here as a general 'authority'.

157. C omits here the moving description in B of the repentance of Haukyn (see XV 194n), suppresses a passus-division, and passes directly to the introduction of the new character. *Liberum Arbitrium*, 'Free Will', is the name given in C to this character, who is called *Anima* in B. The change in name, which leaves some loose ends in the definition originally applied to *Anima* (see below, 182–200), is designed to present the life of Dowel as a more positive act of choice and a more positive *doing* of God's will. Free Will is the highest gift of God to man: it is the whole intellectual and spiritual faculty of man divinely illumined, the seed of God's reason implanted in man. His obedience to the dictates of that reason, in other words his recognition and observance of the will of God, is for him true freedom. For an account of scholastic definitions of *Liberum Arbitrium*, see Schmidt, 1969, and B. J. Harwood in *PQ* 52 (1973), 680–95.

166ᵇ, 167ᵇ, are here interchanged, according to the emendation of Kane-Donaldson (see p. 209) in B XV 16–17.

168. Peter has the keys of the kingdom of heaven (Matt. 16:19), while the falchion or sword is the standard attribute of Paul in medieval art, being the emblem of his martyrdom (he was beheaded with a sword).

That wol defende me heuene dore, dynge y neuere so late.
At mydnyhte, at mydday, my vois is so yknowe   170
That vch a creature þat loueth Crist welcometh me faire.'
    'Whareof serue ȝe?' y saide, 'sire *Liberum Arbitrium?*'
    'Of som tyme to fihte,' quod he, 'falsnesse to destruye,
And som tyme to soffre bothe tene and sorwe,
Layk or leue, at my lykyng chese   175 f.71ª
To do wel or wykke, a will with a resoun,
And may nat be withoute a body to bere me where hym liketh.'
    'Thenne is þat body bettere þen þou?' quod y.
                    'Nay,' quod he, 'no bettere,
Bote as wode were afuyre thenne worcheth bothe
And ayther is otheres hete and also of o will;   180
And so is man þat hath his mynde myd *Liberum Arbitrium.*
    And whiles y quyke þe cors ycald am y *Anima,*
And when y wilne and wolde *Animus* y hatte,
And for þat y can and knowe ycald am y *Mens,*
And when y make mone to god *Memoria* y hatte,   185
And when y deme domes and do as treuthe techeth
Thenne ys *Racio* my rihte name, Reson an Englische.
And when y fele þat folke telleth my furste name is *Sensus*
And þat is wit and wysdoem, the welle of alle craftes.
And when y chalenge or chalenge nat, chepe or refuse,   190
Thenne am y Concience ycald, goddes clerk and his notarie.
And when y wol do or do nat gode dedes or ille

---

184. for U] X *om. Mens* U] X mens thouhte
190. or chalenge U] X *om*

---

177. This may appear to refer more obviously to the relation of the body and soul
(*Anima*) and the fundamental Christian dogma of their inseparability (*Prick of
Conscience* 1848), but the passage (172–81) is in C only and refers aptly enough to
Free Will as the 'form' and informing presence of man's bodily being.
183ff. See below, 200a.
184. *thouhte* is evidently intruded in MS X from a scribal gloss for *mens* (Lat., 'mind,
thought'), which in turn is taken as a gen.pl. 'men's'. Cf. III 140.
185. *make mone to god* is an odd translation of Lat. *recolit* (200a, below). The suggestion is
perhaps of the soul meditating on the thought or remembrance of God (*Jesu dulcis
memoria*) in its supplications.
191. *goddes clerk and his notarie*, i.e. keeping an account of the good and evil deeds.
192–3. Added in C to accord with the change in the speaker's identity. The lines
express the traditional Augustinian idea that man has freedom to choose to do
evil. The definition of Free Will added to the Latin text below, however, expresses
a different idea: that man's will is free only in so far as it chooses to do good
instead of evil. If he does evil, he is not free, but bound by sin. The problem of free
will was a complex one, subjected to much scholarly debate in the Middle Ages
(see Schmidt, 1969, 141–4).

Thenne am y *Liberum Arbitrium*, as lered men telleth.
And when y louye lelly oure lord and alle oþere
Thenne is Lele Loue my name, and in Latyn, *Amor*.   195
And when y fle fro þe body and feye leue þe caroyne
Thenne am y spirit spechelees and *Spiritus* then y hote.
Austyn and Ysodorus, either of hem bothe
Nempned me thus to name; now þou myhte chese
How þou coueytest to calle me, now þou knowest al my names.   200

    Anima pro diuersis accionibus diuersa nomina sortitur:
      dum viuificat corpus, Anima est; dum vult, Animus
      est; dum scit, Mens est; dum recolit, Memoria est;
      dum iudicat, Racio est; dum sentit, Sensus est; dum
      amat, Amor est; dum declinat de malo ad bonum, Liberum
      Arbitrium est; dum negat vel consentit, Consciencia est;
      dum spirat, Spiritus est.'

  'Ȝe beth as a bischop!' quod y, al bourdynge þat tyme,
'For bisshopes yblessed they bereth many names,
Presul and *pontifex* and *metropolitanus*
And oþere names an heep, *episcopus* and *pastor*.'
  'That is soth,' he sayde. 'Now y se thy wille: 205 f.71ᵇ
Thow woldest knowe and conne þe cause of all here names
And of myn yf thow myhteste, me thynketh by thy speche.'
  'Ȝe, sire!' y sayde, 'by so no man were ygreued,
Alle þe sciences vnder sonne and alle þe sotil craftes
Y wolde y knewe and couthe kyndeliche in myn herte.'   210
  'Thenne artow inparfit,' quod he, 'and oen of Pruydes knyhtes;

200a. *accionibus* U] X occacionibus. *viuificat* U] X sinificat. *dum scit, Mens est* B] XUTP *om.*
    declinat U] X declina. *Consciencia* U] X consiencia. *spirat* U] X sperat
203. *metropolitanus* P] XUT metropolanus

200a. '*Anima* is known by different names according to its different functions: when it
gives life to the body, it is Soul; when it expresses volition, it is Consciousness;
when it has knowledge, it is Mind; when it recollects, it is Memory; when it
judges, it is Reason; when it feels, it is Sense; when it loves, it is Love; when it
turns from evil to good, it is Free Will; when it refuses or consents, it is Conscience;
when it breathes (with the divine inspiration), it is Spirit'. This description first
appeared in Isidore's *Etymologiae*, xi.1 (ed. W. M. Lindsay, Oxford, 1911, or *PL*
82:399); it is frequently quoted, as in the standard encyclopaedia of
Bartholomaeus (III.v) or in a stray note in Lambeth MS 306 (ed. EETS 15, 65).
The reference to *Liberum Arbitrium* is added, perhaps from Godfrey of Poitiers
(Schmidt, 1969, 142–3).

203–4. These are all Latin names for a bishop, except that a *metropolitanus*, having
authority over the bishops of a province, is properly an archbishop.

211. The dreamer is prompted by Free Will to reveal his intellectual ambitions, and
immediately and authoritatively rebuked for them. The 'sympathy' we have for
the dreamer (who retains, through all his trials, a characteristic touch of
individuality, as in his little joke above, 201) is the seed of a changing view of the
Faust-story. See XIII 224–8.

For such a lust and lykynge Lucifer ful fram heuene.
> *Ponam pedem meum in aquilone.*

Hit were aʒeyns kynde,' quod he, 'and alle kyne resoun
That eny creature sholde conne al, excepte Crist one.
Aʒenes alle suche Salamon speketh and despiseth here wittes   215
And sayth: *Sicut qui mel comedit multum, non est ei bonum; sic*
> *qui scrutator est magestatis, opprimetur a gloria.*

To Engelische men this is to mene, þat mowen speke and here,
"The man þat moche hony eet his mawe hit engleymeth;
The wittiore þat eny wihte is, but yf he worche þeraftur,
The bittorere he shal abugge, but yf he wel worche."   220
"*Beatus*," saith seynt Bernard, "*qui scripturas legit*
Et verba vertit in opera emforth his power."
Coueytyse to conne and to knowe sciences
Potte out of Paradys Adam and Eue.
> *Sciencie appetitus hominem immortalitatis gloriam spoliauit.*

And riht as hony is euel to defie,   225
Riht so sothly sciences swelleth a mannes soule
And doth hym to be deynous and deme þat beth nat lered.
"*Non plus sapere*," saide þe wyse,
"*Quam oportet sapere*, laste synne of pruyde wexe."

---

216. *qui*² U] X *om.* *opprimetur* P] XUT opprimatur
219. wittiore U] X wittore

212a. See I 110a.

213. *aʒeyns kynde.* Free Will rebukes the dreamer for pretending that the knowledge he seeks *kyndeliche* (210) has any relation to the *kynde knowyng* (I 136n) which is sought for love of God (Davlin, 1971, 5).

216. 'Just as it is not good for anyone to eat much honey, so he who tries to investigate too closely the majesty of God shall be cast down from glory [or, by God, personified as the glory of God: the same text is quoted in a treatise attributed to Rolle, ed. EETS 20, 42, and *a gloria* translated 'of hym-selfe']' (Prov. 25:27). Cf. also Prov. 25:16. and see XIII 195a.

221–2. 'Blessed is he who reads the scriptures and converts words into deeds'. The quotation, with slight variation, is from Bernard's *Tractatus de Ordine Vitae* (*PL* 184:566, see Alford 396), probably through an intermediary. The sentiment is common, based on Matt. 7:24.

223–4. Free Will here echoes an earlier development of this theme by Imaginatyf, XIII 224–6.

224a. 'The desire for knowledge has deprived man of the glory of immortality'. From Bernard's *Sermo IV in Ascensione Domini* (*PL* 183:311). The quotation is also used by Hugh of St Cher (cf. XI 306n) in his commentary on Eph. 4:9–10 (see Alford 396–7), which suggests that it was of general currency.

227. *þat*: 'them that'.

228–9. '(I bid you) not to try to understand more than it is proper to understand' (Rom. 12:3).

Freres fele tymes to þe folk þer they prechen 230
Mouen motyues mony tymes, insolibles and falaes,
That bothe lewed and lered of here beleue douten.
To teche þe ten comaundementz ten sythe were bettere,
And how that folk folliche here fyue wittes myspenen,
As wel freres as oþere folk, foliliche spenden 235
In housynge, in helynge, in high clergie schewynge
More for pompe and pruyde, as þe peple woet wel. f.72ᵃ
That y lye nat, loo! for lordes ȝe plese
And reuerence þe ryche þe rather for here suluer,
Aȝen þe consayl of Crist as holy clergie witnesseth: 240
   Ne sitis acceptores personarum.
  Lo, what holy writ wittnesseth of wikkede techares:
As holiness and honestee out of holy churche
Spryngeth and spredeth and enspireth þe peple
Thorw parfit preesthoed and prelates of holy churche,
Riht so oute of holy churche al euel spredeth 245
There inparfit preesthoed is, prechares and techares.
And se hit by ensample in somur tyme on trees,
Þere som bowes bereth leues and som bereth none;
Tho bowes þat bereth nat and beth nat grene yleued,
There is a meschief in þe more of suche manere stokkes. 250
Riht so persones and prestes and prechours of holy churche
Is þe rote of rihte fayth to reule þe peple;
Ac þer þe rote is roton, resoun woet þe sothe,
Shal neuere flour ne fruyt wexe ne fayre leue be grene.
  For wolde ȝe lettered leue þe lecherye of clothyng 255
And be corteys and kynde of holy kyrke godes,
Parte with þe pore and ȝoure pruyde leue
And þerto trewe of ȝoure tonge and of ȝoure tayl also

---

234. how T] X thorw; U þogh. myspenen U] X myspenenen
236. high U] X holy
245. so U] X *om*
247. se U] X so

---

230. For the friars as preachers, see XV 82n.
231. *insolibles and falaes.* Anglicizations of technical terms in logic (see XIV 192n).
234. *fyue wittes.* See X 144n.
236. *in high clergie schewynge*: 'in displays of lofty erudition'.
238. *loo!* i.e. here is the evidence.
240a. 'Do not be partial to individuals'. Probably a legal maxim: echoes a number of biblical texts, e.g. Prov. 24:23, James 2:1, but perhaps closest to Acts 10:34: *non est personarum acceptor Deus.*
241. *holy writ.* The following lines (242–54) paraphrase parts of the Latin of 271a, below.

And hatien harlotrie and to vnderfonge þe tythes
Of vsererus, of hores, of alle euel wynnynges,   260
Loeth were lewed bote they ȝoure lore folweden
And amenden of here mysdedes more for ensaumples
Then for to prechen and preue hit nat – ypocrisye hit semeth.
Ypocrisye is a braunche of pruyde, and most amonges clerkes,
And is ylikned in Latyn to a lothly dong-hep   265
That were bysnewed al with snowe and snakes withynne,
Or to a wal ywhitlymed and were blak withynne;
Riht so many prestes, prechours and prelates,
That ben enblaunched with *bele paroles* and with *bele* clothes
And as lambes they loke and lyuen as wolues.   270
Iohannes Crisostomus carpeth thus of clerkes: f.72ᵇ

> *Sicut de templo omne bonum progreditur, sic de templo omne*
> *malum procedit. Si sacerdocium integrum fuerit, tota*
> *floret ecclesia; si autem corruptum fuerit, omnium fides*
> *marcida est. Si sacerdocium fuerit in peccatis, totus*
> *populus conuertitur ad peccandum. Sicut cum videris*
> *arborem pallidam et marcidam, intelligis quod uicium*
> *habet in radice, ita cum videris populum indisciplinatum et*
> *irreligiosum, sine dubio sacerdocium eius non est sanum.*

Allas! lewed men, moche lese ȝe þat fynde
Vnkunnynge curatours to be kepares of ȝoure soules.
Ac thyng þat wykkedliche is wonne and with fals sleythes
Wolde neuere oþerwyse god but wikkede men hit hadde,   275

---

266. were U] X were al
271a. *corruptum* P] XUT corupta. *fides* U] X fedes. *videris*[1] U] X viderit

259. *tythes*. For false tithing, see VI 300–308.
264. *braunche*. See VII 70n.
265–7. The origins of this little nexus of images, which are also associated together in the Squire's Tale (*CT* V. 512–20), are the 'whited sepulchres' of Matt. 23:27 (applied to hypocritical scribes and Pharisees) and the proverbial 'snake in the grass' (Virgil, *Ecl.* iii.93). The snakes have found their way into the tomb, which has become a dung-heap covered with snow, while the white lime now disguises merely the surface of the wall.
270. See Prol. 2n.
271. The lines that follow are extracted from a long comparison of the church to the human body in Homily 38 of a series on Matthew wrongly attributed to St John Chrysostom (*PG* 56:839). L evidently takes them from an intermediate source. The text glossed is Matt. 21:12–20.
271a. 'As from the temple proceeds all good, so from the temple proceeds all evil. If the priesthood is sound, the whole church flourishes; if however it is corrupt, the faith of all is withered. If the priesthood is sinful, the whole people are turned to sin. As when you see a tree pale and withered, you know that it has some disease in the root, so when you see a disordered and impious people, without doubt their priesthood is not sound'.

As inparfite prestes and prechours aftur suluer,
Seketours and sodenes, somnours and here lemmanes,
And þat with gyle was gete vngraciousliche be yspened.
Curatours of holy churche and clerkes þat ben auerous,
Lihtliche þat they leue loseles hit deuoureth.   280
Leueth hit wel, lordes, both lewed and lered,
That thus goth here godes at þe laste ende
That lyuen aȝen holy lore and þe loue of charite.'
   'Charite,' quod y tho, 'þat is a thyng forsothe
That maistres commenden moche; where may hit be yfounde?   285
Ich haue yleued in Londone monye longe ȝeres
And fonde y neuere, in faith, as freres hit precheth,
Charite, þat chargeth naught, ne chyt, thow me greue hym,
As Poul in his pistul of hym bereth wittenesse:
   Non inflatur, non est ambiciosa.
I knewe neuere, by Crist, clerk noþer lewed   290
That he ne askede aftur his and oþere-whiles coueytede
Thyng that nedede hym nauhte, and nyme hit, yf a myhte!
For thogh me souhte alle þe sektes of susturne and of brethurne,
And fynde hym, but figuratyfly, a ferly me thynketh;
   Hic in enigmate, tunc facie ad faciem.
And so y trowe treuly, by that me telleth of Charite.'   295

286. Londone X] U londe
294. figuratyfly U] X fuguratyfly

277. *seketours.* For a long diatribe against executors, see *Handlyng Synne* 6229–6508.
   sodenes. See II 187n. *somnours.* See II 59n. For the general sentiment, cf. XII
   215.
280. *Lihtliche* qualifies *deuoureth.*
284. The dreamer's question (cf. XV 274, and 115, above) prompts Free Will to move
   from his attack on false clergy to a more positive discourse on Charity as the life of
   Dowel, which in turn gives way (XVII) to a more comprehensive account of the
   true role of Church and clergy.
286. The corresponding line in B, 'I haue lyued in londe, quod I, my name is longe
   wille' (XV 152), is traditionally regarded as a syllabic anagram of the author's
   name (Kane, 1965, 65–70). See also X 68n.
289a. '(Love) is not boastful, nor is it ostentatious' (1 Cor. 13:4–5).
291. *aftur his*: 'for what was due to him'.
294a. 'Now (we see in a mirror) darkly [i.e. in the form of an enigma or mystery], then
   face to face' (1 Cor. 13:12). The earthly images and experience of God are but
   pale and dim reflections of his divine nature. So here, true charity is found but
   rarely among churchmen, and even when it is found it will be only a pale image
   or reflection of divine charity. L seems to be using *figuratyfly* as a translation of *in
   enigmate*, but the context suggests that the word has a contemptuous ring to it, as if
   the reflection were not only pale and dim but superficial and distorted also.
295. *by that*: 'judging by what'.

'Charite is a childische thyng, as holy churche witnesseth,
  Nisi efficiamini sicut parvuli, etc.
As proud of a peny as of a pounde of golde,
And as glad of a goune of a gray russet   f.73ᵃ
As of a cote of camaca or of clene scarlet.
He is glad with alle glade, as gurles þat lawhen alle,   300
And sory when he seth men sory – as thow seest childerne
Lawhe þer men lawheth and loure þer oþere louren.
And when a man swereth for soth, for sooth he hit troweth;
Weneth he þat no wyhte wolde lye and swerie,
Ne þat eny gome wolde gyle oþere, ne greue,   305
For drede of god þat so goed is, and thus-gates vs techeth:
  Quodcunque vultis vt faciant vobis homines, facite eis.
Hath he no lykynge to lawhe ne to likene men to scorne.
Alle seknesses and sorwes for solaces he hit taketh,
And alle manere meschiefs as munstracie of heuene.
Of deth ne of derthe drad was he neuere,   310
Ne mysliked thogh he lore, or lened þat ilke
That neuere payed peny aȝeyn in places þer he borwede.'
  'Who fynt hym his fode?' quod y, 'or what frendes hath he,
Rentes other richesse to releue him at his nede?'
  'Of rentes ne of oþere rychesse ne reccheth he neuere.   315
A frende he hath þat fynd him þat faylede hym neuere:
Oen *Aperis-tu-manum* alle thynges hym fyndeth;
Fiat-voluntas-tua festeth hym vch a daye.
And also a can clergie, *credo-in-deum-patrem*,
And purtraye wel þe *pater-noster* and peynten hit with *auees*.   320
And oþer-while his wone is to wynde in pilgrimages
There pore men and prisones ben, and paye for here fode,

296a. *sicut* P] XUT sicut et
299. camaca U] X cannaca
310. was T] XU *om*
313. Who U] X He
314. *line supplied from* U (releue T] U rule); X *om*

296a. 'Unless you become like children (you will never enter the kingdom of heaven)'
  (Matt. 18:3).
306a. 'Whatever you wish that men should do to you, do so to them' (Matt. 7:12).
317. *Aperis-tu-manum.* See XV 264a.
318. *Fiat-voluntas-tua.* See XV 250n, 47n.
319. *credo-in-deum-patrem*: 'I believe in God the father', the opening words of the
  Apostles' Creed (see XVII 318). Charity's learning extends to the basic articles of
  the faith.
320. Charity's knowledge of the *pater-noster* and the *Ave Maria* is here momentarily
  envisaged in terms of the work of a manuscript illuminator (cf. IV 140n).
321. *pilgrimages*: 'errands of mercy'. See VII 21n, IV 122.

Clotheth hem and conforteth hem and of Crist precheth hem,
What sorwe he soffrede in ensaumple of vs alle
That pouerte and penaunce, pacientlyche ytake,   325
Worth moche meryte to þat man þat hit may soffre.
And when he hath visited thus fetered folke and oþer folke pore,
Thenne ȝerneth he into ȝouthe and ȝeepliche he secheth
Pruyde, with alle purtinaunces, and pakketh hem togyderes
And laueth hem in þe lauendrie, *laboraui-in-gemitu-meo,*   330
Bouketh hem at his breste and beteth hit ofte,
And with warm water of his yes woketh hit til he white.
    Lauabis me, et super niuem dealbabor.
And thenne syngeth he when he doth so, and som tyme wepynge: f.73[b]
    Cor contritum et humiliatum, deus, non despicies.'
'Were y with hym, by Crist,' quod y, 'y wolde neuere fro hym,
Thogh y my byliue sholde begge aboute at menne hacches.   335
Where clerkes knowe hym nat,' quod y, 'þat kepen holy churche?'
'Peres the plouhman,' quod he, 'moste parfitlyche hym knoweth.
    Et vidit deus cogitaciones eorum.
By clothyng ne by carpynge knowe shaltow hym neuere,
Ac thorw werkes thow myhte wyte wher-forth he walketh.
    Operibus credite.
He is þe murieste of mouthe at mete þer he sitteth,   340
And compenable in companye, as Crist hymsulue techeth:
    Nolite tristes fieri, sicut ypocrite.
Ych haue ysey hym mysulue somtyme in russet,
Bothe in gray and in grys and in gult harneys,

333. wepynge U] X wypynge
334. Crist U] X Criest

330. *laboraui-in-gemitu-meo*: 'I am weary with my groaning' (Ps. 6:7). With characteristically uninhibited concretion (cf. IV 140n), penitence is here imagined as the laundering of the dirty washing of sin (cf. VII 57n). The prompting comes from two of the penitential psalms (III 463n), and from the extensive development of laundry-imagery in medieval sermons (Owst, 1933, 36).
332a. 'Thou shalt wash me, and I shall be whiter than snow' (Ps. 50:9).
333a. Ps. 50:19. See XV 63.
336. *Where*: 'Whether', introducing a question, as in XV 279.
337a. 'And god saw their thoughts' (Luke 11:17, cf. also Matt. 9:4). Piers Plowman's knowledge of Charity is associated with Christ's knowledge of human hearts, as he shows it in the gospels, thus strengthening a developing association between Piers and Christ (see XX 21), which is in fact baldly stated in B XV 212: *Petrus id est christus* (see 1 Cor. 10:4).
339a. 'Believe the works' (John 10:38) – and so recognize God in man, i.e. in Christ and Piers.
341a. 'Do not look dismal, like the hypocrites' (Matt. 6:16).
342–3. i.e. among all classes.

And also gladliche he hit gaf to gomes þat hit nedede.
Edmond and Edward, ayþer were seyntes,   345
And cheef charite with hem, and chaste all here lyues.
Ich haue yseye Charite also syngen and rede,
Ryden, and rennen in raggede clothes;
Ac biddyng als a beggare byhelde y hym neuere.
Ac in riche robes rathest he walketh,   350
Ycalled and ycrimyled and his croune yshaue.
And in frere frocke he was founde ones,
Ac hit is fer and fele зer, in Franceys tyme;
In þat sekte sethe to selde hath he be founde.
Riche men a recomendeth, and of her robes taketh,   355
Of tho that lelelyche lyuen and louen and byleuon.
    Beatus est diues sine macula.
In kynges court a cometh, yf his consaile be trewe,
Ac yf coueytse be of his consaile a wol nat come þerynne.
Amonges þe comune in court a cometh bote selde,
For braulyng and bac-bitynge and berynge of fals witnesse.   360
In constorie bifore commissarie a cometh nat ful ofte,
For ouer-long is here lawe but yf þay lacche suluer.
With bisshopes a wolde be, for beggares sake,
Ac auaris oþer-whiles halt hym withoute þe gate.   f.74ᵃ
Kynges and cardynals knewen hym sum tyme,   365
Ac thorw coueytyse and his consaile ycongeyed is he ofte.
   And ho-so coueyteth to knowe him, such a kynde hym foleweth

352. frocke U] X flokke
354. þat U] X *om*
355. her U] X *om*
365. Kynges U] X kyngels
367. him¹ U] X *om*

344. *also*: 'as, equally'.
345. St Edmund, king of East Anglia (martyred 870), and St Edward the Confessor (d. 1066) – examples to show that Charity can rule kings.
347. *syngen and rede*, i.e. act as a priest.
348. *in raggede clothes*. A perhaps significant echo of XI 196.
350–51. These lines refer most obviously to monks (as well as other higher ecclesiastics, possibly, though see 363 below) and are a reminder of L's respect for the non-mendicant regular clergy (see V 152n).
353. *in Franceys tyme*: in the time of St Francis of Assisi, founder of the Franciscan order of friars.
355. *of here robes taketh*: 'receives gifts of clothes from them'.
356a. 'Blessed is the rich man without blemish' (Ecclus. 31:8).
359. *þe comune in court*, i.e. the common court, the court of the *communitas* of free men (e.g. the County Court), as opposed to the king's court (357, above; cf. II 22, III 472). For the sg. form of *comune*, see Donaldson, 1949, 105.

As y tolde þe with tonge, a litel tyme ypassed;
For noþer he ne beggeth ne biddeth, ne borweth to ȝelde.
He halt hit for a vyce and a foule shame   370
To begge or to borwe, but of god one.
     Panem nostrum cotidianum, etc.

371a. '(Give us this day) our daily bread' (Matt. 6:11).

Passus XVII

Liberum Arbitrium on Charity and the Church

Passus vii de dowel et explicit
'There is no such,' y sayde, 'þat som tyme ne borweth
Or beggeth and biddeth, be he ryche or pore,
And ȝut oþer-while wroeth withouten eny synne.'
    'Ho is wroeth and wolde be awreke, holy writ preueth,' quod he,
'A passeth cheef charite, yf holy churche be trewe.   5
    Caritas omnia suffert.
Holy writ witnesseth þer were suche eremytes,
Solitarie by hemsulue in here selles lyuede
Withoute borwynge or beggynge bote of god one,
Excepte þat Egide a hynde oþer-while
To his selle selde cam and soffred be mylked.   10
Elles foules fedde hem in frythes þer they wonede,
Bothe Antony and Arseny and oþer fol monye.
Paul *primus heremita* hadde yparrokede hymsulue

5a. *suffert* U] X soffert

1. C begins here a new passus where B XV continues. The reshaping of B XIII–XV as C XV–XVIII is partly mechanical, in so far as it is determined by the shifting of B XIII–XIV material relating to Haukyn to C VI–VII (see XV 194n) and by the inordinate length of B XV. But the detail of reshaping, here as at XVI 1 (see also XVI 157, and cf. XIII 1), suggests a desire to emphasize significant stages in the argument (especially with striking opening lines: see Donaldson, 1949, 35–6) rather than the introduction of new 'characters'. Here the dreamer's question prompts a full and comprehensive discussion by Free Will of the relation of Charity and Holy Church. See XVI 284n.
5a. 'Love bears all things' (1 Cor. 13:7, cf. XVI 289a, 294a).
6. *suche eremytes.* The examples that follow are drawn from familiar sources in legendaries such as the *Legenda Aurea*, which in turn derive from the *Vitae Patrum* (*PL* 73–4), a collection of lives of the Desert Fathers, from the lives of whose followers, partly coenobitic, developed the institution of Benedictine monachism in the 6th c.
9. *Egide.* Ægidius is the Latin form of Giles. The story of St Giles the hermit is told in *Legenda Aurea* CXXX.
12. *Antony and Arseny.* St Anthony was one of the first and most famous of the Desert Fathers of Egypt (d. 356). St Arsenius (d. 449) was one of the many who followed him into the Egyptian desert. Their stories are in *Legenda Aurea* XXI, CLXXVIII.
13. *Paul* of Thebes (not the Paul of the NT epistles) is here called the first hermit (as in *Legenda Aurea* XV), i.e. the first of the Desert Fathers (d. 342).

That no man myhte se hym for moes and for leues;
Foules hym fedde, yf frere Austynes be trewe, 15
For he ordeyned þat ordre or elles þey gabben.
Paul aftur his prechyng paniars he made
And wan with his handes al þat hym nedede.
Peter fischede for his fode and his fere Androwe;
Som they sode and som they solde and so they lyuede bothe. 20
Marie Maudeleyne by mores lyuede and dewes;
Loue and lele byleue held lyf and soule togyderes.
Marie Egipciaca eet in thritty wynter
Bote thre litle loues and loue was here soule.
   Y can nat rykene hem riȝt now ne reherse here names 25
That lyueden thus for oure lordes loue monye longe ȝeres
Withoute borwynge or beggynge, or þe boek lyeth, f.74^b
And woneden in wildernesses amonges wilde bestes.
Ac durste no beste byte hem by day ne by nyhte
Bote myldelyche when þey metten maden lowe chere 30
And faire byfore tho men faunede with þe tayles.
Ac bestes brouhte hem no mete bute onliche þe foules
In tokenynge þat trewe man alle tymes sholde

---

21. mores lyuede and dewes XU] T meris mylk lyuede and ewis
30. chere U] X there

15. *Austynes*, adj. with pl. ending (see Prol. 132n, and cf. X 9). The phrase *frere Austynes* can be thought of as a composite plural. The Austin friars, one of the lesser orders of friars (Prol. 56n), claimed to be the earliest foundation, tracing their origin beyond Augustine, from whom they took their name and rule, to the first hermit (they also called themselves the 'hermit-friars'). L's comment on this claim, which is in C only, reflects his growing awareness of the debate which it aroused. See the essays by R. Arbesmann in *Traditio* 1 (1943), 341–53 and by G. Sanderlin in *Speculum* 18 (1943), 358–62.
17. *Paul*. The reference is clearly to Paul of Tarsus (*aftur his prechyng*, e.g. 1 Cor. 4:12, 1 Thess. 4:11, 2 Thess. 3:8), though Paul was by trade a tent-maker (Acts 18:3). The baskets seem to have been transferred from Paul the hermit (see Jerome's *Vita Pauli*, in *PL* 23:28), perhaps under the influence of a famous episode in the early life of Saul/Paul (Acts 9:25). See a note by S. B. Hemingway in *MLN* 32 (1917), 57–8; cf. also *CT* VI. 445.
19. See Matt. 4:18.
21. According to medieval tradition (e.g. *Legenda Aurea*, XCVI, 413) Mary Magdalene spent a period in solitary exile in the wilderness as a penance for her early sinful life (see VII 138, also XI 264, XII 134). L's reference here supports the interpretation of the famous 13th c. song 'Maiden in the moor lay' as a Magdalene poem: see J. Harris in *JMRS* 1 (1971), 59–87.
23. St Mary of Egypt (5th c.) also did penance in the desert for her early sinful life. For the story, and the *tres panes*, see *Legenda Aurea*, LVI, where her name appears as *Maria Ægyptiaca*.

Fynde honest men and holy men and oþer rihtfole peple.
For wolde neuere faythfull god þat freres and monkes   35
Toke lyflode of luyther wynnynges in all here lyf-tyme.
   As wittnesseth holy writ what Tobie saide to his wyf,
When he was blynde, he herde a lambe blete:
"Wyf! be ywar!" quod he, "what haue we herynne?
Lord leue," quod þat lede, "no stole thynge be herynne!"   40
     Videte ne furtum sit. Et alibi: Melius est mori quam
        male viuere.
This is no more to mene bote men of holy churche
Sholde reseue riht nauht but þat riht wolde
And refuse reuerences and raueners offrynges.
Thenne wolde lordes and ladyes be loth for to agulte
And to take of here tenauntes more then treuthe wolde,   45
And marchauntz merciable wolde be and men of lawe bothe,
Wolde religious refuse rauenours almesses.
And thenne grace sholde growe ȝut and grene-leued wexe
And charite þat chield is now sholde chaufen of hymsulue
And conforte alle cristene, wolde holy churche amende.   50
   Iob þe parfite patriarke this prouerbe wroet and tauhte
To make men louye mesure þat monkes ben and freres:
     "*Nunquam,*" *dicit Iob,* "*rugiet onager cum habuerit herbam,*
     aut mugiet bos cum ante plenum presepe steterit?"
     Brutorum animalium natura te condempnat, quia cum
     pabulum comune sufficiat, ex adipe prodiit iniquitas tua.
Yf lewede men knewe this Latyn, a litel they wolden auysen hem
Ar they amorteysed eny more for monkes or for chanons.
Allas! lordes and ladyes, lewede consayle haue ȝe   55

---

38. blynde XU] T blynd as a betil. lambe U] X lannbe
48. leued P] XUT loue
51, 52a. Iob U] X Iop
54. chanons U] X chanoun

35–6. A frequent theme: see VI 287.
40a. 'Look that there be no theft' (Tob. 2:13). And elsewhere: 'It is better to die than to live in sin' (cf. Tob. 3:6). Tobit's wife, Anna, had received a kid as a gift from her employees. Tobit was suspicious. His response to his wife's reproaches was: 'It is better for me to die than to live, since I have heard false reproaches'. This is the third time that L has produced this version of the text (cf. I 143a, VI 290a).
45. Cf. VIII 36.
46. Cf. IX 27–54.
48. For the emendation here, see XVI 249.
52a. 'Does the wild ass ever bray', says Job, 'when he has grass, or the ox low when he stands before a full manger?' (Job 6:5). 'The nature of irrational beasts condemns you, in that your wickedness grows fat on greed, even though the food you have in common is sufficient'. From a commentary on the above, perhaps.
55–7. Cf. V 163.

To feffe suche and fede þat founded ben to þe fulle
With þat ȝoure bernes and ȝoure bloed by goed lawe may clayme!   f.75ᵃ
For god bad his blessed, as þe boek techeth –
> *Honora patrem et matrem* –
To helpe thy fader formost byfore freres or monkes
Or ar prestes or pardoners or eny peple elles.   60
Helpe thy kyn, Crist bid, for þer bigynneth charite,
And afturward awayte ho hath moest nede
And þer help yf thow haste, and þat halde y charite.
    Lo! Laurence for his largenesse, as holy lore telleth
That his mede and his manhede for eueremore shal laste: 65
> *Iusticia eius manet in eternum.*
He gaf goddes men goddes goodes and nat grete lordes
And fedde þat afyngred were and in defaute lyuede.
Y dar nat carpe of clerkes now þat Cristes tresor kepe
That pore peple by puyre riht here part myhte aske.
Of þat þat holy churche of þe olde lawe claymeth   70
Prestes on aparayl and on Purnele now spene.
    Me may now likene lettred men to a Loscheborw oþer worse
And to a badde peny with a gode printe:
Of moche mone þat is mad þe metal is nauhte
And ȝut is þe printe puyr trewe and parfitliche ygraue.   75
And so hit fareth by false cristene: here follynge is trewe,
Cristendoem of holy kyrke, the kynges marke of heuene,

67. afyngred U] X afynred
74. mone U] X noone.   þat is mad T] XUIP *om with subsequent mislineation*

58a. See VII 216a. The commandment, of course, is exactly the opposite of what the context requires, though the matter is smoothed over in line 61: a characteristic example of 'the carefree manner in which the poet's logic goes the wrong direction up a one-way street, emerging triumphantly though scarcely legitimately at its destination' (Donaldson, 1949, 83). C's revisions here are perhaps motivated by a particularly gross misreading in the reviser's copy of the B-text (viz. B XV 307 in Skeat, cf. XV 313 in Kane-Donaldson, and p. 202), which in its turn produced a notably ingenious piece of exegesis in Robertson-Huppé, 1951, 185–6.
65a. 'His righteousness endures for ever' (Ps. 110:3, echoed in the daily grace: see III 339a and note).
66–7. The story was that St Lawrence was martyred (see II 130) for his liberality to the poor (*goddes men*) with the treasure of the church claimed by the emperor (*Legenda Aurea*, CXVII, 489–92).
69. *That*: 'of which'.
71. *Purnele*. See IV 111n.
72. A *Loscheborw* is a spurious coin, imported from Luxembourg, whence the name. The metaphor of the coin is traditional (Raw, 1969, 156–7), and a powerful reminder of the image of God in man, the restoration of which is one of the important themes of the poem (see I 86n).

Ac þe metal, þat is mannes soule, of many of this techares
Is alayed with leccherye and oþer lustes of synne,
That god coueyteth nat þe coyne þat Crist hymsulue printede   80
And for þe synne of þe soule forsaketh his oune coyne.
Thus ar ȝe luyþer ylikned to Lossheborwes sterlynges
That fayre byfore folk prechen and techen
And worcheth nat as ȝe fyndeth ywryte and wisseth þe peple.
    For what thorw werre and wrake and wikkede hefdes,   85
May no preyere pees make in no place, hit semeth.
Lewed men han no byleue and lettred men erren;
Noþer see ne sond ne þe seed ȝeldeth
As they ywoned were – in wham is defaute?
Nat in god, þat he ne is goed, and þe grounde bothe;   90
And þe se and the seed, þe sonne and þe mone   f.75ᵇ
Doen her deuer day and nyhte – dede we so also
Ther sholde be plente and pees perpetuel euere.
Weder-wyse shipmen now and oþer witty peple
Haen no byleue to þe lyft ne to þe lode-sterres.   95
Astronomiens alday in here arte faylen
That whilum warnede men byfore what sholde byfalle aftur.
Shipmen and sheepherdes by þe seuene sterres
Wisten wel and tolde when hit sholde ryne.
Tilyares þat tilede þe erthe tolden here maystres   100
By the seed þat they sewe what þey sulle myhte
And what lyue by and lene, the londe was so trewe.
    Now failleth this folk, bothe follwares and shipmen,
Noþer they ne knoweth ne conneth a cours by anoþer.
Astronamyens also aren at here wittes ende;   105
Of þat was kalculed of þe clymat þe contrarie þey fynde.
Gramer, þe grounde of al, bigileth nouthe childrene,
For is noon of þise newe clerkes, ho-so nymeth hede,
Þat can versifye fayre or formallych endite
Ne construe kyndelyche þat poetes made.   110
    Go we now to eny degre and bote Gyle be holde a maister
And Flaterere for his vscher, ferly me thynketh.

---

    78. of many T] XUI *om*
    88. sond U] X send
    92. also U] X alse
    108. of þis newe clerkes B] XUIT *om with mislineation*; P *substitutes padding*
    109 fayre U] X vayre
    112. ferly U] X and ferly

  78. *of many*: 'by many'.
  85. In the following passage there is allusion to a familiar motif of medieval complaint-poetry, the 'world upside down' topos, as in *Prick of Conscience* 1592–1604.
  98. *þe seuene sterres*, i.e. the planets.

Doctours of decre and of diuinite maistres,
That sholde þe seuene ars conne and assoile a *quodlibet*,
Bote they fayle in philosophie – and philosoferes lyuede   115
And wolde wel examene hem – wonder me thynketh!
Lord lete þat this prestes lelly seien here masse
That they ouerhippe nat for hastite, as y hope they do nat –
Thogh hit suffice for oure sauacioun soethfaste byleue,
As clerkes in Corpus Cristi feste syngen and reden   120
That *sola fides sufficit* to saue with lewede peple.
  Ac ʒif prestes doen here deuer wel we shal do þe bettre,
For Sarrasynes may be saued so yf they so byleued
In þe letynge of here lyf to leue on holy churche.'
  'What is holy churche, chere frende?' quod y.
                          'Charite,' he saide;   125

---

115. Bote] X Bothe; U But
116. *line supplied from* P; XUIT *om*
124. letynge U] X lettynge

114. *þe seuene ars.* See XI 98. *a quodlibet*: a question in theology proposed as an exercise in university disputation. See XIV 192n.
117. Rechelesnesse touched on this point at the end of his discourse (XIII 123). Free Will, however, adds that the people's hope of salvation is dependent only on faith (121) and not on the priest's competence. This is an important rider, since it refutes by implication the Wycliffite position (see also XIII 79n, XIV 65n) that the priestly office is invalid if administered by a sinful priest. He then in turn qualifies this rider in line 122 in order to reaffirm the efficacy of a sound priesthood.
120. *Corpus Christi.* The feast of Corpus Christi, confirmed in 1311, celebrated the gift of Christ's body in the eucharist. It was the day on which the cycles of mystery plays were performed.
121. *Sola fides sufficit*: 'faith alone is sufficient', from the hymn *Pange lingua gloriosi/Corporis mysterium*, sung on Corpus Christi day (Breviary, I. mlxiv). The point of the hymn, again relevant to the refutation of an important Wycliffite doctrine (see Leff, 1967, 549–57, and 117n above), is to affirm the transubstantiation of the communion wafer and wine into Christ's flesh and blood in the sacrament of the eucharist: faith alone can grasp the mystery of transubstantiation, where sense fails (*Praestet fides supplementum/Sensuum defectui*).
124. *letyng*: 'losing', i.e. in the moment of death: an extreme example of *fides sufficit*. It has been argued that L alludes here to the heretical doctrine of Uthred of Boldon, a contemporary theologian, concerning the *clara visio* which was granted at the moment of death to all souls, Christian and heathen alike, and which determined whether they were saved; and furthermore that other changes in C (see XI 196n, XII 74n) have been preparing for this by eliminating references to the absolute necessity of baptism. See Russell, 1966; but cf. XIV 208. It does not seem that L had worked out fully his ideas on the subject.

Lief and loue and leutee in o byleue and lawe,
A loue-knotte of leutee and of lele byleue,
Alle kyne cristene cleuynge on o will,
Withoute gyle and gabbyng gyue and sulle and lene.   f.76ᵃ
Loue lawe withoute leutee allouable was hit neuere;   130
God lereth no lyf to louye withouten lele cause.
   Iewes and gentel Sarresines iugen hemsulue
That lelyche they byleue, and ȝut here lawe diuerseth,
And o god þat al bygan with gode herte they honoureth
And ayther loueth and byleueth in o god almyhty.   135
Ac oure lord aloueth no loue but lawe be þe cause:
For lechours louyen aȝen þe lawe and at þe laste ben dampned,
And theues louyen and leute haten and at þe laste ben hanged,
And lele men lyue as lawe techeth and loue þerof aryseth,
The whiche is þe heued of charite and hele of mannes soule.   140

    Dilige deum propter deum, id est propter veritatem; Et
      inimicum tuum propter mandatum, id est propter legem;
      Et amicum propter amorem, id est propter caritatem.

Loue god for he is goed and grounde of alle treuthe;
Loue thyn enemye entierely, goddes heste to fulfille;
Loue thy frende þat followeth thy wille, that is thy fayre soule.
For when alle frendes faylen and fleen away in deynge
Thenne seweth the soule to sorwe or to ioye   145
And ay hopeth eft to be with here body at þe laste
In murthe or in mournynge and neuere eft to departe.

---

126. and³ P] XUI a; T of
129–30. and lene/Loue lawe XUIP] T lene and loue/Lawe
138. haten U] X hatten

125. Free Will, in a passage new in C (125–49), returns to an argument first broached by Rechelesnesse (XII 78–97). His purpose is to stress the inseparableness of love (of God) and obedience to his law (see Prol. 149n, III 378n), as they are embodied in the life of Holy Church. R tended to interpret the story of Trajan as evidence that love transcended the law. Free Will must make clear the dangers of such a view before passing on to the question of the righteous heathen (briefly anticipated in 132–5).

130. *Loue lawe* is difficult. Skeat suggests 'love's law'; another possibility is 'love-law'. Possibly *loue* should be emended to *lo*. Note the reading of MS T.

140a. 'Love god for the sake of god, that is, for the sake of truth; (love) your enemy for the sake of the commandment, that is, for the sake of law; (love) your friend for the sake of love, that is, for the sake of charity'. The Latin (source not identified) is paraphrased in the next three lines.

142. *Loue thyn enemye.* See XV 141n.

143. *frende* is glossed as *soule*, the agent of free will (cf. XVI 157n). The love of the body for the soul, and its care for their salvation and joint resurrection, is the truest love of a friend, and the truest form of charity.

And þat is charite, leue chield, to be cher ouer thy soule;
Contrarie her nat, as in consience, yf thow wold come to heuene.'
　'Where Sarresynes,' y saide, 'yse nat what is charite?'　　　　150
　'Hit may be so þat Sarresynes haen such a manere charite,
Louen as by lawe of kynde oure lord god almyhty.
Hit is kyndly thyng creature his creatour to honoure,
For þer is no man þat mynde hath þat ne meketh him and bysecheth
To þat lord þat hym lyf lente, lyflode hym sende.　　　　155
Ac many manere men þer ben, as Sarresynes and Iewes,
Louyeth nat þat lord aryht as by þe Legende *Sanctorum*
And lyuen oute of lele byleue for they leue on a mene.
A man þat hihte Makameth for Messie they hym holdeth
And aftur his leryng they lyue and by lawe of kynde,　　　　160
And when kynde hath his cours and no contrarie fyndeth
Thenne is lawe ylefte and leute vnknowe.
Beaute sanz bounte blessed was hit neuere　　　　f.76ᵇ
Ne kynde *sanz cortesie* in no contreye is preysed.
　Me fynde wel þat Macometh was a man ycristened　　　　165
And a cardinal of court, a gret clerk withalle,
And pursuede to haue be pope, prince of holy chirche.
Ac for he was lyk a Lossheborw y leue oure lord hym lette.
Forthy souhte he into Surie and sotiled how he myhte
Be maister ouer alle tho men and on this manere a wrouhte.　　　　170
He endaunted a douue and day and nyhte here fedde;
In ayþer of his eres priueliche he hadde
Corn þat þe coluere eet when he come in places.
And in what place he prechede and the peple tauhte
Thenne sholde þe coluere come to þe clerkes ere,　　　　175

---

154. him U] X *om*
158. leue I] XU loue
163. hit U] X *om*
169. he¹ U] X *om*
173. þat þe U] X *om*

---

150. *Where*: 'Whether', introducing a question (as in XVI 336). C here returns to the matter of B, and the question of the salvation of the righteous heathen (see XI 163, 221, XIV 206n).
157. *as by*: 'according to'. *Legende Sanctorum*. The most widely known saints' legendary was the *Legenda Aurea*, which L uses extensively (e.g. 6, 9, 12, etc., above).
158. *on a mene*: 'in a (false) mediator', i.e. as distinct from Christ (XIV 208n).
163. Proverbial (Whiting B 152).
165. The tradition that Mahomet was a lapsed Christian, who had hoped to be pope, and who afterwards trained a dove to do the office of the Holy Spirit in order to gain authority for himself as a prophet, was widely current. L could have got all he needed from a popular handbook of exemplary stories like the *Alphabetum Narrationum* (15th c. English translation, ed. EETS 126–7, 165).

Menyng as aftur mete, thus Macumeth here enchauntede.
And when þe coluer cam thus then knelede þe peple,
For Macometh to men swaer hit was a messager of heuene
And sothliche þat god sulue in suche a coluere lyknesse
Tolde hym and tauhte him how to teche þe peple.   180
Thus Macumeth in misbileue man and woman brouhte
And on his lore thei lyuen ȝut, as wel lered as lewed.
And seth oure saueour soffrede such a fals cristene
Disceue so the Sarrasyns, sothlyche me thynketh
Holy men, as y hope, thorw helpe of the holy goste   185
Sholden conuerte hem to Crist and cristendoem to take.
   Allas! þat men so longe on Macometh bileueth,
So manye prelates to preche as þe pope maketh,
Of Nasareth, of Nyneue, of Neptalym, of Damaske,
That they ne wente in world as holy writ byd: 190
Ite in vniversum mundum, sethe ȝe wilne þe name
To be prelates, and preche the passioun of Iesus,
And as hymsulue saide so to lyue and deye.
   Bonus pastor animam suam ponit pro ouibus suis.
   Hit is reuthe to rede how riht holy men lyuede,
How they deffouled here flesche, forsoke here owne wille,   195
Fer fro couthe and fro kyn euele yclothed ȝeden,
Baddeliche ybedded, no boek but here consience
Ne no rychesse but þe rode to reioysen hem ynne.
   Absit nobis gloriari nisi in cruce domini nostri.   f.77ᵛ

---

177. cam U] X can
180. him U] X *om*
189. Nyneue] X Vyneue; U Nynyue
190. in world T] XUI *om with subsequent mislineation*
195. deffouled U] X deffoulen

---

187. C omits here a long passage in B (XV 417–91), with much homely imagery, on the proselytizing function of the church.

189. These are towns under Arab rule in the biblical lands, and the seats of imaginary dioceses to which the pope regularly appointed bishops. These bishops *in partibus infidelium* did not of course reside in their diocese; the office was a literal sinecure. For examples of some appointees in the 1360s and 1370s, see Gwynn, 1943, 5–11.

191. 'Go out into all the world (and preach the gospel to the whole creation)' (Mk. 16:15, Christ's injunction to the disciples on his appearance to them after his resurrection). The syntax of the inserted Latin text influences the change of person from *they* to *ȝe*. The MSS mislineate 190–93.

193a. 'The good shepherd lays down his life for his sheep' (John 10:11, with *ponit* for Vg. *dat* on the basis of the first lesson at matins on the second Sunday after Easter: see Adams, 1976, 278).

198a. 'Far be it from us to glory except in the cross of our lord' (Gal. 6:14).

And tho was pees and plente amonges pore and ryche;
And now is reuthe to rede how þe rede noble   200
Is reuerenced byfore the rode and resceyued for the worthiore
To amende and to make, as with men of holy churche,
Thenne Cristes cros þat ouercome deth and dedly synne.
    And now is werre and wo, and who-so why asketh –
For couetyse aftur a cros; the corone stand in golde.   205
Bothe riche and religioues þat rode they honouren
That in grotes is graue and in golde nobles.
For couetyse of that croes clerkes of holi churche
Sholle ouerturne as þe Templers dede, þe tyme approcheth faste.
Minne ȝe not, lettred men, how tho men honourede   210
More tresor then treuthe? y dar nat telle þe sothe
How tho corsede cristene catel and richesse worschipede;
Resoun and rihtfol doem tho religious dampnede.
Riht so, ȝe clerkes, ȝoure coueytise, ar come auht longe,
Shal dampne *dos ecclesie* and depose ȝow for ȝoure pruyde.   215
    Deposuit potentes de sede.
Ȝif knyhthoed and kynde wit and þe comune and consience
Togederes louyen lelelyche, leueth hit, bisshopes,
The lordschipe of londes lese ȝe shal for euer
And lyuen as *Leuitici* dede and as oure lord ȝow techeth:
    Per primicias et decimas.

208. that U] X the
210. not U] X *om*
217. leueth U] X loueth

200. *rede noble*: a gold coin, worth half a mark (6s. 8d.). For the epithet *rede*, not merely conventional, see a note in *Early ME Texts*, ed. B. Dickins and R. M. Wilson (1951), 176. Like other coins, the noble was marked on the obverse with a cross, which is the source of the punning that follows.

205. *For*: '(The answer is) because of'. *aftur a cros*, i.e. the cross stamped on the back of coins, as contrasted with Christ's cross: the play on words is common (see Yunck, 1963, 177–8). *the corone stand in golde*: the crown is stamped in gold coins, with the punning implication that king and state (one sense of *corone*) or clergy (i.e. those who bear the tonsure or *corone*) rely upon and put their faith in (*stand in*) gold.

209. *þe Templers*. The order of Knights Templars, originally founded *c.* 1118 to defend the Christian shrines in the Holy Land, grew corrupt on its wealth and was suppressed by papal decree in 1312. Their fate is prophesied for the friars in the *Song against the Friars* (in Wright, *Pol. Poems*, i.267).

215. *dos ecclesie*: 'the endowment of the Church', as explained in 220, below.

215a. 'He has put down the mighty from their thrones' (Luke 1:52, the Magnificat).

219. *Leuitici*: the priesthood of early Israel, whose duties are prescribed in the book of Leviticus (see also XIV 58n).

219a. 'Upon offerings of first-fruits and tenths [tithes]' (Deut. 12:6).

Whan Constantyn of his cortesye holy kirke dowede   220
With londes and ledes, lordschipes and rentes,
An angel men herde an hye at Rome crye:
"*Dos ecclesie* this day hath ydronke venym
And þat haen Petres power aren apoisened alle."
A medecyne moste þerto þat myhte amende þo prelates   225
That sholde preye for þe pees and possession hem letteth.
Taketh here londe, ȝe lordes, and lat hem lyue by dymes
Yf the kynges coueyte in Cristes pees to lyuene.
For if possession be poysen and inparfit hem make,
The heuedes of holy churche and tho that ben vnder hem,   230
Hit were charite to deschargen hem for holy churche sake
And purge hem of þe olde poysen ar more perel falle.   f.77ᵇ
For were presthode more parfyte, that is, þe pope formost
That with moneye maynteyneth men to werre vppon cristene ·
Aȝen þe lore of oure lord as seynt Luk witnesseth,   235
    Michi vindictam,
His preyeres with his pacience to pees sholde brynge
Alle londes into loue and þat in lytel tyme;
The pope with alle prestes *pax vobis* sholde make.

224. apoisened U] X apousened
234. to U] X do

220. The medieval tradition was that Constantine, in gratitude to Pope Sylvester for
curing him of a fatal illness, gave the Lateran in Rome to the Papacy, thus
securing to the Church its first secular endowment. The story of the angel who
prophesied ruin from the 'donation of Constantine' (cf. III 163) was a favourite
with Lollards (e.g. Wyclif, ed. Arnold, iii.341, 477; ed. Matthew, 122–3, 379–81,
474–5), for whom the disendowment of the Church was an essential requisite of
reform. L shows in this passage how close he is in spirit to many of Wyclif's ideas
and to Lollardy.

224. *þat*: 'those that'.

227. *by dymes*: 'by tithes', i.e. like the early priesthood of Israel. This line embodies a
central tenet of Wycliffite doctrine: see Wyclif, ed. Arnold, i.147, 199, 282,
iii.478–9, 513; ed. Matthew, 364–96, 410, 432–3.

234. The most recent example of this would be the 'crusade' launched by Urban VI in
1379, with mercenary soldiers, against the antipope, Clement VII, after the Papal
Schism of 1378 (see also XV 171n). But already in 1376 there had been a
Commons petition concerning the Pope's maintaining of war in Lombardy (*Rot.
Parl.* ii.339). The allusion begins a passage new in C (233–54), with further
allusion to the story of Mahomet and the dove.

235a. 'Vengeance is mine (I will repay, saith the Lord), (Rom. 12:19 or Heb. 10:30,
not Luke [see XXI 446], but with the wording from the gospel for the third
Sunday after Epiphany: Missale 99).

238. *pax vobis*: 'peace be with you', thrice repeated by Christ on his appearance to the
disciples after the Resurrection (John 20:19, 21, 26), and said, in the sg., with the
kiss of peace in the mass (Missale 624).

And take hede how Macometh thorw a mylde dowue

Hadde al Surie as hymsulue wolde and Sarrasines in equitee. 240

Naught thorw manslaght and mannes strenghe Macometh hadde þe
    maistrie

Bote thorw pacience and priue gyle he was prince ouer hem all.

In such manere me thynketh moste þe pope,

Prelates and prestis preye and biseche

Deuouteliche day and nyhte and withdrawe hem fro synne 245

And crie to Crist a wolde his coluer sende,

The whiche is þe hy holy gost þat out of heuene descendet

To make a perpetuel pees bitwene þe prince of heuene

And alle maner men þat on this molde libbeth.

Yf prestehode were parfyt and preyede thus, the peple sholde
    amende 250

That contraryen now Cristes lawes and cristendoem dispisen.

  For sethe þat this Sarrasines, scribz and this Iewes

Haen a lyppe of oure bileue, the lihtlokour me thynketh

They sholde turne, ho-so trauayle wolde and of þe trinite teche
    hem.

For alle paynyme preyeth and parfitliche bileueth 255

In þe grete god of heuene and his grace asken

And maken here mone to Macometh here message to shewe.

Thus in a fayth lyueth þat folk and in a fals mene,

And þat is reuthe for tho rihtfole men þat in þat reume wonyeth

And a perel for prelates þat þe pope maketh 260

That bereth name of Neptalym, of Niniue, of Damaske.

  For when þe hye kyng of heuene sente his sone til erthe

Mony myracles a wrouhte, men for to torne,

In ensaumple þat men sholde se by sad resoen

That men myhte nat be saued but thorw mercy and grace 265

And thorw penaunce and passioun and parfyt bileue;

And bicam man of a mayde and *metropolitanus* f.78ᵃ

And baptisede and bissheinede with þe bloed of his herte

---

239. how U] X on

254. turne P] XUI *om*

256. grete U] X grethe (the *over erasure*) of. of heuene T] XUIP *om*

262. sone T] XUI soule

267. *metropolitanus* P] XUIT metropolanus

268. bissheinede XUI] TP bisshopid

253. *a lyppe of oure bileue*, i.e. monotheism (see 134–5, 152, above). L's interest in the conversion of the Jews and infidels is orthodox: like bishop Brinton (e.g. Sermons, no. 84, ii.383–4), he offers it as a challenge to a decayed priesthood.

258. *a fals mene*. See 158, above.

261. See 189, above.

267. *metropolitanus* (see XVI 203) is here used of Christ as the head of all bishops.

Alle þat wilnede and wolde with inwit bileue hit.
Mony seynte sethe soffrede deth also,   270
For to enferme þe fayth ful wyde-whare deyede,
In Ynde, in Alisandre, in Armonye, in Spayne,
And fro mysbileue mony men turnede.
In sauacioun of mannes soule seynte Thomas of Canterbury
Amonges vnkynde cristene in holy churche was slawe,   275
And alle holy kirke honoured thorw that deyng.
He is a forbisene to alle bisshopis and a briht myrrour
And souereynliche to suche þat of Surie bereth þe name,
And nat in Ingelond to huppe aboute and halewe men auters
And crepe in amonges curatours and confessen aȝeyn þe lawe,   280
   Nolite mittere falcem in messem alienam.
Many man for Cristes loue was martired amonges Romaynes
Or cristendoem were knowe þere or eny croos honoured.
   Euery bisshope bi þe lawe sholde buxumliche walke
And pacientliche thorw his prouynce and to his peple hym shewe,
Feden hem and follen hem and fere hem fro synne –   285
   baculi forma sit, presul, hec tibi norma:
Fer, trahe, punge gregem, seruando per omnia legem –
And enchaunten hem to charite on holy churche to bileue.
For as þe kynde is of a knyhte or for a kynge to be take
And amonges here enemyes in mortel batayles   290
To be culd and ouercome the comune to defende,
So is þe kynde of a curatour for Criste loue to preche
And deye for his dere childrene to destruye dedly synne,
   Bonus pastor,
And nameliche þer þat lewede lyuen and no lawe ne knoweth.

275. vnkynde U] X vkynde
278. to P] XUIT of
293. destruye U] X defende

278–80. An allusion to the lucrative activities, such as consecration, ordination and
   confession, undertaken by the titular bishops *in partibus infidelium* (see 189, above,
   and Wyclif, ed. Arnold, i.282, iii.300; ed. Matthew, 225).
280a. 'You shall not put a sickle to your neighbour's standing corn' (Deut. 23:25),
   interpreted allegorically here to refer to the 'poaching' of the office of confession
   from the priest who held the cure of souls (cf. VI 119n).
285. *Feden hem.* This has a literal as well as a spiritual sense, since bishops were directly
   responsible for providing the necessities of life for the poor of their diocese
   (Tierney, 1959, 68). Cf. IV 120.
286–7. 'Bishop, let this be your rule (expressed symbolically) in the form of the crosier:
   drive, lead, goad on the flock, keeping the law in all things'. Leonine verses,
   closely resembling three lines copied in B.L. MS Lansdowne 397, f.9ᵛ (Walther,
   Initia, 8828). Cf. X 93–4.
293a. See 193a, above.

Ac we cristene conneth þe lawe and haen of oure tonge 295
Bischopes and bokes the bileue to teche.

    Iewes lyuen in þe lawe þat oure lord tauhte
Moises to be maister þerof til Messie come,
And on þat lawe they leue and leten hit for þe beste.
And ȝut knewe they Crist þat cristendoem tauhte 300
And for a parfit profete that moche peple sauede
And of selcouthe sores saued men fol ofte. f.78ᵇ
By þe myracles þat he made Messie he semede
Tho he luft vp Lasar þat layde was in graue
Quadriduanus coeld, quyk dede hym walke. 305
Iewes sayde þat hit seye with soercerye he wrouhte
And studeden how to struye hym and struyden hemsulue
And her power thorw his pacience to puyr nauht brouhte.

    And ȝut they seyen sothly and so doen þe Sarrasynes
That Iesus was bote a iogelour, a iapare amonges þe comune, 310
And a sofistre of soercerie and a *pseudo-propheta*,
And that his lore was lesynges and lakken hit alle
And hopen þat he be to come þat shal hem releue;
Moises oþer Macometh here maystres deuyneth,
And haen a suspectioun to be saef, bothe Sarresynes and Iewes, 315
Thorw Moises and Macometh and myhte of god þat made al.

    And sethe þat this Sarresynes and also þe Iewes
Conne þe furste clause of oure bileue, *Credo in deum patrem*,
Prelates and prestes sholde preue yf they myhte

---

296. Bischopes U] X Bischope
311. *pseudo* P] XUI seudo

297-8. *þat . . . þerof:* 'of which'. The Jews were reviled by the medieval church because
they rejected Christ (e.g. XVIII 150, XX 109), but respected as those who first
received and obeyed the Law. The conversion of the Jews (see III 479, and 317
below) was a burning issue, even in England (Ames, 1970, 34–6), where the last
Jews had been expelled in 1290.
301. *And for:* 'And (knew him) for'.
305. *Quadriduanus:* 'four days dead' (John 11:39).
311. *pseudo-propheta.* Matt. 24:11.
318. 'I believe in God the father', the first words of the Apostles' Creed (Breviary,
II.2). See 134, 152, 253, above, and III 479–80.

Lere hem littelum and littelum *et in Iesum Christum filium,*
Til they couthe speke and spele *et in Spiritum sanctum,*
Recorden hit and rendren hit with *remissionem peccatorum,*
    Carnis resurrectionem et vitam eternam. Amen.'

320. *et* P] XI and; UT &
322. rendren T] XUI reden
322a. *resurrectionem* U] X resurectoem

320. *littelum and littelum:* 'little by little', lit. 'by littles and littles', where the fossilized
phrase preserves the old dat. pl. in -*um. et in Jesum Christum filium:* 'and in Jesus
Christ his son', a later phrase from the Apostles' Creed. So too with 'and in the
Holy Spirit' in the next line.
322. 'The forgiveness of sins, the resurrection of the body and the life everlasting'. The
last phrases of the Creed.

Passus XVIII

The Tree of Charity and the Meeting with Faith

Passus primus de Dobet
'Leue *Liberum Arbitrium*,' quod y, 'y leue, as y hope,
Thow couthest telle me and teche me to Charite, as y leue?'
  Thenne louh *Liberum Arbitrium* and ladde me forth with tales
Til we cam into a contre, *Cor-hominis* hit heihte,
Erber of alle pryuatees and of holynesse.   5
Euene in þe myddes an ympe, as hit were,
That hihte *Ymago-dei*, graciousliche hit growede.
  Thenne gan y aske what hit hihte, and he me sone tolde.
'The tree hatte Trewe-loue,' quod he, 'the trinite hit sette;
Thorw louely lokynges hit lyueth and launseth vp blosmes,   10
The whiche blosmes buirnes Benigne-speche hit calleth.

7. *Ymago-dei*. The tree that grows in the heart of man (*Cor-hominis*) is the image of God (*Ymago-dei*), a graft (*ympe*) from God's love, set and supported by the Trinity against the winds of the World, the Flesh and the Devil, and bearing the fruit of charitable deeds and charitable souls. The tree is thus the divine potential implanted in man, and also the expression of that potential in history (i.e. the Church). Langland's tree of charity has connections with trees of Knowledge, Life and the Cross (see Frank, 1957, 86; for a study of the cosmological tree of Christian tradition, see E. S. Greenhill in *Traditio* 10, 1954, 323–71), but is probably most directly indebted to pictorial uses of trees as devices for presenting relationships (e.g. trees of the vices and virtues) and sequence (e.g. the tree of Jesse) in spatial terms (see Saxl, 1942, 107–14; Robertson-Huppé, 1951, 192; Bloomfield, 1958, 247–8; Katzenellenbogen, 1964, 63–9), and to the didactic treatises, often illustrated by such pictures, where metaphorical trees are frequently used to organize complex schemes of vices and virtues (cf. VII 70n), as in the *Somme le Roy* of friar Lorens and its English derivatives (e.g. *Ayenbite of Inwyt*, ed. EETS 23, pp. 95–8; *Vices and Virtues* 93–6, 114; and cf. the Tree of Contrition in Chaucer's Parson's Tale, *CT* X. 113). In the treatise, *Vices and Virtues*, the trees planted in the garden of man's heart are *graffes* (cf. *ympe* above) from the tree of Life, being the virtues granted through grace of the Holy Spirit (pp. 93–7, and see Tuve, 1966, 23–4, 108–14).

8. At this point in B (XVI 21), Piers Plowman appears to the dreamer and it is he who conducts the following conversation. The change in C seems to be the product of a desire to hold back the full revelation of Piers (cf. XVI 337a), for both didactic and dramatic reasons, until a later moment. It also removes some confusion in B as to the role of Piers.

And þerof cometh a goed fruyt, þe whiche men calleth werkes
Of holynesse, of hendenesse, of helpe-hym-þat-nedeth,
The whiche is *Caritas* ykald, Cristes oune fode,   f.79ᵃ
And solaceth alle soules sorwful in purgatory.'   15
    'Now, certes,' y sayde, and siȝte for ioye,
'Y thonke ȝow a thousand sethe that ȝe me hider kende,
And sethen þat ȝe fouchensaef to sey me as hit hoteth.'
And he thonkede me tho. Bote thenne toek y hede,
Hit hadde schoriares to shuyuen hit vp, thre shides of o lenghe   20
And of o kyne colour and kynde, as me thoghte,
Alle thre yliche long and yliche large.
Moche merueyled me on what more thei growede,
And askede eft of hym of what wode they were?
    'Thise thre shorriares,' quod he, 'that bereth vp this plonte,   25
Bytokeneth trewely the trinite of heuene,
Thre persones indepartable, perpetuel were euere,
Of o will, of o wit; and herwith y kepe
The fruyt of this fayre tre fro thre wikkede wyndes,
And fro falling þe stok, hit faile not of his myght.   30
The World is a wikkede wynd to hem þat wolde treuthe;
Couetyse cometh of þat wynde, and *Caritas* hit abiteth
And forfret þat fruyt thorw many fayre sihtes;

12. whiche U] X wiche
16–21. *lineation as* U; X *mislineates*
24. eft U] X ofte
30. *line supplied from* U; X *om*
33, 37. sihtes] X shites; U sightes

25–6. There is a reminiscence, in the *thre shorriares*, of the three stems, also symbolic of
the Trinity, which grew from the seeds planted by Seth (see XX 143n), were
found by Moses in Sinai, and went, after various other adventures, to the making
of the true Cross. See *Legends of the Holy Rood* (ed. EETS 46), 70, 77, and *History of
the Holy Rood-Tree* (ed. EETS 103), 2. The direct source for the idea of 'props' is
the assurance of God's support for the good man in Ps. 36:24, quoted in B (XVI
25).
28. *y kepe.* Free Will tends the tree of Charity, since Free Will is 'that part of man
which bears the impress of the image of God to which man was created'
(Donaldson, 1949, 189, cf. XVI 157n).
29. *thre wikkede wyndes*: the World, the Flesh and the Devil (see I 37n). Gregory
provides this allegory in his exposition of Job 13:25 (*PL* 75:980; see Robertson-
Huppé, 1951, 193; Woolf, 1968, 408).
30. *hit faile not of his myght*: 'so that it does not fail in its strength'.
33. *thorw many fayre sihtes*: 'because of the many fair appearances (of the things of the
world)'.

And with þe furste planke y palle hym down, *Potencia-dei-patris.*
Thenne is þe Flesch a fel wynde, and in flouryng-tyme   35
Thorw lecherie and lustes so loude he gynneth blowe
That hit norischeth nise sihtes and som tyme wordes
And many wikkede werkes, wormes of synne,
And al forbet *Caritas* rihte to þe bare stalke;
Thenne sette y þe seconde planke, *Sapiencia-dei-patris,*   40
The which is þe passioun and þe penaunce and þe parfitnesse of
        Iesus,
And þerwith y warde hit oþer-while til hit waxe rype.
And thenne fondeth the Fende my fruyte to destruye,
And leyth a laddere þerto, of lesynges ben þe ronges,
And with alle þe wyles þat he can, waggeth þe rote   45
Thorw bakbitares and brauleres and thorw bolde chidares,
And shaketh hit; ne were hit vnder-shored, hit sholde nat stande.
So this lordeynes lithereth þerto, þat alle þe leues falleth,
And feccheth away þe fruyt som tyme byfore bothe myn yes.
And thenne palle y adoune the pouke with the thridde shoriere,   50
The whiche is *Spiritus-sanctus* and sothfaste bileue,
And that is grace of þe Holy Gost; and thus gete y the maystrye.'   f.79ᵇ
    I toted vpon þat tree tho, and thenne toek y hede
Where þe fruyt were fayre or foul for to loke on.
And þe fruyt was fayre, non fayrere be myhte;   55
Ac in thre degrees hit grewe, grete ferly me thouhte,
And askede efte tho, where hit were all o kynde?
    'Ʒe, sertes,' he sayde, 'and sothliche leue hit,
Hit is al of o kynde, and þat shal y preuen,
Ac somme ar swettore then somme and sonnere wollen rotye.   60
Me may se on an appul-tree, mony tyme and ofte,
Of o kynde apples aren and nat iliche grete,
Ne suynge smale, ne of o swettenesse swete.

---

46. bakbitares U] X bagbitares.   brauleres] XU braules; I brawelers
60. sonnere T] XUI somme
62. and nat] XUIP nat; T and
63. o I] XU *om*

---

34. *Potencia-dei-patris*: 'the power of God the Father'. The prop is immediately trans-
    formed into a weapon, which would of course render it useless as a prop. No subtle
    allegory is intended; it is simply that the dynamic activity of L's imagination will
    not rest content with formal and static allegory. The tree has already begun to
    play a part in the process of history. For an illuminating analysis of the allegorical
    processes at work in this description of the Tree of Charity, see Aers, 1975, 79–107.
40. *Sapiencia-dei-patris*. Sapience, or Wisdom, is traditionally identified with the second
    person of the Trinity, from the interpretation of Prov. 8:22–31.
60. Cf. XII 222.
63. *suynge*: 'in regular gradation'.

Tho that sitten in þe sonne-syde sannore aren rype,
Swettore and saueriore and also more grettore   65
Then tho that selde haen þe sonne and sitten in þe north half;
And so hit fareth sothly, sone, by oure kynde.
Adam was as tre, and we aren as his apples,
Somme of vs soethfaste and some variable,
Summe litel, somme large, ylik apples of oen kynde.   70
As weddede men and wedewes and riht worthy maydones,
The whiche þe Seynt Spirit seweth, the sonne of al heuene,
And conforteth hem in here continence þat lyuen in contemplacoun,
As monkes and monyals, men of holy churche;
These haen þe hete of þe Holi Goest as hath þe crop of tre þe sonne.   75
Wedewes and wedewares, þat here ownere wil forsaken
And chaste leden here lyf, is lyf of contemplacioun,
And more lykynde to oure lorde then lyue as kynde asketh
And folewe þat the flesche wole and fruyt forth brynge,
That *Actiua* lyf lettred men in here langage hit calleth.'   80
'Ʒe, sire,' y sayde, 'and sethen þer aren but tweyne lyues

---

70. oen U] X *om*
75. hete TP] XI Ʒyfte; U sonne. þe⁴ U] X *om*

---

66. *in þe north half.* Cf. I 110a. The metaphor here contradicts that of 60, above. The largest and sweetest apples, here, are those that receive most heat of the sun, i.e. of the Holy Spirit (75, below). The contradiction is resolved in 100, below.

75. Traditionally, monks and nuns and other religious (i.e. members of the regular orders of clergy) were under the special protection of the Holy Spirit (Bloomfield, 1961, 75).

76. Chaste widowhood was placed above marriage and below virginity (i.e. principally the life of celibate religious) in the hierarchy of heavenly reward, as derived from patristic commentary on Matt. 13:3–8: see, for example, *Hali Meidenhad* (in Blake, 1972, 47). Widowhood, and also the celibate life of monks and nuns, are both here associated with the Contemplative life as against the Active life of the Christian in the world (see XV 194n). The association is new in C (like the whole passage, 58–103) and rather confusing, but it may well reflect a certain ambiguity in traditional interpretation of the three grades of chastity, whereby the usual association of widowhood with priests, and of virginity with the contemplative religious (Bloomfield, 1958, 246), was sometimes reversed (Robertson-Huppé, 1951, 13).

81. *tweyne lyues.* The dreamer's remark is at first puzzling, since there is indeed a third quality of life beyond the Active and the Contemplative, namely the Mixed or Apostolic life, which brings the fruits of contemplation into the life of action (see X 78n). But L makes no mention of this third kind of life, neither here nor elsewhere, and unless we assume that he is here introducing in a broad and suggestive way a concept of a third and highest grade of Christian life, which is about to be evidenced, after many hints and anticipations, in the life of Christ (below, 124–78), it would seem that he is merely taking the opportunity to bring in some teaching on the three grades of life – 'There suddenly came up something that

That oure lorde alloweth, as lered men vs techeth,
Actiua Vita and *Contemplatiua Vita*,
Why groweth this fruyt in thre degres?'
         'A goed skil,' he saide;
'Here beneth y may nyme, yf y nede hadde,   85
Matrimonye, a moist fruyt, þat multiplieth þe peple.
And thenne aboue is bettere fruyt (ac bothe two ben gode),
Wydewhode, more worthiore then wedlok, as in heuene.   f.80ᵃ
Thenne is Virginite, more vertuous and fayrest, as in heuene,
For þat is euene with angelis, and angeles pere.   90
Hit was þe furste fruyte þat þe fader of heuene blessed,
And bad hit be, of a bat of erthe, a man and a maide,
In menynge þat the fayrest thyng the furste thynge shold honoure,
And þe clennest creature furste creatour knowe.
In kynges court and in knyhtes, the clenneste men and fayreste   95
Shollen serue for þe lord sulue, and so fareth god almyhty.
Maydones and martres ministrede him here on erthe
And in hey heuene is priueoste and next hym by resoun,
And for þe fayrest fruyte byfore hym, as of erthe,
And swete withoute swellynge, sour worth hit neuere.'   100
   'This is a propre plonte,' quod y, 'and priueliche hit bloweth,
And bryngeth forth fruyt, folk of alle nacion,
Bothe parfit and inparfit; puyr fayn y wolde
Assay what sauour hit hadde,' and saide þat tyme,
'Leue *Liberum Arbitrium*, lat some lyf hit shake.'   105
   And anoon he hihte Elde an hy for to clymbe,
And shaken hit sharpeliche, the rype sholden falle.
And Elde clemp to þe crop-ward, thenne comsed hit to crye.
A waggede Wedewhed, and hit wepte aftur;

94. creatour U] X creature
97. him here T] X here; U him

seemed to need preaching about' (*aliud quod praedicandum videbatur*), as St Bernard
puts it (Spearing, 1972, 125). He may have been influenced by pictures (see 7n,
above) such as that in B.L. MS Arundel 44 (fol. 70a) of the *Speculum Virginum*,
representing a tree of virtues with the three grades of married women, widows and
virgins depicted in its branches in ascending series (see A. Watson in *Speculum* 3,
1928, 351).

86. *a moist fruyt*: sweet and early-ripening, but soonest rotten (as in 60, above).

93. *the fayrest thyng*, i.e. virginity, alluding to the way in which Adam and Eve were
created. *the furste thynge*, i.e. the Prime Cause, God.

96. *and so fareth god almyhty*. The same idea is expressed in *Cleanness* 17–20.

100. *swellynge*, as caused by over-ripeness (or pregnancy: see 86, above).

106. *Elde*. The allegory here takes on its other dimension, of time – time in relation to
man's life and in relation to history.

A meued Matrimonye, hit made a foule noyse;   110
For euere as Elde hadde eny down, þe deuel was wel redy
And gadered hem alle togyderes, bothe grete and smale,
Adam and Abraham and Ysaye þe prophete,
Sampson and Samuel and seynt Iohn þe Baptiste,
And baer hem forth baldly, nobody hym lette,   115
And made of holy men his hoerd *in limbo inferni*,
There is derkenesse and drede, and þe deuel maister.
  Thenne moued hym moed *in magestate dei*,
That *Libera-Voluntas-Dei* lauhte þe myddel shoriare
And hit aftur þe fende, happe how hit myhte.   120
Filius, by þe fadres wille, fley with *Spiritus Sanctus*
To go ransake þat ragman and reue hym of his apples,
That thorw fals biheste and fruyt furste man disseyued.
  And thenne spak *Spiritus Sanctus* in Gabrieles mouthe   f.80ᵇ
To a mayde þat hihte Marie, a meke thyng withalle,   125
That oen Iesus, a iustices sone, moste iouken in here chaumbre,
Til *plenitudo temporis* tyme ycome were
That Elde felde efte þe fruyt, or full to be rype,
That Iesus sholde iouste þer-fore, and by iugement of armes,

---

110. foule U] X foyle

116. *in limbo inferni*: 'in the borderlands of hell', where the souls of the patriarchs and prophets dwelt until released by Christ (XI 221n). We are, at this point in the poem, in the pre-incarnation era, the age of the Law, preparing to enter the time of the gospels (Dobet, XVIII–XX), after which will follow the age of grace (Dobest, XXI–XXII). This is only one of the dimensions in which the allegory of the Tree of Charity – and the poem – exists (see Aers, 1975, 92–107).

118–19. 'Then anger arose in the majesty of God, so that the Free Will of God seized the middle prop', i.e. the Son. *moued hym* is reflexive, 'bestirred himself'. The reference is to the Incarnation. The Free Will of man, keeper of the Tree of Charity, needs in the end the freely willed gift of God's grace through his Son in order to bring the fruit of charity to a proper harvest.

124. The Annunciation is the moment of the intersection of the timeless with time (*Dry Salvages*, 201), the moment of God's second entry into human time. It is the most stupendous moment in Christian history, and Langland, by his sudden and startling shift from allegorical abstraction to historical reality, makes it seem so.

126. *iouken*: 'perch', a technical term in hawking, and very apt to the traditional image of Christ as a bird who descends for a time to the earth (see a note by T. D. Hill in *NQ* 220, 1975, 532). *in here chaumbre*. The Virgin's womb, and the Virgin herself, are often referred to as a chamber, bower or bedroom in which God or the Trinity rested a while (OED, s.v. *chamber*; Gray, 1975, 138–9).

127. *plenitudo temporis*: 'the fullness of time' (Gal. 4:4), referring to the moment that God chose for the Incarnation. 'But when the time had fully come, God sent forth his Son, born of woman, born under the law, to redeem those who were under the law' (Gal. 4:4–5).

128. i.e. the Incarnation was prompted by the events of 106–17, above.

Who sholde fecche this fruyt, the fende or Iesus suluen.   130
The mayde myldeliche the messager she grauntede
And saide hendely to hym, 'Lo, me, his hondmayden
For to worchen his wille withouten eny synne.
    Ecce ancilla domini.
And in þe wombe of þat wenche was he fourty wokes
And bycam man of þat maide, mankynde to saue,
Byg and abydyng, and bold in his barnhoed   135
To haue yfouthte with þe fende ar fol tyme come.
    Ac *Liberum Arbitrium* lechecraeft hym tauhte
Til *plenitudo temporis* hy tyme aprochede,
That suche a surgien sethen ysaye was þer neuere
Ne noon so faythfol fisciscyen, for all þat bysouhte hym   140
A lechede hem of here langour bothe lasares and blynde,
    Claudi ambulant, leprosi mundantur,
And comen wommen conuertede and clansed hem of synne
And luft vp Lazar þat lay in his tombe
Quadriduanus coeld, quyk dede hym rome.   145
    Ac ar he made þat miracle *mestus cepit esse*
And wepte watur with yes, the why weten fewe.
Ac tho that sey that selcouth sayde þat tyme
That he was god or godes sone for þat grete wonder,
And some Iewes saide with sorserie he wrouhte   150

139. hy U] X by

133a. 'Behold, I am the handmaid of the lord' (Luke 1:38).
138. God in his Incarnation must live and suffer as a man (XVIII 202, XX 217) and must learn his job as 'leche of lyf' (I 199, B XVI 118) in terms of the capacities of the human Free Will. He must learn 'creaturely limitation' and refrain from 'a premature exertion of his full Godhead' (Aers, 1975, 108).
139. *plenitudo temporis* (see 127, above) is frequently used in patristic commentary as a reference to the beginning of Christ's public life (Kaske, 1960, 45).
142a. 'The lame walk, lepers are cleansed' (Matt. 11:5, Luke 7:22).
145. *Quadriduanus.* See XVII 305.
146. *mestus cepit esse*: 'he began to be sorrowful' (Matt. 26:37). L has here transferred the words used of the agony of Christ in the garden to the description of his sorrowing (John 11:33, 35, 38) before the miracle of the raising of Lazarus.
147. *the why weten fewe*: 'few know why'. Jesus wept as he was about to perform what he had already recognized (John 11:4) as his greatest miracle. L perhaps wished to believe that he wept because of his humanity, out of human compassion with those who mourned, but his puzzlement was not shared by the allegorists, who declared that Jesus wept 'to make vs to vndirstond how hard it is to anny man to ryse aȝeyn from synne when þat he is fallen þer-in' (Sermons, ed. Ross, 272). Cf. II 32n.

And thorw the myhte of Mahond and thorw misbileue.
　　Demonium habes.
'Thenne is Saton зoure saueour,' quod Iesu, 'and hath ysaued
　　　зow ofte,
As y saued зow sondry tymes and also y fede зow
With fyue fisches and loues, fyue thousendes at ones,
And y lefte basketes ful of broke mete, bere awey ho-so wolde.　　　155
Vnkynde and vnkunnynge!' quod Crist, and with a roep smoet hem
And ouerturned in þe temple here tables and here stalles　　　f.81ᵃ
And drof hem out alle þat þer bouhte and solde,
And saide, 'This is an hous of orysones and of holynesse
And when þat my will is y wol hit ouerthrowe　　　160
And ar thre dayes aftur edefye hit newe.'　　·
The Iewes tolde þe iustice how þat Iesus saide,
Ac þe ouerturnynge of the temple bitokened his resureccioun.
　　Enuye and euel wil ern in þe Iewes,
And pursuede hym priueliche and for pans hym bouhte –　　　165
　　Ne forte tumultus fieret in populo –
Of Ieudas þe Iew, Iesus oune disciple.
This biful on a Fryday, a litel bifore Pasche,
That Iudas and Iewes Iesus thei mette:
'*Aue, raby,*' quod the ribaudes and riht til hym they зede
And kuste Iesus to be knowe þerby and cauht of þe Iewes.　　　170
Thenne Iesus to Iudas and to þe Iewes sayde,
'Falsnesse y fynde in thy fayre speche
And kene care in thy kissyng and combraunce to thysulue.
Thow shalt be myrrour to monye, men to disceue;
Wo to tho þat thy wyles vysen to þe worldes ende!　　　175
　　Ve homini illi per quem scandalum venit.

175a. *scandalum* U] X scandulum

151a. 'You have a demon', frequently said of Jesus by the Jews while he taught in the
temple (John 7:20, 8:48, 52). L transfers the phrase to characterize the general
suspicion of the chief priests and Pharisees after the raising of Lazarus (John
11:47). He continues with a general reminiscence of Jesus's reproach to the Jews
(John 8:39–47) and, on another occasion, to the disciples (Matt. 16:5–12), before
passing to the cleansing of the temple (John 2:13–22).
162. Mk. 11:18.
163. John 2:21–2.
165. *And pursuede*: 'and (they, i.e. the Jews) pursued'.
165a. '(But they said, Not during the feast), lest there should be a tumult among the
people' (Matt, 26:5).
169. *Aue, raby*: 'Hail, Master' (Matt. 26:49).
175a. '(It is necessary that temptations to sin should come into the world), but woe to
that man through whom temptation comes' (Matt. 18:7). Jesus says nothing like
this, or the previous lines, at the taking in the garden.

Sethe y be tresoun am take and to ʒoure will, Iewes,
Soffreth my postles in pays and in pees gange.'
This Iewes to þe iustices Iesus they ladde.

With moche noyse þat nyhte nere frentyk y wakede;
In inwit and in alle wittes aftur *Liberum Arbitrium*   180
Y waytede witterly, ac whoder he wende y ne wiste.
And thenne mette y with a man a Mydde-lentones Sonenday,
As hoer as an hauthorn and Abraham he hihte.
'Of whennes artow?' quod y, and hendeliche hym grette.
'I am with fayth,' quod þat freke, 'hit falleth nat me to lye,   185
An heraud of armes ar eny lawe were.'
'What is his conysaunce,' quod y, 'in his cote armure?'
'Thre persones in o pensel,' quod he, 'departable fram oþere;
O speche and spirit springeth out of alle,
Of o wit and o will, were neuere a-twynne,   190
And sondry to se vpon, *solus deus* he hoteth.'   f.81ᵇ

---

187. conysaunce U] X Iunnesaunces

176–7. John 18:8–9.
179. *With moche noyse*. L's awakening is associated with the noise and tumult of the taking in the garden, which breaks his vision. In B (XVI 160–66) a further seven lines describe briefly the Passion and the triumph of Jesus over death. They are fine lines, but their omission in C is entirely appropriate, since the dreamer must be shown to be not yet fully prepared for the full revelation of Christ's sacrifice. In B, the vision of the Tree of Charity (B XVI 20–167) is an 'inner dream' (cf. XI 168n). L, having eliminated the beginning of the inner dream at the point in B corresponding to 16, above, here inadvertently preserves the waking from the inner dream. The consequence in the text is that he appears to wake twice from the same dream, here and in XIX 331. For convenience, the fifth vision may be said to begin at 182, below.

183. *Abraham*. The epistle for Mid-Lent Sunday (the fourth Sunday in Lent) is Gal. 4:22–31 (Missale 213), one of the many NT texts in which the life of Abraham is taken as the model of the life of Faith under the old dispensation (e.g. Rom. 4, Gal. 3, Heb. 11). An immediate suggestion for the introduction of Abraham is provided by Jesus's debate with the Jews in the temple about the similarity and difference between himself and Abraham (John 8:37–59; see above, 151a), but L's larger purpose is to show the old law in its most perfect life, in Abraham-Faith and Moses-Hope, before demonstrating how that law is both fulfilled and immeasurably transcended in the new law of Christ-Charity.

185. *I am with fayth*. Cf. B (XVI 176): 'I am feiþ'. C shows some initial reluctance to identify the new character by name as Faith (cf. XV 194n, XVI 337a), but accepts the speech-prefix later (e.g. 199, below).

186. *An heraud of armes*: aptly understood as one who runs before his lord, bearing his lord's blazon (here, the Trinity), to announce the coming of his lord into the tournament (see XX 14, and cf. XIX 50). *er eny lawe were*, the law being understood as the commandments given to Moses.

191. *solus deus*: 'one only God' (e.g. Ps. 85:10).

'Suthe they ben suyrelepes,' quod y, 'they haen sondry names?'
'That is soth,' saide he thenne, 'the syre hatte *pater*,
And þe seconde is a sone of þe sire, *filius*;
The thridde is þat halt al a thyng by hymsulue,   195
Holy Goest is his name and he is in all.'
'This is myrke thyng for me,' quod y, 'and for many anoþer,
How o lord myhte lyue o thre; y leue hit nat,' y sayde.
    'Muse nat to moche þeron,' quod Faith, 'til thow more knowe,
Ac leue hit lelly al thy lyf-tyme.   200
Thre bilongeth to a lord þat leiaunce claymeth:
Miȝte, and a mene to se his owne myhte,
Of hymsulue and his seruant, and what soffreth hem bothe.
God, þat bigynnyng hadde neuere bote tho hym goed thouhte,
Sente forth his sone as for seruant þat tyme   205
To ocupien hym here til issue were spronge,
The whiche aren childrene of charite and holy church þe moder.
Patriarches and prophetes and apostles were the childrene,
And Crist and cristendoem and alle cristene, holy churche –
Bitokeneth þe trinite and trewe bileue.   210
O god almyhty þat man made and wrouhte
Semblable to hymsulue ar eny synne were,
A thre he is þer he is and hereof bereth wittnesse
The werkes þat hymsulue wrouhte and this world bothe:
        Celi enarrant gloriam dei.

201. Thre T] XUI That thre
204. þat U] X *om*
207. þe U] X *om*

199. Abraham's explanation of the Trinity is here much abbreviated from B, appro-
priately to his own necessarily limited understanding and to the injunction of XVI
228–9.
202–3. 'Power, and a mediator to recognize [read *shewe* for *se*? B has *knowe*] his own
power in operation [i.e. an executive instrument of his power], as it has to do with
himself and his servant, and (thirdly) what allows mutual existence to them both
[viz. Love]'. This reading treats the lines as a threefold analogy to the activity of
the Trinity (as is more explicitly stated in B), though it is clearly meaningful in
neither original nor transferred sense.
207. *childrene of charite*. There is allusion here to the contrast, developed in the epistle for
Mid-Lent Sunday (see above, 183n), between the 'servants' of the old law, born in
slavery, and the 'children of promise' (Gal. 4:28) of the new law, born in freedom.
208–9. Two constructions seem to have merged here: *holy churche*, originally the
predicate of a verb parallel to *were* in 208, has been made the subject of the verb
bitokeneth in 210, a line new in C.
213. *A*: 'in', prep.
214a. 'The heavens show forth the glory of God' (Ps. 18:1).

That he is thre persones departable y preue hit by mankynde,   215
And o god almyhty, if alle men ben of Adam.
Eue of Adam was and out of hym ydrawe
And Abel of hem bothe and alle thre o kynde;
And thise thre þat y carp of, Adam and Eue
And Abel here issue, aren bote oen in manhede.   220
Matrimonye withoute moylere is nauht moche to preyse,
As þe bible bereth witnesse, a boek of þe olde lawe,
That acorsede alle couples þat no kynde forth brouhte:
    Maledictus sit homo qui non reliquit semen in Israel.
And man withoute a make myhte nat wel of kynde
Multiplie ne moreouer withoute a make louye   225 f.82ᵃ
Ne withoute a soware be suche seed, this we seen alle.
Now go we to godhede: in god, fader of heuene,
Was þe sone in hymsulue in a *simile* as Eue
Was, when god wolde oute of þe wey ydrawe.
And as Abel of Adam and of his wyf Eue
Sprang forth and spak, a spyer of hem tweyne,   230
So oute of þe syre and þe sone þe seynt spirit of hem bothe
Is and ay was and worþ withouten ende.
And as thre persones palpable is puyrlich bote o mankynde,
The which is man and his make and moilere here issue,
So is god godes sone, in thre persones the trinite.   235
In matrimonie aren thre and of o man cam alle thre
And to godhede goth thre, and o god is all thre.
Lo, treys encountre treys,' quod he, 'in godhede and in manhede.'
  'Hastow ysey this?' y seyde, 'alle thre and o god?'
  'In a somur y hym seyh,' quod he, 'as y saet in my porche,   240

---

233. was T] XUI were. and worþ withouten ende T] XUI *om*

---

215. St Augustine mentions this comparison of the Trinity to husband, wife and child in his *De Trinitate*, ii.5 (*PL* 42:1000), but does not think it a good one – which may make it apt to the limited understanding of Abraham.

222. *a boek of þe olde lawe.* The apocryphal gospels of the nativity of Mary (see below, 223a) claimed to be part of the history of the twelve tribes of Israel.

223a. 'Cursed be the man who does not leave behind his seed in Israel'. This reproach (cf. Gen. 30:23, Luke 1:25) is addressed by the Jewish elders to the childless Joachim, and is followed soon by the birth of the Virgin Mary. It appears at the beginning of the apocryphal gospels of the nativity of Mary, such as the *Pseudo-Matthaei Evangelium* (Tischendorf 55), though L's wording is different (and not, *pace* Skeat, closer to *Legenda Aurea* CXXXI, 587).

239. *treys encountre treys*: 'three is set against three'. *treys* is an AN term from dicing, from the game of hazard (cf. *CT* II. 124, VI. 653).

241. The appearance of God in three persons to Abraham, beside the oaks of Mamre, is told in Gen. 18:1–15. The story is memorably treated in *Cleanness* 601–70.

Where god cam gangynge a thre riȝt be my gate.
    Tres vidit et unum adorauit.
Y roos vp and reuerensed god and riȝt fayre hym grette,
Wosch her feet and wypede hem and afturward they eten,
And what y thouhte and my wyf he vs wel tolde.   245
He bihihte vs issue and ayr in oure olde age;
Fol trewe tokenes bitwene vs is when tyme cometh þat y mete hym,
How he fondede me furste – my fayre sone Ysaak
To make sacrefice of hym he heet me, hym to honoure.
I withsaet nat his heste; y hope and bileue   250
Where y walke in this worlde a wol hit me allowe.
Y circumsised my sone also for his sake,
Mysulue and my mayne; and alle þat male were
Bledden bloed for þat lordes loue, y hope to blisse þat tyme.
Myen affiaunce and my faith is ferme in his bileue,   255
For hymsulue saide y sholde haue, y and myn issue bothe,
Lond and lordschip ynow and lyf withouten ende.
    To me and myn issue more he me bihihte,
Mercy for oure mysdedes as many tymes
As we wilnede and wolde with mouthe and herte aske.   260
And sethe a sente me to seyn and saide that y sholde   f.82ᵇ
Worschipe hym with wyn and with breed bothe
At ones on an auter in worschipe of the trinite,
And make sacrefice so – somwhat hit bitokneth;
I leue þat ilke lord thenketh a newe lawe to make.   265
    Fiet vnum ouile et vnus pastor.
Thus haue y ben his heraud here and in helle

244. her U] X hes (s[?] *over erasure*)
256. haue U] X *om*
260. mouthe U] X mouhte
264. make U] X made

242a. 'He saw three and bowed down in worship to one'. From an antiphon sung at vespers on Quinquagesima Sunday (Breviary I. dxlii), and elsewhere widely quoted as an ocular proof of the Trinity (Ames, 1970, 56).
248. Gen. 17:2, 22.
252. *my sone*: Ishmael, his first son, by the slave-woman Hagar. See Gen. 17:23.
256–7. For God's covenant with Abraham, see e.g. Gen. 15, 17:1–8.
258–60. An interpretation of the covenant offered by e.g. Mic. 7:18–20.
262. The bread and wine offered in honour of Abraham by the priest Melchizedek (Gen. 14:18) were commonly interpreted as a prefiguration of the eucharist.
265a. 'There shall be one flock and one shepherd' (John 10:16).
266. *in helle*. Abraham and the other patriarchs and prophets were in hell, or more properly in limbo (see 116, above), awaiting Christ's coming.

And conforted many a carfol þere þat aftur his comyng lokede.
Forthy y seke hym,' he saide, 'for seynt Iohn þe Baptiste
Saide þat a seyh here þat sholde saue vs alle:
    Ecce agnus dei.'
   Thenne hadde y wonder of his wordes and of his wyde clothes,   270
For in his bosome a baer thyng and þat blessede ofte.
And y lokede in his lappe; a lazar lay þerynne,
With patriarkes and profetes pleynge togyderes.
'What waytest thow?' quod Fayth, 'and what wost thow haue?'
'I wolde ywyte,' quod y tho, 'what is in thy lappe?'   275
'Loo!' quod he, and lette me see. 'Lord, mercy!' y saide,
'This is a present of moche pris, what prince shal hit haue?'
'Hit is a preciouse present,' quod he, 'ac the pouke hit hath
      atached,
And me þerwith,' quod the weye; 'may no wed vs quyte
Ne noen bern ben oure borw ne bryngen vs out of þat daunger;   280
Fro þe poukes pondefold no maynprise may vs feche
Til he come þat y carpe of, Crist is his name,
That shal delyuere vs som day out of þe deueles power
And bettere wed for vs wagen then we ben alle worthy,
And þat is lyf for lyf; or ligge thus euere,   285
Lollyng in my lappe thus til suche a lord vs feche.'
   'Allas!' y saide, 'þat synne so longe shal lette
The myhte of goddes mercy that myhte vs alle amende!'
And wepte for his wordes. With þat saw y another
Rappliche renne þe riȝt way we wente.   290
And y fraynede hym furst fro whennes he come,
What he hihte and whoder he wolde, and wihtliche he vs tolde.

270. his² U] X *om*
289. another U] X non other
292. wihtliche] X whithliche; U wightly

269. *þat*: 'one that'.
269a. 'Behold the Lamb of God' (John 1:29).
272. *a lazar*. In fact, the beggar Lazarus, whom the wretched Dives saw in Abraham's bosom (Luke 16:23). See VIII 278n.
278. Cf. 111, above.

Passus XIX

Hope and the Good Samaritan

Passus secundus de dobet
'I am *Spes*, a spie,' quod he, 'and spere aftur a knyʒte
That toek me a maundement vpon þe mont of Synay
To reule alle reumes þerwith in riʒhte and in resoun. f.83ᵃ
Lo, here the lettre,' quod he, 'a Latyn and Ebrew;
That that y sey is soeth se ho-so liketh.' 5
  'Is hit asseled?' y saide; 'may men yse thy lettres?'
  'Nay,' he saide, 'y seke hym þat hath þe seel to kepe,
The which is Crist and cristendoem and croes þer-an yhanged.
Were hit þerwith aseled y woet wel þe sothe
That Luciferes lordschipe lowe sholde lygge.' 10
  'Let se thy lettres,' quod y, 'we myhte þe lawe knowe.'
A pluhte forth a patente, a pece of an hard roche
Whereon was writen two wordes and on this wyse yglosed:
    Dilige deum et proximum.

1. *Spes*: Hope, i.e. Moses. The hope of Israel is in the coming of the Messiah, and this hope is founded in the law of Moses, which Christ fulfils (see e.g. Acts 26:6–7, Rom. 15:4). *a spie*: a scout, spying out the ground. L continues the imagery of preparation for a battle (cf. herald, XVIII 186). At the same time he continues his progress through the liturgical season (the story of Moses occupied the lessons in the week beginning with Mid-Lent Sunday) towards the great events of Palm Sunday (XX 6) and Holy Week. See also XX 471, XXI 201, and Kirk, 1972, 183–7; Adams, 1976, 281–4.

4. *a Latyn and Ebrew*, i.e. the Hebrew original of the Commandments, and the Latin Vulgate version of Jerome. Cf. Wyclif, ed. Matthew, 348: 'God sent a lettre to man by moyses hijs messangere . . . hijs lettre is hijs mawndementis, & grace in moyses soule is hijs priue seel, better þen eny kyngis signe'.

7. *Nay* is the answer to the first question, not the second. The *lettre* may in fact be seen, because it is 'letters patent' (see 12, below, and IX 27n), that is, an open letter, as from the sovereign, for all to see, recording some agreement or contract, here the covenant of the old law. It awaits the seal of Christ, which is hanging from the deed of contract, as seals did, in the form of a cross (see 8, below); this seal is the sovereign's final token of confirmation of the covenant. So Christ comes to confirm and fulfil the law.

8. *The which*, i.e. the seal. *yhanged*, i.e. as the tag of a seal.

12. *a pece of an hard roche*, referring to the tablets of stone on which the Sinaitic law was inscribed (Ex. 31:18).

13a. See XV 135n.

This was the tyxt trewly, y toek ful good gome.
The glose was gloriously writen with a gult penne: 15
   In hiis duobus pependit tota lex.
'Is here al thy lordes lettres?' quod y. '3e, leef me,' he saide,
'And ho worcheth aftur this writ, y wol vndertaken,
Shal neuere deuel hym dere ne deth in soule greue.
For thogh y sey hit mysulue, y haue saued with this charme
Of men and of wommen meny score thousand.' 20
  'He seyth soth,' saide Fayth, 'y haue yfounde hit trewe.
Lo! here in my lappe,' quod Fayth, 'þat leuede vpon þat lettre,
Bothe Iosue and Ieudith and Iudas Macabeus
And six thousand mo,' quod Fayth, 'y can nat seyn here names.'
  '3oure wordes aren wonderfol,' quod y tho. 'Where eny of 3ow be
    trewe
And lele to bileue on for lif or for soule? 25
Abraham saith þat he seyh holly þe trinitee,
Thre persones parselmele, departable fram oþere,
And alle thre bote o god; thus Abraham bereth witenesse,
And hath ysaued þat bileued so and sory for here synnes, 30
He can no certeyn somme telle and somme aren in his lappe.
What nedede hit thanne a newe lawe to brynge
Sethe the furste sufficede to bileue and be saued?
And now cometh this *Spees* that hath aspyed þe lawe,
That of no trinite ne telleth ne taketh mo persones 35
To godhede but o god and on god almyhty
The which alle men aren holde ouer al thyng to honoure; f.83^b
And seth to louye and to lene for þat lordes sake
Alle manere men as moche as ouresulue.
And for to louye and bileue in o lord almyhty 40
Hit is liht for lewed and for lered bothe.
Ac for to bileue in o lord þat lyueth in thre persones

24. can U] X nyl
26. lif T] XUI body
28. departable U] X deparable

15a. 'On these two (commandments) depended [Vg. *pendet*] the whole law' [Matt. 22:40]. L reads this verse as a 'gloss' or commentary (cf. VI 303n), illuminated in gold, on the preceding text. See XIII 118n.
18. See IX 37n.
22. Faith's *lappe* is Abraham's bosom (XVIII 271), the abode in limbo of those righteous under the law.
25. *wonderfol*: 'such as to excite wonder or incredulity'. *where*: 'whether', introducing a question, i.e. 'Can it be that'.
30. *þat*: 'those that'. *and sory*: 'and (were) sorry'.

And lereth þat we louye sholde as wel lyares as lele –
Go thy gate,' quod y to *Spes*, 'so me god helpe,
Tho þat lerneth thy lawe wollen litel while hit vse!'   45
   And as we wenten in þe way thus wordyng of this matere,
Thenne sey we a Samaritaen cam sittynge on a muyle,
Rydynge ful raply þe rihte way we ʒeden,
Comynge fram a contreye þat men callide Ierico;
To ioust in Ierusalem he iaced awey ful faste.   50
Bothe Abraham and *Spees* and he mette at ones
In a wilde wildernesse where theues hadde ybounde
A man, as me tho thouhte, to moche care they brouhte;
For he ne myhte stepe ne stande ne stere foet ne handes
Ne helpe hymsulue sothly, for *semyuief* he semede,   55
And as naked as an nedle, and noen helpe abouten.
   Fayth furst had of hym siht, ac he fleyh asyde

---

57. had T] XUI *om*

43. *as wel lyares as lele*. The dreamer thinks, reasonably enough, that *dilige proximum* is
morally undiscriminating. There is no need to assume that he is thinking of Matt.
5:44, 'Love your enemies' (cf. XV 141n), which would of course be a central
commandment of the new law.

47. The rehandling of the parable of the Good Samaritan (Luke 10:25–37) is one of
the few instances where L's allegorical technique can be analysed usefully in terms
of the traditional four levels of scriptural exegesis (see Owst, 1933, 57–66; Coghill,
1944, 351–7; Robertson-Huppé, 1951, 2–3, 204–8; Salter, 1967, 5–7), though not
in any simple way (see Smith, 1966, 74–93). Literally, it is especially meaningful
in terms of the historical situation of Samaritans as a despised people in Judaea;
allegorically, it demonstrates the precept *dilige proximum*; tropologically (in terms
of abstract morality), it shows the ineffectualness of Faith and Hope without
Charity (1 Cor. 13:13, cf. Rom. 13:10) and of the Old Law of the Priest and
Levite without the New Law of Christ; and anagogically (in terms of spiritual
salvation), it tells with great moving power of Christ's redeeming love for man-
kind, sick of sin. L is aware of all four levels, and uses them, in their context, to
penetrate to the vision of Christ's humanity as the perfect exemplar of Charity.
The interpretation, including the identification of the Good Samaritan as Christ,
is wholly orthodox (see e.g. Wyclif, ed. Arnold, i.32–3), though much of the local
detail is original. The relationship of the treatment of the parable in L to the
preceding appearance of Abraham and Moses and to the subsequent account of
the Passion and Resurrection, and the relationship of the whole sequence to the
liturgy for the 13th Sunday after Trinity (the day on which the parable was read)
is discussed in St-Jacques, 1969.

50. *To ioust in Ierusalem*. See XVIII 186, XIX 1, XX 21. In Luke, the Samaritan is
riding from Jerusalem to Jericho.

55. *semyuief*, Lat. *semivivus*, 'half-alive' (Luke 10:30).

57. The priest and the Levite of the parable are traditionally interpreted as Abraham-
Faith and Moses-Hope (St-Jacques, 1969, 219). For Moses as the Levite, see Ex.
2:1–2.

And nolde nat neyhele hym by nyne londes lenghe.

    Hope cam huppynge aftur, þat hadde so ybosted

How he with Moyses maundement hadde mony men yholpe;   60

Ac when he hadde sihte of this syke, asyde he gan hym drawe

And dredfully withdrow hym tho and durste go no nerre hym.

    Ac so sone so the Samaritaen hadde sihte of this carefole,

A lihte anoen of lyard and ladde hym in his handes

And to this wey a wente, his woundes to byholde,   65

And perseued by his poues he was in perel to deye

And bote if he hadde recouerer the raþer þat ryse sholde he neuere,

And vnbokelede his boteles and bothe he atamede;

With wyn and with oyle his wounds he can lithe,

Enbaumed hym and boend his heued and on bayard hym sette   70

And ladde hym forth to *lavacrum-lex-dei*, a grange,

Is syxe myle or seuene bisyde þe newe marcat,

And lefte hym þere a-lechyng, to lyue yf he myhte;   f.84ᵃ

And toek two pans the hostiler to take kepe to hym,

'And þat more goth for his medicyne y make the good ageynward,   75

For y may nat lette,' quod that lede, and lyard he bystrideth,

And rapede hym to ryde the rihte way to Ierusalem.

Bothe Fayth and his felawe *Spes* folewede faste aftur,

Ac y sewede the Samaritaen and saide how they bothe

Were afered, and flowe fram þe man ywounded.   80

    'Haue hem excused,' quod he, the Samaritaen, 'here helpe
        may nat availe,

Ne no medicyne vnder mone the man to hele brynge,

---

58. nolde T]ˈXUI wolde
69. lithe U] X lihte
71. grange] X grangee; U graunge
73. a-lechyng U] X alechnyg
82. mone B] XUITP molde

---

58. *londes*: the strips or sections into which a ploughed field is divided, for drainage, crop-division or measurement.

71. *lavacrum-lex-dei*: 'the bath of the law of god', i.e. the baptismal font, symbolic of entry into the Law or Church of Christ (a traditional interpretation of the *stabulum* of the parable: see St-Jacques, 1969, 226). *grange* (translating Vg. *stabulum*, 'stable' or 'inn') can mean a group of outlying farm-buildings with barns, belonging to a religious house or feudal lord, where crops were stored. This meaning would be peculiarly apt here if one saw a connection with the great barn of Unity of XXI 319 (see Smith, 1966, 79).

72. *þe newe marcat* would be suggestive of the busy world of getting and spending, the world of the Prologue, from which the life of the Christian must be momentarily detached.

75. *þat more goth*: 'whatever more is required'.

82. *vnder mone*: 'in the sublunary sphere', i.e. of a non-spiritual kind. For this emendation in B XVII 94, see Kane-Donaldson 111.

Noþer Faith ne fyn Hope, so festred aren his woundes.
Withoute þe bloed of a barn he beth nat ysaued,
The whiche barn mote nedes be born of a mayde,   85
And with þe bloed of þat barn enbaumed and ybaptised.
And thouh he stande and steppe, riʒt stronge worth he neuere
Til he haue eten al þat barn and his bloed dronken,
And ʒut be plasterud with pacience when fondynges hym priketh,
(For wente neuere man this way þat he ne was here yruyfled,   90
Saue mysulue soethly, and such as y louede),
And ʒut bote they leue lelly vpon þat litel baby,
That his lycame shal lechen at þe laste vs alle.'
    'A, sire,' y saide, 'shal nat we bileue,
As Faith and his felawe *Spes* enfourmede me bothe,   95
In thre persones a parceles departable fram oþere
And alle thre bote a god? Thus Abraham me tauhte.
And Hope afturward of o god more me toelde
And lered me for his loue to louye al mankynde
And hym aboue alle and hem as mysulue;   100
Noþer lacke ne alose, ne leue þat þer were
Eny wikkedere in þe worlde then y were mysulue,
And moest inparfyt of alle persones, and pacientliche soffre
Alle manere men, and thogh y myhte venge
Y sholde tholye and thonken hem þat me euel wolden.'   105
    'A saide soeth,' quod the Samaritaen, 'and so y rede the also.
And as Abraham þe olde of o god the tauhte,
Loke thow louye and bileue al thy lyf-tyme.
And yf Kynde Wit carpe here-aʒen or eny kyne thouhtes   f.84ᵇ
Or eretikes with argumentis, thien hoend that thow hem shewe. 110
    For god þat al bygan in bigynnynge of the worlde
Ferde furste as a fuste, and ʒut is, as y leue,
        Mundum pugillo continens,

---

89. be U] X he
92. leue U] X loue

---

88. Baptism through the blood of Jesus Christ (1 John 1:7, 5:6) will begin the cure; participation in the sacrament of the eucharist will complete it (John 6:53–8).
89. *ʒut*: 'moreover'. *be plasterud with patience*: 'be prepared to accept a poultice of patience', alluding to the sacrament of penance (see XXII 310, 359n).
90. *wente neuere man this way*. The way to Jerusalem was closed through original sin.
92. *ʒut bote* is parallel to *ʒut* in 89, with change of person from 3 sg. to 3 pl. in the following clause.
103. *And moest inparfyt*: 'And (consider myself) the most imperfect',
112a. 'Holding the world enclosed in his hand': from the hymn *Quem terra, pontus, sidera*, sung in the service of matins in the office of the Annunciation (Breviary III. 235).

As with a fuste with a fynger yfolde togyderes,
Til hym likede and luste to vnlose that fynger
And profered hit forth as with the paume to what place hit
      sholde.   115
The paume is the pethe of the hand and profereth the fyngeres
To ministre and to make þat myhte of hand knoweth,
And bitokeneth trewly, telle ho-so liketh,
The holy goest of heuene: he is as þe paume.
The fyngres þat fre ben to folde and to cluche   120
Bitokneth soethly the sone þat sente was til erthe,
Touchede and tastede, at techyng of the paume,
Seynte Marie, a mayden, and mankynde lauhte.
    Natus est ex Maria virgine.
The fader is thenne as þe fuste, with fynger and with paume
To huyde and to holde as holy writ telleth: 125
    Omnia traham ad me ipsum.
And þat the fynger gropeth he grypeth bote yf hit greue þe paume.
Thus are they alle bote oen as hit an hand were,
A fuste with a fynger and a fol paume.
And as þe fuste is a ful hand yfolde togyderes,
So is þe fader a fol god, the furste of hem alle;   130
As my fuste is furste ar y my fyngores shewe,
So is he fader and formeour, þe furste of alle thynges,
    Tu fabricator omnium,
And al þe myhte with hym is, was and worth euere.
  The fyngeres is a fol hand, for failed they her thombe,
Portrey ne peynte parfitliche, y leue,   135
Sholde ne wright worche were they awey.
Riht so failed þe sone, the syre be ne myhte
Ne holde ne helpe ne hente þat he louede.
    Dextere dei tu digitus.

113. with² U (withowte *with* owte *deleted*)] X withoute
130. furste U] X fuste (furste *with* r *deleted*)
132. So is P] XUIT And
134. her U] X or
136. wright U] X writ

120. One of the traditional names of Christ is *digitus* (Bartholomaeus I. xxi. 30).
123a. 'He was born of the Virgin Mary': from the Apostles' Creed (Breviary II. 2).
125a. 'I will draw all things to myself' (John 12:32).
132a. 'Thou maker of all things': from the hymn *Jesu salvator saeculi*, sung in the office for compline (Breviary II. 234).
135–6. 'No workman would be able to work (so as to) portray,' etc. The work alluded to is that of the manuscript illuminator and scribe (see XIII 118n).
138a. 'Thou finger of the right hand of god': from the hymn *Veni creator spiritus* (see XXI 210).

The paume is puyrliche the hand and hath power by hymsulue
Oþerwyse then þe writhen fuste or werkmanschupe of fyngres.   140 f.85ᵃ
For þe paume hath power to pulte out þe ioyntes
And to vnfolde þe fust, for hym hit bilongeth,
And receue þat the fyngeres recheth and refuse yf him liketh;
Alle þat þe fyngeres and þe fust feleth and toucheth,
Be he greued with here grype, the holy goost lat falle.   145
And thus is the holy goste god, noyther grettore ne lassore
Then is the syre or the sone and of þe same myhte,
And alle thre is bote o god, as myn hoend and my fyngeres,
Vnfolden or folden, a fuste wyse or elles,
Al is hit bote oen hoend, how-so y turne hit.   150
   Ac ho is herte in the hand euene in þe myddes
He may resceyue riht nauhte, resoun hit sheweth;
For þe fyngeres þat folde sholde and þe fust make
For peyne of þe paume power hem fayleth
To cluche or to clawe, to clippe or to holde.   155
Were þe myddel of myn hand withoute male-ese
In many kyne manere y myhte mysulfe helpe,
Bothe meue and amende, thogh alle my fyngeres oke.
Bi this *simile*,' he saide, 'y se an euydence
That ho-so synegeth in þe seynt spirit assoiled worth he neuere   160
Noþer here ne elleswhere, as y herde telle:
   Qui peccat in spiritum sanctum, etc.
For he priketh god as in his paume that *peccat in spiritum
      sanctum.*
For god the fader is as þe fust, þe sone is as þe fynger,
The holy gost of heuene he is as þe paume.
So ho-so synegeth aȝeyn þe seynt spirit hit semeth þat he
      greueth   165
God þerwith he gripeth and wolde his grace quenche.

---

140. fuste U] X furste
143. him U] X hem
145. Be he P] XUIT Bote he be
163. god U] X so (*altered from* go)

161a. 'Whoever sins [Vg. *blasphemaverit*] against the Holy Spirit (never has forgiveness)' (Mk. 3:29). The Vulgate reading makes it clearer that the unforgivable act is not a sin in the everyday sense, but a deliberate, willed refusal of God's proffered forgiveness, a denial of the power and gift of grace (in penitential literature, associated with *wanhope*: see VI 309, VII 80, and Parson's Tale, *CT* X. 695). The rest of the passus is occupied with the matter.

166. *þerwith*: 'in that place wherewith'. *wolde his grace quenche.* Cf. 1 Thess. 5:19.

For to a torche or to a taper þe trinite is likned,
As wexe and a weke were twyned togyderes
And thenne flaumynge fuyr forth of hem bothe.
And as wex and weke and warm fuyr togyderes   170
Fostren forth a flaume and a feyr lye
That serueth this swynkares to se by a nyhtes,
So doth þe sire and þe sone and seynt spirit togyderes
Fostren forth amonges folke fyn loue and bileue
That alle kyne cristene clanseth of synne.   175 f.85ᵇ
And as thow seest som tyme sodeynliche of a torche
The blase be yblowen out, ȝut brenneth þe weke –
Withouten leye and lihte lith fuyr in þe mache –
So is þe holi gost god and grace withouten mercy
To alle vnkynde creatures þat coueyten to destruye   180
Leel lycame and lyf þat oure lord shupte.
And as glowyng gledes gladeth nat this werkmen
That worchen and waken in wynteres nyhtes
As doth a kix or a candle þat cauht hath fuyr and blaseth,
No more doth þe sire ne þe sone ne seynt spirit togyderes   185
Graunten eny grace ne forgeuenesse of synnes
Til þat the holy goest gynne to glowe and blase.
So þat the holy gost gloweth but as a glede
Til þat loue and bileue leliche to hym blowe,
And thenne flaumeth he as fuyr on fader and on *filius*   190
And melteth myhte into mercy, as we may se a wynter
Isekeles in euesynges thorwe hete of the sonne
Melteth in a mynt-while to myst and to water.
So grace of þe holi gost the grete myhte of þe trinite
Melteth al to mercy to merciable and to non oþere.   195
    And as wex withouten more vpon a warm glede
Wol brennen and blasen, be they togyderes,
And solacen þat mowen nat se sittynge in derkenesse,
So wol þe fader forȝeue folke of mylde hertes
That reufulliche repenten and restitucion make,   200

172. se U] X *om*
184. or U] X ar
185. þe¹ U] X *om*
196. vpon U] X vpo

167. *torche* was a name given to a large wax candle. A similar application of the image of the candle (to the triune nature of Christ) is made in *Legenda Aurea* XXXVII, 164–5, while Bartholomaeus (XIX. lxiii.10) comments on the 'wonderful and most couenable vnite' of the three different elements in the candle.
179. The holy spirit is the hot coal of spiritual life in the individual soul; the soul may live, as the wick (*mache*) may still have fire latent within it when it does not burn, but lives in sin until the hot coal is blown into life as a flame.

In as moche as they mowen amenden and payen;
And yf hit sufficeth nat for asseth þat in suche a will deyeth
Mercy for his mekenesse wol maky good þe remenaunt.
And as þe wyke and warm fuyr wol make a fayre flaume
For to murthe men with þat in merke sitten,   205
So wol Crist of his cortesye, and men crien hym mercy,
Bothe forȝeue and forȝete and ȝut bidde for vs
To þe fader of heuene forȝeuenesse to haue.
　Ac hewe fuyr at a flynt foure hundret wynter,
Bote thow haue trasch to take hit with, tender and broches,   210
Al thy labor is loste and all thy longe trauaile;   f.86ᵃ
For may no fuyr flaume make, faile hit his kynde.
So is þe holy gost god and grace withouten mercy
To alle vnkynde creatures, as Crist hymsulue witnesseth:
　　Amen dico vobis, nescio vos.
Be vnkynde to thyn emcristene and al þat þow canst bidde,   215
Dele and do penaunce day and nyht euere
And purchase al the pardoun of Pampilon and of Rome
And indulgences ynowe, and be *ingratis* to thy kynde,
The holy goest hereth the nat ne helpeth the, be thow certeyne.
For vnkyndenesse quencheth hym þat he can nat shine   220
Ne brenne ne blase clere for blowynge of vnkyndenesse.
Paul the apostel preueth where y lye:
　　Si linguis hominum loquar, etc.
　Forthy beth ywar, ȝe wyse men þat with the world deleth,
That riche ben and resoun knoweth – reule wel ȝoure soules.
Beth nat vnkynde, y conseyle ȝow, to ȝoure emcristene.   225
For mony of ȝow riche men, by my soule y lye nat,

202. asseth T] XU1 asech
208. forȝeuenesse U] X forȝeuesse
210. trasch U] X tasch
218. *ingratis* U] X ingrates

212. *faile hit his kynde*: 'if it lacks its natural element'.
213–14. Cf. 179–80, above.
214a. 'Truly I say to you, I do not know you' (Matt. 25:12, said by the lord to the foolish virgins, whose lamps were unprepared; see I 185n).
217. *pardoun of Pampilon*. Indulgences granted by the bishop of Pamplona for issue by the abbot of Roncesvalles were distributed in England from the notorious daughter-house of St Mary's Rounceval at Charing Cross, the home of Chaucer's Pardoner (see an article by M. W. Bloomfield in *PQ* 35, 1956, 60–68).
222a. 'If I speak in the tongues of men (and angels, but have not love . . .)' (I Cor. 13:1). Cf. I 175–80.

Ʒe brenneth ac ʒe blaseth nat and þat is a blynde bekne.

> *Non omnis qui dicit, Domine, Domine, intrabit in*
> *regnum celorum.*

Minne ʒe nat, riche men, to which a myschaunce
That Diues deyede, and dampned for his vnkyndenesse
Of his mete and his mone to men þat hit nedede?   230
Ʒut wan he nat with wrong ne with queynte sleythes,
But riʒtfulliche, as men rat, al his richesse cam hym,
And on hymsulue, as sayth the boek, sotiled how he myhte
Moste lordliche lyue and ʒut on his lycame werie
Clothes of moest cost, as clerkes bereth witnesse: 235

> *Epulabatur splendide et induebatur bisso.*

And for he was a nygard and a nythynge to the nedfol pore,
For godes tretor he is told for al his trewe catel
And dampned a dwelleth with þe deuel in helle.
And sethe he withoute wyles wan and wel myhte atymye
Lordliche for to lyue and lykyngliche be clothed,   240
And is in helle for al þat, how wol riche nouthe
Excuse hem þat ben vnkynde and ʒut here catell ywonne
With wyles and with luyther wittes, and ʒut wollen nat atymye
To go semeliche ne sitte, seth holy writ techeth   f.86ᵇ
That wykkidliche is wonne to wasten it and make frendis?   245

> *Facite vobis amicos de mammona iniquitatis.*

Vch a riche, y rede, reward herof take
And gyueth ʒoure goed to þat god þat grace of aryseth.
For þat ben vnhynde to hise, hope ʒe noen oþer
Bote they dwelle there Diues is, dayes withouten ende.

Thus is vnkyndenesse þe contrarie þat quencheth, as hit were,   250
The grace of the holy goest, godes owene kynde;
For þat kynde doth, vnkynde fordoth, as this corsede theues,

---

232. rat U] X þat
234. on T] XUI *om*
237. told U] X cald
242. catell U] X *om*
243. wittes I] X whites; U wightes
245. *line supplied from* T; XUI *om*
250. þe contrarie þat B] XUI and; TP kid and
252. *lineation as* U; X *mislineates* fordoth/As

227a. 'Not every one who says, "Lord, Lord", shall enter the kingdom of heaven' (Matt. 7:21).
229. *Diues.* See Luke 16:19–31, and VIII 278, XV 301.
231. The same point is emphasized in *Handlyng Synne* 6730: 'And he ne robbed, ne he ne stalle'.
235a. 'He feasted sumptuously and was clothed in fine linen' (Luke 16:19).
245a. See VIII 235a.
248. *hise*: 'his', i.e. God's (servants).

Vnkynde cristene men, for coueytise and enuye
Sleth a man for his mebles with mouthe or with handes.
For that the holy goest hath to kepe tho harlotes distruyeth,   255
The which is lyf and loue, the leye of mannes body.
For euery manere goed man may be likned to a torche
Or elles to a taper to reuerense with the trinite.
And ho-so morthereth a goed man, me thynketh bi myn inwit,
A fordoth the lihte þat oure lord loketh to haue worschipe of.   260
And ȝut in mo maneres men offenden þe holy gost;
Ac this is the worste wyse þat eny wiht myhte
Synegen aȝen þe seynte spirit – assente to destruye,
For coueytise of eny kyne thynge, þat Crist dere bouhte.
How myhte he aske mercy or eny mercy hym defende   265
That wikkedliche and wilfulliche wolde mercy anyente?
Innocence is next god and nyht and day hit crieth
"Veniaunce! veniaunce! forȝeue be hit neuere
That shent vs and shedde oure bloed, forschupte vs as hit
            semede:
      Vindica sanguinem iustorum!"
Thus "veniaunce! veniaunce!" verray charite asketh;   270
And sethe charite, þat holy churche is, chargeth this so sore
Leue y neuere þat oure lord at þe laste ende
Wol louye þat lyf þat loue and charite destruyeth.'
    'Y pose y hadde syneged so,' quod y, 'and sholde nouthe deye,
And now am y sory þat y so the seynte spirit agulte,   275
Confesse me and crye his grace, god þat al made,
And myldeliche his mercy aske, myhte y nat be saued?'
    'ȝus,' saide þe Samaritaen, 'so thow myhtest repente,
That rihtwisnesse thorw repentaunce to reuthe myhte turne.   f.87ᵃ

---

258. to¹ T] XUI *om*
261. offenden U] X affenden
269a. *Vindica* U] X Vindicta
278. þe U] X þe (*or* þo?) þe

---

255. *that the holy goest hath to kepe.* 'Do you not know that your body is a temple of the
    Holy Ghost, which is within you?' (1 Cor. 6:19).
257–8. For the lineation adopted here, see B XVII 281–2 and Kane-Donaldson 206. L
    presses further here the image of man, corresponding to the Trinity, as a taper or
    torch (cf. 179, above).
264. *þat:* 'what'.
269a. 'Avenge the blood of the just!' (Apoc. 6:10, varied, partly as in the versicle sung
    at matins on Holy Innocents' Day, Breviary I. cccvi).
278. *myhtest* is the important word. It is the capacity of the hardened sinner to repent
    that is in question, not God's willingness to grant forgiveness. Cf. VI 331–8, XII
    70–72; Parson's Tale, *CT* X. 91–4; *Speculum Vitae* 965–72.

Ac hit is bote selde yseyen, there sothnesse bereth witnesse,   280
Eny creature be coupable bifore a kynges iustice,
Be yraunsomed for his repentaunce þer alle resoun hym dampneth.
Ther þat partye pursueth the apeel is so huge
That may no kynge mercy graunte til bothe men acorde,
That eyþer partye haue equitee, as holy writ witnesseth: 285
    Nunquam dimittitur peccatum.
Thus hit fareth bi such folk þat folewen here owene will,
That euele lyuen and leten nat til lif hem forsake;
Som drede of disperacion thenne dryueth awey grace
That mercy in here mynde may nat thenne falle.
For goed hope, that helpe thenne scholde, to wanhope þer
    turneth,
                                       290
And nat of þe nownpower of god þat he ne is ful of myhte
To amende al þat amys is, and his mercy grettore
Thenne al oure wikkede werkes, as holy writ telleth:
    Misericordia eius super omnia opera eius.
Ac ar his rihtwisnesse to reuthe turne, restitucion hit maketh,
As sorwe of herte is satisfaccioun for suche þat may nat paye.   295
  Ac thre thynges ther ben þat doth a man to sterte
Out of his oune house, as holy writ sheweth:
That is a wikkede wyf þat wol nat be chasted –
Here fere fleeth here for fere of here tonge;
And if his hous be vnheled and reyne on his bedde   300
A seketh and seketh til he slepe druye;
Ac when smoke and smolder smyt in his yes
Hit doth him worse þen his wif or wete to slepe,
For þorgh smoke and smolder smerteth his sihte
Til he be bler-eyede or blynde and þe borre in his throte,   305

---

283. Ther U] X The
287. til U] X to. lif B] XUITP *om*
287–8 forsake/Som drede XUI] TP forsake synne/Dred
288. awey P] XUIT *om*
294. his U] X this. restitucion U] X restuticon
299. fere[1] U] X fore
302–4. smyt . . . smolder U] X *om*

---

283. *þat partye,* i.e. *resoun,* acting as the plaintiff.
285a. See VI 257a.
291. *And nat of þe nownpower of god*: 'And not because of [i.e. and this has nothing to do with] any lack of power on God's part'.
293a. See XII 72a.
295. *satisfaccioun.* See VI 6n, XVI 31.
297. *as holy writ sheweth.* The illustrative saying that follows is proverbial (Whiting T 187; it occurs in the Wife of Bath's Prologue, *CT* III, 280, and Melibeus, *CT* VII. 1086), but ultimately indebted to Prov. 27:15, with Prov. 10:26, 19:13.
303. *to slepe* is constructed with *doth him worse.*

Coueth and corseth þat Crist ȝeue hym sorwe
That sholde brynge in bettere wode or blowen hit til hit brente.
  Thise thre that y telle of thus ben to vnderstande:
The wyf is oure wikkede flesche, wol nat be chasted
For kynde cleueth on hym euere to contrarie þe soule,   310
And thogh he falle he fynte skiles þat freelete hit made,
And þat is lihtliche forȝeue and forȝete bothe
To man þat mercy asketh and amende thenketh.
The rayne þat rayneth þere we reste sholde
Been seeknesses and oþere sorwes þat we soffren ouhte,   315 f.87ᵇ
As Paul þe apostel in his episteles techeth:
    Virtus in infirmitate perficitur.
And thogh that men make moche deul in here anger
And be inpacient in here penaunces, puyr resoun knoweth
That they haen cause to contrarien bi kynde of here seknesses,
And lihtliche oure lord at here lyues ende   320
Haeth mercy on suche men þat euele may soffre.
Ac þe smoke and þe smolder þat smyt in oure yes,
That is coueytise and vnkyndenesse whiche quencheth godes mercy;
For vnkyndenesse is þe contrarie of alle kyne resoun.
For þer ne is sike ne sory ne non so moche wrecche   325
That he ne may louye, and hym lyke, and lene of his herte
Goed wil, goed word bothe, wischen and wilnen
Alle manere men mercy and forȝeuenesse,
And louye hym yliche hymsulue, that his lyf amende.
  Y may no lengore lette,' quod he, and lyard a prikede   330
And wente away as wynd, and þerwith y awakede.

---

308. to T] XUI *om*
311. þat U] X þat that
329. his lyf] XUIT is lyue and; P hus lyf

311. *freelete hit made.* For a reprehensible use of a similar argument, see III 59–62.
316a. '(My) power is made perfect in weakness' (2 Cor. 12:9), God's words to Paul
    when he complains to him of his bodily infirmity.

Passus XX

The Crucifixion and the Harrowing of Hell

Passus tercius de dobet

Wollewaerd and watschoed wente y forth aftur
As a recheles renk þat recheth nat of sorwe,
And ȝede forth ylike a lorel al my lyf-tyme
Til y waxe wery of the world and wilnede eefte to slepe
And lened me to lenten and long tyme y slepte.   5
  Of gurles and of *gloria laus* greetliche me dremede
And how *osanna* by orgene oelde folke songe.
Oen semblable to þe Samaritaen and somdeel to Pers þe plouhman
Barfoet on an asse bake boetles cam prikynge
Withouten spores oþer spere – sprakeliche he lokede,   10
As is þe kynde of a knyhte þat cometh to be dobbet,
To geten here gult spores and galoches ycouped.

---

1. *Wollewaerd and watschoed*: 'Wearing a garment of rough wool next to the skin [as a form of penance] and with shoes full of water'. Cf. Prol. 2, X 1, XV 3, XXI 2.

5. *to lenten*: 'until Lent'. Cf. XVIII 182. The sixth vision begins here.

6. *gloria laus*: 'glory, praise', the chorus of the processional hymn on Palm Sunday (Missale 260), sung here by *gurles* ('children', in allusion to Matt. 21:15) as if welcoming Christ as king and redeemer to Jerusalem. Much of the opening of this passus is inspired by the liturgy for Holy Week.

7. *osanna*: 'Hosanna', lit. 'Be our saviour, we pray', was shouted by the faithful as Christ entered Jerusalem (Matt. 21:9), and sung repeatedly in the antiphons preceding the processional hymn on Palm Sunday. *by orgene*: not 'to the organ', but 'in *organum*', for which a rough equivalent might be 'in concert'.

11. The imagery of knighting ceremonies prepares for the representation of Jesus's combat with the devil (see below, 27n) as a 'joust' (see XVIII 186n, and 21, 26, below), which is related to the conception of Christ as the 'lover-knight' who does deeds of great prowess and courtesy for his beloved, the human soul (e.g. *Ancrene Wisse*, ed. Shepherd, 21, and see Woolf, 1968, 44–55), but which, since the courtly motive is not at all stressed by L, has more to do with the patristic and liturgical image of Christ the 'warrior-knight' (see R. St-Jacques in *Revue de l'Univ. d'Ottawa* 37, 1967, 146–58).

12. Gilt spurs are a traditional item in the newly-dubbed knight's accoutrements; the *galoches ycouped*, or cut-away shoes, seem to be an allusion to contemporary upper-class fashion – though *gallochis* are specifically associated with the open sandals recommended to the apostles (Mk. 6:9) in *Dives et Pauper* 93.

And thenne was Faith in a fenestre and criede 'A, *filii Dauid*!'
As doth an heraud of armes when auntrous cometh to ioustes.
Olde Iewes of Ierusalem for ioye they songen,   15
    Benedictus qui venit in nomine domini.
  Thenne y afraynede at Fayth what al þat fare bymente,
And ho sholde iouste in Ierusalem? 'Iesus,' he saide,   f.88ᵃ
'And feche þat þe fende claymeth, Pers fruyt þe plouhman.'
  'Is Peres in this place?' quod y, and he prente on me:
'*Liberum-dei-arbitrium* for loue hath vndertake   20
That this Iesus of his gentrice shal iouste in Pers armes,
In his helm and in his haberion, *humana natura*;
That Crist be nat yknowe for *consummatus deus*,
In Pers plates the plouhman this prikiare shal ryde,
For no dount shal hym dere as *in deitate patris*.'   25
  'Who shal iouste with Iesus,' quod y, 'Iewes, or scribz?'
  'Nay,' quod Faith, 'bote the fende, and Fals-doem-to-deye.

---

14. auntrous T] XUIP auntres
25. dount] X doiunt

---

13. *Faith.* It is apt that Faith, the true adherent of the old Law, represented above by Abraham (XVIII 183n), should welcome Jesus with the title of his royal Jewish inheritance. Cf. 'Hosanna to the son of David' (Matt. 21:9).

14. *heraud of armes.* See XVIII 186.

15a. 'Blessed is he who comes in the name of the lord' (Matt. 21:9, but also repeated in the antiphons for Palm Sunday, Breviary I. dcclx).

18. *Pers fruyt þe plouhman*: 'the fruit of Peres Plouhman', i.e. the apples of the Tree of Charity, which have fallen and been seized by the devil (XVIII 112). In C, the tree was looked after by Free Will (XVIII 28), but in B by Piers Plowman (XVIII 8n), whence this reference.

20. *Liberum-dei-arbitrium*: 'the free will of God'. Cf. XVIII 119.

21. *of his gentrice*: 'In accordance with his noble birth'. *in Pers armes*: 'in the coat-armour of Peres' (cf. XVIII 187, and 11n, above), i.e. the flesh. Piers Plowman is clearly seen for a moment as God incarnate, in his manhood (i.e. Jesus, traditionally distinguished by name in this way from Christ, who represented the union of manhood and godhead, the second person of the Trinity; see XXI 14n and Troyer, 1932, 370). To say that Peres 'is' Christ would do scant justice to this subtle and creative handling of the mystery of the Incarnation.

23. *consummatus deus*: 'supreme god'. There is an allusion here to the doctrine of the impassibility of the godhead, i.e. the insusceptibility to injury or suffering of God in his divine nature, which makes the Incarnation necessary.

25. *in deitate patris*: 'in his divine nature as the Father'.

27. *Fals-doem-to-deye*: 'the false judgment of death upon mankind'. The idea of the Crucifixion as a combat between Death and Life is familiar from Heb. 2:14–15 and from the sequence *Victimae Paschali laudes* sung on Easter Sunday (Missale 377), which has the lines: *Mors et vita duello conflixere mirando; dux vitae mortuus, regnat vivus* ('Death and life have met in wondrous conflict; the champion of life is dead, yet lives to reign'). It is the theme of the fine 15th c. alliterative poem *Death and Life* (ed. I. Gollancz, Select Early English Poems, no. V, 1930), which is much influenced by Langland.

Deth saith a wol fordo and adown brynge
Alle þat lyueth or loketh, a londe or a watre.
Lyf saith þat a lyeth and hath leide his lyf to wedde,   30
That for al þat Deth can do, withynne thre dayes to walke
And feche fro þe fende Peres fruyt þe plouhman,
And legge hit þere hym liketh and Lucifer bynde
And forbete adown and brynge bale deth for euere.
    O mors, mors tua ero, morsus!'
Thenne cam Pilatus with moche peple, *sedens pro tribunali*,   35
To se how douhtyliche Deth sholde do, and demen þer beyre rihte.
The Iewes and þe iustices aȝeyns Iesus þey were,
And alle þe court cryede '*Crucifige!*' loude.
Thenne potte hym forth a pelour bifore Pilatus and saide:
'This Iesu of oure Iewene temple iaped and despised,   40
To fordoen hit on a day, and in thre dayes aftur
Edefien hit eft newe – here he stant þat saide hit –
And ȝut maken hit as moche in alle manere poyntes,
Bothe as longe and as large, a loofte and o grounde,
And as wyde as hit euer was; this we witnesseth alle.'   45
  '*Crucifige!*' quod a cachepol, 'he can of wycchecrafte.'
'*Tolle, tolle!*' quod another, and toek of kene thornes
And bigan of grene thorn a garlond to make
And sette hit sore on his heued, and sethe saide in enuye,
'*Aue, raby*,' quod þat ribaud, and redes shotte vp to his yes;   50

---

34. brynge U] X beynge

34. 'And thoroughly beat down (death [*bale*]) and bring death (*bale*) death for ever'.
34a. 'O death, I will be thy death! (O hell, I will be thy) destruction!' (Hos. 13:14, alluded to in 1 Cor. 15:55, and sung as an antiphon on Holy Saturday: Breviary, I. dccci).
35. *sedens pro tribunali*: 'sitting in the judgment seat' (Matt. 27:19).
36. *demen þer beyre rihte*: 'judge the right of both of them (to victory)'. *beyre* is gen. pl., 'of both'.
39. See Matt. 26:61. The account of the Passion is taken chiefly from Matthew, with additions from the other gospels and from Nicodemus, and no doubt some detail from representations in the visual arts and in the mystery plays.
46. *he can of wycche-crafte*. Cf. Nicodemus 1, 2 (*Gesta Pilati*, cap. I, in Tischendorf, p.338: see VI 320n).
47. *Tolle*: 'Away with him' (John 19:15).
50. *Aue, raby*: 'Hail, master', as in XVIII 169. Cf. Matt. 27:29. *redes shotte vp to his yes*: 'thrust sharp reeds at his eyes'. In the gospel account, a reed is first given to Christ as a mock-sceptre and then used to strike him (Matt. 27:29–30). Details such as this (perhaps suggested by Isa. 42:19) are L's only concession to the image of the suffering humanity of Christ, and the emotional identification with that humanity characteristic of 14th c. spirituality. For Langland, Christ is Pantocrator, lord of life and conqueror of death.

And nayled hym with thre nayles naked vpon a rode
And, with a pole, poysen potten vp to his lippes   f.88ᵇ
And beden hym drynke, his deth to lette and his dayes lenghe,
And saiden, 'Yf he sotil be, hymsulue now he wol helpe;'
And 'Yf thow be Crist – and Crist, godes sone –   55
Come adoun of this rode and thenne shal we leue
That Lyf þe loueth and wol nat late the deye.'
   '*Consummatum est*,' quod Crist, and comsed for to swoene.
Pitousliche and pale, as prisoun þat deyeth,
The lord of lyf and of liht tho leyde his eyes togederes.   60
The daye for drede þerof withdrouh and derke bicam þe sonne;
The wal of the temple to-cleyef euene al to peces,
The hard roch al to-roef, and riht derk nyht hit semede.
The erthe to-quasche and quoek as hit quyk were
And dede men for þat dene cam oute of depe graues   65
And tolde why þe tempest so longe tyme durede:
'For a bittur bataile,' þe ded bodye saide;
'Lyf and Deth, in this derkenesse here oen fordoth her oþer,
Ac shal no wyht wyte witturlich ho shal haue þe maistry
Ar a Soneday, aboute the sonne-rysynge,' and sank with þat
      til erthe.   70
Somme saide he was godes sone þat so fayre deyede,
      Vere filius dei erat iste,
And somme saide, 'He can of soercerie; goed is þat we assaie
Wher he be ded or nat ded, down or he be taken.'
   Two theues tho tholed deth þat tyme
Vppon cros bisyde Crist, so was þe comune lawe.   75
A cachepol cam and craked a-to her legges
And here armes aftur, of euereche of tho theues.

67–9. *lineation as* U; X *mislineates*
74. Two U] X Tho
76. cam and U] X of tho theues cam a
77. armes U] X arme

---

53. *his deth to lette and his dayes lenghe.* L introduces this idea (directly contrary to the sense of the corresponding line in B) perhaps as a macabre joke on the part of the tormentors, though there may be some allusion to the role of the tormentors as instruments of the devil, who is trying at this point to prevent Christ dying (see 335, below).

55–7. These three lines, as the alliteration suggests, represent an expansion, probably scribal, of two lines in B XVIII 55–6. They appear thus in all MSS of C.

58. *Consummatum est*: 'It is finished' (John 19:30), i.e. the work of redemption is complete.

65–70. From Matt. 27:52–3, as expanded in Nicodemus.

68. *here . . . her*, pronominal gen. pl., 'of them'.

71a. 'Truly this was the son of God' (Matt. 27:54).

Ac was no boie so bold godes body to touche;
For he was knyht and kynges sone, Kynde forȝaf þat tyme
That hadde no boie hardynesse hym to touche in deynge.   80
   Ac þer cam forth a blynde knyhte with a kene spere ygrounde,
Hihte Longius, as þe lettre telleth, and longe hadde lore his
     sihte;
Bifore Pilatus and oþere peple in þe place he houed.
Maugre his mony teth he was mad þat tyme
Iouste with Iesus, this blynde Iewe Longius;   85
For alle were they vnhardy þat houed þer or stode
To touche hym or to trinen hym or to taken hym down and
     grauen hym,
Bote this blynde bacheler, that bar hym thorw the herte.   f.89ᵃ
The bloed sprang down by the spere and vnspered the knyhte yes;
Tho ful the knyhte vppon knees and criede Iesu mercy –   90
'Aȝeyn my will hit was,' quod he, 'þat y ȝow wounde made!'
And syhed and saide, 'Sore hit me forthenketh;
Of þe dede þat y haue do y do me in ȝoure grace.
Bothe my lond and my licame at ȝoure likynge taketh hit,
And haue mercy on me, riȝtfol Iesu!' and riht with þat a wepte.   95
   Thenne gan Faith fouely þe false Iewes to dispice,
Calde hem caytyues, acorsed for euere:
'For þis was a vyl vilanye; vengeaunce ȝow bifall
That made þe blynde bete the dede – this was a boyes dede!
Corsede caytifues! knyhthoed was hit neuere   100

82, 85. Longius U] X Longies
87. trinen U] X turnen (*over erasure*)
99. *Skeat adds here a line from MS M*

79. *Kynde forȝaf*: 'Nature (i.e. God) granted'.
82. *Longius.* The name Longinus (Longeus) is given in Nicodemus 16 (*Gesta Pilati*, cap. XVI, in Tischendorf, p.387) to the soldier of John 19:34, from the suggestion of the Greek word for 'lance', *longe*, in the verse of John. The story of his blindness, healing and conversion is a later accretion, and appears in the *Legenda Aurea* XLVII; it is derived from the prophecy of Zech. 12:10 alluded to in John 19:37. The representation of Longinus as a Jew (85), rather than the Roman centurion of tradition, demonstrates that an individual Jew received sight (i.e. was converted) at the very moment that the Synagogue (i.e. Jewry, represented in medieval art as a blindfolded female figure) received the blindfold (Ames, 1970, 125–6).
83. *houed*: 'waited in readiness', a term used in descriptions of tournaments in romances.
94. Longinus behaves like a knight defeated in battle (cf. 83, 85, above), yielding himself to his victorious opponent (cf. 103–4, below); but the yielding of his *lond and licame* to Christ is also, of course, symbolic of conversion.
96. Faith again plays the part of the herald (XVIII 186), declaring the outcome of the battle.

To bete a body ybounde, with eny briht wypene.
The gre ȝut hath he geten for al his grete woundes,
For ȝoure chaumpioun chiualer, chief knyht of ȝow alle,
Ȝelde hym recreaunt remyng, riht at Iesu wille.
For be this derkenesse ydo, Deth worth yvenkused,   105
And ȝe, lordeyns, haen lost, for Lyf shal haue maistrie,
And ȝoure franchise þat fre was yfallen is into thraldoem,
And alle ȝoure childerne, cherles, cheue shall neuere,
Ne haue lordschipe in londe ne no londe tulye,
And as bareyne be, and by vsure libbe,   110
The which is lif þat oure lord in all lawes defendeth.
Now ben ȝoure gode dayes ydoen, as Daniel of ȝow telleth,
When Crist thorw croos ouercam, ȝoure kyndoem sholde to-cleue.
    Cum veniat sanctus sanctorum, cessat, etc.'
  What for fere of this ferly and of þe false Iewes
Y withdrow in þat derkenesse to *descendit ad inferna*,   115
And there y seyh sothly, *secundum scripturas*,

---

104. recreaunt T] XUI creaunt.
106. lordeyns U] X lordeyne

105. *be this derkenesse ydo*: 'when this darkness is passed'. The darkness is that of line 61, above. Services in these three days were often held in darkness, *in tenebris* (Breviary I. dcclxxxii).

109. *lordschipe in londe*. Jews were prohibited by law in Christian countries from owning land, which is one reason why they had to turn to moneylending as a profession. Cf. XII 109, XXI 34.

113a. 'When the holy of holies comes, (your anointing) ceases'. This prophecy (usually with verbs *venerit, cessabit*) is derived from Dan. 9:24–7, though the wording is from the pseudo-Augustinian sermon *Contra Judaeos* (*PL* 42:1124) as used in one of the lessons for the fourth Sunday in Advent (Breviary, I. cxxxvii). It alludes to the new law of Christ's cross which supersedes the kingdom of the old law, and is symbolized in the tearing of the curtain of the temple (which veiled the *sanctus sanctorum* of the old law: Ex. 26:33) at the moment of Christ's death (Matt. 27:51).

115. *descendit ad inferna*: 'he descended into hell' (from the Apostles' Creed: see XVII 318n).

116. *secundum scripturas*: 'according to the scriptures' (from the Nicene Creed, Breviary II. 483). The scriptural source for the debate of the Four Daughters of God, which follows, is Ps. 84:11 (see 467a, below). The debate was frequently elaborated in the Middle Ages, providing as it did an effective allegorical means of dramatizing and explaining the reconciliation of the old law and the new law in the doctrine of the Atonement. The treatment in the *Castle of Love* (see 309n, below, VII 232n, and Sajavaara, 1967, 62–90) is an example which may have influenced Langland. On the subject generally, see Owst, 1933, 90–92; Hope Traver, *The Four Daughters of God*, Bryn Mawr College Monographs VI, 1907 (also in *PMLA* 40, 1925, 44–92). It is unusual for the debate to be placed at this point in the Christian story, between the Passion and the Harrowing of Hell.

Out of þe west, as it were, a wenche, as me thouhte,
Cam walkynge in þe way, to hellward she lokede.
Mercy hihte þat mayde, a mylde thynge with-alle
And a ful benyngne buyrde and buxum of speche. 120
Here suster, as hit semede, cam softly walkynge
Euene oute of þe eest, and westward she thouhte,
A comely creature and a clene, Treuthe she hihte; f.89^b
For þe vertue þat her folewede, afered was she neuere.
When this maydones metten, Mercy and Treuthe, 125
Ayþer asked oþer of this grete wonder,
Of the dene and the derknesse and how þe day roued,
And which a lihte and a leem lay bifore helle.
    'Y haue ferly of this fare, in faith,' seide Treuthe,
'And am wendynge to wyte what þis wonder meneth.' 130
    'Haue no merueyle þerof,' quod Mercy, 'murthe hit bitokneth.
A mayde þat hoteth Marie, and moder withouten velynge
Of eny kynde creature, conceyued thorw speche
And grace of the holy gost, wax grete with childe,
Withouten wommane wem into this world brouhte hym; 135
And þat my tale is trewe y take god to witnesse.
Sethe this barn was ybore ben thritty wynter ypassed,
Deyede and deth tholede this day aboute mydday;
And þat is þe cause of this clips þat overcloseth now þe sonne,
In menynge þat man shal fro merkenesse be ydrawe 140
The while this lihte and this lowe shal Lucifer ablende.
For patriarkes and prophetes haen preched herof ofte,
That was tynt thorw tre, tre shal hit wynne,
And þat deth down brouhte, deth shal releue.'

132. and U] X a

117. *Out of þe west.* The four daughters come from the four poles (see 122, 167, 170), in allusion to Isa. 43:5–6, and the two pairs (of Ps. 84:11) from opposite poles. There is no clear symbolic significance in this of the kind suggested for Prol. 14, 16, I 110a, though the two more austere figures do come from the colder quarters.

143–4. 'What was lost through the tree (of Knowledge), the tree (of the Cross) shall win back, and those that death cast down, (Christ's) death shall lift up again'. These lines echo lines (e.g. *Ipse lignum tunc notavit,/Damna ligni ut solveret*) from a famous hymn, *Pange lingua gloriosi/Lauream certaminis* (not to be confused with the hymn of XVII 121n), sung on Passion Sunday (Breviary I. dccxvii) and in the office of the Veneration of the Cross on Good Friday (Breviary III. 276). The same idea was developed in a different way in the legends of the Holy Rood (XVIII 25n), according to which the wood for the Cross was taken from trees which had grown from *kirnels* from the tree of Knowledge, fetched by Seth from paradise and 'planted' under Adam's tongue after his death.

'That thow tellest,' quod Treuthe, 'is bote a tale of Walterot!   145
For Adam and Eue and Abraham with oþere
Patriarkes and prophetes þat in peyne liggen,
Leue hit neuere that ӡone liht hem alofte brynge
Ne haue hem out of helle – holde thy tonge, Mercy!
Hit is bote truyfle þat thow tellest; y, Treuthe, woet þe sothe,   150
That thyng þat ones is in helle out cometh hit neuere.
Iob þe parfit patriarke repreueth thy sawes:
    Quia in inferno nulla est redempcio.'
  Thenne Mercy fol myldely mouthed this wordes:
'Thorw experiense,' quod she, 'y hope they shal ben saued;
For venym fordoth venym, þer feche y euydence   155
That Adam and Eue haue shullen bote.
For of alle fretynge venymes the vilest is the scorpioun;
May no medecyne amende the place there he styngeth   f.90ᵃ
Til he be ded and do þerto, and thenne he destruyeth
The verste venemouste thorw vertu of hymsulue.   160
And so shal this deth fordo, y dar my lyf legge,
Al þat Deth and þe deuel dede formost to Eue.
And riht as the gylour thorw gyle bigiled man formost,
So shal grace, þat bigan al, maken a goed ende
And bigile þe gilour, and þat is a goed sleythe: 165
    Ars vt artem falleret.'
  'Now soffre we,' saide Treuthe; 'y se, as me thynketh,
Out of þe nype of þe north, nat ful fer hennes,

---

152. Iob U] X Iop
154. she] XUIT·he; P heo
159. be ded and do B] XUIT ded ydo; P be ded ydo

---

145. *a tale of Walterot*: 'a far-fetched tale, an idle tale of no significance'. The usual form is *trotevale* (OED): see Skeat's note.
152a. 'For there is no release from hell': a response in the Office of the Dead (Breviary II. 278), originally suggested by Job 7:9, and widely quoted, e.g. *Prick of Conscience* 2833, 7249, *Parl. of the Thre Ages* 642. But there were of course two regions of 'hell': the region of those who were damned for ever through sin or misbelief, and the other region, limbo (*Vices and Virtues* 7–8). This will answer Truth's immediate objection, since she speaks in OT terms and knows nothing of the time of grace. But for those who have sinned in the time of grace and been consigned to hell at the particular judgment, things will be more difficult: L has his answer, later (420, below).
159. *do*: 'applied'. Bartholomaeus, in his encyclopaedia (VII. 68 and XVIII. 98), describes how this is done.
163–5. The word-play here (cf. 326–7, 382, 392, below) is proverbial. See Whiting G 491, and cf. Reeve's Tale, *CT* I. 4321; Gower, *Conf. Am.* VI. 1379–81.
165a. 'One cunning stratagem in order to deceive another' (from the same hymn as in 143n, above). For the 'stratagem', see 327, below.
166. *Now soffre we*: 'Now let us be patient and quiet'.

Rihtwisnesse come rennynge. Reste we the while,
For she woet more then we – she was ar we bothe.'
'That is soth,' saide Mercy, 'and y se here bi southe   170
Where cometh Pees pleiynge, in pacience yclothed;
Loue hath coueyted here longe – leue y non oþere
Bote Loue haue ysente her som lettre what this liht bymeneth
That ouerhoueth helle thus; she vs shal telle.'
    Whenne Pees, in pacience yclothed, aproched her ayþer oþer,   175
Rihtwisnesse reuerenced Pees in here rich clothyng
And preyede Pees to tellen hire to what place she sholde
And in here gay garnementes wham she gladie thouhte?
    'My wil is to wende,' quod Pees, 'and welcomen hem alle
That many day myhte y nat se for merkenesse of synne,   180
Adam and Eue and other mo in helle.
Moises and many moo mery shal synge
And y shal daunse þerto – do thow so, sustur!
For Iesus ioustede wel, ioy bigynneth dawe.
     Ad vesperum demorabitur fletus, et ad matutinum leticia.
Loue, þat is my lemman, such lettres he me sente   185
That Mercy, my sustur, and y mankynde shal saue,
And þat god hath forgyue and graunted to alle mankynde,
Mercy, my suster, and me to maynprisen hem alle;
And þat Crist hath conuerted the kynde of rihtwisnesse
Into pees and pyte, of his puyr grace.   190
Loo, here þe patente!' quod Pees, '*in pace in idipsum* –
And that this dede shal duyre – *dormiam et requiescam.*'   f.90^b
    'Rauest thow?' quod Rihtwisnesse, 'or thow art riht dronke!
Leuest thow þat ȝone lihte vnlouke myhte helle
And saue mannes soule? suster, wene hit neuere!   195
At the bigynnynge of the world, god gaf the doem hymsulue
That Adam and Eue and al his issue

169. she, she] XUIT he; P hue; *so in 174*
177. hire U] X *om*
178. in P] XUIT *om*
182. mery B] XUITP mercy
188. my suster U] X *om*

177. *she sholde*: 'she was going'.
184a. 'In the evening weeping shall have place, and in the morning gladness' (Ps. 29:6).
187. *forgyue*: 'fully granted' (as in 79, above); 'give and grant' is a legal phrase (MED, s.v. *graunten*, v. 4a).
191–2. 'Look, here is the letter of open authorization [cf. XIX 7n, 12]: "In peace in the selfsame" – and to prove that the deed of gift is permanently binding – "I will sleep and rest secure"' (Ps. 4:9). This psalm was sung in matins on Holy Saturday, with this verse divided thus as versicle and response (Breviary I. dccxcv).
197–8. Cf. XVIII 113. *Rihtwisnesse* (Justice), like Truth, represents and supports the old law.

Sholde deye down-riht and dwellen in payne euere
Yf that thei touched þat tre and of þe fruyt eten.
Adam afturward, aȝenes his defense,   200
Freet of the fruyt and forsoke, as hit were,
The loue of oure lord and his lore bothe,
And folewede þat þe fend tauhte and his flesch will,
Aȝeynes resoun; y, Rihtwysnesse, recorde hit with treuthe
That her peyne is perpetuel – no preyer may hem helpe.   205
Forthy let hem chewe as they chose and chyde we nat, sustres,
For hit is boteles bale, the byte that they eten.'
   'And y shal preue,' quod Pees, 'here payne moet haue ende,
And þat her wo into wele moet wende at þe laste.
For hadde they wist of no wo, wele hadde thay nat knowen;   210
For no wiht woet what wele is þat neuere wo soffrede,
Ne what is hoet hunger þat hadde neuere defaute.
Ho couthe kyndeliche with colour descreve
Yf all þe world were whit or swan-whit all thynges?
Yf no nyht ne were, no man, y leue,   215
Sholde ywyte witterly what day is to mene;
Ne hadde god ysoffred of som oþer then hymsulue,
He hadde nat wist witterly where deth were sour or swete.
For sholde neuere riȝt riche man, þat lyueth in rest and in hele,
Ywyte what wo is, ne were þe deth of kynde.   220
So god, þat bigan al, of his gode wille

---

198. dwellen U] X down
199. touched U] X touchen
206. let T] XUI *om.*   chewe T] XUI cheue
208. preue B] XUITP preye
213. with T] XUI whit

---

210. The argument is perhaps inspired by the paradox of the *felix culpa* (VII 127n); also by John 16:21–2. Cf. *Roman de la Rose* 21537–8: 'N'onc nus ne sot quel chose est ese/S'il n'ot avant apris mesese'. The need for contrast is one of Bradwardine's explanations of the existence of sin in the world (see Leff, 1957, 59–60, and VII 269n).
217. *of*: 'at the hands of'. The argument of lines 217–18 owes some debt to Heb. 2:9. However theologically naive it may seem, and however simply supported by arguments for experience defined 'by contraries' (cf. Boethius, *De Cons. Phil.*, IV, pr. 2.2–3; *Roman de la Rose* 21532–52; *Troilus and Criseyde* i.637–44; Lydgate's *Temple of Glass* 1250–56 and the edition thereof by J. Norton-Smith, Oxford, 1966, p. 177), this is an important (and unusual) positive view of the Incarnation – that God became man in order to share fully in man's humanity – to set beside the strategy of duplicity (see 165, above, and 327, below).
220. *ne were þe deth of kynde*: 'if there were no natural death'.

Bycam man of a mayde, mankynde to saue,
And soffred to be sold to se þe sorwe of deynge,
The which vnknytteth alle care and comsyng is of reste.
For til moreyne mete with vs, y may hit wel avowe, 225
Ne woet no wyht, as y wene, what is ynow to mene.
　Forthy god of his goednesse þe furste gom Adam
Sette hym in solace furste and in souereyne merthe; f.91ᵃ
And sethe he soffrede hym to synne, sorwe to fele,
To wyte what wele was ther-thorw, kyndeliche to knowe. 230
And aftur, god auntred hymsulue and toek Adames kynde
To wyte what he hath soffred in thre sundry places,
Bothe in heuene and in erthe – and now to helle he thenketh,
To wyte what al wo is, þat woet of alle ioye.
　　Omnia probate; quod bonum est tenete.
So hit shal fare bi this folk: here folye and here synne 235
Shal lere hem what loue is and lisse withouten ende.
For woet no wiht what werre is þer as pees regneth
Ne what is witterliche wele til wel-a-way hym teche.'
　Thenne was ther a wihte with two brode yes;
Boek hihte þat beau-pere, a bolde man of speche. 240
'By godes body,' quod this Boek, 'y wole bere witnesse,
Tho þat this barn was ybore þer blased a sterre
That alle þe wyse of the world in o wit acordede
That such a barn was ybore in Bethleem þe citee
That mannes soule sholde saue and synne distruye. 245

---

227. gom T] XUI man
230. was U] X wat (*marked for correction*)
239. was U] X wast
241. bere I] XU here
242. þer blased U] X þat blased as

224. Though speaking of the 'sorrow of dying', Pees alludes momentarily to a different view of death, stoical or post-redemptive, as 'an ende of every worldly soore' (Knight's Tale, *CT* I. 2849).
226. *what is ynow to mene*: 'what is the meaning of "enough" '.
234a. See III 488n.
239. *two brode yes*, i.e. the two Testaments (and the two Laws), or perhaps the power of seeing both literal and spiritual truth. The debate is wound up with Scripture's evidence of the divinity of Jesus Christ, based, as he says, on the witness of the elements: air (247), water (251), fire (254) and earth (256). L follows here a well-known homily of Gregory on Matt. 2:1–12, delivered at Epiphany (Breviary I. cccxxv: see R. E. Kaske in *Anglia* 77, 1959, 117–44, and Kaske, 1960, 35–40). His introduction of 'Book', at the very moment when the Old Law and Testament are to be shown crowned in the New, dramatizes the unity of the truth of the bible's testimony, both literal and spiritual.

And all þe elementis,' quod the Boek, 'hereof bereth witnesse.
That he was god þat al wrouhte the welkene furste shewede:
Tho þat weren in heuene token *stella comàta*
And tenden hit as a torche to reuerensen his burthe;
The lihte folewede þe lord into þe lowe erthe.   250
The water witnesseth þat he was god, for a wente on hym druye:
Peter þe apostel parseyued his gate
And as he wente on þe watur wel hym knewe, and saide,
     "*Domine, iube me venire ad te.*"
And lo, how þe sonne gan louke here lihte in heresulue
When she sye hym soffre, þat sonne and se made!   255
Lo, þe erthe for heuynesse þat he wolde soffre
Quakid as a quyk thyng and also to-quasch þe roches!
Loo, helle myhte nat holde, bote opened tho god tholede
And lette out Symondes sones to sen hym honge on rode.
     Non visurum se mortem.
And now shal Lucifer leue hit, thogh hym loeth thynk;   260

---

253. *Skeat adds here a line from MS F*
255. she B] XUITP he
260. hit U] X lihte

248. *stella comata*: 'a star trailing fire (lit. long-haired)', i.e. a 'comet'. This was the usual interpretation of the star of Matt. 2 (Alford 397). 'For þis stere was no fix stere in heven, noþur no planete, as is mevynge shewed well, but it was a comete, *stella comata*, new made by þe myghty powre of almyȝthy God' (Sermons, ed. Ross, 227).

253a. 'Lord, bid me come to you (on the waters)' (Matt. 14:28).

254. Luke 23:45, Matt. 27:45.

257. Matt. 27:51.

259. *Symondes sones*. In the gospel of Nicodemus (*Descensus Christi ad Inferos*), the two sons of Simeon (the 'just and devout man' of Luke 2:25) are released from death and hell by Christ (Nicod. 17; *Descensus*, cap. I, in Tischendorf, p. 390). They give an eye-witness account of Christ's descent into hell to release the souls of the righteous (the 'Harrowing of Hell'); this account is the substance of the *Descensus*, which forms the second part of the apocryphal gospel of Nicodemus (see VI 320n), a composite narrative deriving from the 4th c. and attributed in the 12th c. to the Nicodemus mentioned in John 19:39 as Joseph of Arimathea's helper. It was regarded in the Middle Ages as an important supplement to the Passion narrative, and was extensively drawn upon for the powerful representations of the Harrowing of Hell in the mystery plays, which may have influenced Langland. See also VII 134a. L has also used the very widely known version of the story in *Legenda Aurea* LIV.

259a. 'He should not see death' (before he had seen Christ), the promise made to Simeon in Luke 2:25.

For Iesus as a geaunt with a gyn cometh ȝende   f.91ᵇ
To breke and to bete adoun all þat ben agaynes hym
And to haue out of helle alle of hem þat hym liketh.
And ȝut y, Boek, wol be brente bote he aryse to lyue
And comforte alle his kyn and out of care brynge   265
And alle þe Iewene ioye vnioynen and vnlouken,
And bote they reuerense this resurexioun and þe rode honoure
And bileue on a newe lawe, be ylost lyf and soule.'
   'Soffre we,' sayde Treuthe; 'y here and se bothe
A spirit speketh to helle and bit to vnspere þe ȝates.'   270
     Attollite portas.
   A vois loude in þat liht to Lucifer saide:
'*Princepes* of this place, prest vndo this gates,
For here a cometh with croune, þe kynge of all glorie!'
   Thenne syhed Satoun and saide to Helle,
'Suche a lyht aȝenes oure leue Lazar hit fette;   275
Care and combraunce is come to vs all.
Yf this kyng come in, mankynde wol he fecche
And lede hit þer Lazar is and lihtliche me bynde.

263. of helle T] XUI *om*
268. bileue U] X bilewe

261. *as a geaunt.* The reference is to the *gigas* ('giant') of Ps. 18:6 ('He rejoiced like a giant in the running of the race'), who was traditionally identified with Christ in patristic commentary (see R. E. Kaske in *JEGP* 56, 1957, 177–85, and Kaske, 1960, 38).

264. 'And I, even I, the Book, will gladly be burnt if he does not rise again to life'.

266. *vnioynen* and *vnlouken* are infinitives (like *be* in 268) transitional from the preceding subjunctives *aryse, comforte* and *brynge* (see Donaldson, 1966).

267. *they*, i.e. the Jews. The conversion of the Jews to the New Law (by Enoch and Elias: see XI 221n) was a traditional part of millennial prophecy (cf. III 479).

270a. 'Lift open (your) gates, (O princes)': from Nicodemus 18 (*Descensus*, cap. V, in Tischendorf, p. 397), as based on Ps. 23:7, another psalm sung in matins on Holy Saturday.

271. *þat liht*: alluding to Isa. 9:2 (see VII 134a).

272. *Princepes* (properly *Principes*): 'Princes'.

274. *Helle.* Hell is personified (Lat. *inferus*) in Nicodemus 19 (*Descensus*, cap. IV, in Tischendorf, p. 394). He represents the power of hell, to which Satan himself is subject. L seems to identify Hell with Lucifer, and makes also the traditional distinction between Lucifer and Satan, in accordance with an exegetic tradition established by Jerome in his commentary on Isa. 14:12 (*PL* 24:219). Lucifer represents the fallen angel, Satan the totally corrupted spirit of evil, or devil.

278. *þer Lazar is*: 'where Lazarus is'. But Lazarus was brought back to life, not led into paradise. Perhaps Satan does not understand the difference between life and eternal life; it is unlikely that he recognizes the raising of Lazarus as a type of the resurrection.

Patriarkes and prophetes haen parled herof longe
That such a lord and a lihte shal lede hem all hennes.   280
Ac arise vp, Ragamoffyn, and areche me all þe barres
That Belial thy beel-syre beet with thy dame,
And y shal lette this loerd and his liht stoppe.
Ar we thorw brihtnesse be blente, go barre we þe ȝates.
Cheke we and cheyne we and vch a chine stoppe   285
That no liht lepe in at louer ne at loupe.
Astarot, hoet out, and haue out oure knaues,
Coltyng and al his kyn, the castel to saue.
Brumstoen boylaunt brennyng out cast hit
Al hoet on here hedes þat entrith ney þe walles.   290
Setteth bowes of brake and brasene gonnes
And sheteth out shot ynow his sheltrom to blende.
Set Mahond at þe mangenel and mullestones throweth
And with crokes and kalketrappes acloye we hem vchone!'
   'Lustneth,' quod Lucifer, 'for y this lord knowe;   295
Bothe this lord and this lihte, ys longe ygo y knewe hym.   f.92ᵃ
May no deth this lord dere, ne no deueles quentyse,
And where he wol is his way – ac waer hym of þe perelles:
Yf he reue me of my rihte, a robbeth me of his maistrie.

284. blente U] X brente
285. we¹ T] XUI *om.* chine U] X shine
288. castel] XU car; IT care; P catel
293. mangenel P] XUI mangrel; T magnail
294. with] XUIT *om*; P whith.   acloye P] XUIT and cloye
297. no² I] X do; U *om*

281. *Ragamoffyn*: a fanciful name for a demon. This passage (281–94), with its lively
   detail, is an addition in C, of a somewhat uncharacteristic kind.
286. *louer*: a 'louver' was a lantern-like turret in the roof of a hall to let smoke out and
   light in.
287. *Astarot*: Ashtaroth, another demon, originally the Phoenician moon-goddess. Hell,
   as in Milton, and in accordance with tradition, is peopled with pagan deities
   (including also Mahomet, 293).
288. *Coltyng*: another demon (perhaps the name is from *colt*, with its association with
   wantonness and lechery?).
291. *bowes of brake*: cross-bows with a winding mechanism to give tension.
292. *sheltrom*. Christ has no *sheltrom*, or body of troops, but to Satan's incurably literal
   way of thinking this is how he will conquer hell.
294. *kalketrappes*: 'caltrops', spiked iron balls used to impede and maim horses in battle.
   acloye refers strictly to the laming of horses by driving nails into their hooves while
   shoeing them. Satan now seems to assume that Christ is leading a cavalry charge.
299. *my rihte*. The theory of the 'devil's rights' (for a brief and lucid exposition, see R.
   Woolf in *MÆ* 27, 1958, 137–53, esp. p. 144) was evolved to provide a legalistic
   framework for the act of Redemption. The devil was granted the right of legal
   possession (see 309, below) to the souls of all sinful men after the Fall. He might

For bi riht and by resoun þe renkes þat ben here 300
Body and soule beth myne, bothe gode and ille.
For hymsulue said hit, þat sire is of heuene,
That Adam and Eue and all his issue
Sholde deye with doel and here dwelle euere
Yf they touched a tre or toek þerof an appul. 305
Thus this lord of liht such a lawe made,
And sethe he is a lele lord y leue þat he wol nat
Reuen vs of oure riht, sethe resoun hem dampnede.
And sethen we haen ben sesed seuene thousand wynter,
And neuere was þer-aȝeyne and now wolde bigynne, 310
Thenne were he vnwrast of his word, þat witnesse is of treuthe.'
    'That is soeth,' saide Satoun, 'bote y me sore doute,
For thow gete hem with gyle and his gardyn breke;
Aȝeyne his loue and his leue on his londe ȝedest,
Not in fourme of a fende bote in fourme of an addre 315
And entisedest Eue to eten by here one –
    Ve soli! –
And byhihtest here and hym aftur to knowe
As two godes, with god, bothe goed and ille.
Thus with treson and tricherie thow troyledest hem bothe
And dust hem breke here buxumnesse thorw fals bihestes, 320
And so haddest hem out and hiddere at þe laste.'
    'Hit is nat graythly ygete ther gyle is þe rote,

forfeit this right by 'abuse of power', that is, by attempting to seize a sinless soul; or it might be annulled by ransom, the offer of soul for soul. L alludes to both schemes of Redemption (see below, 327n, 386), even though the theory of 'devil's rights' had been repudiated by Aquinas (see Sajavaara, 1967, 58–61) and was now old-fashioned theologically. The doctrinal patterns of the English mystery cycles are very similar to Langland's: see e.g. T. Fry, 'The Unity of the *Ludus Coventriae*,' *SP* 48 (1951), 527–70. *of his maistrie*: 'by his power', i.e. by might alone, and not by right.

309. *ben sesed*: 'have been in legal possession'. Early uses of the verb *seize* refer to the acquisition of legal possession of a feudal holding. The technical term *seisyne* is introduced at the corresponding point in the closely parallel debate on the Redemption in the *Castle of Love* (line 1049), an early 14th c. translation of Grosseteste's *Chateau d'Amour* (see VII 232n, and Sajavaara, 1967, 294). *seuene thousand*. Conventionally arbitrary: the usual figure is nearer four or five thousand.

310. 'And there was never (any objection) against this, and now he would begin (to raise objections)'.

313. The Temptation in the Garden would usually be assigned to Satan.

316. *by here one*: 'on her own, by herself'.

316a. 'Woe to him who is alone (when he falls)' (Eccl. 4:10).

And god wol nat be gylde,' quod Gobelyne, 'ne byiaped.
We haen no trewe title to hem, for thy tresoun hit maketh.
Forthy y drede me,' quod þe deuel, 'laste Treuthe wol hem fecche.   325
And as thowe bigyledest godes ymages in goynge of an addre,
So hath god bigiled vs alle in goynge of a weye.
For god hath go,' quod Gobelyne, 'in gome liknesse
This thritty wynter, as y wene, and wente aboute and prechede.
Y haue assayled hym with synne, and som tyme ich askede   330
Where he were god or godes sone? He gaf me short answere.
Thus hath he trolled forth like a tydy man this two and thritty
      wynter;   f.92^b
And when y seyh hit was so, y sotiled how y myhte
Lette hem þat louede hym nat, laste they wolde hym martre.
Y wolde haue lenghed his lyf, for y leued, yf he deyede,   335
That if his soule hider cam hit sholde shende vs all.
For þe body, whiles hit on bones ȝede, aboute was hit euere
To lere men to be lele and vch man to louye oþer;
The which lyf and lawe, be hit longe y-vysed,
Hit shal vndo vs deueles and down bryngen vs all.'   340
  'And now y se where his soule cometh sylinge hidward
With glorie and with gret lihte – god hit is, ich woet wel.
Y rede we flee,' quod the fende, 'faste all hennes,
For vs were bettere nat to be then abyde in his sihte.
For thy lesinges, Lucifer, we losten furst oure ioye,   345

323. ne T] XUI no
338. be U] X *om*
342. gret U] X *om*·

323. *Gobelyne* seems to be used by L as another name or an *alter ego* for Satan, since he assumes responsibility for the temptation of Christ (Matt. 4:1–11) in 330, below. In the allocation of speeches here, he is treated as a separate speaker, synonymous with *þe deuel*.

327. *in goynge of a weye*: 'in adopting the gait and manner of a man'. The doctrine of Atonement had to be justified according to law (see 385a, below) and the theory of the 'devil's rights' (see 299n, above), and for these purposes the Incarnation was interpreted as a piece of divine deception (see 165, above). The devil was to be trapped (the image of a baited hook was often used, e.g. *Castle of Love* 1129–32 in Sajavaara, 1967, 297; *Northern Homily Cycle* 413–40; *Cursor Mundi* 16931–2) into forfeiting his rights by transgressing his agreement with God, namely, by compassing the death of a sinless soul, that of Jesus, whom the devil did not recognize as God. In accordance with this doctrine the Temptation of Christ was interpreted as the devil's attempt to find out whether Christ was the Son of God: see 331, below, Wyclif, ed. Arnold, i.109, and the essay by D. L. Wee in *MP* 72 (1974–5), 1–16.

335. The reference is to the dream that Satan sent to Pilate's wife, warning her to persuade her husband not to condemn Christ. The legend grew from Matt. 27:19; it was extensively developed in the mystery cycles.

337. *aboute was hit euere*: 'it was always busy'.

And out of heuene hidore thy pryde made vs falle;
For we leued on thy lesynges, þere loste we oure blisse.
And now, for a lattere lesing þat thow lowe til Eue,
We haen ylost oure lordschipe a londe and in helle.

    Nunc princeps huius mundi, etc.'

   Sethe þat Satan myssaide thus foule   350
Lucifer for his lesynges, leue y noen oþer
Bote oure lord at þe laste lyares here rebuke
And wyte hem al þe wrechednesse that wrouhte is her on erthe.
Beth ywaer, ȝe wyse clerkes and ȝe witty men of lawe,
That ȝe belyen nat this lewed men, for at the laste Dauid   355
Witnesseth in his writynges what is lyares mede:

    Odisti omnes qui operantur iniquitatem; perdes omnes qui
      loquuntur mendacium.

(A litel y ouer-leep for lesynges sake,
That y ne sygge nat as y syhe, suynde my teme!)
   For efte þat lihte bade vnlouke, and Lucifer answeride.
'What lord artow?' quod Lucifer. A voys aloude saide: 360
'The lord of myhte and of mayne, þat made alle thynges.
Dukes of this demme place, anoen vndoth this ȝates
That Crist may come in, the kynges sone of heuene.'
   And with þat breth helle braek with alle Belialles barres;
For eny wey or warde, wyde open þe ȝates.   365
Patriarkes and profetes, *populus in tenebris*,   f.93ᵃ
Songen with seynt Iohan '*Ecce agnus dei!*'
Lucifer loke ne myhte, so liht hym ablende;
And tho that oure lord louede forth with þat liht flowen.
   'Lo! me here,' quod oure lord, 'lyf and soule bothe,   370

347–8. þere loste . . . lesing T] XUI *om*
359. and Lucifer answeride T] XUI *om*

349a. 'Now the ruler of this world (shall be cast out)' (John 12:31).
350–58. This digression on lying is in C only. Like much else in the poem, it is reminiscent of the practice of preachers, who are told by Gregory to follow their theme where it needs takes them, like a river – an image which seems very appropriate to *Piers Plowman*, 'with its combination of urgent pressure and unforeseen direction' (Spearing, 1972, 124).
356a. 'Thou hatest all evil-doers; thou destroyest all who speak lies' (Ps. 5:7).
360–62. These lines paraphrase the question (*Quis est iste rex glorie?*) and reply (*Dominus fortis et potens*) that follow the command of 270a, above, in Ps. 23:8.
362–3. See above, 270a.
365. *For eny wey or warde*: 'For all that any man or guard could do'.
366. *populus in tenebris.* See VII 134a. Cited in Nicodemus 18 (*Descensus*, cap. II, in Tischendorf, p. 392).
367. *Ecce agnus dei*: 'Behold, the Lamb of God' (John 1:36), John the Baptist's address to Jesus. Cited in Nicodemus 18 (*Descensus*, cap. II, in Tischendorf, p. 393).

For alle synfole soules to saue oure bothe rihte.
Myne they were and of me; y may þe bet hem clayme.
Althouh resoun recordede, and rihte of mysulue,
That if they ete þe appul alle sholde deye,
Y bihihte hem nat here helle for euere.   375
For the dedly synne that they dede, thi deseite hit made;
With gyle thow hem gete agaynes all resoun.
For in my palays, paradys, in persone of an addere
Falsliche thou fettest there þat me biful to loke,
Byglosedest hem and bigiledest hem and my gardyne breke   380
Aȝeyne my loue and my leue. Þe olde lawe techeth
That gylours be bigiled and yn here gyle falle,
And ho-so hit out a mannes eye or elles his fore-teth
Or eny manere membre maymeth oþer herteth,
The same sore shal he haue þat eny so smyteth.   385
     Dentem pro dente, et oculum pro oculo.
So lyf shal lyf lete ther lyf hath lyf anyented,
So þat lyf quyte lyf – þe olde lawe hit asketh.
Ergo, soule shal soule quyte and synne to synne wende,
And al þat men mysdede, y man to amenden hit;
And þat deth fordede my deth to releue   390
And bothe quykie and quyte that queynte was thorw synne,
And gyle be bigyled thorw grace at þe laste.
     Ars ut artem falleret.
So leue hit nat, Lucifer, aȝeyne þe lawe y feche
Here eny synfole soule souereynliche by maistrie,
Bote thorw riht and thorw resoun raunsome here myn lege.   395
     Non veni solvere legem, set adimplere.

379. thou B] XUITP *om*
382. be T] XUI *om.*   yn U] X *om*
386. lete U] X lede.   anyented U] X anended
392. be T] XUI *om*

371. *to saue oure bothe rihte*: 'to preserve the right of both of us', i.e. to honour the just claim on all sinful souls of both Christ and Satan.
382. See 163-5, above. Cf. Ps. 9:16.
385a. 'Tooth for tooth, and eye for eye' (Ex. 21:24). This is the old law (381, 387) which Christ himself criticizes in Matt. 5:38. But his concern at the moment is to prove (e.g. 386–90) that the new law is grounded in the fulfilment of the letter of the old, and to prove that no law is being broken (see 395a, below).
386. 'So a living man must lose his life wherever a man has destroyed a life'.
388. *synne to synne wende*: 'one sin [the Crucifixion] go to balance another [the Fall]'.
389. 'And I (become) man to make amends for all that man did wrong'.
392a. See 165a, above.
394. *by maistrie.* See above, 299.
395a. 'I have not come to destroy the law, but to fulfil it' (Matt. 5:17).

So þat with gyle was gete, thorw grace is now ywonne.
And as Adam and alle thorwe a tre deyede,
Adam and alle thorw a tre shal turne to lyue.
And now bygynneth thy gyle agayne on the to turne   f.93ᵇ
And my grace to growe ay wyddore and wyddore.   400
The bitternesse þat thow hast browe, now brouk hit thysulue;
That art doctour of deth, drynke þat thow madest!
    For y þat am lord of lyf, loue is my drynke,
And for þat drynke today y deyede, as hit semede.
Ac y wol drynke of no dische ne of deep clergyse,   405
Bote of comune coppes, alle cristene soules;
Ac thy drynke worth deth and depe helle thy bolle.
Y fauht so, me fursteth ʒut, for mannes soule sake.
    Sicio.
May no pyement ne pomade ne preciouse drynkes
Moiste me to þe fulle ne my furst slokke   410
Til þe ventage valle in þe vale of Iosophat,
And I drynke riht rype must, *resureccio mortuorum.*
And thenne shal y come as kynge, with croune and with angeles,
And haue out of hẽlle alle mennes soules.
    Fendes and fendekynes byfore me shal stande   415
And be at my biddynge, at blisse or at payne.
Ac to be merciable to man thenne my kynde asketh,

408a. *sicio* P] XUT scicio
412. I B] XUITP *om*

397–8. See 143, above.
401. Proverbial: 'Let hem drynk as they hanne brewe' (Whiting B 529).
402. *That*: 'Thou that'. For the tradition of the image of the bitter cup of death, see
    C. Brown in *Speculum* 15 (1940), 389–99; and for parallels which include the con-
    trast of Christ's offer of life-giving drink, see G. V. Smithers in *EGS* 4 (1951–2),
    67–75.
403–12. From the image of the drink of death brewed by the devil, and the allusion to
    the bitter drink offered to Jesus on the cross (Matt. 27:48), grows this magnificent
    elaboration of the image of the drink of love and life, of Christ thirsting (408a) for
    man's love. For an analysis of the complex patterns of repetition and echo in this
    passage, see Salter, 1962, 49–52.
405. *deep clergyse*: 'profound learning', conceived of momentarily as a deep (and elabor-
    ate) drinking-vessel, in contrast to the homely cups of ordinary Christian souls.
408a. 'I thirst' (John 19:28).
411. *Til þe ventage valle*: 'until the time of the grape-harvest comes'. *þe vale of Iosophat*.
    The vale of Jehoshaphat is taken as the future scene of the resurrection of man-
    kind (so *Prick of Conscience* 5150), in accordance with the prophecy of Joel 3:2,
    12–13.
412. *must*: 'new wine'. *resureccio mortuorum*: 'the resurrection of the dead' (from the
    Nicene Creed: see 116, above).

For we beth brethrene of o bloed, ac nat in baptisme alle.
Ac alle þat beth myn hole brethrene, in bloed and in baptisme,
Shal neuere in helle eft come, be he ones oute.   420
  Tibi soli peccaui, et malum coram te feci.
Hit is nat vsed on erthe to hangen eny felones
Oftur then ones, thogh they were tretours.
And yf þe kynge of þe kyngdoem come in þe tyme
Ther a thief tholie sholde deth oþer iewyse,
Lawe wolde he ȝoue hym lyf and he loked on hym.   425
And y þat am kynge ouer kynges shal come such a tyme
Ther þat doem to þe deth dampneth alle wikkede,
And if lawe wol y loke on hem hit lith in my grace
Where they deye or dey nat, dede they neuere so ille.
Be hit enythyng abouhte, the boldenesse of here synne,   430

---

419. brethrene U] X brethene

---

418. *brethrene of o bloed*, i.e. fellow human beings, because of Christ's Incarnation (a different sense from that of VIII 217, XII 108). *nat in baptisme*: referring to those who have not been baptized into the Christian faith in the age of the new law (as well as the pagans who lived in the time of the old law) rather than to those who lived under the old law, since the latter have already been brought out of hell.

419. *hole brethrene*: 'full brothers', i.e. Christians. *in bloed* here could refer to the blood of redemption (VIII 217n).

420. *be he ones oute*: 'once he is out'. The reference, since it is to Christians, seems to be to the release, for general judgment at Doomsday, of those consigned to hell by particular judgment at their death. For an orthodox account of the two judgments, see *Prick of Conscience* 2593–2650; L's theology here is extraordinarily flexible, and he makes little mention of purgatory, which is a cornerstone of orthodox eschatology, as described at length in the *Prick of Conscience* 2692–3965 (where the geography of the nether regions is made very clear, 2786–2815, with the hell of unbaptised children between hell proper and purgatory, and limbo above the three, nearest to earth). Nothing could be more different than the gloomy certainty of the *Prick of Conscience* (e.g. 5150, 5354) and the optimistic manoeuvring of Langland in their accounts of Doomsday.

420a. 'Against thee alone have I sinned, and done what is evil in thy sight' (Ps. 50:6). Therefore Christ's forgiveness cancels the debt.

422. *Oftur then ones* clearly refers to cases of imperfect hanging, where the victim was left alive as well as kicking. A famous instance at Leicester in 1363, where the king pardoned the hanged man (who revived on the way to the graveyard), was recorded in Knighton's Chronicle (see Skeat's note), and probably prompted L's use of the secular analogy.

425. 'The law would require that he should grant him a reprieve, if he were there to see him'.

430. *Be hit enythyng abouhte*: 'If it be at all adequately paid for' (i.e. by Christ's sacrifice). Whilst scrupulously observing the law, Christ is here evolving, through his own compassionate meditation, a doctrine and means of universal salvation (not in itself totally heterodox: see Hort 118–26) which will turn the Last Judgment into a

Y may do mercy of my rihtwysnesse and alle myn wordes trewe.

   For holy writ wol þat y be wreke of hem þat wrouhte ille,

As *nullum malum impunitum, et nullum bonum irremuneratum.*

And so of alle wykkede y wol here take veniaunce.   f.94ᵃ

And ȝut my kynde in my kene ire shal constrayne my will –   435

    Domine, ne in furore tuo arguas me –

To be merciable to monye of my halue-bretherne.

For bloed may se bloed bothe afurst and acale

Ac bloed may nat se bloed blede, bote hym rewe.

    Audivi archana verba, que non licet homini loqui.

Ac my rihtwysnesse and rihte shal regnen in helle,

And mercy al mankynde bifore me in heuene.   440

For y were an vnkynde kyng bote y my kyn helpe,

And namliche at such a nede þat nedes helpe asketh.

    Non intres in iudicium cum seruo tuo.

   Thus by lawe,' quod oure lord, 'lede y wol fro hennes

Tho ledis þat y louye and leued in my comynge.

Ac for þe lesynge þat thow low, Lucifer, til Eue,   445

Thow shal abyye bittere,' quod god, and bonde hym with chaynes.

Astarot and alle oþere hidden hem in hernes;

They dorste nat loke on oure lord, the lest of hem alle,

Bote leten hym lede forth which hym luste and leue which hym

    likede.

Many hundret of angels harpeden tho and songen,   450

---

431. Y U] X or
435. in U] X and
440. al B] XUITP and
444. ledis T] XUI *om*
446. bonde U] X boynde

---

day of mercy rather than wrath. Traditional theology, in its attempt to find a place for both God's justice and his mercy, held the view that God's mercy was supreme in this life and at the particular judgment at the moment of death, but that at the Last Judgment all would be ordered in accordance with justice alone (see Woolf, 1969, 66).

433. See IV 140.

435a. 'O Lord, rebuke me not in thy anger' (Ps. 37:1).

436. *halue-bretherne.* See 418, above. *bloed* in the following lines refers, in the same way, to kinship.

438. *bote hym rewe*: 'without taking pity'.

438a. 'I heard [Vg. *audivit*] words which cannot be told, which man may not utter' (2 Cor. 12:4). L transfers Paul's words, of the man (evidently Paul himself) caught up into the third heaven, to his dreamer, suggesting that he is aware of the limits to which his vision of Christ's promise of mercy can be taken. Like much of L's Latin quotation, the words are not dramatically part of the surrounding speech.

440. *And mercy al mankynde*: 'And mercy (shall reign over) all mankind'.

442a. 'Enter not into judgment with thy servant' (Ps. 142:2). This supplication is not of course appropriate to be spoken by Christ.

Culpat caro, purgat caro, regnat deus dei caro.
Thenne piped Pees of poetes a note:
Clarior est solito post maxima nebula Phebus;
Post inimicitias clarior est et amor.
'Aftur sharpest shoures,' quod Pees, 'most shene is þe sonne;   455
Is no wedore warmore then aftur watri cloudes,
Ne no loue leuore, ne no leuore frendes,
Then aftur werre and wrake when loue and pees ben maistres.
Was neuere werre in this world ne wikkedere enuye
That Loue, and hym luste, to louhynge it ne brouhte,   460
And Pees thorw pacience alle perelles stopede.'
    'Trewes,' quod Treuthe, 'thow tellest vs soeth, by Iesus!
Cluppe we in couenaunt and vch of vs kusse oþere!'
    'And lat no peple,' quod Pees, 'parseyue þat we chydde,
For inposible is no thynge to hym þat is almyhty.'   465
    'Thowe saiste soeth,' saide Rihtwisnesse, and reuerentlich
            here custe,
Pees, and Pees here, *per secula seculorum.*
    Misericordia et veritas obuiauerunt sibi; iusticia et
        pax osculate sunt.   f.94ᵇ
Treuth trompede tho and song *Te deum laudamus,*
And thenne lutede Loue in a loude note,
    Ecce quam bonum et quam jocundum est, etc.
Til þe day dawed thes damoyseles caroled   470
That men rang to þe resureccioun, and riht with þat y wakede

---

453. *post . . . Phebus* P] XUIT *om*
460. it ne T] XUI *om*

451. 'The flesh sins, the flesh atones for sin, the flesh of God reigns as God': from the hymn *Æterne rex altissime,* sung on the vigil of Ascension day (Breviary I. dcccclviii).
453–4. 'The sun is wont to be brighter after the darkest clouds; and love is stronger after strife'. More or less in this form in the *Liber Parabolarum* of Alain of Lille (*PL* 210:581–2; see Alford 397), but also of general proverbial currency (Walther 2794 and, for English examples, Whiting C 315).
460. *and hym luste:* 'if he wanted to'.
467. *Pees here:* 'Peace (kissed) her'. *per secula seculorum:* 'for ever and ever' (see III 432n).
467a. 'Mercy and truth have met together; righteousness and peace have kissed' (Ps. 84:11). See 116n, above.
468. *Te deum laudamus:* 'We praise thee as god'. Sung at matins on Sundays (Breviary II. 27).
469a. 'Behold, how good and pleasant it is (for brothers to dwell in unity)' (Ps. 132:1).
471. The dreamer awakens to the ringing of the bells on Easter morning, a return to time which confirms in reality the truth of his vision, in striking contrast to the rueful earlier cry of XIII 215–16.

And calde Kitte my wyf and Calote my douhter:
'Arise, and go reuerense godes resureccioun,
And crepe to þe croes on knees and kusse hit for a iewel
And rihtfollokest a relyk, noon richore on erthe.
For godes blessed body hit baer for oure bote,
And hit afereth the fende, for such is þe myhte
May no grisly goest glyde þer hit shaddeweth!'

475

477. the U] X th

472. *Kitte my wyf*. See V 2n. *Calote my douhter*. The proverbial association of this name
with the name Kit (Mustanoja, 1970, 73–4), itself a type-name, suggests that the
daughter too may be fictitious.

474. 'Creeping to the cross' (i.e. shuffling forwards on the knees), and kissing it, were
enjoined as penitential and devotional exercises, especially for Good Friday.

Passus XXI

The Founding of Holy Church

Explicit dobet et incipit dobest
Thus y wakede and wrot what y hadde ydremed
And dihte me derely and dede me to kyrke
To here holly þe masse and to be hoseled aftur.
In myddes of þe masse, tho men ȝede to offrynge,
Y ful eftesones aslepe and sodeynliche me mette   5
That Peres þe plouhman was peynted al blody
And cam in with a cros bifore þe comune peple
And riht lyke in alle lymes to oure lord Iesu.
And thenne calde y Consience to kenne me þe sothe:
'Is this Iesus the ioustare,' quod y, 'þat Iewes dede to dethe?   10
Or hit is Peres þe plouhman? who paynted hym so rede?'
    Quod Conciense and knelede tho: 'This aren Peres armes,
His colours and his cote armure, ac he þat cometh so blody

3. be U] X *om*
11. who U] X *om*
12. Peres B] XUITP Cristes

2. *dihte me derely*. The dreamer's dress symbolizes the change in his spiritual state (cf.
XX 1, and see Robertson-Huppé, 1951, 217). He is now robed as a true wedding-
guest (Matt. 22:11), ready to enter into communion with Christ.
5. The seventh vision begins here. The moment is a striking one, as L dramatizes in
his dream the presence of the body and blood of Christ in the sacrament of the
eucharist.
6. *peynted al blody*. In addition to the obvious reference to the Passion, there is here an
allusion to the image of the 'Christ of the Winepress', derived from patristic
interpretation of Isa. 63:1–7 (a reading for Wednesday in Holy Week: Missale
286), beginning with the question (cf. 10, below), 'Who is this that comes from
Edom?' See D. Gray, *Themes and Images in the Medieval English Religious Lyric*
(London, 1972), 12–17, and Woolf, 1968, 199–202.
8. See XX 8, 19–25.
12. *and knelede tho*: as was enjoined (Mirk, *Instructions*, 284) at the ringing of the bell at
the consecration of the host.

Is Crist with his croes, conquerour of cristene.'
    'Whi calle ȝe hym Crist, sennes Iewes callede hym Iesus?   15
Patriarkes and prophetes profecied bifore
Þat alle kyn creatures sholde knelen and bowen
Anoon as men nemned þe name of god Iesu.
Ergo is no name to þe name of Iesus
Ne noen so nedfol to nemnie by nyhte ne by day,   20
For alle derke deueles aren drad for to heren hit
And synfole ben solaced and saued by þat name.
And ȝe callen hym Crist – for what cause, telleth me?   f.95[a]
Is Crist more of myhte and more worthiore name
Then Iesu or Iesus, þat all oure ioye cam of?'   25
    'Thow knowest wel,' quod Concience, 'and þou kunne resoun,
That knyht, kyng, conquerour may be o persone.
To be cald a knyht is fayr, for men shal knele to hym;
To be cald a kyng is fairor, for he may knyhtes make;
Ac to be conquerour cald, þat cometh of special grace,   30
And of hardiness of herte and of hendenesse,
To make lordes of laddes of lond þat he wynneth
And fre men foule thralles þat folleweth nat his lawes.
The Iewes, þat were gentel men, Iesu thei dispisede,
Bothe his lore and his lawe – now are they lowe cherles;   35
As wyde as þe worlde is wonyeth þer none
Bote vnder tribuyt and talage as tykes and cherles.
And tho þat bycome cristene bi consail of þe Baptist
Aren frankeleynes and fre men thorw follyng þat they toke

17. Þat U] X To
20. nedfol U] X medfol
36. wyde U] X wydes

14. *conquerour of cristene.* The following argument is based on the assumption that *Christ*
means 'conqueror' (62, below), an assumption that fits naturally with the por-
trayal of Christ as the conqueror of death (XX 27n, 50n, and below, 50–62). The
actual meaning of the Greek word from which *Christ* is derived is '(the one)
anointed of God', and it is used as an equivalent of the Hebrew word *Messiah*
(John 1:41), though there is no conflict of meaning, since 'the anointed one' is also
the anointed king of the Jews, aptly represented as 'conqueror' in David, a type of
Christ (see 102, below). Conscience also alludes here to the traditional distinction
of the names Jesus and Christ (XX 21n).

17–18. See Phil. 2:10.

32. *of laddes* is constructed with *make*, i.e. 'to make laddes lordes of lond'.

34–40. The secular conqueror has power to promote his faithful followers into the
aristocracy and degrade those who oppose him; those who follow Christ are
likewise raised in spiritual rank and become *fre men*, while those who reject
him are degraded, even if they were formerly *gentel men*. Cf. XII 109, XX
107.

And ientel men with Iesu, for Iesu was yfolled 40
And vpon Caluarie on cros ycrouned kyng of Iewes.
   Hit bicometh for a kyng to kepe and to defende
And conquerour of his conqueste his layes and his large.
And so dede Iesus þe Iewes: he iustified and tauhte hem
The lawe of lyf that laste shal euere, 45
And fended hem fro foule eueles, feueres and fluxes,
And fro fendes þat in hem was and false bileue.
Tho was he Iesu of Iewes cald, gentel profete,
And kyng of here kyngdoem and croune baer of thornes.
And tho conquerede he on cros as conquerour noble; 50
Myhte no deth hym fordo ne adown brynge
That he ne aroos and regnede and raueschede helle.
And tho was he conquerour cald of quyke and of dede,
For he ȝaf Adam and Eue and oþere mo blisse
That longe hadden leye bifore as Luciferes cherles 55
And toek Lucifer the loethliche þat lord was of helle
And bonde him as he is bounde with bondes of yre.
Ho was hardior then he? his herte bloed he shedde
To make alle folk fre þat folweth his lawe.
And sethe he ȝeueth largeliche all his lele lege 60 f.95ᵇ
Places in paradys at here partyng hennes
He may be wel called conquerour, and that is Crist to mene.
  Ac the cause that he cometh thus, with his cros and his passioun,
Is to wissen vs þerwith þat when we ben ytempted
Therwith to fihte and fende vs fro fallyng into synne, 65
And se bi his sorwe þat ho-so loueth ioye
To penaunce and to pouerte he mot putte hymsuluen
And moche wo in this world wilnen and soffren.
  Ac to carpe more of Crist and how he cam to þat name,
Faythly for to speke, his furste name was Iesus. 70
Tho he was bore in Bedlehem, as þe boek telleth,
And cam to take mankynde, kynges and angeles
Reuerensed hym riht fayre with richesses of erthe.

---

48. cald U] X *om*
48–51. *lineation as* U; X *mislineates*
57. him U] X *om*
58. shedde U] X shewede

40. *for Iesu was yfolled.* In continuation of the secular analogy, baptism is here treated as the means by which man becomes free (cf. Gal. 5:1).
69. Here begins a life of Christ and a history of the delivery of the new law (69–198), in which further explanation of the name of Jesus Christ is merged with another exposition of Dowel, Dobet and Dobest.

Angels out of heuene come, kneled and songe,
> *Gloria in excelsis deo.*

Kynges cam aftur, knelede and offrede sense,   75
Mirre and moche gold, withouten mercy askynge
Or eny kyne catel, bote knoweleched hym souereyn
Bothe of sand, sonne and see, and sennes þei wente
Into here kyngene kuth by consail of angelis.
And þer was þat word fulfuld þe which þou of speke: 80
> *Omnia celestia, terrestria, flectantur in hoc nomine Iesu.*

For alle þe angelis of heuene at his burthe knelede
And al þe wit of the world was in tho thre kynges.
Resoun and rihtfulnesse and reuthe thei offrede;
Wherefore and why wyse men þat tyme,
Maistres and lettred men, *Magi* hem calde.   85
> That o kyng cam with resoun, ykyuered vnder ensense.

The secounde kyng seth soethliche offrede
Rihtwisnesse vnder reed gold, resones felawe;
Gold is likened to lewetee that laste shal euere
And resoun to richeles, to riht and to treuthe.   90
The thridde kyng cam and kneled to Iesu
And presented hym with pyte, apperynge bi mirre,
For mirre is mercy to mene and mylde speche of tonge.
Ertheliche honeste thynges was offred thus at ones
Thorw thre kyne kynges knelyng to Iesu.   95
> Ac for all this preciouse presentes oure lord prince Iesu

Was noþer kyng ne conquerour til he comsed wexe   f.96ᵃ

---

74. Angels U] X Angele
75. sense B] XUITP *om*
82. tho U] X *om*
86. o] X a; U oen
90. richeles] XUITP riche golde

74a. 'Glory to God in the highest' (Luke 2:14).
76. *mercy*, 'thanks', is unusual. Kane-Donaldson (p. 160) suggest *mercede*.
79. *by consail of angeles*. See Matt. 2:12.
80a. 'All things [Vg. *omne genu*] in heaven and earth bow down at the name of Jesus' (Phil. 2:10). See 17–18, above.
83. The gifts of the three Magi, frankincense, gold and myrrh, were frequently and variously interpreted as allegorical symbols of Christ-like qualities (e.g. *Legenda Aurea* XIV, p. 93). Here they represent reason, justice and mercy, attributes of Christ the king-to-be (96–7, below).
86. *ykyuered vnder*: 'hidden under', i.e. symbolized by.
90. *resoun to richeles*. The close association of reason and justice (*resones felawe*, 88) might have led to some transfer of symbolism, but the line as it appears in the MSS makes poor sense. Kane-Donaldson emend B XIX 90 to *For it shal turne tresoun*, etc. (see p. 161).

In þe manere of a man, and þat by moche sleythe,
As hit bicometh for a conquerour to conne mony sleythes
And many wyles and wyt þat wol be a ledare.   100
And so dede Iesu in his dayes, who-so durste tellen hit.
Som tyme he soffrede and som tyme he hudde hym
And som tyme he fauht faste and fley oþer-while
And som tyme he gaf goed and graunted hele bothe;
Lyf and lyme, as hym luste, he wrouhte.   105
As kynde is of a conquerour so comesede Iesu
Til he hadde all hem þat he fore bledde.
    In his iuuentee this Iesus at Iewene feste
Turned watur into wyn, as holy writ telleth;
And þer bigan god of his grace to dowel.   110
For wyn is likned to lawe and lyf-holinesse,
And lawe lakked tho, for men loued nat her enemyes,
And Crist consayleth vs and comaundeth bothe,
Bothe to lered and to lewed, to louye oure enemyes.
So at þat feste furste, as y before tolde,   115
Bigan god of his grace and goodnesse to dowel.
And tho was he cleped and calde not only Crist but Iesu,
A fauntekyn ful of wyt, *filius Marie.*
For bifore his moder Marie made he þat wonder
That she furste and the formoste sholde ferme bileue   120
That he thorw grace was gete and of no gome elles.
He wrouhte þat by no wyt bote thorw word one,
Aftur þe kynde þat he cam of. Þer comsede he dowel.
    And when he was wexen more, in his moder absence
He made lame to lepe and ȝaf liht to blynde   125

117. only U] X my
120. she T] XU þe

98. For the emphasis on *sleythe*, see XX 327.
102. In these allusions to Christ's life, L seems to be exploiting the typological associa-
tion of Christ with David (cf. 14n, above, and 132–9, below) who, as guerrilla
leader and fugitive king, had these very experiences (see a note by T. D. Hill in
NQ 221, 1976, 291–4).
105. *wrouhte*: 'made whole'.
107. *hadde*, i.e. 'possessed, had at his will'.
108. *Iewene feste*: the marriage at Cana (John 2:1–11).
114. *to louye oure enemyes.* This universal active charity was formerly part of Dobest (e.g.
XI 161). 'Dowel has, as it were, been raised to a higher power by the transforming
fact of the incarnation – just as the water has been transformed into wine' (Kean,
1969, 94; and see X 78n). The turning of the water into wine was traditionally
interpreted as the transformation of the old into the new law.
119–21. Jesus's words to Mary in John 2:4 were traditionally interpreted as a declara-
tion to her of the Godhead (Robertson-Huppé, 1951, 219–20).

And fedde with two fisches and with fyue loues
Sore afyngered folk, mo then fyue thousend.
Thus he comfortede carefole and cauhte a grettere name,
The which was Dobet, where þat he wente.
For deue thorw his doynges and dombe speke and herde   130
And all he heled and halp þat hym of grace asked.
And tho was he cald in contreye of þe comune peple,   f.96ᵇ
For þe dedes þat he dede, *fili Dauid, Iesus.*
For Dauid was the douhtiest of dedes in his tyme;
The buyrdes tho songe *Saul interfecit mille, et Dauid decem milia.*   135
Forthy þe contre þer Iesu cam calde hym *fili Dauid*
And nempned hym of Nazareth, and no man so worthy
To be cayser or kyng of the kyngdoem of Iuda
Ne ouer Iewes iustice as Iesus was, hem thouhte.
    Hereof hadde Cayphas enuye and oþer Iewes   140
And for to do hym to dethe day and nyhte they casten
And culden hym on cros-wyse at Caluarie on a Fryday
And sethen burieden his body and beden þat men sholde
Kepen hit fro nyhte-comares with knyhtes y-armed
For no frende sholde hit fecche; for profetes hem tolde   145
That þat blessed body of buyrielles sholde ryse
And goen into Galilee and gladien his apostlis
And his moder Marie – thus men bifore deuyned.
The knyhtes þat kepten hit biknewen hemsuluen
That angeles and archangeles, ar the day spronge,   150
Comen knelyng to þat cors and songen
Christus resurgens, and hit aroos aftur,
Verray man bifore hem alle, and forth with hem ʒede.
The Iewes preyed hem of pees and preyede tho knyhtes
Telle þe comune þat þer cam a companie of his apostles   155
And bywiched hem as they woke and away stelen hit.
Ac Marie Maudeleyne mette hym by þe weye,

130. and² T] XU he
143. burieden U] X burden
153. hem¹ U] X *om*
156. hem U] X *om*

126. Matt. 14:17.
133. Matt. 9:27, etc.
135. 'Saul has slain a thousand, and David ten thousand' (1 Reg. 18:7).
145. *profetes hem tolde.* See Matt. 27:62–6 and, for use of prophecy, Matt. 12:40 (referring to Jon. 1:17; cf. also Hos. 6:2 and Luke 24:45–6).
152. *Christus resurgens*: 'Christ being raised (from the dead)' (Rom. 6:9), sung as an antiphon on Easter day (Breviary I. dcccvii).
154–6. Matt. 28:13.
157. *by þe weye.* In the garden around the tomb, according to John 20:11.

Goynge toward Galilee in godhede and in manhede
And lyues and lokynge, and aloude criede
In vch a companye þer she cam, *Christus resurgens!*   160
Thus cam hit out þat Crist ouerkam, rekeuerede and lyuede –
    Sic oportet Christum pati et intrare, etc. –
For þat woman witeth hit may nat wel be conseyl!
    Peter parseyued al this and pursuede aftur,
Bothe Iames and Iohan, Iesu to seke,
Taddee and ten mo, with Thomas of Ynde.   165
And as al thise wyse weyes weren togyderes   f.97ᵃ
In an hous al bishut and here dore ybarred,
Crist cam in – and al closed, bothe dore and ȝates –
To Peter and to his apostlis and saide *Pax vobis,*
And toek Thomas by the hoende and tauhte hym to grope   170
And fele with his fyngeres his flescheliche herte.
Thomas touched hit and with his tonge saide:
    "*Dominus meus et deus meus.*
Thow art my lord, y bileue, god, lord Iesu,
Deyedest and deth tholedest and deme shalt vs all
And now art lyuynge and lokynge and laste shalt euere."   175
Crist carpede thenne and corteysliche saide:
"Thomas, for thow trowest this and treweliche bileuest hit
Yblessed mote thow be and be shalt for euere.
And yblessed mote they be in body and in soule
That neuere shal se me in sihte as thowe seste nowthe   180
And leelliche bileuen al this – y loue hem and blesse hem.
    Beati qui non viderunt et crediderunt."
    And when this dede was doen, dobest he thouhte

---

160. she U] X he
161a. *oportet* T] XU *om*
162. may U] X *om.* wel be U] X be wel
166. togyderes U] X two togyderes
176. corteysliche U] X corteyliche
180. That U] X Tha

---

160. For Mary Magdalene as a preacher, see *Legenda Aurea* XCVI, p. 409.
161a. 'Thus it was necessary that Christ should suffer and enter (into his glory)'. The translation is completed here from *gloriam suam* in MS P. The Vulgate (Luke 24:46) concludes, *pati et resurgere a mortuis.*
162. *conseyl*: 'a secret'. A conventionally sly remark, very inappropriate in the context.
165. *Thomas of Ynde.* According to legend, St Thomas preached and converted in India.
169. *Pax vobis*: 'Peace be with you' (John 20:19).
172a. 'My lord and my god' (John 20:28).
181a. 'Blessed are those who have not seen and yet have believed' (John 20:29).

And ȝaf Peres power and pardoun he graunted
To alle manere men, mercy and forȝeuenesse;
Ȝaf hym myhte men to assoyle of alle manere synnes   185
In couenaunt þat they come and knoleched to pay
To Peres pardoun þe plouhman *Redde quod debes.*
Thus hath Peres power, be his pardoun payed,
To bynde and to vnbynde bothe here and elles
And assoile men of alle synnes, saue of dette one.   190
Anoon aftur an heyh vp into heuene
He wente, and woneth there, and wol come at þe laste
And rewarde hym riht wel that *reddet quod debet,*
Payeth parfitly as puyr treuthe wolde.
And what persone payth hit nat punischen he thenketh   195
And demen hem at domesday, bothe quyke and dede,
The gode to godhede and to grete ioye
And wikked to wonye in wo withouten ende.'
    Thus Consience of Crist and of þe cros carpede
And conseyled me to knelw þerto; and thenne cam, me thouhte,   200   f.97^b
Oen *Spiritus paraclitus* to Peres and to his felawes.
In liknesse of a lihtnynge a lihte on hem alle
And made hem konne and knowe alle kyne langages.
Y wondred what þat was and wagged Consience
And was afered for the lihte, for in fuyres liknesse   205
Spiritus paraclitus ouerspradde hem alle.

185. Ȝaf P] XUT *om*

183. *Peres*: St Peter, the rock on which Christ founded his church (Matt. 16:18); but also, now, Piers Plowman.
183–5. For a suggested rearrangement of these lines as they appear in B XIX 183–5, see Kane-Donaldson 120.
186. *knoleched to pay*: 'acknowledged their responsibility to pay'. Cf. 188, 389–90, below.
187. *Redde quod debes*: 'Pay back what you owe' (see VI 316n). The Latin text is treated as the grammatical object of *pay* (cf. 259, 390, below), as if in itself it meant 'debt'. The emphasis in this passage, which deals with the power granted to Peter and to the Church to absolve from sin (the *pardoun* of Piers Plowman, cf. IX 3n, and see Matt. 16:19), is on the necessity of restitution (VI 6n, 309n) as the necessary prerequisite of pardon. Restitution is not to be understood solely or primarily in material terms: it is, in a larger sense, the rendering of the debt of love to God and one's neighbour. For its importance as a theme in *Piers Plowman*, see Frank, 1957, 106–9; Bloomfield, 1961, 130–32.
193. See 187, above.
201. *Spiritus paraclitus*: 'the Spirit (and) comforter (or intercessor)', i.e. the Holy Spirit, who descended in the form of fire upon the apostles at Pentecost (Acts 2:1–4), as prophesied in John 14:16, 26, 15:26.
204. *wagged*: 'shook', i.e. shook Conscience by the arm, a nervous gesture to get his attention and ask him to explain what is going on.

Quod Consience and knelede: 'This is Cristes messager
And cometh from the grete god, Grace is his name.
Knele now,' quod Consience, 'and yf thow canst synge
Welcome hym and worschipe hym with *Veni creator spiritus*.'   210
And y sang þat song and so dede many hundret
And criden with Consience, 'Helpe vs, god, of grace!'
  And thenne bigan Grace to go with Peres the plouhman
And conseilede hym and Consience the comune to sompne:
'For y wol dele today and deuyde grace   215
To alle kyne creatures þat can his fyue wittes,
Tresor to lyue by to here lyues ende
And wepne to fihte with þat wol neuere fayle.
For Auntecrist and hise al the world shal greue
And acombre þe, Consience, bote yf Crist the helpe.   220
And false profetes fele, flateres and glosares,
Shal come and be curatours ouer kynges and erles.
And thenne shal pryde be pope and prince of holy chirche,
Coueytise and vnkyndenesse cardynales hym to lede.
Forthy,' quod Grace, 'or y go y wol gyue ȝow tresor   225
And wepne to fihte with þat wol neuere fayle.
And ȝaf vch man a grace to gye with hymsuluen
That ydelnesse encombre hem nat, ne enuye ne pryde.
    Diuisiones graciarum sunt.
  Som men he ȝaf wyt with wordes to shewe,

---

224. to U] X *om*

---

208. *Grace* is the name given to the Holy Spirit, the mediator to men of Christ's new law
   (cf. Rom. 6:14).
210. *Veni creator spiritus*: 'Come, creating spirit' (the first words of a hymn sung at the
   beginning of the Ordinary of the Mass, and specially at Pentecost: Breviary II.
   481, I. mviii).
219. *Auntecrist.* The name of Antichrist is derived from the epistles of St John (1 John
   2:22, 2 John 7), where it is applied to those who deny the divinity of Christ. The
   concept was enriched by association with the demoniacal beasts of apocalyptic
   writing (Dan. 7, Apoc. 13) and with Paul's 'son of perdition' (1 Thess. 2:3), and
   out of this emerged the medieval belief in Antichrist as a kind of 'incarnation' of
   Satan, human, and yet the embodiment of evil. His coming was to inaugurate the
   tyranny of the Last Days, which in turn would precede the Second Coming of
   Christ. The name Antichrist was thus often applied, in reference to the prophecy,
   to any particularly wicked king or pope, though the term was often used in the
   more abstract way, as here. See Reeves, 1969, 295–303 and, for a lengthy account
   of his role, *Prick of Conscience* 4047–4612.
227. *gye with hymsuluen*: 'guide himself with'.
228a. 'There are varieties of gifts' (1 Cor. 12:4). With these words, Paul introduces an
   enumeration of the spiritual gifts of the Holy Ghost. L extends this mediation of
   the Holy Spirit (see 208, above) to cover not only discipleship but the work of all
   men, religious and secular. In the passage that follows (229–49), with its enumera-

To wynne with treuthe þat the world asketh, 230
As prechours and prestes and prentises of lawe:
They leely to lyue bi labour of tonge
And bi wit to wissen oþere as grace hem wolde teche.
And somme he kende hem craft and konnynge of syhte,
With sullyng and buggynge here bileue to wynne. 235 f.98ª
And som he lered to laboure a londe and a watre
And lyue by þat laboure a leele lyf and a trewe.
And somme he tauhte to tulye, to þecche and to coke,
As here wit wolde when þe tyme come.
And somme to deuyne and to deuyde noumbres, 240
To kerue and to compace and coloures to make.
And some to se and to saye what sholde bifalle
Bothe of wele and of wo and be ywaer bifore,
As astronomens thorw astronomye, and philosopheres wyse.
And somme to ryde and somme to rekeuere that vnrihtfulliche was 245
    wonne;
He wissede men wynne hit aȝeyn thorw wihtnesse of handes
And fechen hit fro false men with Foleuiles lawes.

---

238. þecche T] XU teche
240-1. noumbres/To kerue and to T] XU noumbres to kenne/And
244. As U] X And.   astronomens U] X astronmens
246. wihtnesse] XU whitnesse; T wiȝtnesse

---

tion of professions and trades, L returns to the world of the *Visio*, now seen as the Christian community living as Christ's Church. The rest of the poem is essentially concerned with the life of this community. It is the field full of folk (Prol. 19) again, but now a field of battle, not a *mase* (I 6), with the lines of battle clearly drawn. The life of the Christian community (*ecclesia*) on earth has in fact been L's concern throughout the poem. The long sections of the poem in which the life of the community seems to recede into the background are mainly attempts to explore the ways in which that community is to be truly founded in the perfecting of the individual soul. They are not, for instance, concerned with the search of the individual soul for God.

230. *þat the world asketh.* Cf. Prol. 21.
239. B, which corresponds very closely in these last two passus (unrevised in C), has here a completely different line, 'To wynne wiþ hir liflode bi loore of his techynge' (B XIX 239).
240. *deuyde noumbres.* Three chapters of the encyclopaedia of Bartholomaeus (XIX. cxxiv-vi) are devoted to 'division [i.e. classification] of numbers'.
247. *Foleuiles lawes* had evidently become a nickname for the administration of 'private justice' by local bands and brotherhoods as a means of circumventing the law's delay (and improving on its provisions). L seems to admire such justice, as a rough and ready substitute for the inefficiency and corruptness of the law, though the activities of the original Folville gang, whose exploits in Lincolnshire in the 1330s are well documented (see E. L. G. Stones in *TRHS*, 5th series, 7, 1957, 117-36, and R. H. Bowers in *NQ* 206, 1961, 327-8), might seem from the record little more than local banditry and feuding.

And somme he lered to lyue in longyng to be hennes,
In pouerte and in pacience to preye for alle cristene.
And al he lered to be lele, and vch a craft loue oþere,   250
Ne no boest ne debaet be among hem alle.
   'Thouh somme be clenner then somme, ȝe sen wel,' quod Grace,
'That all craft and connyng cam of my ȝefte.
Loke þat noen lacke oþere bute loueth as bretherne
And he þat moest maistries can, be myldest of berynge.   255
And crouneth Consience kyng and maketh Craft ȝoure styward
And aftur Craftes consail clotheth ȝow and fedeth.
For y make Peres the plouhman my procuratour and my reue,
And registrer to reseyuen *Redde quod debes*.
My prowour and my plouhman Peres shal ben on erthe   260
And for to tulye treuthe a teme shal he haue.'
   Grace gaf Peres a teme, foure grete oxen:
That oen was Luc, a large beste and a lou-chered,
And Marc, and Mathewe the thridde, myhty bestes bothe,
And ioyned til hem oen Iohan, most gentill of all,   265
The pris neet of Peres plouh, passynge alle oþere.
   And sethe Grace of his goednesse gaef Peres foure stottes,
All þat his oxes erede they to harwen aftur.
Oen hihte Austyn and Ambrosie anoþer,

248. lered U] X rered
258. procuratour U] X procreatour
268. to harwen P] X two harwed; U harowed; T to harewide

258. Piers Plowman acts as the mediator of the law of the Holy Spirit, as the inheritor of St Peter, and as the leader of the Church (cf. VII 188n). The ploughing scene which follows (262–335), which can be seen as a commentary on passus VIII (see VIII 2n, 112n, and cf. XII 165a), is allegorical of the establishment and life of the Christian community under the regulation of the Church. The allegorical connection between agricultural labour and the office of the clergy (with the soul as the field, and the preachers tilling the earth with the plowshare of the tongue: see X 199) was elaborately developed by the commentators, from many scriptural suggestions (see Barney, 1973), but especially Matt. 13:24.

259. *Redde quod debes*. See above, 187n.

262. *foure grete oxen*. The evangelists are the oxen (commonly used as draught-animals in medieval England, as well as horses: see H. G. Richardson, 'The Medieval Plough-Team', in *History* 26, 1942, 287–94) which draw the plough of the Scriptures, and prepare man's soul (275, below) for harrowing and planting. The idea was perhaps prompted by the fact that Luke is represented by an ox in the traditional symbolism derived from Ez. 1:10 and Apoc, 4:7 (Matthew by a man, Mark by a lion and John by an eagle), but the association of oxen with apostles and preachers was traditional in the agricultural imagery of the commentators (Barney, 1973, 267, 275).

269–70. The four greatest of the Church Fathers (see XV 45n), who are seen here primarily in their role as biblical commentators and exegetes.

Gregory the grete clerk and Ieroem þe gode.   270
Thise foure, the fayth to teche, folewede Peres teme
And harwed in an hand-while al holy scripture   f.98ᵇ
With two aythes þat they hadde, an oelde and a newe,
    Id est vetus testamentum et nouum.
    And Grace gaf Peres graynes, cardinales vertues,
And sewe hit in mannes soule, and sethe he toelde here names.   275
    Spiritus prudencie the furste seed hihte,
That ho-so ete þat, ymageny he sholde,
Ar he dede eny dede deuyse wel þe ende;
And lered men a ladel bugge with a longe stale
That caste for to kele a crok and saue þe fatte aboue.   280
    The seconde seed hihte *Spiritus temperancie*;
He þat eet of that seed hadde such a kynde,
Sholde neuere mete ne meschief maken hym to swelle,
Ne sholde no scornare out of skille hym brynge;
Ne neuere wynnynge ne welthe of wordliche richesse,   285
Waste word of ydelnesse ne wikede speche meue.
Sholde no curious cloth comen on his rugge
Ne no mete in his mouth þat maister Iohan spyced.
    The thridde seed that Peres sewe was *Spiritus fortitudinis*
And ho-so ete of þat seed hardy was euere   290
To soffre al þat god sente, seeknesse and angeres.

271. folewede U] X folewe
281. seed T] XU sethe
285. of U] X or
286. Waste T] XU Wasten
290. þat U] X þa

273a. 'That is, the old testament and the new'. *Id est* suggests the language of biblical exegesis and allegory.

274. *cardinales*. See Prol. 132n. The four cardinal virtues, prudence, temperance, fortitude and justice (see Tuve, 1966, 57–76), are distinguished from the three theological virtues, faith, hope and charity (XIX 47n), but the two groups are sometimes combined to form a seven, on the analogy of the seven deadly sins. These in turn are distinguished from the seven Christian virtues (VII 270n). The cardinal virtues are the social virtues (Bloomfield, 1961, 134), and their introduction here reinforces the emphasis on the life of the community (see note to 228a, above).

277. *ymageny*: 'have foresight'.

279. *lered*: '(it) taught'.

280. *That*: 'who', antecedent *men*. *kele* refers to the action of cooling a pot by stirring its contents, for which a long-handled ladle is prudent (cf. Knight's Tale, *CT* I. 2020), and necessary too for preserving the fat that floats to the top (which would otherwise bubble over into the fire).

288. *maister Iohan*: a contemptuous name for a cook.

Myhte no lyare with lesynges ne losse of worldly catel
Makyn hym, for eny mornynge, þat he ne was murye in soule,
And bold and abidynge busmares to soffre;
And pleded al with pacience and *Parce michi, domine*,   295
And keuered hym vnder consayl of Caton the wyse:
Esto forti animo cum sis dampnatus inique.

   The ferthe seed that Peres sewe was *Spiritus iusticie*,
And he þat ete of þat seed sholde be euene trewe
With god, and nat agast bote of gyle one   300
(For gyle goth so priueyly þat goed fayth oþer-while
May nat be aspyed thorw *Spiritus iusticie*).
Spiritus iusticie spareth nat to spille hem þat ben gulty
And for to corecte the kyng, and the kyng falle in any agulte.
For counteth he no kynges wreth when he in court sitteth,   305 f.99ª
To demen as a domesman; adrad was he neuere
Noþer of deuk ne of deth þat he ne dede þe lawe,
For presente or for preyere or eny prinses lettres;
He dede equite to alle euene-forth his knowyng.

   Thise foure sedes Peres sewe and sennes he dede hem harewe   310
With olde lawe and newe lawe that loue myhte wexe
Among thise foure vertues and vices distruye.
'For comunliche in contrayes cammokes and wedes
Fouleth the fruyt in the feld ther thei growe togyderes,
And so doth vices vertues; forthy,' quod Peres,   315
'Harweth alle þat conneth kynde wit bi consail of þis doctours
And tulieth aftur here techynge the cardinal vertues.'

   'Aʒeynes thy graynes,' quod Grace, 'bigynneth for to rype,
Ordeyne the an hous, Peres, to herborwe in thy cornes.'

---

292. lesynges U] X lesynge
295. pleded U] X plede
303–4. *lineation as* B; XUTP *mislineate*
311. lawe² U] X *om*
313. comunliche U] X cominliche
316. þat U] þa. þis U] X *om*
319. Peres U] X quod Peres. to U] X in to

---

295. *Parce michi, domine*: 'Spare me, O lord' (Job 7:16), the beginning of the first lesson at matins in the Office of the Dead (Breviary II. 273). See III 463n, V 46n.
297. 'Be resolute of spirit when you are judged unfairly' (*Disticha Catonis* ii.14: see IV 17n).
308. *For*: 'for any', i.e. despite.
315–17. Piers has authority to deal with special problems within the general directives given by Grace.
319. *an hous*. The house is at first a barn, called Unity or Holy Church, founded in Christ's Passion, in which may be gathered (as in Luke 3:17) the ripened corn of properly prepared human souls (cf. the fate of the fruit of the Tree of Charity, XVIII 111). The name 'Unity' is used to suggest the union of God and man in Christ and through him in his church (cf. John 17:11). It would not be appro-

'By god! Grace,' quod Peres, 'ȝe moet gyue tymber   320
And ordeyne þat hous ar ȝe hennes wende.'
   And Grace gaf hym þe cros with croune of thornes
That Crist vpon Caluary for mankynde on peyned;
And of his bapteme and bloed þat he bledde on rode
He made a manere morter, and mercy hit hihte.   325
And þerwith Grace bigan to make a goode foundement
And wateled hit and walled hit with his paynes and his passioun,
And of all holy writ he made a roof aftur
And calde þat hous Vnite, Holy Chirche an Englisch.
And when this dede was doen Grace deuysed   330
A cart hihte Cristendoem to carie hoem Peres sheues,
And gaf hym caples to his carte, Contrissioun and Confessioun,
And made presthoed hayward the while hymsulue wente
As wyde as the world is with Peres to tulye treuthe
And þe londe of bileue, the lawe of holi churche.   335
   Now is Peres to the plouh – Pryde hit aspiede
And gadered hym a grete oeste; greue he thenketh
Consience and alle cristene and cardinale vertues,
Blowe hem doun and breke hem and bite a-to þe mores;
And sente forth Surquidous, his seriaunte of armes,   340
And his spye Spille-loue, oen Speke-euele-bihynde.   f.99ᵇ
Thise two cam to Consience and to cristene peple
And toelde hem tydynges, þat tyne thei sholde
Þe sedes that sire Peres sewe, þe cardinale vertues:
'And Peres berne worth broke, and þei þat ben in Vnite   345
Shal come oute, and Consience and ȝoure two caples,
Confessioun and Contricioun, and ȝoure carte the bileue
Shal be coloured so queyntly and keuered vnder oure sophistrie
That Consience shal nat knowe (be contricioun ne bi confessioun)
    ho is cristene or hethene,

---

339. breke U] X bleke. bite U] X bete
340. Surquidous B] XUTP Surquidours. seriaunte B] XUTP seriauntes
343–4. *lineation as* P; XUT *mislineate* sholde þe sedes/That
346. and¹ U] X of
348. oure U] X ȝoure

---

priate to associate it with the mystical use of 'Unity' to describe the highest of the
three stages of the fully contemplative life (purgative, illuminative, unitive), as is
suggested by H. Meroney in *ELH* 17 (1950), 1–35, esp. p. 12.
323. *on peyned*: 'suffered on' (i.e. the Cross).
336. *Now is Peres to the plouh*. Cf. VIII 112. Here the meaning is that he leaves the
vicinity of Unity to till truth elsewhere. *Pryde*, as the chief of the seven deadly sins,
acts as commander of the host of Antichrist. Cf. XXII 70.
342. *Thise two*. Retention of this reading demands emendation in 340, above.
349. *be contricioun ne bi confessioun* seems to be an undigested addition to the original line:
it may be scribal.

Ne no manere marchaunt þat with moneye deleth   350
Where he wynne with riht, with wrong or with vsure!
With such colours and queyntises cometh Pruyde y-armed,
With the lord þat lyueth aftur the lust of his body,
To waston on wel-fare and in wikked kepynge
Alle the world in a while thorw oure wit,' quod Pruyde.   355
     Quod Consience to alle cristene tho, 'My consayl is þat we wende
Hastiliche to Vnite and holde we vs there.
Preye we þat a pees were in Peres berne þe plouhman,
For witterly y woet wel we be nat of strenghe
To goen agayn Pruyde bute Grace were with vs.'   360
     And thenne cam Kynde Wit Consience to teche,
And cryede and comaundede alle cristene peple
To deluen a dich depe aboute Vnite
That holi churche stoed in holinesse as hit were a pile.
     Consience commaundede tho alle cristene to delue   365
And make a moche moet þat myhte be a strenghe
To helpe holi churche and hem þat hit kepeth.
Thenne alle kyne cristene, saue commune wommen,
Repenteden and refused synne; saue thei one –
And a sisour and sompnour þat weren forsworen ofte;   370
Wytyng and wilfully with the false thei helden
And for suluer weren forswore, soth thei wisten hit –
Ther ne was cristene creature that kynde wit hadde
That he ne halpe a quantite holinesse to wexe,
Somme thorw bedes-biddynge and bi pilgrimages   375
Or oþer priue penaunses and somme thorw pans-delyng.   f.100ᵃ
And thenne walled watur for wikked werkes,
Egrelich ernynge oute at menne yes.
Clannesse of þe comune and clerkes clene lyuynge

---

364. pile P] XU pole; T piler
365. tho T] XU to
374. quantite U] X quatite

---

355. *quod Pruyde.* The speech began as one by Pride's outriders, who are the most
appropriate speakers still in 352.

363. *a dich.* Digging the moat of holiness about the barn of Unity turns it into a kind of
fortress, and prepares for the allegory of castle and siege in the next passus (XXII
70).

377–8. The suggestion seems to be that the tears of repentance fill the moat of holiness.
There is a striking parallel here with the *Ancrene Wisse* (Nero MS, ed. EETS 225,
109–10: see a note by G. L. Wilkes in *MS* 27, 1965, 334–6), where the scalding
tears of repentance which drive back the devil (alluding to Ps. 73:13) are com-
pared to the showers of boiling water with which the defenders of a castle drive
back the assailants. A second *uorbisne*, immediately following, speaks of the moat of
humility, watered by such tears, which surrounds the castle.

Made Vnite holi churche in holinesse stande. 380
   'Y care nat now,' quod Consience, 'thow Pryde come nouthe;
The lord of lust shal be ylette al this lente, y hope.
Cometh,' quod Consience, 'ȝe cristene, and dyneth,
That haen labored lelly al this lenten tyme.
Here is bred yblessed and godes body þerunder. 385
Grace thorw godes word gaf Peres plouhman power,
Myhte to make hit and men for to eten hit
In helpe of here hele ones in a monthe
Or as ofte as they hadden nede, tho þat hadden payed
To Peres pardon þe plouhman *Redde quod debes*.' 390
   'How?' quod alle þe comune, 'thow conseylest vs to ȝelde
Al þat we owen eny wyhte or þat we go to hosele?'
   'That is my conseil,' quod Consience, 'and cardinale vertues;
Or vch man forȝeue oþer, and þat wol þe *pater-noster*,
    Et dimitte nobis debita nostra,
And so to ben assoiled and sennes to be hoseled.' 395
   'ȝe? bawe!' quod a breware, 'y wol nat be yruled,
By Iesu! for al ȝoure iangelyng, aftur *Spiritus iusticie*
Ne aftur Consience, bi Crist, while y can sulle
Bothe dregges and draf and drawe at on hole
Thikke ale or thynne ale; and þat is my kynde 400
And nat to hacky aftur holinesse – hold thy tonge, Consience!
Of *Spiritus iusticie* thow spekest moche an ydel.'
   'Caytyf!' quod Consience, 'corsede wreche!
Vnblessed art thow, breware, but yf the god helpe.
Bote thow lyue bi lore of *Spiritus iusticie*, 405
The cheef seed þat Peres sewe, ysaued worst þou neuere.
Bote Consience thy comune fynde and cardinale vertues,

---

390. *debes* U] X debet
398. while y can T] XU y couthe
406. worst U] X woest
407. fynde] XUT fode; P fede

---

390. See 187, above.
393. *and cardinale vertues*: 'and (also the counsel of the) cardinal virtues'.
394. *Or vch man forȝeue oþer*. This is an alternative form of preparation for the eucharist, for those who have no debts to pay.
394a. 'And forgive us our debts (as we also have forgiven our debtors)' (Matt. 6:12).
397. *aftur*: 'according to'.
400. *Thikke ale or thynne ale*. For the brewer's practice, see VI 226.
401. *hacky aftur*: 'dig around for, grub about for', suggestive of something not worth bothering with, and perhaps with some allusion to what the brewer considered forced labour on the moat of holiness (365, above). The response of the brewer to Conscience's exhortations repeats, like much else in this passus, the pattern of earlier sequences in the *Visio* (e.g. VII 283, VIII 149).

Leue hit, þow art lost bothe lyf and soule.'
   'Thenne is many man ylost,' quod a lewed vicory.
'Ich am a curatour of holi churche and cam neuer in my tyme   410
Man to me þat me couthe telle of cardinales vertues   f.100^b
Or þat acounted Consience a cokkes fether or an hennes.
Y knewe neuere cardinale þat he ne cam fro þe pope
And we clerkes when they come for here comunes paieth,
For here pelure and palfrayes mete and pelours þat hem folweth.   415
The comune *clamat cotidie*, vch a man to oþer:
"The contreye is þe corsedore þat cardinals cometh ynne
And þer they lygge and lenge moest lecherye þer regneth."
Forthy,' quod this vicory, 'bi verray god y wolde
That no cardinal come among þe comune peple,   420
Bote in here holinesse holden hem stille
At Auenon among Iewes (*cum sancto sanctus eris, etc.*)
Or in Rome, as here reule wolde, þe relikes to kepe;
And thow, Consience, in kynges court and sholdest neuer come thennes,
And Grace, that thow gredest so of, gyour of all clerkes,   425
And Peres with his newe plouh and also his olde
Emperour of al þe world þat all men were cristene.
   Inparfit is þat pope þat all peple sholde helpe
And soudeth hem þat sleeth suche as he sholde saue.

408. þow art B] XUTP we been

409. *a lewed vicory*: an uneducated parish priest, ill-paid deputy to the *persone*. His opinions, though bluntly expressed, are not to be despised: he is the latest in a line of figures (including the dreamer and Rechelesnesse) who have questioned the relation between the Church's teaching and the Church's practice, between cardinal virtues and cardinals' virtue. His role seems to be to test and challenge the ecclesiastical orthodoxy of Conscience, and also to confirm it in significant ways, especially in his account of Piers Plowman (430–41).

413. *cardinale*. The *lewed vicory* takes advantage of the same pun as is exploited in Prol. 132–4. There may be allusion here to a specific embassy (Gwynn, 1943, 13). A Commons petition of 1376 speaks in bitter complaint against the cardinals who devour the land (*Rot. Parl.* ii.339).

416. *clamat cotidie*: 'cries out daily'.

422. *Auenon*. Avignon was the seat of the papacy from 1309 to 1377, and of the antipope during the period of the schism (XV 171n). *among Iewes*. Jews, as one of the classes of professional moneylenders, would have an important role at such a financial centre as the papal court (Bennett *MÆ*, 1943, 62–3). *cum sancto sanctus eris*: 'with the holy thou shalt be holy' (Ps. 17:26, used ironically).

424. For Conscience at the *kynges court*, see III 149.

428–9. For another reference to the schismatic wars of the popes, see XVII 234n, and see also Huppé, 1941, 41–4. Attacks on papal war-mongering are an insistent feature of Wycliffite writing, e.g. Wyclif, ed. Arnold, i.243–7, ii.314, 319, iii.141, 246.

Ac wel worth Peres the plouhman þat pursueth god in doynges,   430
Qui pluit super iustos et iniustos at ones,
And sente þe sonne to saue a corsed mannes tulthe
As brihte as to þe beste man or to þe beste womman.
Rihte so Peres the plouhman payneth hym to tulie
As wel for a wastour or for a wenche of the stuyves   435
As for hymsulue and his seruauntes, saue he is furste yserued.
So yblessed be Peres the plouhman þat peyneth hym to tulie
And trauaileth and tulieth for a tretour also sore
As for a trewe tydy man, alle tymes ylyke.
And worschiped be he þat wrouhte all, bothe gode and wicke,   440
And soffreth þat synnefole be til som tyme þat þei repente.
   And god amende þe pope þat pileth holi churche
And claymeth bifore þe kynge to be kepare ouer cristene
And counteth nat thow cristene be culde and yrobbed
And fynde folke to fihte and cristene bloed to spille,   445
Aȝen þe olde lawe and þe newe lawe, as Luk bereth witnesse:
   Non occides. Michi vindictam.   f.101[a]
Hit semeth, bi so hymsulue hadde his wille,
He rekketh riht nauht of þe remenaunt.
And Crist of his cortesye þe cardinals saue
And turne here wit to wisdoem and to wele for þe soule.   450
For the comune,' quod this curatour, 'counteth ful litel
The conseyl of Consience or cardinals vertues
Bote hit sowne, as bi sihte, somwhat to wynnynge.
Of gyle ne of gabbynges gyueth they neuer tale

432. sonne T] XU soule
441. som U] X com
450. wit U] X with
451. For U] X And

430. *wel worth.* See XIII 1n.
431. 'Who sends the rain on the just and the unjust' (Matt. 5:45, referring to the generous impartiality of God in his gifts).
432. *And sente*: 'And (who, i.e. *qui*, God) sends'.
436. *saue he is furste yserued.* Allegorically, there is a reference here to the hierarchy of heavenly reward (XIV 135n).
443. There is clearly a sceptical reference here to the doctrine of papal dominion, though this should not be regarded as a clear expression of Wycliffite opinion (Leff, 1967, 532–6), since there was but lukewarm acceptance for the doctrine in England.
445. See 428–9, above.
446a. 'Thou shalt not kill' (Ex. 20:13, quoted in Luke 18:20). 'Vengeance is mine' (also attributed to Luke in XVII 235).
454. *gyueth they neuer tale*: 'they never take account'.

For *Spiritus prudencie* among þe peple is gyle   455
And al tho fayre vertues as vises thei semeth.
For vch man sotileth a sleythe, synne to huyde,
And coloureth hit for a connyng and a clene lyuynge.'
    Thenne lowh ther a lord and 'Bi this lihte!' saide,
'Y halde hit riht and resoun of my reue to take   460
Al þat myn auditour or elles my styward
Conseileth me bi here acounte and my clerkes writyng.
With *Spiritus intellectus* they toke þe reues rolles
And with *Spiritus fortitudinis* fecche hit, wolle he, null he.'
    And thenne cam þer a kyng and bi his corone saide: 465
'Y am kyng with croune the comune to reule
And holy kyrke and clerge fro cursed men to defende.
And yf me lakketh to lyue by, þe lawe wol þat y take hit
Ther y may hastilokest hit haue, for y am heed of lawe
And 3e ben bote membres and y aboue alle.   470
And sethe y am 3oure alere heued y am 3oure alere hele
And holy churche cheef helpe and cheuenteyn of þe comune
And what y take of 3ow two y take hit at þe techynge
Of *Spiritus iusticie*, for y iuge 3ow alle.
So y may boldely be hoseled for y borwe neuere   475
Ne craue of my comune bote as my kynde asketh.'
    'In condicioun,' quod Consience, 'þat þou þe comune defende
And rewle thy rewme in resoun riht wel and in treuthe,

463. toke T] XU cote
469. may T] XU may hit
477. þe B] XUTP *om*

459–64. The lord seems to take it for granted that the activity of a reeve (cf. Chaucer's
Reeve, *CT* 1. 593–612) is a characteristic example of deceit and self-seeking
masquerading as prudence. He exonerates himself from blame by assigning the
responsibility for checking the reeve's *rolles*, or statements of account, to this
auditor and steward, who have the intelligence to understand them and the
authority to enforce repayment from the reeve if the accounts are shown to be
false. Like the brewer, the priest (in his criticisms) and the king (465–76), he
shows how self-interest challenges and may pervert the cardinal virtues, and
prepares us for the catastrophes of the next passus.

464. *wolle he, null he*: 'whether he likes it or not' ('willy-nilly').

465. *bi his corone*: 'with reference to his crown', i.e. in the right of his kingship.

471. *alere*, gen. pl., 'of (you) all'.

477. Conscience may seem a little apprehensive in his response to the king, but the king
is claiming no more for his regality than was offered, e.g. in the Wycliffite exalta-
tion of kingship (Workman, ii.29). See V 168.

Than haue thow al thyn askyng as thy lawe asketh.

 Omnia sunt tua ad defendendum sed non ad deprehendendum.'

The vicory hadde fer hoem and fair toek his leue,   480

And y wakned þerwith and wroet as me mette.   f.101^b

479. Than haue thow] XU That thow haue; T Trewþe wile þat þou haue; P Than that
thow haue

480. fair U] X *om*

481. me U] X *om*

479a. 'All things are thine to be defended but not to be exploited for gain'. Source not
identified. A similar sentence appears in a treatise on the Seven Deadly Sins which
may be a part-source of Chaucer's Parson's Tale (see S. Wenzel, in *Traditio* 30,
1974, 367); it was probably a familiar expression, going back to some legal dic-
tum.

Passus XXII

The Coming of Antichrist

Passus secundus de dobest
And as y wente by the way when y was thus awaked,
Heuy-chered y ȝede and elyng in herte,
For y ne wiste where to ete ne at what place.
And hit neyhed neyh þe noen and with Nede y mette
That afrounted me foule and faytour me calde: 5
'Couthest thow nat excuse the, as dede the kyng and oþere,
That thow toke to lyue by, to clothes and to sustinaunce,
Was bi techyng and by tellyng of *Spiritus temperancie*
And þat thow nome no more then nede the tauhte?
And nede ne hath no lawe ne neuere shal falle in dette   10
For thre thynges þat he taketh his lyf for to saue:
That is mete, when men hym werneth for he no money weldeth,
Ne wyht þat now wol be his borwe ne no wed hath to legge;
And he cacche in þat caes and come therto by sleithe
He synegeth nat sothlich þat so wynneth his fode.   15
And thow he come so to a cloth and can no bettere cheuesaunce,
Nede anoen-riht nymeth hym vnder maynprise.
And yf him lust for·to lape the lawe of kynde wolde
That he dronke at vch a dysch ar he deye for furste.
   So nede at greet nede may nyme as for his owne   20
Withouten consail of Consience or cardinale vertues,

---

2. elyng U] X helyng
11. his U] X is
18. him U] X *om*

---

1. For other waking episodes, see V 1, X 1.
7. *That*: 'that what'.
10. *nede ne hath no lawe.* Proverbial (Whiting N 51). Cf. XIII 43a.
15. Medieval theology taught that a man has a right to the necessities of life (I 20): 'in extreme need, a man is even bound under pain of sin to take them wherever he can get them' (Dunning, 1937, 33). But the nature of God's provision for the faithful has already been made clear (e.g. XVI 369–71, XVII 1–34; also below, 210–11), and its moral content is spelt out in Wyclif, ed. Arnold, i.37: 'No man shulde faile of mete unto harmynge of his soule, but ȝif his synne be cause þerof, and so þat it be good and just þat he faile þus of mete'.
17. The argument of necessity serves to release him from the full rigours of the law.

So þat he sewe and saue *Spiritus temperancie.*
For is no vertu be ver to *Spiritus temperancie,*
Noyther *Spiritus iusticie* ne *Spiritus fortitudinis.*
For *Spiritus fortitudinis* forfeteth wel ofte;   25
He shal do more þen mesure mony tymes and often
And bete men ouer-bitere and som body to litel
And greue men grettore then goed faith hit wolde.
And *Spiritus iusticie* shal iugen, wol he, nel he,
Aftur þe kynges conseyl and þe comune lyke.   30
And *Spiritus prudencie* in many a poynt shal faile
Of þat he weneth wolde falle yf his wit ne were.
Wenyng is no wisdoem ne wyse ymaginacioun:
    Homo proponit, deus disposuit;
God gouerneth all gode vertues.
   And Nede ys nexst hym, for anoen he meketh   35 f.102ᵃ
And as louh as a lamb for lakkyng þat hym nedeth,
For Nede maketh neede fele nedes louh-herted.
Philosopheres forsoke welthe for they wolde be nedy
And woneden wel elyngly and wolden nat be riche.
And god al his grete ioye goestliche he lefte   40
And cam and toek mankynde and bicam nedy.
So he was nedy, as saith the boek in mony sondry places,

26. þen U] X þe
34–6. *lineation as* U; X *mislineates*
35. ys U] X as

23. Need's selection of Temperance as the chief of the cardinal virtues might make us suspect special pleading, especially in so far as it involves deprecation of the other virtues. But Holy Church likewise emphasised *mesure* (I 33), and Need's argument may reflect an overriding concern with the life of the community (see Bloomfield, 1961, 135–43).

30. *and þe comune lyke*: 'and similarly (according to the counsel of) the commons'. Need suggests that the exercise of justice is inevitably influenced by political considerations, whether the influence is exerted by king or commons.

31–2. Prudence's mistake, according to Need, is in assuming that what is to come can be foreseen or prepared for.

34. 'Man proposes, God has disposed'. Usually *disponit*; cf. XI 306.

35. *Nede is nexst hym*, i.e. nearest to Temperance (see 23, above).

37. *nedes*: 'of necessity'. The argument, that it is necessity that forces men to be humble (and not patience that teaches them to be so), seems specious (though cf. the defence of poverty in XVI 44–98). The authority of Need as a witness in this episode is in fact throughout debatable. Even his use of the life of Christ as a model of Need (40–50, below) is suspect, being based on similar arguments falsely used by the friars in the controversy about poverty (see XII 99n, Wyclif, ed. Arnold, iii.410–15, and Frank, 1957, 113–17). Perhaps L is setting before us the *reality*, not the authority, of Need (cf. 232–41, below), so that we understand why friars must have a *fyndynge* (383, below).

That he saide in his sorwe on þe sulue rode:
"Bothe fox and foule may fle to hole and crepe
And þe fisch hath fyn to flete with to reste,   45
There nede hath ynome me þat y moet nede abyde
And soffre sorwes ful soure, þat shal to ioye torne."
Forthy be nat abasched to byde and to be nedy
Sethe he þat wrouhte al þe worlde was willefolliche nedy,
Ne neuere noen so nedy ne porore deyede.'   50
    Whenne Nede hadde vndernome me thus, anoen y ful aslepe
And mette ful merueylousely þat in mannes fourme
Auntecrist cam thenne, and al the crop of treuthe
Turned hit tyd vp-so-down, and ouertulde þe rote,
And made fals sprynge and sprede and spede menne nedes;   55
In vch a contrey ther he cam, kutte awey treuthe
And garte gyle growe þere as he a god were.
    Freres folewed þat fende, for he ȝaf hem copes,
And religious reuerensed hym and rongen here belles
And al þe couent cam to welcome a tyraunt   60
And alle hise as wel as hym, saue onelich foles;
The whiche foles were wel gladere to deye

---

49. he U] X *om*
51. me T] XU *om*
55. spede U] X speke
62. The whiche foles T] XU *om with subsequent mislineation*

44–7. Matt. 8:20. The words were actually spoken by Christ, according to the gospels, on an earlier occasion, but they were often associated with the words from the Cross.
50. Cf. X 193, XII 99, 130.
51. The eighth vision begins here.
53. *Auntecrist.* See XXI 219n. Antichrist now follows up the first attack of Pride (XXI 336), which was temporarily thwarted by the digging of the moat of holiness. The presence of Antichrist, whose coming, it was believed, would precede the Second Coming, gives to this last passus a powerful apocalyptic quality (cf. Prol. 62n, III 477, VIII 343, and Bloomfield, 1961, 9), in which the pattern of contemporary events is read as a premonition of the Last Days. The sense of impending doom was particularly strong in the later Middle Ages, and was reflected in an increasing volume of vaticinations foretelling the imminent coming of Antichrist (Leff, 1967, 5).
54. L continues here with the imagery of field and harvest (from Matt. 13:25) before turning to the allegory of the siege.
55. *spede menne nedes*: 'satisfy men's desires (of the things of the world)'.
57. *gyle.* See XXI 455.
58. The friars are systematically identified with Antichrist in the Wycliffite writings.
61. *foles* is used here, ironically (as often by Paul: see IX 105n), of faithful Christians. 'Þe world clepeth hem fooles þat goon Goddis weyes, and men clepeth hem "goode felawes" and worsshipful þat goon in þe feendis weyes' (Clanvowe, *The Two Ways*, ll. 601–4: see IX 136n).

Then to lyue lengere, sethe leautee was so rebuked
And a fals fende Auntecrist ouer all folke regnede.
And þat were mylde men and holy þat no meschief dradden, 65
Defyede all falsenesse and folke þat hit vsede,
And what kyng þat hem confortede, knowynge here gyle,
Thei corsede, and here consail, were hit clerk or lewed.
    Auntecrist hadde thus sone hondredes at his baner
And Pryde hit baer baldly aboute 70
With a lord þat lyueth aftur likyng of body,
That cam aȝen Consience, þat kepar was and gyour
Ouer kynde cristene and cardinale vertues. f.102^b
    'Y consail,' quod Consience tho, 'cometh with me, ȝe foles,
Into Vnite holi churche, and halde we vs there. 75
And crye we to Kynde þat he come and defende vs
Foles fro this fendes lymes, for Peres loue the plouhman;
And crye we on al þe comune þat thei come to Vnite
And þere abyde and bikere aȝeyn Beliales childrene.'
    Kynde Consience tho herde and cam oute of the planetes 80
And sente forth his forreours, feueres and fluxes,
Cowhes and cardiacles, crampes and toeth-aches,
Reumes and radegoundes and roynouse scabbes,
Byles and boches and brennynge aguwes;
Freneseyes and foule eueles, forageres of Kynde, 85

65. *And þat*: 'And those ("fools")'.

67. *hem*, i.e. the 'folk that used falseness'.

70. *Pryde* bears the banner, as the chief of the seven deadly sins (cf. XXI 336). The scene that follows, in which the vices besiege the barn-fortress of Unity (XXI 319, 363), is a form of *psychomachia*, or battle of vices and virtues (cf. VII 271n, and see C. S. Lewis, *The Allegory of Love*, Oxford, 1936, 66–73). The motif is perhaps too commonplace to make it worthwhile looking for parallels in particular OF allegorical poems such as Rutebeuf's *La Voie de Paradis* (see VII 205) or Huon de Meri's *Tournoiement* (see XV 47).

71. *a lord*, i.e. 'Pride of Life' (XI 177), the man dedicated to the pleasures of the world, like the 'King of Life' in the morality play *The Pride of Life* (ed. EETS, Supp. 1).

74. *ȝe foles*. See 61, above.

76. *Kynde*. Conscience calls on Nature to help, assuming that man's human nature, which he shares with Piers Plowman, or Christ incarnate (see XX 21n, 418n), is itself a defence against evil. Nature's help takes an unexpected form.

80. *oute of the planetes*. The incidence of disease, in nature, was controlled by planetary influence (as Chaucer's Doctor understands, *CT* I. 414). Nature's allies in the fight against sin are disease, age and death, since these reminders of mortality most surely bring man to an understanding of the nothingness of the things of the world. But coercion is a desperate expedient, and no substitute for spiritual reformation, as Piers Plowman found earlier when he called in Hunger to discipline the people (VIII 168). There is historical reference in both passages to the failure of the people to take notice of God's warning in the visitation of famine and plague (e.g. the Black Death) in the 14th c.

Hadde ypriked and preyed polles of peple;
Largeliche a legioun lees the lyf sone.
　　There was 'Harow!' and 'Help! here cometh Kynde
With Deth þat is dredful to vndoen vs alle!'
The lord þat lyuede aftur lust tho aloud cryede　　　　　　　90
Aftur Conforte, a knyhte, come and beer his baner.
'Aiarme! alarme!' quod þat lord, 'vch lyf kepe his owene!'
Thenne mette thise men, ar munstrals myhte pype
And ar heroudes of armes hadden descreued lordes,
Elde þe hore; he was in þe vawwarde　　　　　　　　　　95
And baer þe baner bifore Deth – bi riht he hit claymede.
Kynde cam aftur hym with many kyne sores,
As pokkes and pestilences, and moche peple shente;
So Kynde thorw corupcions kulde fol mony.
Deth cam dryuyng aftur and al to duste paschte　　　　　100
Kynges and knyhtes, caysers and popes.
Lered ne lewed he lefte no man stande
That he hitte euene, þat euere stured aftur.
Many a louly lady and here lemmanes knyhtes
Swowened and swelte for sorwe of dethes duntes.　　　　105
　　Concience of his cortesye tho Kynde he bisouhte
To sese and soffre, and se wher they wolde
Leue pruyde priueyliche and be parfyt cristene.
And Kynde sesede tho, to se þe peple amende.　　　　f.103ᵃ
　　Fortune gan flateren thenne tho fewe þat were alyue　110
And bihihte hem long lyf, and Lecherye he sente
Amonges alle manere men, wedded and vnwedded,
And gaderet a greet oest alle agayn Consience.
This Lecherye leyde oen with lauhyng chere
And with priue speche and paynted wordes,　　　　　　115
And armed hym in ydelnesse and in hey berynge.
He baer a bowe in his hoend, and many brode arwes,
Weren fythered with fayre biheste and many a fals treuthe,

---

103. hitte U] X hihte
105. swelte U] X swelde
110. tho T] XU to

92. 'To arms! to arms! Every man for himself!'
94. *descreued*: 'described', i.e. introduced the combatants by name and blazon (XVIII 186). In other words, this is a battle in earnest, not a chivalric exercise.
100. *Deth cam dryuyng aftur*. Perhaps we should imagine a skeleton astride a horse: the fourth rider, on 'a pale horse', of Apoc. 6:8 was often portrayed thus in Apocalypse illustration (Woolf, 1968, 336–7).
110. There was, to the disgust of moralists, no general improvement in people's morals in the years after the Black Death (cf. X 269).

And with vntidy tales he tened ful ofte
Consience and his companye, of holy churche þe techares.   120
   Thenne cam Couetyse and caste how he myhte
Ouercome Consience and cardinal vertues;
And armed hym in auarice and hungriliche lyuede.
His wepne was al wyles, to wynnen and to hyden;
With glosynges and gabbynges he gyled þe peple.   125
Symonye hym suede to assaile Consience
And presed on þe pope and prelates their made
To holde with Auntecrist, here temperaltee to saue;
And cam to þe kynges consail as a kene baroun
And knokked Consience in court bifore hem alle,   130
And gert Goed Faith fle and Fals to abyde
And baldeliche baer adoun, with many a brihte noble,
Moche of þe wyt and wisdoem of Westministre halle.
He iogged til a iustice and iustede in his ere
And ouertulde al his treuthe with 'Taek this on amendement';   135
And into þe Arches in haste he ȝede anoen aftur
And turnede syuyle into symonye, and sethe he toek þe official
And for a meneuer mantel he made leele matrimonye
Departen ar dethe come, and a deuors shupte.
   'Allas!' quod Consience tho, and cryede, 'Wolde Crist of his grace   140
That Coueytyse were cristene þat is so kene to fihte,
And bolde and abydynge þe while his bagge lasteth.'
   And thenne lowh Lyf and lette dagge his clothes,
And armed hym in haste in harlotes wordes,
And helde Holinesse a iape, and Hendenesse a wastour,   145 f.103ᵇ
And leet Leautee a cherl, and Lyare a freman;
Consience and conseil, he counted hit folye.

---

125. and U] X and be
128. mantel U] X mandel

129. There is reminiscence here of scenes in II 202ff.
133. *Westministre halle*, where the law-courts were (II 174).
134–5. The image, as Skeat points out, is that of a mock-joust, with the judge's ideas of truth and justice being overturned by the offer of a bribe to 'see things right'.
136. *þe Arches*. See II 61n.
137. *turnede syuyle into symonye*: 'subordinated Civil law to the practice of simony'. See II 63n. *toek*: 'gave (something) to', i.e. bribed.
139. *Departen ar dethe come* alludes to the words of the marriage-service (*Manuale ad usum Sarum*, ed. A. J. Collins, 1960, 48).
143. *Lyf*, i.e. the lord of 71, 90, above. *lette dagge his clothes*: 'had his clothes cut with slits or serrations in the hem'. This extravagant fashion was in vogue at the time, and much attacked by moralists (e.g. Chaucer's Parson's Tale, *CT* X. 418, 421).
146. 'And accounted loyalty a form of bondage and lying the only true freedom'.

Thus relyed Lyf for a litel fortune
And priketh forth with Pruyde – preyseth he no vertue
Ne careth nat how Kynde slowh and shal come at þe laste   150
And culle all erthely creature, saue Consience one.
 Lyf lepte asyde and lauhte hym a lemman:
'Hele and y,' quod he, 'and heynesse of herte
Shal do the nat drede noþer Deth ne Elde,
And to forȝete þouȝt and ȝeue nat of synne.'   155
This likede Lyf and his lemman Fortune
And geten in here glorie a gadlyng at þe laste,
Oen þat moche wo wrouhte, Sleuthe was his name.
Sleuthe wax wonder ȝerne and sone was of age
And wedded oen Wanhope, a wenche of þe stuyves;   160
Here syre was a sysour þat neuere swoer treuthe,
Oen Tomme Two-tonge, ateynt at vch enqueste.
This Sleuthe was sley of werre and a slynge made,
And throw drede of dispayr a doysayne myle aboute.
 For care Consience tho cryede vpon Elde   165
And bad hym fonde to fihte and afere Wanhope.
And Elde hente gode hope and hastiliche shroef hym
And wayued away Wanhope, and with Lyf he fihteth.
And Lyf fley for fere to Fisyk aftur helpe
And bisouhte hym of socour, and of here salue hadde,   170
And gaef hym goelde goed woen þat gladede here hertes,
And they gyuen hym agayne a glasene houe.
Lyf leuede þat lechecraft lette sholde Elde
And dryue awey Deth with dyaes and drogges.

148. fortune U] X folye
155. þouȝt T] XUP ȝouthe
162. tonge U] X to tonge
164. throw] X thorw; U þorgh; T þreuȝ
171. gladede U] X gladde

154. There is reminiscence here of the dream of the land of longing (e.g. XI 197), where Wanhope is also (XI 199, cf. 160, below) a consequence of following Fortune.
158. The submission of Life to the attractions of worldly Fortune produces a slothfulness in the works of the spirit which then issues in Wanhope, despair of grace and amendment (see VII 59n).
162. *Tomme Two-tonge*. Cf. IV 18.
167. 'Age took hope (of amendment and salvation) and quickly shrove himself'. Skeat's note here, which suggests that Elde formerly fought on the side of the vices (95, above), is mistaken (see 80n).
172. *a glasene houe*: 'a glass hood', a proverbial metaphor (Whiting H 218) for an imaginary protection, here a useless 'cure' (cf. *Troilus*, ii.867, v.469).

And Elde auntered hym on Lyf, and at þe laste he hitte 175
A fisician with a forred hoed that he ful in a palesye,
And þere deyede þat doctour ar thre dayes aftur.
'Now y see,' saide Lyf, 'that surgerie ne fysyke
May nat a myte avayle to medlen aȝen Elde.'
And in hope of his hele gode herte he hente 180
And roed so to Reuel, a ryche place and a murye, f.104ᵃ
(The compeny of Comfort men clepede hit som tyme),
And Elde aftur hym, and ouer myn heued ȝede
And made me balled bifore and baer on þe crowne;
So harde he ȝede ouer myn heued hit wol be sene euere! 185
  'Syre euele-tauȝt Elde,' quod y, 'vnhende go with the!
Sennes whanne was þe way ouer menne heuedes?
Haddest thow be hende,' quod y, 'thow wost haue asked leue.'
  'Ȝe, leue? lordeyne!' quod he, and leide on me with age,
And hitte me vnder þe ere – vnnethe may ich here. 190
He boffeded me aboute þe mouthe and beet out my wang-teeth,
And gyued me in gowtes – y may nat go at large.
And of þe wo þat y was ynne my wyf hadde reuthe
And wesched wel witterly þat y were in heuene.
For þe lyme þat she loued me fore and leef was to fele 195
(A nyhtes, nameliche, when we naked were),
Y ne myhte in none manere maken hit at here wille,
So Elde and she hit hadde forbete.
  And as y saet in this sorwe y say how Kynde passede
And Deth drow ney me; for drede gan y quaken 200
And cryede to Kynde out of care me brynge:
'Lo, how Elde þe hore hath me byseye;
Awreke me, ȝif ȝoure wille be, for y wolde be hennes.'
  'Yf thow wolde be wreke, wende into Vnite
And halde the there euere til y sende for the, 205
And loke thow conne som craft ar thow come thennes.'

---

186. tauȝt U] X ythouȝte
198. she U] X hee

---

175. *auntered hym on Lyf*: 'ventured himself (in an attack) on Life'. A jousting term.
176. *A fisician with a forred hoed*. Cf. VIII 291.
180–82. Enjoying the pleasures of life puts away for a while thoughts of growing old.
183. In this strange interlude (183–213), the life of the dreamer, growing old and bald, materializes momentarily in his dream in a matter-of-fact and slightly comical way. Though the dreamer has no proper part in the action, and though, in a larger way, it is not possible to relate the poem's sequence to the chronology of the dreamer's life (see XI 189, XII 1, and cf. J. F. Adams, '*P.Pl.* and the Three Ages of Man', *JEGP* 61, 1962, 23–41), the interlude gives a poignant personal focus to the vision of the world running down to destruction.
189. *Ȝe, leue?*: 'Oh yes, (ask) leave, eh?'

'Consaileth me, Kynde,' quod y, 'what craft be beste to lere?'
'Lerne to loue,' quod Kynde, 'and leef all othere.'
'How shal y come to catel so, to clothe me and to fede?'
'And thow loue lelly, lacke shal the neuere   210
Wede ne worldly mete while thy lif lasteth.'
And y bi conseil of Kynde comsed to rome
Thorw Contricion and Confessioun til y cam to Vnite.
And there was Consience constable, cristene to saue,
And biseged soethly with seuene grete geauntes   215
That with Auntecrist helden harde aȝeyn Consience.
  Sleuthe with his slynge an hard sawt he made.   f.104ᵇ
Proute prestes cam with hym – passyng an hundred
In paltokes and pikede shoes and pissares longe knyues
Comen aȝen Consience; with Couetyse they helden.   220
'By þe Marie,' quod a mansed prest, was of þe march of Ireland,
'Y counte no more Consience, bi so y cache suluer,
Then y do to drynke a drauht of goed ale!'
And so sayde syxty of þe same contreye,
And shoten aȝeynes hym with shotte, many a shef of othes,   225
And brode-hokede arwes – goddes herte, and his nayles –
And hadden almost Vnite and holynesse adowne.
  Consience cryede, 'Helpe, Clergie, or y falle
Thorw inparfit prestes and prelates of holy churche!'
Freres herde hym crye and comen hym to helpe,   230
Ac for they couthe nat wel here crafte Consience forsoek hem.

217. an U] X and
225. with U] X *om*
231. Ac P] XU And; *line om* T

208. An emergency summary of the poem's argument. Cf. I 141–200.
209. The dreamer is uneasily conscious of what Need was saying earlier (6–50, above): love is all very well, but surely a certain enlightened self-interest is proper?
213. *Contricion and Confessioun*, the first two stages of the act of penance, the third being Satisfaction or Amendment. They were horses in XXI 346.
214. *Conscience constable.* Cf. X 143.
215. *seuene grete geauntes*: the seven deadly sins.
219. *and pissares longe knyues.* We should expect this phrase to be introduced by *with* rather than *in*, and the expression is in other ways awkward. Kane-Donaldson emend the corresponding half-line in B to '[purses and] longe knyues' (see their Introd., p. 184), but this does not completely remove the awkwardness. *pissare* is attested as a term for 'man' and is used (see OED) to translate Lat. *mingentem* in 4 Reg. 9:8. It might suggest lechery; it might be a cant term for a long knife. What is clear is that knives are as inappropriate to priests as peaked shoes (see B XV 124). Translate: 'and carrying long knives like common men'.
226. Oaths by God's heart, or the nails of the Cross, are like weapons used against the Church and God. Cf. Pardoner's Tale, *CT* VI. 474, 651; Parson's Tale, *CT* X. 591.

Nede neyhede tho ner and Conscience he toelde
That they cam for couetyse to haue cure of soules:
'And for thei aren pore, parauntur, for patrimonye hem faileth,
Thei wol flatere, to fare wel, folk þat ben riche.   235
And sethen thei chosen chele and cheytyftee
Late hem chewe as thei chose and charge hem with no cure!
For lomere he lyeth þat lyflode moet begge
Then he þat laboreth for lyflode and leneth hit beggares.
And senne freres forsoke the felicite of erthe   240
Lat hem be as beggares or lyue by angeles fode!'
   Consience of this consail tho comesed for to lawhe,
And corteysliche confortede hem and calde hem in, all freres,
And saide, 'Syres, soethly welcome be ȝe alle
To Vnite and holi churche, ac o thyng y ȝow preye –   245
Holdeth ȝow in Vnite and haueth noen enuye
To lered ne to lewed, but lyueth aftur ȝoure reule.
Y wol be ȝoure borwh; ȝe shal haue breed and clothes
And oþere necessaries ynowe; ȝow shal no thyng lakke
With þat ȝe leue logyk and lerneth for to louye.   250
For loue lefte they lordschipe, bothe lond and scole,
Frere Fraunceys and Domynyk, for loue to be holy.
   And yf ȝe coueiteth cure, Kynde wol ȝow telle   f.105ᵃ
That in mesure god made alle manere thynges
And sette hit at a serteyne and at a syker nombre   255
And nempned hem names and nombred þe sterres.
   Qui numerat multitudinem stellarum.
Kynges and knyhtes, þat kepen and defenden,
Haen officerys vnder hem and vch of hem a certeyne.

236. cheytyftee] XU cheytyftee pouerte; TP chaitif pouerte
240. felicite T] XU felice
243. corteysliche U] X corteyliche
254. manere U] X *om*
257. kepen U] X kepten

233. *cure of soules.* In assuming the role of confessors (Prol. 62n), friars had laid claim to the cure of souls, the responsibility of the parish priest, and to endowment.
241. *by angeles fode,* i.e. on nothing.
242. Conscience laughs at Need's advice because it is so obviously at variance with Christian charity. He suggests that friars, provided they keep their rule, should have what is necessary to live on. The poem ends (383, below) on the same question.
250. *With þat:* 'provided that'. *ȝe leue logyk.* Friars were criticized for their over-ingenious interpretation of the scriptures (Prol. 58n).
252. *Fraunceys and Domynyk,* the founders of the two main orders of friars.
256a. 'Who determines the number of the stars (and gives to all of them their names)' (Ps. 146:4). Not to be numbered is to be lost from God's sight (270, below).

And yf thei wage men to werre thei writen hem in nombre;
Wol no tresorer taken hem wages, trauayle they neuere so sore,　260
Bote hy ben nempned in þe nombre of hem þat been ywaged.
Alle oþere in bataile been yholde brybours,
Pilours and pike-harneys, in vch a parsch acorsed.
Monkes and monyales and alle men of religioun,
Here ordre and here reule wol to haue a certeyne nombre.　265
Of lewed and of lered the lawe wol and asketh
A certeyne for a certeyne – saue oenliche of freres!
Forthy,' quod Consience, 'bi Crist, kynde wit me telleth
Hit is wikked to wage ʒow, ʒe wexeth out of nombre.
Heuen hath euene nombre and helle ys withouten nombre;　270
Forthy y wolde witterly þat ʒe were in registre
And ʒoure nombre vnder notarie sygne and noþer mo ne lasse!'
　Enuye herde this, and heete freres go to scole
And lerne logyk and lawe and eke contemplacioun,
And preche men of Plato and preuen hit by Seneca　275
That alle thynges vnder heuene ouhte to be in comune.
　He lyeth, as y leue, þat to þe lewed so precheth,
For god made to men a lawe and Moyses hit tauhte:
　Non concupisces rem proximi tui.
And euele is this yholde in parsches of Yngelond,
For persones and parsche prestes, þat sholde þe peple shryue,　280
They ben curatours cald, to knowe and to hele,

268. Forthy U] X For they
270. *line supplied from* U; X *om*
276. ouhte] X oute; U ought
281. They ben T] XU And they ben

263. *pike-harneys*: those who steal armour from the dead after a battle.
265. *wol*: 'require (them)'. *a certeyne nombre.* The number on the establishment of a
　religious house was usually regulated.
267. *A certeyne for a certeyne*: 'a certain number for a certain job'.
270. The suggestion for this is in texts like 256a, above, and Job 10:22 (cf. Parson's
　Tale, *CT* X. 217–18), set against Apoc. 20:8, but there are many contradictory
　texts (e.g. Apoc. 7:9, Jer. 33:22). Commentary on Job 10:22 was apparently first
　applied to the friars by the great anti-mendicant propagandist, archbishop
　Fitzralph (see Prol. 62n; Bloomfield, 1961, 146, and *Defensio Curatorum*, 59–60).
　England swarmed with friars, according to the Wife of Bath (*CT* III. 866) and
　Wyclif (ed. Arnold, iii.400).
275. *Plato, Seneca.* Quoted as general 'authorities' (XII 172n).
276. Friars preached the virtues of communal possession as an extension of their doc-
　trine of voluntary poverty. L sees it as a way of poaching on people who earn their
　living honestly, and a result of Envy. An instance in 1371 of friars petitioning
　parliament and asking for the disendowment of the monasteries for the common
　good is mentioned in Bloomfield, 1961, 80.
278a. 'Thou shalt not covet anything that is thy neighbour's' (Ex. 20:17).

Alle þat been here parschienes penaunses enioynen
And be aschamed in here shryft; ac shame maketh hem wende
And fle to þe freres, as fals folk to Westmynstre,
That borweth and bereth hit theddere and thenne biddeth frendes   285
ȝerne of forȝeuenesse or lengore ȝeres leue.
Ac while he is in Westmynstre he wol be bifore   f.105^b
And maken hym murye with oþere menne godes.
And so hit fareth with moche folke þat to freres shryuen,
As sisours and secutours; they shal ȝeue þe freres   290
A parcel to preye for hem, and make hem merye
With þe remenaunt that oþere men biswonke,
And soffren þe dede in dette to þe day of dome.
     Enuye herfore hatede Consience,
And freres to filosophye he foend hem to scole,   295
The while Couetyse and Vnkyndenesse Consience assailede.
In Vnite holi church Consience heeld hym
And made Pees porter to pynne þe ȝates
Of all tale-tellares and titerares an ydel.
Ypocrisye and they an hard sawt they ȝeuen.   300
Ypocrisye at þe ȝate harde gan fyhte
And wounded wel wykkedly many a wys techare

---

283. hem U] X *om*
291–3. *lineation as* P; XUT *lineate as two lines*

283–93. L recurs to one of the fundamental themes of the poem – the way in which friars, by taking over the role of confessors, have undermined the efficacy of confession and the penitence that must accompany it (Prol. 62n). People evade the real soul-searching of confession, the shame and repudiation of sin, the consequences as to penance and amendment, by making superficial formal confession to friars, who have little interest in the matter apart from money. As swindlers borrow money to go to law (for purposes such as those described in 131–9, above) and get the loan waived or extended while they have a good time on the proceeds, so those who confess to the friars are increasing their debt of sin, not repaying it, at the same time that they live lives of worldly pleasure on the presumed strength of improper confession. The last line of the comparison (288) reminds L of another practice associated with those who confess to friars: in their capacity as jurymen and executors they pay off a trifle from a dead man's estate to friars to pray for their souls, or that of the dead man, and spend the rest on themselves, leaving the dead man to bear the full burden of his debt of sin (which might otherwise be reduced by the prayers of the faithful) in purgatory until doomsday.
283. *And be aschamed*: 'and (to enjoin them also) to be ashamed'.
285. *hit*, i.e. what they borrow.
291–2. *make . . . biswonke*. Kane-Donaldson read '[pleye] wiþ þe remenaunt', regarding the rest as scribal padding.
294. L picks up again from 273, after his digression.
299. *Of*: 'with regard to', i.e. against.

That with Consience acordede and cardinal vertues.
Consience calde a leche þat couthe wel shryue
To salue tho þat syke were and thorw synne ywounded.   305
Shrift schupte scharp salue and made men do penaunses
For here mysdedes that thei wrouht hadde,
And þat Peres pardon were ypayd, *redde quod debes.*
    Somme liked nat this leche and letteres they sente
Yf eny surgien were in þe sege that softur couthe plastre.   310
Sire Lyf-to-lyue-in-lecherye lay þer and groned;
For fastyng of a Fryday a feerde as he wolde deye.
'Ther is a surgien in the sege that softe can handele,
And more of fysyk bi fer, and fayror he plastereth;
Oen frere Flatrere is fiscicien and surgien.'   315
Quod Contricion to Consience, 'Do hym come to Vnite,
For here is many man hert thorw Ypocrisye.'
'We haen no nede,' quod Consience; 'y woet no bettere leche
Then person oþer parsche prest, penytauncer or bischope,
Saue Peres the plouhman, þat haeth power ouer alle   320
And indulgence may do, but yf dette lette hit.
Y may wel soffre,' sayde Consience, 'sennes ȝe desiren,
That frere Flaterare be fet and fisyk ȝow seke.'
    The frere herof herde and hyede faste   f.106ᵃ
To a lord for a lettre, leue to haue to curen   325
As a curatour a were, and kam with his lettre
Baldly to þe bishope and his breef hadde
In contreys þer he cam confessiones to here;
And cam þer Consience was and knokked at þe ȝate.
Pees vnpynned hyt, was porter of Vnite,   330
And in haste asked what his wille were?
    'In fayth,' quod this frere, 'for profyt and for helthe,
Karpe y wolde with Contricioun and þerfore y cam heddere.'
    'He is syke,' saide Pees, 'and so ar many other;
Ypocrysye haeth herte hem – ful hard is yf thei keuere.'   335
    'Y am a surgien,' saide the frere, 'and salues can make;
Consience knoweth me wel and what y can bothe.'
    'Y preye the,' quod Pees tho, 'ar thow passe forþere,
What hattest thow? y praye the, hele nat thy name.'

---

331. asked U] X eschete
335. herte] X herde; U hirt

---

308. *And þat*: 'and (to make sure) that'. *redde quod debes.* See XXI 187n.
321. *but yf dette lette hit.* See XXI 190.

'Certes,' saide his felawe, 'sire *Penetrans-domos*.' 340
'3e? go thy gate!' quod Pees, 'bi god, for al thi fisyk,
Bote thow conne eny craft thow comest nat here-ynne!
Y knewe such oen ones, nat eyhte wynter passed,
Cam ynne thus ycoped at a court þer y dwelte,
And was my lordes leche and my ladyes bothe. 345
And at þe laste this lymytour, tho my lord was oute,
He salued so oure wymmen til some were with childe!'
    Hende-speche heet Pees tho opene the 3ates:
'Lat in þe frere and his felawe and make hem fayere chiere.
He may se and here here, so may bifalle, 350
That Lyf thorw his lore shal leue Couetyse
And be adrad of Deth and withdrawe hym fro Pruyde
And acorde with Consience and kusse here ayther oþer.'
    Thus thorw Hende-speche entred the frere
And cam to Consience and corteyslich hym grette. 355
'Thow art welcome,' quod Consience; 'can thow hele syke?
Here is Contricioun,' quod Consience, 'my cosyn, ywounded;
Conforte hym,' quod Consience, 'and taek kepe to his sores.
The plasteres of the persoun, and poudres, ben to sore,
And lat hem lygge ouer-longe and loeth is to chaungen; 360 f.106ᵇ
Fro lente to lente he lat his plastres byte.'
    'That is ouer-longe,' quod this lymitour, 'y leue. Y schal amenden
        hit';
And goeth gropeth Contricion and gaf hym a plastre
Of a pryue payement and 'Y shal preye for 3ow,
And for hem þat 3e aren holde to, al my lyf-tyme, 365

---

355. corteyslich U] X corteylich

---

340. *Penetrans-domos.* 'Among them (i.e. those whose presence will be perilous "in the last days") are those who *insinuate themselves into households*, and subdue to their purposes weak and foolish women' (2 Tim. 3:6). The apocalyptic prophecies of 2 Tim. 3:1–10 (cf. also XV 76a) had been associated with the coming of the friars by William of St Amour (see Prol. 62n). The accusation of spiritually seducing women made by him (see Williams, 1953, 512) was readily extended to charges of physical seduction. For a lively example, see the *Song against the Friars* in Wright, *Pol. Poems* i.265–6.

345. *my lordes leche.* Friars of course had a reputation as bodily as well as spiritual physicians, and could take advantage of both (see Wyclif, ed. Matthew, 10).

351. *Lyf.* The central figure in the allegory of this passus. See above, 71n, 90, 143–83, 311.

359–61. The plasters of true shrift (cf. XIX 89) are the painful kind of poultices which 'draw' as they draw out the evil of a wound or a sore (like the *drawyng salue* of *Jacob's Well*, 178–9); but these plasters have been left on too long (Contricion only confesses once a year, at Easter, the time of obligation) and the wound is reinfected. Cf. IX 262–3; Parson's Tale, *CT* X. 998.

And make ȝow my Ladye in masse and in matynes
Of freres of oure fraternite, for a litel suluer.'
Thus he goeth and gedereth and gloseth þer he shryueth
Til Contricioun hadde clene forȝete to crye and to wepe
And wake for his wikkede werkes, as he was woned bifore.   370
For confort of his confessour, Contricioun he lefte,
That is the souereyne salue for alle kyne synnes.
    Sleuth seyh þat, and so dede Pruyde,
And comen with a kene wil, Consience to assaile.
Consience cryede efte Clergie come help hym,   375
And baed Contricioun to come to helpe kepe þe ȝate.
'He lyeth adreint,' saide Pees, 'and so doth mony oþere;
The frere with his fisyk this folk hath enchaunted
And doth men drynke dwale, þat men drat no synne.'
    'By Crist,' quod Consience tho, 'y wol bicome a pilgrime,   380
And wenden as wyde as þe world regneth
To seke Peres the plouhman, þat Pruyde myhte destruye,
And þat freres hadde a fyndynge, þat for nede flateren
And countrepledeth me. Consience. Now Kynde me avenge,
And seende me hap and hele til y haue Peres plouhman.'
And sethe he gradde aftur Grace tyl y gan awake.

373. sleuth U] X sleyth

366. *my Ladye*, i.e. a particular object of my prayers as a member of our fraternity (III
51n), with some hint that he will be equal to Our Lady in the zeal with which
they pray for him. Kane-Donaldson substitute *memoria* (see their Introd., p. 160).
For this use of *my Ladye*, cf. *Cleanness* 1084.
382. Conscience goes out to seek Piers Plowman, the founder of Holy Church, who last
appeared in the poem as he left to till truth in all the world (XXI 336). In other
words, the Church's strength can only be restored by a return to the principles on
which it was founded.
383. *And þat*: 'and (ensure) that'. Holy Church, the Unity of the Christian community,
is threatened by the friars, whose lack of a *fyndynge*, or provision for their necessary
livelihood (cf. V 175), drives them into a flattering and false misuse of confession,
which undermines the act of penance and destroys all hope for men of winning
Piers's pardon.
386. For the relation of Piers Plowman to Grace (the Holy Spirit), see XXI 208n,
258n. *tyl y gan awake*. This last episode (228–386) – closely detailed, bitterly
specific, dry, toneless, unheroic, almost comic – makes an extraordinary ending to
a long Christian poem, as L focusses his vision of the world's ills with desperate
clarity upon the friars. The ending is abrupt, but to us, as to Skeat, he will seem
'to have ceased speaking at the right moment, and to have managed a very
difficult matter with consummate skill'. Above all, the ending of the poem is a
beginning, the beginning of a new search, but with the nature of the quest now
clearly identified (cf. Prol. 4) and the object of the quest known and loved (cf. X
2). There is no end to the searching. 'We shall not cease from exploration/And the
end of all our exploring/Will be to arrive where we started/And know the place for
the first time'.

Alphabetical Reference-List

This list serves as a key for the abbreviated references to books and articles used in the Introduction and in the Notes to the Text. Such references are normally employed for works which are referred to more than once. For a recent annotated bibliography to the poem, see K. Proppe, in *Comitatus* 3 (1972), 33–88.

Adams 1976   R. Adams, 'Langland and the Liturgy Revisited', *SP* 73 (1976), 266–84

Aers 1975   D. Aers, *Piers Plowman and Christian Allegory* (London, 1975)

Alan of Lille   *Anticlaudianus*, in *Anglo-Latin Satirical Poets of the Twelfth Century*, ed. T. Wright, Rolls series 59 (1872), ii. 268–428

——   *De Planctu Naturae*, in *ibid.*, ii. 429–522

Alford   J. A. Alford, 'Some Unidentified Quotations in *Piers Plowman*', *MP* 72 (1974–5), 390–99

Alford 1977   J. A. Alford, 'The Role of the Quotations in *Piers Plowman*', *Spec.* 52 (1977), 80–99

Amassian 1971   M. Amassian and J. Sadowsky, 'Mede and Mercede: A Study of the Grammatical Metaphor in *Piers Plowman* C. IV. 335–409', *NM* 72(1971), 457–76

Ames 1970   R. M. Ames, *The Fulfillment of the Scriptures: Abraham, Moses, and Piers* (Evanston, 1970)

Ancrene Wisse   *The English Text of the Ancrene Riwle*, ed. J. R. R. Tolkien, EETS 249 (1962)

——, ed. Shepherd   *Ancrene Wisse*, Parts Six and Seven, ed. G. Shepherd, Nelson's Medieval and Renaissance Library (London and Edinburgh, 1959)

Axton 1974   R. Axton, *European Drama of the Early Middle Ages* (London, 1974)

Barney 1973   S. A. Barney, 'The Plowshare of the Tongue: The Progress of a Symbol from the Bible to *Piers Plowman*', *MS* 35 (1973), 261–93

Bartholomaeus   *On the Properties of Things*, John Trevisa's translation of *Bartholomaeus Anglicus De Proprietatibus Rerum*, general editor M. C. Seymour, 2 vols. (Oxford, 1975)

Bennett   Langland, *Piers Plowman*, The Prologue and Passus I–VII of the B-text, ed. J. A. W.

	Bennett, Clarendon Medieval and Tudor Series (Oxford, 1972)
Bennett *MÆ* 1943	J. A. W. Bennett, 'The Date of the B-text of *Piers Plowman*', *MÆ* 12 (1943), 55–64
Bennett *PMLA* 1943	J. A. W. Bennett, 'The Date of the A-text of *Piers Plowman*', *PMLA* 58 (1943), 566–72
Blake 1972	*Middle English Religious Prose*, ed. N. F. Blake, York Medieval Texts (London, 1972)
Bloomfield 1958	M. W. Bloomfield, '*Piers Plowman* and the Three Grades of Chastity', *Anglia* 76 (1958), 227–53
Bloomfield 1961	M. W. Bloomfield, *Piers Plowman as a Fourteenth-Century Apocalypse* (New Brunswick, N.J., 1961)
Boethius	*De Consolatione Philosophiae* (The Consolation of Philosophy), ed. L. Bieler, Corpus Christianorum Series Latina XCIV (Turnhout, 1957). English trans. by V. E. Watts (Penguin, 1969)
Breviary	*Breviarium ad usum insignis ecclesiae Sarum*, ed. F. Procter and C. Wordsworth, 3 vols. (Cambridge, 1882–6)
Bright 1928	A. H. Bright, *New Light on 'Piers Plowman'* (London, 1928)
Brinton, Sermons	*The Sermons of Thomas Brinton, Bishop of Rochester (1373–1389)*, ed. Sister Mary Aquinas Devlin, 2 vols., Camden Third Series, vols. LXXXV–VI (London, 1954)
Burrow 1965	J. Burrow, 'The Action of Langland's Second Vision', *EC* 15 (1965), 247–68
Carnegy 1934	F. A. R. Carnegy, *An Attempt to Approach the C-Text of Piers the Plowman* (London, 1934)
Castle of Love	see Sajavaara 1967
Cato's *Distichs*	see *Disticha Catonis*
Chambers 1924	R. W. Chambers, 'Long Will, Dante, and the Righteous Heathen', *E & S* 9 (1924), 50–69
Chaucer	*The Works of Geoffrey Chaucer*, ed. F. N. Robinson (1933; 2nd ed., Cambridge, Mass., 1957). For abbreviated titles of poems, see List of Abbreviations
Cleanness	Ed. (as *Purity*) R. J. Menner (New Haven, 1920)
Coghill 1933	N. K. Coghill, 'The Character of Piers Plowman considered from the B Text', *MÆ* 2 (1933), 108–35
Coghill 1944	N. Coghill, 'The Pardon of Piers Plowman', *PBA* 30 (1944), 303–57
Cursor Mundi	Ed. R. Morris, EETS 57, 59, 62, 66, 68, 99, 101 (1874–93)

Davlin 1971   Sister Mary C. Davlin, O. P., '*Kynde Knowyng* as a Major Theme in *Piers Plowman* B', *RES*, n.s. 22 (1971), 1–19

Defensio Curatorum   Richard Fitzralph's Sermon: 'Defensio Curatorum' (as translated by John Trevisa), pp. 39–93 in Trevisa, *Dialogus inter Militem et Clericum*, etc., EETS 167 (1925)

Disticha Catonis   Ed. M. Boas (Amsterdam, 1952). English trans. in *Minor Latin Poets*, ed. J. W. and A. M. Duff (Loeb Classical Library, 1934)

Dives et Pauper   Ed. P. H. Barnum (Part I: Text of Commandments I–IV), EETS 275 (1976)

Dobson 1970   *The Peasants' Revolt of 1381*, ed. R. B. Dobson (London, 1970)

Donaldson 1949   E. Talbot Donaldson, *Piers Plowman: The C-Text and Its Poet*, Yale Studies in English 113 (New Haven, 1949)

Donaldson 1966   E. Talbot Donaldson, 'The Grammar of Book's Speech in "Piers Plowman"', in *Studies in Language and Literature in Honour of Margaret Schlauch* (Warsaw, 1966), pp. 103–9

Dunning 1937   T. P. Dunning, *Piers Plowman: An Interpretation of the A-Text* (London, 1937)

Dunning 1943   T. P. Dunning, 'Langland and the Salvation of the Heathen', *MÆ* 12 (1943), 45–54

English Gilds   *English Gilds*, ed. Toulmin Smith and Lucy Toulmin Smith, EETS 40 (1870)

Frank 1957   R. W. Frank, *Piers Plowman and the Scheme of Salvation*, Yale Studies in English 136 (New Haven, 1957)

Friedberg   *Corpus Iuris Canonici*, ed. A. Friedberg, 2 vols. (Leipzig, 1879)

Goodridge 1959   Langland: *Piers the Ploughman*, trans. J. F. Goodridge (Penguin, 1959)

Gray 1975   *A Selection of Religious Lyrics*, ed. D. Gray, Clarendon Medieval and Tudor Series (Oxford, 1975)

Grosseteste, *Chateau d'Amour*   see Sajavaara 1967

Gwynn 1943   A. Gwynn, S. J., 'The Date of the B-text of *Piers Plowman*', *RES* 19 (1943), 1–24

Handling Synne   Robert [Mannyng] of Brunne's '*Handlyng Synne*', ed. F. J. Furnivall, EETS 119, 123 (1901–3)

Hill 1968   T. D. Hill, 'The Tropological Context of Heat and Cold Imagery in Anglo-Saxon Poetry', *NM* 69 (1968), 522–32

Hort   Greta Hort, *Piers Plowman and Contemporary Religious Thought* (London, n.d.)

Huppé 1939	B. F. Huppé, 'The A-Text of *Piers Plowman* and the Norman Wars', *PMLA* 54 (1939), 37–64
Huppé 1941	B. F. Huppé, 'The Date of the B-Text of "Piers Plowman" ', *SP* 38 (1941), 34–44
Hussey 1965	S. S. Hussey, 'Langland's Reading of Alliterative Poetry', *MLR* 60 (1965), 163–70
Hussey 1969	*Piers Plowman: Critical Approaches*, ed. S. S. Hussey (London, 1969)
Jacob's Well	*Jacob's Well*, An Englisht Treatise on the Cleansing of Man's Conscience, ed. A. Brandeis (Part I), EETS 115 (1900)
Kane 1965	G. Kane, *Piers Plowman: The Evidence for Authorship* (London, 1965)
Kane-Donaldson	*Piers Plowman: The B Version*, ed. G. Kane and E. Talbot Donaldson (London, 1975)
Kaske 1960	R. E. Kaske, 'Patristic Exegesis in the Criticism of Medieval Literature: The Defense', in *Critical Approaches to Medieval Literature*, Selected Papers from the English Institute 1958–9, ed. D. Bethurum (New York and London, 1960), pp. 27–60.
Kaske 1963	R. E. Kaske, ' "Ex vi transicionis" and its passage in *Piers Plowman*', *JEGP* 62 (1963), 32–60
Kaske 1968	R. E. Kaske, '*Piers Plowman* and Local Iconography', *JWCI* 31 (1968), 159–69
Katzenellenbogen 1964	A. Katzenellenbogen, *Allegories of the Virtues and Vices in Mediaeval Art* (1939; trans. A. J. P. Crick, New York, 1964)
Kean 1964	P. M. Kean, 'Love, Law, and *Lewte* in *Piers Plowman*', *RES*, n.s. 15 (1964), 241–61
Kean 1965	P. M. Kean, 'Langland on the Incarnation', *RES*, n.s. 16 (1965), 349–63
Kean 1969	P. M. Kean, 'Justice, Kingship and the Good Life in the Second Part of *Piers Plowman*', pp. 76–100 in Hussey 1969
Kellogg 1935	E. H. Kellogg, 'Bishop Brunton and the Fable of the Rats', *PMLA* 50 (1935), 57–68
Kellogg 1949	A. L. Kellogg, 'Satan, Langland and the North', *Spec.* 24 (1949), 413–14. Reprinted in A. L. Kellogg, *Chaucer, Langland and Arthur: Essays in Middle English Literature* (New Brunswick, N.J., 1972), pp. 29–31
Kellogg 1951	A. L. Kellogg and L. A. Haselmayer, 'Chaucer's Satire of the Pardoner', *PMLA* 66 (1951), 251–77. Reprinted as above, pp. 212–44
Kellogg 1958	A. L. Kellogg, 'Langland and Two Scriptural Texts', *Traditio* 14 (1958), 385–98. Reprinted as above, pp. 32–50

Kellogg 1960   A. L. Kellogg, 'Langland's "Canes Muti": The Paradox of Reform', in *Essays in Literary History in honor of J. M. French*, ed. R. Kirk and C. F. Main (New Brunswick, N.J., 1960). Reprinted as above, pp. 51–8

Kirk 1972   E. D. Kirk, *The Dream Thought of Piers Plowman*, Yale Studies in English 178 (New Haven, 1972)

Knowles   Dom David Knowles, *The Religious Orders in England*, 2 vols. (Cambridge, 1956–7)

Krochalis and Peters 1975   *The World of Piers Plowman*, ed. and trans. J. Krochalis and E. Peters (Univ. of Pennsylvania Press, 1975)

Lawlor 1962   J. Lawlor, *Piers Plowman: An Essay in Criticism* (London, 1962)

Leff 1957   G. Leff, *Bradwardine and the Pelagians: A Study in his 'Causa Dei' and its opponents*, Cambridge Studies in Medieval Life and Thought, n.s.5 (Cambridge, 1957)

Leff 1967   G. Leff, *Heresy in the Later Middle Ages: The Relation of Heterodoxy to Dissent, c. 1250-c. 1450*, 2 vols. (Manchester and New York, 1967)

Legenda Aurea   Jacobus a Voragine, *Legenda Aurea*, ed. Th. Graesse (3rd ed., 1890; repr. Osnabrück, 1969)

Liber Albus   *Liber Albus: The White Book of the City of London*, compiled A.D. 1419 by John Carpenter, common clerk, and Richard Whittington, mayor, trans. H. T. Riley (London, 1861)

Lipson 1959   E. Lipson, *The Economic History of England*, vol. I: The Middle Ages (1915; 12th ed., London, 1959)

Lyndwood, *Provinciale*   William Lyndwood, *Provinciale seu Constitutiones Angliae*, cui adjiciuntur *Constitutiones Legatinae D. Othonis et D. Othoboni* (Oxford, 1679; repr. 1968)

Mills 1969   D. Mills, 'The Rôle of the Dreamer in *Piers Plowman*', pp. 180–212 in Hussey 1969

Mirk, *Instructions*   John Myrc, *Instructions for Parish Priests*, ed. E. Peacock, EETS 31 (1868)

Missale   *Missale ad usum Sarum*, ed. F. H. Dickinson (Oxford, 1861–83)

Mitchell 1939   A. G. Mitchell, 'Notes on the C-text of *Piers Plowman*', *London Medieval Studies* 1 (1937–9), 483–92

Mitchell 1956   A. G. Mitchell, *Lady Meed and the Art of Piers Plowman*, Chambers Memorial Lecture, 1956. Reprinted in *Style and Symbolism in Piers*

	Plowman, ed. R. J. Blanch (Knoxville, 1969), pp. 174–93
Muscatine 1972	C. Muscatine, *Poetry and Crisis in the Age of Chaucer* (Notre Dame, 1972)
Mustanoja 1970	T. F. Mustanoja, 'The Suggestive use of Christian Names in Middle English Poetry', pp. 51–76 in *Medieval Literary and Folklore Studies in honor of F. L. Utley*, ed. J. Mandel and B. A. Rosenberg (New Brunswick, N. J., 1970)
Northern Homily Cycle	*The Northern Homily Cycle*, ed. S. Nevanlinna, Mémoires de la Société Néophilologique de Helsinki 38 (1972), 41 (1973). Continuing
Owst 1926	G. R. Owst, *Preaching in Medieval England* (Cambridge, 1926)
Owst 1933	G. R. Owst, *Literature and Pulpit in Medieval England* (Cambridge, 1933; 2nd ed., Oxford, 1961)
Pantin 1955	W. A. Pantin, *The English Church in the Fourteenth Century* (Cambridge, 1955)
Prick of Conscience	Ed. R. Morris, Philological Society (Berlin, 1863)
Quirk 1953	R. Quirk, 'Langland's Use of *Kind Wit* and *Inwit*', *JEGP* 52 (1953), 182–8
Reeves 1969	M. Reeves, *The Influence of Prophecy in the Later Middle Ages. A Study in Joachimism* (Oxford, 1969)
Riley's *Memorials*	*Memorials of London and London Life in the XIIIth, XIVth and XVth Centuries*, ed. H. T. Riley (London, 1868)
Raw 1969	B. Raw, 'Piers and the Image of God in Man', pp. 143–79 in Hussey 1969
Risse 1966	R. G. Risse, 'The Augustinian Paraphrase of Isaiah 14:13–14 in *Piers Plowman* and the Commentary on the *Fables* of Avianus', *PQ* 45 (1966), 712–17
Robbins 1959	*Historical Poems of the XIVth and XVth Centuries*, ed. R. H. Robbins (New York, 1959)
Robertson-Huppé 1951	D. W. Robertson, Jr., and B. F. Huppé, *Piers Plowman and Scriptural Tradition*, Princeton Studies in English 31 (Princeton, 1951)
Roman de la Rose	Guillaume de Lorris and Jean de Meun, *Le Roman de la Rose*, Classiques Français du Moyen Age, 3 vols. (Paris, 1966–70)
Rot. Parl.	*Rotuli Parliamentorum* (Rolls of Parliament), 6 vols. (London, 1783)
Russell 1966	G. H. Russell, 'The Salvation of the Heathen. The Exploration of a Theme in *Piers Plowman*', *JWCI* 29 (1966), 101–16

Russell 1969 — G. H. Russell, 'Some Aspects of the Process of Revision in *Piers Plowman*', pp. 27–49 in Hussey 1969

St-Jacques 1969 — R. St-Jacques, 'The Liturgical Associations of Langland's Samaritan', *Traditio* 25 (1969), 217–30

Sajavaara 1967 — The Middle English Translations of Robert Grosseteste's *Chateau d'Amour*, ed. K. Sajavaara, Mémoires de la Société Néophilologique de Helsinki 32 (1967)

Salter 1962 — E. Salter, *Piers Plowman: An Introduction* (Oxford, 1962)

Salter 1966 — E. Salter, '*Piers Plowman* and *The Simonie*', *Archiv* 203 (1966–7), 241–54

Salter 1967 — *Piers Plowman* (Selections from the C-text), ed. E. Salter and D. Pearsall, York Medieval Texts (London, 1967)

Saxl 1942 — F. Saxl, 'A Spiritual Encyclopaedia of the later Middle Ages', *JWCI* 5 (1942), 82–142

Schmidt 1969 — A. V. C. Schmidt, 'Langland and Scholastic Philosophy', *MÆ* 38 (1969), 134–56

Sermons, ed. Ross — *Middle English Sermons* (from MS Royal 18 B.xxiii), ed. W. O. Ross, EETS 209 (1940)

The Simonie — 'Poem on the Evil Times of Edward II: *The Simonie*', in *The Political Songs of England*, ed. T. Wright, Camden Society (1839), pp. 232–45.

Skeat — *The Vision of William concerning Piers the Plowman*, in three parallel texts, together with *Richard the Redeless*, by William Langland, ed. W. W. Skeat, 2 vols. (vol. I: Text, vol. II: Introduction, Notes and Glossary, Oxford, 1886). Reprinted, with addition of Bibliography by J. A. W. Bennett (1954)

Smith 1966 — B. H. Smith, *Traditional Imagery of Charity in Piers Plowman* (The Hague and Paris, 1966)

Spearing 1972 — A. C. Spearing, 'The Art of Preaching and *Piers Plowman*', pp. 107–34 in *Criticism and Mediaeval Poetry* (London, 1964; 2nd ed., 1972)

Speculum Christiani — Ed. G. Holmstedt, EETS 182 (1933)

Speculum Vitae — The Middle English *Speculum Vitae*: a Critical Edition of part of the text [viz. the second quarter, *c.* 4000 lines] by V. Nelson (unpublished Ph.D. thesis, Univ. of Sydney, 1974). A specimen (lines 1–370) is printed by J. Ullmann in *EStn* 7 (1884), 468–72

Statutes — *Statutes of the Realm*, 11 vols. (London, 1810–28; repr. 1963)

Taitt 1971	P. Taitt, 'In Defence of Lot', *NQ* 216 (1971), 284–5
Tawney 1926	R. H. Tawney, *Religion and the Rise of Capitalism* (London, 1926)
Thomas of Erceldoune, ed. Murray	*The Romance and Prophecies of Thomas of Erceldoune*, ed. J. A. H. Murray, EETS 61 (1875)
Tierney 1959	B. Tierney, *Medieval Poor Law* (Berkeley, 1959)
Tischendorf	*Evangelia Apocrypha*, ed. C. de Tischendorf, 2nd ed. (Leipzig, 1876). English trans. in *The Apocryphal New Testament*, by M. R. James (Oxford, 1924)
Trower 1973	K. B. Trower, 'Temporal Tensions in the *Visio* of *Piers Plowman*', *MS* 35 (1973), 389–412
Troyer 1932	H. W. Troyer, 'Who is Piers Plowman?' *PMLA* 47 (1932), 368–84
Tuve 1966	R. Tuve, *Allegorical Imagery: Some Medieval Books and their Posterity* (Princeton, 1966)
Vasta 1965	E. Vasta, *The Spiritual Basis of Piers Plowman* (The Hague, 1965)
Vices and Virtues	*The Book of Vices and Virtues*, ed. W. Nelson Francis, EETS 217 (1942)
Vulgate (Vg.)	*Biblia Vulgata*, ed. A. Colunga and L. Turrado, Biblioteca de Autores Cristianos, 4th ed. (Madrid, 1965). Translated by the English Colleges at Douay 1609 (OT) and Rheims 1582 (NT) as the Douay-Rheims Bible (rev. and repr., London, 1899). N. B. The translations in the notes to the present edition are eclectic, based partly on Douay-Rheims and partly on the AV and its revisions, but adapted to Langland's versions of the texts
Walther	*Proverbia Sententiaeque Latinitatis Medii Ævi* (*Lateinische Sprichwörter und Sentenzen des Mittelalters*), ed. H. Walther, 6 vols. (Göttingen, 1963–9)
Walther, *Initia*	*Initia Carminum ac Versuum Medii Ævi Posterioris Latinorum* (*Alphabetisches Verzeichnis der Versanfänge mittellateinischer Dichtungen*), ed. H. Walther (Göttingen, 1969)
Wells 1929	H. W. Wells, 'The Construction of *Piers Plowman*', *PMLA* 44 (1929), 123–40
Whiting	*Proverbs, Sentences and Proverbial Phrases from English Writings mainly before 1500*, by B. J. Whiting, with the collaboration of H. W. Whiting (Cambridge, Mass., 1968)
Whitworth 1972	C. W. Whitworth, 'Changes in the Roles of Reason and Conscience in the Revisions of "Piers Plowman"', *NQ* 217 (1972), 4–7

Williams 1953	A. Williams, 'Chaucer and the Friars', *Spec.* 28 (1953), 499–513
Winner and Waster	Ed. I. Gollancz, Select Early English Poems III (London, 1930)
Wittig 1972	J. S. Wittig, '*Piers Plowman* B IX–XII: Elements in the Design of the Inward Journey', *Traditio* 28 (1972), 211–80
Woodcock 1952	B. L. Woodcock, *Medieval Ecclesiastical Courts in the diocese of Canterbury* (Oxford, 1952)
Woolf 1968	R. Woolf, *The English Religious Lyric in the Middle Ages* (Oxford, 1968)
Woolf 1969	R. Woolf, 'The Tearing of the Pardon', pp. 50–75 in Hussey 1969
Workman	H. B. Workman, *John Wyclif: a Study of the English Medieval Church*, 2 vols. (Oxford, 1926; repr. 1966)
Wright, *Pol. Poems*	*Political Poems and Songs*, ed. T. Wright, 2 vols., Rolls Series 14 (1859)
Wright, *Pol. Songs*	*The Political Songs of England*, ed. T. Wright, Camden Society (1839)
Wyclif, ed. Arnold	*Select English Works of John Wyclif*, ed. T. Arnold, 3 vols. (Oxford, 1869–71)
Wyclif, ed. Matthew	*The English Works of Wyclif hitherto unprinted*, ed. F. D. Matthew, EETS 74 (1880)
Yunck 1963	J. A. Yunck, *The Lineage of Lady Meed: The Development of Medieval Venality Satire*, Univ. of Notre Dame Publications in Mediaeval Studies XVII (Notre Dame, 1963)

Glossary

In the alphabetization, ʒ is placed after g, þ with th, and u/v are not discriminated. There is no attempt at a full reconciliation of forms. Common words of consistent meaning are glossed without line-reference. Parsing is provided only where it is necessary to avoid ambiguity.

a *adj.* one, a single III. 473
a *prep.* in III. 51, 259, IX. 154, XVIII. 213, XIX. 149; on II. 56, XI. 255, XIV. 131, 141
a *pron.* he, she, they
abasched,-et ashamed VI. 17, IX. 86
abate assuage the swelling of, heal I. 146
abaue deter, put off VIII. 226
a-beggeth a-begging VIII. 138, 246
abite garb, attire Prol. 3
abiteth bites off, bites away at XVIII. 32
ablende *inf.* blind XX. 141; *pa.t.3sg.* XX. 368
aboughte, abouhte *see* abugge
a-bribeth a-begging VIII. 246
abugge(n), abygge(n), abyye pay dearly (for) II. 141, VIII. 41, 83, XVI. 220, XX. 446 **aboughte, abouhte** *pa.t.3sg.* X. 232, XIII. 15, XX. 430
ac but
acale *pp.* oppressed by cold XX. 437
accidie sloth, fit of sluggishness VI. 417
acloye hinder progress of, impede XX. 294
acombre encumber, hinder, burden II. 52, XXI. 220 **acombreth** XIV. 17 **acombred** *pp.* I. 31, 191, 198
acordaunde agreeing III. 394
acorse curse, condemn Prol. 127
acounten take account of X. 95
adaunte subdue III. 440
adrencheth drown X. 162 **adreint, adreynt** *pp.* drowned X. 243; drowned (in physic) XXII. 377
afayte tame, train by taming VIII. 30
afelde brought down, ruined III. 162
aferes affairs, doings VI. 152
affayten tame, subdue VI. 7
affiaunce trust, reliance XVIII. 255
afraynede asked XX. 16
afrounted accosted XXII. 5
after, aftir, aftur *prep.* after, according to; in the direction of Prol. 14
afurst(e) *pp.* oppressed by thirst IX. 85n, XI. 43, XVI. 15, XX. 437
afyng(e)red *pp.* oppressed by hunger IX. 85n, XI. 43, 50, XVI. 15
agast *pp.* (*adj.*) frightened II. 221, XXI. 300
agayne *prep.* against IX. 65
ageynward *adv.* in return XIX. 75
aglotye fill the stomachs of IX. 76
agulte *n.* sin XXI. 304

agulte *inf.* offend against, commit sin VI. 17, XVII. 44 *pa.t.1sg.* XIX. 275
aʒen(es), aʒeyn(e) *prep.* against; in return for VII. 43
aʒeyn(e) *adv.* back, again
aʒeynes *conj.* in readiness for the time when XXI. 318
aitheres *pron.gen.sg.* of either, of each XII. 137
aknowe *pp.* known, acknowledged IX. 86
al *adv.* entirely I. 30, VI. 292, XXI. 295
alayed alloyed XVII. 79
ale ale; alehouse Prol. 43, VII. 19
a-lechyng being healed, getting better XIX. 73
alere *pron.gen.pl.* of all XXI. 471
alery *adv.* twisted backwards VIII. 129n
aliens foreign merchants or mercenaries III. 266
Alisa(u)ndre Alexandria VII. 173, XVII. 272
allowe *inf.* give credit for XVIII. 251 **alloueth** *pres.3pl.* approve XVI. 144 **alloued, allowed** *pp.* praised, commended VIII. 250, XII. 193, XIV. 212
almaries aumbries, cupboards XVI. 88
almesfull charitable VI. 48
almesse alms IX. 141
almest almost III. 208
almusse alms IX. 96
almyhten *adj.* almighty Prol. 218
alose *inf.* praise XIX. 101
alouede, alowed *pp.* praised III. 204, VII. 96
alowed *adv.* aloud II. 131
also *adv.* as, equally XVI. 344
althey, althow although II. 121, IX. 201
amayster, amaystrye *inf.* master, compel, exert power over II. 161, VIII. 221 **amaystred** *pp.* II. 167
amis *adv.* amiss, wrongly I. 173
amorteysed mortgaged XVII. 54
amorwe *n.* the morrow III. 307
a-morwen *adv.* on the morrow VII. 13
an *prep.* in XIV. 14, XVI. 187; on II. 134, V. 186, VI. 124
ancre anchoress III. 140
and and; if II. 204, III. 44, 139, IV. 134, VI. 91, 289, VIII. 160, IX. 19, 71, XII. 71, 191, etc.
angre *n.* affliction, distress, trouble VI. 79; **angres** *pl.* VI. 114, XXI. 291

angry *inf.* injure XVI. 86
anhengede hanged I. 64
ankeres,-us anchorites Prol. 30, VIII. 146
anon, anoen, anon ryhte straightway
anyente *inf.* destroy, deny XIX. 266 **any-
ented** *pp.* XX. 386
aparayle *n.* dress VI. 30
apartye *adv.* apart, on one side XV. 54
apayed pleased, content, satisfied II. 45, VIII.
115, IX. 178, XV. 64
apayre harm, injure VII. 211, VIII. 167; im-
pair, reduce V. 144 **apayred** *pp.* VIII. 229
apeel appeal, call for justice XIX. 283
apendeth belongs, pertains I. 97
apertly openly III. 313
apose ask XIV. 154 **aposed of** questioned
concerning I. 45
appereth is seen to be, reaches XVI. 84
appeyreth impairs, harms III. 163
appose ask, question III. 5, XV. 105 **ap-
posede** V. 10
ar *conj.* before
arate rebuke, tax, reproach XII. 34 **aratede**
V. 11
aray dress, order, arrangement **out of aray**
not in proper dress or form V. 157
arere *adv.* backwards VI. 405
aresenede, aresounede argued with XIII.
128, 193
Armonye Armenia VII. 173, XVII. 272
arrerage arrears, debt IX. 274, XI. 299
ars arts XI. 98, XII. 92
arste *adv.* first VI. 308
arwed frightened, made cowards of III. 236
as *adv.* likewise, accordingly VI. 422
as *conj.* as, as if; *enclitic with preps.* e.g. VIII. 88,
97
asaye examine III. 5
ascuth ask(s) Prol. 21, I. 34, VI. 56
aseled sealed II. 114, XIX. 9
askape escape II. 215, III. 61
aspele spare, save VI. 432
aspye see, examine II. 235, III. 109, VI. 152
assay try, ask XVI. 163
asseled sealed XIX. 6
asseth *n.* compensation, amends XIX. 202
assoile, assoille, assoyle(n) absolve; solve,
explain XI. 157, XIV. 155, XVII. 114 **as-
soiled** *pp.* absolved; *pa.t.* resolved, sorted out
XII. 136
Astarot Ashtaroth XX. 287n, 447
asterte escape XIII. 209
at *prep.* at; of, from I. 204, II. 176, 191, III.
375, VI. 56, VII. 57, etc; according to, by
XIX. 122
atache arrest II. 211 **atached** laid claim to
XVIII. 278
a-take *pp.* taken III. 139
atamede opened, broached XIX. 68
ateynt attained, accused XXII. 162
athynketh (*impers.*) grieves, causes regret VI.
100
a-to in two, apart VIII. 64
attacheth claims jurisdiction over XI. 308 **at-
tached** arrested II. 252
attese at ease I. 19

atwene in twain Prol. 114
atyer attire II. 15
atymye attain (possibly *atyniye?*) XIX. 239
243
avauncen *inf.* advance, make prosper X. 253
avaunsed *pp.* advanced to preferment I.
188; put in position of authority XIII. 103
auer wealth, possessions VI. 32
auerous avaricious I. 88, XIV. 21, (*as n.*) X.
86
auȝte possessions XIII. 7
auht anything, at all VI. 111, VII. 177, XVII.
214
auncel balance for weighing VI. 224
aunpolles ampules, phials VII. 165
auntur chance **an auntur** lest perchance III.
70, 433, VIII. 40 **good auntur** by good luck
VIII. 79
auntreth (*refl.*) ventures X. 215 **aunt(e)red**
ventured XX. 231; (*refl.*) ventured (oneself)
in battle XXII. 175
auntrous *adj. as n.pl.* adventurous knights
XX. 14
Austyn Augustine
auters altars V. 164
autor authority XI. 150
auysen (*refl.*) be advised, consider XVII. 53
auyseth IV. 21
awayte(n) attend to VI. 279; look to see
XVII. 62; obtain by stealth and with
anxiety X. 297
awreke *imp.sg.* avenge VIII. 158, 170; (*refl.*)
satisfy (thyself) **awreke, awroke** *pp.*
avenged
axen ask VII. 181
ay always, ever XV. 246
ayr always, ever XV. 246
ayr heir XVIII. 246 **ayres** *pl.* III. 321, IX. 4
aysches ashes III. 125
ayther, ayþer *pron.* either, each **her ayþer
oþer** each other of them XX. 175 **aytheres**
gen.sg. of either, of each **here aytheres** of
each of them XII. 136
aythes harrows XXI. 272

baburlippid thick-lipped VI. 198
bacheler knight XX. 88 **bachelers** *pl.* bach-
elors of divinity Prol. 85
baches valleys VII. 159
baer bore XVIII. 271 **baer adoun** overcame
XXII. 132
bakkes clothes to cover the back XIII. 71
balayshed beaten with a rod VI. 157
baldeliche boldly XVI. 56
baldere,-ore bolder IV. 102, IX. 336
bale offence, harm, suffering, misery
baleyse stick XI. 124
balkes strips of unploughed land VIII. 114n
balled bald XXII. 184; bald, devoid of signifi-
cance XI. 38
bane destruction VIII. 351
banne(th) curse(s)
bar bore; pierced XX. 88
barn child, son II. 3 **barnes** *pl.* III. 188, V.
70
barnhoed childhood XVIII. 136

barones important city men Prol. 220
barres bars of the law-courts IV. 132
baslard sword worn by a private person III. 457
bastardus *adj.pl.* bastard V. 71
bat lump XVIII. 92
batauntliche *adv.* pressing forward with eager and clumsy haste XVI. 56
bat-nelde pack-needle (large strong needle used for coarse stitching) VI. 218
bawe *interj.* bah! exclamation of contempt XII. 73, XXI. 396
bayard a common name for a horse (properly a bay)
be *pp.* been Prol. 62, V. 80
be *prep.* by; according to VI. 382; during VII. 9
beau fitz fair son IX. 313
beau-pere good father, reverend father XX. 240
bed-bourde bed-play, sexual intercourse X. 290
bedel beadle II. 111 **bedeles** *pl.* III. 2
bedemen *see* **bedman**
beden *inf.* offer X. 265
beden *pa.t.3pl.* bade III. 28, XV. 27 *pp.* bidden, invited II. 56
bedes prayers VII. 16
bedes-biddynge saying of prayers XII. 83, XXI. 375
Bedlem Bethlehem
bedman beadsman (one who prays for another for money) III. 43, 48 **bedemen** *pl.* III. 274
bedredene bedridden VII. 108, IX. 34
beel-syre grandfather XX. 282
been-feet good deed VII. 42 **been-fetes** *pl.* VII. 264
begeneldes beggar's X..261
begge buy III. 86, VIII. 303 **beggeth** III. 82
begrucheth grumbles VIII. 155
begyneld beggar's IX. 154
beȝende beyond, abroad III. 145
behote *pres.1sg.* promise VIII. 301 **behyte** *pa.t.3sg.* III. 30
bekne beacon XIX 227
beknowe acknowledge V. 92
bele (*Fr.*) fine, fair XVI. 269
belsyre grandfather II. 121 **belsires** forefather's X. 232
belyen deceive by lies XX. 355
ben *inf.* be *pres.pl.* are
Benet Benedict
bere *inf.* low XIII. 149
beren *pa.t.3pl.* bore VI. 416
berkeres barkers, dogs IX. 260
bern(e) *v.* burn III. 237, 422
bern *n.* man XVIII. 280
bernes children XVII. 57
bernes barns VIII. 179 **bernys** barns' IV. 60
berw hill VII. 227
best shalt be VII. 236
bet *pa.t.3sg.* beat Prol. 115
bet better
beten relieve VIII. 246
Betene Betty V. 135; Betty's VI. 353

betrauaile work hard for XV. 210
bette better
bew-pere good father IX. 248n
beygh necklace, collar Prol. 180, 191
beyre *pron.gen.pl.* of both of them XX. 36
beyers necklaces, collars Prol. 178
bid(e), bidde pray; beg VI. 49; ask for, solicit VI. 69
biddares, bidders beggars Prol. 41, IX. 61
biful befell **me biful** it befell me, I happened Prol. 7
bigerdeles purses X. 85
bigruchen begrudge, grumble at VIII. 68
biheste *n.* promise XII. 13, XVIII. 123 **bihestes** *pl.* XX. 320
bihote *v.* promise VII. 69, VIII. 238 **bihihte, bihyhte** promised VI. 5, XVIII. 246
bihoueth (*impers.*) it behoves **me bihoueth** I must VII. 295
bikere *v.* fight XXII. 79
biknowe confess VI. 206 **biknewe(n)** admitted XXI. 149 **biknewe on** acknowledged belief in XI. 257
bileue *n.* faith
bileue *inf.* remain XII. 211
bille petition IV. 45
bilyue food, sustenance I. 18
bionales biennials IX. 322n
bireue take away VIII. 258
bisowte besought III. 115
bissheinede beshined, polished bright, made radiant (Cf. MSS TP *bisshopid*: confirmed in baptismal vows) XVII. 268
biswynketh gain by working, work for VIII. 260 **biswonke** worked for XXII. 292
bitelbrowed with beetling or prominent brows VI. 198
bitit (*impers*) betides **hym bitit** it befalls him XIII. 210
Bitte var. of Bet, dim. of Bartholomew VI. 379
bittorere more bitterly XVI. 220
blaunmanger a fancy dish made of bland meats (poultry, fish) pulped and blended with cream, eggs, etc. XV. 100
blenche turn aside VII. 227
blende blind XX. 292 **blente** blinded VII. 135, XX. 284
blered *pat.3sg.* dimmed the vision of **blered here yes** deceived them Prol. 72 *pp.as adj.* bleared (with the oozing of gummy secretions) VI. 198
blesseth consecrates, arranges consecration of III. 185
blew livid, lead-coloured III. 125
blisse bless, be thankful for XVIII. 254
blody in blood XII. 108, 114
bloed-chedyng blood-shedding XIV. 207
blynde invisible XIX. 227
blyne cease VIII. 176
bochere butcher VI. 379 **bocheres** *pl.* Prol. 222, III. 80
boches lumps, boils, tumours XXII. 84
boende *adj. as n.* bondman XV. 14
boest noise, outcry XVI. 89; self-vaunting XXI. 251
boetles without boots XX. 9

bokkes bucks, deer VIII. 29
bolk *n.* belch VII. 6
bollares drunkards (lit. 'bowlers') IX. 194
bolle drinking-bowl VII. 164, XX. 407
bollyng swelling VIII. 226
bommode tasted VI. 229
bond *n.* straw binding (for sheaves) V. 14
bond(e) *adj.* bound **bond oen** bound one, i.e. bondwoman X. 261 *adj.as n.* bondwoman X. 265 *adj. as n.pl.* bondmen III. 200
bondemen *n.pl.* bondmen, 'servile' men, bound to the service of a feudal lord through customary obligation Prol. 220, V. 65 **bondemannes** *gen.sg.* VI. 201 **bondemen** *gen.pl.* V. 70
bone request, prayer III. 417, XII. 83
boost boastfulness XVI. 65
borde boat-board, side of a boat X. 40
bordiours jesters IX. 136
bordles without a table XIV. 140
bordoun pilgrim's staff VII. 162
bordor jester VII. 108
borre burr, huskiness XIX. 305
borw(e), borwh pledge, surety IV. 85, XVIII. 280, XXII. 13; guarantor XXII. 248 **borewes** *pl.* I. 74
borw borough II. 92 *pl.* IX. 189
borwen borrow II. 176
boske hasten X. 223 **boskede** hurried III. 15
boste *v.* boast II. 85 **bostede** threatened boastfully VIII. 152
bote *conj.* but **bote yf** unless
bote *n.* remedy, cure, relief, recompense **to bote** in compensatory cash adjustment XVI. 109
bote *v.* compensate VI. 382
boteles without remedy XX. 207
botened cured VIII. 188
bothe *pron.gen.pl.* of both of them II. 67, XX. 371
bothe *adv.* also, too XVI. 113
bouketh bleaches, 'buck-washes', i.e. steeps in alkaline lye as first process in cleansing XVI. 331
bounchede beat, 'bonked' Prol. 72
bounte goodness VIII. 49
bour(e) bower, private room III. 11, 15
bourdynge joking XVI. 201
bourdyors jesters IX. 127
bowen ready II. 173
bowhe bough V. 134
boy rascal, fellow, layabout Prol. 78, XII. 110 **boys** *pl.* VIII. 265
brake *inf.* vomit VI. 431
brake *n.* cranking mechanism XX. 291n
brede breadth II. 93, III. 259
breedcorn (coarser) grain used for bread (also for sowing) VIII. 61
breef letter, written authority XXII. 327
breere briar II. 28
breke didst break IX. 278
brenne(n) burn XII. 66, XIX. 197, 221
breres briars VI. 402
bretful brimful Prol. 42
bretil brittle, frail X. 47
breuet letter XIII. 54

breuh-wyf alewife VI. 354
brewestere female brewer, alewife VI. 353
bridale bride-ale, bridal ceremony II. 56
brocage business deal done by brokers, especially marriage-agreement XVI. 108 **brocages** *pl.* II. 92
brochen sew together coarsely with large stitches VI. 218
broches thin sticks, matches XIX. 210
broches brooches Prol. 73
broke maimed V. 33
broker, brokor broker, agent, match-maker, procurer II. 66, VI. 95 **brokeres** *pl.* II. 60
brolle brat III. 261
brouk(e) enjoy, make trial of, receive XII. 55, XX. 401
brouth brought Prol. 67
browe brewed XX. 401
brugge bridge VII. 213
bruttene break in pieces III. 237
bruttenynge destruction XV. 156
brybours robbers XXII. 262
bugge(n) buy IV. 85, IX. 28, XVI. 73 **buggynge** XXI. 235
buirnes men XVIII. 11
bulle papal letter of authority Prol. 67 **bulles** *pl.* Prol. 71
burgages tenements III. 85, 105
burgeys *n.pl.* burgesses, important citizens Prol. 220, III. 200 **burgeis** *gen.sg.* XIV. 91
busmares slanders XXI. 294
but(e) but; unless **but yf** unless
buth are IX. 160
Butte *var.* of Bat, Bart, dim. of Bartholomew II. 111, V. 134
buxum obedient III. 417; modest XX. 120
buxumliche obediently XIV. 57
buxumnesse obedience VII. 239
buyrde lady, maiden III. 15, XX. 120 **buyrdes** *pl.* XXI. 135
buyrielles sepulchre XXI. 146
buyrn(e), buyren man III. 473, VI. 247, XV. 156, 163
buyth buys XV. 302
by *prep.* by; according to I. 87, II. 122, IX. 17, XI. 271; concerning VI. 162, X. 164, XI. 11, XIII. 111; during VII. 112; in comparison with XVII. 104; with reference to XVI. 8 **by so** provided that
bycometh is becoming, is fitting III. 264, V. 61 **bycam** was gone XV. 150
byde pray VII. 240
bydels beadles II. 60n
byfalleth is proper, befits, belongs I. 48, IX. 129 **byful(l)** was fitting XIII. 108; became(of) VI. 326; (*impers.*) befell VI. 27
bygge(n) buy Prol. 183, III. 33
bygeten begotten X. 208
byglosedest didst deceive XX. 380
byȝete begotten II. 144
byheste *n.* promise X. 248
byhihtest promised XX. 317
byhofte in need, use XII. 186
byhoueth is needful IX. 89
byiaped deceived, tricked I. 63, XX. 323
bykenne commend(to) II. 51, X. 58

byknowen *inf.* admit, acknowledge Prol. 210 **byknowe** *pp.* acknowledged, known XIII. 10; recognized, welcomed III. 36

byles boils XXII. 84

byleue belief, faith IX. 218, XIII. 89

byleue, byliue food, living V. 21, XVI. 335

bylongeth (*impers.*) befits **thyse bylongeth** it befits these V. 66

bylowe slandered IX. 181

bylyueth believe X. 167

bylyue food V. 29, VIII. 260

bymene *inf.* signify, mean I. 56 **bymeneth** *pres.3sg.* Prol. 217, I. 1, XX. 173 **bymente** *pa.t.3sg.* XX. 16

bynyme *inf.* take away from III. 320 **byno(e)m** *pa.t.3sg.* took away (from) VIII. 254; seized, abducted XIII. 8

    ytten *pa.t.3pl.* shut up II. 223

bysette(n) bestow VI. 254, 346

byseye treated XXII. 202

byswynke(n) gain by labour, work for VIII. 140, 224

byt *pres.3sg.* bids III. 306, XV. 77

byteche commend, deliver XV. 183

bythenke think up VI. 108

bytrauayle gain by labour, work for VIII. 242

bytulye gain by tilling the ground, till the ground for VIII. 242

cachepol officer of the court XX. 46, 76

caes case, circumstance IX. 155; mishap IX. 48

cald *pp.* called Prol. 132

cam out happened XXI. 161

camaca rich (silken) cloth XVI. 299

cammokes tough-rooted weeds ('rest-harrow') XXI. 313

can know(s); has power over XXI. 216 **can on** knows about II. 236

canoen *n.* canon law XV. 85

canonistres experts in canon law IX. 305

cantel portion XIV. 163

capel horse IV. 24 **caples** *pl.* XXI. 332, 346

capped endorsed (ref. to the caps worn by masters of divinity) XI. 80

carde *inf.* card wool (i.e. prepare it for spinning by combing it out) IX. 80 **cardet** *pp.* combed out XI. 15

cardiacle heart-attack, heart-disease VI. 78 **cardiacles** pl. XXII. 82

cardinales *adj.pl.* cardinal, chief Prol. 132n, XXI. 274

carefole *adj.as n.pl.* men burdened with care I. 198, XII. 102

careyne flesh XIV. 178

carfol worried, full of care XIII. 109

carneles crenallations VII. 235

caroled sang (while dancing) XX. 470

caroyne body, corpse VIII. 100, XVI. 196

carpen speak **carpeth carped(e)**

carse cress XI. 14

cast *n.* contrivance III. 20

caste(n) *inf.* plan, plot XI. 16; calculate XII. 65 **cast** *pres3sg.* (*refl.*) plans IX. 151 **caste(n)** *pa.t.* planned, devised Prol. 143, XXII. 121;

intended XXI. 280; plotted XXI. 141; calculated XI. 127; set to work, exercised VI. 264

catel property, wealth; ready money V. 129

Cato(u)n Cato IV. 17, VII. 34, IX. 69, 305, XIII. 211, XXI. 296 **Catones** *gen.sg.* VIII. 337

caudel mess VI. 412

cauke tread, (of birds) copulate XIV. 161 **caukede** XIII. 169

Caym Cain

cayren go, wander Prol. 31

cayser emperor III. 314, XXI. 138

caytif, caytyf *n.* miserable wretch, outcast, low person VIII. 244, XII. 63 **caytyfs** *gen.sg.* XIV. 90 **caytifues, caytyues** *pl.* XX. 97, 100

caytif, caytyue *adj.* mean, wretched, vile X. 219, XIII. 109

caytifliche abjectly III. 241; wretchedly, meanly (*non-pej.*) XII. 126

caytiftee wretched villainy IX. 255

certes indeed IX. 257

certyne *adj.as n.* certain number XXII. 258

cesseth cease IV. 1

chaffare *n.* trading deal, trade, bargain Prol. 33, VI. 380 **chaffares** *pl.* II. 60

chaffare(n) *v.* trade, make deals VIII. 249, XII. 226 **chaffared** VI. 252

chalenge(n) lay formal claim to Prol. 91, XVI. 190 **chalenged** accused VI. 136, 156

chalengynge accusing VI. 68

chaleniable open to challenge XIII. 116

chancerye chancery, the chancellor's court Prol. 91

chanons canons V. 156, 170

chapitre cathedral or monastic chapter (meeting of clergy) III. 472

chapitre-hous chapter-house VI. 156

chapman merchant, tradesman Prol. 62 **chapmen** *pl.* V. 136, VI. 235

chapun-cote hen-house VI. 136

charge *n.* responsibility IX. 258

charge *v.* burden with the responsibility of XXII. 237 **chargeth** worries, is burdened with care XVI. 288; demands, insists upon as a responsibility XIX. 271

charite charity **pur charite** for charity's sake

chaste(n) chastise, punish **chasteth chasted**

chastel castle II. 89

chatel property XII. 60

chaufen grow warm XVII. 49; incite, enrage XIV. 68

chaunce good fortune VI. 85

chees *see* **chese**

cheke let us arrest (their progress) XX. 285

cheker the office of the royal exchequer, which dealt with the receipt of revenue and the audit of accounts Prol. 91, IV, 185

chele cold VIII. 249, XXII. 236

chepe *v.* buy, bargain XVI. 190

chepyng market VIII. 322 **chepynges** *pl.* IV. 59

cher(e) *adj.* dear XVII. 125; fond, anxious XVII. 148

chere *n.* countenance, appearance

cherl bondman, villain, base fellow

chersyng *n.* cherishing, indulging IV. 112
chese(n) *v.* choose Prol. 33, XVI. 175 **chees** chose XIII. 3
chesibles chasubles, church vestments worn at mass VIII. 11
cheste strife, dissension Prol. 105, II. 89, X. 272, XIV. 68
chetes escheats, revenues that revert to the crown IV. 169n
cheue win, thrive, prosper VIII. 249, XX. 108, **cheued** VI. 252
cheuenteyn chief, leader XXI. 472
cheuesaunces money-lending contracts, i.e. payments for loans as a concealed form of usury VI. 252
cheyne *v.* chain (the gates) XX. 285
cheueth prosper, get on Prol. 33; (*impers.*) XVI. 69
cheytyftee the wretchedness of poverty XXII. 236
chibolles small onions VIII. 310
chield chilled XVII. 49
chine chink XX. 285
chingled clinker-built, having the outer timbers overlapping like roof-tiles X. 231
chiruulles chervil (a pot-herb) VIII. 310
choppes blows X. 272
chyht, chyt chides, argues, gets angry I. 176, XVI. 288 **chydde** argued VI. 147
claumsest art numb XV. 252
clees claws Prol. 172
clemp *pa.t.* climbed
clemynge guttering (of a candle), i.e. through being clogged (MED *clemen*, 3) III. 106
cleped(e) called
clergialiche in a scholarly manner VII. 34
clergie, clergyse learning, the body of learned men **Clergices** *gen. sg.* XI. 99
clerkes clerics, scholars **clerkene** *gen.pl.* IV. 114
clerkysh clerical (i.e. to do with clerics) VI. 42
cler-matyn fine white bread VIII. 327
cleuth clings VII. 304, XIX. 310 **cleuynge** joining XVII. 128
clingest art shrivelled or parched XV. 252
clippe embrace, hold XIX. 155
clips eclipse XX. 139
cloches clutches Prol. 172
clokke hobble, lag III. 37
cloute *inf.* patch clothes IX. 80
cloutes *n.pl.* patched or ragged clothes II. 230
cluppe embrace XX. 463
clycat latch(-key) VII. 252
clymat one of the (seven) belts of the earth's surface between given latitudes, presided over by the seven planets XVII. 106
cockes cockles IX. 95
coest cost, expense
coffes mittens VIII. 59
coke *inf.* put hay into cocks XXI. 238
coke *n.* cook
cokeney small egg (lit. cock's egg) VIII. 308
cokeres haycockers, haymakers V. 13
cokeres leggings VIII. 59
coket fine white bread VIII. 327

cokewold(e) cuckold IV. 159, VI. 134
coler collar Prol. 184 **colers** *pl.* Prol. 209
colhoppes, colloppes eggs fried on bacon, dishes of fried meat VIII. 308, XV. 68
collateral additional XVI. 135
coltur coulter, plough-share III. 460, VIII. 65
coluer(e) *n.* dove **coluere** *gen.sg.* XVII. 179
comaunded commended XI. 278
combraunce burden, disadvantage, trouble, misfortune XII. 244, XX. 276 **combraunces** *pl.* V. 190
combre encumber, entangle I. 67
comen *pa.t.3pl.* came
comen *adj.* common XVIII. 143
comeneres citizen members of the city council IV. 188
comeseth begins **comesed** began
commen, commune *adj.(as n.)* common **in commen** generally XII. 166
commissarie bishop's officer II. 190n, III. 179, XVI. 361
compace *inf.* make measurements XXI. 241
compacience fellow-feeling, compassion XV. 88
compenable agreeable, companionable XVI. 341
comseth begins
comsyng *n.* beginning XX. 224 **comsynges** *pl.* XI. 95
comune *adj.* common, mutual, general *adj.as n.pl.* (also **comunes**) the commons; the common people; the commonalty or commonwealth; the community Prol. 95, 144, 145, etc.
comune(s) *n.* commons, food, allowance of provisions Prol. 143, V. 144, VIII. 292, XXI. 407
comuners commoners V. 183
comyn *adj.* common, accessible III. 167
conclude refute XI. 282
congeie, congeye say goodbye to, dismiss, get rid of **conieyod** *pa.t.* XV. 176
conne(th) can; know how to Prol. 35, VIII. 69
connyng *n.* knowledge XI. 225
connynge *adj.* clever **connyngest** *superl.* VI. 42
consayl(e), conseil, conseyl *n.* advice; confidential information VI. 165; secret XXI. 162; council Prol. 167, III. 127 **be my conseil** if you take my advice Prol. 207
conseile, conseyle *v.* advise **conseilede** *pa.t.*
consenteth concedes, agrees to give (MED *consenten*, 2b[b]) II. 90
conseyue understand X. 56
conspire plot XI. 80
constorie consistory court Prol. 127n, III. 34, 178, 472, XVI. 361
contenue continue, persevere V. 39
contina(u)nce outward appearance, show Prol. 26; facial expression VI. 165; meaningful look, a 'face' XI. 164, XV. 120
continence appearance, looks *or* self-restraint XI. 178n
contrarieth contradicts II. 22 **contraryed** *pa.t.* Prol. 59

contre country **contrees** *pl.* districts, areas of jurisdiction II. 63
contreplede argue against, contradict Prol. 138
contrerollor one who keeps the counter-roll so as to check the person in charge of accounts XI. 300
contreued(e) devised, invented Prol. 144, VI. 39
contuimax *adj.* wilfully disobedient to authority XIII. 84
contynue continue; be continent X. 281n
conysaunce a heraldic mark or device by which a person is distinguished, especially as to his allegiance XVIII. 187
copes, copis *n.pl.* hooded cloaks
cope *inf.* provide with a cope VI. 288 **copeth** III. 179 **copeden** *pa.t.3pl.* II. 240
cople *inf.* yoke II. 190
coppe cup
coppe-mele cup-fuls VI. 231
corleu curlew XV. 242
cornel kernel XII. 145, 148
corone crown XXI. 465
cors process XIII. 144
cors corpse XV. 11, XVI. 182
cor-seynt sainted person, saint VII. 177
coruen *pa.t.3pl.* cut VIII. 185
cost expense III. 72
costes districts X. 12
costumes customs XIV. 73
cote cottage, hovel V. 2, IX. 151 **cotes** *pl.* IV. 123, IX. 72
coterelles cottars, cottagers IX. 97, 193
coteth provides coats for III. 179
cotte-pors cut-purse, thief VII. 283
couayteth wants, desires I. 180
coueityse covetousness
couent convent, religious house (not in ME restricted to a nunnery) V. 151, VI. 39
couerour coverer, maker of roofs V. 175
couert court I. 104
coueth coughs XIX. 306
coueyten desire Prol. 31
coueytise covetousness
counte county, count's domain II. 90
counteth reckons as important XXI. 305
countreplede oppose VIII. 53, 88 **countrepledeth** XXII. 384
countresegge contradict XI. 225
coupable found guilty XIX. 281
coupe guilt VI. 328
coupes large drinking-bowls III. 23
cours process III. 60; pattern of movement XVII. 104
court castle VII. 232
courtepies short jackets VIII. 185
couthe *v.* could; knew (of), knew how to
couthe *adj.as n.* kith, family XVII. 196
cowed, cowhede *v.* coughed VI. 412, XV. 109
cowhes *n.pl.* coughs XXII. 82
cowpe guilt VI. 351
crabbed cross, peevish XIV. 100
crache scratch Prol. 200, VI. 140; claw back, clutch XII. 77

craft skill, knowledge; trade, profession
crafty skilled in a craft, skilful
craym cream VIII. 305, 321
creaunt, cryant yielding, 'believing' XIV. 132, 153
crocer cross-bearer V. 113
croddes curds VIII. 305, 321
croft small enclosed field VII. 219, VIII. 31 **croftes** *pl.* VIII. 314
crok cooking-pot XXI. 280
crokes hooks XX. 294
crompe cramp VI. 78
crop top XVIII. 75
crope crept Prol. 200
crose bishop's crook, crosier X. 92
crouch (emblem of the) cross VII. 167
croumes crumbs VIII. 279, 288
crouneth *v.* marks with the tonsure XIII. 124 **crouned** *pp.* V. 63
crounes *n.pl.* tonsured crowns V. 177
crownyng tonsure Prol. 86
cryant *see* **creaunt**
culle kill **culde(n)** killed
culorum conclusion III. 432n, XI. 249
curatour holder of a 'cure' of souls, parson XXI. 410 **curatours, curatores** *pl.* XI. 249, XV. 16
cure *n.* cure (of souls), pastoral care Prol. 86, XXII. 233, 237
cure(n) *inf.* have 'cure' of souls XIV. 70, XXII. 325
custe kissed XX. 466
custume custom III. 373 **custumes** *pl.* III. 206
cuuere cover, provide a roof for III. 64

daffe fool I. 138, X. 177, XIII. 233
dagge *inf.* cut with slits or serrations XXII. 143
Damascle, Damaske Damascus VII. 173, XVII. 189, 261
dame mother
dampne condemn XVII. 215
dar (*impers.*) needs **dar þe** you need XV. 257
dawe *inf.* dawn XX. 184
Dawe Dave, dim. of David VI. 369, VIII. 353
decre the body of canon law as set out in decretals XVII. 113
decretistre student of the decretals (decrees) of canon law XV. 85
ded *adj.* dead *adj.as n.* dead man XXII. 293
dede *pa.t.* did; made, caused to; (*refl.*) made my way XXI. 2
dedeynous disdainful, proud X. 81
dees dice VIII. 72
defaute want, lack; fault XII. 35
defendeth forbids III. 68, XX. 111
defense prohibition **his defense** the prohibition laid upon him XX. 200
defie, defye(n), deffye digest
degre rank, grade
dele give (away) I. 196, XI. 71, XIX. 216 **delest** III. 76 **deleth** XI. 69
delitable delicious, delightful I, 32
deluare digger VIII. 353 **deluares, deluers** *pl.* Prol. 225, VIII. 114

deluuye deluge (Lat. *diluvium*) XI. 252
deme(n) judge, deliver judgment
demme *adj.* dark XX. 362 *adv.* dimly XI. 128
demynge judgment, exercise of justice XII. 78
dene din, commotion II. 217, XX. 65, 127
Denote Dennet, dim. of Denise VIII. 72
dentiesliche dainteously (on dainties) VIII. 323
depraue slander III. 224
dere *n.* harm VIII. 158
dere *inf.* harm, injure IX. 38, XIX. 18, XX. 25, 297
dere *adj.* expensive X. 197
derely richly, in my best clothes XXI. 2
derfly violently III. 415
derne secret III. 291, X. 292, XIII. 154
dernely secretly XIII. 162
derste durst Prol. 193
derworth(e) precious, beloved I. 83, VI. 89, XIII. 17
descreue describe VI. 196, XX. 213
deseyte deceit II. 128 **in deseyte of** to deceive Prol. 77
despene spend, make use of VIII. 235
despeyre cause to despair IX. 38
desseyue deceive I. 40
destrueth destroy Prol. 24
deth-deynge death-dying, i.e. hour of death VII. 86, 111
deue *adj.as n.pl.* deaf (people) XXI. 130
deuer duty, job XVII. 92, 122
deuinede explained, interpreted X. 101
deul sorrow, lamentation VIII. 127, XIX. 317
deuors divorce XXII. 139
deuoutours *adj.pl.or n.pl.* adulterous, adulterers II. 184
deux dew VII. 265
deuyne *inf.* explain XV. 98 *imp.pl.* divine, work out Prol. 218 **deuyneth** *pres.3pl.* interpret, base their theology upon XVII. 314 **deuynede** *pa.t.3sg.* interpreted IX. 307
deuynours divines XV. 123
dewe *adj.* due III. 304
dey(e) die
deyes high table, dais XI. 40
deyneth designs XI. 61 **deynede** VIII. 331
deynous disdainful, proud XVI. 227
deynte value, importance XI. 314
deys dais XV. 66
Dido a useless tale
diffoule damage, spoil VIII. 31
dighte, dihte dressed XXI. 2; had sexual intercourse with I. 27
dikere ditcher VI. 369 **dikares** *pl.* VIII. 114
discerue deserve XIII. 85
disceue deceive XVII. 184
discret discerning, judicious V. 84
dispice despise II. 84
disshere dish-maker or seller VI. 372
distruye destroy Prol. 213
diuerseth is different, varies XVII. 133
do, don(e), doen do; (*with inf.*) cause to (do, or be done); make III. 469; execute upon III. 446; appeal for confirmation (to) II. 39; (*refl.*) betake (oneself) X. 273 **do** *pp.* done; put, lodged X. 137

dobbed, dobbet dubbed I. 101, XX. 11
dobelares platters XV. 91
doem judgment IX. 343
doen *see* **do**
doke duck VI. 174
dome judgment, exercise of justice VI. 299, 347, XII. 87; (day of) judgment IX. 340 **domes** *pl.* 16. 186
domesman judge XXI. 306
dompynges dabchicks XIII. 167
don(e) *see* **do**
donet elementary lesson-book VI. 215n
doom judgment II. 129, III. 470
doseyne, dosoyne dozen IV. 38, VI. 369
dotede foolish, stupid I. 138
doth does; causes to, makes; prepares II. 221
doumbe dumb II. 39
dount blow, injury XX. 25
doute *n.* fear, anxiety VI. 284, XIV. 69
doute *v.* fear X. 126, XX. 312
douue dove XVII. 171
dowe endow III. 319 **dowede** XVII. 220
down-riht definitely, without question XX. 198
dowue dove XVII. 239
doysayne dozen XXII. 164
dradd *pa.t.3sg.* (*refl.*) feared XV. 284
draf refuse, pigswill XI. 9; lees, remains XXI. 399
drat *pres.3sg.* fears VII. 73, XII. 150, XXII. 379
drawe *pp.* taken away VIII. 288
dremeles *n.* dream XV. 17
dreuele slobber XI. 9; talk sloppily and ignorantly XI. 40
dronklewe given to drink X. 81
drosenes dregs VIII. 193
drouthe drought, lack of water, dry season V. 149, VIII. 312, XV. 252
drow *pa.t.1sg.* (*refl.*)betook (myself) VI. 215
druerie object of affection, prized thing I. 83
druie *adj.* dry **drynke druie** drain the pot IX. 145
druyeth *pres.3pl.* dry XIV. 22
ducherie duchy III. 244
duntes blows VIII. 187, XXII. 105
dure last, live
dust *pa.t.2sg.* madest XX. 320
duyren last, live, endure
dwale opiate, sleeping-potion XXII. 379
dyaes medicinal remedies XXII. 174
dyhte *inf.* make ready VIII. 315
dykers ditchers Prol. 225
dykke ditch XIII. 233
dymes tithes XVII. 227
dynge *v.* bang, knock XVI. 169
dysors popular reciters **dysores** *gen.sg.*
dyuer duty, work XVI. 5
dyuynour expert in divinity XV. 85

Ebrew Hebrew XIX. 4
echone each one, all
edefien, edefye build IX. 203, XVIII. 161, XX. 42
edwitede reproached, accused VI. 421
eer *adv.* before I. 201

eft(e), eefte again; afterwards IV. 102
eftesones soon after again VI. 328, XXI. 5
eggede urged, egged on I. 61
egre better, angry XV. 89
egrelich bitterly, painfully XXI. 378
eg-toel sharp-edged weapon or tool III. 475
elde old age
eleue eleven II. 238
elles else, otherwise; at other times Prol. 89; elsewhere XXI. 189
elyng(e) sad, miserable, bereft Prol. 204, XXII. 2
elyngly wretchedly XXII. 39
emcristen(e) *adj.as n.pl.* fellow-Christians II. 99, VII. 46, X. 79 *see* **euen-cristene**
emforth *prep.* in proportion to, to the full extent of XV. 142, XVI. 222
enbaumed anointed XIII. 106, XIX. 70
enblaunched whitened, made outwardly attractive XVI. 269
enchesoun reason VI. 40
endaunted tamed XVII. 171
ende (i.e. hende) gracious, courteous X. 145
endit *pp.* ended III. 303
endite indict XV. 119; compose a letter XVII. 109
enferme make firm XVII. 271
engendrure engendering, procreation XIII. 143
engleymeth chokes, cloys XVI. 218
enioynen unite in marriage II. 150 **enioyned** combined X. 130
enleuene eleven III. 226, XII. 173
enpugneth impugns, rejects XIII. 117
enqueste legal court of inquiry XXII. 162 **enquestes** *pl.* XIII. 84
ensaumple, ensaunple example, demonstration, edifying story
entermetynge *n.* meddling XIII. 223
eny any
enys-kyn(n)es any kind of (*lit.* of any kind) II. 212, III. 113
equitee voluntary subjection XVII. 240
erber garden, arbour XVIII. 5
erede ploughed XXI. 268
eremites, ermytes hermits
ergo (Lat.) therefore
ern *pa.t.3sg.* ran **ern in** pervaded the minds of XVIII. 164
ernde errand, commission III. 48
ernynge running XXI. 378
ers arse V. 160, VI. 157
erye *v.* plough
ese ease, comfort
espirit spirit XIV. 27
euaungelie gospel XI. 205, XII. 100
euen-cristene *adj.as n.pl.* fellow-Christians (i.e. 'neighbours', trans. Lat *proximus*) VI. 75
euene *adj.* equal XVIII. 90; fixed, definite XXII. 70
euene *adv.* fairly IV. 178; steadily, consistently XVI. 54, XXI. 299; squarely XXII. 103
euene-forth *prep.* in proportion to XXI. 309
euereche *pron.* each XX. 77
euesynges eaves XIX. 192

ewangelie gospel I. 195
exitede urged, excited VI. 20
eye *interj.* eh! alas! XII. 1
eyres heirs
eyus eyes VII. 57

fader father *gen.sg.* XVI. 27
falaes *n.pl.* fallacious questions XVI. 231
falewe *inf.* plough VII. 295
fallas *n.pl.* crafty tricks, spurious logical arguments XI. 22
falle befall, happen **falleth** befalls; belongs I. 162 **falle** *pp.* Prol. 63
falsnesses failures of true observance Prol. 69
famed defamed, slandered III. 231
Farao Pharaoh IX. 315
fare *v.* go, fare, live **faren** *pp.* VIII. 112
fare *n.* business, goings-on XX. 16, 129
fast(e) *adv.* quickly, vigorously, etc. (contextually intensive)
fauchen sword XVI. 168
Fauel deceit, fraud
fauht fought
fauntekyn infant XXI. 118 **faunt(o)kynes** *pl.* IX. 35, X. 182
fauntes children IX. 170
fauten *v.* lack X. 182
fay doomed to die XV. 2
fayful faithful I. 15
fayfulleche faithfully VIII. 70
fayn glad
faytest beggest falsely V. 30 **fayteth** IX. 100 **fayteden** Prol. 43
faythly truly XXI. 70
faytour *adj.* deceitful IX. 64
faytour *n.* false beggar, malingerer, lying vagabond VIII. 73 **faytours** *pl.* II. 193, VIII. 128
faytrye falseness, deceit VIII. 138
feet deed I. 182
feffament feoffment, deed of gift or endowment II. 73
feffe endow II. 160, III. 369, XVII. 56 **feffeth** II. 83 **feffed** II. 137
fel, felle fierce, harsh, stern
fele many
fend(e) *n.* devil
fende *v.* defend I. 99
fendekynes lesser fiends XX. 415
fenestre window XX. 13 **fenestres** *pl.* XVI. 42
fenkelsedes fennel-seeds VI. 360
fer far, far away
ferddede gathered together XIII. 147
ferde(n) happened, was XIV. 141; acted XIX. 112; fared, behaved X 233
fere mate, spouse, companion XIII. 163, XVII. 19, XIX. 299 **feres** *pl.* II. 219
fere make afraid XVII. 285
ferie feast-day IV. 113
ferly marvel, wonder XI. 229, XX. 114 **ferlyes** *pl.* Prol. 63 **ferly me thynketh** I shall be very surprised XV. 118
ferlyede marvelled XIII. 171
ferne-ȝer formerly VII. 46
fers eager VI. 7

ferthe fourth IX. 56
festene incorporate, join XII. 8
fette *inf.* fetch **fette(n)** *pa.t.* **fet** *pp.*
feye doomed to die XVI. 196
fiscuth wanders IX. 153
fithele play on the fiddle VII. 107
flateres flatterers VII. 83, 90, XXI. 221
flatte dashed, cast quickly VII. 58
flete float, swim XXII. 45
fley, fleyh *pa.t.3sg.* flew XVIII. 121; fled, hurried II. 220, XIX. 57
floreynes florins (gold coins worth 6s. 8d.)
florischeth causes to prosper, preserves XVI. 132
flowen *pa.t.3pl.* flew, escaped XX. 369; fled II. 249, VIII. 179
flux discharge VI. 161
fly *pa.t.3sg.* flew I. 118
fobbes cheats, impostors II. 193
fode food
foel *adj.* foolish VII. 83
foel *n.* fool XII. 210
foende *pa.t.3pl.* provided for V. 36
fol *adj.* full
fol *adv.* full, very
folde earth
foles birds XI. 251
fol(i)liche foolishly XVI. 234, 235
follen baptise XVII. 285
follwares servants, farm-labourers XVII. 103
follyng(e) baptism XIV. 207, XVII. 76, XXI. 39
fond(e) *inf., imp.* try XV. 144, XXII. 166 **fondeth** *pres.3sg.* tests XIV. 119
fond(e) *pa.t.* found, perceived, discovered
fondement foundation XVI. 42
fondlynges foundlings X. 295
fondynges temptations X. 42, XVI. 137, XIX. 89
fonge take, get, grasp VII. 202, IX. 91, XV. 202
fonk spark VI. 335
for *conj.* for; because XII. 105, XX. 184; so that VI. 23
for *prep.* for; despite, in spite of, to prevent
forbar spared, let go III. 426
forbede forbid IX. 329
forbet bites away, eats away XVIII. 39
forbete *inf.* beat thoroughly XX. 34 *pp.* worn down by exertion, enfeebled XXII. 198
forbisene example, illustrative story X. 32; example, model XVII. 277
forbodene forbidden III. 188
forbere go without I. 99
forbrenne burn up III. 125 **forbrent** *pa.t.* burnt to pieces III. 107
force matter, consequence XIV. 10
fordo, fordo(e)n *inf.* destroy, bring to destruction V. 122, XX. 41, 161 **fordoth** *pres.3sg.* XIX. 252, 260, XX. 155 **fordo** *pp.* XV. 230
fore track, course VI. 118
forel box XV. 103n
foreynes strangers, unrelated persons IX. 199
forfare perish VIII. 234
forfeteth offends XXII. 25

forfret eats away XVIII. 33
forglotten swallow up XI. 66
forgoere fore-goer (*see* II. 61n) II. 198
forgyue *pp.* fully granted XX. 187
forȝaf granted XX. 79
forȝeld repay, reward VIII. 298
forȝet *pa.t.* passed right through XII. 12n
forȝeten *pp.* forgotten VII. 13
forleyn *pp.* lain with wrongfully IV. 46
forlong balk of unploughed land VII. 32n
formeste, formost *adv.* first, first of all I. 73, VI. 15, XX. 162, 163
foroward agreement, promise IV. 13
forreours foragers XXII. 81
forschupte unmade, undid the work of creation, destroyed XIX. 269
forsleuthed wasted by idle carelessness VII. 52
forst frost XII. 191 **forstes** *pl.* XII. 187
forstalleth buys up goods in advance IV. 59n
for-strenede procreated with painful effort XIII. 170
forth *n.* way, free course III. 194
forthenketh (*impers.*) it makes repent XX. 92
forthere more widely VIII. 76
forthi, forthy *adv.* therefore
forthynketh (*impers*) it makes repent **me forthynketh** I repent X. 250
forto *conj.* until VII. 214
forw furrow VI. 268 **forwes** *pl.* VIII. 65
forwanyen spoil by indulgence V. 137
fouchensa(e)f vouchsafe, warrant (me) V. 49; grant XVIII. 18
foul *adj.* foolish VII. 104
foul *n.* bird
founded *pp.* endowed, provided for XVII. 56
fram *prep.* from
Franceys *see* **Fraunceys**
frankeleyn franklin, man of free but not noble birth holding land by freehold X. 238 **frankeleynes** *pl.* V. 64, XXI. 39
Fraunceys Francis (St) IV. 117, XXII. 252 **Franceys** *gen.sg.* XVI. 353
frayned(e) asked
fraytour refectory V. 173
freek man XV. 81
freel frail, fickle X. 48
freelete frailty, weakness of the flesh XIX. 311
freet ate XX. 201
freke man IX. 153 **frekes** *pl.* VI. 152
frele frail, weak III. 157
frelete frailty III. 59
fremde *adj.as n.pl.* unrelated persons, strangers XII. 154
frendes friends; relations V. 36n, X. 183, XII. 154
frentyk frantic XVIII. 179
frere friar *gen.sg.* friar's
frete eat II. 100
fretynge devouring, destructive XX. 157
frithed fenced VII. 228
frithes woods IX. 224
fro *prep.* from
fryth wood XIV. 158 **frythes** *pl.* woods, wild places XVII. 11

ful(l) *pa.t.3sg.* fell; befell XVIII. 128 **fullen**
   pa.t.3pl. fell I. 125
fulle *inf.* fill VI. 390
fullyng baptism XIV. 208
fundement foundation III. 344, 345
furste *adj., adv.* first
furste *n.* thirst VI. 438, XX. 410
fursteth (*impers.*) it makes thirsty **me fur-
   steth** I thirst XX. 408
fust(e) fist
fuyr fire
fyle concubine VI. 135
fyn subtle XI. 159
fynde find; provide (for) **fynt** *pres.3sg.*
fyndynge provision for livelihood VI. 293,
   XXII. 383
fythele *n.* fiddle
fythelen *inf.* play on the fiddle XV. 206

ga go **ga we** let us go Prol. 228
gabbe(n) *v.* lie, tell lies III. 225, XVII. 16
gabbyng *n.* lying XVII. 129 **gabbynges** *pl.*
   lies XXI. 454, XXII. 125
gadlyng vagabond, worthless fellow XXII.
   157 **gadelynges** *pl.* X. 294
gaf gave
galoches shoes XX. 12n
galpe *v.* yawn XV. 97
Galys Galicia IV. 124, VII. 166
gan *pa.t.3sg.* began; did (i.e. *as pa.t.aux.*) **gonne**
   pa.t.3pl.
gange *inf.* go XVIII. 177
gangynge going, walking XVIII. 242
garnement garment IX. 119 **garnementes**
   pl. XX. 178
gart(e) *pa.t.3sg.* made, caused (to) V. 146,
   VIII. 324, XXII. 57
gate way, passage; manner of walking XX.
   252
gentel(e) noble, well-born
genteliche courteously III. 14
gentrice noble birth XX. 21
gert *pa.t.3sg.* made, caused to XXII. 131
geste story, tale VII. 107 **gestes** *pl.* XI. 23,
   XV. 205
gete *pp.* got VI. 342; begotten X. 294
geterne gittern (a kind of guitar) XV. 208
geuen *pa.t.3pl.* gave VI. 375
gileth deceives IX. 65
gladie *inf.* gladden XX. 178
glase glaze, provide glass for III. 52
glasene made of glass XXII. 172
glede glowing coal XIX. 188 **gledes** *pl.* XIX.
   182
gleman minstrel XI. 104
glosares deceivers XXI. 221
glose *n.* gloss, qualification III. 328
glosed *adj.* equipped with commentary VI.
   303n
glosede *pa.t.* glossed, interpreted (speciously)
   Prol. 58
glosynge *adj.* flattering IV. 138
glosynge *n.* deceitful words, deceit VI. 259
   glosynges *pl.* XXII. 125
gnedy niggardly XV. 86
go *pp.* gone

gobet small portion V. 100
gode, goed, good(e) *n.* goods, wealth,
   property; good birth II. 145
goestliche spiritual XXII. 40
goky fool XIII. 119, 120
gome *n.* man **gomus** *pl.* Prol. 44
gome *n.* heed, notice XIX. 14
gommes *n.pl.* gums (as used in spices and per-
   fumes) II. 236
gon(e) go
gonne *see* **gan**
good *adv.* well Prol. 58
good(e) *see* **gode**
goodliche liberally I. 178
gorge throat XI. 41n
gossip friend, crony VI. 357 **gossipes** *pl.* VI.
   47
gost spirit
gothelen, gothly *inf.* rumble VI. 398, XV. 97
gott stomach I. 34 **gottes** *pl.* XI. 41
gradde cried out aloud XXII. 386
graffe graft, engrafting I. 200
grange group of farm-buildings XIX. 71n
gras grace VI. 84
grat cry out aloud VIII. 284
graþest most direct I. 200
graue *inf.* bury XX. 87; engrave III. 52 *pp.*
   engraved XVII. 207
grauynge *n.* engraving, painting III. 68
graynes seeds (of corn) XXI. 274
grayth, grayeth exact, true III. 89, VI. 230,
   X. 240
graythly, graytheliche directly, without
   delay VII. 296; duly, properly XI. 139, XX.
   322
gre prize, honour of the day XX. 102
greden cry out aloud IX. 76 **gredest** XXI.
   425 **gredeth** XIV. 133
gredyre gridiron II. 130
greeut earth XIII. 175
grene green; unripe VIII. 304
gret *adj.as n.* much III. 89
gret(e) *adj.* great
grette *pa.t.3sg.* greeted IV. 42, XII. 206
grettere more fiercely Prol. 122
greut earth XIII. 22
gries *see* **grys**
groche *v.* grumble Prol. 171 **grochede** *pa.t.*
   VI. 111
gromes men VIII. 227
grote groat (silver coin worth 4d.) VI. 230
   grotes *pl.* III. 174, XVII. 208
gruche grumble, complain VIII. 227, 337
grydy greedy VI. 398
grype, grypeth *v.* grab, grip, seize III. 89,
   282 **grypen** *pp.* III. 227
grys, gries *n.pl.* pigs, piglets Prol. 228, IV. 49,
   VIII. 304
gult(e) *n.* sin, guilt
gult *adj.* gilt XVI. 343, XIX. 15
gulte *pa.t.* sinned VII. 151
gurdeth strike (off) II. 213
gurles children I. 29n, IX. 76, XVI. 300,
   XX. 6
gye(n) *inf.* guide II. 198, XXI. 227
gyle guile, trickery, deceit

Gyle Giles (St) VIII. 54
gylle gill (quarter-pint) VI. 397
gylours deceivers, cheaters III. 100, 302
gyn siege-engine XX. 261
gyour guide XXI. 425, XXII. 72
gyue *v.* give **gyue of** respect IV. 37 **gyue** *pp.* given
gyued *pa.t.* set in gyves XXII. 192
gyues *n.pl.* gyves, leg-shackles XV. 253

ȝaf gave
ȝe yes, yea, indeed
ȝe you
ȝede(n) went
ȝeepliche eagerly XVI. 328
ȝefte gift **to ȝefte** as a gift XI. 104 **ȝeftes** *pl.*
ȝelde(n) *v.* repay, pay back **ȝeld(e)** *pa.t.* yielded, acknowledged, surrendered XIV. 132, 153, XX. 104
ȝeme *inf.* care for X. 304
ȝeme *n.* heed III. 484
ȝemen *n.pl.* yeomen, servants III. 269
ȝende yonder XX. 261
ȝent *adj.* noble XV. 131
ȝep vigorous, fresh X. 284, XI. 180
ȝer year(s)
ȝerd land, country VIII. 207
ȝerde(s) *n.pl.* sticks IV. 112; yards VI. 220
ȝerne *adv.* eagerly, readily, earnestly IV. 53, VII. 36, VIII. 320, XXII. 286; quickly, vigorously XXII. 159
ȝerne *v.* run III. 269 **ȝerneth** runs XVI. 328
ȝerne *v.* yearn, desire
ȝeuan Evan VI. 310
ȝeue(n) *v.* give **ȝeue** or reckon of importance XXII. 155 **ȝeue** *pp.* given
ȝokes yokes (of oxen) VII. 295
ȝone yon XX. 148
ȝonge young
ȝorn ran, passed XII. 12
ȝoue gave XX. 425
ȝoure your
ȝow you
ȝowsuluen yourselves
ȝowthe youth I. 139
ȝus yes (in response to negative questions) VI. 91, 235, XIX. 278
ȝut yet, nevertheless, furthermore, further, moreover, even

haberion coat of mail XX. 22
hackenayman one who hires out horses VI. 365, 378
hacky grub about XXI. 401
hadde *pa.t.subj.* might have XXII. 383
haen *pres.pl.* have III. 172, V. 70
haiward *see* **hayward**
hakeneys horses II. 175
halde(n) *v.* hold; consider **halden with** support I. 94
haldyng *pres.p.as adj.* under obligation (OED, s.v. *beholding*) VI. 299
hales *see* **hals**
halewe consecrate XVII. 279
halie drag, pull back X. 93
hals(e), hales neck

halsede besought, conjured I. 70
halsyng embracing VI. 187
halt *pres.3sg.* holds
haluendele half, half-portion VII. 29
han *v.* have
hand-while short while XXI. 272
handy-dandy exchange game IV. 68n
hansull gift VI. 375n
hap fortune, good luck III. 297, XXII. 385
hapeward a travelling entertainer with a performing monkey VII. 284
happe *v.* happen, befall III. 438, XVIII. 120 **happed** *pa.t.* (*impers.*) it befell **hym happed** he happened V. 95
hardiloker, hardyore more boldly, more confidently VI. 306, XVI. 102
harlotes rogues, scoundrels
harlotrie, -rye ribaldry, coarse story (-telling)
harow *interj.* alas! XXII. 88
harwen *inf.* harrow
hastilokest most quickly, most readily XXI. 469
hastly quickly XII. 162
hastow hast thou
hater garment III. 157
hatte is called **hattest** art called XXII. 339
haued *pa.t.* had
haunt *n.* custom, frequentation XVI. 93
haunten, haunteth practise, indulge in
hawes haws, hawthorn berries XI. 8, 82
haylsede bowed down to, greeted IX. 311, X. 10
hayre hair-shirt VI. 6
hayward, haiward hayward (the man who watched over enclosures and prevented animals straying among the crops) V. 16, VI. 368, XIII. 44n
hed(e) heed *n.* head
heddere hither XXII. 333
heet(e) *pa.t.* commanded XVIII. 249, XXII. 273, 348
hefdes *n.pl.* heads, leaders XVII. 85
heggen make and trim hedges V. 19
hehte, heihte *pa.t.* was called VIII. 80, XVIII. 4
heiliche devoutly VIII. 90
helden *pa.t.3pl.* **helden with** supported I. 108
hele *n.* health, salvation, security, prosperity **to his hele** on his side III. 297
hele *inf.* cover, conceal IX. 157, XXII. 339 **helede** *pa.t.* XIII. 162
helle-pouke goblin of hell XV. 164
hellerne elder-tree I. 64
helynge roofing XVI. 236
hem them; themselves
hemself themselves
hende gracious, courteous VIII. 47, XI. 44
hendely, hendeliche, hendly graciously, courteously III. 30, X. 10, XVIII. 132
hendenesse grace, courtesy II. 81, XI. 13, XVIII. 13, XXI. 31
hengen *pa.t.* hanged I. 170
hennes hence
hente(n) seize, take VI. 8, XVI. 81, XIX. 138 *pa.t.* VII. 152
hep(e) heap, crowd **to hepe** together X. 189n, 191

her *adv.* ere, before III. 393
her *see* **here**
herborw *n.* harbour, refuge XI. 248
herborwe *inf.* harbour, provide refuge for VII. 258; store XXI. 319 **herberwed** *pp.* lodged VI. 235
her(e) *poss.adj.3pl.* their
her(e) *pron.3gen.pl.* of them X. 270, XIV. 105, XVI. 81, XX. 68, 175, XXII. 353
here *v.* hear
here-agayn here-against, contrary to this X. 234
herly early VI. 374
hernes corners, hiding-places II. 249, XX. 447
herrore higher II. 30
herte heart
heruost harvest VIII. 314
heste command III. 148, XVIII. 250 **hestes** *pl.* II. 87, VIII. 213, IX. 336
hette *pa.t.* commanded I. 17
heued head
heuegeste heaviest VI. 242
heuegore heavier XIV. 105
heuenriche *gen.sg.* heavenly kingdom's Prol. 29
heuy sad IV. 160
heuynesse pain, suffering XX. 256
Hewe Hugh VI. 365
hewe *n.* labourer, servant III. 307, VII. 196 **hewen, hewes** *pl.* I. 123, IV. 58, 102, XVI. 3
hey(e), heyh high, devoutly VII. 226
heye-festes high festivals (of the Church) VI. 182
heyliche generously, nobly III. 251; at a high rate VIII. 335
heynesse pride XXII. 153
heyres heirs
hidward hitherward XX. 341
hihte *pa.t.3sg.* commanded VII. 14, 247, XVIII. 106
hihte *pa.t.3sg.* was called VII. 299, VIII. 81, 82
hit it **hit ben, hit are(n), hit beeþ** they are V. 59, VIII. 52, 217, IX. 118, 126
hit *pa.t.* flung down (as a wager) VI. 378
hitsilue itself
ho who, whoever
hoed hood
hoer grey- or white-haired VIII. 92, 18.183
hoes whose I. 46
hoet *v.* hoot, shout XX. 287
hoet *adj.* intense, sharp XX. 212
hokkerye (fraudulent) retail dealing VI. 233
holde *v.* hold, consider **holdeth togederes** go together, are inseparable I. 53, **holde(n)** *pp.* held, considered; beholden, obliged XIX. 37, XXII. 365; carried on, practised VI. 233
holde *adj.* faithful VIII. 195
holdyng *adj.* under obligation (*see* **haldyng**) VIII. 103
hole *adj.* entire VII. 258; full XX. 419
holly wholly, entirely
holpen helped
hongen hang

hoor grey-haired VI. 193
hoores whores III. 300
hope think, expect, hope
hopur hopper, sower's seed-basket VIII. 60
hore whore **horen** *gen.pl.* XIV. 21
horedom whoring VII. 76
hors horses II. 176
hosebonde husbandman, farmer XII. 197
hosele *n.* communion XXI. 392
horseled *pp.* housled **be hoseled** receive communion XXI. 3, 395, 475
ho-so who-so
hostiele inn, lodging XIII. 63
hote, hoteth *v.* command **hote** *pp.* commanded
hote *v.* am called XVI. 197 **hoteth** is called II. 31, XVIII. 18 **hote(n)** *pp.* called II. 20, XI. 1
houe hood, skull-cap tied under the chin as worn by lawyers III. 447, XXII. 172 **houes** *pl.* Prol. 159
houed hung around, waited in readiness Prol. 159, XX. 83, 86
houped whooped, shouted VIII. 168
hous, hows *n.pl.* houses VII. 52, 237
hudde(n) hid XIII. 162, XXI. 102
hulles hills
huppe hop XVII. 279
huppynge hopping, walking jauntily XIX. 59
hutte hit XIV. 51
huydeth conceals X. 240
huyre *n.* hire, reward, wage, payment
huyre *inf.* hire II. 175
hye high
hyhte *pa.t.* commanded III. 9, VI. 212
hyhte *pp.* called VI. 310
hym him; himself
hyne servant VI. 262

iaced rode XIX. 50
iang(e)le talk idly or argumentatively II. 99, X. 118, XV. 92
iangelynge *n.* arguing, quarrelling VI. 133
iape *inf.* play tricks, tell jokes XV. 207; mock, jibe II. 99
ich I
Iewene *gen.pl.* Jews' I. 63, XX. 40
iewyse penalty XX. 424
ilk(e) *adj.* same III. 456, VII. 245 *pron.* same thing, very thing I. 79
ilych *prep.* like VII. 129
ingang entrance VII. 282
ingratis (Lat, *ingratus*) ungrateful XIX. 218
inlyche inwardly III. 370
inpugne call in question Prol. 136 **inpugnede** *pa.t.* IX. 303, XV. 131
insolibles *n.pl.* insoluble problems XVI. 231
inwit(t), inwyt conscience: more specifically, the faculty of intellect which distinguishes right and wrong and precedes the acts of conscience V. 10, VI. 10, 421, IX. 117, XI. 143n
iogele juggle XV. 207
Iohan, Ion John
Ionet Janet
Iosepes Joseph's
Iosue Joshua

iouken perch XVIII. 126
iourne day's work XVI. 5
ioutes soups, stews VI. 133
is his (*to form gen.sg.*) VI. 329
isekeles icicles XIX. 192
iuge, iugge judge, give a judgment
iurdan chamber-pot XV. 92n
iuuentee youth XXI. 108
iuyste *n.as adj.* pot, wine-jar XV. 92

kaes case, instance III. 432
kalketrappes caltrops XX. 294n
kayes keys VII. 167
kayres (*refl.*) betakes (himself), goes VI. 351
kaytif wretch VI. 206
kele *inf.* cool XXI. 280
kembe(n) *v.* comb IX. 80, XI. 15
kene sharp; harsh, bitter
kenne, kenneth, kenet teach(es)
kepe, kepeth *v.* keep, guard, protect; care, be concerned III. 432, XIII. 231
kepe *n.* heed XIII. 144, 164
kepynge *n.* living XXI. 354
kerne *inf.* become corn, harden into grain XII. 179
kerue *inf.* cut VIII. 65
keruers carvers XI. 126
keuere *v.* recover XXII. 335 **keuereth** recovers, protects XIV. 118
keuereth *pres.3sg.* covers IX. 249 **keuered** *pp.* covered, hidden IX. 138, XXI. 348; protected, fortified XXI. 296
kix rushlight XIX. 184
knaue lad, servant, workman, low-born man
knet knitted, joined III. 210
knowe *v.* know; recognize IX. 232 *pp.* known; well-known, distinguished Prol. 54, XI. 96
knowelecheth *v.* acknowledges XIII. 89
knowlechede, knoleched(e) *pa.t.* acknowledged responsibility XXI. 186; confessed VI. 328, VII. 148
knowlechyng *n.* understanding X. 56
knowyng *n.* recognition II. 240
knyhtes-fees estates of land held by a knight (under original obligation of armed service) V. 77
koke put hay into haycocks V. 13
kud *pa.t.* showed VII. 46
kulde *pa.t.* killed III. 232
kunnyng knowledge XI. 228
kusse *v.* kiss
kuth country, people III. 260, XXI. 79
kyn kind **alle kyn** all kinds (of)
kynde *adj.* natural; ordinary V. 56; proper, right X. 69 **kynde wytt** natural intelligence Prol. 141n, 144, 147, I. 51, XIV. 236, XV. 17, 30, 163, XXII. 361 **kynde knowyng** natural understanding I. 136n, 141, 161, etc.
kynde *n.* nature; natural vigour VI. 193, XII. 145; lineage, birth II. 81; kinship II. 27; creature XIII. 150; (grammatical) kind III. 336, 346
kyndly *adj.* natural XVII. 153
kynd(e)ly, kyndeliche *adv.* naturally; intimately, intuitively I. 78, 159, VII. 183; properly, according to its nature, rightly IX.

213, XVII. 110; in ordinary language (i.e. in plain English) IV. 147
kyndore more natural, more intimate X. 108
kyne kind, sort (of) **eny kynes** any kind of (*lit.* of any kind) V. 20 (cf. *enys-kynes*)
kynedom kingdom
kyneriche, kyneryche kingdom
kyngene *gen.pl.* kings' XXI. 79
kynrede kindred X. 256
kyrke-ward church-ward **to kyrke-ward** towards the church VI. 351

labbe blab XII. 38
labory *v.* work
lacche, lache *v.* get, obtain, seize, catch
lacchesse, lachesse idleness
lach(e)-draweres latch-pickers, sneak thieves VIII. 287, IX. 192
lacke, lacky, lakke *v.* blame, reprimand, speak ill of, slander, find fault with
lacles blameless XIII. 208
ladde *pa.t.* led
laghte *pa.t.* seized Prol. 169
laghynge laughing III. 55
lakke *see* **lacke**
lakke *v.* lack, be lacking
lambren *n.pl.* lambs III. 411
land-tulyng land-tilling XI. 296
langour illness XVIII. 142
lape *inf.* drink VI. 414, XXII. 18
large *adj.* liberal, generous; broad
large *n.* bounty, power of patronage XXI. 43
largeliche liberally, generously, freely II. 138, IV. 67, XXI. 60
largenesse generosity XVII. 64
largesse bounty VII. 109
Lasar Lazarus
lasares lepers XVIII. 142
lasse *adj.* less *adj.as n.pl.* lesser folk
lassore lesser XIX. 146
lat(e), laton *v.* let; cause to
lat, latte *pres.3sg.* leads XV. 276; carries XIII. 55
lat *pa.t.1sg.* considered VI. 261
lauendrie laundry, washing-place XVI. 330
laueth washes XVI. 330
lauhe *v.* laugh
lauhfollyche lawfully IX. 59
lauhte *pa.t.,pp.* seized, took (taken); took on, assumed XIX. 123
lauhyng laughing VI. 23
launceth grow, spring XII. 184
launde field, open meadowland Prol. 8, X. 64
launseth grows, springs XII. 221; shoots forth XVIII. 10
lawen, lawhe(n) *v.* laugh IV. 101, VII. 84, XVI. 300
layes laws XXI. 43
layes fallow-lands IX. 5
layȝe *pp.* lain VI. 330
layk(e) *inf.* play Prol. 187, XVI. 175
layk *n.* sport, wrestling-match XVI. 85
layn *v.* conceal II. 18
Lazar Lazarus
lazar leper XVIII. 272n

leaute truth, loyalty XII. 23 *see also* **leute, lewte**
lecche, leche *n.* physician
leche *inf.* heal XV. 220
ledare leader, organizer, controller I. 155 **ledares** *pl.* V. 158, VIII. 251
lede *n.* man
lede *v.* lead, govern, carry
ledes *n.pl.* lands, properties, possessions XI. 69, XV. 304, XVII. 221
ledene cry, voice XIII. 171, XIV. 178
leed *n.* lead VII. 238
leef, lef *n.* page; (*fig.*) bit XV. 104
leef, lef *n.* leaf; thing of little value V. 97
leef, lef *adj.* fain, glad willing; dear, precious
leef, lef *adv.* dearly, gladly
leef, lef *imp.sg.* believe I. 36, 194, X. 303
leege *adj.* loyal, liege III. 414
leel(e) *adj.* loyal, true, faithful; lawful V. 103
leeliche, leely truly, faithfully, properly
lees *pa.t.3sg.* lost VII. 132, X. 195, XIII. 151
leet *pres.3sg.* leads III. 195
leet *pa.t.3sg.* considered to be XXII. 146 *pp.* esteemed XI. 34
lef *see* **leef**
lege *adj.* liege IV. 178 *adj.as n.pl.* liege-servants III. 316, 317, XX. 395, XXI. 60
lege, legge *v.* lay, wager, pledge IV. 191, VIII. 290, 292, XX. 161, XXII. 13
legityme *adj.as n.pl.* legitimate ones (Lat. *legitimi,* the form recorded in MS U) X. 210
leiaunce allegiance XVIII. 201
leide laid **leide on** struck, set about beating XXII. 189
lele *adj.* true, faithful, loyal *adj.as n.pl.* loyal and true men
leliche, lel(l)y, lellyche truly, certainly
lemman lover, mistress
lene *v.* give, lend
lened *pa.t.1sg.* reclined, rested Prol. 8, X. 64, XX. 5
lenge *v.* dwell, remain XXI. 418
lenger, lengore, lengur longer
lenghe *n.* length II. 93, III. 259, XIII. 38
lenghe *inf.* lengthen XX. 53 **lenghed** *pp.* XX. 335
lente *pa.t.3sg.* gave XI. 47 *pp.* given XV. 239
lente-sedes Lent-seeds, i.e. seeds for the spring crop of wheat XII 189
lenton Lent Prol. 89 **lentones** *pl.* XIII. 80
leode man X. 7
lep, lepen leapt, dashed
lere *v.* teach, instruct, guide; learn
lere *n.* face I. 3
lered *adj.as n.pl.* the learned
lerne learn; teach VIII. 340
lese(n) lose
leste least, least important
lesyng *n.* lie
lete(n) *v.* let, leave, give up III. 263, VI. 101, XI. 23, XIX. 287; allow, cease VI. 312; grant XVII. 117; consider V. 167, XI. 78, XVII. 299 **leteth** leaves, yields II. 104 **lette** *pa.t.3sg.* caused to, had XXII. 143; esteemed, valued IV. 156, VI. 243 **leten**

pa.t.3sg. caused to, let II. 172; considered, reckoned Prol. 195
lette, let *v.* hinder, delay, prevent I. 154, 203, III. 35, X. 160, XI. 60, XIX. 76, XX. 53; keep, stop VI. 349 **letteth, lettith** II. 38, III. 193, IV. 170, etc. **lette** *pa.t.* III. 238
lettere hinderer, destroyer I. 65
lettrure, letrure learning Prol. 137, IX. 195, 198; scripture XI. 26; written precept XIV. 127
lettyng(e) delay VIII. 5, XI. 137
letynge leaving, losing XVII. 124
leue *adj.* dear *adj.as quasi-subst.* pleasure IX. 146
leue *n.* leave, permission
leue *v.* leave, give up; grant, allow
leue *v.* believe
leue, leuen(e) *v.* live IV. 194, V. 44, VIII. 16, XII. 227, XIV. 9, XV. 179, 245 **leueth** III. 281, 419, XIII. 192
leuele level for checking horizontality XI. 127
leuer(e) *adj.* more pleasing
leuere *adv.* rather
leues leaf's, page's III. 489
leuest dearest, most dearly
Leuey Levi IX. 212
Leute(e) loyalty II. 20, 49 *see* **Lewte**
leuyte priest, deacon II. 130n **leuytes** *pl.* XIV. 58n
lewed(e) *adj.* ignorant, unlearned, lay; useless I. 185 *adj.as n.pl.* the unlearned, the laity
lewedenesse ignorance, illiteracy III. 35
lewete, Lewte loyalty Prol. 149n, III. 378, VI. 195
ley *v.* lay, stake XII. 91 **ley on** attack XV. 147
leye *n.* flame XIX. 178, 256
leye-land fallow-land X. 216
leyen *pa.t.* lay
leyhing laughing VI. 394
libbe *v.* VI. 125, XX. 110 **libbeth** VIII. 70
libbyng living IX. 58
liche *prep.* like VII. 124
licketh (*impers.*) pleases III. 19
liflode means of life, food, sustenance
liggeth *pres.3sg.* lies III. 221
lightliche, lihtliche quickly, readily, easily
lihtloker, -our more easily, more lightly VII. 216, XVII. 253
lik *v.* (*impers.*) please XI. 135 **liketh** *pres.3sg.* pleases **likede** *pa.t.* pleased
likene compare (odiously) VII. 23, XVI. 307
likerous luxurious, pleasant Prol. 32; tasty I. 25
lippe portion II. 37
lisse joy, bliss X. 154, XX. 236
liste strip of cloth VII. 162
lithe *inf.* soothe by anointing XIX. 69
lithereth throw things XVIII. 48
lipeth listen to VII.98
litte little IX. 207
littelum *n.dat.pl.* by little stages XVII. 320n
lixt liest VI. 138
lobies lazy hulking fellows, louts Prol. 53
loef loaf VIII. 286
loes loss XVI. 148

loeth reluctant XVI. 261

logh low, humble X. 83

loke look, see, keep an eye open, be attentive; inspect II. 234; watch over, keep VIII. 85 **loketh** looks; decides, provides II. 209 **loketh after (aftur)** waits for, expects III. 248, XIV. 120 **lokede** looked; (*impers.*) seemed **hym lokede** he seemed VI. 197

lokes locks (of hair) XV. 8

lokynge opinion, judgment, witness II. 122

lollare idler V. 2n **lollares** *pl.* V. 4, VIII. 74, 287, IX. 101, 107 *gen.sg.* IX. 103 **lollarne** *gen.pl.* V. 31, IX. 140

lolleth rests, lounges XIV. 152 **lolled** hung, made to swing XIV. 130

lombe lamb VII. 197 **lombren** *pl.* lambs IX. 260

lome often X. 165, XII. 120

lomere more often XXII. 238

lomes tools V. 45

londe land, earth **londes** *pl.* field-strips XIX. 58n

lone *n.* moneylending IV. 194; gift from a superior VIII. 196

long(e) long; tall

longe *v.* dwell, remain VI. 158, IX. 130

longe-lybbynge long-living (a patriarchal attribute) XIV. 168

longes lungs VIII. 189

longeth belongs, is attached III. 247

loo see, behold

loofte air

loos good fame, praiseworthiness VII. 109

Loot Lat

lope leapt (away) IV. 101

lordene *gen.pl.* lords' I. 95

lordeyne lazy rascal, villainous blockhead V. 162 **lordeyn(e)s** *pl.* XVIII. 48, XX. 106

lore teaching, doctrine, practice

lorel lazy worthless fellow VI. 314 **lorel(l)es** *pl.* Prol. 75, VIII. 129, IX. 137

loren, lorn lost

loresman teacher XIV. 122

los fame, renown, praise XIII. 110

Loscheborw, Lossheborw spurious coin imported from Luxembourg XVII. 72, 168 **Lossheborwes** *pl.* XVII. 82

loseles wastrels VIII. 74, XVI. 280

losliche uneasily XIV. 152

lossum lovesome, desirable X. 257

Lote Lot

lotebyes concubines III. 187

loteth (*refl.*) bows down, humbles (himself) XII. 156

loth difficult XV. 137

lotheth (*impers.*) is loathsome Prol. 173

louable praiseworthy V. 103

lou-chered of humble countenance XXI. 263

loue (*refl.*) humble (thyself) X. 302

loued *pp.* praised XI. 34

loueday III. 196, XI. 17 **louedayes** *pl.* III. 195n

loueliche *adj.* humble, modest X. 83, XII. 128

loueliche *adv.* pleasantly, charmingly III. 55

louelokest loveliest I. 106, VI. 44, 192

louelyche humbly XVI. 70

louer louver, latticed opening in roof XX. 286n

louh *adj.* low, humble VI. 227, VII. 197, XVI. 153

louh *pa.t.3sg.* laughed XII. 23, XVIII. 3

louhliche humbly IX. 141

louhnesse humility V. 155

louie *inf.* love

louke lock, enclose XX. 254

loupe loop-hole XX. 286

loure *v.* frown, scowl

loute(n) *v.* kneel in prayer or intercession, bow

louye(n), louyon *v.* love **louyet** *pres.3.pl.* love VI. 142

low(e) *pa.t.2sg.* lied XX. 348, 445

lowe *n.* flame, blazing light XX. 141

lowe *v.* (*refl.*) humble (thyself) XIV. 9 **lowede** *pa.t.* VIII. 194

lowh *pa.t.3sg.* laughed XXI. 459, XXII. 143

Lucas Luke

luft *adj.* left

luft *pa.t.3sg.* raised XVIII. 144

Lukes Lucca IV. 194, VIII. 109

luppen *v.* leap I. 112 **lup** *pa.t.3sg.* leapt II. 69, VII. 135

lust(e) *n.* desire

lust(e) *pres.3sg.* (*impers.*) pleases **luste** *pa.t.* pleased

lutede played on the lute XX. 469

luther, luyther bad, wicked

luyred lured VII. 45n

lyard a common name for a horse (properly one of a grey colour) XIX. 64

lybbe *inf.* live III. 202

lycame body, flesh

lycour juice XII. 219

lye flame XIX. 171

lyf person, man, body

lyflode food, sustenance, means of life

lyft *adj.* left III. 75

lyft *n.* sky XVII. 95

lygge(n) *v.* lie; lie idle VIII. 160

lygge *adj.* laid flat XII. 231n

lyggynge lying II. 53

lyhtliche, lyhtlych quickly, readily

lyhtloker more readily XIV. 101

lyketh *pres.3sg.* (*impers.*) pleases **lykede** *pa.t.* pleased

lykynde, lykyng *adj.* pleasing X. 283, XI. 134, XVIII. 78

lykynge *n.* pleasure XI. 12

lykyngest most pleasing VI. 44

lykyngliche pleasingly, according to his pleasure XIX. 240

lymes limbs

lym-ȝerd lime-twig X. 283

lynage lineage, good birth IX. 195

lynde linden-tree, lime-tree I. 151, X. 64

lyne measuring-line XI. 127

lynnen(e) linen

lyn-sed linseed (i.e. flax-seed) XII. 189

lyppe small portion, bit VI. 245, XI. 227, XVII. 253

lyppeth leap II. 188

lysse happiness VI. 315; relief, release I. 199

lyst edge of a piece of cloth VI. 216

lyte little
lyth tells lies III. 193
lythe(n) *v.* listen to VI. 194, VII. 79 **lythed**
pa.t. VII. 116
lyther wicked X. 165
lyue *n.* life **lyues** *pl.* living creatures VI. 424
lyues *gen.sg.as adj.* alive XXI. 159
lyuynge *n.* leaving, i.e. what was left on the
ground VI. 414

ma more II. 250
Machameth, Macometh Macumeth
Mahomet
mache wick XIX. 178
madden are mad, become mad IX. 108
made made; caused XX. 376; made verses V.
5
Mahond Mahound (i.e. Mahomet) III. 481,
XVIII. 151, XX. 293
maistres masters
maistrie, maistry sovereignty, power
Makameth Mahomet
make *n.* mate
make, maky *v.* make; cause to be so XII. 110
male bag, saddlebag XIII. 55 **makes** *pl.* VI. 236
malecolie melancholy VI. 77
male-ese, mal-ese pain, misery, injury VIII.
233, XV. 84, XIX. 156
Malkyn dim. of Mary or Matilda I. 180n
mamele mutter, prate on V. 123 **mamelede**
prated XIII. 225
manascheth threatens IV. 62 **manased**
threatened XV. 6
manere manner, kind; kind(s) of; habit
maneres manors, country residences V. 159
manged eaten VIII. 271
mangenel mangonel, siege-engine for hurling
stones XX. 293
mangerye feast XII. 45
mankynde man's nature XI. 146, XXI. 72,
XXII. 41
manschipes acts of courtesy, compliments
XII. 104
mansed cursed II. 41, XXII. 221
manslaght, manslauht manslaughter IV.
182, XVII. 241
marcat market-town XIX. 72
marchaunde *v.* trade VI. 280
marchaundise *n.* trade
marchen (1) go, progress (2) have a common
boundary Prol. 61n
mare more IV. 93
mareys marshes XIII. 166
margerie-perles margarite-pearls (*margarite*
is another word for *pearl*) XI. 7
markede observed, noted down XIV, 74
Mary *gen.sg.* Mary's II. 2
mase maze, confused turmoil I. 6; confusion,
frustration III. 197
mas-pans mass-pence III. 278
mataynes, mat(e)ynes matins (the earliest of
the daily services, held between midnight and
daybreak) Prol. 125, III. 53, VII. 67, etc.
maugre, maugrey *prep.* despite II. 214, VIII.
38, 68 **maugre his teth** despite all he could
do XX. 84

maumettes idols (i.e. images associated with
the worship of Mahomet or any pagan
religion) Prol. 119
maundement commandment XIX. 2, 60
maydones virgins (of either sex) X. 278
mayne *n.* strength XX. 361
mayne *n.* retinue, household III. 25, XVIII.
253
maynpernour *n.* surety IV. 107
maynprise *n.* bail, security IV. 84, XVIII.
281, XXII. 17
maynprise *v.* go bail for IV. 173, XX. 188
mayntenaunce *n.* support (in ill-doing) VI.
248
maynteneth, maynteyneth *v.* support, abet
III. 186
mayntenour *n.* supporter, abettor III. 286
mayr(e) mayor
maystres masters
maystrie sovereignty VI. 77
me, men *impers.pron.* man, one (unstressed
form of *man*) III. 407, 412, 477, IV, 121, etc.
mebles movable possessions, property
mechel great VI. 333
meddeled mixed VI. 260
mede reward
medlen *v.* combat XXII. 179
meke *adj.* meek; tame XV. 292
meke(n) *inf.* (*refl.*) act meekly IV. 90 humble
(oneself) VI. 10, VII. 248
memorie commemorative mention VII. 27,
VIII. 104
men *see* **me**
men *gen.pl.* men's III. 7, V. 29, XIV. 168
mendena(u)nt *adj. and n.* mendicant, beggar
Prol. 60, XV. 3 **mendenant(e)s, menden-
antz** *pl.* beggars V. 76, IX. 179, XIII. 78
mendes amends, recompense IV. 97
mendynantz orders of friars XV. 81
mene *adj.* common, poor, lowly *as n.pl.* the
poor
mene *n.* mediator
menede *v.* (*refl.*) complained III. 215
menege mention, commemorate VIII. 104
meneuer miniver, fur XXII. 138
menne *gen.pl.* men's
Menores Minors X. 9n
menske *inf.* honour III. 229
menyng *pres.p.* intending XVII. 176
menynge *n.* symbolic token Prol. 99
menynges *pl.* intentions; intellectual
capacities I. 137n
mercede due reward III. 290, 332
mercement fine, tax I. 158n, IV. 182
mercy *n.* thanks XXI. 76n
mercyede thanked III. 21
mere boundary, boundary-marker III. 380
merke *adj.* dark I. 1
merke *n.* darkness XIX. 205
merkeness darkness XX. 140, 180
mersyen *v.* fine VIII. 37
mery(e) pleasant; cheerful
merytorie suitable in terms of merit IX. 68
mesch(i)ef misfortune, disease, evil Prol. 65,
XI. 233, XVI. 250 **mescheues** *pl.* troubles,
misfortunes XII. 200

mesels lepers IX. 179
meseyse trouble XV. 159
meson-dewes hospitals (run by religious), i.e. *maisons de dieu* IX. 30
Messie Messiah
mester job IX. 7
met *pp.* dreamed XIII. 214
mete *n.* food
meteles *n.* dream Prol. 217, IX. 298, 299, XV. 4
meten *v.* measure Prol. 163 **meteth** I. 173
mette *pa.t.* (*impers.*) it came as a dream (e.g. **me mette** I dreamed) Prol. 9, 219, V. 109, 110, IX. 310, etc.
mette *n.* table-companion XV. 55 **mettes** *pl.* XV. 41
mette *n.* measurement XI. 127
metyng dreaming II. 54
meue(n) *v.* move, stir XIV. 67; introduce move X. 118 **meued(e)** stirred to anger XIII. 178; raised for discussion XII. 40, XV. 130
meuynge moving IX. 110
meyntene maintain (in wrongdoing) III. 271 **meynteyneth** IV. 58
Mihel-masse Michaelmas
minne remember XVII. 21p, XIX. 228
mirre myrrh XXI. 76, 92, 93
misbede injure, harm VIII. 42
mitigacioun relaxation of the strict penalty of the law VI. 324
mo *adj., pron.* more **opere mo** others besides XXI. 54
moche(l) much, great
moder *gen.sg.* mother's VI. 173
modiliche angrily IV. 167
moed anger XVIII. 118
moes moss XVII. 14
moet must XI. 234, 300, XVI. 71
moet-halle council-chamber IV. 163
moilere *adj.* of legitimate birth II. 120n *as n.* legitimate offspring XVIII. 235
Moises Moses
mok muck, wealth X. 96
molde earth, world
molde mould XIII. 160
mone money II. 170, III. 263, XIII. 97
mone prayer of petition XVI. 185, XVII. 257
monekes monks III. 168
moniales, monyals nuns V. 76, 170, XVIII. 74
mony, moneye many
more *n.* root XVI. 250, XVIII. 23 **mores** *pl.* XVII. 21, XXI. 339
more *adj.* more *as n.pl.* (the) great and powerful folk
moreyne, morreyne murrain, plague III. 97, XX. 225
mornyng *n.* mourning XII. 202
morthere *v.* murder IV. 58 **morthereth** XIX. 259
mortrewes stews of minced meat XV. 47, 67
moskeles mussels IX. 94
moste *adj.* greatest
moste *pa.t.* must; might XVII. 243; must (go), must (be applied) XVII. 225

mostre show, display VI. 260
mot(e) *v.* must; may II. 117, VII. 157, XV. 148
mote *v.* plead or debate a case in law I. 172, III. 197
mot-halle council-chamber IV. 148
motoun gold coin (stamped with an image of a sheep) III. 25
motyef question, theme for discussion XV. 130 **motyues** *pl.* XVI. 231
motyng(e) pleading at law IV. 132, IX. 54
mouen raise, bring up for discussion XVI. 231
mouhte *pa.t.* might XI. 160, 267
mowe(n) *v.* may **mowe(n) with** may endure XII. 187, 190
moylere, moylo(u)re *adj.* of legitimate birth II. 145, X. 209 *as n.* legitimate offspring XVIII. 221
Moyses Moses, Moses's
muche(l) *adj.* great VII. 149; big, tall X. 68
muche *adv.* very much IV. 170
mullere miller II. 113
mum any sound or mumble resembling a word Prol. 164
Munde (prob.fr. ON Asmundar) II. 113
murthe *n.* mirth
murthe *v.* make merry XIX. 205
murye pleasant; cheerful
musels lepers III. 168
musons measurements (of time and interval) in music XI. 120
must *n.* new (unfermented or partly fermented) wine XX. 412
muster trade, profession III. 110
muynde mind VI. 284
muys mice Prol. 166, 213
myddel waist III. 10
Myddelerd, Myddelerthe Middle-Earth XI. 171, XIII. 131n
myht(e) *pa.t.* might
myhte *n.* power
myhtfull mighty I. 169
myhtow might thou I. 168
myhty mighty
mynistre monastery V. 91
mynne *adv.* less III. 395
mynt(e)-while, mynte-whyle *n.* very short while XII. 216, XIII. 197, XIX. 193
myrke *adj.* dark, obscure XVIII. 197
mysbileue *n.* wrong belief Prol. 102
mysdede did amiss XX. 389 **mysdo** *pp.* IV. 86
myseyse *adj.* unfortunate IX. 30
mysfare go astray, meet with misfortune X. 161
myspenen *v.* misuse, misspend XVI. 234 **myspeneth** X. 174 **myspened** V. 93
myssaide *pa.t.* berated XX. 350 **mysseyde** *pp.* slandered VI. 9
myssomer midsummer XVI. 13
mystiloker mistier, more confusing XI. 130
mysulue myself
myswonne won by evil means XV. 48
myte mite, very small amount of money XIII. 96
mywen stack the mown swathes V. 14

na no, not
Nabugodonasor Nebuchadnezzar IX. 308
nameliche especially
nat not
nauhte, nautht nothing
nawher nowhere
ne not
nedes *adv.* of necessity XX. 442, XXII. 37
nedfole *adj.* needful, needy *as n.* (the) needy XIII. 76
nedlare needle-maker VI. 365
neet ox XXI. 266
nelde needle I. 153
nelle will not Prol. 136, I. 122, VI. 312, XI. 185, etc.
nemn(i)e, nemnen *inf.* name, mention I. 21, 122, XXI. 20 **nemned, nempned(e)** *pa.t.* named XXI. 18; nominated VI. 377, 388
neodefole needful IV. 121
Neptalym Naphtali (N.W. of the sea of Galilee: see Matt. 5:13) XVII. 189, 261
ner *adv.* nearly, almost VIII. 175
nere *pa.t.* were not
nere *adv.* never
nerre nearer XIX. 62
nese niece V. 176
neste did not know XIII. 217
neyh *prep.* near VIII. 322
neyhele come near XIX. 58
nidefole needful I. 21
Niniue Nineveh XVII. 261
nise foolish XVIII. 37
niuilynge snivelling, running with mucus VI. 102
niyed harmed, hindered II. 19
no *conj.* nor III. 395, VI. 166
no *pron.* none IX. 123
noble gold coin III. 47, XVII. 200n **nobles** *pl.* III. 391
Noe Noah **Noes** Noah's
noen *adj.* no III. 433
noen *n.* noon VI. 434; midday meal VIII. 289
noght not
noȝt not
nolde would not
nome *pa.t.* took XXII. 9
nones *n.* noon VI. 429, VIII. 146
noon *pron.* none
notarie *gen.sg.* lawyer's, notary's XXII. 272 **notaries** *pl.* II. 139, 156
note song XX. 452 **notes** *pl.* points, degrees I. 117
nother, noþer *conj.* neither
nouȝt not, nothing
noumper umpire VI. 388
nouthe now
nownpower lack of power XIX. 291
noyther(e) neither
nulle wilt not VIII. 153
nuye *v.* harm VII. 221 **nuyede** *pa.t.* caused trouble III. 433
ny nigh, nearly
nyhed approached VIII. 322
nyhtes *gen.sg.as adv.* of a night, at night V. 16
nyme(n), nym *v.* take, receive **nyme** *pp.* III. 402

Nyneue Nineveh XVII. 189
nype *n.* piercing cold XX. 167
nythynge *n.* a miserly person XIX. 236

o *adj.* one, a single
o *prep.* in
obediencer one owing obedience to a religious house (and as such licensed to beg) V. 91
oen *adj., pron.* one
oeste army XXI. 337
of *adv.* off
Offnies *gen.sg.* Ophni's Prol. 107, 123
of-helden withheld II. 238
of-walked exhausted with walking Prol. 7n
oke *pa.t.* ached XIX. 158
on *adj., pron.* one
on *prep.* in Prol. 51, V. 51, VIII. 103, XIX. 233
ondynge smelling XV. 256
one *adj.* alone **myn one** by myself, on my own X. 61, XI. 201
onelyche only XVI. 154
ones *adv.* once
ones *adj.* alone III. 181
onswerie *inf.* answer VI. 347
oon, ooen *adj.* one, a certain
oon *prep.* on IV. 31
ope *prep.* upon XII. 239
opelond in the country V. 44
or *conj.* before I. 70, XVII. 282
or *conj.* either VI. 125, XV. 204
ordeyne arrange for the building of XXI. 319, 321
orgene organum XX. 7n
Oseye Alsace Prol. 230
oste host, army III. 251, 418
other(e), oþer *conj.* or
oþere *pron.pl.* others XVI. 302
oþergates otherwise X. 294
other-while, oþer-while from time to time V. 50, XVII. 9
othes oaths
ouer *prep.* over; beyond III. 307, VII. 196
oueral everywhere II. 228
ouerhippe skip over parts XVII. 118
ouerhoueth hangs over XX. 174
ouerkarke overburden, exploit III. 468
ouerlep pounced on Prol. 169
ouerseye looked over, perused XI. 116
ouertulde overtilted, overturned XXII. 54, 135
ouerward about to cross IV. 128
ouht *pron.* anything, something
ouhte *pa.t.* ought; owned III. 72
oune *adj.* own
oures *n.pl.* the canonical hours, i.e. the seven times in the day allocated for the saying of the divine office; the services held or prayers said at those times Prol. 125, I. 179
outen *adv.* out, alive, in existence XIV. 190
outryderes members of religious orders licensed to leave the cloister IV. 116
ownere *pron.gen.pl.* own XVIII. 76

palays enclosed place (OED *palis*) XX. 378
paleis *n.* palace **paleis** *pl.* X. 16

palle beat XVIII. 34, 50
palmere pilgrim VII. 180 **palmers** *pl.* Prol. 47n
paltokes cloaks XXII. 219
Pampilon Pamplona XIX. 217
panes pence
paniars baskets XVII. 17
paniter keeper of the pantry XVI. 150
panne skull IV. 74
pans pence
pans-delyng giving of money XXI. 376
papelotes *n.pl.* porridge IX. 75
parail *n.* apparel X. 116, XII. 123
paramours *n.* lover XVI. 106; matters of sexual love VI. 186
parauntur *adv.* perhaps, by chance
parayle *inf.* dress VIII. 56 **parayled(e)** *pa.t.* Prol. 25, II. 224
parcel a small portion (of money) XXII. 291 **parceles** *pl.* separate parts XIX 96
parede clipped VI. 242
par-entrelynarie with interlineation XIII. 118
parfay by my faith, indeed XVI. 118
parfourme perform; fulfil, bring to fruition XV. 173
parled spoken XX. 279
paroles(*Fr.*) words XVI. 269
parsceyued perceived Prol. 128
parsche parish
parschien(e)s parishioners VI. 120, XXII. 282
parsel part XI. 48 **parseles** *pl.* bits, parts XIII. 118
parselmele in small quantities III. 86; separately XIX. 28
parsilie parsley VIII. 309
parte(n) share, divide
partie, party(e), parteyƷe part, portion I. 7, III. 382, XV. 157; party, faction III. 379 **parties** *pl.* parties (to a transaction) III. 389
Pasche Passover, Easter XVIII. 167 **paske-woke** Easter week XII. 121
paschte dashed down XXII. 100
passeth goes beyond, transgresses against I. 98, XVII. 5
passioun suffering (as of a saint or martyr) VII. 79, XV. 99
pastours shepherds XI. 295
patente letter of authority, letter patent XIX. 12, XX. 191
patrones patrons, i.e. those holding advowson, or right of presentation to a living V. 78
paueloun (lawyer's) coif or hood III. 448
paume palm XIX. 115, 116, 119, etc.
pay(e) *n.* pleasure, satisfaction III. 348 **to paye** to (his) pleasure or satisfaction VII. 190, 193, XIII. 159, XVI. 94
pay *inf.* please VIII. 332
payn(e) bread
paynyem *n.* heathen VII. 161 **paynyme** *adj.as n.pl.* pagans XVII. 255
pays peace XVIII. 177
peccunie *n.* money III. 389
peccuniosus (*Lat.*) *adj.* moneyed XII. 10

pees peace; the spirit of reconciliation XX. 171
pelour accuser XX. 39
pelours pillagers, thieves XXI. 415
pelur(e) fur
pennes feathers XIV. 179
pensel pennon, banner XVIII. 188
pentauncers penitencers, confessors VI. 256
peny-ale thin or feeble ale, cheap ale VI. 226n, IX. 92
penytauncer penitencer, confessor XXII. 319
pere *n.* equal III. 261, IX. 308, XVIII. 90 **peres** *pl.* IX. 20
pere-ionettes sweet early pears XII. 220
Peres Piers, dim. of Peter VI. 367n, etc.
permutacioun exchange III. 313
permuten exchange benefices II. 185n
persaunt piercing I. 153
persen pierce, penetrate XI. 297
persoun parson, incumbent of a living VII. 30 **persones** *pl.* Prol. 81n, II. 185, III. 186, etc.
pertliche openly, clearly V. 117
perye jewellery XI. 10
pes(e) pea VIII. 166, IX. 347
pesecoddes peascods, pea-pods XII. 220
pethe pith, central part XIX. 116
petyt small IX. 53
peynted drawn, inscribed XIII. 118
peyse *n.* weight (as used in weighing) VI. 242
peysed *pa.t.* weighed VI. 223
peytrele *inf.* protect with breast-plate IV. 23
piche *inf.* pitch (sheaves) V. 13
pikede peaked, pointed XXII. 219
pike-harneys stealers of armour from the dead XXII. 263n
pikois mattock, pick-axe III. 461
pile *n.* fort, stronghold, 'peel' XXI. 364
pilede *adj.* bald-headed VI. 370
pileth *v.* pillages XXI. 442
pilours robbers, strippers of the dead XIII. 2, XXII. 263
pissares *gen.pl.* common men's XXII. 219n
pistul epistle XVI. 289
places country residences (on monastic estates) V. 159
plates pieces of plate-armour XX. 24
platte (*refl.*) threw flat VI. 3
playne complain
plede *v.* plead at law IV. 57 **pldeden** *pa.t.* Prol. 161
plenere fully XII. 46
pleye *v.* play, amuse oneself
pleyne *v.* complain
pleynt complaint III. 213
plihte, plighten *v.* plight, pledge III. 469; (*refl.*) join in agreement Prol. 47
plihte *pa.t.* plucked XII. 47
plonte plant
pluhte *pa.t.* plucked, drew XIX. 12
plyhte *pa.t.* pledged, plighted II. 124
Pocalips Apocalypse XV. 99n
pocok peacock XIV. 172
poddyng-ale thick or strong ale VI. 226n
pohen peahen XIV. 174
poke *n.* bag XV. 247 **pokes** *pl.* XVI. 87

poketh *v.* urges, incites VII. 263 **pokede** *pa.t.* I. 128, VII. 287

pol *n.* head XII. 10 **polles** *pl.* XXII. 86

pole *inf.* pull, pull back, restrain IV. 23n

polettes pullets VIII. 303

polleden pulled II. 229

pomade drink made from apples XX. 409

pondefold pound, pinfold (a place for confining stray animals) XVIII. 281

popeiay parrot XIV. 172

pop-holy affecting to be as holy as the pope, i.e. hypocritical VI. 37

pore poor

porfiel furred or embroidered trimming of a dress IV. 111

Porfirie Porphyry XII. 172, XIV. 189

porore poorer XXII. 50

pors *n.* purse VI. 199

pors *v.* purse up, put in one's purse XII. 163

port bearing, conduct VI. 30

portatif 'portable', light I. 153

pose suppose, put the case XIX. 274

postles apostles

pot *v.* put

potage soup

potager cook, maker of stews VI. 132

pote *n.* stick VIII. 64n

potel pottle (i.e. two quarts) VI. 399

potte(n) *v.* put

pouert *n.* poverty

poues pulse XIX. 66

pouhe-ful pouchful, sackful IX. 344

pouke devil XVIII. 50, 278

Poul Paul

pound-mele pound's-worths II. 232

poynt point, cause V. 117; precise obligation, article of agreement I. 98

predestinaet *adj.as n.pl.* ·those who are predestined XI. 208

preiers prayers

preisede appraised VI. 384

prente looked significantly XX. 19

prenties, prentises, prentys *n.pl.* apprentices II. 224, III. 279, VI. 279

prentished apprenticeship VI. 251

prescient *adj.as n.pl.* (those who are) foreknown XI. 209

presed brought pressure to bear XXII. 127

pressoures presses, stretching frames VI. 219

prest *n.* priest

prest *adj.* eager, quick XVI. 63

prest, prestly *adv.* promptly, immediately III. 305, VIII. 102, XV. 41, XX. 272

presteste promptest VII. 195

preue(n), preueth *v.* prove, demonstrate, exemplify Prol. 39, V. 141, VI. 119, XV. 88, XIX. 222; test, try X. 120, XVII. 319 **preuede(n)** *pa.t.* V. 115, VI. 186

preuete secrets XIII. 228

preyede preyed upon, injured XXII. 86

preynte looked significantly XV. 121

preyse appraise, assess VI. 380

prikeare, prikiare horseman, cavalier X. 134, XX. 24

priketh rides XXII. 149

prime nine a.m. VIII. 119

prior priory V. 91

pris *adj.* prize, best XXI. 266

prisones prisoners III. 173, VII. 277, IX. 34, etc.

priue *adj.* secret, confidential III. 117, IV. 189; familiar, intimate III. 183

priue(i)liche, priueyliche secretly, quietly VI. 266, XII. 47, XV. 150, XVIII. 101

priueoste most intimate XVIII. 98

procuratour proctor, agent XXI. 258 **procuratours** *pl.* VII. 90

proed, proued proud III. 224, X. 134

propre proper; fine XVIII. 101; belonging to it, contained in it IX. 303

prouendres *n.pl.* prebends, benefices III. 32

prouendreth *v.* provides prebends for III. 186

prouincial *adj.* of a province XII. 9 **prouinciales** *adj.pl.* emanating from the provincial (superior of a province) of a religious order IX. 344

prouisour provisor IV. 130 **provisores, prouysours** *pl.* I. 182n, 186, III. 183

prout(e) proud VI. 46, XXII. 218

prowour provider, purveyor XXI. 260

pruyde pride

Pruys-lond Prussia VI. 279

pryke ride (hurriedly)

prymer private prayer-book V. 46n

pryuatees secrets, mysteries XVIII 5

pryue secret, familiar, intimate

pues pews VI. 144

pulte push, beat X. 94; activate XIX. 141 **pult** *pp.* thrust XI. 209

purfiled edged, dressed in a robe edged II. 10

purfyel V. 128 *see* **porfiel**

Purnele dim. of Petronilla V. 128, VI. 3, 135, 367n, XVII. 71 *gen.sg.* IV. 111n

pursueth *v.* prosecutes XIX. 283 **pursuede** *pa.t.* endeavoured XVII. 167

pursward purse-ward **into pursward** in the direction of your purses Prol. 101

purtinaunces things associated with (it) XVI. 328

putour lecher VI. 172

putrie lechery, whoring VI. 186

puttes pits IX. 72

puyr *adj.* pure, mere, very, true, sheer

puyre *adv.* very VII. 20

puyreliche *adv.* completely XV. 230

puyrere of finer quality II. 10

pyche *inf.* pick VIII. 64

pye-hele pastry base of a pie IX. 347

pyement piment, sweet drink made with wine, honey and spices XX. 409

pyk *n.* pointed end X. 94; pike-staff VII. 180

pykares pilferers V. 17

pylie *v.* peel IX. 81n

pyne *n.* punishment V. 131; suffering XI. 275

pynnes pegs VIII. 199

pynyng stoles punishment chairs III 79

pyonie (seeds of the) paeony, used as a spice VI. 359

pytaunce special allowance of food IX. 92n, XV. 61

pyuische peevish VIII. 151

quene quean (common woman, or prostitute) VIII. 46
quentyse cunning trickery XX. 297
queste inquest, court of inquiry; collecting mission II. 110n **questes** *pl.* legal courts of inquiry XI. 22
queyne *adj.* cunning IV. 161, XIX. 231
queynte *pp.* quenched, destroyed XX. 391
queyntises cunning tricks XXI. 352
quite *v.* requite, repay XII. 103
quod said
quodlibet question in theology XVII. 114n
quoek quaked XX. 64
quoer choir V. 60
quyk *adj.* alive XVIII. 145, XX. 64, 257
quyk(i)e *v.* quicken, inspire with life, bring to life XVI. 182, XX. 391
quyte(n) *v.* repay, pay for, requite XII. 106, XIII. 75, XVIII. 279, XX. 388, 391 **quyt** *pp.* quit, satisfied IV. 98

raap reaped VI. 270
radde(n) *pa.t.* advised, directed; read III. 487 **rad** *pp.* read III. 495
radegoundes running sores XXII. 83
rageman roll of parchment tagged with seals Prol. 73
ragman cowardly devil XVIII. 122
rakeare street-sweeper VI. 371
rape *vv.* hasten **rapede** *pa.t.* (*refl.*) XIX. 77
rape, raply, rappliche *adv.* quickly VI. 383, XVIII. 290, XIX. 48
rappe *v.* strike; hasten I. 91n
rat *pres.3sg.* reads III. 406, XII. 209, XV. 268
rathe *adv.* early X. 139, XI. 90
rather rather; sooner VIII. 44, 125, X. 54, etc.
rathest soonest, most readily VI. 392, IX. 148
rato(u)n rat **ratones** *pl.*
ratoner rat-catcher VI. 371
raueners, rauenours *gen.pl.* robbers' XVII. 43, 47
raughte, rauhte reached out for, raked in Prol. 73; was stretched IV. 179
rayes striped cloths VI. 217
rayme reach after, obtain (OED, s.v. *ream*) XIII. 95
Raynald Reynold II. 111
reame realm Prol. 192
rebaudes worthless sinners XV. 232
rech(e) *v.* care, worry, take heed, (*refl.*) worry oneself **reccheth** care III. 387
recheles reckless, uncaring XII. 63, XX. 2
rechelesnesse recklessness XI. 196n, etc.
recheth seizes, lays hold of III. 497
reclused *pp.* enclosed IV. 116
recouerer *n.* remedy, means of recovery XIX. 67
recreaunt *adj.* defeated XX. 104 *see* **creaunt**
rect *adj.* direct III. 333, etc.
rectores rectors II. 184n
red *n.* advice VI. 270
rede, redon *v.* advise; describe, esplain; read **redde** *pa.t.* VII. 120
redyng-kynge VI. 372 **redyng-kynges** *pl.* II. 112n

reed *n.* advice IV. 29
refte deprived III. 326
regne reign, rule, prevail
regrater retail trader VI. 232 **regraters** *pl.* III. 113, 118
regraterye the retail trade III. 82n
reherce, reherse recount, recite, declare, repeat
reik way Prol. 216n
rekene reckon, list
rekeuere *v.* recover XXI. 245 **rekeuerede** *pa.t.* XXI. 161
relacion, relacoun relation **relacions, relacoynes** *pl.*
rele *inf.* reel IX. 81n
releue *inf.* restore to life XX. 390; lift up again XX. 144; assist IX. 36
religioun *n.* the body of those in religious orders III. 202, V. 143, 150, etc.
religious *adj.as n.pl.* those in religious orders V. 147, 164, etc.
relyed recovered heart XXII. 148
remyng crying out, weeping XX. 104
rendren *v.* construe, interpret XVII. 322 **rendred(e)** *pa.t.* X. 88; recited off from memory VI. 217
reneyed *pp.as adj.* renegade XII. 63
reng man X. 24
reninde running III. 333
renke man
rennares runners, voyagers IV. 125
renne(n) *v.* run, go, go about II. 193, XII. 62, XVI. 348
rennynge running XX. 168
renoye renounce, abjure XII. 58, 59
rente *n.* rent, i.e. property bringing in an income from rent III. 322 **rentes** *pl.* III. 82
renten *v.* endow IX. 36
repe *pa.t.* reaped VI. 270
repreueth proves wrong III. 385, XX. 152
rescettour receiver, one who harbours criminals or receives stolen goods III. 497
resonede argued with XIII. 182
resoun reason, argument **out of resoun** unreasonable, improper
restitucioun restitution VI. 234n, 237, etc.
restitue make restitution (of) VI. 299, 344, X. 54, etc.
ret *pres.3sg.* reads III. 412, XIII. 5
retenance retinue II. 55
retribucoun paying back III. 337
reuares robbers XIII. 57
reue(n) *v.* rob, take away XVI. 1, XVIII. 122, XX. 299, 308
reue *n.* reeve, farm-bailiff II. 112, III. 308, etc.
reueled wrinkled X. 263
reuerences flattering obeisances XVI. 47
reuerentloker in a more honoured place VIII. 44
reueth deprive of IV. 180
reufulliche sorely XIX. 200
reule *v.* rule, govern
reule *n.* rule; rule of life
reule *n.* space in bedroom between main bed and wall IX. 79

Reule La Reole Prol. 231
reume *n.* realm
reumes *n.pl.* rheums, catarrhal colds
reuthe *n.* pity
reward *n.* regard, notice IV. 40, XIX. 246
rewe *v.* have pity VI. 322; (*impers.*) it causes to pity XX. 438
rewe *n.* row (of houses) III. 107 **by rewe** in order I. 22
rewme realm III. 190
riche *v.* grow rich VI. 126
richeles incense XXI. 90
riȝt *adj.* very same XVIII. 290
riht *adv.* right, exactly, directly
riht(e) *adj.* right; exact XIX. 48
riht *pres.3sg.* rides Prol. 186
rihtfollokest most rightfully XX. 475
rikene reckon, give account XIII. 34
Robardus knaues robbers Prol. 45n
Rochele La Rochelle Prol. 231
rodded *pp.* reddened XV. 108
rode *n.* rood, cross
roen *pa.t.* rained XV. 268
Romaynes Romans XVII. 281
rome, rometh *v.* roam, wander, walk Prol. 186, XII. 47, XVIII. 145
romede *pa.t.* stretched VII. 7
ronde *n.* round IX. 48
roost *n.* roast meat Prol. 231
ropere rope-maker VI. 372
roteth, rotieth rots, decays V. 150, XII. 222
roteyed copulated XIII. 145
rotheth (*refl.*) root themselves, are firmly established II. 55
rotte snored VII. 7, XIV. 95
rotye rot, die III. 357, XVIII. 60
roued sent out rays, began to dawn XX. 127
rouhte cared XII. 21
roume *v.* leave clear, avoid Prol. 181, 189
roun(n)ed whispered IV. 14, VI. 383
rounynge whispering IV. 25
rousty filthy VIII. 75
route *n.* crowd
roweth shows streaks of light, shines, beams I. 113
roxlede stretched VII. 7
roynouse dirty, scurfy XXII. 83
ruche, rusche rush (thing of little value) III. 178, XII. 195
ruet small horn VI. 400
rufol miserable, wretched VI. 237
rug, rugge back IX. 144, XVI. 55, XXI. 287
rusche *see* **ruche**
russet coarse cloth X. 1, XVI. 298
ruyflare robber VI. 316 **ruyflares** *pl.* IV. 125
ruyfle *inf.* rob IV. 54 **ruyfled** *pp.* X. 194
ruylen govern IX. 10
ruylynge *n.* rule Prol. 150
ryalte pomp, royal state XVI. 52
rybauder teller of coarse tales, scurrilous buffoon VIII. 75 **rybaudes** *pl.* VI. 435, VII. 150
rybaudie, rybaudrye filthy jokes and stories Prol. 45, VI. 435, XI. 200
rybbe scrape IX. 81n

rybibour player on the rubible (a small stringed instrument) VI. 371
rychen grow rich III. 82
rygebones backbone's VI. 400
ryȝt *pres.3sg.* rides IV. 25
ryhte *n.* right; rights III. 367
ryhte *adv.* right; justly III. 324
rykene *inf.* reckon, count, keep accounts, settle II. 62, IV. 171, XI. 300, etc.
rykenynge reckoning VI. 348
ryne *v.* rain V. 164, XVII. 99
rypereue head-reaper V. 15

sad steadfast, firm **saddere, saddest**
Salamon, Salomon Solomon
salue healing ointment
sam-rede half-red (i.e. half-ripe) VIII. 310
sannore, sannour sooner III. 62, XVIII. 64
sarmon sermon III. 121
Sarrasyn Saracen, pagan XII. 86n **Sarrasynes, Sar(r)esines, Saresynes** *pl.* III. 480, XII. 53, XIV. 200, XVII. 123, 132, etc.
sarrore more sorely XV. 284
sauac(i)oun salvation
saue save; preserve XXII. 22
Sauel Saul III. 408
saueriore tastier XVIII. 65
sauery *v.* please by taste VIII. 273 **sauereth** please, satisfy X. 107
sauete safety, salvation XII. 54
sauhtene make peace, be reconciled IV. 2
sauhter psalter III. 287
saumplare model, exemplar XIV. 47
saunbure comfortable litter or saddle II. 178
sauter psalter
sautrien play on the psaltery XV. 208
sawes sayings, remarks X. 107, XX. 152
sawt *n.* assault XXII. 217, 300
say, sayh *pa.t.sg.* saw
sayle *v.* dance XV. 208
sayn *inf.* say Prol. 202
saynt *adj.* holy, blessed I. 80
scale shell XII. 144
scathe, schathe injury, wound IV. 75, 92
schaef sheaf VIII. 350
schawes woods X. 159
schoppe *inf.* chop, strike XIV. 68
schoriares props XVIII. 20
schupestares dress-maker's VI. 75
schupte prescribed XXII. 306
schyreues sheriffs III. 78
sclayre veil (as worn over or round the sides of the face under a hat) VIII. 5
scole school, university V. 36n, 153, 155, XV. 129, XXII. 251
screueynes scribes XI. 97
scribz scribes (i.e. Jewish law-interpreters) XVII. 252, XX. 26
scrippe, scryppe scrip, pilgrim's bag VII. 180, VIII. 60
se *v.* see **se to** look upon I. 55
secatours executors II. 189
secheth seeks; looks in III. 493
secte suit of clothes, apparel XII. 131; (i.e. the flesh) VII. 130; following, retinue XVI. 97

seden beget offspring X. 249

see *n.* sea

seel *n.* seal

seem *n.* horse-load III. 42

seet *pa.t.* sat VIII. 122 **seete** *pa.t.subj.* might sit, might be VI. 99

seg(g), segge *n.* man

sege *n.* place, town which is seat of government XXII. 310

segge *v.* say

seggyng saying V. 107

seigh *pa.t.sg.* saw

seke *adj.* sick

seke *v.* seek

seketoure executor (of a will) VI. 254 **seketours** *pl.* XVI. 277

sekte suit of clothes (i.e. flesh) VII. 137, 141

selcouthe *adj.* strange, rare, enigmatic XII. 44, XVII. 302

selcouthe *n.* marvel, wonder XIII. 176 **selcouthes** *pl.* XIII. 173, XIV. 75

selde *adv.* seldom

seleth seal III. 184

selk(e) silk

selkouthe *adj.* strange, marvellous Prol. 5

selles cells Prol. 30, XVII. 7

sellies marvels, strange things Prol. 5

seluer silver

selys seals Prol. 67

semblant looks, appearance X. 117

semeth is fitting XVI. 8

semyng with the appearance, intimating XI. 87

semyuief (*Lat.*) half-alive XIX. 55

sende *pa.t., pp.* sent II. 197, XVII. 155

sendel fine silk VIII. 10

senes, sennes *prep., conj.* since I. 55, XXII. 322

senes, sennes *adv.* then, afterwards

seneschalles high stewards Prol. 93

sense incense XXI. 75

sent *pres.3sg.* sends XIV. 27, XXI. 432

seriaunt serjeant-at-law, professional lawyer III. 447 **seriauntes, seriantz** *pl.* Prol. 160, III. 78

serk shirt, shift I. 99, VI. 6

sertes certainly, indeed V. 22

serteyne *adj.as n.* certain number XXII. 255

serued *pp.* deserved XII. 117, XIV. 136

seruicie duty III. 447

sese *inf.* cease II. 165

sesed *pp.* seized, established in full legal possession XX. 309

sesoun season

Sesse Cissy, dim. of Cicely, Cecilia VI. 362

sete(n) *pa.t.* sat VI. 396, XIV. 2

seth(e) *conj.* since II. 134, V. 40, etc.

sethe(n) *adv.* since, since then, then, afterwards III. 50, 408, V. 140, 143, VII. 47, 54, 145, etc.

sethe *n.pl.* times XVIII. 17

setteth set store (by) IX. 304

settynge planting Prol. 23

sewe(n) *v.* follow, accompany XI. 184, XIII. 142, 179, XXII. 22 **seweth** III. 352 **sewede** *pa.t.* III. 325, XIX. 79

sewe *inf.* sue, make claim III. 367

sewe *pa.t.* sowed VI. 271, XVII. 101, XXI. 406

sey(e) *inf., pres.* say

seyn *v.* see IV. 154 **sey, seyh(e)** *pa.t.sg.* saw **seyn, seyen** *pp.* seen

seynede made the sign of the cross on (himself) VII. 63

seynt *adj.* holy XI. 154, 205

seyntwarie sanctuary, holy place V. 79

shabbede scabbed IX. 264

shape *inf.* devise, arrange III. 18 **shapeth** *pres.3sg.* determines I. 157; impels IX. 62

shar plough-share III. 460

sharpeliche severely, sternly VI. 13

sharre scissors, shears VI. 75

sheltrom body of armed troops XX. 292

shendeth *pres.3sg.* ruins, corrupts III. 192 *pres.3pl.* ruin, defile XIII. 114 **shent** *pp.* ruined, destroyed III. 171, XIX. 269

shene bright XX. 455

shentfolyche shamefully III. 429

shereue sheriff II. 177

shette *pa.t.* shut VII. 250

sheware shower, revealer XIV. 96

shewe *v.* show; appear X. 159 **sheweth** looks upon X. 61

shewe *v.* follow, keep on with

shides planks X. 221, XI. 240, XVIII. 20

shille shrilly VI. 46

sholle(n) *v.* shall **sholde** *pa.t.* should; intended (to go) XX. 177

shon shoes V. 18

shop(e), shoop *pa.t.sg.* made, formed, created VI. 424, XI. 240; arranged II. 177; (*refl.*) dressed Prol. 2; (*refl.*) shaped, got ready XIII. 244

shoriar prop XVIII. 119 **shorriares** *pl.* XVIII. 25

shost shouldest III. 135

shrapede scraped VI. 90

shrewe wicked person, rascal IV. 105, VI. 173, 318, XIII. 232

shrewed wicked, cursed Prol. 122, 124, VI. 75

shrof(e) shrove, confessed XI. 257; (*refl.*) VI. 422

shroudes (woollen) outer garments Prol. 2

shryuars confessors Prol. 64

shryue *pp.* shriven VI. 356

shupte *pa.t.* shaped, created XIX. 181; fixed, arranged XXII. 139

shuyuen *inf.* prop XVIII. 20

shyreues, shyryues sheriffs II. 59, III. 171 **shyreues** *gen.sg.* sheriff's IV. 164

shyt *pres.3sg.* befouls IX. 264

sib *adj.* kin, akin, related VII. 278, 289, XI. 98

sicurly certainly X. 26

sigh *pa.t.* saw

signes signatures II. 156

si3te *pa.t* sighed XVIII. 16

siht sight; witness I. 201

siker sure, certain

sikerliche truly, certainly; in security IV. 51

sikerore *adj.comp.* securer, freer from care I. 116

sikorere *adv.comp.* more securely XII. 149

simile (*Lat.*) likeness XIX. 159

Simond Simon XIV. 142n
simonye simony II. 63n, etc.
Sinoye Sinai VII. 171
sismatikes schismatics, heretics XII. 48
sisour juryman XXI. 370
sit *pres.3sg.* sits, is placed (of the moon: according to its phase) IX. 108
sith(en) *conj.* since
sithe *prep.* since
sithe *n.pl.* times VII. 37
sitte *inf.* beset, oppress II. 154
skalones scallions, shallots VIII. 309
skathe harm III. 61
skil, skille reason, reason why, pretext VI. 22, XVI. 121, XVIII. 84; reason, good sense, self-control VI. 25, XXI. 284 **skiles, skilles** *pl.* reasonable arguments, reasonable sounding explanations V. 153, XI. 163 XIII. 129, XIX. 311
sklaundre slander II. 86
sle *inf.* slay III. 419, 439 **slawe** *pp.* slain Prol. 113, XI. 267, XVII. 275
sleep *pa.t.sg.* slept VI. 418 **slepen** *pa.t.pl.* slept XV. 270
slewthe sloth
sley cunning XXII. 163
sleyliche by stealth VI. 108
sleylokests most slyly XI. 267
sleythe trick, stratagem XX. 165 **sleythes, sleythus** *pl.* II. 91, VI. 73, 108, etc.
slokke slake XX. 410
sloo earth XII. 178
slowh slew XXII. 150
smauhte smelt VI. 414
smerte painfully XIII. 241
smethen *v.* forge III. 476
smolder dense suffocating smoke from a smouldering fire not burning properly XIX. 302, 304
smylle *v.* smell VII. 50
smyt *pres.3sg.* strikes XIII. 241 **smyte** *pp.* smitten III. 476
smythe *v.* forge III. 459
so *conj.* provided that II. 125, III. 388, X. 43, etc.; as VII. 231; so that X. 185 **by so** provided that X. 306, etc.
so *adv.* so; so much VII. 41
sode *pa.t.* cooked, boiled *pp.as adj.* boiled IX. 149
sodenes sub-deans II. 187n, XVI. 277
Sodoume Sodom XV. 231
soend sand XIV. 40
soethnesse truth XII. 80
soffraunce forbearance, indulgence, allowing Prol. 124, III. 207
soffre(n) *v.* suffer, allow, endure, be patient **soffre we** let us be patient XX. 166, 269
sofistre false teacher XVII. 311
softe softly; gently, slowly IV. 54
sokene soke, district II. 111
soleyn *adj.as n.* solitary XIV. 144
solfe *inf.* sing the sol-fa (scale of notes) VII. 31
somde(e)l *adv.* somewhat VII. 190, XX. 8
somer, somur summer
somme some

somne, sompne summon II. 172, III. 468, XXI. 214 **sompned** *pp.* XII. 45
somnour, sompnour summoner IV. 162, XXI. 370 **somnours, sompnores** *pl.* II. 59n, 187, III. 170, XVI. 277
sond sand, earth XVII. 88
sonde *n.* sending, what is sent, gift VI. 111, IX. 178, XVI. 135
sone soon, straightway
Sonendayes Sundays II. 231
songen *pa.t.3pl.* sang
sonne sun
sonnere sooner
sonnest soonest
Sortes Socrates XIV. 192
sorughe sorrow XVI. 29
soth(e) truth
sothliche, sothly truly, indeed
sothnesse truth
sotil subtle, clever IV. 149, X. 207, XX. 54
sotileth *pres.3sg.* devises cunningly XXI. 457 **sotiled** *pa.t.3sg.* cunningly devised or contrived VI. 189, XVII. 169, XIX. 233, XX. 333
sotiltees cunning tricks XII. 239, XIV. 76
souche *v.* devise II. 26, XII. 239
soudeth pays XXI. 429
souerayne *adj.* sovereign
souereynly above all VI. 92
souhteres female shoemaker VI. 362
souke suck XII. 54
soule savoury relish XVII. 24
soune *v.* tend, have to do (with) XI. 79 **souneth** *pres.3sg.* tends, has to do with, contributes VI. 59, IX. 216
sounore sooner, more readily XIV. 111
soutere cobbler, shoemaker VI. 83 **soutares** *pl.* V. 72
Southewerk Southwark VI. 83
sowl any food eaten as a relish with bread VIII. 285
sowne *v.* tend XXI. 453
sowngewarie dream-interpretation IX. 304
spare *v.* save IX. 74; desist VI. 151
spede *v.* prosper, get on; (*impers.*) VIII. 42 **spedde** *pa.t.*
speke *pa.t.* spoke IV. 44
spele save up XIII. 76
spelle relate, spell out XVII. 321
spendour spendthrift V. 28
spene spend, give freely, spend wastefully
spensis expenses, spending XVI. 40
spere enquire XIX. 1
spie *n.* scout XIX. 1
spiek ear of corn XII. 179
spille *v.* waste, ruin, destroy; die XI. 43 **spilde** *pa.t.* VI. 432
spille-tyme time-waster V. 28
spir blade (of corn) XII. 179
spiritualte *n.* endowments (a) appropriated to the religious, or (b) of a purely religious nature VI. 125
spores spurs XX. 10, 12
spousehod married state XIII. 10
sprakeliche lively, sprightly XX. 10
spryg stick, rod V. 138

sputeden dug VIII. 184
spyer *n.* shoot XVIII. 231
spyre *v.* enquire III. 109
spysours sellers of spices II. 235
squire square for calculating measurements (e.g. set-square, etc.) XI. 127
stale *n.* handle XXI. 279
stale *pa.t.* stole VI. 265
stande *v.* stand; cost III. 51
stede place **stedes** *pl.* places, estates V. 145
stere stir, move XIX. 54
sterlynges *adj.pl.* of English money XVII. 82
sterue starve to death, die
steryng movement X. 36
stewed restrained, governed V. 145
stottes horses XXI. 267
stounde while, space of time X. 64
strayues *n.pl.* lost property, specifically strayed animals, to which the crown laid claim Prol. 92n
strenghe *n.* strength; stronghold III. 344 **strenghtes** *pl.* strongholds, fortresses III. 237
strenghe *inf.* strengthen III. 345
strikares wanderers IX. 159
strok *pa.t.* moved abruptly Prol. 197
struye(n) destroy, ruin VII. 27, XVII. 307
stryk *v.* press on VII. 224
stunte stint, stop II. 166
stured stirred XXII. 103
sturnely boldly, resolutely Prol. 197
stuyues, stuyves brothels VIII. 71, XIII. 74, XVI. 93, etc.
styfliche stoutly, firmly III. 345
styhlede organized everything XV. 40
stynte stop VII. 223
styuest stiffest, bravest VI. 43
sue(n), suewen follow, accompany; attend to VII. 187
suffraunce forbearance, indulgence IV. 189
sull(e) *v.* sell
sullers sellers, traders III. 116
sullyng selling XXI. 235
sulue *pron.* self, himself XII. 135
sulue *adj.* very, own VII. 255, XXII. 43
suluer silver
sum, summe some
sumdel somewhat VII. 44
sunnere sooner XI. 258
supersedeas (*Lat.*) II. 187n, IX. 263
suppriour sub-prior VI. 153
Surie Syria XVII. 169, 278
surquidous *adj.* arrogant XXI. 340
suspectioun expectation XVII. 315
sustantif substantive, noun III. 335, 342, 352
suynde, suynge *pres.p.* following XX. 358; regularly XVIII. 63
suyrelepes *adj.pl.* separate, distinct XVIII. 192
swelte *v.* die VI. 129 *pa.t.* died XXII. 105
swere(n), swerien swear
swete *v.* sweat Prol. 36
sweuene *n.* dream IX. 312
swoene *inf.* sink into the coma of death XX. 58
swoet *n.* sweat VIII. 241

swonken worked Prol. 23
swowe *inf.* swoon VI. 129
swynkares workers VIII. 259, XIX. 172
swynke *v.* work
swynke *n.* work
swythe *adv.* very, very much; quickly XIII. 52
syb *adj.* kin VII. 280 **sybbe** *adj.as n.pl.* kinsfolk XII. 154
syddore lower VI. 200
sye, syhe *pa.t.* saw XIV. 75, XX. 255, 358
syg, sygge *v.* say
syke *v.* sigh III. 399 **syhed** *pa.t.* sighed XX. 274
syhte *n.* sight **by syhte** in the sight II. 115
syker *adj.* safe IX. 333; sure, definite XXII. 255
sykeren *v.* promise VII. 185
sykerloker more confidently VII. 142
sykerost safest V. 39
sylinge gliding XX. 341
Symme Sim, dim. of Simon VI. 207
Symondes Simon's (Simon Magus). V. 79
symonye, syimonye simony (the purchase or sale of an ecclesiastical office or preferment)
Synay Sinai XIX. 2
synege *v.* sin
synguler exceptional, excelling VI. 36
syre father *gen.sg.* father's III. 366
Syse Assisi VII. 166
syse assize II. 178
sysour assize-man, juryman IV. 162 **sysores** *pl.* II. 59, 63, 179, III. 170, etc.
sythe *n.pl.* times VI. 428, XVI. 233 **sythes** *pl.* times
sythe *conj.* since
Syuile *n.* Civil law II. 63n, 67 **Syuyles** *gen.sg.* II. 115

tabard loose coat, usually sleeveless or with wide, open sleeves VI. 203
tabre *v.* play on the tabor (a small drum) XV. 205
Taddee Thaddeus XXI. 165
take(n) *v.* take; give, deliver, bestow I. 52, III. 87, etc.; catch (fire) XIX. 210; (*refl.*) take counsel (among themselves) VI. 154 **taken on** behave, 'carry on' XIII. 153 **taketh** *pres.3sg.* takes; gives; seizes, afflicts VI. 80
talage taxation XXI. 37
tale account, importance, consideration I. 9, III. 390, XXI. 454
talewys given to tale-telling and gossip III. 166
tauhte taught
tayl retinue II. 196
tayl tallying, reckoning (often punning: sexual organs) IV. 61n, X. 80n, XVI. 258
taylende reckoning, sum of qualities III. 369
tecche, teche teach, direct
telde *pa.t.* dwelt (*lit.* pitched his tent) XIV. 149
telde *pa.t.* told VIII. 76
tell, telle(n) tell; count, reckon Prol. 90, XII. 174
teme theme, text, subject VI. 1, VIII. 20, XII. 43, XV. 82, XX. 358
Themese Thames VI. 335, XIV. 104

tenden lighted XX. 249

tender tinder (any dry inflammable stuff that readily takes fire) XIX. 210

tene *v.* harm, oppress, annoy III. 139, VIII. 36, XIV. 8, XV. 160 **teneth** *pres.3sg.* III. 159 **tened** *pa.t.* harmed, annoyed III. 474, XXII. 119; troubled, worried XI. 129; (*refl.*) grew angry II. 116 *pp.* VII. 38

tene *adj.* ten I. 104

tene *n.* suffering, misery, trouble I. 165, XII. 48, XIII. 7, XVI. 174; anger VIII. 124

teneful painful, worrying III. 494

Teologie Theology II. 116

termisones terminations III. 405

termyned determined, passed verdict on I. 93

teyen tie, bind I. 92

thankes *gen.sg.* of choice, of will **his thankes** willingly IX. 66

than(ne) *adv.* then

thare where

that, þat *rel.pron.* who, that; that which, what; those that; he that

theche *inf.* thatch XXI. 238

theder thither

thedom prosperous or thrifty activity VII. 53

þei, thei they

thekynge thatching VIII. 199

then *conj.* than

thenke *v.* intend I. 21

thennes thence

ther(e), þer(e) there; where

ther, þer their

þer-tyl thereto

thewes manners, traits of character VI. 141

this(e), þis(e) this; these

tho, þo *adv.* then *conj.* when *pron.* those

thogh though

thoghte thought

tholye *inf.* suffer IV. 80, XIX. 105 **tholieth** *pres.3pl.* XVI. 33 **tholede(n)** *pa.t.* XII. 203, XV. 73

thonkynge thanking II. 162

thorlede pierced I. 170

thorpes villages Prol. 220

thorw(e), þoruȝ *prep.* through, because of

thoughte, thouhte *pa.t.* thought; (*impers.*) it seemed; intended (to go) XX. 122

thow *conj.* though, if

thresfold threshold VI. 408

threttene thirteen VI. 220

threw fell VI. 408

thridde third VII. 137

thromblede staggered, stumbled VI. 408

thus-gates in this way, thus XVI. 306

thwytinge cutting, whittling VIII. 199

thynketh (*impers.*) it seems

tidiore more proper, more worthy XII. 186

tikel wanton III. 166

til *prep.* to

tilion till, cultivate IX. 2

tilyares tillers (of the land) XVII. 100

titerares tittle-tattlers XXII. 299

tixst, tixt text II. 129, III. 492

to *prep.* to; as, for VI. 128, XII. 205, 210; on VI. 155; until XX. 5

to *adv.* too, too much I. 139, V. 23, 24, VI. 166, XVI. 354

Tobie Tobias

tobroke, tobroken(e) broken in pieces X. 85; broken down IX. 32; maimed IX. 99

to-cleue *inf.* split asunder XIV. 84, XX. 113 **to-cleyef** *pa.t.* was cleft asunder XX. 62

toek took; gave XIII. 105, XIX. 2, XXII. 137

tofore *prep.* before V. 114

tofte hill I. 12

toged(e)res, togyderes together

togrynt grinds XI. 62

tok(e) *pa.t.* took; gave III. 47 **tok on** engaged in trade III. 84 *pa.t.subj.* should take III. 294

tol toll, tax, tribute Prol. 98, XIII. 72

told(e) *pa.t.* told; reckoned XIX. 237; stretched, were drawn VI. 220

tolle *inf.* pay toll XIII. 50

to-logged pulled about II. 226

Tolomeus Ptolemy XII. 174

tome leisure II. 196

tomorwe tomorrow

tookene sign, token XIII. 11

to-quasch(e) *pa.t.* was (were) shaken to pieces XX. 64, 257

tore torn VI. 203

to-reueth robs, plunders III. 202

to-roef was riven asunder XX. 63

torne turn; convert XVII. 263

toted looked XVIII. 53

touore tougher, hardier XII. 186

tour tower

toward *adj.* ready at hand, about Prol. 215

transuerseth transgresses III. 445

trasch twigs and wood-shavings and other inflammable refuse XIX. 210

trauaile *v.* work

trauaile, trauayle *n.* work **trauayles** *pl.* works (imposed as a form of penance) IX. 234

trauersede transgressed XIV. 209

trede *inf.* tread, copulate with XIV. 161 **treden** *pa.t.* trod XIII. 164

tresor treasure

tretor traitor XIX. 237

treuthe truth; troth, promise II. 124, VIII. 33

treuthliche truthfully XIII. 72

trewe(s) *n.* truce, respite VIII. 354, XX. 462

treweliche truly, honestly

treys three XVIII. 239n

triacle medicine I. 146n

tric(c)herye treachery

trinen *v.* touch XX. 87

trionales triennials, masses for the dead said for three years IX. 322n, 332, 335

trist *n.* trust **trist of** dependence on III. 159

trist *v.* trust VI. 333, XIII. 101 **tristeth** *pres.3sg.* I. 66

Troianes Trajan XII. 74, XIV. 149, 205

trolled walked unhindered, strolled XX. 332

trompy *inf.* play on the trumpet XV. 205 **trompede** *pa.t.* XX. 468

trowe *v.* believe

troyledest deceived XX. 319

trusse *inf.* leave, pack off II. 228

Tullius Cicero XII. 174

tulthe cultivated land or its produce XXI. 432

tulye cultivate XX. 109

tulyers tillers, cultivators Prol. 224

tumbe thumb VII. 45

turne turn; overturn, pervert III. 49

tutor guardian, keeper I. 52

twene, tweye two

Tybourne Tyburn, in London, where public executions were held VI. 368, XIV. 129

tyd *adv.* quickly XXII. 54

tydy *adj.* honest III. 474, XXI. 439; proper, well set up XX. 332

tykes (*fig.*) dogs, churls XXI. 37

tylie, tylye *inf.* till, cultivate Prol. 87, VIII. 244 **tyl(e)de** *pa.t.* XV. 265, 269

tymbred timbered, built wooden houses III. 84

Tymme Tim, dim. of Timothy VI. 364

tyne *v.* lose X. 275, XI. 198, XXI. 343; waste XIV. 8 **tynt** *pp.* lost XX. 143

tythe(n) *inf.* pay or offer tithes VI. 306, XIII. 72

tyxst, tyxt text III. 494, XII. 48, XIX. 14

valle befall, take place XX. 411

vansche *inf.* cause to vanish XV. 8 **vanscheαe** *pa.t.* vanished XIV. 217

vaunsed advanced, promoted III. 36

vaw(w)arde vanguard V. 58, XXII. 95

vch(e), vcche *adj.* each **vch a** each

vchon(e) *pron.* each (one)

veile *n.* the watchful one VII. 57n

vele many VI. 74

velynge feeling, touch XX. 132

venemouste venomousness XX. 160

ventage vintage, grape-gathering XX. 411

ver far **be ver** by far, anywhere near in importance XXII. 23

vernicle vernicle VII. 168n

verset little verse XIV. 128

vertu power XX. 160

vicory vicar (the poorly paid deputy of the parson, or holder of the living of a parish) XXI. 409, 480

vigilies vigils, fasts VII. 25, IX. 232

vitailes victuals II. 191

vitalers traders in victuals II. 61n

Vmbletee humility VII. 272

vmbywhile from time to time VI. 396

vnbuxum disobedient II. 87, VI. 16, 17

vnconnynge unwise, stupid III. 243

vnconnyngliche unwisely, stupidly III. 262

vncrounede without the tonsure V. 62

vndede expounded IX. 307

vnderfongen *v.* receive, accept III. 270, IX. 129 **vnderfeng, vndirfenge** *pa.t.sg.* I. 73, XII. 51 **vnderfonge** *pp.* III. 111, VII. 279; accepted, granted XII. 83

vndernome corrected, reproved XXII. 51

vnder-nymynge reproof VI. 35

vndertake *inf.* receive Prol. 98 **vndertoke** *pa.t.* reproved XII. 31

vndoth explains, provides a commentary on II. 40

vngracious without grace, unlikely to be favoured X. 296

vnheled unroofed, uncovered XVI. 75, XIX. 300

vnhende *n.* ill-grace XXII. 186

vnhynde *adj.* ungracious XIX. 248

vnkun(n)ynge ignorant XV. 16, XVI. 273

vnkynde unnatural VI. 296

vnlek unlocked VII. 251

vnlele untrue, unfaithful XIII. 68

vnlossum undesirable X. 260

vnloueliche unpleasant XIV. 178

vnmeble(s) *n.pl.* non-movable property (e.g. land) III. 421, X. 186

vnnethe *adv.* hardly IV. 63, XXII. 190

vnredy improvident, unadvised XII. 215

vnsauerly *adv.* with an unpleasant taste XV. 49

vnsittyng inappropriate, improper III. 207, IV. 189

vnskilful unreasonable, wantonly neglectful of reason VI. 25

vnspere *v.* unbar, open XX. 270 **vnspered** *pa.t.* XX. 89

vntydy inadequate, unsatisfactory III. 87; improperly made, unsuitable IX. 262; filthy XXII. 119

vnwittiliche unwisely III. 133

vnwrast deceitful XX. 311

voketes advocates II. 61n

vorgoers purveyors II. 61n

vp *prep.* upon, on, in I. 157, II. 75, IV. 128, 179, etc.

vphalderes, vpholderes second-hand clothes dealers VI. 374, XII. 217

vrete ate, gnawed VI. 74

Vrye Uriah XII. 266

vsererus usurers XVI. 260

vycary vicar (*see* **vicory**) XIV. 70

vysen *pres.3pl.* use XVIII. 175

wafrestere female cake-seller VII. 285n

wafrrer wafer-seller XV. 199

wage(n) *inf.* pay wages (to) IV. 192, XXII. 269; give security, promise IV. 93; lay down as security XVIII. 284 **waged** *pp.* given security IV. 96

waggeth *pres.3sg.* shakes XVIII. 45 **wagged(e)** *pa.t.sg.* shook XXI. 204; shook (in anger and denial) XII. 18

wagyng tossing X. 34

wake *inf.* keep awake at nights (as a penance) XXII. 370

wakere watchful IX. 259

walch Welsh flannel (a cheap cloth) VI. 205

waleweth toss, move, fluctuate X. 46

walkeres cloth-fullers (i.e. those who treated the woollen cloth after weaving) Prol. 223

walled welled, gushed forth XXI. 377

Walshe *n.* Welshman VI. 373

Walterot something of no value XX. 145n

wang-teeth 'cheek-teeth', molars XXII. 191

wanhope despair II. 103n, VII. 81, etc.

wanne pale VI. 419

war aware, ready

warde gatekeeper XX. 365

wardemotis ward-meetings Prol. 92n

wardes, wardus wardships, responsibilities Prol. 92n, V. 185
Wareyn(e) Warren IV. 27, 31
warien *v.* curse VIII. 336
warrokye restrain (a horse) with a girth IV. 21
warth *pa.t.sg.* became, fell XI. 168; befell V. 98
wasche *pp.* washed, scoured VI. 402
wastel cake VI. 341
wateled walled, fenced XXI. 327
watres waters, urine II. 234
watschoed wet-shoed XX. 1n
Watte Wat, dim. of Walter V. 132, VI. 363
waye *inf.* weigh VI. 210 **wayed** *pa.t.* VI. 224
wayke weak V. 23
wayte(n) *v.* see to, look after VI. 208, VII. 188
    wayten after look for, expect I. 123, II. 78
    waytest lookest at XVIII. 274 **wayteth** looks, is on the watch IV. 52 **waytede** *pa.t.sg.* looked (around) Prol. 16, IX. 295, XVIII. 181
waytynge *n.* ogling look VI. 177 **waytynges** *pl.* II. 94
wayued *pa.t.* drove XXII. 168
wayues *n.pl.* lost property to which the crown laid claim Prol. 92n
wawes waves X. 45
wax *pa.t.sg.* grew, became III. 482
webbe weaver VI. 221 **webbes** *pl.* IX. 204
webbesteres female weavers Prol. 223
wed, wedde *n.* pledge, security III. 258, VI. 243, XIII. 43, 44n, XVIII. 279, XXII. 13
    to wedde as security V. 73, XX. 30
wedde *v.* pledge, wager II. 136, IV. 143
weder, wedore *n.* weather VI. 113, XX. 456
    wederes *pl.* storms X. 46, XII. 188
wedes clothes VI. 177, XIII. 188
wedewes widows III. 160
wedy *inf.* weed VIII. 66
weel *adv.* well
weet-shoed wet-shoed XVI. 14
weke wick XIX. 168, 170, 177
wel *adj.* good III. 69
wel-a-way, welowo *interj.as n.* alas, misery XVI. 78, XX. 238
welde wield, have control over XII. 20
wele *n.* happiness
wel-fare fine living XXI. 353
welkene sky XX. 247
welowo *see* **wel-a-way**
wem stain, uncleanness XX. 135
wenche maidservant VI. 415
wende(n) go
wene *v.* think **wente** *pa.t.* thought VI. 32, 41
wentes *n.pl.* twists, contrivances, stratagems VI. 263
weps *n.* sprig VI. 402
wer troubled state, perplexity XII. 49
werie *inf.* wear III. 447, XIX. 234 **wered** *pp.*
    wered out passed away with the passing of time V. 81
werkmanschip ability to do the job II. 96
wernardus liars, deceivers II. 142
wernare keeper of a warren, gamekeeper VI. 363

werneth refuse XXII. 12
werre war
weschen *inf.* wish X. 266 **wesched** *pa.t.* VI. 402
wesches *n.pl.* wishes, desires VI. 66
weschynges wishings, desires II. 95
wete(n) *v.* know IV. 100, XVIII. 147
wethewynde wild convolvulus VII. 163
wex, wexe(n) *v.* grow, become; fall, begin to be XII. 49 **wexe** *pa.t.* grew XV. 262
wex *n.* wax
wey(e) *n.* man III. 225, VI. 105, XIII. 13, 156, XIX. 65 **weyes** *pl.* XIV. 195
weye *inf.* weigh VI. 242 **weye** *pp.* weighed I. 174, IX. 273
weyhtes weights VI. 258
wham *rel.pron.* whom
whan(ne) *conj.* when
whare *adv.* where
wher(e), wheder *conj.* whether Prol. 186, I. 137, II. 149, III. 296, IX. 240, XII. 50, XIV. 193, XIX. 222
where *pron.* which of the two (in interrog.) XVI. 89, etc.
which(e) *adj.* what, what sort of IV. 26, XI. 26, XX. 128
whicche *n.* clothes-box ('hutch') IV. 111
while *adv.* meanwhile IV. 16
whil(e) *n.* while, time X. 289 **þe whiles** whilst, meanwhile
whith *n.* bit III. 130
whoder whither XVIII. 181 **whoder out** forth in what direction VII. 178
whodeward whither VI. 354
whyes *n.pl.* why's, reasons XIV. 156
wightes weights XVI. 129
wiht(e) *n.* man, one X. 4, XX. 239
wihtliche quickly, promptly XVIII. 292
wihtnesse strength, force XXI. 246; smartness, cleverness XI. 286
wille *n.* will, disposition; sexual desire II. 96
willefolliche willingly XXII. 49
wilnen *v.* desire, wish
wilnynge desiring
wirdes fortunes, destiny XII. 208
wisse(n) guide, direct, instruct, advise
wissyng guidance, advice XII. 11
wiste *pa.t.* knew **wist** *pp.* known XX. 210
wit(t), wyt(t) wisdom, cleverness, intelligence; mind, reason; trick, piece of cleverness
with that, with þat *conj.* provided that VI. 173, XXII. 250
withoute *conj.* unless IV. 176
withsit(t)e, withsytte *inf.* oppose Prol. 174, VIII. 202, X. 97 **withsaet** *pa.t.* XVIII. 250
witte *pa.t.sg.* blamed I. 30, VI. 113
witterliche, witterly truly, for certain
withes withies, restraining bands for a horse IV. 23n
wittiliche skilfully, properly VIII. 18
wittiore wiser, cleverer V. 188
witturlich truly, for certain XX. 69
witty *adj.* wise, clever II. 151, VI. 24 *as n.pl.* wise men XI. 229
wittyly cleverly X. 130
woen dwelling, place III. 141

woen quantity XXII. 171

woet *pres.3sg.* knows IV. 37, V. 181, VI. 163, VII. 245, IX. 70, etc.

woke *n.* week VIII. 269, IX. 253 **wokes** *pl.* XVIII. 134

woky *v.* moisten, soften by moistening XIV. 25 **woketh** moistens XVI. 332

wol *pres.3sg.* will

wolde(n) *pa.t.* would, wished, would wish, would like (to)

woldes *n.pl.* wishes II. 95n

wolle wool VIII. 12, XI. 15

wollene *adj.as n.* woollens I. 18

wolleth *pres.3pl.* will, wish to

wollewaerd dressed in wool only XX. 1n

woltow wilt thou

wombe stomach

wommane *gen.sg.* woman's XX. 135

wonden *pa.t.* wound, dressed II. 230

wonder *adj.* wondrous I. 125

wonderly wonderfully II. 9

wone, wonye(n) *v.* dwell **won(y)eth** *pres.3sg.* dwells **woned** *pa.t.* dwelt **woned** *pp.* accustomed, wont VIII. 164

wone *n.* custom, habit IV. 22, XVI. 321 **wones** *pl.* dwellings, quarters Prol. 18

woot *pres.3sg.* knows

wopen *pa.t.* wept IX. 41

worche *v.* work, make; bring about

wordes *n.pl.* words; precepts XIX. 13

wordes *n.pl.* destinies, chances V. 98; destinies, inherent qualities XIV. 32

world-ryche *gen.sg.* worldly kingdom's XVI. 16

worliche *adj.* worthy, excellent III. 368

wormes snakes XIII. 136

worre war XI. 267

worschip(e) honour, renown

wortes vegetables VIII. 331

worthe(n) *inf.* become XI. 24, 89, XV. 148; be, remain undisturbed I. 49 **worth** *pres.2sg.* shalt be VII. 265 *pres.3sg.* will be, shall be, is going to be; becomes III. 123; will come to XII. 231n *pres.subj.3sg.* may be XIII. 1

worthily *adj.* worthy VIII. 9

woschen washed II. 230

wose ooze, mud XII. 228

wost *pa.t.2sg.* wouldest XVIII. 274, XXII. 188

wost *pres.2sg.* knowest III. 225

wot *pres.3sg.* knows

woware wooer XII. 19

wowes walls III. 65

woxe *pp.* grown III. 211

wrake destruction XVII. 85, XX. 458

wrang *pa.t.* wrung (her hands) II. 252

wrath(e) *v.* make angry II. 118; (*refl.*) grow angry VIII. 149 **wrathest** *pres.2sg.* (*refl.*) get angry III. 228 **wratheth** *pres.3sg.* (*impers.*) angers **hym wratheth** he is angered Prol. 189 **wrathed** *pa.t.* angered I. 26, VI. 148

wrecche wretch II. 41

wreth wrath XXI. 305

wriht(e) workman, carpenter XI. 241, XIII. 159 **wrihtes** *pl.* XI. 253

Wring-lawe law-perverter IV. 31

writhen tightly folded together, clenched XIX. 140

wroeth angry XVII. 3

wroghte, wroghton *pa.t.* acted I. 26; did, would do I. 13 **wroft** *pp.* wrought, done III. 133

wroken *pp.* **ar wroken** have forced their way IX. 259

wroth *pa.t.* twisted, clenched VI. 66

wrother more angry Prol. 117

wroþer-hele ill fate XV. 299n

wrouhte *pa.t.* did, worked, caused *pp.* done, brought about

wrouhtestou wroughtest thou III. 137

wrytes carpenters XI. 244

Wy Weyhill VI. 211

wycche witch VI. 81

wyddore more widely, further II. 213

wyde-whare far and wide X. 61, XVII. 271

wye man VII. 158

wyghte, wyht(e) *n.* creature, man I. 59, IX. 116, XIII. 59, 217

wyghtliche quickly II. 218

wyht(e) *adj.* vigorous, strong X. 146, XV. 172

wyke wick XIX. 204

wykke *adj.as n.pl.* wicked men XIV. 164, 166

wykkede *adv.* wickedly I. 26

wynde *inf.* go, wend XVI. 321

wynkyng *pres.p.* with eyes closed in sleep Prol. 11

wynkynge *n.* doze XI. 168

wynne win; earn a livelihood I. 175

wynnynge prosperity gained by trade V. 137

wypne weapon III. 458

wyrdus fates, destinies III. 240

wyse *n.* manner, way, fashion **a fuste wyse** in the manner of a fist XIX. 149

wyssen *v.* guide, direct, advise

wyste *pa.t.* knew

wyt(t) *see* **wit**

wyte(n) *v.* know **wyten** *pres.subj.3pl.* let them know II. 79

wyte *v.* blame for XX. 353

wytterly truly, certainly I. 71

wyue *n.dat.sg.* wife **to wyue** as wife III. 146, 368, IV. 158, etc. **wyuene** *gen.pl.* wives' V. 131

y *pron.* I

ybete beaten, punished IV. 89

yblessed consecrated IX. 13, XVI. 202

ybore born II. 144

ybosted boasted XIX. 59

ybrent burnt III. 105

ycalled wearing a cap XVI. 351

ychaffared traded, made deals V. 94

ych *pron.* I

ycheueled trembled, quivered, wobbled VI. 200

yclyketed fastened with a latch VII. 266

ycongeyed dismissed XVI. 366

ycoped coped, clothed III. 38

ycouped cut away XX. 12n

ycrimyled anointed with holy oil XVI. 351

ycrouned crowned with the tonsure V. 56, 59

ydel *adj.as n.* **an ydel** in vain, idly VII. 218, XIV. 7
ydo *pp.* done
y-ered ploughed VIII. 3
yes *n.pl.* eyes
ye-syhte eyesight IX. 102
yfolled baptized XXI. 40
yfonde found III. 491; provided for III. 41
yglobbed gulped down VI. 397
ygrounde sharpened XX. 81
ygyue given II. 162
yȝoten begotten, taken flesh I. 150
yhapsed hasped, padlocked I. 192
yheled roofed VII. 237
yholde held, kept V. 157; considered, esteemed I. 80; bound, obliged XIV. 196
yholpe helped XIX. 60
yhote told, commanded II. 228
yhouted hooted at II. 228
yhuyred hired VIII. 335
ykald called, summoned III. 149
yknowe recognized, brought to notice IV. 71
ykud known, acknowledged XII. 195
ykuld killed Prol. 199
ykyuered covered, hidden XXI. 86
ylered learned X. 10
ylet hindered, delayed XIII. 36
ylet allowed **ylet by** esteemed III. 204, V. 3
yley lain XI. 260
yliche, ylyche *adv.* alike, equally XIV. 148, XVI. 20
ylike, ylyche *adj.* like, alike VI. 183, X. 68
ylle evil, wickedness
ylore, ylost lost
ylow lied **ylow on** lied against II. 20
ylyche *see* **yliche, ylike**
ymageny have foresight XXI. 277
ymaginacioun prudent forethought XXII. 33

ymedled mixed X. 129
ymorthred murdered XII. 241
ympe graft, shoot, scion XVIII. 6
Ynde India XVII. 272, XXI. 165
ynne lodging X. 4
ynome seized XXII. 46
ynow(e) *adj.* enough, plentiful
yparayled dressed VII. 161
yparroked(e) enclosed VI. 144, XVII. 13
yplyht bound, indentured VI. 208
ypresed praised X. 307, XII. 194
yren iron Prol. 97
yreuestede vestmented, dressed V. 112
yrobed robed, given robes XI. 21
yruyfled robbed XIX. 90
Ysaye Isaiah XI. 259, XVIII. 113
ysaye seen XVIII. 140
yschape prepared, planned XV. 299
yse *imp.sg.* see XIV. 103
ysey *pa.t.* saw II. 67, XII. 82 *pp.* seen XVI. 342, 347
Ysodorus Isidore XVI. 198
yspilde wasted VII. 48
ytayled tallied VII. 35n
ythryueth *pres.3pl.* thrive Prol. 34
ytynt lost, wasted V. 93
yvenkused vanquished XX. 105
ywar, ywaer wary, cautious, careful; aware, forewarned
ywete *inf.* know Prol. 181
ywitted with good wits, intelligent XI. 236
ywonne won, derived, begotten XII. 108
yworded spoken XV. 149
yworthe *inf.* be, be left alone Prol. 201, VIII. 86, X. 163
ywrithe twisted VII. 163
ywrouhte worked, done
ywrye twisted, awry XVI. 75
ywyte *inf.* know III. 76